Social Problems:
A Critical Approach

Fifth Edition

Kenneth J. Neubeck

The University of Connecticut

Mary Alice Neubeck

Davita Silfen Glasberg

The University of Connecticut

Boston   Burr Ridge, IL   Dubuque, IA   Madison, WI   New York
San Francisco   St. Louis   Bangkok   Bogotá   Caracas   Kuala Lumpur
Lisbon   London   Madrid   Mexico City   Milan   Montreal   New Delhi
Santiago   Seoul   Singapore   Sydney   Taipei   Toronto

Higher Education

SOCIAL PROBLEMS: A CRITICAL APPROACH

Published by McGraw-Hill, a business unit of The McGraw-Hill Companies, Inc., 1221 Avenue of the Americas, New York, NY, 10020. Copyright © 2007, 1997, 1991, 1986, 1979 by The McGraw-Hill Companies, Inc. All rights reserved. No part of this publication may be reproduced or distributed in any form or by any means, or stored in a database or retrieval system, without the prior written consent of The McGraw-Hill Companies, Inc., including, but not limited to, in any network or other electronic storage or transmission, or broadcast for distance learning.

Some ancillaries, including electronic and print components, may not be available to customers outside the United States.

This book is printed on acid-free paper.

1 2 3 4 5 6 7 8 9 0 DOC/DOC 0 9 8 7 6

ISBN-13: 978-0-07-296804-0

ISBN-10:   0-07-296804-4

Vice President and Editor-in-Chief: *Emily Barrosse*
Publisher: *Phillip A. Butcher*
Sponsoring Editor: *Sherith H. Pankratz*
Senior Marketing Manager: *Daniel M. Loch*
Managing Editor: *Jean Dal Porto*
Senior Project Manager: *Diane M. Folliard*
Art Editor: *Emma C. Ghiselli*
Photo Research Coordinator: *Natalia C. Peschiera*
Photo Researcher: *Inge King*

Cover Designer: *JoAnne Schopler*
Lead Designer: *Gino Cieslik*
Designer: *Marianna Kinigakis*
Cover Credit: *Abstract #13 by Diana Ong, 1976. Private Collection/Super Stock, Inc.*
Production Supervisor: *Jason I. Huls*
Composition: *10.5/12 Times New Roman, Interactive Composition Corporation*
Printing: *45 # New Era Matte, R.R. Donnelley & Sons*

Credits: The credits section for this book begins on page 657 and is considered an extension of the copyright page.

Library of Congress Cataloging-in-Publication Data
Neubeck, Kenneth J.
    Social problems : a critical approach / Kenneth
J. Neubeck, Mary Alice Neubeck, Davita Silfen Glasberg.—5th ed.
        p. cm.
    Includes bibliographical references and indexes.
    ISBN-13: 978-0-07-296804-0 (softcover : alk. paper)
    ISBN-10: 0-07-296804-4 (softcover : alk. paper)
    1. Social problems. 2. Social history—20th century.
    3. United States—Social conditions—1980- I. Neubeck, Mary Alice. II. Glasberg, Davita Silfen. III. Title.
HN18.N47 2007
361.1—dc22   2005056142

The Internet addresses listed in the text were accurate at the time of publication. The inclusion of a Web site does not indicate an endorsement by the authors or McGraw-Hill, and McGraw-Hill does not guarantee the accuracy of the information presented at these sites.

www.mhhe.com

To Lucy, Harper, and Dylan Neubeck,
and in loving memory of Yssis Neubeck

To Morgan Silfen Glasberg,
and Gillian and Raymond Arnott, Jr.

about the authors

Kenneth J. Neubeck is a Professor Emeritus of Sociology at the University of Connecticut, where he served as director of the university's undergraduate minor in human rights. He is coauthor (with Noel A. Cazenave) of *Welfare Racism: Playing the Race Card Against America's Poor* (Routledge, 2001) and the author of *When Welfare Disappears: The Case for Economic Human Rights* (Routledge, forthcoming). Professor Neubeck has authored or coauthored four previous editions of *Social Problems: A Critical Approach,* two of which were published by McGraw-Hill, and he is coauthor of *Sociology: Diversity, Conflict, and Change* (McGraw-Hill, 2005), written with Davita Silfen Glasberg.

Mary Alice Neubeck served as the Director of Undergraduate Studies for the University of Connecticut's School of Family Studies. A sociologist by training, Ms. Neubeck taught in the university's Women's Studies Program before holding the position of Lecturer in Human Development and Family Studies. She oversaw undergraduate internships and was active in promoting service learning programs as well as diversity training for students entering careers in the social services. Ms. Neubeck is coauthor, with Kenneth J. Neubeck, of *Social Problems: A Critical Approach* (McGraw-Hill, 1997).

Davita Silfen Glasberg is Professor and Department Head of Sociology at the University of Connecticut-Storrs. She received her Ph.D. in Sociology from the State University of New York at Stony Brook in 1983. She has authored or coauthored several books and more than two dozen journal articles on issues of finance capital, the state in finance capitalism, and political economy. Professor Glasberg's most recent books were *Sociology: Diversity, Conflict, and Change* (coauthored with Kenneth J. Neubeck) (McGraw-Hill) and *Corporate Welfare and the Welfare State: Bank Deregulation and the Savings and Loan Bailout* (coauthored with Dan Skidmore) (Aldine de Gruyter). She is currently working on a book about power, oppression, and the state, as well as a study of predatory lending and the Community Reinvestment Act. Her special interests are political sociology, political economy, and systems of inequality.

brief contents

contents

chapter four

The Global Context: Population and Underdevelopment   96

chapter five

Environmental Abuse   126

part II   Group Problems

chapter six

Economic Inequality and Poverty   162

chapter seven

Racism   196

chapter eight

Sexism   238

chapter nine

Heterosexism   268

chapter ten

Ageism   298

chapter eleven

The Changing Structure of Work   326

chapter sixteen

Mental Illness   508

chapter seventeen

Substance Abuse   540

chapter eighteen

Suicide   586

preface

ocial Problems: A Critical Approach is now in its fifth edition. Our goal is to encourage students to seriously analyze some of the causes and implications of many of the most pressing social problems confronting people today. The text is intended to provoke spirited thought, discussion, and debate among students rather than to simply present a series of dry facts. Out of this process should come new views, knowledge, and awareness; and for some students, the will to act when possible to help attack those social problems of greatest concern to them.

As the table of contents indicates, *Social Problems: A Critical Approach* opens with an introductory chapter that presents traditional approaches to the study of social problems and then describes the approach taken in this book. Our approach involves examining four different types of social problems: societal; groups; institutional; and problems of individuals. We analyze causes and effects and—in many cases—posit possible solutions or steps toward mitigating the problems. These solutions or steps toward mitigation may themselves invite healthy debate.

In the first part of the text, students are introduced to four "societal problems"—dynamics of society that are to us demonstrably harmful to millions of people. In the second part, students are presented with five "group problems" with attention to how groups are socially constructed in power hierarchies and how these hierarchies produce social problems for subordinate members of groups. In the following section students are introduced to four "institutional problems:" we explore how institutions are structured and how they intersect with other institutions to create problems for people in them. Finally, students are provided four chapters covering "individual problems"—individual behaviors that have an adverse impact on other people and/or are self-harmful.

The text is organized to make it possible for instructors to assign the chapters they wish to use in the sequence they prefer. However, it is our feeling that the problems involving individual behaviors are most logically handled after—and thus in the context of—societal, group, and institutional problems.

As a learning device, a textbook must be comprehensible to students and must engage their interest. Like the first four editions, this text presents information in a straightforward and highly readable manner, even when rather complex and abstract ideas are being addressed. Conflicting and contrasting views on problems are clearly delineated. Tables, figures, and photographs are directly linked to the text in order to underscore important ideas. Specialized terms and concepts are defined and illustrated in the text.

Another feature of this text that will promote student involvement in discussing the subject matter is the series of provocative questions at the end of each chapter. These questions can form the bases of classroom or small-group discussions, or they may be used in conjunction with outside assignments. Many of the questions are designed to encourage debate and to get students to consider different positions or viewpoints on social problems. We have used the discussion questions with great success and highly recommend class assignments and/or panels around them.

Many instructors will want to know how this fifth edition differs from the fourth. We begin by saying that very little was removed from the fourth edition (basically outdated events and data). The extremely favorable reception accorded the fourth edition led instead to our expansion of what we were—according to users and reviewers—already doing right. We have reorganized the book, grouping the chapters to more explicitly reflect the four main types of social problems. The chapter on work is now called "The Changing Structure of Work" to more accurately reflect the chapter's new focus on how the current organization of work and labor markets create problems for workers. Moreover, we have added a number of new topics to original chapters. For example, we have introduced materials on terrorism, the current war in Iraq, voting and democracy (including a discussion of events in Florida in the 2000 national election in the United States), the role of the globalization of production in world development, and the question of the effect of welfare reform.

Other new topics include the rise of club drugs and steroid abuse, same-sex marriage and civil unions, the effect of No Child Left Behind federal education policy, family violence as a matter of power inequalities rather than an individualized matter of stress and anger, identity theft and computer crime, death row syndrome, euthanasia, and political suicide.

Many people have selflessly contributed to the successful completion of the fifth edition. Our appreciation goes to the wonderful staff of McGraw-Hill, especially to Sherith Pankratz, Diane Folliard, Laurie McGee, and Inge King, and to Pat Forrest at Carlisle Communications. It was indeed a pleasure to work with you all. We are also grateful to friends and colleagues at the University of Connecticut and at other institutions who took time to make suggestions about the fifth edition.

We are greatly indebted to Angie Beeman for helping us with the library research and general legwork that was required to complete this edition. She displayed good humor in the face of numerous and often hectic demands, and the fruits of her labors are visible throughout this text. Many thanks, Angie.

We wish also to thank our undergraduate students. Their reactions—both in and outside the classroom—helped guide the direction and development of this edition.

Together with McGraw-Hill, we would like to thank the following reviewers for their helpful comments and suggestions: Dean Rojeck, University of Georgia; Jerome McKibben, Eastern Connecticut State University; Michael R. Nusbaumer, Indiana University–Purdue; Joseph D. Yenerall, Duquesne University; and Kathlyn Fritz, Newberry College.

Thanks go to Michael, Kara, and Christopher Neubeck, and to Morgan Silfen Glasberg and Gillian Arnott for their continued love and support. Finally, we thank one another for continued coauthoring success that reflects almost two decades of friendship and professional collaboration. Right up the road or on opposite coasts, it still survives!

Kenneth J. Neubeck
Mary Alice Neubeck
Davita Silfen Glasberg

Social Problems:

A Critical Approach

chapter 1

Introduction

What would you say is the most important issue facing the United States today? Public opinion pollsters ask this question of voters before presidential elections in an attempt to estimate what is likely to affect how people will vote. Some issues that voters identify change from one election to another while other issues remain high on people's lists. During the 1968 election, for example, the primary concerns of voters included the war in Vietnam, civil rights, and the state of the economy. By the 1976 election, energy and the environment rose as a concern and war receded as a concern; but the state of the economy remained as an important issue. In 2004 war was once again a significant issue for voters, as was the state of the economy and health care. And throughout the last several decades, although racism and civil rights, sexism and women's rights, homophobia, crime, and poverty have been important issues to at least some segments of the population, they rarely if ever top the list.

The polls that survey voters' concerns are identifying what people perceive to be social problems. The ebb and flow of issues that emerge out of these polls raises important questions: What is a social problem? What affects the cycle of defining social problems as significant or unimportant? What causes something to become a social problem? Who gets to define social problems and what to do about them? How do we discover information that shapes people's perceptions of social problems?

Identifying the existence of social problems does not necessarily mean there is nothing positive to be said about society. Over the last hundred years alone, there have been many astounding technological and medical breakthroughs that have significantly improved life in the United States and around the world. Many movements for freedom and liberation have also raised consciousness, changed social relations, and contributed to better conditions for many people. At the same time, equally striking are the many serious social problems that continue to plague people. These problems, far from being resolved, provide a bothersome contrast to the many positive tendencies and accomplishments that characterize U.S. and global society.

Social Problems: A Critical Approach analyzes some of today's social problems, ranging from the concentration of political and economic power in the hands of a few to substance abuse. The book looks at the causes and effects of these problems and considers solutions to many of them. None of the social problems analyzed in this text has a simple solution, and all pose challenges to our collective wisdom and ingenuity. We begin this introduction with a review of the various approaches sociologists have traditionally taken toward the study of social problems. Next, we outline the approach taken in this book—a **critical approach** to social problems. We then discuss some reasons for change in the level of societal concern with particular problems over a period of time. Finally, we comment on sociological methods of research that help to shed light on many social problems.

Traditional Approaches to the Study of Social Problems

Sociologists around the world have long been interested in the problematic aspects of social life. In fact, the nineteenth-century scholars who pioneered in the development of sociology within the United States did so out of deep concern over social conditions, particularly the problems in the nation's rapidly expanding cities. During the 1800s this society experienced the almost simultaneous impact of industrialization, urbanization, and the arrival of millions of immigrants from abroad. Property crime, violence, alcoholism, and mental troubles seemed to be on the increase. The early sociologists hoped that a better understanding of U.S. society's problems might provide clues on how to improve conditions. The new discipline of sociology was not simply an academic exercise; rather, its proponents saw sociology as a means to an end: the reduction of suffering, strife, and destructive behavior.

Historically, there have been two major approaches to the study of social problems (Rubington and Weinberg 2002). The first, the **social pathology approach,** was popular primarily during the nineteenth and early twentieth centuries. Social pathologists were largely concerned with individuals whose behavior they thought deviant. They assumed that this deviant behavior was to a large degree due to biological or psychological deficiencies. After World War I, the social pathology approach gave way to a second orientation toward the study of social problems—the **social disorganization approach.** This approach also focused on the deviant behavior of individuals. But somewhat more attention was given to the influence of the social environment in explaining deviance.

It is important to stress that these two approaches reflect a fundamental division in social science thinking that in one or another form continues even today; that is, to some the only social problems of true importance are those revolving around the behavior of individuals. Both the problems and their causes are reducible to the individual level. In contrast, those who would take a more "structural" approach tend to view the organization and operation of society itself (or particular institutions within society) as problematic. The system poses problems for those who live within it. The social pathology approach tends toward the first, whereas the social disorganization approach is somewhat more concerned with matters of societal structure.

The Social Pathology Approach

The approach to the identification of social problems taken by the scholar-reformers of the nineteenth and early twentieth centuries has earned them the title of *social pathologists.* Borrowing ideas from the biological sciences, these sociologists preferred to conceive of U.S. society as an organism. Like living organisms, said the social pathologists, society is subject to the dangers of disease and illness—in this case, such undesirable behavior as criminality and mental disorders. Social pathologists defined as social problems those behaviors which, in their judgment, ran contrary to the maintenance of a healthy society—a society that harbored little or no deviance. The social pathologists typically cast the blame for such behaviors onto the individuals involved. They explained phenomena like criminality largely in terms of such presumed personal weaknesses as character deficiency and psychological inadequacy. Many suggested or implied that criminals and other "undesirable" individuals were genetically or biologically inferior to "normal" people. While social pathologists were aware of the unsettling changes under way in the United States, they were less concerned with the effect of these changes on individuals than they were with the effect of "defective" people on U.S. society. As social pathologist Samuel Smith suggested, "defective" people created more "defective" people:

In social pathology the interrelation of the abnormal classes is one of the most impressive facts. Paupers often beget criminals; the offspring of criminals become insane; and to such an extent is the kinship of the defective, dependent, and delinquent classes exhibited, that some have gone so far as to hold that under all the various forms of social pathology there is a common ground in the nervous morbid condition of individuals. (Smith 1911:8–9; cf. Rubington and Weinberg 2002)

Although Smith and other social pathologists were concerned with what they called "bad environment," they believed that social problems primarily involved "weakness of the individual mind or will, the lack of development and the lack of self-control" among certain groups of people in society (Smith 1911:8–9; cf. Rubington and Weinberg 2002).

Carefully selected family histories were often used by pathologists to support their views. One such history, which was to become widely cited, concerned the Jukes family (Dugdale 1877). Max Jukes, a backwoodsman born in 1720, was described as an extremely ignorant man who married an equally ignorant woman. Allegedly, most of their descendants between 1740 and 1874 turned out to be criminals, paupers, or mentally troubled individuals.

Another family history concerned the Kallikaks (Goddard 1914). Martin Kallikak, a soldier in the Revolutionary War, married a young girl who was said to be feebleminded. Of their 480 descendants, all but 46 were criminals, prostitutes, "illegitimate" children, or other types of "deviates." In his second marriage, Kallikak took a wife who was said to come from "good stock." This marriage produced 496 descendants, almost all of whom were doctors, lawyers, and other well-regarded members of their communities. Such family histories were regarded as proof that "defective" people produced offspring whose behavior constituted the social problems of the day.

Modern-day scholars have harshly criticized such family studies as scientifically worthless (Chase 1977:138–75). For example, the studies are said to have reflected bias in the choice of families investigated and in the categorization of various family members as defective. The most common criticism is that social pathologists failed to address the impact of social, cultural, and economic influences on those whose behaviors were singled out for scrutiny.

Nonetheless, social pathologists used their findings as the basis of their proposals for solutions to social problems. According to these scholars, individuals whose behavior interfered with societal health had to be dealt with. Depending on the illness, the cure might entail education, counseling and moral guidance, disciplinary punishment and forced labor, or even involuntary confinement. Since the social pathologists blamed many social problems on the growing immigrant population, they frequently suggested denying various "defective" ethnic groups entry into the country. In fact, this idea influenced federal legislation; the Immigration Act of 1924 drastically reduced the legal quotas of Jews, Italians, Russians, Poles, Hungarians, Spaniards, Greeks, and other eastern and southern Europeans, who, along with people of color, were considered "racial defectives" (Chase 1977:289–91).

These early analysts of U.S. society clearly were making moral and political judgments about who and what were to be considered social problems. These judgments seem to have been based on social class biases and rigid personal moral codes that viewed anything other than native-born white, Protestant, middle-class attitudes and behavior as "bad." What we would today call *racism,* directed against southern and eastern Europeans and people of color, also appeared to guide their judgments. The social pathology approach was consistent with widespread public beliefs in *social Darwinism* (Hofstadter 1965). This body of ideas was based on the belief that people's social-class position was linked to their biological quality. Those living at the bottom levels of the socioeconomic scale were thought to be less fit for survival than the more affluent.

The approach taken by the social pathologists also implicitly embodied a belief that the United States—a rapidly growing, industrial, capitalist society—was basically benign and wholesome, as social orders go. Certainly, no major overhaul or transformation of U.S. institutions was thought to be needed. Instead, certain defective individuals were seen as the real social problems of the day. Though there were "bad environments," these were localized conditions of an exceptional nature, and they could easily be eradicated. The major reform efforts, then, were to focus on the troublesome populations. Thus, social pathologists defined social problems in such a way as to make them solvable within the boundaries of the prevailing social order.

The social pathology approach still lingers on, although only among a minority of social thinkers. Edward Banfield's work on the urban poor is perhaps the best example. In *The Unheavenly City* Banfield—a former White House adviser on urban affairs—explained the plight of poverty-stricken slum-dwellers in terms of their alleged personal deficiencies:

The lower class individual lives in the slum and sees little reason to complain. He does not care how dirty and dilapidated his housing is, either inside or out, nor does he mind the inadequacy of such public facilities as schools, parks and libraries; indeed, where such things exist he destroys them by acts of vandalism. Features that make the slum repellant to others actually please him. (Banfield 1970:62; see also Banfield 1974; Mead 1992)

Banfield, with such incorrect and misleading "facts," both promotes and panders to existing ignorance about the poor (see Massey and Denton [1998] for an alternative analysis). His ideas are embarrassing in their naïveté and reflect no contact with low-income people. Yet Banfield's proposed solutions to urban poverty are consistent with the social pathology approach. He suggested the involuntary sterilization of poor people and the removal of newly born infants from their parents for placement in more "normal" middle-class surroundings. Such solutions are virtually identical to those proposed to handle so-called defective European immigrant groups in the not-so-distant past. Unlike his predecessors, though, Banfield did not expect his ideas to be carried out, since few would see them as politically feasible.

The Social Disorganization Approach

After World War I a number of sociologists had grown dissatisfied with the biological analogy that social pathologists used to discuss the workings of U.S. society. They also began to feel that the deviant behaviors identified as social problems by the social pathologists were not totally the fault of those involved. Seeking an alternative way to explain such behaviors, sociologists moved toward a new approach involving the concept of *social disorganization.* As we shall see, this concept enabled scholars to pay more attention to the immediate environments within which problematic behaviors were found. As they focused on such environments, they discovered that "deviant" behavior was more likely to be expressed under some kinds of societal conditions than others.

This shift in scholarly focus was not only an advance toward a better understanding of deviance; it was also a step forward in the intellectual sophistication of the new discipline of sociology. During the post–World War I period, sociologists were increasingly concerned with establishing credibility as *scientists.* To obtain greater scholarly recognition and respect within the academic world, they needed to separate the study of social problems from reformist moralizing. A more objective approach was deemed desirable—one in which sociologists might consciously stand back and examine problems within the context of basic social laws and processes, just as other scientists objectively study physical phenomena. The concept of social disorganization was thought to provide a scientifically neutral and value-free approach to social phenomena. In focusing on the workings of society, rather than on presumed psychological or biological traits of individuals, the new approach was also more distinctly *sociological.* This fit well with the desire of sociological practitioners to clarify the boundaries of their new academic field.

▲ Normlessness and Social Disorganization

Those who emphasized the social disorganization approach rejected the social pathologists'

biological conception of society. Rather, they saw society as a complex organizational unit—a *social system*—whose parts were all interrelated and interdependent. The organization of society was facilitated by sets of *social norms,* or rules for appropriate behavior. Norms were dictated by and flowed from the dominant culture. If all members of society accepted and adjusted their behavior to these norms, that is, if they fulfilled their appropriate *social roles,* the social system would function smoothly. In that case, the social system would be in a state of equilibrium and would grow and progress by means of natural evolutionary tendencies.

Against this theoretical background, sociologists still had to explain why all was not well in the United States. Why did such phenomena as violence, property crime, and alcoholism exist, and why did U.S. society's growing urban centers particularly seem to be the scenes of these problems? Their answer was that certain sectors of the population were overwhelmed by the very difficult demands associated with change. Deviant behaviors were due to the existence of social disorganization within parts of the social system.

For example, the progressive movement of people from rural areas to crowded cities that accompanied industrialization meant that many migrants had to make great life adjustments. The norms that regulated interpersonal relationships and lifestyles in a small town were often inapplicable to fast-paced city living, much to the surprise of new migrants. Urban life often meant daily contact with strangers, new and stressful living conditions, and subservience to the impersonal demands of officialdom at work and in the realm of law. Past experiences provided little support and few guidelines for a quick adjustment to the city, it was suggested. In the absence of clearly defined norms, or with the failure of migrants to internalize existing norms readily, deviant behavior was likely to occur. Deviance was thus viewed as an indication of *normlessness,* a response to the confusion and disorientation associated with being caught up in change.

As a result of such ideas, sociologists began to examine the United States' urban scene and tried to relate its features to nonconforming behavior. A famous series of studies was carried out in Chicago (Faris and Dunham 1939; Shaw and McKay 1942). Urban sociologists noted that Chicago consisted of several ecological zones, each of which differed in terms of economic status, neighborhood stability, and the degree to which relations among residents were closely knit. They found that such phenomena as mental disorders and juvenile delinquency appeared most frequently in unstable areas of the city—neighborhoods that were in a constant state of flux because most of the inhabitants were new arrivals and transients. They concluded that neighborhood instability caused social disorganization—the absence of norms to guide people's behavior—and that, as a result, deviant behavior abounded.

Similar difficulties were said to confront new immigrants from abroad. Many people immigrating to the United States came from rural backgrounds and followed others of their national origins into ethnic enclaves in the nation's cities. Also, sociologists suggested, the native cultures of many immigrants were at variance with the dominant U.S. culture that had largely been fashioned by native-born white Anglo-Saxon Protestants. The demands of "Americanization" meant that many immigrants had to shed their traditional and taken-for-granted ways of living. Often they were caught between wanting to learn and adapt to the "American way" and wanting to cling to the ethnic identities and ancestral lifestyles with which they felt most comfortable. Many norms of behavior in the old country seemed out of place in the United States. Hence, sociologists saw the *culture conflict* arising out of immigration as yet another source of deviant behavior. Culture conflict was also thought to be a result of change processes taking place within U.S. society.

Perhaps the most influential study in this area was *The Polish Peasant in Europe and America,* by William I. Thomas and Florian Znaniecki (1927). Basing their findings primarily on an analysis of letters to and from Polish immigrants, these researchers documented the personal troubles many Polish people experienced in their dealings with the dominant culture. This society's emphasis on individualism, competition, and material gain, for example, ran counter to traditional Polish communal values. The stresses associated with adapting to a new culture and its norms frequently led to marital problems and family instability. Conflict between generations was common, as children came into contact with dominant cultural values at school. The Polish immigrant was finding it hard to become integrated into U.S. society, and deviant behavior was often the result.

▲ Merton's Anomie Theory

The concept of social disorganization also led some sociologists to look at the opportunity structure of the United States and its role in nurturing deviant behavior. The best example is Robert K. Merton's (1938; see also Durkheim 1965) influential *anomie theory.* The dominant culture, Merton observed, supports such goals as getting ahead and attaining material success. Yet the means for pursuing these cultural goals are not equally distributed within the population. People do not have the same family resources, access to educational opportunities, and important social connections. Some people are discriminated against because of their racial or ethnic backgrounds. Moreover, aside from race and class membership, not everyone has internalized the approved norms governing the pursuit of material success equally.

If an individual has the means to pursue cultural goals and has internalized the socially approved norms for doing so, deviance is unlikely. In Merton's terms, such a person will be a *conformist.* Otherwise, an individual may experience *anomie* (normlessness) and act in accordance with other norms of behavior.

Anomic individuals may respond to their situations in any one of four ways, according to Merton (1964:140–57). (1) In *innovation,* a person pursues cultural success goals by socially disapproved means. This category encompasses, among others, those who commit crimes against property—from purse-snatching to white-collar offenses by government and corporate executives. (2) *Ritualism* takes place when an individual slackens the pursuit of material success by lowering aspirations and rejecting the pressures to compete and get ahead, but still accepts the societal means. The low-level bureaucrat who has little hope for upward mobility and simply plods along year after year, enforcing the bureaucratic rules, exemplifies the ritualist. (3) In *retreatism* a person rejects and abandons both the goals and the means of pursuing them, simply withdrawing from the "game." The seriously mentally troubled, the chronic alcoholic, the drug addict, and the Skid Row vagrant are examples. (4) Finally, *rebellion* involves the attempt to change both the cultural goals and the means by which they are pursued. This category includes individuals who have committed themselves to radical revolutionary change in the values and structure of social life.

In sum, Merton and other social disorganization theorists blamed social problems on the uneven workings of the societal opportunity structure, industrialization, urbanization, and immigration, which, they said, carried disruptive consequences for some segments of the U.S. population. Changes taking place in society often rendered norms unclear, difficult to learn and adjust to, and even of questionable utility. Persons caught up in situations of social disorganization that led to deviance were problems. But the explanation for deviant behavior went beyond questions of individual character and personality deficiency. Instead, the major problem was social disorganization itself, which meant that parts of the social system were out of kilter and in need of some minor adjustment.

▲ Social Disorganization and the Ideal Society

Like the social pathologists, those sociologists who turned to the social disorganization approach made certain moral and political judgments about the nature of social problems in U.S. society. Despite claims to the contrary, their approach was not totally scientific and objective. Rather, it reflected a set of assumptions about the ideal state of society. These sociologists believed that society *should* be a well-organized social system characterized by relative homogeneity in cultural beliefs, individual conformity to the norms of the dominant culture, and the absence of behavior that deviated from accepted norms.

As we have seen, *the way in which a social problem is defined has a great deal to do with consideration of possible solutions.* For theorists of social disorganization, the solutions seemed to require a twofold strategy. First, the norms of the dominant culture had to be clarified and efforts had to be made to bring deviants in line with these norms. Second, means had to be found to slow down change or, at least, to reduce the harmful effects of change and to take some of the kinks out of the opportunity structure. In practical terms, the first strategy was probably easier. It was also consistent with the solutions to social problems that had already been advanced by the social pathologists.

Thus, the focus of those employing the social disorganization approach was largely on deviant individuals, although there was sympathetic consideration of the difficulties imposed by their immediate environments. Consequently, solutions to social problems were essentially viewed as matters of administration. Deviant behaviors could be taken care of by proper intervention, without reorganizing or transforming the entire social system. Some minor adjustments to some parts of the system were perhaps necessary, but for all practical purposes it would be much easier if the deviants were to do most of the adjusting.

The social disorganization approach continues to have a following among sociologists. During the 1960s, for example, Daniel Moynihan wrote a federal report that attempted to explain why African Americans continued to be disproportionately represented among the poor (most poor people in the United States were then, and are today, white) (see Rainwater and Yancey 1967). Moynihan argued that the era of slavery created a tradition of family instability and disorganization among African Americans. The African American family, he alleged, was still in a state of breakdown; "illegitimacy," crime, delinquency, unemployment, and welfare dependency were among the results of this breakdown. Only if the African American family were strengthened and stabilized would equality with whites be achieved.

Critics pointed out that Moynihan was talking about a minority of African American families, that he was ignoring the many poor and working-class families that functioned well even in the face of hardships, and that he was ignoring the continuing existence of white racism as a hindrance to African American advancement. Instead, Moynihan was subtly blaming African Americans for their historical and current position of social, economic, and political subordination. Consistent with the social disorganization approach, Moynihan's solution was for African Americans to become better adjusted to society and model their families after an ideal that many whites have failed to achieve.

Interestingly, ideas similar to those expressed by Moynihan and his critics reemerged in the 1990s in debates surrounding urban crime and welfare policy. Much of the debate focused upon the behavior of African American youth. While many politicians once again bewailed the alleged breakdown of the African American family, others assessed the situation quite differently:

Despite their overrepresentation among poor and "at risk" adolescents, the majority of black youths stay in school, avoid drugs and premarital pregnancy and childbearing, are employed or eager to work, are not involved in crime or other forms of self-destructive behavior, and grow up to lead normal and productive lives, in spite of serious social and economic disadvantages. (Taylor 1995:6)

Once again, critics have accused politicians of racial stereotyping and of "blaming the victims" of large-scale societal inequalities (Ryan 1976).

Both the social pathologists and the social disorganization theorists have tended to view various forms of deviant behavior as the principal focus for the study of social problems. Proponents of both approaches have, to one degree or another, failed to see the organization and operation of society itself as problematic. In reaction to this, an increasing number of sociologists have moved away from the more traditional approaches (Eitzen and Baca Zinn 2003; Soroka and Bryjak 1999). These sociologists contend that scholars should not simply accept the prevailing order as a given but should instead treat it as worthy of examination and critical review. Few would deny that the troublesome and troubled behavior of individuals continues to merit serious attention. But certain key features of society are at least as problematic as individual deviance.

In the next section we shall set forth the critical approach to social problems that is followed in the remaining chapters of this book. This approach focuses not only on problems associated with the behavior of individuals but also on societal features that are harming millions of people.

A Critical Approach to Social Problems

In identifying social problems, a sociologist's own values are inevitably brought into play. In particular, it is impossible to state that a specific phenomenon is a social problem without making implicit reference to an assumed ideal societal state. The social pathologists valued a "healthy" society, one in which the illness of socially undesirable behavior was absent. Proponents of social disorganization theory valued a smooth-working, culturally homogeneous social system in which people adapted their behavior to accepted norms (Mills 1943:165–80). All these theorists possessed a vision of the ways in which a society should work. It was against this vision that they determined who and what were to be identified as social problems.

Is it possible not to have a vision of the ideal society somewhere in your mind whenever you say X, Y, or Z is a social problem? No. In fact, all authors of social problems textbooks possess such a vision, even if they do not directly acknowledge the values leading them to choose certain problems for inclusion in their books (Horton 1966).

The *critical approach* taken in this book is likewise based on a vision or ideal against which the status quo is judged. This vision has informed and guided the identification of social problems that are addressed in the chapters that follow. By placing this vision in full view, we are making it possible for readers to determine whether the critical approach furthers understanding of the realities of contemporary life.

Our vision or ideal possesses the following characteristics:

1. Our relationship with poor, underdeveloped nations is nonexploitative and supportive of movements to secure basic human rights.

2. Members of society are able to participate actively in or influence directly those political and economic decisions that affect them.

3. Our government provides international leadership and sets a strong example for other nations in its approach to nuclear disarmament and the cooperative, nonviolent settlement of differences.

4. Resources are devoted to the preservation and conservation of the natural environment, and technological decisions take into account the well-being of future generations.

5. Work is freely available to all. It is organized cooperatively, with special attention to providing meaning, dignity, and satisfaction.

6. Gross differences in personal wealth and income are greatly reduced, so that the life chances of all members of U.S. society are relatively equal and all are able to share in the abundance of goods and services being produced.

7. Each individual has ready and continuing access to the education and training needed to develop his or her interests and capabilities to the fullest extent.

8. There is no personal and institutionalized discrimination against individuals on the basis of group membership (e.g., race, ethnicity, sex, age, or sexual orientation).

9. Adequate health care is understood to be a human right and thus is made accessible and affordable to all.

10. Special attention and support are freely given to troubled families and their members, including single-parent households. Moreover, the bases for violence and abuse within families of all types are absent.

11. Members of U.S. society are at peace with themselves and with one another. The vicarious rewards associated with such activities as crime, violence, and substance abuse have no attraction, and the social factors that provoke mental troubles and suicide are absent.

We might view our list of features as constituting something similar to what German sociologist Max Weber (1968) called an "ideal type." To Weber an ideal type is simply an abstract description of some form of social organization that is put together by a sociologist on the basis of examining examples of it. No particular case fits the description exactly, but the description contains the essential features that are to be found in reality. Although we have no examples of societies that in reality fit our vision or ideal, by considering our list of features as adding up to an "ideal type" we are in a position to see how closely U.S. society (or any other society for that matter) approximates it.

After this much has been said, it should be obvious that the approach to be taken in this text to social problems is necessarily "critical." Given the gap between our vision and the stark realities, we are forced to find fault with and judge severely the very structure and operation of U.S. society as a whole, as well as its relationships with poorer, weaker societies. We do not take our society as a given; we instead see it as problematic in and of itself. At the same time, we find ourselves looking with understanding— though not always with approval—at the variety of troubled and troublesome behaviors of

individuals who find themselves cast as deviants within the prevailing order.

Our vision of the ideal society is, obviously, rather utopian. No society in the world today comes close to matching its features, though we expect that some society will someday manage to do so. Our vision of the ideal society is simply a tool, a measuring rod that provides a set of criteria by which to assess the real-life status quo. In line with the critical approach, we adopt Mills's (1959) distinction between personal troubles and public issues. **Personal troubles** concern problems that people face as a result of their own individual behaviors. Individuals more or less can exert some control over their own behaviors to affect the troubles they encounter. Personal troubles, then, are not likely to be widespread and may be changed by altering how individuals behave.

Contrast this to **public issues,** which are typically widespread and pervasive, affecting large proportions of the population. Public issues are problems that derive from the way society is organized; as such, individuals have very little control over the circumstances that produce the problems they confront. Problems that are public issues are unlikely to change unless the way key features of social arrangements become altered.

Using Mills's distinction between personal problems and public issues, we examine four major categories of problems in this book. *Macro problems* encompass key features of how society is organized that are problematic. These include problems that can be categorized as societal problems, group problems, and institutional problems.

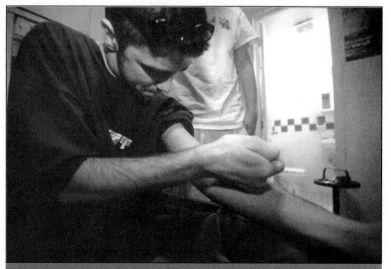

Micro problems—or problems involving individual behaviors— touch a wide range of people. Drug abuse, for example, has been of particular concern because of its effects. Here, a young drug abuser injects himself intravenously while a friend watches.

Micro problems include forms of individual behavior that may be harmful to others and/or to the person, which we categorize as individual problems.

Macro Problems

Certain very fundamental organizational or structural features of society stand in the way of our individual and collective development as human beings. That is, certain economic, political, social, and technological arrangements that have come to prevail are problematic because they harm millions of people. We categorize macro problems as societal problems, group problems, and institutional problems.

Societal problems involve arrangements of social structures that have a vast impact on how societies operate and the effect of this on the life chances of millions of people. These problems include population and underdevelopment; the concentration of political and economic power; militarism, war, and terrorism; and environmental abuse. Social arrangements and relations also produce **group problems.** These are social problems that affect the life chances of millions of people based on their ascribed statuses, particularly class and poverty, racial and ethnic heritages, gender, sexual orientation, and age. **Institutional problems** derive from the way that social institutions are arranged to address the basic needs of social survival. These arrangements often benefit some members of society more than others, or unintentionally may produce unequal opportunities for people. We will examine institutional problems within education, the structure of work, family, and health care.

Because macro problems are rooted in societal organization and group relationships, their reduction or elimination may well require an eventual transformation of the prevailing order. Macro problems will not yield to minor technical or administrative reforms. They can be dealt with only if men and women work consciously and collectively to bring about change. To do so, people must analyze, plan, and seek to reorganize society with a vision in mind. The kind of transformation our own vision suggests cannot come about by wishful thinking. Nor is it likely to happen if we simply back away and trustingly leave our future in the hands of societal elites and their appointed "experts." We must all be involved in the solution of macro problems.

Micro Problems

Although our critical approach emphasizes the harmful effects of key features of society, we cannot ignore the troublesome and troubled behavior of individual societal members. Millions of people in the United States are engaging in behavior that adversely affects other people and/or is at times self-destructive. Though theories on the causation of such behavior abound, we have a great deal to learn about criminal behavior, mental illness, and substance abuse.

We shall refer to these micro-level social problems as **individual problems.** The term *micro* is not used to belittle the significance of this behavior. Rather, it simply underscores the difference between problems largely involving the macro order—the structure of society—and those arising from the actions of individuals, or the micro order. In the traditional approaches to social problems, the behaviors we consider micro problems were seen as forms of *deviant behavior.* We wish to avoid this term, for it carries unnecessarily negative connotations. Those whose behavior is troubled or troublesome can in many instances be considered to be acting normally, given the life situations with which they may be faced.

Moreover, the concept of deviance implies that people are being judged unacceptable and that they should be made to adjust to society and its norms. Yet the behavior in question could be viewed in quite a different manner. In ways we are still seeking to fully understand, some forms of deviance may be caused by the organization of society and its institutions. It is senseless to ask people to adjust or conform to societal conditions that may be harming them. The more logical solution is to alter these conditions.

Analysis of the relationship between features of society at the macro level and people's behavior at the individual level has come to be viewed as a central challenge facing sociologists (Ritzer and Goodman 2003). Our ability to fathom many micro problems may well await progress on this front by contemporary theorists of society.

The Life Cycle of Social Problems

For decades sociologists have claimed that social problems have a natural history or *life cycle*. As early as the 1940s, attempts were made to specify the general stages through which problems were believed to go. One such early attempt, which still influences contemporary thinking on the matter, was developed by Richard Fuller and Richard Myers (1941). According to this approach, the cycle begins when people become aware of some objective situation that, in their estimation, is problematic. They are not quite sure what to do about it, and they begin to communicate their concern to others. What often follows is public debate over the problem, with conflicting ideas put forth as to why the situation exists and what is to be done. In the course of public debate, the various groups whose interests are affected by the problem and/or its solution make their positions known. Finally, we come to the stage of reforms. Official policies for dealing with the problem, which were hammered out through debate and influenced by the jockeying of various interest groups, are finally implemented.

Not too long ago two sociologists—Robert Ross and Graham Staines—attempted to update and extend earlier efforts to specify problem life cycles. Many of their ideas are supportive of our

critical approach. According to these sociologists, the following process takes place during the career of a social problem:

Private or interest group recognition of the social problem; political recognition of the problem as an appropriate issue for public discussion; public debate and social conflict about the causes of the problem; a set of political outcomes of this sequence. (Ross and Staines 1972:18)

Defining a Social Problem

Ross and Staines (1972) noted that an individual or group defines a given phenomenon as problematic in terms of the person's or group's *ideology* or sense of what the ideal state of affairs should be (see also Hilgartner and Bosk 1988). (This is much like what we have been calling a vision against which objective reality can be compared.) They suggested that social problems are defined largely in terms of an individual's or group's perceived self-interest. Thus, the initial definition of a social problem can be a highly political event, particularly when opposing interests get involved.

Take, for example, the denial of voting rights that until fairly recently confronted many African American citizens in the southern and border states. Unrealistic qualifications were often set up to prevent African Americans and other people of color from voting, and persons who pushed too hard to exercise the franchise were frequently threatened or harmed. The civil rights movement of the 1950s and 1960s denounced the discrepancy between African American voter participation and the rights granted to all citizens under the Constitution. As members of the civil rights movement saw it, African Americans should be voting and electing political representatives who would respond to their interests. Many whites, on the other hand, viewed African American involvement in politics as an erosion of their monopoly over political affairs. Opposing interests were thus involved in the definition of racism in politics as a social problem.

Transformation into a Public Issue

The next stage in the sequence involves the transformation of a problem into what Ross and Staines (1972) call a *public issue*. In their opinion, this transformation will take place only if the privately recognized problem is seen as publicly important and legitimate for public consideration. A number of different "social actors" are typically involved as a problem becomes an issue. Coverage by the mass media is critical in terms of making a problem visible and in determining its importance and legitimacy.

The changes demanded by the civil rights movement required that racism in politics be seen as a public issue. Hence, large-scale demonstrations were organized in the early 1960s—demonstrations that drew thousands of African Americans, along with other people of color and sympathetic whites. The demonstrations were covered in the national news media, and they were considered even more newsworthy because of the violent responses they frequently met. Television viewers saw peaceful sign-carrying marchers being beaten with police batons, shocked by cattle prods, set upon by dogs, battered by the spray from high-pressure hoses, and trampled by horses. Other violent events during the early 1960s, including the murders of African American and white civil rights workers and deaths of children and adults resulting from the bombing of African American churches, simply underscored the issue of racism in politics.

Ross and Staines see the reaction (or even nonreaction) of public officials as an element in the equation. Sometimes there is conflict between media representatives and public officials over whether a given problem deserves the status of public issue. Again, this may be a matter of perceived self-interest, as officials can attempt to downplay the importance of problems and provide their own interpretation of events. For example, many southern politicians, who had been elected with white votes, saw civil rights as nothing to get excited about. In their view, a handful of "outside agitators," racemongers, and riffraff who did not understand or appreciate the "southern way" were stirring up trouble. While the media brought racism in politics and white resistance to change into the limelight, many southern officials tried to deny there was any issue deserving such concern.

Debating Causes and Solutions

Once a privately recognized social problem becomes a public issue, according to Ross and Staines, debate about its causes begins. This stage is extremely important, for perceived causes have a definite relationship to the types of solutions that are considered. Ross and Staines distinguish between two different causal interpretations commonly brought to bear on social problems. On the one hand, a problem may be given a *systemic attribution;* that is, the system itself is problematic and/or generates difficulties for individuals. Our critical approach leans toward this category. On the other hand, a problem may simply be blamed on the people involved; it is their deficiency, their irresponsibility that "causes" the social problem. This second causal interpretation is termed *personal attribution.* Earlier we saw how the social pathology approach and, to a lesser extent, the social disorganization approach tend to lead in such a direction.

For participants in and supporters of the civil rights movement, the lack of African American participation in elections was a result of a well-organized system of racist exclusion and denial of voting opportunities. The outcome was African American political powerlessness and the election of white candidates who served only white interests. Engaging in systemic attribution, the civil rights movement demanded that this system be changed and that African Americans' efforts to exercise the franchise be protected. Many southern officials, on the other hand, claimed that African Americans could vote if they were "qualified," but that most were not really interested in doing so. If the "outside agitators" and "liberal media" had not come in to stir up trouble, there would be no problem. Here the causal interpretation of personal attribution was being employed; those demonstrating and demanding change were the *real* problem, not the "southern way."

Different groups find either systemic or personal attribution in line with their perceived self-interest. Ross and Staines observe that public officials often prefer to blame the people facing problems for their troubles, rather than to encourage a belief that the prevailing order is itself somehow problematic and deserving of transformation. It seems likely that all dominant groups will tend to favor personal attribution, for they manage, control, and profit from the system that could be called into question.

After the opposing groups make public their interpretation of the causes, serious debate begins. As Ross and Staines put it: "Since causal diagnoses of social problems are reached by different people in different political situations, conflict between alternative patterns of attribution becomes inevitable" (Ross and Staines 1972:32). The result is a complex bargaining process between authorities and the "partisans" of the social problem that eventually results in a compromise between the groups. The political outcome is often in the form of legislation or administrative changes through which the problem, as it has come to be defined, is addressed.

In the case of the demands of the civil rights movement, the compromise was debated and reached at the national level. The Voting Rights Act of 1965 outlawed the formal procedures used by many southern states to block African American voter participation, and the federal government provided observers at polling places to check on overt efforts to intimidate voters. Though the law could not address the more informal means by which whites attempted to discourage African Americans from voting, it did put the force of national policy behind those who wanted to enter the polling booth. Whites still dominate the political scene in the southern and border states, except in communities in which African Americans predominate. And Congress found enough rights violations occurring to justify expanding the protections provided by the Voting Rights Act in 1970, 1975, and 1982. Nonetheless, the civil rights movement won something—even if it was only a slow acquiescence to the presence of African Americans in the voting booth. Southern political leaders have to take African American votes into account and to curry African American support by avoiding or being very careful in their exploitation of racial issues, long a major theme in southern politics.

The Role of Power

The message implicit in Ross and Staines's discussion is that *power* determines how problems are ultimately defined and, thus, what solutions are likely to be considered and implemented. By *power* sociologists usually mean the probability that individuals or groups can implement their desires even though they may be resisted. Groups have different self-interests to advance or protect, and those that cannot mobilize power (even if only to disrupt the status quo) are likely to lose out to those whose dominance is well established.

People or groups who possess power are in the best position to

1. Determine whether a privately recognized problem will be permitted to become a public issue,

2. Advance their self-interested version of the sources or causes of a problem,

3. Control the ways in which a given problem will come to be defined, and

4. Determine what, if anything, will be done to solve the problem.

The power of the civil rights movement lay in its ability to mobilize public opinion against racism in politics, thus pressuring government officials to take steps against denial of constitutional rights for people of color.

The life cycle of social problems and, especially, the role of power have direct implications for the critical approach. The macro problems discussed in this book can be reduced or eliminated. But attempts to do so are a threat to the perceived self-interests of those who benefit from the ways in which U.S. society is now organized. Thus, those who derive power and special privilege from maintaining the status quo will prefer to keep macro problems from becoming public issues. If the problems do become issues, dominant groups will actively push for solutions that are consistent with their self-interests. To the degree to which they are successful either nothing will change or those changes that are made will be easily incorporated into the prevailing order.

Take, for example, the problem of economic inequality and poverty (addressed in Chapter 6), according to U.S. Census data, about a fifth of the U.S. population is poor or near-poor, while a small minority lives in almost unimaginable affluence. Since the early 1980s, the economic gap between U.S. society's affluent and its poor has noticeably grown; indeed, the percentage share of family income and wealth held by the nation's poorest 20 percent of families has actually diminished. Consequently, homelessness, hunger, and health problems among poor people have increased. The sharp reduction of economic inequality and improvement in the situation of the poverty-stricken would require a drastic shift in the ways in which income and wealth are distributed in the United States, with the most affluent giving up much of their economic advantage.

Certainly the affluent prefer to keep the problem of economic inequality and poverty from becoming a public issue; they are not about to engage in efforts to impress this problem upon the public, nor are they likely to champion a

Those in power tend to blame social problems on the people involved. Homeless persons, such as this man shown sleeping on the streets of New York, are often portrayed as, by definition, personally responsible to their plight, thus avoiding the question of why the supply of affordable housing for low-income people is so inadequate that individuals and whole families are living in the nation's streets.

movement for redistribution of income and wealth. Such a position would not be in their self-interest. The affluent will, however, throw their support toward definitions of and "solutions" to the situation of the poor that do not make serious inroads on their own economic privilege.

A good example of this occurred during the mid-1990s. Growing numbers of people were living below the federal poverty line. This trend was accompanied by growth in the nation's welfare rolls, as many poor people who were eligible had little choice but to apply for income assistance (Rank 1995). Political elites from both major parties worked together to control the way in which this problem would be defined, and thus the solutions that would logically follow. Thus the problem, as ultimately defined for the U.S. citizenry by state governors, members of the U.S. Congress, and the president (offices of and recipients of campaign contributions from the affluent), was not economic inequality and poverty. Instead, the problem was said to be the poor themselves. Poor people were condemned for "welfare dependency" and for their alleged failure to work hard to attain economic self-sufficiency and rise out of poverty (Gordon 1994; Piven 1995).

Playing upon negative stereotypes about and prejudices against poor people, legislative debate and proposals at both the state and the federal level focused almost entirely on the need for "welfare reform." As one might expect, this reform did not call for drastic increases in benefits so that the incomes of those receiving welfare might be brought up near the federal poverty line. Rather, welfare reform typically meant sharply restricting the terms, conditions, and time periods under which poverty-stricken individuals and families would be allowed to receive assistance (Norris and Thompson 1995).

Through such initiatives, political elites successfully kept the problem of economic inequality and poverty from becoming a public issue. Instead, public attention was diverted to debates over the best measures to discourage the alleged lack of work effort on the part of the poor. A systemic problem—economic inequality and poverty—was transformed into one of personal attribution, as welfare recipients' character became the problem to be solved. Meanwhile, the growing economic advantage of the affluent remained unaddressed and untouched.

The preceding example implicitly suggests that it *is* in the interests of dominant groups to permit micro problems to enter public awareness and to be seen as the *real* problems of the day. Micro problems are easily blamed on the traits of individuals rather than on the character of the system—in other words, they lend themselves to personal attribution. Each year resources are earmarked for handling micro problems as economic, political, and social elites throw their support behind crime control and campaigns against substance abuse, among other programs. The point is that these social problems are widely considered amenable to administrative and technical adjustments—more research, more tax money, more experimental programs, and more surveillance and control of people. Since none of these strategies threatens the existing order from which dominant groups draw benefits, societal elites obviously see it as better for the public to focus on "deviance" when they reflect on problems of U.S. society. In this way public attention is diverted from the societal arrangements that are harmful and that may even contribute to the generation of the "deviant" behavior.

Methods of Research

To learn more about social problems—their nature, extent, effects, and causes—social scientists conduct research using different methods. Unlike those people who lay claim to knowledge of conditions or groups with which they have had little or no contact, sociologists and other social scientists doggedly go after facts. Such researchers develop a healthy skepticism toward everyday taken-for-granted ideas about society and its members. They prefer to base statements on the best available evidence gained through systematic, objective inquiry. In sharing descriptions of their work with others, including the general public, social scientists open both their methods and findings to critical scrutiny. Much of this text revolves around information elicited by sociologists and other social scientists, used in this case to shed as much light as possible on serious social problems.

Three methods of research are of interest. First, there is **survey research,** wherein a carefully selected sample of individuals is asked to respond to a set of questions. Second, there is **field research,** which involves direct contact with and observation of people whose behavior and thinking are the subject of study. Third, there is **experimental research,** wherein a comparison is made between the behavior of two (or perhaps more) groups, each of which is subjected to different conditions. In this section we use examples to illustrate each of these methods. The examples are from research on the topic of poverty, a topic taken up in more detail in Chapter 6.

Survey Research

The survey research method can be used to gather descriptive information about people's characteristics, including their attitudes and behaviors. Public opinion polls are a case in point. But survey research can be undertaken for reasons that go beyond a desire for description. Sociologists and other social scientists often conduct surveys to gain information that would shed light on the adequacy of a particular theory or to help develop new theories. In either case survey research commonly requires that the researcher choose a representative sample of the population about which he or she wishes to generalize.

Typically a survey is a "onetime" exercise. That is, those included in the sample are asked

Researchers have used various methods to understand some of the factors responsible for widespread poverty in the United States. Surveys have found that one of the most common reasons families fall into poverty is job loss by the principal wage earner, a situation that befell the woman pictured here.

to respond to a set of questions on a onetime basis. If a researcher is particularly interested in changes taking place among people over a period of time, it may be preferable to conduct a type of survey known as a "panel study." Here the people in the original representative sample are questioned more than once, that is, at periodic time intervals. Panel studies are more difficult to administer and more expensive to conduct than onetime surveys, but they can provide very useful information. Our example of survey research is a panel study.

In 1968 researchers at the University of Michigan Survey Research Center began the Panel Study of Income Dynamics. Each year 5,000 U.S. families, chosen to serve as a representative sample, provide information about their employment and economic circumstances as well as other events in their lives. Even as family members leave the household (e.g., divorced spouses or grown children) they remain on the panel of people surveyed. Hence it has been possible to document important changes in U.S. families in recent years.

In his book *Years of Poverty, Years of Plenty,* researcher Greg Duncan (1984) reported on a selection of findings for the years 1969–1978. In this case Duncan was interested in those families that experienced poverty. Many people believe that "the poor" are a homogeneous and stable group whose membership is pretty much the same from year to year. It is also common to find people believing that most poor people live in poverty generation after generation. Using the survey research method, and employing a panel study for its advantages in studying change in people's lives, Duncan proved the common wisdom was wrong.

His work revealed that there is a very high degree of turnover—people moving in or out of poverty—from year to year. Most poverty-stricken people are what Duncan calls the "temporarily poor." Two-thirds of those living in families with incomes under the government-defined poverty line in any given year were still poor the following year, meaning a full one-third were not.

Duncan defined as "persistently poor" individuals who were poor for at least 8 of the 10 years for which he was examining data. Only one-third of the poor fell into this category, or some 3 percent of the U.S. population. Clearly, relatively few people experience generations of poverty.

Moreover, the research revealed that far more members of U.S. society have experience with poverty than anyone previously had realized. Annual statistics from the U.S. Census portrayed poverty rates in the 1969–1978 period typically in the 11–12 percent range, slightly below where it has been in recent years. But Duncan found that fully a quarter of the U.S. population lived in poor families in one or more years over that time period. The census data had simply masked the true extent to which people in the United States must deal with economic deprivation.

Nor was Duncan able to find any particular characteristic that distinguished the vast majority of poor, who have relatively brief contact with poverty, from everyone else. In his words:

Few people are immune to such events as personal illness, adverse local or national economic conditions, or the death or departure of a spouse; and for a substantial proportion, these events can precipitate a year or two of severe hardship. (Duncan 1984:61)

This opening up of new facts about poverty, through the survey research method, obviously provides badly needed guidance to policymakers concerned with attending to the needs of both the temporarily and persistently poor. Unfortunately, political elites (like many other people) often choose to ignore facts that run counter to their priorities or preferred ways of viewing problems, meaning that sociological research findings do not necessarily influence decisions that they make.

Field Research

There are times when the direct observation of people is the best (and perhaps the only) route to obtaining information about their thinking and behavior. Field research may vary in the degree to which one must actually get involved with those being studied. At one extreme, the researcher may play the role of a nonparticipant observer, simply recording what is going on and attempting to make sense of it. At another extreme, the researcher may play the role of participant observer, being directly immersed in the activities of those whose thinking and behavior are to be understood. In some cases it may be possible and desirable for someone to participate without his or her role as a researcher being known, so as to avoid that having an impact on the behavior observed. But often people do not mind knowing they are of interest to researchers and can be of great assistance in understanding the unfamiliar.

One of the most important decisions a field researcher must make is the choice of research site. Whereas survey researchers can choose individuals to serve as research subjects on the basis of certain statistical procedures and assumptions about their representing a larger population, often field researchers face much more limited degrees of freedom. Generalizability of research findings may be an issue, at least until other researchers (perhaps even using other research methods) come up with confirming data.

On the other hand, the field research may be aimed at obtaining information about a group or organization that is for some reason unique. This situation raises an issue that is common to most field research. Would a different researcher have been likely to come up with the same or similar findings? This issue arises because of the amount of judgment left in the hands of field researchers in determining what will be considered data and how data will be interpreted.

Field research, like survey research, may be a way of gaining a set of descriptive information about people. It may also be oriented toward assessing an existing theory or producing a new one. In the example of field research we consider here, what began as an exploratory effort with descriptive goals produced findings with important theoretical implications. When this occurs, no doubt the researchers find the tremendous amount of labor and personal sacrifice that can go into spending time "in the field" to have been very worthwhile.

Between 1998 and 2000 researcher Barbara Ehrenreich (2001) conducted participant observation among low-wage workers, taking jobs such as hotel housekeeper in Florida, nursing home aide in Maine, and an "associate" at Wal-Mart in Minnesota. Her findings, reported in *Nickel and Dimed: On (Not) Getting By in America,* illustrated in concrete terms the seeming contradiction of the "working poor" that other research could not: What is it like to work for minimum or very low wages? How does one pay rent and buy food on such meager wages? What happens when one becomes ill (often from the conditions of one's job) but has no health insurance? Why can't the poor simply leave these jobs if they pay so poorly and do better?

The purpose of Ehrenreich's field research was to record and interpret the everyday lives of low-wage workers, a group about which social scientists felt they knew very little. Her research was to be exploratory; she did not start out with the goal of assessing some theory about low-wage workers. Rather she began with a conversation as a journalist with her editor at *Harper's Magazine* at a fairly lavish lunch during which she was discussing potential topics for stories. She mused about how one possibly managed to live on the low wages that were so common in the United States, and she wondered how welfare recipients who lost their benefits under welfare reform were going to survive on such poor wages, saying, "Someone ought to . . . go out there and try it for themselves" (Ehrenreich 2001:1). She wanted to try to understand their lives in their terms, from their point of view.

Ehrenreich left behind her relatively comfortable middle-class life and began the task of struggling to find a place she could afford to live and a job in each place she moved. She lived and worked as those in low-wage jobs do, without resorting to her previous financial resources and without telling people around her who she really was or what she was doing. To them, she was simply doing what they always do: struggling to make ends meet day after day.

As weeks and months went by, Ehrenreich worked at wearying and low-paying dead-end jobs, meeting other hardworking but poor people in each job setting. Slowly she made friends and built close personal relationships. All along she knew that she was an outsider: She knew that when her research was done she had a more comfortable life to which to return; not so the many people with whom she had worked and come to know.

At the time that Ehrenreich was conducting her field research, a number of social scientists were debating the problem of poverty and its relationship to welfare reform and low-wage work. Does welfare encourage the poor to be lazy and not value hard work? Does welfare reform that sharply reduces the amount of time people may remain on public assistance instead motivate the poor to get jobs and thus stimulate their development of the work ethic that the middle class presumably already embraced? The so-called culture of poverty theory argued that low-income people had a unique set of cultural values that set them apart from middle-class people and that in effect kept them poor. For example, it was suggested that low-income people have different values pertaining to work and that this gets in the way of economic success.

Ehrenreich's in-depth, day-in-and-day-out experiences as a low-wage worker herself and her contact with other low-wage workers produced unique and invaluable data bearing on the culture of poverty theory. Unlike culture of poverty theorists (and other outsiders), she had firsthand knowledge of how these workers viewed work and their values surrounding it.

Briefly, she found that low-wage workers shared the values of the larger society pertaining to work. They saw work as important, both as a source of economic gain and security and as a source of self-identity and self-respect. The problem was that the type of work available to them offered very little in these areas. In taking any jobs they were able to find, they struggled to subsist, often having to choose between eating a meal or paying some other pressing expense. What might appear to an outsider as a lazy or poor choice to stay with a low-paying job instead of leaving it for a better-paying one was actually the result of factors over which people had little control; some, for example, did not have transportation to get to the better job. Others lacked sufficient education or skills. Ehrenreich's subjects clearly revealed they did not possess a unique set of cultural values with regard to work that kept them poor. She concluded that the problem of poverty was not one of a failure of the poor to value the work ethic: "You don't need a degree in economics to see that wages are too low and rents too high" (Ehrenreich 2001:199).

While Ehrenreich's work, like many other pieces of field research, produced findings about which one must be cautious in making wide generalizations, these findings illustrate the pain often accompanying poverty. This could be readily missed or simply assumed not to exist were our knowledge of poor people to be informed by less intensive methods of research.

Experimental Research

Sociologists and other social scientists at times have used experimental studies, similar in principle to experiments in the natural sciences, to study human beings. Such research has most commonly been conducted in laboratory settings and involved a limited number of individuals or small groups of people as subjects. Less common, though of interest to us here, are experiments conducted in "natural" (that is, nonlaboratory) settings.

Experimental research involves, in its simplest form, the creation of two groups of participants. The first group, known as the "experimental group," is treated to carefully controlled conditions designed by the researcher. He or she is interested in the impact of these conditions on the thinking and/or behavior of members of the experimental group.

The second group, known as the "control group," is purposely *not* exposed to the researcher-designed conditions, which are commonly called the "experimental treatment." Nonetheless, the control group's members' thinking and/or behavior are also monitored. This is because the researcher wants to be sure what happens in the experimental group is due to the conditions he or she introduced and probably would not have occurred otherwise. The control group is thus very important to making that determination.

In short, those doing experimental research seek to ensure that the conditions introduced, and not some other factor or "variable," account for what is observed in the experimental group. Hence it is very important that characteristics of the members of both experimental and control groups not differ in any important way. By randomly assigning individuals to one or the other group, it is hoped that such differences will be minimized.

Typically, experimental research is conducted with some kind of theory in mind, which guides researchers' choice of the conditions to impose on the experimental group. This is the case whether the research is taking place in the laboratory or in a natural setting. Exploratory goals are possible but generally are limited by the theory of interest to the researcher.

Laboratory experiments are most frequently employed by researchers who need to maximize their hold over the conditions to which both experimental and control groups are exposed. Precision may thus be attained, but observations made in a laboratory setting, involving a relatively small number of people, may be open to questions about the "real-life" applicability of the findings. This is somewhat similar to the

issue of generalizability often faced by those conducting field research.

On the other hand, conducting experimental research in nonlaboratory or natural settings may sacrifice the quest for precision laboratory researchers enjoy. Moreover, there may be practical, administrative, financial, or ethical reasons why research in a natural setting cannot be done. For such reasons, this type of research is less common than that conducted in the laboratory.

Probably the most common type of experimental research in a natural setting involves the attempt to assess the impact or effectiveness of government programs. In the example presented here, data were gathered to help policymakers project the possible effects of introducing a guaranteed minimum income for people living in poverty. Both the experimental findings and their interpretation proved to be quite controversial, as different groups jockeyed to use this research to support their own views on how poverty should be addressed.

In the 1960s federal government officials declared a "war on poverty." It was hoped that by providing more services to low-income people—from early childhood education, to job-training programs, to legal aid—poverty could be defeated. This "service approach," which came to characterize much of the war on poverty, was questioned by critics who saw poverty as a straightforwardly economic matter. They favored an "income approach" that would put more money, not simply services, in the hands of the poor. They argued that all families should be guaranteed a minimum income that would help them avoid poverty.

At that time little was known about the possible effects of an income approach, particularly its effects on the incentive of people to work and on marital stability. To investigate such matters the federal government began sponsorship of a series of experiments in the late 1960s. The largest, known as the Seattle-Denver Income Maintenance Experiment (SIME/DIME), began in 1970 and continued for almost a decade

(U.S. Department of Health and Human Services 1983).

Like the other experiments in the series, SIME/DIME involved a particular form of guaranteed income: the negative income tax, or NIT. The NIT has two important features. First is the "maximum benefit"—the annual amount of money a family is guaranteed if it has no other source of income. Second is the "benefit reduction rate," or tax rate at which the maximum benefit is reduced in response to a family's employment earnings. At a certain point, when the employment earnings become high enough, the tax rate reduces the cash benefit from the program to zero.

SIME/DIME involved almost 5,000 low-income families residing in Denver and Seattle. These families were randomly assigned to experimental and control groups. In the experimental group, families were exposed to one or another of 11 maximum benefit and tax rates, as the researchers were interested in comparing the impacts of different versions of an NIT. The control group was not subject to NIT treatment but simply received income from any employment opportunities and/or government programs to which its members had access. Families in both experimental and control groups were periodically interviewed on a wide variety of matters it was thought could be affected by an NIT. These interviews took place during and immediately after the experiment.

A principal focus of the researchers was on work effort. It was theorized that a guaranteed income would be likely to reduce work effort, but there was only speculation as to how much. The results of the experiment did reveal some reduction, varying by participants' role in the family, type of NIT benefit/tax rate, and other factors. For example, husbands in families receiving NIT treatment worked fewer hours annually than husbands in the control group. Yet controversy has arisen over how to interpret this statistical finding. It would seem that few persons who were employed left their jobs in response to the experimental treatment. Rather, experimental group husbands who became unemployed (defined as out of work but looking for a job) took more time to find work than did control group husbands. Whereas some read this as a sign of lower incentive to work, others argued it was rational behavior given the very undesirable jobs and negative job experiences persons forced to take low-wage positions routinely faced.

A second focus of the researchers was on marital stability. Critics of welfare in the United States have long argued that its bureaucratic regulations help to break up intact families. At the time of this research, half of all states refused welfare benefits to homes with children in which both parents were present. Critics suggest this often forces desperate fathers to abandon their wives and children in return for their getting welfare assistance. Because the NIT experiment made income available to intact low-income families as well as single-parent families, researchers anticipated it would be a stabilizing force for families.

Did the NIT treatment help to keep families from breaking up? The answer is no. Marriages ended more frequently for couples in the experimental group than in the control group. Again, there was variation depending on the NIT plan to which the subjects were exposed and other factors. Still, controversy arose over these findings. Did families break up that never should have? Does an income guarantee provide women with economic security that allows escape from an unhappy marriage? Is marital dissolution for many a positive event as opposed to, by definition, a negative one?

The researchers made their findings public, subjecting both the findings and the research methods that led to them to critical scrutiny. They were scrupulous in underscoring the fact that the SIME/DIME sample is nationally unrepresentative and that their findings, although suggestive, cannot simply be extrapolated to a permanent national NIT program. The researchers also acknowledged the difficulty of interpreting findings such as those we have looked at here. In stark contrast, politicians and others with relatively little sympathy for the plight of poor people proved uninterested in the researchers' wise cautions (Neubeck and Roach 1981). To them the message of the findings was that an NIT broke up families and fostered laziness. The cautions and ambiguity surrounding the findings were thus put to political use to derail further consideration of an "income approach" to reduce the economic distress of poor people. But the uses to which findings from this particular research were put notwithstanding, experiments in natural settings offer another method for studying how people deal with their environment and its problems.

Summary

In this introduction we have looked at various approaches to the study of social problems and have set forth the approach that will be followed in this text. We began with an overview of the two approaches that have dominated the field. The *social pathology approach* saw deviant behavior as the major social problem and blamed this behavior on biological and psychological deficiencies of the people involved. The *social disorganization approach,* on the other hand, focused on disruptions in social life as the cause of social problems. Like the social pathology approach, this approach tends to focus on deviant behavior of individuals.

The *critical approach* to social problems looks mainly at problems in the structure and organization of society. Sociologists using the critical approach adopt Mills's distinction between *personal troubles* and *public issues*. Personal troubles affect relatively few people and result from behaviors over which individuals may exert some control. In contrast, public issues are widespread and come from the way society is organized.

Like the social pathology and social disorganization approaches, the critical approach identifies social problems on the basis of moral and political judgments. Such judgments are inevitable when deeming something to be a "problem." The judgments behind our critical approach are set forth within the context of our ideal vision of or hope for society.

Macro problems result from organizational features of society that do harm to millions of people. These include societal problems that derive from large-scale social arrangements, group problems that affect people because of their ascribed statuses, and institutional problems resulting from the way social institutions are structured to address basic social needs. In contrast, *micro* or *individual problems* involve people's behaviors that are self-harmful or have an adverse impact on others. The reduction or elimination of macro problems may well require an eventual transformation of the ways in which society is organized.

The *life cycle* or career of a social problem is a political process in which power plays a decisive role. As problems enter public awareness, those who benefit from the maintenance of the status quo have a stake in ensuring that the accepted causes and solutions do not infringe upon their perceived self-interest. In practical terms, this means that macro problems—even when they somehow are brought into public awareness—may fail to be "solved." Since preferred solutions tend to be those that do not disrupt the prevailing order, macro problems tend to remain with us.

The degree to which a solution to a macro problem can be incorporated into the prevailing order will affect what is done about it. At the same time, dominant groups have no real reason to discourage public awareness and concern with micro problems involving individuals, since attacks on these problems can more easily be accommodated without appreciably altering the status quo.

Sociologists and other social scientists, in seeking to learn more about social problems, conduct research using different methods. Surveys, field research, and experiments in natural settings provide means for objective, systematic inquiry. The findings may be of theoretical importance and at times become politically controversial.

Key Terms

Critical approach 4
Experimental research 19
Field research 19
Group problems 13
Individual problems 13
Institutional problems 13

Personal troubles 12
Public issues 12
Social disorganization approach 4
Social pathology approach 4
Societal problems 13
Survey research 19

Discussion Questions

1. What is the most serious social problem facing us today? Discuss the criteria you used to choose this problem.

2. Are people who are poor, or mentally troubled, or involved in heavy drug use, "normal"? What assumptions or set of values does your answer to this question reflect?

3. Edward Banfield blames the plight of U.S. Society's urban slum-dwellers on their attitudes and behavior—a case of personal attribution. What factors would one look to if trying to explain the slum-dwellers' plight in terms of systemic attribution?

4. Look at the front page of today's newspaper. What "social problems" are reported? Take one problem and discuss alternative solutions to it, considering the individual or group self-interests the various solutions would affect.

5. The mass media, according to Ross and Staines, play a major role in rendering problems into public issues. What does this suggest about the significance of the attitudes and values of those who own or work for the mass media?

6. It is not necessary that you share the same vision of the ideal society that the authors set forth. Where do you disagree? What elements or characteristics of the ideal society would you eliminate or add? Why?

Suggested Readings

Babbie, Earl. *The Practice of Social Research*. 9th ed. (Belmont, CA: Wadsworth, 2000). Comprehensive overview of different sociological research methods that can be used to study social problems.

Horton, John. "Order and Conflict Theories of Social Problems." *American Journal of Sociology* 71 (May 1966): 701–713. Classic statement on the assumptions underlying opposing views of who and what are social problems.

Lewontin, R. C., Stephen Rose, and Leon J. Kamin. *Not in Our Genes* (New York: Pantheon Books, 1984). Critique of theories that reduce explanations for complex human behaviors down to biological factors.

Nock, Steven L., and Paul W. Kingston. *The Sociology of Public Issues* (Belmont, CA: Wadsworth, 1990). Uses sociology to critically evaluate public issues as presented in the mass media.

Rubington, Earl, and Martin S. Weinberg, eds. *The Study of Social Problems*. 6th ed. (New York: Oxford University Press, 2002). Examination of several alternative perspectives on social problems, with illustrative readings.

Ryan, William. *Blaming the Victim*. Rev. ed. (New York: Vintage Books, 1976). Explores examples of the tendency to blame individuals for the social problems in which they are caught up (e.g., blaming poor people for poverty).

part I

Societal Problems

chapter 2

Concentration of Political and Economic Power

Members of society should be able to actively participate in or directly influence those political and economic decisions that affect them.

It is common to refer to the United States as a democracy. From kindergarten on, children are taught about the democratic character of the U.S. political system. Ours, it is often said, is a government "of, by, and for the people." Students are encouraged to study the Constitution and to learn about the various branches of government. Frequently, the U.S. political system is favorably contrasted with others that are called totalitarian or dictatorial. In short, the schools act as agencies of political socialization; they function to provide future adult citizens with a belief in the noble origins and operation of our political system and to urge faith in its democratic workings.

Unfortunately, the schools too often fail to distinguish between democratic ideals and political realities. Everyday observations and practical experiences have led many people in the United States to doubt the democratic character of their political system. Many contend that political power has become concentrated in the hands of a select few and that to the degree such concentration exists, we do not have a government of, by, and for the people. Instead, decisions affecting us all are made by persons primarily concerned with the pursuit of their own self-defined interests.

This chapter begins by examining the conventional **pluralist perspective** on the distribution of political power. This perspective holds that power is equitably distributed and that the United States is a democratic nation in which no one group is politically dominant. Although this conventional view is widely held, we point to indications of doubt and disagreement that have emerged in recent years among the public. Next we set forth three alternative perspectives on the distribution and use of power. The **power elite perspective** sees power as having become concentrated among those holding top positions in the United States' largest bureaucratic organizations. The **business dominance perspective** emphasizes the power-wielding capabilities of the wealthy and their representatives. The **structuralist perspective** reminds us that needs

31

of our economic system may constrain political decision making. Finally, we consider some of the consequences of the concentration of power for political participation and suggest some steps that might move the U.S. political system closer to the democratic ideal.

Power in the United States: Who Rules?

Is the United States a democratic society? Those holding the *pluralist perspective* would say that it is. In this section we present the views of David Riesman, whose book *The Lonely Crowd* cogently expresses the pluralist position (Riesman 1961; also see Alford and Friedland 1985, Part I). We then look at survey results that indicate that many people in the United States entertain doubts about the validity of this perspective.

The Pluralist Perspective

In *The Lonely Crowd* sociologist David Riesman commented on U.S. politics while making a large-scale assessment of our nation's culture and personality. Riesman argued that great changes took place in the political system during the twentieth century. At various times during the nineteenth century, Riesman noted, wealthy businessmen and industrialists exercised an inordinate amount of power over the federal government and its policies. It almost appeared that an economic upper class ruled in the United States. Riesman contended that upper-class domination over government disintegrated in the twentieth century and that our society has become pluralistic in its national politics. That is, there are now many other groups capable of countering the political powers historically held by men of great wealth and high incomes. Riesman used the term *veto groups* in referring to those organized bodies

strong enough to make a direct impact on key national policy decisions. In his view, farm groups, labor and professional organizations, and ethnic and regional groups, among others, have all developed the political strength to veto policies that might adversely affect their interests. To a somewhat lesser extent, such groups can also initiate actions and mobilize pressures to gain the adoption of policies they want.

The pluralist perspective, as espoused by Riesman and others, essentially contends that political power is dispersed and distributed among a multitude of competing and contending interest groups. No group is capable of dominating at all times, nor is any group even interested in all questions of national policy. The distribution of power in the United States is a constantly shifting and rather amorphous phenomenon. Occasionally, political alliances form among different interest groups, only to be dissolved when new issues revive conflicting interests. The federal government is assumed to be a neutral body—an arbitrator, a compromiser—which soothes conflict and works out matters in the best interests of all. It is responsive to all groups and dominated by none.

Thus, from the pluralist perspective, the United States is a democratic society. All persons are free to join or otherwise support organized groups that promise to represent their interests in the national political arena. The leaders of such groups, in order to gain strength and make themselves felt at the national level, must appeal to the citizenry for support. Organizations representing great business interests, according to the pluralist perspective, are just like any other group in this respect.

Not coincidentally, *The Lonely Crowd* dismissed the idea that there are continuing, large-scale economic inequalities in U.S. society. In fact, according to Riesman, "America is a middle-class country." He asked rhetorically "whether one would not find, over a long period of time, that decisions in America favored one group or class . . . over others." He answered that this was not the case. "Does not wealth exert its pull in the long run? In the past this has been so; for the future, I doubt it" (Riesman 1961:222). The rise of a multitude of veto groups has neutralized the historical power of wealth, according to Riesman. The wealthy are just like any other group: They must compete and struggle to be heard.

We are thus presented with an orthodox picture of the national political scene, one that coincides with the content of many standard social studies textbooks. Riesman in his own way expressed the dominant teachings about the distribution of power in the United States. But is political power really so completely dispersed throughout U.S. society? Is the federal government just a neutral body that responds to the best interests of the nation's people? Is political decision making at the national level divorced from the interests of wealth and ownership? Is the upper economic class just one among many groups constantly scrambling for influence? Does one group or class really run things in this society? Let us look at public beliefs about these issues.

People's Beliefs about Political Power

Over the years, there have been several major surveys of people's beliefs about political and economic power in the United States. These surveys, which have been conducted on both the local and national levels, have found that a significant proportion of respondents do not believe in the pluralist position. Instead, the results indicate that many people in the United States feel that they are powerless and that the country is run by a small group of powerful people.

▲ The Muskegon Studies
During the 1960s William Form and Joan Rytina conducted a well-known survey on beliefs about

the way power is distributed in the United States. They carried out a series of interviews with a sample of persons residing in the city of Muskegon, Michigan. The researchers selected participants from three economic groups: the rich, the middle class, and the poor (Form and Rytina 1969; Huber and Form 1973).

During the course of interviews, participants were asked to decide which of the following three statements best described the national distribution of power:

A. No one group really runs the government in this country. Instead, important decisions about national policy are made by a lot of different groups such as labor, business, and religious and educational groups. These groups influence both political parties, but no single group can dictate to the others, and each group is strong enough to protect its own interests.

B. A small group of men at the top really run the government in this country. These are the heads of the biggest business corporations, the highest officers in the Army, Navy and Air Force, and a few important senators, congressmen, and federal officials in Washington. These men dominate both the Republican and Democratic parties.

C. Big businessmen really run the government in this country. The heads of the large corporations dominate both the Republican and Democratic parties. This means that things in Washington go pretty much the way big businessmen want them to. (Form and Rytina 1969:22)

Three-fifths of those interviewed selected statement A, which is a summary of the pluralist perspective. But there was not an overwhelming consensus. Roughly one-fifth selected statement B, and the remaining fifth chose statement C. An intriguing finding emerged when the researchers matched the economic level of the participants with the statements they chose. The higher their family income, the more likely persons were to state that pluralism best described our national system of power. Lower-income persons and people of color among the poor and middle classes were far more likely to select the alternative statements.

Form and Rytina concluded that persons in different economic positions see the structure of power from different vantage points and in terms of their own perceived interests. Those at higher income levels, finding that the political system generally works for them and in their class interests, are likely to voice the conventional view that this is a democratic society. On the other hand, the poor and people of color have not found the political system so responsive to their needs and perceived interests; they have experienced domination and thus feel the absence of a pluralist democracy. Statements B and C, which suggest dominance, fit quite well with the everyday reality of their lives.

A decade after the study by researchers Form and Rytina, sociologist Steven Stack (1978) focused once again on Muskegon. Stack wanted to see if views on the distribution of political power had changed. Although his research method differed quite a bit from that of the original study, Stack's findings—along with other surveys to be discussed shortly—indicate a remarkably widespread rejection of the pluralist perspective as time has passed.

In the Form and Rytina study three-fifths of those surveyed saw pluralism as an accurate depiction of the distribution of power in the United States; in Stack's study this was not the case. Indeed, three-quarters of his respondents agreed with the following statement (similar to statement B in the earlier study): "Big business executives, top governmental officials, and the military brass hold the real power in the U.S." (Stack 1978:227). Once again low-income people were most likely to agree with this view, but clearly it had spread dramatically upward to other classes in the decade since the Form and Rytina study. More recent surveys, conducted nationally,

underscore the powerlessness many people in the United States have come to feel. These national surveys reveal that such feelings extend well beyond the poor and people of color.

▲ Polls on Attitudes toward Government

Since the mid-1960s national surveys of public attitudes toward government officials and institutions have revealed an extraordinary degree of dissatisfaction (Lipset and Schneider 1983). People in the United States have decried dishonesty in government and claimed that their interests were being sacrificed in favor of powerful special-interest groups.

In a 2003 poll 70 percent of respondents agreed "this country's political system is so controlled by special interests and partisanship that it cannot respond to the country's real needs" (Princeton Survey Research Associates/*Newsweek* 2003). A later survey found that 40 percent of respondents identified "major corporations like pharmaceutical and auto companies" as the special interest "present[ing] the biggest problem because of their influence on decisions in Washington," more than any other special interest (NBC News/*Wall Street Journal* 2004). Another survey found that 75 percent of respondents agreed "elected officials in Washington lose touch with the people pretty quickly" (2003 Values Update Survey 2003). In another, 60 percent of respondents believed that "you can trust the government in Washington to do what is right" only some of the time, and another 6 percent believed it could never be trusted (Women's Voices, Women's Vote Survey 2003).

Many of those polled describe themselves as alienated and disenchanted, unable to influence the actions of their government. Sixty-three percent of those polled in 2003 said they were "angry" or "dissatisfied" when asked to pick a phrase "which best describes how you feel about the way the political process works" (ABC News/*Washington Post* 2003). In another poll, 59 percent of respondents disagreed with the statement, "most elected officials care what people like me think" (2003 Values Update Survey 2003). When asked "how much say do you think people like yourself have about what the government does," 56 percent of respondents in one survey said, "not much" (CBS News/*New York Times* 2003). Still another survey found that 67 percent of respondents believed that "people in Washington are out of touch with the rest of the country" (Harris Poll, Dec. 10–16, 2003). Such expressions of alienation have generally been on the increase since at least 1966.

In addition to political alienation and loss of respect for and trust in those who run governmental institutions, people in the United States have become less confident in the government. In 2003 one poll indicated that 57 percent of respondents agreed that "when something is run by the government it is usually inefficient and wasteful" (2003 Values Update Survey 2003). Another survey suggested at least one element behind this cynicism: 60 percent of respondents agreed that "governments and the energy industry are just exaggerating about energy shortages to support their political or financial goals" (IPSOS-Public Affairs 2004). But surveys also have indicated that members of U.S. society continue to believe that their government could be made to work effectively and to meet their needs. They are not ready to toss the political system out the window (Lipset and Schneider 1983:375–412). Indeed, candidates for the presidency and Congress have frequently appealed to such sentiments, claiming that if elected they would make government more efficient and more responsive to the common people. Such claims seem to have had little effect on changing public opinion.

A society in which the people feel that they cannot influence their governmental leaders, one in which so few have great confidence in those who run government, does not seem to be a *democratic* society. Instead, it appears to be a society marked by the erosion of political democracy and the concentration of power in the hands of a few.

▲ Polls on Attitudes toward Business

One of the other key participants in the exercise of power over people in the United States—the corporate world—has also undergone a crisis of faith in recent years (Lipset and Schneider 1983:163–98). Most people continue to believe in the basic principles of the capitalist economic system—for example, that business and industry belong under private control and ownership. Survey reports indicate that people in the United States oppose the notion of nationalization, or federal takeover, of industries (by a government that many distrust or believe to be incompetent). But most believe that the federal government should be "tougher" on big business. In 2004, 61 percent of adults surveyed felt dissatisfied with "the size and influence of major corporations" (Gallup Poll, Jan. 12–15, 2004). In that same poll, 60 percent of respondents said they "would like to see major corporations have less influence in this nation." In another poll, 69 percent of respondents complained that corporations "are paying too little in federal taxes" (Gallup Poll, April 5–8, 2004). The fact that relatively few believe that corporate power will actually be curbed demonstrates the public's sense of impotence in the face of both their national government and the power now believed to be wielded by the corporate world.

Between 1966 and 2003 the percentage of people in the United States expressing a "great deal of confidence" in major companies dropped from 55 to 8 percent (Gallup/CNN/*USA Today* 2003). Public confidence in the quality of goods and services being sold also dropped markedly, and people expressed an ever stronger belief that they were paying out more and receiving less for their money. There were more complaints about the failure of the corporate world to provide enough steady jobs for people. Fewer people thought business offered young people a chance to get ahead or that it allowed people to utilize their full creative talents. Survey results show that few people in the United States agree that business really cares about the individual.

At the same time, the majority of people in the United States believe that business could and should be doing more to improve the public welfare. Despite public expectations, the corporate world has failed to respond. In a 2003 survey over half of the respondents disagreed with the statement, "Business corporations generally strike a fair balance between making profits and serving the public interest" (2003 Values Update Survey 2003). Sixty-two percent in that same survey felt that business corporations make too much profit.

As a result, public respect for the corporate world has markedly declined. While the public has in past years looked to business and industry to fill the vacuum created by government ineffectiveness, the corporate world has chosen to concentrate on the pursuit of narrow economic goals. From the perspective of members of U.S. society, the corporate world is unresponsive to their needs and too far outside the realm of popular control through governmental restraint. In 2003 more than half of the respondents in one survey agreed that "most people on Wall Street would be willing to break the law if they believed they could make a lot of money and get away with it," and that "Wall Street only cares about making money and absolutely nothing else" (Harris Poll, Oct. 14–19, 2003). Another survey found that 77 percent agreed "there is too much power concentrated in the hands of a few big companies" (2003 Values Update Survey 2003).

Americans hold negative attitudes toward government and business, with a majority feeling themselves powerless in the face of corporate and governmental interests. It seems clear that the pluralist perspective does not coincide with the views and experiences of millions of people. In the view of a significant proportion of citizens and of many scholars, the United States is not working as a democracy of, by, and for the

people. "One person, one vote" notwithstanding, political power—like economic wealth—is not distributed anywhere near equally.

The Power Elite Perspective

Shortly after the publication of David Riesman's *The Lonely Crowd,* another sociologist, C. Wright Mills (1956), directly challenged the pluralist perspective, offering a different version of the way power is distributed in U.S. society (see also Domhoff and Ballard 1968; Miliband 1969). His work, *The Power Elite,* provoked a debate that has not yet ceased. Mills's study caused many sociologists to take a new and more critical look at the national political system.

The Attack on Pluralism

In *The Power Elite,* C. Wright Mills (1956) attacked the pluralist perspective as a form of romanticism. The position taken by scholars like Riesman, Mills felt, reflected what we might like U.S. society to be rather than what it is. The United States is not a democratic society, despite whatever vestiges of pluralism might be said to exist. Rather, in Mills's eyes, it is a society dominated by a set of *elites*—the men (and in rare instances, women) who hold the very highest offices in the large-scale bureaucratic hierarchies that have come to prevail in the United States.

Mills did not deny the existence of farm groups, labor and professional organizations, and other interest groups. Such groups clearly exist, but Mills felt they exist at a secondary level of power. The power to make decisions of national and international significance is on another level altogether, a level above and beyond the reach of the multitude of veto or interest groups deemed so significant by Riesman. It is *the power elite* alone that makes the decisions that shape the nature and course of the society in which we live. To Mills, Congress is not part of this power elite. It too exists on the secondary level of power. The decisions made by Congress—often under the buffeting pressures of one or another set of interest groups—are ordinarily made within an overarching political and economic framework determined and promoted by the power elite.

Identifying the Power Elite

Who are the members of the power elite? Mills answered this question by tracing the historical ascendancy of three major components of U.S. society. The first component is *big business and the corporate rich*. Unlike Riesman, Mills denied that the political significance of economic elites underwent a decline in the twentieth century. To Mills, the persons who sit at the very highest levels in this nation's giant corporations and financial institutions retain enormous political strength. Whether through direct participation in national government, campaign contributions to political candidates, or other forms of political activity, economic elites work to ensure that their particular interests are met.

Second, Mills identified the *military* as a bureaucratic entity whose top officials possess membership in the power elite. Mills traced the historical ascendancy of the U.S. military from a marginal arm of civilian government, important only in times of war, to a vast hierarchical institution that has become an enduring and integral part of U.S. society. Reaching preeminence during World War II, it has maintained much of its wartime political and

economic importance, even as military threats to the United States and its allies have grown more remote. As do members of the nation's economic elite, the highest officers in the military establishment have particular personal and institutional interests to pursue and protect. Their positions at the very top provide them with the means to do so.

Third, Mills focused on the *executive branch* of the federal government. Top officials of this branch, including the president, have come to reign over an immense bureaucratic network. The office of the president and the cabinet agencies under this office have progressively expanded in size and importance. In Mills's view, the executive branch overwhelms Congress in terms of power, and Congress largely responds to initiatives and decisions that flow from the executive branch. The two governmental bodies are not coequal, in Mills's estimation, and those persons in the top positions of the executive branch are prominent members of the power elite.

When the affluent and powerful make contributions to political campaigns it earns them greater access to lawmakers to press their interests in legislation. Here, a Dow Corning lobbyist meets with a senator and a Legislative Council Bureau member to discuss a bill of interest to the company.

Thus, Mills presented a complex of elites in which there is a three-way sharing of power, a triumvirate that sits in judgment over major national and international decisions of the day. No segment of the elite—economic, political, or military—dominates, though a close reading of Mills's study can easily lead one to conclude that he saw economic elites as first among equals. Nevertheless, each segment of the power elite has definite interests it wishes to pursue. These interests can be met only by close cooperation with the others:

The power to make decisions of national and international importance is . . . seated in the political, military, and economic institutions. As each has assumed its modern shape, its effects on the other two have become greater and the traffic between the three has increased. As each of these domains has coincided with the others, as decisions have become broader, the leading men of each . . . have tended to come together to form the power elite of America. (Mills 1956:9)

The persons who participate in this powerful triumvirate, in Mills's judgment, form a self-contained, cohesive social group. In his study, Mills attempted to show the bases of their group cohesion. The members of the power elite, he argued, come from similar social origins. It is not surprising, then, to find that the power elite members are typically white male Protestants educated at prestigious institutions. Analyzing the power elite in 2000, for example, Thomas R. Dye found that only 10 percent of the top 7,314 economic and political institutional positions in the power elite were filled by women; and people of color were almost nonexistent among the power elite, where African American representation was almost entirely restricted to high-level government positions but not found among the chief executives in major American corporations. Dye also found that 54 percent of the

corporate elite and 42 percent of the state elite were graduates of the 12 most exclusive private universities. And more than two-thirds of the institutional elite were members of exclusive social clubs; more than one-third belonged to one or more of a few prestigious social clubs (Dye 2002). Together, these data suggest a strong race, class, and gender bias among the power elite.

Given their common class identity, it is not surprising to find evidence of an overwhelmingly white, male, relatively affluent network of individuals mentoring, supporting, and promoting new elites much like themselves. Yet there is also evidence that this network is not powerful enough to be entirely closed; it is possible for someone outside the network to break into elite ranks. While there are still few women holding executive-level positions in the powerful institutions of society, it is reasonable to expect to see more women in these positions in the future. Note, however, that in spite of the limited progress of women and people of color in their representation among the power elite to date, there has been even less progress in terms of class; the power elite remain firmly drawn from among the most economically privileged in society (Zweigenhaft and Domhoff 1998).

Close personal and family ties exist among those whose bureaucratic positions provide elite status. And there is a frequent interchange of personnel between the hierarchies commanded by the elite. Top corporate executives are tapped for key appointments in the executive branch, and persons of wealth are routinely invited to take on ambassadorial posts around the world. Such persons move in and out of government with ease. High-ranking executive branch officials and retiring military officers frequently enter key offices in business and industry. The ease of movement, to Mills, is a visible indication of the close ties among those at the top, as well as an indication that elites tend to think alike. To Mills, members of the power elite are of a similar social type, thereby contributing to the unity of the power elite as a group.

The Erosion of Public Involvement

As we have seen, Riesman argued that members of U.S. society exert political influence through the medium of organized veto or interest groups. Mills did not have so optimistic a view of the role of the public. According to Mills, dominance by the power elite produced the **massification** of the U.S. citizenry. By this he meant that the public, in succumbing to manipulation by the powerful, had become increasingly unable to define and act on its own political interests. In Mills's terms, the majority of people in the United States comprised a *mass society* and existed on the third or lowest level of power.

The power elite manipulates members of U.S. society through careful orchestration of the mass media, the major means by which people find out what is going on. By selective censorship of information, by limiting the realm of national debate, by emphasizing entertainment over messages that inform, the mass media minimize serious political discussion and controversy. This is to be expected, since the national media are owned, controlled, and financed (through advertising) by the economic component of the power elite. The public is not properly informed and thus cannot participate in deciding the issues that affect all people. Thus, Mills argued, members of the mass society are progressively less capable of understanding issues and comprehending decisions that are allegedly made in their interest by those at the top.

As a result of manipulation from above and their powerlessness over important national decisions, citizens of the mass society have become less and less interested in politics. Political democracy becomes less possible, and the majority of people in the United States find themselves at the mercy of forces they can neither understand nor control. Slowly but perceptibly, the members of the power elite have become more inaccessible and less accountable to those affected by their high-level decisions.

Inaccessibility and lack of accountability open the way for abuses of power. Such abuses no doubt often go undetected and unreported, thus remaining uninvestigated. But many fail to remain hidden. In his book *The Criminal Elite,* James William Coleman (1995) surveys many such abuses both in government and in the business world (see also Coleman and Hagan 1994). If we restrict our attention to events involving political officials at the national level, examples examined by Coleman include:

Acceptance of illegal campaign contributions in return for political favors;

Illegal surveillance and harassment of civil rights and other protest organizations;

Burglary of political opponents' offices and the illegal tampering with the U.S. mail;

Maintenance of secret lists of "potentially dangerous" subversives who would be picked up and imprisoned in times of "national emergency";

Spreading harmful "disinformation" (false information) to discredit and defame political opponents or to create divisiveness and discord among them;

The use of agents provocateurs to incite others to commit crimes or to provoke others to violence so as to secure arrests; and

Involvement in or encouragement of assassination attempts on foreign leaders with whose policies there was disagreement.

These are not the kinds of behaviors common sense tells us we should expect from responsible members of government in a democratic society. (Additional examples of governmental power abuses may be found in Chapter 3.)

The Business Dominance Perspective

C. Wright Mills's concept of the power elite—wherein leaders of corporations, the executive branch of government, and the military were seen as coequal wielders of power—sidesteps one central issue of interest to sociologists, that of the relationship between *class inequality* and the distribution of political power. By focusing on bureaucratic elites and their self-interests in maintaining their institutional positions, Mills seemed to overlook the possibility that government actually functions in the interests of a particular social class. Is government, while purporting to represent the interests of *all* people in the United States, really a servant of the upper class? Is it dominated by that class, used as an *instrument* to cater to its interests even at the expense of others? Some would say yes. This "business dominance" perspective, as it has been called, is revealed in the works of G. William Domhoff (McQuarie and McGuire 1994). His first major study in this area appeared in the late 1960s under the title of *Who Rules America?* (Domhoff 1967), and his subsequent work has been part of an ongoing debate over the true nature of governance in nominally democratic societies (Domhoff 2002, 1995).

The Social and Economic Upper Class

Domhoff began by trying to establish the existence of a social upper class of national dimensions—that is, an exclusive social grouping that reigns supreme in terms of status and prestige. As evidence of the existence of such a class, Domhoff pointed to the social registers that have long been maintained in a score of major U.S. cities. The individuals and families listed in these registers are there by virtue of family pedigree and economic circumstance. They are members of "high society."

Domhoff also identified a set of institutions and events that cater to the exclusive tastes and interests of upper-class individuals. These include private schools, elite universities and colleges, clubs and resorts, and parties and balls. Domhoff argued that they provide a basis for cohesiveness among members of the upper class, for it is at such institutions and events that these people mingle with one another (Cookson and Persell 1985; Ostrander 1984). The outcomes are the formation of friendships, the establishment of business and social contacts, and the exposure of upper-class youth to potential marriage partners of the "right kind." Adults and children of this class readily sense their high status and are easily able to differentiate themselves from others who do not "belong."

Having established to his satisfaction that such a social upper class exists, Domhoff turned to another question: Is this *social* upper class also an *economic* upper class? He found a great overlap between those with the greatest wealth and highest incomes and those who are considered at the top in social terms across the United States. Members of the social upper class are, for the most part, wealthy businessmen and their families or descendants of such men. They comprise that component of society that C. Wright Mills called the economic elite.

Does the United States Have a Governing Class?

Domhoff was particularly interested in discovering whether this national social and economic upper class is also a ruling or *governing class* in a political sense. Domhoff defined a governing class as "a social upper class which owns a disproportionate amount of a country's wealth, receives a disproportionate amount of a country's yearly income, and contributes a disproportionate number of its members to the controlling institutions and key decision-making groups of the country" (Domhoff 1967:9). Thus, Domhoff looked at the ways in which members of the social and economic upper class participate in the nation's major institutions.

One place major decisions are made is in the dominant economic institutions that, by virtue of their overall size, sales, and assets, are the foundation of the U.S. economy. Decisions made at the top levels of these institutions often have an impact on the economic well-being of the entire nation. The largest corporations and financial institutions, according to Domhoff, are under the control of the upper class. Upper-class individuals either play the roles of directors and managers of such institutions themselves or handpick persons from non-upper-class backgrounds for such important decision-making roles.

Obviously, high-ranking officials in the federal government also hold a great deal of power. In Domhoff's words, "Members of the American upper class and their employees control the Executive Branch" (Domhoff 1967:84). To support this assertion, he examined the ways in which presidential nominees are controlled. The key here is money. Financing a national political campaign has become an increasingly expensive proposition. Candidates are generally unable to bear most of the costs themselves, and contributions by the public are generally insufficient. Thus, private benefactors must be sought out. Upper-class individuals and corporate contributors are most likely to support candidates who best articulate upper-class goals and values and who are unlikely to threaten upper-class economic interests. Donations, or loans, or campaign services rendered implicitly mean favors in return, and the debts of successful presidential candidates to wealthy benefactors are reflected, in Domhoff's view, in key policy decisions.

Furthermore, the president appoints individuals to key posts in the federal bureaucracy and the judiciary, including the U.S. Supreme Court. Appointees to such positions of importance, according to Domhoff, tend to come from the social and economic upper class in far greater frequency than one would expect, given its small size. Those individuals who lack upper-class backgrounds, Domhoff suggests, are appointed on the basis of their past demonstrated performance in understanding and serving upper-class interests. They are, in effect, "co-opted" upward. Through this and through data on financial contributions, Domhoff was able to support his argument that the upper class is, in reality, a governing or ruling class.

Pluralism Below

Congress is heavily influenced but not controlled outright by the upper class, in Domhoff's view. Members of Congress (many of whom are themselves millionaires) often depend on upper-class contributions for their election campaigns. (Table 2.1 provides an overview of campaign contributions.) They are also directly subject to influence by the powerful, well-financed lobbies that represent upper-class economic interests. However, Congress is also subject to pressures from many groups that do not represent upper-class interests. Thus, senators and representatives are very much subject to influence but are not under absolute upper-class control.

It is with regard to Congress and on the local and state levels of government that Domhoff feels the pluralists may have a point. While decisions and policies made in the executive branch of the federal government and in the corporate world may be under the control of upper-class individuals or their representatives, more political diversity exists below. Domhoff saw no incompatibility between top-level control by the upper class and pluralism at another level. Here he seems to be siding with Mills, who also conceptualized a secondary level of power operating within a framework of domination imposed from above.

But Domhoff departed from Mills by insisting that despite the existence of a governing class, the United States is still democratic. He argued that the governing class is not monolithic

Table 2.1 — Congressional Campaign Finances—Receipts and Disbursements: 1995 to 2000

Item	House of Representatives — Amount (mil. dol.)			House of Representatives — Percent distribution			Senate — Amount (mil. dol.)			Senate — Percent distribution		
	1995-96	1997-98	1999-2000	1995-96	1997-98	1999-2000	1995-96	1997-98	1999-2000	1995-96	1997-98	1999-2000
Total receipts[1]	**505.4**	**493.7**	**610.4**	**100**	**100**	**100**	**285.1**	**287.5**	**437.0**	**100**	**100**	**100**
Individual contributions	272.9	253.2	315.6	55	52	52	166.9	166.5	252.1	59	58	58
Other committees	155.0	158.5	193.4	31	32	32	45.6	48.1	52.0	16	17	12
Candidate loans	42.0	46.8	61.9	8	10	10	40.3	52.2	89.0	14	18	20
Candidate contributions	7.0	5.3	6.3	1	1	1	16.4	1.3	18.7	6	(Z)	4
Democrats	233.1	233.4	286.7	46	47	47	126.5	134.1	230.4	44	47	53
Republicans	266.9	255.8	317.7	53	52	52	157.7	153.0	203.8	55	53	47
Others	5.4	4.5	6.0	1	1	1	0.9	0.4	2.8	(Z)	(Z)	1
Incumbents	279.8	293.6	361.8	56	60	59	81.8	135.5	130.6	29	47	30
Challengers	119.1	92.8	127.4	24	19	21	79.2	113.9	99.6	28	40	23
Open seats[2]	101.1	102.7	121.1	14	21	20	124.1	37.7	206.7	44	13	47
Total disbursements	**477.8**	**452.5**	**572.3**	**95**	**100**	**100**	**287.4**	**287.9**	**434.7**	**100**	**100**	**100**
Democrats	221.1	211.1	266.8	44	47	47	127.4	134.6	226.3	44	47	52
Republicans	251.4	237.2	299.7	50	52	52	159.1	152.9	205.7	55	53	47
Others	5.3	4.2	5.7	1	1	1	0.9	0.4	2.7	(Z)	(Z)	1
Incumbents	258.1	257.2	327.0	51	57	57	85.4	137.3	130.2	30	48	30
Challengers	119.6	94.7	125.6	24	21	22	78.9	112.5	99.3	27	39	23
Open seats[2]	100.2	100.6	119.7	20	22	21	123.1	38.1	205.1	43	13	47

Note: Covers all campaign finance activity during two-year calendar period indicated for primary, general, run-off, and special elections. For 1987–88 relates to 1,582 House of Representatives candidates and 210 Senate candidates; for 1989–90 to 1,580 House of Representatives candidates and 179 Senate candidates; for 1991–92 to 2,580 House of Representatives candidates and 365 Senate candidates. Data have been adjusted to eliminate transfers between all committees within a campaign.

Z Less than $50,000 or 0.5 percent. [1]Includes other types of receipts, not shown separately. [2]Elections in which an incumbent did not seek re-election.

Source: U.S. Department of Commerce, Bureau of the Census, *Statistical Abstract of the United States, 2003* (Washington, D.C.: U.S. Government Printing Office, 2004), p. 274.

According to the business dominance perspective, it is at the state and local levels that the people are most likely to have a voice in political policies and decisions. In this photograph, Arnold Schwarzeneggar speaks at a town hall meeting during his gubernatorial campaign in California.

and that there are splits and divisions within it. Not all members of the upper class agree on just what policies and decisions will best coincide with their short-term and long-term interests. Domhoff suggested that competing factions within the upper class may find themselves forced to indirectly seek support from non-upper-class groups in order to meet their self-defined needs. Thus, members of the upper class may be divided over whether to throw their weight behind Democratic or Republican candidates for national office. It is a question of which party and candidate promises to best protect those aspects of the societal status quo the upper class wishes to preserve. Domhoff suggests that

democracy in U.S. society is based primarily on cleavages within the governing class itself, at the same time that this class effectively shapes the nature and course of societal members' lives.

The Structuralist Perspective

Since the power elite and the business dominance perspectives have been put forth, yet another view has surfaced to raise important issues about the use of power by those in whose hands it may be concentrated. The so-called structuralist perspective does not deny that political power is concentrated in the hands of a few. The perspective acknowledges Domhoff's findings that in the United States the "few" are by and large members of the social and economic upper class or their helpers. What the structuralist perspective does suggest is that the wielders of political power are constantly constrained by the need to attend to the demands of our corporate capitalist economy (Gold, Lo, and Wright 1975). Such constraints have implications for decision making, no matter what group manages to ascend to elected or appointed political office (Domhoff, 1990).

Let us look briefly at the nature of the United States' capitalist economic system and then at the structuralist perspective as it relates politics to economics. As we shall see, governmental elites, no matter what their class background now or in the future, may have problems not serving the upper class over and above all other members of the citizenry.

From Free Enterprise to "Corporate Capitalism"

The United States has a capitalist economy. For the most part its "productive apparatus" (i.e., its means of producing goods and services for sale in the marketplace) is privately owned. Moreover, production is undertaken first and foremost to make profits. Private owners are prone to reinvest much of their profits so as to make even more profits in the future. This general picture of what capitalism looks like could fit the U.S. economy at almost any point in its history.

Until the mid-nineteenth century the U.S. economy consisted largely of numerous individual productive units, small and often organized around the extended family. Each unit provided goods and services for sale in localized markets and for self-consumption. The majority of U.S. workers were self-employed, primarily in agriculture but also in various crafts, trades, professions, and sales activities. This was the system of "free-enterprise" capitalism—small

entrepreneurs, often engaged in competition with one another—that was glowingly described by Adam Smith in his 1776 classic, *The Wealth of Nations.*

Large-scale changes in the nature of economic organization began to take place after the Civil War and have continued until this day. Industrialization reduced self-employment and diminished the number of competing entrepreneurs. Only the most successful survived and grew; most others fell by the wayside. The modern large corporation was born as the wealthy combined their resources to purchase the new machine technology that would make regional and national markets possible. Such firms drove the less well endowed competitors out of business. Free-enterprise capitalism thus slowly gave way to **corporate capitalism**—a capitalist economy in which a few large firms came to dominate most product and service areas.

Michael Parenti (1995:10) underscores the degree to which our economy has become concentrated: "Less than 1 percent of all corporations account for over 80 percent of the total output of the private sector. In 1992 the combined sales of goods and services of the corporate giants totaled $4 trillion."

Likewise, Thomas Dye (1995:15) points out how a relatively small number of individuals are in a position to make decisions that affect the economic affairs and well-being of tens of millions of people:

Economic power in America is highly concentrated. Indeed, only about 4,300 individuals—two one-thousandths of 1 percent of the population—exercise formal authority over more than one half of the nation's industrial assets; two thirds of all banking assets; one half of all assets in communications and utilities; and more than two thirds of all insurance assets. . . . The reason for this concentration of power in the hands of so few people is found in the concentration of industrial and financial assets in a small number of giant corporations.

Dye tends to use a business dominance perspective in his interpretation of these data as evidence of the power elite. But they also suggest evidence of a structure in which the increasingly dominant economic position of *corporations,* not simply the elite positions of *individuals* in institutions, strongly shapes everyone's life chances. When corporations become such a central dominating force that controls financial and production assets, as well as jobs, it becomes less important who the elites are; what does become crucial is the security of the conditions that keep corporations economically healthy in the interest of protecting and preserving the nation's assets and people's jobs. Therefore, the very structural position of corporations as the controllers of resources shapes and constrains the range of political decisions governmental leaders may make.

Corporate Capitalism and Politics

From the business dominance perspective, government at the national level largely serves as an instrument of the upper class (a class primarily made up of rich businessmen, their families, and their descendants, according to G. William Domhoff). This implies that if non-upper-class groups could capture control over high-level government positions, they too could make government an instrument. Interests other than those of the upper class could be served.

However, those holding to a structuralist perspective would take issue with such possibilities. For government may be seen as somewhat of a captive of the ongoing needs of corporate capitalism. The maintenance of a healthy economic order—on which not only large corporations and the rich but also everyone else depends—must take precedence in policymaking, no matter who runs the government.

Martin N. Marger (1987:43) succinctly summarizes the structuralist position:

Since the viability of the state is dependent upon a healthy economy . . . state leaders must promote the interests of big business (that is, the corporations) regardless of who they are or what their views may be. If the economy declines, tax revenues dry up, imperiling government programs and weakening public support for elected officials and other government leaders. The general interests of the capitalist class are thus naturally served. Indeed, state leaders may be more aware of the general need for maintaining a stable social order (that is, a capitalist system) than profit-oriented capitalists.

Since the needs of capitalism (e.g., a lower tax burden on corporations to enhance profits) are often at odds with the needs of the population at large (e.g., a higher tax burden on individuals to offset corporate tax reductions), trade-offs must be made (O'Connor 1973). The structuralist perspective is suggesting that no matter who is in charge of our governmental institutions, the needs of capitalism by necessity overwhelm all others. To the degree to which this is true in practice, and it is clear from survey data that the public senses that this is what goes on, it is small wonder that so many persons are disillusioned with and alienated from this deformed version of political democracy.

The structuralist perspective provides a context within which we can interpret federal policymakers' actions in recent years. For example, during the Reagan administration (1981–88) numerous actions were undertaken to serve the interests of large corporations and the wealthy upper class. Income tax rates were lowered in ways that disproportionately favored the rich, while firms were allowed new tax reductions, deductions, and write-offs to increase their economic health (Phillips 1990). Huge sums were spent to buttress the well-being of the aerospace-defense industry, a central component of the United States' "permanent war economy" (see Chapter 3) on which many private fortunes depend. In these and other ways, federal policymakers sought to enhance even further the economic advantage of those among whom U.S. society's economic assets have become highly concentrated (Barlett and Steele 1992). In this way, the policymakers believed, investment in economic activity and growth would be encouraged, and ultimately the benefits would "trickle down" to the general population.

As the U.S. government acted to meet the needs of our capitalist economy in the ways mentioned, it balanced these actions with various cost-cutting initiatives. In particular, it decided that the costs associated with encouraging economic growth would be borne by cutting back spending on programs for the nonwealthy.

Unfortunately, this all was taking place during a period when many members of U.S. society were in greater need of such programs than ever (Parenti 1995; Phillips 1990). More people, especially women and children, were experiencing economic dislocation and poverty. For the first time since the 1960s widespread hunger began to be reported. Homeless people began to appear on the nation's streets. But federal policymakers cut back spending on low-income housing. They moved to reduce expenditures on government food programs and income assistance to poor individuals and families. Eligibility requirements were tightened to discourage participation in programs ranging from social security for the disabled to medical care for low-income children. Federal policymakers resisted efforts to increase the minimum wage and dismissed proposals for government subsidization of day care, which would allow more mothers to work outside the home.

Nor has the middle class been spared a share of the burden from federal policymakers' fixation with the need to promote the welfare of those at the top (Phillips 1993). Besides being asked to shoulder a larger part of the tax burden (since the rich and corporations are shouldering less), those in the middle have seen their real incomes fall in the face of rising costs of living with which wages and salaries fail to keep pace.

While the costs of higher education have zoomed, federal policymakers tightened eligibility for student financial aid and substituted loan programs for those providing outright grants. Meanwhile, escalating rents and prices of houses have forced members of the middle class (and those less affluent) to spend an ever higher percentage of income on shelter. Many young adults from middle-class families despair at ever being able to afford to buy their own homes (Crispell 1994).

U.S. capitalism as a system may be working, as government policies provide economic incentives and rewards to its key operatives and owners. As the system benefits, so by definition does the upper class. This, in the 1980s, was made possible only by escalating the level of sacrifice, deferred dreams, and outright suffering among the majority, from the middle class down to the poor. By 2004 the Congress was pushing for even more sacrifice, cutting back scores of social programs in order to address the enormous federal fiscal deficit. This deficit was created in large part by huge income tax cuts (more than a third of which benefited the most affluent 1 percent of the population) and corporate tax cuts, and by high levels of military spending in 2003–2004 during war against Iraq waged by George W. Bush's administration. As our political apparatus makes such trade-offs, which at times it *must* from the structuralist perspective, estrangement from this apparatus can only be reinforced.

Political Alienation

Political Nonparticipation

Democratic societies rely on the participation of individuals in processes of selecting leadership. That participation is predicated on the assumption of a fully informed public who know their interests and who participate accordingly. The ability of the public to be fully informed relies on a the existence of a free and independent press, an academic community engaged in unfettered research, open and critical discussion of any and all issues, and the ability of the public to openly and freely discuss issues and challenge leadership. However, as we have seen, many people in the United States are asking whether the political system is truly democratic and whose interests political representatives are serving. Feeling that their voices are not being heard, a significant proportion of citizens have become alienated and have withdrawn from participation in national politics. People who are politically alienated frequently feel the electoral process does not address issues that are vitally important to them, and so they see no reason to participate. That is not the same thing as **political apathy.** When people are politically apathetic they simply do not care about the outcome of an election. Public opinion polls do indeed indicate a significant level of voter apathy: More than one-fourth of the respondents to one poll in 1999, for example, indicated that "it doesn't make much difference how I vote because all politicians are pretty much alike" (Hart and Teeter/NBC/*Wall Street Journal,* 1999, available at www.publicagenda.org/issues).

Unofficially, the United States maintains a two-party system. The Democratic and Republican parties dominate elections for national office. In the past several decades, an ever-increasing percentage of the voting population has been unwilling to identify with either major party. According to Gallup poll data (reported periodically in *Gallup Opinion Index),* substantial numbers of people are choosing to call themselves independents. The growth of this bloc reflects numerous factors, among which is the substantial dissatisfaction that has developed over the conduct of national politics.

Even more serious a reflection of **political alienation** is the apathy of eligible voters. Over one-third of the U.S. citizens who are eligible are not registered to vote. And participation of eligible voters in elections has been low for a long time (Piven and Cloward 2000; Teixeira 1992). In every national election since 1972 barely more than half of all eligible voters participated in the choice of the new president. (See Table 2.2.) Ronald Reagan's 1980 "landslide," as the media called it, was provided by little more than one-quarter of those eligible to vote. The number of voters choosing him in 1984 was somewhat higher but still constituted a minority of eligible voters. George Bush was likewise elected by a minority in 1988, as were Bill Clinton in 1992 and 1996 and George W. Bush in 2000. An even greater level of voter indifference is discernible with regard to the election of persons to the U.S. Congress.

The relatively low voting participation rate in the United States stands in contrast to the participation rates in most other established and high-population democracies around the world (see Figure 2.1). Only Switzerland had a lower voter participation rate than the United States in recent national elections. Since participation is a key feature of democracy, what do low voter participation rates mean? Why might so few people exercise their right to participate in decision making about power, policy, and leadership?

Low voter turnout could simply be due to satisfaction (or dissatisfaction) with all competing candidates. But given the other indices of political alienation we have mentioned, it seems more likely that declining turnouts represent cynicism and disgust over the workings of the political system in general (Marger 1987:239–41). Indeed, the 2000 presidential elections may have contributed to a corrosion of voter confidence in the process, especially among people of color. Many people of color in Florida complained that they were harassed by police as they waited in line to vote, or they were told by election monitors that they were at the wrong voting district and could not vote there. Others were simply denied the right to vote because their names were similar to those on a list of felons (convicted felons in Florida lose their right to vote); subsequent investigations

Table 2.2	Participation in Elections for President and U.S. Representatives: 1960 to 2000

| Year | Resident population (incl. aliens) of voting age[1] (1,000) | Votes cast | | | |
		For President[2] (1,000)	Percentage of voting-age population	For U.S. Representatives (1,000)	Percentage of voting-age population
1960	109,672	68,838	62.8	64,133	58.5
1962	112,952	(X)	(X)	51,267	45.4
1964	114,090	70,645	61.9	65,895	57.8
1966	116,638	(X)	(X)	52,908	45.4
1968	120,285	73,212	60.9	66,288	55.1
1970	124,498	(X)	(X)	54,173	43.5
1972	140,777	77,719	55.2	71,430	50.7
1974	146,338	(X)	(X)	52,495	35.9
1976	152,308	81,556	53.5	74,422	48.9
1978	158,369	(X)	(X)	55,332	34.9
1980	163,945	86,515	52.8	77,995	47.6
1982	169,643	(X)	(X)	64,514	38.0
1984	173,995	92,653	53.3	83,231	47.8
1986	177,922	(X)	(X)	59,619	33.5
1988	181,956	91,595	50.3	81,786	44.9
1990	185,812	(X)	(X)	61,513	33.1
1992	189,524	104,425	55.1	96,239	50.8
1994	193,650	(X)	(X)	69,770	36.0
1996	196,789	96,278	48.9	89,863	35.7
1998	201,270	(X)	(X)	65,897	32.7
2000	205,813	105,397	51.2	97,226	47.2

Note: As of November. Estimated resident population 21 years old and over, 1932–70, except as noted, and 18 years old and over thereafter; includes Armed Forces. Prior to 1960, excludes Alaska and Hawaii. District of Columbia is included in votes cast for president beginning 1964 and in votes cast for representatives from 1972 to 1992.

X Not applicable. [1]Population 18 and over in Georgia, 1944–70, and in Kentucky, 1956–70; 19 and over in Alaska and 20 and over in Hawaii, 1960–70. [2]Source: 1932–58, U.S. Congress, Clerk of the House, Statistics of the Presidential and Congressional Election, biennial.

Source: U.S. Department of Commerce, Bureau of the Census, Statistical Abstract of the United States, 2003 (Washington, D.C.: U.S. Government Printing Office, 2004), p. 270.

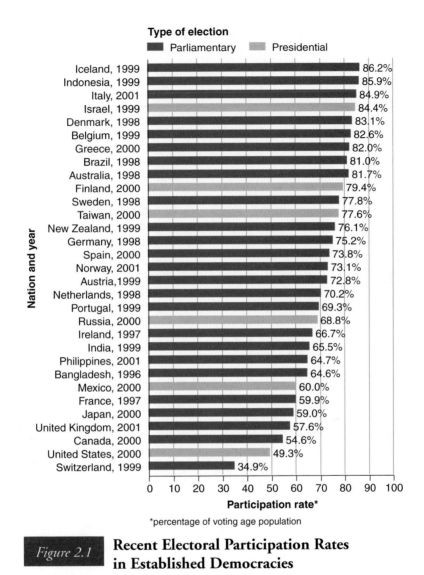

Type of election

■ Parliamentary   ▨ Presidential

Nation and year	Participation rate*
Iceland, 1999	86.2%
Indonesia, 1999	85.9%
Italy, 2001	84.9%
Israel, 1999	84.4%
Denmark, 1998	83.1%
Belgium, 1999	82.6%
Greece, 2000	82.0%
Brazil, 1998	81.0%
Australia, 1998	81.7%
Finland, 2000	79.4%
Sweden, 1998	77.8%
Taiwan, 2000	77.6%
New Zealand, 1999	76.1%
Germany, 1998	75.2%
Spain, 2000	73.8%
Norway, 2001	73.1%
Austria,1999	72.8%
Netherlands, 1998	70.2%
Portugal, 1999	69.3%
Russia, 2000	68.8%
Ireland, 1997	66.7%
India, 1999	65.5%
Philippines, 2001	64.7%
Bangladesh, 1996	64.6%
Mexico, 2000	60.0%
France, 1997	59.9%
Japan, 2000	59.0%
United Kingdom, 2001	57.6%
Canada, 2000	54.6%
United States, 2000	49.3%
Switzerland, 1999	34.9%

Participation rate*

*percentage of voting age population

Figure 2.1   **Recent Electoral Participation Rates
in Established Democracies**

Source: Adapted from Wattenberg 2002:15; International Institute for Democracy and
Electoral Assistance, available at www.idea.int

revealed that this list was highly inaccurate, often included people convicted of misdemeanors rather than felonies, and contained many names shared by more than one person. In addition, thousands of ballots in that state, particularly in voting districts heavily populated with people of color, remained uncounted because the use of cardboard punch ballots produced unclear results when "chads" (the piece of cardboard that gets pushed out to select a candidate) did not fully break off. Ballots in these districts were designed in a side-by-side butterfly fashion that seriously confused voters as to which chad corresponded with which candidate. These irregularities in

Florida resulted in an extended delay in declaring a presidential winner there for weeks while the courts tried to decide what to do. Although Al Gore won more votes nationwide than George W. Bush, the Supreme Court declared Bush the winner in Florida, which gave Bush enough electoral votes to win the election. That was because this presidential election was a very tight race, and therefore Florida's electoral votes would determine the outcome. The Supreme Court thus effectively appointed the president by declaring a winner of the state. In the end, then, it was the Supreme Court, not the voters, who decided the winner in Florida. Many voters became quite cynical in the aftermath of the 2000 elections, a cynicism that could easily translate into political alienation.

The term **democracy** refers to a political system through which it is possible—and in which members of society want—to have some input into those decisions that affect them. In such a system, the people themselves play an informed and active role in determining the nature and course of their society. Power rests in the hands of the people, and government expresses their will. It seems clear that the U.S. political system is not meeting these criteria. As Richard M. Valelly (Skocpol and Campbell 1995:200) put it, "Our electoral politics now fails to realize the empowering possibilities of democratic life."

The concentration of power in the hands of a few—be it a power elite or a governing class—means that many of the crucial issues of our times are decided for us, if they are even raised at all. The consequences are felt in terms of how, for example, questions such as the following get answered: Shall we have a more equitable system of taxation, one that minimizes economic inequalities? Shall we set up mechanisms to redistribute wealth and income in the interests of eliminating poverty? Shall we reorganize this society's productive apparatus so as to eliminate unemployment and fully utilize our productive capabilities? Are there particular elements of business and industry that should be taken out of

private hands and placed under public ownership and control? Shall we limit defense expenditures in favor of improving the quality of life? Would the resources devoted to space exploration be better used for more earthly needs? Shall we require corporations to bear the full costs of ending their pollution and environmental destruction, instead of passing the costs on to the consumer and taxpayer? To what degree are we to share our wealth and technology with underdeveloped nations around the world?

In a democratic society these issues should be debated and decided by the majority of people. In the United States they may be decided by a minority, many of whom have more than a passing interest in protecting the status quo. With power concentrated in the hands of a few, the majority of society's members cannot help but feel powerless and alienated from their rulers. People become objects rather than actors, victims of history rather than makers of it.

The Influence of the "New Right"

The alienation that has led many citizens in the United States to abandon voting and other forms of political participation has created a vacuum in recent years into which a conservative numerical minority of the U.S. voting population has stepped or been led. By the mid-1990s this minority, which is collectively referred to as the "New Right," had become influential in advancing parts of its agenda in many states, as well as in Congress and in presidential campaign politics.

The New Right agenda includes less government control over and regulation of corporate activities; reduced taxes, particularly on corporations and wealthy individuals; maintenance of near–Cold War levels of military spending on troops and weapons systems; sharp cutbacks or restrictions on government spending on welfare, health, and education; increased spending on crime control; easier implementation of capital punishment; abolition of the right of women to obtain legal abortions; restrictions on government's role in promoting civil rights protections for people of color, women, and homosexuals; an end to public school sex education; government support for those who wish to attend private (including religious) schools; and, expansion of the right to pray in public schools.

The New Right's roots can be traced back to the Depression of the 1930s, when conservatives unsuccessfully opposed Democratic president Franklin D. Roosevelt's "New Deal" policies. Among other things, New Deal policies provided the beginnings of a U.S. "welfare state" similar to (but subsequently never as well developed as) those existing in most European capitalist democracies. The New Deal involved unprecedented federal intervention in and control over the operation of the U.S. economy, recognized the rights of workers to form unions and collectively bargain with employers, and created a variety of new programs to provide a minimal "safety net" to aid people who were jobless, poverty-stricken, or otherwise in need.

In the 1960s the federal government added social programs to those begun during the New Deal era. It responded to the demands of a militant civil rights movement by ending legal forms of racial segregation, provided programs to address health problems of the elderly and poor, vastly expanded its expenditures on public education from preschool through university level, and launched a "war on poverty." In the 1970s the federal government addressed the quality of the environment, implementing a series of new laws intended to reduce some of the most obvious and dangerous environmental contaminants whose source was largely corporate polluters.

The goals of the New Right have included the elimination of New Deal and subsequent "liberal" laws and programs such as those just enumerated that, in its view, undermine the U.S. economy, restrict the productive use of assets by individuals and corporations, and substitute government bureaucratic decision making for individual responsibility and initiative. Many

New Right conservatives see such laws and programs as "socialistic," arguing that by extending and enhancing the influence of government they reduce the rights of citizens. The New Right wishes to radically roll back the role of the federal government in everyday life, abolish most of its activities, and increase societal emphasis and individual reliance on other institutions such as the family and church.

The agenda of the New Right has been shaped by a loose coalition composed of three components (Himmelstein 1990). One component is made up of a segment of the United States' religious community, primarily in this case white Christian fundamentalists and evangelists. Church leaders and their followers are concerned with what they see as a decline in family and religious values in U.S. society and are politically energized by issues such as abortion and school prayer.

A second component of the New Right is the corporate sector, discussed by C. Wright Mills and G. William Domhoff. Parts of this sector, facing increased international competition in the last couple of decades, have increased their funding for conservative policy study centers or "think tanks" generating policy and legislative ideas that, if adopted, benefit corporations and their stockholders. The corporate sector also has chosen to heavily focus its campaign contributions and other resources on those political candidates (especially incumbents) who are the most probusiness and antiunion and who are in favor of military spending and reducing corporate taxes and regulation.

The third component of the New Right is the conservative wing of the Republican Party, which has been successful in moving party candidates to the fore who embrace the agenda issues of both the religious groups and the corporate sector, and in mobilizing party resources for conservative candidates who find themselves in close races. Together, these three components have formed an informal alliance that has resulted in substantial fund-raising, managed to focus political discourse on New Right issues, and advanced the New Right agenda by winning a number of elections.

The ability of a numerical voting minority to advance its particular agenda in the United States, and to greatly influence the content of political discourse, is facilitated by others' withdrawal from political involvement. The danger is that groups with narrow views may be able to gain a foothold in promoting policies that are harmful to other members of society. Aside from the harm that may flow from the New Right's efforts to restrict or abolish laws and programs on which many people's lives and opportunities depend (such as those concerned with poverty and welfare, health, education, environmental regulation, and civil rights), the anti-federal-government rhetoric emphasized by the New Right may be harmful. This rhetoric may contribute to a political environment in which highly troubled citizens feel justified in engaging in extremist acts, even to the point of violence against their own government.

Political Extremism

When people are alienated politically, they are unlikely to participate in the electoral process. But that does not necessarily mean that they withdraw from any attempts to change what they see as problematic about the nation, particularly if they see the problems as stemming from an overbearing concentration of political and economic power that erodes the preconditions of democracy. When people believe the routine institutional avenues to affect their government and redress their grievances are inaccessible or ineffective for them, they may channel their political energy into acts of extremism. In April 1995, for example, a huge bomb exploded in Oklahoma City, destroying a federal office building and taking the lives of 168 people, including a dozen children. Hundreds of people were maimed and injured. Speculation over the perpetrators of the violence, which was subsequently described as the most serious act

of terrorism in U.S. history prior to September 11, 2001, began immediately. Some people leaped to the conclusion that a group from outside the United States was probably responsible, and some—with overtones of racism—said it had to be people from the Middle East. The suspects almost immediately arrested, however, were U.S. citizens, members of the white majority, and people with possible ties to a shadowy collection of paramilitary and white supremacist groups. In recent years many such groups have been increasing their recruitment and organizing activities across the nation (Southern Poverty Law Center 1995b). Some are even using modern technology such as the Internet computer communications system and cable television's public access channels to spread their ideas and gain converts.

Prior to the Oklahoma bombing the mass media paid little attention to groups like the paramilitary Michigan Militia Corps and white supremacist Aryan Nations. News coverage focused on them intensely after the arrest of the suspects in the bombing. The media tended to depict those who participate in such groups as deviants—marginal people with warped ideas and interests. Many people who knew of or were made aware of these organizations were ready to view their participants as mentally troubled. In a poll done shortly after the Oklahoma City bombing 55 percent of the respondents described the members of militia groups as "crazy," and an even higher percentage described members as "dangerous" and "a threat to our way of life" (Smolowe 1995:60).

When one examines some of the beliefs that have circulated among the members of paramilitary and white supremacist groups, the term "crazy" may not seem too far-fetched. For example, these common themes have been reported:

- The United Nations, with the cooperation of officials in the federal government, has plans to conquer the United States and create a "new world order."

Paramilitary citizens groups around the United States went largely unnoticed until law enforcement officials and the news media focused on the possibility they were linked to the 1995 bombing of a federal office building in Oklahoma City. In this photograph members of one such paramilitary group, Alpha 66, gather for training near the Everglades in Florida.

- There are already foreign troops under U.N. command in the United States, and they have been using black helicopters for surveillance of the citizenry.

- Bar codes on the backs of road signs are intended to guide invading troops, and the federal government plans to brand citizens with bar codes to monitor their movements and behavior.

- The federal government has rigged auto ignitions to stall all over the United States on the day the invaders launch their attack to impose the new world order.

- Political dissidents and resisters will be housed in concentration camps or destroyed in a giant crematorium (Smolowe 1995: 62–63; see also Shapiro 1995:38).

Believers in these ideas not only hold that the federal government is an enemy, but that it is necessary for people to arm themselves and be prepared to go to war against it. Indeed, the first suspect detained in the Oklahoma City bombing represented himself to arresting authorities as a "prisoner of war." Federal efforts aimed at gun control, as well as government surveillance and police powers directed at potentially dangerous organizations, are seen as consistent with the idea that the United States is moving toward abandonment of the Constitution, martial law, and oppression of the citizenry.

Are we talking only about a handful of kooks and nuts? One media account put it this way:

How many people have reached that breaking point with their Federal Government—and are they acting alone or together? If you count just the people who are arming themselves against the day when U.N. tanks roll through the heartland to establish the one-world order, estimates range only as high as 100,000. But if you include all the people in as many as 40 states who respond to the patriotic rhetoric about a sinister, out-of-control federal bureaucracy—all the ranchers fed up with land- and water-use policies, all the loggers who feel besieged by environmentalists, all the underemployed who blame their plight on NAFTA (North American Free Trade Agreement) and GATT (General Agreement on Tariffs and Trade) [both international economic agreements between the United States and other nations]—then the count soars upwards of 12 million. (Smolowe 1995:61)

In truth we really have no idea how many people hold these kinds of views. But how are we to make sense of the anger and paranoia that afflicts such people in the United States, in some cases to the point where they are ready to use violence against their own government? In our view these phenomena cannot simply be dismissed as expressions of craziness or the outcome of mental disturbances. They must be understood in the context of the distribution of power in the United States that we have been discussing in this chapter.

The concentration of power in the hands of a few, together with the growing political alienation of a citizenry that feels incapable of influencing decisions that affect it, has created a societal environment in which many people have become extremely frustrated. Frustrations are worsened when, as has been occurring, millions of people find themselves faced with economic insecurities and problems in living over which they have no control, and sense they are losing ground when they should be enjoying the American Dream. Some of these insecurities and problems in living are directly linked to government policies or the failure of the government to recognize and act on people's needs.

Antigovernment rhetoric, even that which is odd or extreme, is to be expected in a society in which federal officials are increasingly seen as dishonest, incompetent, and uninterested in the problems and plight of the average person. White supremacist organizations, militias, and patriot groups play upon widespread political alienation and economic frustrations, capturing attention and support for many of their ideas, if not always the most outlandish ones (Berlet 1994). They are joined by radio talk show hosts and highly articulate spokespersons for the New Right who churn and reinforce the alienation. Such an environment may foster political extremism, and it thus should not surprise us when "true believers" in extremist ideas adopt terrorist violence as what is, in their view, a legitimate and justifiable means of bringing about change.

Toward the Democratic Ideal

The concentration of political and economic power can be arrested and reversed. For this to happen, popular myths that counsel cynicism or quiescence, such as "You can't fight city hall" or "Our leaders know best," must be rejected (Parenti 1994). Persons must inject themselves into the political arena and make their concerns heard and felt. Staying silent is equivalent to sanctioning the status quo. People in the United States must take greater advantage of the lessons of the 1960s, when the collective political activities of people committed to change had a significant impact on national policies (Boggs 1995).

In the early 1960s centuries of tradition were overturned by the efforts of an active and aggressive grassroots civil rights movement. African Americans, other people of color, and whites entered into the political arena, stirring up a major shift in race relations in this country. Governmental elites, as indifferent to racism as their predecessors, were pressured into providing federal legislation to protect and enhance opportunities for people of color (as well as women). If those who dared to launch and join that civil rights movement had written off change as hopeless, governmental indifference would have continued.

By the late 1960s a series of presidential decisions, made secretly and without reference to the public, had embroiled the United States in a war in Southeast Asia. As U.S. involvement escalated and as the costs of the war became clear, tens of millions of people voiced their outrage in the national political arena. Governmental elites were forced to alter their stance on the war and withdraw from involvement in it, in response to the popular pressures placed upon them. If those who attacked the U.S. presence in Southeast Asia had not done so, the wartime carnage might have continued far longer.

It is not correct to assume that participation in political activity will make no difference. In fact, as the preceding examples indicate, the fabric of national politics is much more delicate and vulnerable to change from below than we often recognize. Much can be done when people cease being spectators to decisions of national consequence and seek ways to help shape such decisions. Many people in the United States seem ready for change.

College students are in an excellent position to analyze and reflect on major political issues. Indeed, students played key roles in the initiation and conduct of the civil rights movement of the 1960s and antiwar movements of the 1960s and early 1970s. By joining or creating organizations that are outspokenly dedicated to progressive societal change, students can help generate the public discussion necessary for such change to be realized. Such discussion and the

pressures for change to which it is likely to give rise are unlikely to be generated from other than grassroots directions. Certainly those whose political and economic power depends on maintaining the status quo are unlikely to stimulate discussion of change.

Along with grassroots movements for change must come major alterations in the conduct of government. In the mid-1970s, in the aftermath of the Watergate scandal of the Nixon administration, Congress passed campaign financing laws to limit direct private contributions to presidential candidates and to collect public funds for use in campaigns. These laws should be progressively strengthened and loopholes should be eliminated. For example, wealthy candidates can still use their own personal funds to outspend less affluent ones in political campaigns. **Political action committees** (PACs), allowable under the law, permit powerful corporate and trade groups to make campaign contributions of such a magnitude that incumbents' favoritism is easily bought (Clawson, Neustadtl, and Weller 1998). (See Table 2.3.) This must cease.

Many in Congress recognize the problems that PACs create for the political process, and they periodically raise the specter of campaign finance reform. However, Congress has still not passed significant legislation that effectively addresses campaign financing issues. Most particularly, in recent years it has become very clear that perhaps an even larger problem is "soft money" in campaign financing, which is not limited by the legislation that created PACs. **Soft money** refers to any contributions that are used for "party building" activities, "get out the vote" efforts, and political education campaigns. These terms are so broad that a good deal of spending on campaign activities that would otherwise be limited by law is allowed to go unchecked. Indeed, as the likelihood increases that legislators will be forced to further control PACs and their abuses, soft money has continued to grow to alarming levels. Thus far, no legislation has addressed the problem of soft money, a situation

Table 2.3   **Contributions to Congressional Campaigns by Political Action Committees (PAC), by Type of Committee: 1993 to 2002**

Type of committee	In millions of dollars					
	Total	Democrats	Republicans	Incumbents	Challengers	Open seats[1]
House of Representatives						
1993–94	132.4	88.2	43.9	101.4	12.7	18.3
1995–96	155.8	77.3	77.7	113.9	21.4	20.5
1997–98	158.7	77.6	80.9	124.0	14.9	19.8
1999–2000	193.4	98.2	94.7	150.5	19.9	23.0
2001–02, total[2]	**206.9**	**102.6**	**104.2**	**161.0**	**13.8**	**32.1**
Corporate	68.2	23.6	44.6	59.7	1.6	6.9
Trade association[3]	57.2	23.0	34.2	47.1	2.1	8.0
Labor	44.4	39.9	4.3	31.5	5.2	7.7
Nonconnected[4]	32.2	14.0	18.1	18.5	4.8	8.9
Senate						
1993–94	47.2	24.0	23.2	26.3	5.7	15.1
1995–96	45.6	16.6	29.0	19.4	6.9	19.3
1997–98	48.1	20.7	27.3	34.3	6.6	7.2
1999–2000	51.9	18.7	33.2	33.5	7.1	11.3
2001–02, total[2]	**59.2**	**25.4**	**33.8**	**37.0**	**14.2**	**8.1**
Corporate	23.4	7.0	16.4	15.8	4.3	3.4
Trade association[3]	14.3	4.9	9.3	9.5	3.1	1.7
Labor	7.5	7.0	0.5	4.1	2.4	1.1
Nonconnected[4]	12.5	5.8	6.6	6.6	4.1	1.8

Note: Covers amounts given to candidates in primary, general, run-off, and special elections during the 2-year calendar period indicated.

[1]*Elections in which an incumbent did not seek reelection.* [2]*Includes other types of PACs not shown separately.* [3]*Includes membership organizations and health organizations.* [4]*Represents "ideological" groups as well as other issue groups not necessarily ideological in nature.*

Source: U.S. Department of Commerce, Bureau of the Census, *Statistical Abstract of the United States, 2003* (Washington, D.C.: U.S. Government Printing Office, 2004), p. 274.

that will need careful and vigorous attention sooner rather than later.

All candidates for national political office and all elected and appointed officials and their staffs should be required by law to make regular full disclosure of their economic interests. Members of Congress, for example, should not be permitted to sit on committees or vote for bills that are connected to their economic holdings. The tie between economic self-interest and political behavior must be completely broken if the concerns of the U.S. public are to be addressed effectively.

It is also important to facilitate greater public involvement in national politics. The federal government should be working much harder to encourage all citizens to register to vote. It should be subsidizing regular television coverage of significant congressional debates and committee hearings. Election procedures should be simplified so that anyone can run for public office without going through a great deal of red tape. Presidential primaries and elections should be conducted on a national basis, rather than state by state. All such changes would bring more people into politics and increase the probability that democracy will become more than a symbolic ideal in this society.

Summary

There are four major perspectives on the workings of the U.S. political system. The conventional view is that the United States is democratic and pluralistic and that no one group or class dominates politics at the national level. Yet many people in the United States feel dominated and see themselves as powerless to affect decisions that affect them.

Two alternative perspectives suggest that political power has become concentrated in the hands of a few. The power elite perspective emphasizes the important role played by those in top positions in the corporate world, the military, and the executive branch of government. The business dominance perspective emphasizes the power-wielding capabilities of the rich as they participate in or otherwise influence government decisions. While differing in their emphases, these two perspectives seem closer to the reality experienced by many people than does the pluralist view. Meanwhile, the structuralist perspective calls our attention to the constraints on governmental leaders—even were they to be from nonelite or non-upper-class origins—stemming from the requirements of corporate capitalism.

To the degree to which political power is concentrated in the hands of a few, abuses of power can be expected. With such concentration and abuses comes political alienation. Members of U.S. society must overcome this sense of alienation, which can be linked to expressions of political extremism and violence against government. They must challenge concentrated power in aggressive but nonviolent and constructive ways, seeking changes and reforms at all levels of government that will bring the political system closer to the democratic ideal.

Key Terms

Business dominance perspective 31
Corporate capitalism 44
Democracy 50
Massification 39
Pluralist perspective 31
Political action committees 55

Political alienation 47
Political apathy 47
Power elite perspective 31
Soft money 55
Structuralist perspective 31

Discussion Questions

1. How were you taught to view the workings of the U.S. political system in elementary school? In high school? How much of what you were taught seems to fit with reality?

2. How important is it for people to vote in elections? Do you feel that voting or not voting makes a difference? In what way?

3. How do your family and friends view politics and politicians at the national level? To what degree and in what ways do you share their views?

4. While the 1960s and early 1970s were years of widespread protest, especially by college students, very little of this kind of activity is going on now. Why do you think this is the case?

5. Are you optimistic or pessimistic about whether the U.S. political system can be moved closer to the democratic ideal? On what do you base your optimism or pessimism?

Suggested Readings

Coleman, James William. *The Criminal Elite.* 5th ed. (New York: W.H. Freeman, 2002).
Analysis of criminal behavior by economic and political elites and its impact on the less privileged strata of U.S. society.

Domhoff, G. William. *Who Rules America? Power and Politics.* 4th ed. (New York: McGraw-Hill, 2002).
Mobilization of evidence that the United States is ruled by and in the interests of the economic upper class.

Parenti, Michael. *Democracy for the Few.* 7th ed. (New York: Wadsworth, 2001).
  Exploration of ways in which the forces of democracy and modern-day capitalism are contradictory and often clash.

Phillips, Kevin. *The Politics of Rich and Poor.* (New York: Random House, 1990).
  How elite political decision making that favors the affluent has increased wealth and income inequalities.

Piven, Frances Fox, and Richard A. Cloward. *Why Americans Still Don't Vote: And Why Politicians Want It That Way.* (Boston: Beacon Press, 2000).
  Reasons why so many U.S. citizens—in contrast to those in other industrial democracies—fail to exercise their voting rights.

Sklar, Holly. *Chaos or Community?* (Boston: South End Press, 1995).
  Explores the political and economic forces that are actively undermining access to the American Dream and presents ideas for changing this situation.

chapter 3

Militarism, War, and Terrorism

To an irrational degree the United States devotes resources to military aggression and violence against other peoples of the world. Instead, our nation and others must move toward disarmament and the peaceful settlement of differences.

In the spring of 1975 the U.S. military officially withdrew from South Vietnam, a small peasant society located 8,000 miles away in Southeast Asia. Vietnam was reunited under a socialist government that the United States had failed to defeat in a decade of military action that left over 58,000 U.S. military personnel dead and hundreds of thousands more maimed and disabled. Still others are "missing in action." The impact on those native to the war zone was even more staggering: More than 3 million people perished, including some 2 million civilians.

Many U.S. survivors of the Vietnam experience continue to suffer greatly. Mental troubles among Vietnam veterans have been both common and similar enough to have been termed *posttraumatic stress syndrome.* Still other veterans are trying to deal with the long-term aftereffects of exposure to Agent Orange, a herbicide used to kill foliage and thus minimize enemy hiding places in Vietnam. One of the aftereffects of exposure to this chemical is cancer.

The war in Vietnam also caused years of unprecedented domestic political unrest. It cost U.S. taxpayers an estimated $150 billion and created a cycle of inflation and recession in our overall economy. The devastating impact of the war on the Vietnamese people, as well as on those to whom the war traveled in Laos and Cambodia, will probably never be calculated in full.

Yet, while the United States retreated in defeat from Vietnam, the domestic institutional forces that had helped to bring about and sustain our military involvement there remained intact. The U.S. government warned the world at that time that the setback it experienced in Southeast Asia was not to be interpreted as a sign of weakness. Indeed, in the years since the Vietnam War ended in 1975, the United States has repeatedly used her military power within or against other nations.

Almost immediately after the Vietnam War, President Gerald Ford sent military forces to free the merchant ship *Mayagüez* from temporary Cambodian capture. In 1980 President Jimmy Carter sent troops and helicopters in a failed attempt to rescue 60 U.S. citizens held hostage by the government of Iran. In 1983 President Ronald Reagan sent naval warships and marines to Lebanon, partly in an effort to shape the outcome of a long-term civil war in that country. In the same year, U.S. troops were ordered to the small Caribbean island of Grenada, where they ended that nation's short-lived experiment with socialism. In 1986 U.S. planes were sent to bomb the living quarters of Colonel Muammar al-Qaddafi, head of socialist Libya, on the basis of allegations of Libyan involvement in European terrorist incidents. Meanwhile, President Reagan also had uniformed military advisers in El Salvador to guide that country's army in a civil war involving peasant revolutionaries and was openly using mercenaries trained by the U.S. Central Intelligence Agency in an effort to overthrow the government of Nicaragua.

In 1989 President Bush employed 12,000 troops in a U.S. invasion of Panama, searching out General Manuel Antonio Noriega for arrest and prosecution on drug trade–related charges. President Bush also issued the call to other nations that led to the initiation of the Persian Gulf War in response to Iraq's invasion of Kuwait in August 1990. Over a half million U.S. troops were mobilized. The brief war, involving forces on land, in the air, and at sea, directed high-tech, extremely destructive weaponry against Iraq, whose actions threatened to disrupt access to supplies of Middle Eastern oil. In 1994 President Bill Clinton raised the possibility that U.S. military force might be required if North Korea did not cease apparent efforts to develop nuclear weapons. President Clinton also involved U.S. military forces in peacekeeping operations on different continents, in Somalia, Rwanda, Haiti, and Bosnia. By 2003 President George W. Bush had deployed troops to Afghanistan in response to the September 11, 2001, terrorist attacks on

the United States, and to Iraq to depose Saddam Hussein.

When the 45-year-old Cold War and monumental arms race with the Soviet Union slowed in the late 1980s and then abruptly ended with the dissolution of that nation in 1991, many citizens saw an opportunity to shift substantial amounts of funds away from military-related expenditures to programs that would improve the quality of life within U.S. society. Billions of dollars could be diverted from Cold War expenditures to, for example, rebuild the nation's deteriorating central cities or expand opportunities for education and training in the job skills to be needed in the twenty-first century.

However, the hoped-for "peace dividend" has not been realized to date. Instead, the United States has retained its powerful Cold War–level nuclear and conventional warmaking stance. And it has emerged as the world's largest arms exporter, selling weapons systems to developed and underdeveloped nations and thus helping to increase the level of violence with which the world is afflicted when weapons are used to resolve conflicts. To understand this situation we must examine the constellation of institutional forces that underlie the United States' militaristic posture.

For many years critics have characterized the United States as a "weapons culture" and a "warfare state" (Cook 1962; Lapp 1968). Retired Marine Colonel James A. Donovan once wrote, "America has become a militaristic and aggressive nation embodied in a vast, expensive, and burgeoning military-industrial-scientific-political combine which dominates the country and affects much of our daily life, our economy, our international status, and our foreign policies" (Donovan 1970:1). The "combine" to which Colonel Donovan refers is more popularly called the **military-industrial complex,** a term coined by President Dwight D. Eisenhower in his farewell address in 1961. It is an ongoing human creation that contributes to this society's predisposition to police the world and to help

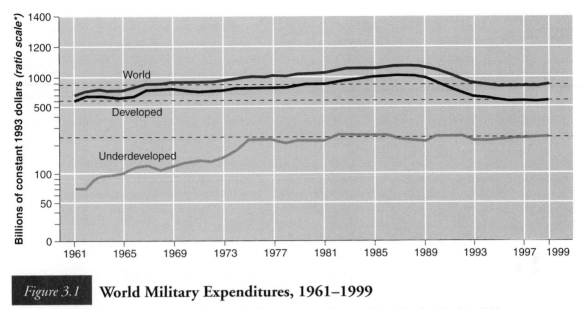

Figure 3.1   **World Military Expenditures, 1961–1999**

Source: U.S. Arms Control and Disarmament Agency, *World Military Expenditures and Arms Transfers*. 4th ed. Available at: www.state.gov/documents/organization/18723.pdf.

saturate it with the technology of violence. As more nations acquire nuclear weapon capabilities or more powerful conventional arms, the probability they will be used rises. But the U.S. military-industrial complex, which contributes to the technology of destruction that is spreading worldwide (see Figure 3.1), grinds on. Let us examine this complex and its components.

The Military-Industrial Complex

As the Vietnam War began to escalate in 1965, Marc Pilisuk and Thomas Hayden (1965) wrote an article that asked, "Is there a military-industrial complex which prevents peace?" Their conclusion—still relevant some four decades later—was that "American society *is* a military-industrial complex." The complex is usually said to have emerged at the time of World War II (Hooks 1991; Markusen et al. 1991). It consists of several components: the

uniformed military, the aerospace-defense industry, the civilian national security managers, and the U.S. Congress.

Each component of the military-industrial complex promotes and protects its own interests while reinforcing the interests of the other components:

Each institutional component of the military-industrial complex has plausible reasons for continuing to exist and expand. Each promotes and protects its own interests and in doing so reinforces the interests of every other. That is what a "complex" is—a set of integrated institutions that act to maximize their collective power. (Barnet 1969:59)

The uniformed military jockeys for the resources required to sustain, if not increase, U.S. warmaking capabilities. The aerospace-defense industry presses for a continuing flow of procurement contracts, under which it can pursue profits at low risk. The civilian national security

Table 3.1	Federal Budget Outlays for National Defense Functions: 1970 to 2003							
Defense function	1970	1980	1985	1990	1995	2001	2002	2003 est.
Total	**81.7**	**134.0**	**252.7**	**299.3**	**272.1**	**305.5**	**348.6**	**376.3**
Percent change[1]	10.1	15.2	11.1	−1.4	−3.4	3.7	14.1	8.0
Defense Dept., military	80.1	130.9	245.2	289.8	259.4	291.0	332.0	358.2
Military personnel	29.0	40.9	67.8	75.6	70.8	74.0	86.8	92.7
Operation, maintenance	21.6	44.8	72.4	88.3	91.1	112.0	130.0	136.3
Procurement	21.6	29.0	70.4	81.0	55.0	55.0	62.5	63.2
Research and development	7.2	13.1	27.1	37.5	34.6	40.5	44.4	52.8
Military construction	1.2	2.5	4.3	5.1	6.8	5.0	5.1	6.0
Family housing	0.6	1.7	2.6	3.5	3.6	3.5	3.7	4.2
Other[2]	−1.1	−1.1	0.6	−1.2	−2.4	1.1	−0.5	3.0
Atomic energy activities[3]	1.4	2.9	7.1	9.0	11.8	13.0	14.9	16.3
Defense-related activities[4]	0.2	0.2	0.5	0.6	0.8	1.5	1.7	1.8

[In billions of dollars, except percent. For fiscal year ending in year shown; minus sign (−) indicates decline.]
[1]*Change from prior year; for 1970, change from 1965.*
[2]*Revolving and management funds, trust funds, special currency program, allowances, and offsetting receipts.*
[3]*Defense activities only.*
[4]*Includes civil defense activities.*

Source: U.S. Department of Commerce, Bureau of the Census, *Statistical Abstract of the United States, 1995* (Washington, D.C.: U.S. Government Printing Office, 1995), p. 356; U.S. Department of Commerce, Bureau of the Census, *Statistical Abstract of the United States, 2003* (Washington, D.C.: U.S. Government Printing Office, 2004), p. 342.

managers champion the military expenditures central to their definition of national security and the formulation of foreign policy. And members of Congress provide the tax dollars that keep the military-industrial complex humming, taking credit when military expenditures have a positive impact on the economic life of their states and districts. The magnitude of spending is huge, as indicated in Table 3.1.

The Rise of the Military-Industrial Complex

Before World War II the United States did not routinely maintain large numbers of men and women in uniform, nor did it devote much in the way of national resources to the maintenance of massive warmaking capabilities. During World War I, for example, people and matériel (equipment and supplies) were mobilized as needed. When the war had been won, the military establishment was virtually dismantled, and war industries were converted back to peacetime operations. With World War II this pattern of mobilization and postwar demilitarization was to change.

During World War II the United States became a highly efficient war machine. The U.S. economy, which had been unable to break out of years of peacetime depression in the

1930s, boomed as a consequence of wartime production demands. Depression-level unemployment—wherein 13 million people, or over 25 percent of the labor force, were out of work—ceased to be a problem, given the labor requirements of industry and the uniformed military services. A sense of national purpose and unity grew in response to the challenge of achieving victory overseas. By the war's end, the United States had demonstrated a level of military power unequaled in history. It had developed and shown a willingness to use nuclear arms. And it had escaped the war intact and (unlike many of its European and other allies) virtually unscathed because of its geographic isolation from military action.

At the end of World War II, the war machine was not wholly dismantled. High-ranking U.S. military officers, having gained great public honor from the victory and enjoying command over an unprecedentedly huge military establishment, campaigned to keep their powers and responsibilities intact. Governmental and corporate elites feared that a full-scale military demobilization and industrial conversion would lead the United States back into an economic depression. Moreover, corporate chieftains had learned that a lot of money could be made from government contracts for military weapons, equipment, and supplies.

A further justification for maintaining a permanent war economy was simultaneously provided by the outbreak of the Cold War with the Soviet Union—a war in which both nations jockeyed for world dominance without ever actually using their enormous military arsenals directly against each other. After World War II U.S. elites saw the Soviet Union as constituting a political and military threat. They pointed to the spread of Soviet domination within Eastern Europe as evidence of that threat. Further, they warned that Soviet socialism posed a real danger to all governments committed to maintaining capitalist economies. When the Soviet Union demonstrated its potential as a nuclear

power in the 1940s, and when mainland China moved toward building a socialist society in 1949, it seemed clear to the elites that socialism could be held in check only by the threat or use of military power.

For 45 years (1945–1990) U.S. society's military-industrial complex rode on the fears of expanding socialism, the Soviets—with their nuclear might—being of central concern. During this period U.S. military and paramilitary (e.g., Central Intelligence Agency) interventions took place across the globe and a spiraling nuclear arms race with the Soviet Union occurred. At the same time, more and more nations, particularly those in the economically underdeveloped areas of the world, experimented with various types of socialist economic systems.

By the 1990s major socialist nations had begun to undergo significant internal transformations involving the adoption of capitalist economic principles, including China, Russia, and former Soviet bloc nations in Eastern Europe. Socialism continued to be defined as a threat by U.S. elites (witness the U.S. government's harsh economic boycott on socialist Cuba, maintained in the hopes of forcing an uprising against the Castro government). But the collapse of the Soviet Union and changes under way in major socialist nations forced U.S. officials to reassess U.S. defense needs and priorities. As we shall see in a later section, these officials quickly came up with new potential dangers that, in their view, justified maintaining enormous military expenditures in the post–Cold War era. The uniformed military would be a key beneficiary of this reassessment process.

The Uniformed Military

Among the institutional components central to the military-industrial complex is the uniformed military. The United States Air Force, Army, Navy, and Marine Corps are all under the authority of a civilian-headed umbrella organization, the Department of Defense (DOD). Since

World War II the military services have taken the form of vast bureaucracies commanded by professional career officers who make up an **officer class.** The services receive tens of billions of dollars annually from the federal government in order to carry out their domestic and foreign operations. While trimmed down somewhat in the post–Cold War era, they continue to control property and weapons systems valued in the hundreds of billions of dollars, and to maintain military bases and installations around the world. At a signal from the president, who is the commander in chief of the military, the civilian head of DOD can call any or all of the 1.6 million members of the active-duty uniformed military into immediate action—to move people and equipment or even to obliterate whole segments of the earth's population. The duty of the uniformed military is to follow orders.

Since World War II each of the military services has carved out its own roles or *missions* in defense and active warfare. Each service competes with the others for new responsibilities and resources and the "honor" of being used first in or being the centerpiece of military action. The officer class of each service tries to justify the strategic importance of its activities and plans. In a word, each of the services is continually striving to *sell* the notion of its flexible capabilities and indispensability.

Selling has meant working to persuade governmental civilians and the public that there are serious military dangers for which this society must be prepared. Top-ranking officers pressure their civilian DOD overseers and the White House to prepare budgets that will maintain the authority and prestige of their respective services. Military personnel join DOD and White House officials in briefing Congress, which provides funds for these budgets. Interservice rivalries have at times revolved around identifying new dangers to be guarded against, whether immediate or potential, to back up funding requests.

As mentioned, reductions in defense expenditures occurred in the 1990s, leading to some military base closings, cutbacks in corporate defense contracts, and fewer men and women in uniform. But these reductions came into being only after a significant escalation in U.S. defense spending had taken place in the 1980s, one purpose of which was to put overwhelming pressure on the leadership of the Soviet Union to abandon the arms race. Despite the reductions, Congress still allocates billions in tax funds each year for guns, tanks, planes, bombs, missiles, ships, submarines, and communications devices for undersea and outer-space use. Additional funds go for research, development, and production of new weapons systems to strengthen the U.S. military arsenal and to replace the obsolete. Since military threats and weapons technology alter with time, obsolescence is often under way before the new tools of warfare are finished and in place. In 2002 an estimated 17 percent or $348.6 billion of the federal government's total annual expenditures went toward defense, down from a high of 27 percent ($299 billion) in 1985 (U.S. Bureau of the Census, *Statistical Abstracts of the United State,* 1995, 2004). Many more billions go each year for military-related activities not counted in the "defense" portion of the budget, such as the operations of secret intelligence agencies, missile development and space exploration projects of the National Aeronautics and Space Administration, and nuclear weapons manufacture funded by the federal Department of Energy.

Since most people in the United States take military use of their tax dollars for granted, the uniformed military services are in a position to press their institutional self-interests. How many of us are expert enough to judge the importance of missions and the consequent military claims on the federal budget? How many of us can assess accurately the validity and seriousness of military dangers alleged to exist around the world? Even if we were experts, we would find it hard to get the facts, for the uniformed military and its civilian overseers in the DOD and White House are able to maintain a ring of secrecy around such matters. Even Congress often finds this secrecy hard to counter.

The resources provided to the uniformed military include funds for public relations efforts. Officers may appear at public events to remind the U.S. public of the patriotism of those who serve and to raise the specter of dangers that presumably make military power deserving of support. Community public opinion leaders are known to have been invited to tour military facilities, where they receive VIP (very important person) treatment. Armed Forces Day is celebrated at military bases and installations each year, often with demonstrations of military weaponry for the public to enjoy. Mobile informational displays on military missions and technology are installed in shopping centers. Tapes and films dealing with military matters are mass-produced for use by schools and citizens' organizations. Local newspapers regularly receive news releases from military press units. Civilian advertising agencies are hired to promote the virtues of military service. And DOD has cooperated with Hollywood to produce war extravaganzas that reflect well on U.S. military prowess. In brief, millions of tax dollars are used each year to promote the uniformed military and legitimate its activities.

But perhaps the best "advertisement" for public consumption is success in warfare. The Persian Gulf War provided the uniformed military with an opportunity to influence public opinion toward it in positive ways. It was portrayed as a "just" war. This was done by careful attention to news control. Unlike the Vietnam War, and despite media complaints, news correspondents and journalists were largely kept out of the Gulf War zone and severely limited in their access to and use of interviews, news releases, films, and photographs other than those permitted by military public relations officials. The U.S. public thus saw what the military wanted it to see and no more (Fialka 1992; MacArthur 1992). The grotesque human horrors of the war, its impact on hundreds of thousands of Iraqi troops and civilian noncombatants, and a sense of the absolute physical devastation that was wreaked in cities such as Baghdad were filtered out (Clark et al. 1992; United Nations 1991).

Instead, public understanding of the war largely derived from periodic television appearances by President Bush and high-ranking military leaders, daily briefings by military spokespersons, and news portrayals of aerial and air-to-ground warfare that closely resembled electronic video games. The military's informational emphasis was on success, an outcome that was predictable. The most militarily powerful nation in the world, mobilizing over a half million of its troops, was using some of its most destructive nonnuclear weapons—weapons that were originally developed for continent-wide battles with the Soviet superpower and its allies. Iraq, a comparatively minor world military power, had no chance to win from the start. The degree to which the public's perceptions of the war were successfully "managed" through manipulation of the mass media was unique in comparison with past wars (Chomsky 1991).

Subsequent revelations concerning "Gulf War Syndrome," however, undid some of the good public relations achieved by the uniformed military. The syndrome frequently involves serious illnesses. There have, for example, been complaints of unusual neurological problems, reproductive difficulties and births of infants with defects, skin disorders, and cancers among tens of thousands of the over half a million men and women who served in the Gulf War zone. Military officials both denied and resisted any acknowledgment that these illnesses might be war related. The scandal of a possible military cover-up of the causes of the illnesses (e.g., exposure to Iraqi chemical or biological warfare agents, toxic effects of medications taken by the U.S. forces in case of exposure, poisoning by exposure to burning oil fires or to radioactive armament debris) marred the "victory" for many participants. The victory was further tarnished by the fact that the Iraqi leader who ordered the invasion of Kuwait, Saddam Hussein, escaped the war unharmed, remained in power, and continued to issue further military threats and engage in provocations years after the war ended.

Public understanding of U.S. involvement in war was similarly shaped in 2003 when President George W. Bush declared war against Iraq. He began to mobilize support for the war by first announcing that an "axis of evil" existed in Iraq, Iran, and North Korea. He asserted that these nations had developed weapons of mass destruction, posing a clear and present threat to the United States and to the world. Although world opinion strongly resisted Bush's insistence that Iraq and its alleged weapons of mass destruction needed to be forcibly brought under control (and the Security Council in the United Nations clearly denied his proposal for a military action against Iraq), he sent thousands of U.S. troops to that country and staged a massive invasion. To bolster public support in the United States, if not in the world, for the war, Bush allowed journalists to be embedded with the troops as they deployed deep into Iraq. Journalists were supposed to report on the bravery of the troops, their successful incursions into the country, the defeat of Saddam Hussein, and (he hoped) their discovery of the much-sought weapons of mass destruction. They were not supposed to report on mass civilian casualties, massive defeats of U.S. troops, or declining morale among the troops. The Bush administration thus sought to control what the media reported and hence what the public understood about the war. Indeed, the Bush administration termed the publication of film footage and photographs of scores of flag-draped coffins of U.S. casualties returning home as unpatriotic and as aiding and abetting the enemy, an echo of attempts to silence critics against the war in Vietnam.

When it became apparent that no weapons of mass destruction were to be found, the Bush administration shifted the rationale for the war from the need to root out these weapons to the need to punish Saddam Hussein and Iraq for their supposed role in the September 11, 2001, terrorist attacks against the United States. Using the media as the conduit of this new shaping of public perception, several spokespersons in the administration invited media coverage of speeches and held press conferences during which they invoked the public's anger, resentment, and great fear of terrorism and vowed to make the world safer by deposing Saddam Hussein. Amid triumphant images of the destruction of Saddam's statue and his palaces, President Bush declared "mission accomplished." However, increasing evidence suggested that there was no clear or direct connection between Saddam Hussein or Iraq to the September 11 attacks; rather, the link appeared to be with Saudi Arabia, a staunch ally and major supplier of oil to the United States.

Once again, the rationale for the war shifted, to one of "liberating Iraq" from the dictator Saddam Hussein, with promises that the Iraqi people would greet U.S. troops not as occupiers but as welcome liberators who would secure the country and then hand over control to a grateful population. However, spiraling violence and growing instability in Iraq, sharply increasing animosity to U.S. military and civilian occupation of the country, and growing U.S. casualties made it difficult to maintain that rationale, as well. By mid-2004, unsettling reports of U.S. military abuse of Iraqi prisoners and the indefinite detention of hundreds of prisoners tarnished the U.S. mission amid charges of violations of the Geneva Convention and its international accords concerning the human rights of prisoners of war. And, sadly, lost in all the rhetoric about duty to country, the moral war against terrorism, and national self-interest were the needs and interests of those who put their lives in jeopardy to serve.

The officers of the respective military services thus have personal and institutional self-interests to pursue, and have day-to-day contact

U.S. involvement in the war in Iraq was as much a public relations event as it was a military operation, as military and civilian government officials strove to mold public opinion in support of entering and continuing military actions there. Here, U.S. Marines carry out their mission in Fallujah, Iraq in 2004.

with the means to enact enormous violence. Yet, unlike some other nations, the uniformed military in the United States is under firm civilian control. The influence of the military within the military-industrial complex is indeed strong, but it appears to be fed by—and feeds—other institutional components, which also have a major stake in keeping the complex going.

The Aerospace-Defense Industry

U.S. militarism is big business (Klare 1984; Stubbing and Mendel 1986). The billions upon billions in tax dollars spent annually by the military establishment have been the mainstay of the permanent war economy since the 1940s. Handsome stockholder revenues for members of the ownership class (see Chapter 6) are one result of such expenditures. In addition, the livelihoods of millions of U.S. workers have become dependent on the permanent war economy. Indeed, many have found their livelihoods disrupted as military-related expenditures have undergone reductions in the post–Cold War era. Between 1989 and 1993, some 440,000 defense workers were laid off, more than the combined job losses due to major nondefense cutbacks by America's largest corporations in that period (Smith 1993).

Each year the DOD enters into contracts for the purchase and procurement of weapons, ammunition, equipment, supplies, and services. The recipients of these contracts include 25,000 to 30,000 principal firms classified as "primary contractors" and 50,000 subcontractors. Production of goods and services for the DOD is highly concentrated. For many years, most of the DOD procurement budget has gone to a mere 100 large corporations, and the top 10 among them have taken a major share of that.

For example, in 2002 the U.S. Department of Defense awarded $170.8 billion in prime (i.e., over $25,000) contracts. Over $107.2 billion, or 62.8 percent of the money awarded, went to 100 large U.S. corporations and their subsidiaries. Most of the contracts were for aircraft, missile/space systems, ships, and electronic and communications equipment (U.S. Department of Defense 2003, available at www.dior.whs.mil/peidhome/procstat).

The top 10 defense contractors were Lockheed, Martin Marietta, Boeing, Northrop, Raytheon, General Dynamics, United Technologies, Science Applications International, TRW, Health Net, and L-C Communications Holdings. In 2002 alone, these firms received contracts valued at $67.4 billion—almost two-thirds of the contract dollars that were awarded to the entire top 100 contracting corporations (U.S. Department of Defense 2003, available at www.dior.whs.mil/peidhome/procstat). For most of these 10 firms the DOD is their largest customer by far. The highly concentrated and economically powerful aerospace-defense industry has, understandably, developed an outlook on military spending comparable to that of the uniformed services (Boies 1994).

▲ Pentagon Capitalism

The relationship between the aerospace-defense industry and the DOD has been characterized as **Pentagon capitalism** (Melman 1974). Among other things, this term denotes the rather special relationship between the department and its contractors. Doing business with the department is quite different from operating in the civilian marketplace and selling consumer goods to the public.

Corporations that produce goods and services for the civilian marketplace often must compete for customers' attention and dollars. They must adjust their production to actual and anticipated public demand. There is a degree of risk involved in dealing with the public—there will be no profits if goods and services cannot be sold. Errors in production may prove quite costly. Such risks are taken for granted by firms that service the public, though efforts are constantly made to minimize them.

Under Pentagon capitalism, on the other hand, procurement contracts are often issued to principal contractors without requiring competition among them. Aerospace-defense firms frequently develop their products and services in close cooperation with their military customers. The amounts to be produced are specified in advance, and the demand is guaranteed. In contrast to doing business in the civilian marketplace, production for the military establishment involves relatively few risks and assured profits. Even if the goods and services turn out to cost more than originally anticipated (*cost overruns*), the aerospace-defense contractor can request and usually get supplemental funds. If errors in production occur, or if the time schedule for delivering goods and services cannot be observed, DOD cooperates, waits, and often shoulders any extra costs involved (Boies 1994).

The highly dependable and lucrative nature of DOD procurement contracts—under which cost overruns, errors, waste, and assured profits are taken for granted—has made aerospace-defense firms strong backers of U.S. militarism. The aerospace-defense industry serves its own interests by responding to the perceived needs and plans of the officer class, supporting its constant pursuit of new missions, responsibilities, and budgetary resources. On its own initiative, the industry develops products and services that might encourage the military to push for new missions not yet in existence. Under the drive for profits, the industry has engineered a community of interest with the military establishment within which each embellishes the strivings of the other.

▲ The Community of Interest

The community of interest between industry and the military has been cemented through the circulation of personnel. Executives from the aerospace-defense industry have, with startling frequency, moved into important civilian positions in DOD. Top-ranking military officers, as well as lesser members of the officer class, have retired and moved into positions in the industry. In the latter case, contractors have been able to exploit the specialized knowledge and skills of former officers as well as their familiarity with people and procedures involved in procurement contracting at DOD. The circulation of military personnel to aerospace-defense corporations raises the concern that some military officers may be tempted to bestow favors on particular firms in order to ensure themselves employment upon retirement from active duty. The same potential conflict of interest exists for persons holding key civilian positions in the DOD (Boies 1994:34–35).

More than 30 years ago, Senator William Proxmire (March 24, 1969) gave a speech before Congress in which he pointed out some of the issues involved in the "community of interest" that has continued to evolve between industry and the military establishment:

When the bulk of the budget goes for military purposes; when 100 companies get 67 percent of the defense contract dollars; when cost overruns are routine and prime military weapon system contracts normally exceed their estimates by 100 to 200 percent; when these contracts are let by negotiation and not by competitive bidding; and when the top contractors have over 2000 retired high-ranking military officers on their payrolls; there are very real questions as to how critically these matters are reviewed and how well the public interest is served.

Today the same very real questions remain. The "community of interest" between industry and the military establishment may easily lead to corruption, given the huge amounts of money at stake. In 1988 the news media learned of a massive scandal involving federal defense expenditures that was uncovered in an investigation begun secretly two years earlier. Investigators charged that defense contractors, acting through intermediaries, bribed top DOD civilian staff members to steer prime defense contracts their way. Offices searched for evidence by the Federal Bureau of Investigation included the headquarters of some of the nation's largest contractors. Those calling for criminal prosecution claimed that the case could involve tens of billions of dollars (Church 1988). By 1993, when the investigation was winding down, it had resulted in the conviction of 9 government officials, 42 private consultants and corporate executives, and 7 corporations (including giant United Technologies) (Ross 1993). Given the "community of interest" that exists between the uniformed military and the aerospace-defense industry, there is a high likelihood such criminal behavior will reoccur.

The National Security Managers

As we have stated, the uniformed military services are under civilian control within the Department of Defense. The ultimate responsibility for safeguarding national security and for formulating foreign policy outside the White House is held by executives in DOD and civilian representatives from such other agencies as the Department of State and the Central Intelligence Agency.

Who are the people who have determined that militarism is in the interest of national security? Richard J. Barnet has attempted to identify the backgrounds and hint at the worldview of the United States' civilian **national security managers,** the top-level civilian executives of the federal agencies already mentioned. When Barnet examined the backgrounds of 91 individuals who held key executive posts between 1940 and 1967, he found that 70 "were from the ranks of big business or high finance" (Barnet 1969:88). He took this to mean that military policy was formulated largely on the basis of business interests:

Defining the national interest and protecting national security are the proper province of business . . . . For a National Security Manager recruited from the world of business, there are no other important constituencies to which he feels a need to respond. (Barnet 1969:89, 100)

While national security managers to this day tend disproportionately to come from the business elite (Chomsky 1982; Kaplan 1982), it would be wrong to conclude that business interests are always the sole consideration in the process of formulating policy. Nevertheless, the fact that the national security managers are commonly drawn from business does constitute another case of conflict of interest. Since massive military expenditures are the mainstay of this nation's permanent war economy, the national security managers recruited from big business and high finance are unlikely to tamper significantly with the status quo. This is particularly so in that national security managers often move in and out of governmental service, using it as a means of enhancing their career chances in the business world. The potential of conflict of interest is highest in the case of executives recruited from the aerospace-defense industry, an industry to which they are likely to return.

As we saw in Chapter 2 the U.S. business community has progressively taken on multinational dimensions. Many of the economy's largest corporations have increasingly come to depend on profits generated by investments and sales abroad. A global military posture can readily be rationalized as a means of protecting U.S. corporate interests around the world. National security managers who come from big business and high finance can be expected to be sensitive to such matters, insofar as the national interest can be equated with the well-being of the large corporations that dominate the U.S. economy.

The Militarized Congress

The uniformed military, the aerospace-defense industry, and the national security managers are the main institutional components of the military-industrial complex. But for this complex to exist, billions of tax dollars must be given it every year. The national security managers and the uniformed military prepare annual budget requests and justifications for proposed expenditures. These are then presented to Congress, which alone has the authority to appropriate the funds requested. As the controller of the purse strings that must be loosened for U.S. militarism to continue unhampered, Congress has virtually become an institutional component of the complex; in other words, it has become a **militarized Congress.**

In past years the U.S. Senate and House of Representatives have, almost without exception, responded favorably to requests for funds to support the military establishment and its procurement contracts. Periodic investigations by congressional committees and individual senators and representatives have sometimes resulted in harsh criticism of the costs of military procurement and errors and waste on the part of contractors. But when it comes time to vote on military budgets, most members of Congress support high spending levels. An annual ritual in Congress involves hearings on the military budget. During these hearings a few legislators pose some sharp questions, pare some money off the requests, and end up approving most of the funds requested.

There are several reasons for congressional support of the permanent war economy. Many members of Congress are themselves veterans and retired or reserve officers, so they identify favorably with the military as an institution. Despite their positions of responsibility, many are as uninformed as most citizens when it comes to judging national security needs, the relevance of missions, the necessity for weapons systems, and the dangers against which military power must be poised. There is thus a tendency to accept the authoritative judgments of the national security managers and top-ranking military officers.

Many members of Congress are affluent, which means that they are likely to own stock in U.S. corporations, including aerospace-defense firms. And even if they do not, certainly many of those who provide contributions for their campaign expenses do. Hence, their stand on military budget requests may make the difference between being reelected or finding a new job, especially since DOD money is channeled into the states or districts of most members of Congress. There is obviously little political incentive to vote down military expenditures if this means the loss of bases, procurement contracts, and employment for constituents. Rather, there is even more reason to approve such expenditures and, especially in an era of budgetary reductions, to use political influence to get such expenditures directed in ways that benefit their own voters.

Sidney Lens (1970:45), author of *The Military-Industrial Complex,* once posed this rhetorical question:

Who can tell in this game of quid pro quo *how many legislators vote for a weapons system they don't think is necessary in order to get a contract for their own business community, and how much pork is put into the budget by the Pentagon to lure a congressional vote?*

In response to the "pork" (extra proposed expenditures), to lobbying efforts by the various institutional components of the military-industrial complex, and to pressures from such special-interest groups as organized labor and veterans' associations, Congress goes along with the game. But when public outrage over military spending and its uses arises and becomes intense, as in the later stages of the Vietnam War, we have seen Congress adjust its stance on U.S. militarism.

Protecting U.S. Economic Interests Abroad

Our economic system has often been labeled *corporate capitalism* in recognition of the key role that large corporations have come to play within it. According to U.S. government income tax data, there were 25 million active business enterprises in 2000. But most of the nation's business is done by a very tiny percentage of these enterprises. In 2000 a mere 3.8 percent of these firms had receipts of $1 million or more. Yet this tiny percentage of firms accounted for 81.7 percent of all business receipts that year (U.S. Bureau of the Census; *Statistical Abstract of the United States,* 2004:495).

Another way to underscore the significance of large corporations to our economy is to look at the industrial sector. In 2000 there were 288,506 manufacturing corporations in the United States, with total assets of $5.7 trillion. But the largest 1,595 manufacturing firms— those with assets of $250 million and over— possessed 76 percent of the total. Such concentration of economic assets in the hands of relatively few firms is also found in such economic sectors as mining, transportation, public utilities, insurance, and banking (U.S. Bureau of the Census; *Statistical Abstract of the United States,* 2004:501). The economic well-being of these large corporations is crucial to the United States. To the degree they are successful in meeting their objectives of profit and growth, this society's capitalist economy avoids stagnation.

To grow and profit, U.S. corporations have found it necessary to extend their activities well beyond the political boundaries of the nation. In the years since World War II we have witnessed the growth (both in size and numbers) of multi-national firms, corporations headquartered in the United States but with properties, plants, and offices around the world (Barnet and Cavanaugh 1994). Between 1960 and 2002, direct corporate investments in foreign nations grew from $31.9 billion to more than $1.5 trillion (U.S. Bureau of the Census; *Statistical Abstract of the United States,* 1995:811; 2004:808). Most of this money has been channeled into the developed economies of Canada and Western Europe, where U.S.-owned enterprises cater to markets for manufactured goods. The rest has gone to Middle East petroleum suppliers and to a num-ber of economically underdeveloped nations in Latin America, Africa, and Asia. (See Fig-ure 3.2.) For the most part, investments in the Middle East and elsewhere in underdeveloped nations have been made to obtain natural re-sources to be used in production in the United States and other industrialized economies. Even though U.S. corporate investment dollars have gone primarily into Canada and Western Europe, the rates of return on investments in un-derdeveloped nations have proved to be higher.

Earnings from foreign operations constitute an increasing percentage of the annual net in-comes of many of the United States' largest firms. It seems fair to conclude that the eco-nomic health of the United States has come to depend, to a significant degree, on the multina-tionals' ability to penetrate the economies of other nations. In doing so, the multinationals gain access to and control over valuable raw ma-terials, including many materials utilized by such key industries as aerospace-defense. Many of these raw materials are in short supply or would be more expensive to extract in the United States. In addition, multinational corporations

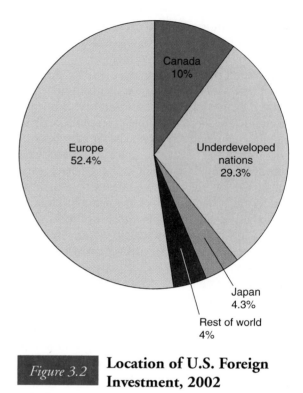

Figure 3.2   **Location of U.S. Foreign Investment, 2002**

Source: U.S. Department of Commerce, Bureau of the Census, *Statistical Abstract of the United States, 2003* (Washington, DC: U.S. Government Printing Office, 2004), p. 808.

are able to cultivate new markets for products manufactured in this country and in their plants abroad. Particularly in underdeveloped nations, such firms are able to take advantage of large pools of cheap labor, thus cutting costs. The profits from such operations flow back to corpo-rate headquarters in the United States, where they can be used to reward stockholders and/or provide a basis for further investments.

The Corporate-Governmental Partnership

The spread of U.S. economic interests across the globe has been greatly facilitated by the federal government—or, more specifically, by the national security managers (Magdoff 1978;

Williams 1980). Given their background in business and finance, it is not surprising that these managers have often tailored foreign policy to protect corporate operations abroad.

For example, after World War II the government financed what came to be called the Marshall Plan, a program of aid designed to help rebuild the war-torn nations of Western Europe. The Marshall Plan was initiated during the emergence of the Cold War, at a time when the expansion of Soviet socialism was perceived as a growing danger to Western European capitalist nations. At a cost of $13 billion, the aid program succeeded in revitalizing these nations' economies within a capitalist framework. This revitalization provided immense investment and market opportunities for U.S. corporations, thus helping stimulate their increased involvement abroad.

At the same time, U.S. national security managers entered into a military pact with these and other friendly nations, a pact calling for mutual cooperation in the event of outside aggression (e.g., by the Soviet Union). This involved the creation of the North Atlantic Treaty Organization (NATO) in 1949. Through NATO, the United States maintained permanent military capabilities in Europe and elsewhere. This society's involvement in NATO has helped to protect U.S. economic interests in Western Europe and enabled our military-industrial complex to benefit from overseas demands for troops and weapons systems.

The national security managers have also provided foreign economic and military aid to many underdeveloped nations. Economic aid has often taken the form of loans that require the recipients to purchase goods and services from U.S. corporations. Such aid has also been used to encourage poor nations to allow multinational corporations access to raw materials and low-wage labor.

Since underdeveloped nations have been prone to political upheaval and on occasion revolutionary change, corporate investments have also required protection. U.S. military aid has enabled the governments of such poor nations to purchase military equipment produced by this nation's military-industrial complex. The United States exported arms and weapons systems worth $13.1 billion to both developed and underdeveloped countries in 2001, an amount constituting 45.8 percent of the world arms export market. These exports make the United States the world's single leading arms supplier (www.fas.org). Military aid directed into poor nations has often been designed to help governments contain internal movements for change—e.g., movements toward socialism. (See Table 3.2.)

Defending the World against Socialism

Why has U.S. militarism often been used as a means of protecting the world from socialism? And what are military strategies to which the fear of socialism has led?

Michael Tanzer (1971:66) argues in *The Sick Society* that the threat posed by socialism is not wholly, or even necessarily, a military one:

Once granted that economic interests play the major role in foreign policy, then it makes a great deal of difference whether a country is . . . socialist or capitalist, even if the country is totally incapable of threatening us militarily. Each country that shifts from the capitalist world to the socialist world is a country where the United States loses valuable existing investments as well as potential outlets for profitable future investments (and possibly trade).

After all, the United States has the power to destroy any nation that poses a military threat.

Moreover, socialism is not a threat to democratic freedoms and civil liberties in some of the nonsocialist societies with which the United States is or has been allied. The federal government has often provided economic and military

Table 3.2

United States: Military Deliveries to Selected Developing Countries, by Recipient*
(Million US $)

	1975–1988	1989	1990	1991	1992	1996
Total	**106,400**	**8,946**	**7,575**	**8,805**	**8,674**	**12,731**
North Africa and Middle East	**76,453**	**3,198**	**2,999**	**4,862**	**5,270**	**5,498**
Of which:						
Egypt	6,248	574	654	644	1,112	1,261
Israel	13,270	1,229	546	384	710	388
Jordan	2,164	83	56	24	21	16
Kuwait	1,099	62	56	113	256	651
Morocco	953	41	44	32	42	22
Oman	121	2	8	45	8	5
Saudi Arabia	39,259	1,044	1,245	3,107	2,778	2,937
Tunisia	566	26	33	28	21	19
Sub-Saharan Africa	1,318	93	58	50	32	27
Latin America	**3,905**	**378**	**504**	**413**	**363**	**344**
Of which:						
Brazil	413	108	48	32	75	169
Colombia	160	10	39	10	21	46
El Salvador	610	92	88	58	66	19
Mexico	434	50	60	37	19	4
Venezuela	868	106	31	35	20	21
Asia	**20,843**	**4,385**	**3,447**	**3,239**	**2,796**	**3,244**
Of which:						
Indonesia	598	67	227	24	37	11
Malaysia	504	35	20	20	5	42
Pakistan	2,122	244	425	24	3	4
Philippines	617	88	74	99	97	90
Singapore	1,098	119	146	136	66	107
South Korea	5,627	551	590	784	347	393
China (Taiwan)	5,302	433	687	717	917	1,192
Thailand	2,342	238	209	268	134	350
Europe	**3,881**	**892**	**567**	**241**	**213**	**3,536**
Portugal	528	81	94	51	54	21
Spain	3,353	811	473	190	159	435

*Fiscal years. Including deliveries under the following programs: (1) Military Assistance Program grants under the various Mutual Security Acts; (2) Foreign Military Sales, which consist of U.S.-financed arms, U.S.-guaranteed private arms credits, and U.S.-approved commercial sales; and (3) Military assistance excess stocks, which involved surplus equipment that has been valued at 33 percent of the original acquisition value.

Source: U.S. Central Intelligence Agency, *Handbook of Economic Statistics, 1989* (Washington, D.C.: CIA, 1989), pp. 182–183, and U.S. Central Intelligence Agency, *Handbook of International Economic Statistics, 1993* (Washington, D.C.: U.S. Government Printing Office, 1993), p. 165; http://www.umsl.edu/services/govdocs/hies97/j/tab127.htm.

Soldiers carry the body of a fallen comrade to an evacuation helicopter in Vietnam in 1965. Their unit suffered the largest U.S. losses in the Vietnam War.

aid to harsh dictatorships, so long as they in turn have been friendly to U.S. corporate interests. Such regimes have received U.S. support in Argentina, Brazil, Chile, Colombia, the Dominican Republic, El Salvador, Ethiopia, Greece, Guatemala, Haiti, Indonesia, Iran, Laos, Morocco, Nicaragua, Pakistan, Paraguay, Peru, the Philippines, Portugal, Saudi Arabia, South Korea, South Vietnam, Spain, Tunisia, Turkey, and Uruguay (Cohen and Rogers 1983).

What, then, has been the threat of socialism to the United States? It would seem that it has been largely economic. U.S. militarism is one means by which corporate capitalist economic interests—so often subtly equated with national interests—can be served, protected, and extended.

Several different military strategies were developed to battle against socialism (Klare 1972, 1981). In the post–World War II period, the Cold War was expected to result in possible military aggression by the Soviet Union and its allies around the globe. In response, the military-industrial complex came up with the means of "massive retaliation." The idea was that U.S. nuclear arms, visibly poised for use, would act as a deterrent against Soviet military adventure. When it became known, shortly after World War II, that the Soviet Union was also developing a nuclear capability, the United States began to strengthen its military arsenal to make possible a "first strike." The idea here was that the Soviet Union would be deterred from using its weapons, since the United States could put nuclear arms to use first.

To combat the Soviet Union's growing nuclear strength, President Ronald Reagan ordered the DOD to proceed with a controversial research and development project called the Strategic Defense Initiative (SDI) or "Star Wars" project. SDI, projected to eventually cost hundreds of billions of dollars, was to be an outer-space defense system intended to protect the United States from incoming Soviet missiles while allowing our military to shoot off its own. Many critics doubted such a system could be made to work. Needless to say, the need for U.S. massive retaliation, first strikes, and Star Wars was dealt a major blow when the Soviet Union broke up into independent states in 1991. Although the development of Star Wars has been slowed, the U.S. military continues to spend billions of dollars maintaining its readiness to engage in a full-scale, global nuclear war, even though it is not clear with whom such a war could now be fought.

In recent years a number of nations have joined the "nuclear club," thereby increasing concerns over the prospects of future nuclear warfare. This nuclear club includes the United States, Russia (which also controls nuclear weapons in Belarus, Kazakhstan, and Ukraine), Britain, France, and China. Nations believed to have nuclear weapons, but which have not officially declared their possession, include India, Pakistan, and Israel. Other nations are known to have been working on obtaining nuclear weapons, such as Algeria, Iran, Iraq, Libya, North Korea, and Syria (*Time* 1993:38). The nations mentioned are either engaged in friendly relations with the United States or are so small and comparatively weak militarily that they are unlikely to risk nuclear war with a superpower. Nonetheless, many today fear that weaker nations might choose to use such weapons against one another in regional clashes, for example, in the Middle East or Far East, unleashing enormous and perhaps irreparable damage to the earth, its environment, and its population (Klare 1993a).

A second type of military strategy has been "limited warfare," the direct use of military power involving conventional, rather than nuclear, arms. U.S. involvements in Korea in the 1950s and later in Southeast Asia were defined as limited wars, in both these cases against the encroachment of socialism. In each case the costs were extremely high in terms of lives lost, but both were considered the only acceptable alternative to the use of nuclear force.

A third type of military strategy has been "counterinsurgency warfare," utilizing the resources of such paramilitary agencies as the CIA (Klare and Kornbluh 1988). Here the approach has been to combat the threats posed by socialism through secret, disruptive tactics. In 1953 the CIA organized the overthrow of the government of Iran, where U.S. corporate oil interests had been threatened. The following year the CIA was involved in overturning the elected government of Guatemala, which was encroaching on U.S. investments and hampering explorations for oil. Oil interests were also at stake in the CIA's participation in overthrowing the government of Indonesia in 1958.

In the 1960s, before becoming a major participant in the war in Southeast Asia, the CIA participated in organizing the abortive Cuban Bay of Pigs invasion and has since been implicated in attempts to assassinate Cuban socialist leader Fidel Castro. The government of Cuba had appropriated a billion dollars worth of U.S. corporate investments shortly after its succession to power in 1959. In 1974 the elected government of Chile, whose socialist program effected a takeover of U.S.-owned copper production, was "destabilized" and overthrown with the assistance of the CIA. In the 1980s Nicaragua received similar CIA attention. Since the activities of the CIA are supposed to be secret, it is impossible to know when and where other efforts at destabilization have been attempted.

It has not always been the absolute dollar value of U.S. economic interests abroad that provokes militaristic responses to socialism. Certainly the United States had no corporate investments in South Vietnam even remotely worth the $150 billion spent on fighting socialism there. Rather, the national security managers have often feared that movements toward socialism in a given country can set an example for others. The so-called domino theory of foreign affairs interpreted any successful move toward socialism in one part of the world as inviting experimentation elsewhere. Socialism in South Vietnam was viewed as unacceptable, not because that country was a military threat to the United States or because of corporate investments there, but because of what that could mean in terms of the future of Southeast Asia as a whole. Socialism in Cuba, Chile, and Nicaragua promised similar threatening developments in the rest of the underdeveloped nations of Latin America.

Hence, from the perspective of our national security managers, dominoes could not be allowed to fall, because if they did, the United States might become progressively economically isolated and forced to deal with other nations on less advantageous terms. Counterinsurgency, limited warfare, and the threat of all-out nuclear annihilation—all made possible by a well-financed military-industrial complex—have been used to make the world "safe" for U.S. corporations to do business. The irony behind using war to create peaceful business conditions has rarely been questioned within U.S. society, despite the dangers to which it gives rise.

With the demise of the Soviet Union, and changes taking place within many socialist nations that include adoption of capitalist economic principles, where do the military threats to vital U.S. interests now lie? What military strategy is needed in order for the United States to meet these threats? The national security managers have developed answers to these questions that are compatible with the interests of each of the institutional components of the military-industrial complex. They have, as we shall see, found grounds to keep the permanent war economy going indefinitely even as the perceived worldwide threats posed by socialism are apparently diminishing or at least seriously in abeyance.

Military Readiness in the Post–Cold War Era

When the Cold War with the Soviet Union and its allies ended, the United States' post–World War II enemy—the superpower whose nuclear and conventional weapons capabilities provided the principal rationale for massive military spending by the United States—disappeared. Yet the possibility that we must engage in war at any moment, DOD officials tell us, requires that the U.S. continue to spend hundreds of billions of dollars for this purpose annually.

The end of the Cold War, together with the federal government's need to address the huge fiscal deficit created in large part by the escalated military-related expenditures of the 1980s, required that DOD reassess its annual budget and begin some cost-cutting, downsizing, and streamlining. This has produced modest reductions in military-related expenditures. At the same time as these reductions have occurred, however, U.S. defense officials have insisted that the United States remains heavily endangered. Moreover, as indicated in Figure 3.3, U.S. military expenditures remain higher than those of any other nation. One top defense official put it this way:

There are still unstable and hostile areas in the world where vital U.S. interests could be threatened and U.S. military involvement cannot be ruled out in these regions. . . . The reason that the defense budget savings are not larger today have to do with the need to preserve readiness. (Deutch 1995)

These comments reflect the results of a so-called bottom-up review, a DOD study of U.S. defense needs whose results were made public in 1993. This review set out plans for military missions in the post–Cold War era. The review provided a basis for determining war-readiness priorities and thus the need for additional or lesser amounts of military-related expenditures.

Michael T. Klare (1993b:348), who has chronicled post–Cold War era developments at the Department of Defense, argues that in order for the DOD to justify maintenance of the war machine, which of course is in its interests to do, "the United States must be threatened (or appear to be threatened) by an enemy force that roughly approximates the Soviet threat in scale and technology." The Persian Gulf War provided a model for the kind of wars DOD decided the

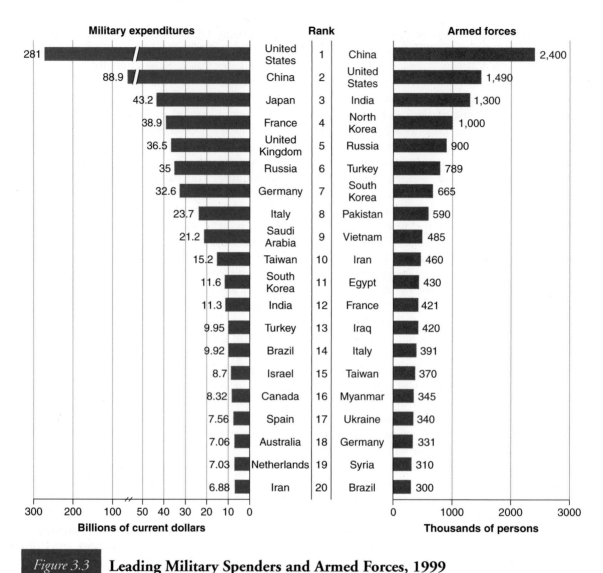

Source: U.S. Arms Control and Disarmament Agency, *World Military Expenditures and Arms Transfers: Country Rankings.* Available at www.state.gov/documents.

Figure 3.3   **Leading Military Spenders and Armed Forces, 1999**

United States needed to be ready for—actions against underdeveloped regional powers equipped with highly advanced conventional and possibly, in the future, nuclear weaponry (Klare 1991). The military would have to be ready for anything such nations might use against it, including biological and chemical weapons.

After much discussion with top officers of the uniformed military, DOD officials decided that the United States needed to be ready to go to war against not one but a continuing succession of underdeveloped nations. Further, it needed to be able to overwhelm and defeat two such enemy nations simultaneously (Klare 1993b). Nations like Iraq, Iran, Libya, Syria, and North Korea were catapulted into prominence in DOD's new assessment of dangers for which the United States must be prepared. Such nations rapidly began to be referred to as "rogue" states (as in rogue elephants), a phrase that carries connotations of dangerous unpredictability and a threat to all others around (Klare 1995a; 1995b).

Terrorism

While the Department of Defense identified "rogue" states as the new threat to the United States after the Cold War, September 11, 2001, forcibly shifted the definition of the threat to international networks of terrorists. These attacks have also raised the question of the role the international arms market may play in contributing to the dangers posed by terrorists around the world. The State Department estimates that 28 terrorist organizations operate from 18 nations. The United States does not directly sell arms to these terrorist groups, but it has sold weapons and provided military assistance and training for more than a decade to 16 of the 18 governments that host these organizations and tolerate them, including Saudi Arabia, Algeria, Iraq, Lebanon, and Sri Lanka (www.cdi.org). Although it may have seemed like a good idea at one time to sell arms to these nations, September 11 must surely raise some concerns for reassessing it. Consider, for example, the significant role the United States played in arming and training the Taliban military in Afghanistan in the early 1990s in support of its resistance to the invasion by the former Soviet Union. That role represented a common feature of U.S. foreign policy wherein "the enemy of my enemy is my friend." In this particular case, the weapons surely helped the Taliban fend off the Soviet invasion of

Afghanistan, but the imported weapons and the Afghanis' training expertise remained long after. These became critical elements strengthening the international al Qaeda network, which was identified as the terrorist perpetrator of the September 11, 2001, attacks against the World Trade Center, the Pentagon, and other targets.

Global economic and political inequalities, international arms trade, and U.S. military support for "friendly" militaristic regimes throughout the world have enhanced the growth of international terrorism. U.S. officials insisted that the September 11 attacks represented acts of war against the United States, requiring a military response. What is the difference between "war" and "terrorism"?

War is an organized, armed conflict between nations (Palen 2001). It is a perennial aspect of world history and of the United States, which has participated in more than 200 major wars, "peacekeeping missions," and other assorted armed conflicts (Leckie 1992). **Terrorism** is the use of unpredictable violence as a strategy to gain political objectives and may be used by individuals or groups who usually have relatively little power otherwise. When used by those with little power, terrorism has been called a "weapon of the weak" (Scott 1985) and "diplomacy from below" (Kumamoto 1991). The power of terrorism is its ability to provoke people's tremendous sense of fear and vulnerability as a result of unpredictable, seemingly random acts of violence against individuals or against society's important institutions, leaders, and symbols. Terrorism disrupts the routines of life by altering people's freedom of movement, comfort in their surroundings, and confidence in the state to protect them. It can thus create a legitimacy crisis for the state and destabilize existing governments. Terrorism also has the potential to challenge the privileges of living in the core, where life without the threat of the violence that is so common elsewhere in the world can be taken for granted, including the ability to go to work every day, to shop, to travel, to vote, to simply open the daily mail, without fear of loss of life and limb.

Terrorism is commonly a weapon of the weak, but it can also be used by the state, which enjoys the sole legitimate use of force and violence as social control mechanisms. Governments can use all the weapons at their disposal to conquer resistant or dissenting populations and to eliminate challengers to state power. For example, the military in Argentina and Chile in the 1970s kidnapped, murdered, and tortured substantial numbers of people in a violent purge of leftist critics there; thousands of the victims of these purges remain among the "disappeared." In 1999 former President of Yugoslavia Slobodan Milosevic endorsed the use of terrorist tactics, including rape, murder, and kidnapping to "ethnically cleanse" Kosovo of Albanians by scaring them into leaving or by killing them.

Terrorism has clearly intensified globally in the last few years; but, like war, it is not new or rare. Terrorist bombings have routinely occurred in Great Britain, Northern Ireland, the Middle East, and elsewhere throughout the 1980s and 1990s. The use of terrorism is also not restricted to "others" outside the United States. The Ku Klux Klan and other white supremacist groups have often used terrorist tactics in their struggles against civil rights, as have antiabortionists, and extremists such as the Weather Underground in the antiwar movement in the 1960s. When a bomb killed 168 people in the destruction of the Federal Building in Oklahoma City in 1995, many in the United States immediately assumed that the bombers were probably Middle Eastern terrorists, a viewpoint repeated in the press. But it quickly became evident that those responsible were U.S. citizens participating in local militia groups devoted to violently challenging the federal government. In fact, Timothy McVeigh, who was eventually convicted and executed for the bombing, was a U.S. Marine veteran. As this case illustrates, terrorist tactics can be used by a wide variety of groups in any nation as a strategy for achieving their political objectives. Despite their differences in origin, cause, or location, what they often have in common is the possession of far less power than the governments they seek to challenge.

Are all acts of random violence terrorism? The answer to this question is not necessarily clear-cut; that is, not everyone agrees on what actions should be defined as terrorism. What some may define as "terrorism" others may call "patriotism." What is the difference? U.S. citizens involved in domestic terrorism are often part of a loose network of groups referring to themselves as the "Patriot" movement. They share a belief that the federal government routinely violates the Constitution, and they consider it their patriotic duty to subvert and challenge that government wherever and however possible (Berlet and Lyons 1995; Wills 1995). Members of the Irish Republican Army (IRA) similarly consider themselves to be patriots defending the right of Northern Ireland to self-determination against Great Britain; and members of the radical Islamic jihad movement believe they are patriotic when they attack states and communities that violate their interpretation of Islamic law. For that matter, colonists in the American Revolution saw the Boston Tea Party as an act of patriotism, and that view is reinforced in historical representations of that incident. These examples illustrate how one person's terrorism may be another's patriotism. While we don't suggest that terrorist crimes against humanity are justifiable if they're defined as acts of "patriotism," it is useful to consider these issues in order to approach some understanding as to why terrorist acts occur.

Despite President George W. Bush's insistence that the world is starkly defined by "evil doers" on one side and "us" on the other, the world is in reality much more complex. Terrorism may not simply be a matter of the evil that some people may inexplicably do to good people. It is useful, for example, to appreciate the relationship between the United States and other core nations on one hand, and underdeveloped and oppressed populations on the other. Increased expenditures on conventional military responses to terrorism against the core that arise out of that context are unlikely to provide increased security. Viable solutions to terrorism have a better chance to develop when people more fully understand the global context in which it occurs. Important questions to consider include: What social, political, and economic factors are likely to influence the growth of international terrorism? Some research suggests that many international terrorist groups have in common feelings of alienation, social isolation, threatened survival, and a heightened sense of religious imperative in the intensification of ethnic and religious rifts (Hoffman 1995). Other researchers identify widening global economic inequality, the increasingly dominant military role of the United States, and the global expansion of the culture-invasive Internet as critical trends to watch (Jensen 2001).

The DOD's assessment is that underdeveloped nations and international networks of terrorists may pose serious threats to vital U.S. interests, threats requiring warfare. How accurate and realistic is this assessment? How effective will conventional military responses and weaponry be against the threat of international terrorism, especially when its source is not a defined and identifiable nation but rather a loose configuration of groups across nations? Are there more effective nonmilitary preventive measures that can address the motivations underlying the appeal of terrorism for some? Does the U.S. defense budget really need to be frozen at near–Cold War heights to meet such threats? How valid are the assumptions that underlie DOD's assessment, which, after all, seems extremely speculative? Are there not ways that defense against the alleged threats could be shared with other nations, so the costs to the United States would be far less? The U.S. citizenry has not been invited to debate these matters but has been asked to accept DOD's assessment and its cost implications. A consensus has been forged within the military-industrial complex around the threat scenarios and what is needed to meet these threats. The result is a level of annual military-related spending that is not radically below that of the Cold War era and the absence of any "peace dividend" to help meet pressing domestic needs.

Defending the World against Terrorism

The world watched in horror as the World Trade Center towers collapsed on September 11, 2001, and shared a collective reality that the world would never be the same again. Suddenly, the "enemy" was no longer rooted in the Cold War rhetoric of communism; rather, the enemy was now more amorphous, harder to identify as a single nation, and trickier to defend against. Unfortunately, the narrow thinking of the Cold War remained a governing force in shaping national defenses against this new enemy. Violent, militaristic responses were the familiar, although questionably effective, reactions to accelerating terrorist attacks. The United States launched a conventional military assault on Afghanistan in search of Osama bin Laden and his al Qaeda followers. Later, although the war in Afghanistan was hardly over and Osama bin Laden remained elusive and although the rest of the world refused to participate, the United States embarked on a war against Iraq. President George W. Bush offered a strong statement outlining the rationale for opening a second front in the "war against terrorism": Saddam Hussein was an "evil-doer" who surely was behind the September 11 attacks; Iraq was allegedly stockpiling weapons of mass destruction, which Saddam Hussein would not hesitate to use; and Saddam Hussein was allegedly attempting to become a nuclear power, a goal that needed to be thwarted to prevent nuclear terrorist attacks in the future.

While the United Nations Security Council and many allies of the United States argued forcefully against the prospect of a protracted war against Iraq, the United States determined to go to war with or without international support. That decision has served to alienate the United States politically from much of the international community. Conventional military action was treated by the president and by Congress as the only viable response; alternative responses were never considered. Nor did anyone question the validity of the evidence presented to the United Nations in support of the war by U.S. Secretary of State Colin Powell. That evidence has subsequently been found to be thin at best. To date, no weapons of mass destruction have ever been found, nor is there any evidence that such weapons existed in recent years. And no evidence has emerged linking Saddam Hussein to the terrorist attacks on September 11. Indeed, the only national links to terrorists in general and al Qaeda in particular appeared to come from Saudi Arabia. However, the economic ties between the United States and Saudi Arabia make it unlikely that the United States will embark on a militaristic assault there.

Meanwhile, by the end of 2005, the war against Iraq continued to rage, with thousands of Iraqi citizens and over 2,000 U.S. troops killed, thousands more on both sides wounded, no weapons of mass destruction found, and Iraq itself in political and economic turmoil with no end in sight. It would appear that conventional militaristic responses are unlikely to suffice in the war against terror.

The Effects of Militarism

U.S. militarism affects more than the nature of our relations with other nations. It has negative influences on the civilian economy of the United States and the quality of life of citizens. It also may even provoke others into inflicting violence upon our own society.

Military Expenditures and the Civilian Economy

Since World War II U.S. military, political, and economic elites have claimed that large military expenditures benefit the United States in many ways. Often such expenditures are portrayed as a positive force in promoting domestic economic health—even apart from their relationship to the protection of U.S. corporate interests abroad. In the words of Seymour Melman (1974:18), "the belief that war brings prosperity has served as a powerful organizing idea for generating and cementing a cross-society political consensus for active or tacit support of big military spending." This belief has been just as influential in keeping the military-industrial complex going as perceived external threats. Critics of post–Cold War expenditures on new weapons systems cynically refer to them as a "jobs program," suggesting the weapons are not really needed but building them keeps people employed. But as Melman and others have argued, a number of rarely considered negative consequences are associated with big military spending. No society can maintain a permanent war economy without some adverse internal effects (see also Melman 1965; Pascall and Lamson 1991).

Many members of the U.S. labor force are, directly or indirectly, dependent on military-related expenditures. But the goods and services produced through these expenditures do not really serve basic needs of the U.S. population. We cannot consume nuclear submarines, supersonic fighter planes, or tanks. The funds spent on maintaining and equipping people in uniform do not enhance the quality of everyday life. The vast productive apparatus that military expenditures support—laboratories, plants, equipment, tools—is isolated from civilian-oriented use. Thus a significant segment of the U.S. economy, from people to matériel, is nonproductive in terms of public well-being.

Another effect of the permanent war economy has been the creation of firms that have little knowledge of business other than their ability to exist on tax funds. As we have seen, many aerospace-defense firms depend on continued military expenditures for their economic survival. They cannot operate successfully in the civilian marketplace but have instead geared their products and talents toward the security provided by Pentagon capitalism. Their managerial and professional personnel have had no need to gain experience in advertising, marketing, and product planning to meet the needs of civilian consumers. Many aerospace-defense firms would find it exceedingly difficult to convert to non-military-related business.

Related to this has been the **brain drain** of technically educated workers, wherein people have been siphoned away from civilian industry into nonproductive aerospace-defense jobs. This brain drain has been encouraged by military expenditures that have provided employment opportunities in the military-industrial complex. Thus, scientific and engineering talent that could have been put to use in other productive settings has been usurped. Moreover, the skills and technical knowledge possessed by many such persons are often not easily transferred elsewhere. Even the nation's universities have been affected, as federal research and development funds—important sources of income for many institutions—have heavily gone to meet military-related requirements.

Seymour Melman has argued that non-war-related industries have become progressively underdeveloped—both in terms of their productive potential and in comparison with industries in other nations (e.g., in Western Europe and Japan) that spend relatively little on militarism (Melman 1974:74–104, 1983). With parts of the U.S. economy's labor force and productive apparatus engaged in keeping up our status as the world's number one military power, our production of peacetime goods and services has suffered. Important sectors of the civilian economy are afflicted with low levels of productivity, inefficiency and the need for modernization, inability to maintain quality, and unnecessarily high production costs that inflate prices. Inflated prices then stimulate worker demands for higher wages, thereby increasing the cost of living.

One result is that the United States is finding it increasingly difficult to compete successfully with other nations in world trade. Many U.S.-made products cannot find foreign buyers, and the United States has to import finished goods that formerly had been produced domestically. The United States has become more and more dependent on selling its agricultural products abroad, much like an underdeveloped country. (While Japan exports electronic entertainment equipment to the United States, we send Japan soybeans.) And the United States has, as we have seen, become involved in selling billions of dollars' worth of military weapons systems and equipment—also to help balance off the value of imported goods. (See Figure 3.4.)

The deteriorating state of domestic civilian industry has made it necessary for U.S. corporations to invest outside this country in order to keep profits high (Bluestone and Harrison 1982; Craypo and Nissen 1993). By opening up plants elsewhere, corporations can cut transportation and labor costs so as to render their products more competitive with those of other nations. This strategy exacerbates domestic economic problems. Corporate investments abroad mean that these dollars are not being utilized to update and improve deteriorating stateside industries. Moreover, such investments often function to ship jobs abroad, putting more U.S. residents out of work. Finding it difficult to afford higher-priced, domestically made goods, unemployed people, and many who are employed, turn to cheaper imported products. This then throws more people in the United States out of work.

One need not be an economic genius to understand that the foreign investments of the last several decades have been developing a cumulative effect that is just beginning to be felt. By allocating massive societal resources to militarism, other activities that are important to our daily lives have been allowed to go into decline. Military expenditures, in Seymour Melman's (1974:260) judgment, have "become a major

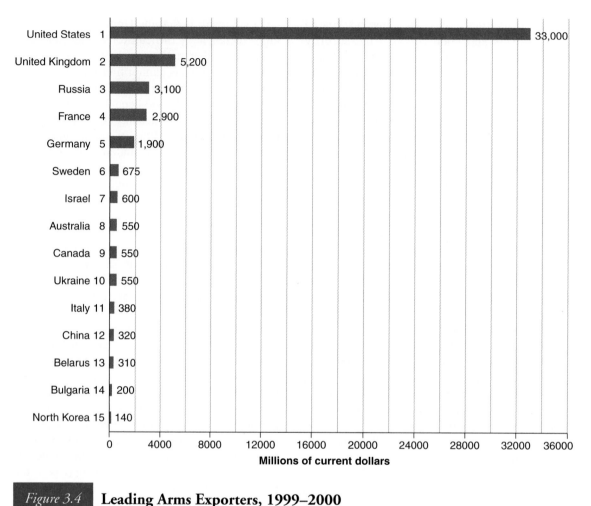

Figure 3.4   **Leading Arms Exporters, 1999–2000**

Source: U.S. Arms Control and Disarmament Agency, *World Military Expenditures and Arms Transfers, 1999–2000.* Available at www.state.gov.

source of corrosion of the productive competence of the American economy as a whole."

The Quality of Life

High military expenditures have also created underdevelopment in the area of social welfare. The money allocated toward military expenditures could be used to improve the quality of life for millions.

For example, the Center for Defense Information, an organization that tracks military spending, has determined that the total purchase price for aircraft procurement by DOD in 2003 was $46.7 billion (www.dod.mil/comptroller/defbudget). In contrast, the federal government's annual expenditure on Temporary Assistance to Needy Families, a major welfare program on which some 5 million poverty-stricken people—primarily women and children—depend, was only $16.8 billion in 2003 (www.cbo.gov). Even with help from TANF, these families still lived far below the federal poverty line. The total costs for new military aircraft would abolish poverty among these 5 million people for almost three years! While politicians have made the high costs of welfare a political issue and raised allegations of welfare fraud, far less political attention has been paid to the huge amounts of tax monies flowing to aerospace-defense contractors and the added costs of illegal or unethical behavior in which they have been found to be involved.

It is not hard to think of other examples. The areas of environmental pollution control and cleanup, education, medical and health care, housing, public transportation, recreation, assistance to the aged, and child care, among others, are all underdeveloped, while government spending, even with reductions in recent years, remains highly skewed toward maintaining the permanent war economy.

Militarism affects the quality of life in more than just economic ways. It also interferes with our democratic rights and civil liberties. It is not surprising that a militarized government committed to a warlike posture toward external enemies should attempt to repress imagined threats from within. President Dwight D. Eisenhower warned of this possibility in his farewell address on January 17, 1961:

In the councils of government we must guard against the acquisition of unwarranted influence, whether sought or unsought, by the military-industrial complex. . . .

We must never let the weight of this combination endanger our liberties or democratic processes. We should take nothing for granted. Only an alert and knowledgeable citizenry can compel the proper meshing of the huge industrial and military machinery of defense with our peaceful methods and goals so that security and liberty can prosper together. (U.S. Dept. of State 1961)

Since the early 1960s the U.S. military and paramilitary apparatus has been used at times against lawful activities by citizens. Many of the internal "enemies" were individuals and groups who actively protested military expenditures, the uses to which they have been put (particularly in Southeast Asia), and the adverse effects of all this for U.S. society. Among the activities carried out under the rationale of protecting internal security were wiretapping and spying; organized disruption of dissident groups; the employment of agents provocateurs; burglary and violation of the mails; infiltration of campuses and classrooms; maintenance of secret dossiers on thousands of innocent people; and legal harassment and intimidation (Churchill and Wall 1990; Donner 1980; Theodoris 1991).

After public exposure and widespread condemnation of these abuses in the 1970s, it was hoped that such treatment of citizens would not occur again. Yet not only was the machinery for the violation of democratic rights and civil liberties not dismantled by the federal government—it was used again in the 1980s. In early 1988 it was revealed that the FBI had conducted a lengthy and aggressive surveillance effort against persons opposed to the Reagan administration's policies in Central America. Over 100 church, civil rights, union, education, and political organizations were encompassed in the surveillance, which began in 1983 (Gelbspan 1991).

Like earlier government violations of U.S. citizens' rights, surveillance operations in the 1980s were found to have included the use of secret informants and undercover agents. Thus, when an antigovernment bombing killed 168 adults and children in a federal building in Oklahoma City in 1995, President Clinton's proposal to remove congressionally imposed restrictions on federal investigations of groups not known to be involved in criminal activities raised immediate concerns among people aware of previous abuses of power.

These concerns have not been alleviated in the aftermath of the September 11 attacks. In fact, these concerns have intensified, as the Patriot Act has given the federal government broad powers that violate individuals' civil rights and intimidate the free expression of dissent as unpatriotic. The American Civil Liberties Union has repeatedly charged that the Patriot Act allows the violation of individuals' rights to privacy, including federal surveillance; examination of personal records, including bank accounts, credit card use histories, school records, and library borrowing histories; and the ability to arrest and hold individuals indefinitely without charge (www.aclu.org). While people were largely supportive of the Patriot Act and its promises of enhanced national security after September 11, more are beginning to question the abuse of power it poses, particularly in the absence of evidence that it has enhanced national security in any measurable way.

The Nuclear Threat

All macro problems cause harm to and limit the life chances of millions of people. But as tragic and wasteful of human potential as they are, none of these problems can create anywhere near the carnage that would result from the use of nuclear arms (Chivian et al. 1982; Riordan 1982). It is amazing that we can go about our daily lives either ignorant of or apathetic to the life-threatening dangers to which militarism contributes.

Nagasaki and Hiroshima are reminders of the monumental horrors that would be associated with any further nuclear warfare. The United States is the only nation ever to use nuclear weapons, the effects of which are seen in this photograph taken in Hiroshima in 1945.

strategies—all made possible by a well-financed military-industrial complex—are used to make the world safe for U.S. multinational corporations.

Critics have pointed to negative effects of militarism on the U.S. civilian economy. That sector of the economy that produces military-related goods and services is said to be nonproductive, in that it does not serve basic needs of the civilian population. Many firms that have grown dependent on producing for the DOD would find it exceedingly difficult to convert to production for civilian consumption. Many technically educated persons have been siphoned away from civilian industry into aerospace-defense jobs, creating a "brain drain" or loss of talent that could have been used in other settings. Finally, investment in militarism is said to have caused the underdevelopment of sectors of the civilian economy, leading to inefficiency and higher production costs. The productive competency of the civilian economy has become corroded, and this has begun to interfere with our ability to compete in the world market.

Militarism also has negative effects on the quality of life in the United States. Tax funds going to support the military-industrial complex could be used for other purposes—cleaning the environment, ending poverty and hunger, rebuilding the nation's cities, and so on. The maintenance of a militaristic posture also affects domestic civil liberties. A government oriented toward the use of force against external enemies is prone to repress imagined threats from within. Since the early 1960s the U.S. military and paramilitary apparatus has at times been used against citizens engaged in lawful activity—for example, persons and groups protesting militarism.

One final negative effect of militarism is the constant possibility of nuclear warfare. Despite treaty agreements, nuclear weaponry threatens to proliferate around the world. As more nations join the "nuclear club," the likelihood that nuclear weapons will actually be used increases. Should nuclear warfare occur, the carnage is likely to be immense. Whether such warfare is global or limited to regional conflicts, there is no way of telling what kind of world the survivors—if there were any—would inherit. Despite our massive military expenditures, there is no real way this society can be protected from nuclear attack so long as others possess both the will and means to inflict such damage.

Hence, in the interests of human survival, efforts to bring about worldwide multilateral disarmament must take place, and expenditures on militarism must be directed into peace-oriented activities. The United States must cease selling weaponry to other nations. Ultimately, this and other societies must perfect nonviolent means of resolving conflicts.

Key Terms

Discussion Questions

1. What arguments can be made for and against resolving disagreements through violence? Are there circumstances under which the ends justify violent means?

2. In all past wars, at least some U.S. citizens have refused to be inducted into military service. Should people have the right to decide whether they will follow the demands of a government that engages the nation in warfare?

3. In what ways and to what degree is your community or state dependent on military expenditures? Discuss what would happen if these expenditures were to suddenly cease.

4. Who ultimately benefits the most from the maintenance of a permanent war economy in the United States? In what ways?

5. The U.S. military, a ruled-from-the-top, nondemocratic institution, is admired today to a far greater extent than democratic institutions such as the Congress and the presidency. Why? What does this situation imply about the directions in which our society is going?

6. Is the propensity to engage in warfare a part of human nature? Or is it the outcome of socioeconomic and political forces? Give evidence in support of your answer.

7. Is terrorism ever justified? If yes, when? If no, why not? If conventional military responses are not effective to counter terrorism, what alternatives might be more useful?

Suggested Readings

Barnet, Richard J., and John Cavanagh. *Global Dreams* (New York: Simon & Schuster, 1994). The power and significance of large multinational corporations whose operations run throughout the global economy.

Boies, John L. *Buying for Armageddon* (New Brunswick, NJ: Rutgers University Press, 1994). Explores the institutional forces encouraging massive U.S. military expenditures.

Cohen, David B., and John W. Wells, eds. *American National Security and Civil Liberties in an Era of Terrorism* (New York: Palgrave Macmillan, 2004). A collection of readings that explores the tension between attempts to secure national security in the aftermath of the September 11, 2001, terrorist attacks and the need to maintain the protection of individuals' civil liberties.

Fisher, David E. *Fire and Ice* (New York: Harper and Row, 1990). The potentially catastrophic impact of an outbreak of nuclear warfare on the earth's atmosphere, climate, and weather.

Klare, Michael T. *Rogue States and Nuclear Policy*
(New York: Hill and Wang, 1995).
The defense establishment's identification of
post–Cold War threats to U.S. security and their
use to justify continuing high levels of military
spending.

Makhijani, Arjun, Howard Hu, and Katherine Yih.
Nuclear Wastelands (Cambridge, MA: M.I.T.
Press, 1995).
How nuclear weapons production has already
seriously poisoned the earth's environment and
is causing untold damage to human health.

chapter 4

The Global Context: Population and Underdevelopment

Our relationship with poor, underdeveloped nations should be nonexploitative and supportive of movements to secure basic human rights.

Introduction

If you have been fortunate enough to travel abroad and happened to be exposed to the mass media in nations you visited, you may have seen substantial news space devoted to the United States. The reverse is less often the case: U.S. media tell us comparatively little about what is going on in the countries you may have visited. Citizens elsewhere often are very interested in and surprisingly aware of U.S. affairs. They are also often very sensitive to the political and economic relationships between their own nations and others, including our own. In contrast, we seem myopic.

Ignorance and lack of awareness are dangerous. Catchphrases such as the "global village" and "spaceship earth," popular in recent years, underscore an important fact: Humanity's 5.6 billion members occupy a relatively small planet with finite resources. The fate of any one segment of that population is tied to that of every other segment. In effect, a society's fortunes are determined to a large degree by the global context within which it operates. The United States is not an exception.

Ignorance of the global context within which U.S. society functions is at times accompanied by a rather distorted view of our role in the world at large. In its extreme this view may hold that the United States has produced the best society that has ever existed, that no other way of life even approaches ours, that all other nations should emulate us, and that our superiority as a people gives us the right (and responsibility) to police the rest of the world, using force when necessary to protect our vested interests. This is more than patriotism, which involves love of and loyalty to one's country, and it goes beyond nationalism, which emphasizes devotion to the interests of one's nation. Rather, it is a type of *ethnocentrism,* which is the inability to understand other societies except in terms of one's own. In ethnocentric terms, the "American Way" becomes the revered standard against which other nations are measured and by definition fall short. In this way indifference toward, and even maltreatment of, other nations can be justified. As Ian Robertson (1987:72–73) points out,

[Ethnocentrism] can encourage racism, it can cause hostility and conflict between groups, and it can make a people unwilling to recognize the need for changes in their own culture.

The global context in which our society functions is not always apparent to us, but it involves problems that are reaching crisis proportions and inflicting incredible suffering on hundreds of millions of our fellow human beings. Ethnocentrism poses obstacles to the rational discussion of these problems and gets in the way of the pursuit of solutions. Yet the handling of such problems now may well determine the human prospect for generations to come (Heilbroner 1996).

Our first concern in this chapter is world population growth, with primary attention paid to underdeveloped nations (often referred to as the "Third World"), where most of humanity lives. Then we focus on the life chances now available to citizens of such nations. Their life chances are severely limited by hunger, malnutrition, and starvation; by ill health and susceptibility to preventable disease; and by extremely high rates of infant mortality and low life expectancy.

Many would argue that high rates of population growth, and thus overpopulation, cause life chances to be limited in underdeveloped nations. However, we approach these topics from a different angle. High population growth rates and severely limited life chances among citizens of underdeveloped nations will be understood largely as *outcomes* of a fact that too often is ignored: the gross economic inequality in these nations and the widespread poverty resulting from the policies of a small ruling political elite.

Yet underdeveloped nations exist in a world context. Thus, in the final pages of this chapter we discuss some of the relationships between underdeveloped nations and developed nations such as our own. Does the United States contribute in any way to the underdevelopment of other nations? Does the United States benefit from world poverty? What is our position toward movements seeking fundamental change—political, economic, and social—in underdeveloped nations? This chapter closes with comments on the instabilities inherent in the relationships between developed nations and their poverty-stricken counterparts.

World Population Growth

The earth's population is growing relentlessly, currently at an estimated rate of 1.5 percent annually, which means that each year there are 90 million or more human beings than there were the year before (Brown 1987; United Nations 2003b). (These statistics are estimates because of the unreliability of census figures.) This fact has caused some to fear that humanity is beginning to tax the resources of the planet and has raised the specter of widespread struggles between have and have-not nations.

The 5.6 billion people who occupy this planet will likely grow to over 6 billion in the beginning of the twenty-first century and to over 8 billion by the year 2025. To understand what is going on we must explore briefly some of the dynamics of world population growth. It is particularly important to see where this growth is most rapid. As we shall see, "technological" solutions, such as increased use of birth-control devices, are likely to have only limited impact on overall growth rates.

The phrase **population explosion** is an apt description of the real situation. Indeed, it was not until the 1960s that world population growth even became a serious international issue. The rapidity and abruptness with which the population increase burst on the world have been underscored by Erik Eckholm (1982:37):

Two thousand years ago humans scarcely numbered 250 million; only in the early 1800s did the figure reach one billion. A second billion was added in one hundred years, a third in thirty years, and a fourth in just the fifteen years from 1960 to 1975.

To get from that 4 billion in 1975 to over 8 billion people in the year 2025 involves a doubling of the earth's population in a mere 50 years!

The statistics denoting population growth are based on two factors that deserve attention: (1) **birthrate** (expressed as the number of births per 1,000 members of the population in a given year) and (2) **death rate** (the number of deaths in a given year per 1,000 members of the population). When one subtracts the number of deaths from the number of births, the result is usually expressed as an annual percentage called the **population growth rate.** As mentioned earlier, the world population growth rate is now 1.5 percent annually. (This is down from a high of 2 percent in 1970).

An annual growth rate of 1.5 percent may seem modest, but the growth is exponential (i.e., each year's growth rate is applied to the size the population grew to the previous year), so that the so-called doubling time of a population is relatively short. For example, at a 1 percent rate of growth a population doubles in 70 years; at 2 percent only 35 years is required.

Growth in Developed versus Underdeveloped Nations

It is important to emphasize the differences in rates of population change among nations. The developed nations—the most affluent, heavily consumer-oriented societies—are located primarily in the Northern Hemisphere and tend to have low growth rates. For example, the U.S. growth rate is 0.6 percent, and in Europe there are about a dozen nations where the annual births and deaths are roughly equal, resulting in nearly zero population growth. Overall, the average annual growth rate for developed nations is 0.3 percent.

In contrast, the "underdeveloped" nations tend to have much higher population growth rates. (See Figure 4.1.) These are generally poor nations with very limited industrial activity and low levels of consumption and are located mostly in the Southern Hemisphere. Most human beings—*some 81 percent*—live in underdeveloped nations! The population growth rate for such nations now averages almost 2 percent annually. If present trends continue, an even higher percentage of the world's population—*84 percent*—will live outside the nations of affluence by the year 2025. (See Table 4.1.) Many will be our near neighbors in Latin America.

Some differences in population growth rates do exist among underdeveloped nations. For instance, the People's Republic of China, a nation of over 1 billion people, has a growth rate of 0.7 percent annually. However, countries in sub-Saharan Africa show growth rates of almost 3.0 percent per year. At this rate of growth sub-Saharan Africa will almost double the size of its population in only 21 years. This sharply contrasts with Western Europe, where it would take 500 years to double the population at present growth rates.

Differences in population growth rates reflect in part the population age distributions within developed and underdeveloped nations. By the year 2001, 83 percent of those under 25, persons of prime childbearing age, lived in underdeveloped countries (www.prcdc.org/summaries/worldpop/worldpop.html). In contrast, developed nations will see a significant graying of their populations, as well as an increase in the "oldest old"—persons aged 80 and over. Overall, the current world total of 425 million people over 65 will grow to a projected 585 million by 2015. Developed countries are already feeling the social and political impact of this demographic shift; underdeveloped

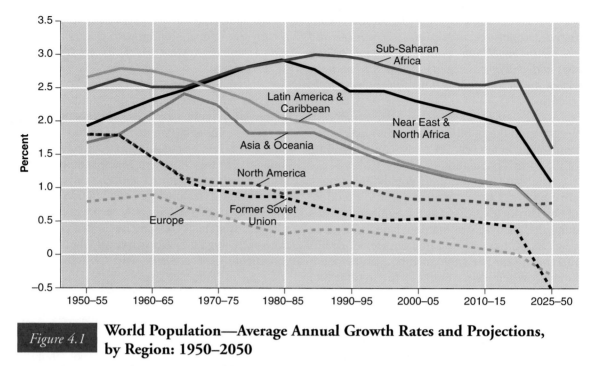

Figure 4.1   **World Population—Average Annual Growth Rates and Projections, by Region: 1950–2050**

Source: U.S. Department of Commerce, Bureau of the Census, *World Population Profile, 1994* (Washington, DC: U.S. Government Printing Office, 1994); U.S. Department of Commerce, Bureau of the Census, *Global Population Profile: 2002*. Available at www.census.gov (Table A.2).

countries will feel it, too, in the years to come (Kinsella 1994; United Nations 2000).

We shall turn shortly to some of the major reasons for high population growth rates and the concerns over an increasing world population. But first let us focus on the life chances now available to many people in those nations where population is growing most rapidly.

Life Chances and Underdevelopment

We have seen that four-fifths of humanity live in the underdeveloped nations of the world, where population growth rates are typically quite high. In this section we discuss two interrelated factors that limit life chances for hundreds of millions of people: chronic malnutrition or "undernutrition" and poor health.

Hunger may afflict people for different reasons. Historically, periods of famine have been relatively common. Famine may occur as a result of a natural catastrophe (e.g., severe flooding or prolonged drought) or of human actions (as when people are involuntarily displaced from their homes and lands during war). Famines occur for these reasons today, although with modern communication and transportation it is at times possible to limit their devastating effects somewhat by timely relief efforts.

In late 1984 United Nations disaster relief officials and officials of the International Red Cross drew attention to severe drought-related famines in 27 African nations (while noting that food shortages exist in all areas of Africa).

Table 4.1	World Population and Vital Statistics, by Region, 1960–2002, and Projections, 2025 (in Millions)				
	Midyear population (millions)				
Region	1960	1980	1994	2002	2025
World	3,038	4,456	5,642	6,228	7,834
Underdeveloped	2,093	3,319	4,402	5,030	6,582
Developed	945	1,137	1,240	1,199	1,252
Africa	282	469	701	839	1,247
Sub-Saharan Africa	226	379	572	687	1,036
North Africa	56	91	130	152	211
Asia	1,685	2,600	3,345	3,518	4,375
Asia, excluding Near East	1,628	2,500	3,195	3,339	4,095
Near East	57	99	149	179	280
Latin America and the Caribbean	218	362	474	539	690
North America	199	252	289	320	388
Europe	425	484	509	513	515
(Former) Soviet Union	214	266	296	121	117
Baltics	6	7	8	9	10
Commonwealth of Independent States	204	253	282	290	300
Georgia	4	5	6	6	7
Oceania	16	23	28	32	40

Seventeen of these were said to be especially hard hit, with over 35 million people desperately hungry. In Ethiopia alone 6 million to 7 million human beings were facing starvation and death. In the 1990s, war-related famines threatened the lives of an estimated 4.5 million people in Somalia, and 1.7 million Rwandan refugees lacked sufficient sources of food and water. Television news programs showed the dead and dying in living color. Private relief agencies increased their efforts. The United Nations and the United States provided protection for relief efforts. Yet aid experts indicated that even with relief on the way, the death toll would be high. The weakest—infants and children—would die first and in large numbers.

But hunger is not always a matter of emergent conditions that create temporary food scarcity. Hundreds of millions of human beings live routine daily lives in which they are in no danger of outright starvation. Yet they are in a state of chronic malnutrition or "undernutrition." For such persons food scarcity is a never-ending way of life.

Table 4.1   (*Continued*)

Average annual rate of growth (percent)				Birthrate 2002	Death rate 2002	Total fertility rate (number)		Life expectancy (years) 2002
1960–70	1980–90	1990–2000	2010–25			2002	2020	2002
2.0	1.7	1.4	0.9	21	9	2.7	2.5	64
2.4	2.1	1.7	1.1	23	9	2.9	2.7	62
1.0	0.6	0.4	0.1	11	10	1.6	1.8	76
2.4	2.9	2.5	1.6	36	14	4.9	3.9	50
2.4	2.9	2.6	1.7	39	16	5.3	4.2	47
2.4	2.6	2.3	1.6	24	5	2.9	2.5	70
2.3	1.9	1.7	1.1	25	9	3.0	2.4	63
2.2	1.8	1.4	0.9	19	8	2.4	2.3	66
2.6	3.0	2.3	1.9	28	6	3.8	3.4	69
2.7	2.0	1.7	1.1	21	6	2.5	2.1	71
1.3	0.9	1.2	0.8	14	8	2.0	2.1	77
0.8	0.3	0.3	(Z)	10	10	1.6	1.7	79
1.3	0.8	–0.1	–0.2	16	11	1.4	1.9	73
1.2	0.7	0.7	0.6	14	12	1.3	1.8	69
1.3	0.8	0.2	(Z)	13	13	1.7	1.9	66
1.2	0.8	0.9	0.4	16	9	1.5	1.9	65
2.1	1.6	1.5	0.9	17	7	2.3	2.0	74

Birthrate, number of births during 1 year per 1,000 persons (based on midyear population). Death rate, numbers of deaths during 1 year per 1,000 persons (based on midyear population). Total fertility rate, average number of children that would be born per woman if all women lived to the end of their childbearing years and, at each year of age, they experienced the birthrates occurring in the specified year.

Key: Z less than 0.05 percent.

Source: U.S. Department of Commerce, Bureau of the Census, *World Population Profile, 2002* (Washington, DC: U.S. Government Printing Office, 2004).

We who live in developed nations are often worried about being overweight. For many in the underdeveloped world, however, the average person consumes two-thirds of our calorie intake and one-half of our protein consumption. The average person in the United States takes in a hefty 3,600 or more calories per day; hundreds of millions of people elsewhere must function with far less.

It is difficult for experts to determine the extent of chronic malnutrition. One difficulty lies in objectively defining malnutrition. How

Hunger and malnutrition are widespread in most underdeveloped nations. Famine situations have become commonplace in many parts of the African continent. In this photo, a hungry vulture stalks a starving Sudanese child.

many calories are needed for people to function up to their physical and mental potential? How much protein must a diet have to be adequate? Nutritional experts disagree over the answers to such questions, but the numbers of people considered to be in dietary need depend on these answers.

In the 1960s the United Nations Food and Agriculture Organization (FAO) estimated that some 1.5 billion people were malnourished—at that time nearly half of the world's population. Later, in the mid-1970s, the figure was reduced to less than 0.5 billion people. Was chronic malnutrition miraculously reduced? Hardly. The FAO simply revised downward its definition of the amount of calories and protein needed in an

adequate diet. Still, the lower figure encompassed a quarter of the population of underdeveloped nations (Murdoch 1980).

Chronic malnutrition may not be as visible as famine-related hunger, but its effects are severe. One such effect is a much greater susceptibility to disease. Those who are particularly at risk include women attempting to breast-feed, infants, and small children. Almost one-third of the children in the underdeveloped world suffer from protein-energy malnutrition caused by the interaction of poor diet and frequent illness. The absence of simple nutrients in diets can have a profound impact. For example, because of iodine deficiency disorders it is estimated that 5.7 million people are afflicted with cretinism and 26 million people are brain damaged. The solution to iodine deficiency is simple: the use of iodized salt at a cost of 5 U.S. cents per person per year.

So long as there is an absence of ample and nutritionally sufficient food for hundreds of millions, we will continue to see the impact of malnutrition in

the child who looks to be 7 years old but turns out to be 10 or 11, . . . the child who is sitting in the shade, dull eyed, without even the energy to ward off flies, . . . the child who rarely joins in the games and adventures of others, . . . the child whose eyes are glazed over behind a school desk and who does not understand or remember what he or she is being taught. For poor nutrition in the early years of life . . . means disruption in the miraculous process by which neurons migrate to the right location in the brain and begin to form the billions of subtle synapses that make lifelong learning possible. (United Nations Children's Fund, 1995:16–17)

The life chances of the poorest world citizens are reduced by poor health. Lost battles with illness and disease are reflected in statistics on life expectancy. (See Table 4.2.) In developed nations average life expectancy is in the seventies. Yet there are many countries in Africa and Asia where on average people die in their forties and fifties. Our middle age is old age to others. Moreover, the very young die at astonishing rates (United Nations Children's Fund 2002). Consider the following:

In many industrialized nations the death rate among infants in their first year of life is less than 1 in 100; in some African and Asian nations it is 1 in 4.

In industrialized nations deaths during childhood are infrequent (1 per 1,000 persons in the population annually), and most are due to accidents. Children under five

account for half of *all* deaths in underdeveloped nations, with most dying from disease.

Seventeen million infants and children under five die each year in underdeveloped nations; if these nations' health-care resources were equivalent to those in northern Europe, most of these deaths would be prevented (Eckholm 1977, Chapter 4).

A simple doctor's prescription written not for medicine but for *food* is often the first requirement for the prevention of disease. Malnourished children do not fight disease well; moreover, some diseases reduce the body's ability to assimilate food.

As recently as 1980 less than 10 percent of the world's children were immunized against common childhood diseases such as measles, whooping cough, tetanus, and diphtheria. These diseases were claiming the lives of more than 13,000 children every day, with many of those who survived left deaf, blind, or disabled. The World Health Organization (WHO) and the United Nations International Children's Education Fund (UNICEF) set a goal to immunize 80 percent of the world's children by 1990. By 1999, they came close to achieving that goal for measles and polio, with 73 percent of children under 12 months immunized (World Development Indicators 2002:108); but children and their families continue to be at risk because of other conditions that affect the health of people in underdeveloped nations. Such conditions often include:

Extreme shortages of uncontaminated water, so necessary for personal hygiene, drinking, cooking, and the cleansing of eating and cooking utensils and clothing.

Nonexistent or inadequate means of disposing of human and animal excrement and other wastes that are linked to disease.

Daily exposure to numerous infectious parasites that thrive in water and in soil, including hookworm and roundworm.

Table 4.2	Key Differences between a Selected Group of the Poorest and Richest Nations			
	GNI per capita, 2000 (dollars)	Life expectancy at birth, 2000 (years)	Infant mortality, 2000 (per 1,000 live births)	Maternal mortality, 1995 (per 100,000 live births)
Fifteen Poorest Nations				
Mozambique	210	42	129	980
Ethiopia	100	42	98	1,800
Tanzania	270	44	93	1,100
Haiti	510	53	73	1,100
Bangladesh	370	61	60	600
Lao PDR	290	54	92	650
Malawi	170	39	103	580
Nepal	240	59	74	830
Chad	200	48	101	1,500
Burundi	110	42	102	1,900
Sierra Leone	130	39	154	2,100
Madagascar	250	55	88	580
Nigeria	260	47	84	1,100
Uganda	300	42	83	1,100
Zambia	300	38	115	870
Fifteen Richest Nations				
Netherlands	24,970	78	5	10
Kuwait	18,030	77	9	25
Belgium	24,540	78	5	8
Austria	25,220	78	5	11
France	24,090	79	4	20
United Arab Emirates	>9,266	75	7	30
Canada	21,130	79	5	6
Germany	25,120	77	4	12
Denmark	32,280	76	4	15
United States	34,100	77	7	12
Sweden	27,140	80	3	8
Finland	25,130	77	4	6
Norway	34,530	79	4	9
Japan	35,620	81	4	12
Switzerland	38,140	80	4	8

Source: World Bank, *World Development Indicators, 2002* (Washington, DC: International Bank for Reconstruction and Development, 2002), and United Nations Development Programme, *Human Development Report, 2000* (New York: Oxford University Press, 2000).

As a result of such conditions, diarrhea and other intestinal illnesses are rampant in the underdeveloped world, resulting in tens of millions of deaths annually. Once again the impact on children is greatest: "On average, a child under five years of age in the [underdeveloped] world experiences at least three bouts of diarrhea per year. That means each year there are some 1.4 billion episodes worldwide, resulting in more than 3 million deaths" (United Nations 1992:56).

Diarrhea often leads to severe dehydration, inability to assimilate nutrients, and loss of strength to fight off new disease. In the mid-1980s health organizations began utilizing oral rehydration therapy to combat the dehydration. This is a simple solution of salt, sugar, and clean water. However, successes in combating one problem are often offset by the appearance of others. For example, there has been a dramatic rise in reported cases of cholera in underdeveloped nations (one of the most easily treated and least deadly of the diarrheal diseases), with death rates of 30 to 40 percent due to people's lack of access to treatment facilities with trained health workers and basic supplies.

Debilitated people are vulnerable to diseases that most of us will never experience. In tropical climates these include malaria and schistosomiasis (a disease caused by parasites in the blood vessels and involving disorders of the liver, bladder, lungs, or central nervous system). Finally, new diseases at times arise that may go misdiagnosed or inadequately treated because of the poor quality of the health-care systems available to most people in underdeveloped nations. Some of these new diseases may find their way into developed nations, as did acquired immune deficiency syndrome (AIDS), believed to have originated in Africa and now taking its most devastating toll in the underdeveloped world. Sub-Saharan Africa, which has the fastest-growing rate of new adult HIV infections, has been particularly hard-hit by the AIDS epidemic; by 2002 almost three-fourths of all cases of HIV in the world occurred in the region (www.allafrica.com). In Zimbabwe alone, more than 30 percent of everyone older than 15 is HIV-positive (World Bank 2003).

A major goal of the World Health Organization had been "Health for All by the Year 2000." This past decade, however, we have witnessed a worsening of conditions throughout the underdeveloped world as wealthy nations, in a shift of priorities, decreased their official development assistance to poor countries to the lowest point in 20 years. Meanwhile, governments in underdeveloped nations have had to reduce their budgeting for food subsidies and funding for health and education in the name of "fiscal reform," required in exchange for desperately needed loans from international lending agencies (United Nations Children's Fund 1995:2, 34). Given these trends, the World Health Organization's praiseworthy goal seems hopelessly far-fetched.

Relationship between Poverty and Population Growth

How is one to make sense of spiraling population growth? What is its relationship to the poverty-stricken conditions in which so many suffer in underdeveloped nations? Does population growth result in poverty, or does poverty lead to population growth? The answers will dictate the appropriate strategies for bringing growth rates under control.

The conventional wisdom is that it is population growth that produces poverty. This perspective is based on **Malthusian logic.** Thomas Malthus, a British clergyman and economist writing in the late 1700s and early 1800s, argued that the geometric growth of the world's population would result in the inability of the earth to provide sustenance for its members. Famine, pestilence, and wars would ultimately result from unfettered growth.

Modern-day Malthusians argue that too many people are engaging in sexual relations without effective birth control, resulting in high birthrates. The problem is exacerbated by the preponderance of young people, capable of procreation, in underdeveloped nations (Hartman 1995). This view goes on to suggest that the numbers of people to be fed are overwhelming food-producing resources, creating food scarcity and subsequent health problems, as well as endangering the global environment by depleting the earth's natural capital (Brown 2000). The solution that follows from this conventional wisdom is to emphasize family planning. Ignorance, superstition, and any other source of resistance to family planning must be overcome. The focus of this argument on the procreative behavior of people in underdeveloped nations ignores the threat of population growth in highly developed nations like the United States and those in Western Europe, which consume substantially disproportionate amounts of the world's resources. Large populations in the developed nations, then, may pose an even larger threat to global resources more because of their consumption patterns than their sheer numbers.

On the other hand, few would argue that population growth is irrelevant to a nation's economic circumstances. It seems obvious that any effort to overcome underdevelopment in a poverty-stricken nation might well include close attention to family planning as a positive measure. But is population growth really the cause of world poverty? Some would say no, that such logic is simplistic and naive.

Many have challenged the conventional wisdom. Among its severest critics are Frances Moore Lappé and Joseph Collins (1979, 1986), best known for their research on food and hunger. They believe that the conventional wisdom is based on a number of myths. Consequently, the solutions put forth, which largely blame the poor for their own plight, will not work. Here we consider three of these myths,

along with the gist of Lappé and Collins's rebuttals. While their primary focus is on hunger, their analysis does provide some significant insights into the relationship between population growth and poverty in underdeveloped nations.

Myth 1: "People Are Hungry because of Scarcity"

The concept of scarcity deserves to be questioned as it is currently applied. Enough food to nourish all people on earth adequately is being produced now. We must carefully examine how this food is currently distributed and consumed. Inequitable distribution and consumption among nations are definitely part of the problem. But inequitable distribution *within* nations can be an important factor underlying what, on the surface, looks like absolute scarcity.

In most underdeveloped nations a small, elite class is overfed at the same time that many others go hungry. Scarcity may be maintained, at least to some degree, by a political power structure that assumes it is within its right to determine who will consume and under what conditions. (Even in the United States there are millions of people who suffer from hunger [Schwartz-Nobel 2002]. No one would try to explain this in terms of a scarcity of food in the nation.) Thus, it is possible for "scarcity" to exist in a nation when it could be eliminated if food were shared. Moreover, the assumption of scarcity as the cause of hunger sidesteps the problem of inadequate resources to buy food. Nations like the United States certainly have access to more than adequate supplies of food, but millions of people living there simply do not have adequate resources to purchase it. The problem, then, is less one of scarcity of food and more one of poor distribution of financial resources to ensure everyone has sufficient ability to buy this basic necessity.

In addition to purchasing power and distribution problems is the problem of political leaders who may use food access as a weapon against their own populations. Zimbabwe, for example, was world renowned until recently as the region's breadbasket, and its farms in 2004 were reputed to have been producing a bumper crop of food. Yet millions of Zimbabweans are now literally starving to death, because the nation's president, Robert Mugabe, has seized the farms under a violent strategy of awarding the land to his supporters. His actions have concentrated the power to control land and crops among a small elite of his loyalists; at the same time he has refused to allow the United Nations World Food Program to continue providing food relief to nearly 6 million starving people there (Neier 2004). Zimbabwe, then, illustrates how the problem of extreme hunger and starvation can be a matter of distribution and political power rather than scarcity of food for too many people.

Myth 2: "Hunger Results from Overpopulation"

The relation between population size and the availability of food is not simple. Lappé and Collins offer China as a dramatic example. With a population over a billion, it has more people than any other country in the world. Yet, after the Chinese socialist revolution of 1949, its leaders managed to bring hunger under control in a couple of decades. This is the case despite a population that continues to grow at a rate that is much higher than the average for developed nations. China has sought to maximize the utilization of existing food resources while developing systems of distribution that try to provide all groups within the society with adequate nutrition. Large population size alone cannot explain hunger.

In addition to the artificial scarcity created by the ways in which food (and the financial resources to purchase it) is distributed, many nations appear nowhere near to full utilization of existing cultivable land (Lappé and Collins 1986). Perhaps less than half of the world's cultivable land is now being used for crops. Moreover, crop yields from the land that is being utilized are often well below their full potential, particularly in underdeveloped nations. Why are resources underutilized in underdeveloped nations? To begin to answer this question, one must examine patterns of land ownership.

Myth 3: "To Solve the Problem of Hunger We Must Grow More Food"

Lappé and Collins cite evidence that per capita food production in a nation can increase simultaneously with an increase in the number of persons who are hungry! How can such a contradiction exist?

First, it must be understood that land ownership in underdeveloped countries is concentrated typically in the hands of a small but wealthy propertied class. Landholdings are retained within families through inheritance and gifts and within the class itself through intermarriage and the merging of business interests. Much of the land available for cultivation, and usually the best land, is monopolized by this class.

Second, land ownership carries with it the prerogative of deciding if the land will be planted and if so, with what; the decision of what technology to use in the growing process is also the owner's. These kinds of decisions are made with profit considerations in mind. The impact of such decisions, however, is felt by the majority of the population, for in underdeveloped nations agricultural activities are generally the core of the economy.

Landowners' policies often contribute to poverty, malnutrition, and ill health. For example, chemicals and machines bought from developed nations are used to increase production while reducing labor costs. Agricultural laborers, on the other hand, are left to suffer from exposure to toxic pesticides and from unemployment resulting from the new technology, which is replacing traditional methods of agriculture, transforming cultivable lands into corporate food factories.

Production of specialized goods for export, usually to developed nations, often means using the best lands to grow luxury commodities (e.g., cocoa, tea, coffee). Meanwhile locally needed foodstuffs are underproduced. For example, grain may be grown and then used to fatten cattle for beef export to developed nations; this grain is then unavailable for local consumption. Indeed, many countries, because of landowners' production priorities, have become *importers* of grain and other foodstuffs they have produced or could produce.

Landowners' profits from such practices are frequently used to increase landholdings, thereby limiting even further the ability of families to engage in production for local markets or for their own subsistence. The plight of small growers has been exacerbated in recent years as rising petroleum prices have driven up the costs of fuel and fertilizer. Many small producers have been forced to sell out to the heavily capitalized large landowners. The desperation of rural families, increasingly finding themselves landless and without opportunities for employment, drives many to the city. There they attempt to subsist in massive, overcrowded, unsanitary slums, often claiming squatters' rights to a few square feet of city property in order to erect a bare shack. In fact, the largest population growth rates, now and in the foreseeable future, are in urban areas of the underdeveloped world.

Lack of *control* over food-producing resources by those who most need food helps to explain why food production and hunger can increase simultaneously. These types of considerations help us to put the issue of population growth in underdeveloped nations in perspective. To Lappé and Collins, high birthrates are symptoms of the "insecurity and poverty of the majority resulting from the monopolizing of

productive assets by a few" (Lappé and Collins 1986:11).

If you live in an agricultural society but do not own land and have no employment security, children may be one of your only assets. Whether in rural settings or in the urban shantytown, children provide extra hands to help make survival possible. They may perform household tasks (including care of younger siblings) that free adults to work, or they may earn enough to help those who cannot find work.

Underdeveloped nations are not "welfare states," with social security and retirement plans. Children must be around to help parents and other family members, particularly as they face infirmity from illness and aging. Given the high probability that many of those born will die quite young, high birthrates are a must. These needs obviously place tremendous demands on females in underdeveloped nations. Poverty forces women into high-risk childbearing and traditional family roles. They often have no other options.

Economic Security and Reduction of Family Size

The solution to poverty—and the hunger and ill health typically accompanying it—is not simply birth control, as the conventional wisdom has it. Efforts in that direction can have only limited impact on birthrates, given the quite rational incentives that move poor people to have many children. Moreover, even when such efforts do appear to have a significant effect on population growth rates, they may unintentionally produce other social problems. China, for example, has maintained a policy limiting each family to only one child as a measure to curb the escalating growth in its population. The government enforced this policy with institutional incentives and privileges for compliant families, including preferential treatment for jobs and promotions, housing, educational advantages, and access to health-care services; those families that did not comply were refused access to these privileges, and only the first child would receive educational opportunities and health care. While this policy did indeed contribute to a dramatic decline in the rate of population growth, it had several unintended consequences so debilitating that the government began in the late 1990s to relax enforcement of the policy. One consequence was an alarming increase in female infanticide, abortion of female fetuses, and abandonment of female newborns because of the cultural preference for males. Since most families determined to have boys as their single child, the nation faced the unforeseen problem of a shortage of females in the potential marriage pool for the first generation of males conceived under the one-child per family policy. Furthermore, families in China have traditionally relied upon a network of children in the extended family to care for aging parents; the one-child policy meant that the burdens of caring for four elderly parents of each couple could not be shared among many siblings (Lev 2000). Thus, although China's birth control policy certainly did have the effect of reducing the rate of population growth, it also produced serious social problems.

While birth control alone is a problematic approach to population growth, population growth rates can be changed by combining family planning programs with fundamental political, economic, and social changes. An example lies with Kerala, a southern state in India. There we find not only birthrates down to population replacement level, but other social indicators demonstrating a quality of life not matched throughout the rest of India (Hartman 1995; Repetto 1995; Stevens 1994). Today one out of six of the world's people live in India, making it the most populous country after China. But while China's current population growth rate is 0.6, India's is 1.5, and by 2035 India will surpass China in total population count. However, the Indian state of Kerala has made a "demographic transition," wherein the average number of births per woman of 1.9 is at replacement level, compared to 4 births to the average Indian woman. What accounts for this dramatic contrast in population growth rates between Kerala and the rest of India?

First, the state of Kerala has a history of participatory democracy that has led to the redistribution of wealth. In the late 1950s and early 1960s land reforms were legislated *and implemented* because of both massive social movements and a progressive state government. While Kerala has one of the lowest per capita incomes of any state in India, its more equal distribution of land-based wealth has led to better food distribution, increased production, and overall nutritional improvements. The presence of strong labor unions combined with enabling legislation has created employment for agricultural workers and has provided them with benefits and pension funds.

Second, the state of Kerala invests in its people through funding of primary and secondary education and by meeting the demand for health-care services. What is most noteworthy is the retention of girls in grades 1 to 5 in primary school. This contrasts sharply with the rest of India's dropout rate for girls of 50 percent, and it also points to the third and perhaps the most important reason for Kerala's success—the improved status of women.

Families in Kerala have long supported both the primary and secondary education of daughters. Some sections of Kerala have also had a tradition of matrilineal inheritance of land and property (i.e., inheritance through the mother's family line). This respect for and support of women is reflected in the area's higher-than-average ratio of women to men: In Kerala the ratio is 104 to 100 while, for all of India, the ratio is 93 to 100. This latter rate reflects sex-selective abortion, female neglect, and female infanticide that occurs as a response to the traditional Indian desire for sons.

In those underdeveloped nations where governments have made sure people receive a just share of income and wealth, population growth rates drop and health conditions improve. These Chinese shoppers enjoy a day of shopping in a new store in Shanghai. They have far greater economic well-being and security than their counterparts in most other poor nations.

Families in Kerala have access to the same family planning resources as the rest of India, but 37 percent more families in Kerala engage in fertility control. Fertility control is linked to women's active participation in the paid labor force in Kerala. Because they are able to obtain educations and jobs that help improve their own and their families' quality of life, it makes sense to women in Kerala to take advantage of the family planning services provided by the state (Mahmud and Johnston 1994; Sen 2000). Kerala thus provides an important model of factors that must be addressed to reduce population growth rates and improve people's well-being in underdeveloped nations.

The interrelatedness of (1) the status of women, (2) economic development across all societal groups, and (3) family planning to lower fertility rates in underdeveloped nations was made a major point of focus in the 1995 United Nations Conference on Population and Development in Cairo, Egypt. This was the third world population conference in 20 years, but it was the first to include the word *development* in its title and the first to systematically address women's rights in reproductive choices and health care.

More than 20,000 participants from 180 countries worked over a period of nine days to draft a nonbinding document, "Program of

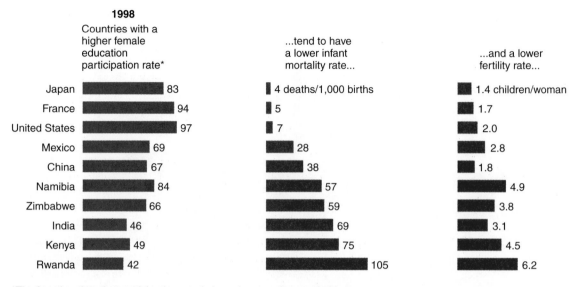

1998

Countries with a higher female education participation rate*

...tend to have a lower infant mortality rate...

...and a lower fertility rate...

Country	Education rate	Infant mortality	Fertility rate
Japan	83	4 deaths/1,000 births	1.4 children/woman
France	94	5	1.7
United States	97	7	2.0
Mexico	69	28	2.8
China	67	38	1.8
Namibia	84	57	4.9
Zimbabwe	66	59	3.8
India	46	69	3.1
Kenya	49	75	4.5
Rwanda	42	105	6.2

*The female education participation rate is based on enrollment of girls in primary, secondary, and tertiary school.

Figure 4.2   **Female Education Index in Relation to Infant Mortality Rate and Fertility Rate in Developed and Underdeveloped Nations**

Source: United Nations, *Human Development Report, 2000* (New York: Oxford University Press, 2000), Tables 2, 9, and 19.

Action," that included support for women's rights to make their own decisions regarding their families and their relationships, to decide the number of children they will have and when they will have them, and to condemn the practice of female genital mutilation (a cultural tradition in a number of societies). The document also called for men to be equally responsible for family planning and the prevention of sexually transmitted diseases. The ability to get women's issues centrally on the agenda came from the work of over 2,000 women's organizations and individuals throughout the world (Sen, Germaine, and Chen 1994).

Implementation of the kinds of principles being pursued in Kerala, India, and deemed important by the United Nations conference must take place if population growth rates in underdeveloped nations are to decrease. The education of women can play a key role, as Figure 4.2 indicates.

Earlier we talked about the rapid population growth predicted for sub-Saharan Africa in the next century. A possible scenario for the future lies in current growth patterns there:

The danger in such growth is that economies have to move full steam ahead just to avoid standing still. And in Africa, they hardly moved at all; in the 1980s per capita income declined by almost 2 percent a year, leaving everyone except for a tiny elite significantly poorer by the end of the decade.

According to a World Bank report published in 1992, some 220 million Africans south of the Sahara—more than one out of three—now live in "absolute poverty," meaning that they are unable to meet their most basic needs. Some studies predict that half the population will be in poverty by the end of the century. (Darnton 1994)

Lappé and Schurman (1990:67–68) comment as follows on their research on societies showing declining birthrates:

We have suggested that within each of these societies, shifts in power relations in key aspects of family, community, and national life have made lowered fertility possible: the enhanced power of women—through basic literacy, education, and employment; the heightened power of peasants to provide food and income for themselves because reforms have widely dispersed access to land; the bolstered power of consumers to secure adequate nutrition . . . the enhanced capacity of people to protect their health . . . the heightened power of women to limit their births through birth control. These are some vital measures of changes needed for people to be able to choose fewer children.

However, in most of the underdeveloped world, resources are *not* shifting toward the poorest groups, nor are birthrates in significant decline. Who or what stands in the way of the steps necessary for fundamental change in underdeveloped nations? Naturally, the wealthy, propertied classes in these nations resist such change, for they benefit from the status quo. But ironically, rich, developed nations—including the United States—stand in the way of any change that could threaten their own interests. It is to this topic that we now turn.

Development, Underdevelopment, and the Colonial Legacy

The economic gap between affluent developed nations such as the United States and poor underdeveloped nations is on the steady increase.

In 2000 the per capita income for persons in the United States was $34,100. In contrast, the per capita income of our nearest underdeveloped neighbor, Mexico, was $5,070. In India per capita income was $450. In Ethiopia per capita income was $100 (World Development Indicators 2002). As rich nations hold their population growth rates down at the same time that so many poor nations cannot, the gap in per capita income widens progressively.

But population growth rates alone do not fully explain the disparities that exist. One must also have some sense of history to account for the present. Until quite recently, most peoples of the underdeveloped world were subjected to colonialism and other forms of outside domination. A group of what were to become some of today's developed nations implemented and enforced this domination through the exercise of greater military, political, and economic power. As recently as World War I, most of the earth's inhabitants were subject to colonial rule, and many nations gained independence only in the last five decades. (See Table 4.3.) The external rulers were joined by coopted (and thus cooperative) native elites *within* underdeveloped societies. The purposes of colonization—in Africa, Asia, Latin America, and elsewhere—included the exploitation of cheap labor, the extraction of raw materials and agricultural products, and the creation of new markets.

It is important to understand that these colonized and otherwise dominated societies were coerced into adopting forms of economic and political organization that would best serve the interests of those who ruled. The cultural traditions and ways of life that had enabled these societies to live self-sufficiently were progressively destroyed. To those who ruled, the needs of the colonized were secondary. In effect, the ability of these nations to develop, except as dictated from afar, was blocked. Poverty, hunger, ill health, and limited life chances were manufactured, while local discontent was typically put down by military force.

Table 4.3   **Chronological List of 119 Newly Independent Nations (Since 1943)**

Year	Date	Country	Year	Date	Country
1943	Nov. 22	Lebanon	1960	Aug. 15	Congo
1944	Jan. 1	Syria		Aug. 16	Cyprus
	June 17	Iceland		Aug. 17	Gabon
1946	Mar. 22	Jordan		Aug. 20	Senegal
	July 4	Philippines		Sept. 22	Mali
1947	Aug. 14	Pakistan		Oct. 1	Nigeria
	Aug. 15	India		Nov. 28	Mauritania
1948	Jan. 4	Myanmar	1961	Apr. 27	Sierra Leone
	Feb. 4	Sri Lanka		June 19	Kuwait
	May 15	Israel		Dec. 9	Tanzania
	Aug. 15	Korea	1962	Jan. 1	Western Samoa
1949	Mar. 8	Vietnam		July 1	Burundi
	July 19	Laos		July 1	Rwanda
	Nov. 8	Cambodia		July 5	Algeria
	Dec. 28	Indonesia		Aug. 6	Jamaica
1951	Dec. 24	Libya		Aug. 31	Trinidad and Tobago
1956	Jan. 1	Sudan		Oct. 9	Uganda
	Mar. 2	Morocco	1963	Dec. 12	Kenya
	Mar. 20	Tunisia	1964	July 6	Malawi
1957	Mar. 6	Ghana		Sept. 21	Malta
	Aug. 31	Malaysia		Oct. 24	Zambia
1958	Oct. 2	Guinea	1965	Feb. 18	Gambia, The
1960	Jan. 1	Cameroon		July 26	Maldives
	Apr. 27	Togo		Aug. 9	Singapore
	June 27	Madagascar	1966	May 26	Guyana
	June 30	Zaire		Sept. 30	Botswana
	July 1	Somalia		Oct. 4	Lesotho
	Aug. 1	Benin		Nov. 30	Barbados
	Aug. 3	Niger	1967	Nov. 30	Yemen (South)
	Aug. 5	Burkina Faso	1968	Jan. 31	Nauru
	Aug. 7	Ivory Coast		Mar. 12	Mauritius
	Aug. 11	Chad		Sept. 6	Swaziland
	Aug. 13	Central African Republic		Oct. 12	Equatorial Guinea

Year	Date	Country	Year	Date	Country
1970	June 4	Tonga	1983	Sept. 19	Saint Kitts and Nevis
	Oct. 10	Fiji	1984	Jan. 1	Brunei
1971	Aug. 14	Bahrain	1986	Oct. 21	Marshall Islands
	Sept. 3	Qatar		Nov. 3	Micronesia, Federated
	Dec. 2	United Arab Emirates	1990	Mar. 21	States of Nambia
1972	Apr. 4	Bangladesh		May 22	Yemen
1973	July 10	Bahamas, The	1991	April 9	Georgia
1974	Feb. 7	Grenada		June NA	Croatia
	Sept 10	Guinea-Bissau		June 25	Slovenia
1975	June 25	Mozambique		Aug. 24	Russia
	July 5	Cape Verde		Aug. 25	Belarus
	July 12	São Tomé and Principe		Aug. 27	Moldova
	Sept. 16	Papua New Guinea		Aug. 30	Azerbaijan
	Nov. 11	Angola		Aug. 31	Kyrgyzstan
	Nov. 25	Suriname		Sept. 6	Estonia
	Dec. 31	Comoros, The		Sept. 6	Latvia
1976	June 28	Seychelles		Sept. 6	Lithuania
1977	June 27	Djibouti		Sept. 9	Tajikistan
1978	July 7	Solomon Islands		Sept. 23	Armenia
	Oct. 1	Tuvalu		Oct. 27	Turkmenistan
	Nov. 3	Dominica		Dec. 1	Ukraine
1979	Feb. 22	Saint Lucia		Dec. 1	Uzbekistan
	July 12	Kiribati		Dec. 16	Kazakhstan
	Oct. 27	Saint Vincent and the Grenadines	1992	April NA	Bosnia and Herzegovina
1980	Apr. 18	Zimbabwe	1993	Jan. 1	Slovakia
	July 30	Vanuatu		Jan. 1	Czech Republic
				May 24	Eritrea
1981	Sept. 21	Belize	1994	Oct. 1	Palau
	Nov. 1	Antigua and Barbuda	2002	May 20	East Timor

Source: U.S. Department of State, Bureau of Intelligence and Research, *Geographic Notes,* No. 1 (Washington, DC: Department of State, Spring 1992), special issue devoted to "Status of the World's Nations," and U.S. Central Intelligence Agency, *The World Factbook, 1993* (Washington, DC: CIA, 1993); www.aneki.com/independence.html.

In the twentieth century sweeping changes occurred. In all areas of the world colonial relations have been severed, often after long-lasting warfare and rebellion against the colonial powers and their native representatives. In most instances, however, the end of formal colonization left underdeveloped nations in extremely poor condition. Although independent politically, they had been so ravaged by the colonial experience that economic self-sufficiency was difficult. For many such nations it would be an elusive goal.

In recent decades we have seen new tactics from many developed nations, including the United States. Such nations have at times taken advantage of the vulnerability of underdeveloped nations, subtly re-creating relations of dominance and exploitation. What might be called **neocolonialism** has emerged, in many cases promoting the continuing poverty and suffering to which attention was drawn earlier in this chapter. The United States has been a participant in this process.

The United States and the Underdeveloped World

As other chapters in this text note, the economic system of the United States has become increasingly global. It is a central part (if not *the* central part) of what some describe as a world capitalist system. This system dominates economic activity and influences political policy in most of the developed and underdeveloped nations of the world (Sklair 1995; Wallerstein 1979).

The United States has developed widespread economic vested interests outside its political boundaries but within the world capitalist system. One indicator of these interests is direct investments made by U.S. firms abroad. In 2002 the value of these investments was more than $1.5 trillion, a figure that represents substantial growth since the years after World War II and more than a doubling of investments in the 1980s alone. Almost two-thirds of this $1.5 trillion have been invested in nations in the developed world, largely in Europe and Canada (U.S. Bureau of the Census 2004:808). While investments worth $572 billion have been made in underdeveloped nations, their dollar value does not indicate their full significance to U.S. firms. This is because the rate of return from investments in underdeveloped nations is usually quite a bit higher than returns from, say, Europe and Canada. On the other hand, the investment risks are often also higher.

While investments by U.S. firms (so-called multinational corporations) span the globe, when it comes to underdeveloped nations these investments are relatively concentrated. Nearly half in 2002 were in Latin America (U.S. Bureau of the Census 2004:808), where the United States has acted as a self-appointed overseer (even if not a colonial power) for many generations. Here is Thomas Jefferson writing to James Monroe in 1801:

However our present interests may restrain us within our limits, it is impossible not to look forward to distant times when our rapid multiplication will expand itself beyond those limits, and cover the whole northern, if not the southern continent, with a people speaking the same language, governed in similar form, and by similar laws. (cf. Chace 1984:11)

Since Jefferson's time the U.S. government has viewed Latin America as within its "sphere of influence." The United States has not hesitated to intervene politically, and even militarily, in Latin American nations to influence developments thought to bear on our national interest.

Today the large-scale investments that have been made in Latin America are an important component of this national interest. U.S.

multinational business firms have developed a strong dependency on profits from this area of the underdeveloped world. The average rate of return from dollars invested in Latin America is about 20 percent, whereas the international average is barely a third of that (see U.S. Department of Commerce, *Survey of Current Business;* for periodic updates see www.bea.gov/bea/pubs.htm). The needs of today's multinational firms are quite similar to those of the traditional colonial powers: cheap labor, inexpensive raw materials and agricultural goods, and markets for manufactured goods.

Production can be quite cheap in underdeveloped nations, where unemployment is rife,

unions virtually nonexistent, and people so desperate for wages that health, safety, and environmental practices outlawed in the United States are common. The profits from such production find their way back to the developed world. U.S. officials hope that such profit gains will occur as an outcome of the North American Free Trade Agreement (NAFTA), negotiated with Mexico and Canada and put into effect in 1994. NAFTA reduces trade barriers between the United States and our neighbor to the south, and it also opens the door further for U.S. multinational corporations to profit from access to inexpensive Mexican labor and new consumer markets. To date, investment by U.S. firms in underdeveloped

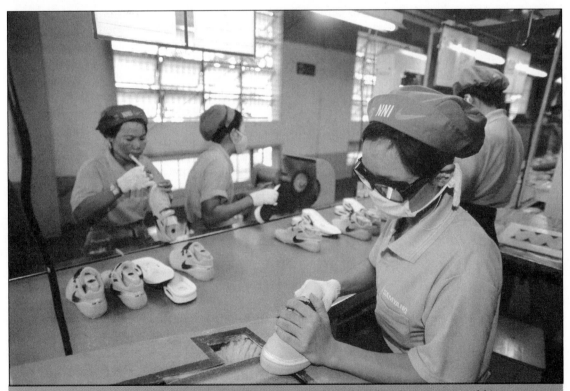

Many products that could be made in the United States are produced and sometimes sold in underdeveloped nations by branches of U.S. multinational corporations. These firms obtain low-wage labor from persons in need of work and direct the profits from their operations back to U.S. headquarters.

nations has not really aided their overall economic development or spread meaningful benefits to the large low-income sectors in such nations. For the most part those who prosper are those native elites chosen by U.S. firms to participate in management and supervisory positions. The local population derives nowhere near the benefits that accrue to the investing firms.

In many cases the impact of investment may actually contribute to further underdevelopment. Raw materials extracted from the ground are ordinarily irreplaceable. In the long run this is a form of material impoverishment (a fact that helped to motivate the dramatic price increases of oil-producing nations in the 1970s). Agricultural production devoted solely to the most technologically efficient production of items for export can, as we have seen, adversely affect local employment opportunities and food supplies. Indifference to health and safety needs of workers and abuse of air, water, and land with dangerous pollutants that affect the general population create further serious problems in living. The movement of the rural poor to urban areas in the remote hope of finding work contributes to congestion, housing shortages, public health problems, and further cycles of birth and impoverishment.

The acceleration of the globalization of the economy has intensified the widening gap between life in developed nations and life in underdeveloped nations. Multinational firms have been searching the world over for the cheapest, most exploitable labor, and they commonly find it in the poorest countries. Beyond globalizing corporate culture in the McDonaldization of the world (Ritzer 1996), multinational corporations increasingly are globalizing unequal production and power relationships that benefit the firm but have dire consequences for people in underdeveloped nations. Although these firms do provide employment for people in the poorest nations, it comes at wages that are below subsistence even by local standards of living. In China, for example, production workers who make products for Wal-Mart are paid

an average wage of 13 cents an hour per worker, even though the minimum wage there is 31 cents an hour (which itself is below subsistence) (Hightower 2002). Such low wages threaten workers' health because they cannot afford to live in anything other than squalid and overcrowded conditions that lack adequate access to clean water and sewers, and their severely insufficient wages deprive them of enough food.

Workers' health is also compromised by unsafe work conditions. For example, young women who work in electronics factories in the Philippines squint into microscopes for 8 to 12 hours each day, severely straining their eye muscles and endangering their eyesight. The health and well-being of garment factory workers (who are primarily women) is often threatened because of the extremely long hours and severely overcrowded conditions of the sweatshops in which they work (Soyer 1999). In factories where workers make toys for Wal-Mart in China's Guangdong Province, headaches and nausea from paint dust, unsafe handling of paint thinner and other toxic solvents, and 100-degree factory temperatures are chronic (Hightower 2002). Exposure in some factories to toxic chemicals and fumes causes lung and respiratory diseases, miscarriages, cancer, and other life-threatening diseases. Moreover, slave labor continues to be a common and rapidly growing feature of production in the global economy (Bales 1999). Some corporations respond to workers' complaints of less-than-living wages and unsafe work conditions by automating, replacing people with technology. This only increases unemployment, poverty, and hunger among workers in the underdeveloped world.

In addition to the globalization of production, underdeveloped nations find that economic aid also often generates problems. Economic foreign aid provided to many underdeveloped nations through the U.S. government in cooperation with banking institutions has generally been in the form of loans. Underdeveloped nations, desperate for resources, take these loans, but economic circumstances are such that new loans must be negotiated simply to pay the interest rates on old ones. Now caught up in heavy, inescapable debt, underdeveloped nations become captives of a world economic system in which they possess practically no influence. Their dependence on outside loans and investments means that the developed world, including the United States, can dictate internal economic, and thus political, policies.

Underdeveloped nations, with very few exceptions (e.g., China), are entrapped; their economic development is systematically stymied. Much as in colonial days, there are classes within underdeveloped nations that are willing to cooperate with the neocolonial powers in return for privileges and lifestyles that most of their fellow citizens cannot enjoy. Thus, a minority within most underdeveloped nations, a **transnational capitalist class,** benefits from the status quo, as do the investing multinational firms. Commenting on the transnational capitalist class, Leslie Sklair (1991:8) notes:

This class consists of people who see their own interests, and/or the interests of their nation, as best served by an identification with the interests of the capitalist global system, in particular the interests of the countries of the capitalist core and the transnational corporations domiciled in them.

The profitability of multinationals' investments contributes to their prosperity and to the prosperity of their home nations. Thus, the profitability of U.S. multinationals operating in the underdeveloped world contributes to the prosperity of the United States, which interferes with change in our relations with poor countries. Daniel Chirot (1977:9), author of *Social Change in the Twentieth Century,* put it this way:

Rich societies have not been, and are not presently, interested in turning poorer societies into independent and prosperous ones. Rather they are interested in keeping the poorer areas dependent, and overspecialized in the production of certain cheap goods. Balanced development in any poor society, therefore, is likely to meet the active resistance of the rich societies.

Thus, movements for broad change that episodically flow from the poorer population segments within underdeveloped nations are commonly interpreted by U.S. government officials as dangerous to our national interest. In reality, such movements represent aspects of those societies that are dangerous simply because they are not under our control. U.S. officials (to the degree to which they express concern about it) discuss world poverty in terms of the need for more effective birth control. They tend not to discuss it in terms of unjust systems of political and economic inequality that must be transformed.

Modern-day threats to the United States and its interests abroad have undergone a major reassessment by U.S. officials since the breakup of the Soviet system in 1991 and the end of the Cold War. (See Chapter 3.) Yet U.S. officials remain concerned with stemming change movements in underdeveloped nations, especially those whose goals are to replace capitalism with some form of socialism. That suffering peoples may have just reasons for seeking fundamental reordering of their societies becomes irrelevant. Since it is against the interests of developed nations such as the United States to help the poor overturn systems from which the developed nations profit, it should not be surprising that movements toward socialism are met with force and oppression. The harsh economic boycott and stranglehold that the United States has held on socialist Cuba for many years, and U.S. military and paramilitary interventions in other Latin American nations where political revolts have threatened, are intended as lessons of what can happen when underdeveloped nations undertake an internal reordering that impedes the developed nations' ability to dominate and exploit them.

U.S. government policies have helped to prop up and protect existing systems of political and economic inequality in many underdeveloped nations so that U.S. corporations can pursue profits from their operations in those nations. But in propping up and protecting inequalities, such policies have also contributed to the legal and illegal migration of millions to the United States (as well as to Europe). In the 1980s the U.S. took in over 7 million immigrants, one-third of them from Mexico. The majority of the remainder came from other underdeveloped countries in Latin America and from Asia (United Nations Population Fund 1993:17–19).

Migration to escape intolerable conditions is a pattern that is repeated elsewhere. Throughout the world, 145 million people live outside of their homelands (Epstein, Graham, and Nembhard 1993; Gould and Findlay 1994; Population Reference Bureau, available at www.prb.org). While a small proportion of these are refugees—20 million in 2003—many are individuals and families seeking improved economic possibilities and political refuge in the developed world (United Nations 2003a). The controversy over the growing numbers of immigrants to the United States from underdeveloped nations that erupted in the 1990s often ignores the role played by this country in creating or maintaining the conditions elsewhere from which so many migrants are attempting to escape.

Another type of movement—that of illegal drugs—has helped to fashion relationships between the United States and a number of underdeveloped nations. The U.S. Drug Enforcement Agency estimates that people in the United States spend tens of billions of dollars for such drug imports as cocaine, marijuana, and heroin. A 1989 U.S. Senate report estimated that 60 percent of all illegal drugs produced around the world are consumed in the United States (U.S. Senate 1989). By 2001 the illegal drug market in the U.S. totaled $60 billion (www.economist. com). Latin America is a major exporter and pipeline for illegal drugs, only a fraction of which are seized while being smuggled into the United States. Other exporters of illegal drugs are located in the Near and Middle East and in Asia.

A great deal of public attention has come to focus on cocaine use in the United States and its connection to underdeveloped countries in Latin America. We in this country spend an estimated $12 billion a year on cocaine, most of which comes from Colombia, Peru, and Bolivia (www.whitehousedrugpolicy.gov/publications/drugfact). Our demand has helped to exacerbate the economic and political difficulties faced by such countries. They have suffered tragic costs as a direct consequence of large-scale involvement in the drug trade (Honderich 1993).

The cultivation of coca (the raw material of cocaine) and its transformation into a marketable product have provided economic benefits to some segments of the exporting countries. The illegality of cocaine in the United States helps to keep its price high. Hence, many farmers in Colombia, Bolivia, and Peru find they can earn more money by growing coca for the drug trade than they can by cultivating other crops; it is hardy, pest-free, and very easy to grow. In addition, employment opportunities are provided by virtue of the need to process, transport, and provide security for the product. But most of these people benefit only indirectly. The bulk of the profit goes to the key actors in a small number of well-organized crime cartels (known as *narcotraficantes*), who monopolize the trafficking of cocaine to the United States and take advantage of the highly inflated prices it brings.

Thus far we have spoken only of the economic benefits cocaine brings to certain segments of the underdeveloped nations involved. These benefits are being dwarfed by a number of tragic costs (Honderich 1993). These include increased cocaine use by youth in Colombia, Bolivia, and Peru; traffickers' corruption of officials—from police officers to cabinet ministers—who either ignore the drug industry or actively assist in it; and the shift of political power to enormously wealthy criminal groups whose willingness to use extortion and violence has rendered them makers of their own laws. The power these groups have been able to accrue has a chilling effect on those who would seek to combat the drug trade through governmental action. Key law enforcement officials (supreme court judges, attorneys general, police chiefs) have been subject to death threats and murdered with impunity.

The appetite for illegal drugs in the United States sustains a steady traffic: 19.5 million people, or 8.3 percent of the population, use such drugs on a regular basis, and 2 million of these are cocaine users (www.oas.samhsa.gov). Ironically, users' drug purchases help to promote widespread corruption, violence, and lawlessness in nations already burdened with wrenching poverty, hunger, malnutrition, and ill health. While drug users in the affluent United States take their pleasures, it is at the cost of some of the most vulnerable of the world's people.

Where Is It All Going?

The situation described in this chapter seems overwhelming. We prefer to be optimistic about problems, believing that they can somehow be solved, and grow very frustrated when ready (even easy) solutions do not offer themselves or when they do, they are, incomprehensibly, not fully implemented.

Today a fifth of the world's people share less than 1.5 percent of the world's income, while the richest fifth has about 85 percent of the world's gross national product (GNP). As a consequence, the United Nations Children's Fund (1995:2) points out, "An underclass is being created, undereducated and unskilled, standing beneath the broken bottom rungs of social and economic progress."

In Latin America alone, real income has fallen as much as 20 percent in some countries (United Nations Children's Fund 1995:3). The situation in sub-Saharan Africa today can only give us a glimpse of the problems to come if extreme levels of inequality within and between nations continue and the needs of people go unheeded. People in such underdeveloped lands, if history is our guide, may increasingly welcome death resulting from the struggle for change to the passive death to which they have been condemned. Or they may flock to cities and other countries, putting pressure on existing populations. We are likely to see more and more movements for change develop, with an escalation of violence, terrorism, and repression. This is part of the global context in which we operate. Is this the way we want to live? Is this the only way we are capable of relating to the desperate conditions of most of the rest of the world? The answers to these questions must be no.

Solutions lie at a variety of different levels, as implied by our discussion in this chapter. At the international level, investment, finance, trade, as well as military and economic aid, must be directed so as not to just serve the interests of the wealthy few. At the national level, underdeveloped nations' public spending priorities must put people first and they must seek to redistribute wealth more evenly through more equitable land policies and tax systems. Citizens' human rights and civil liberties must also be protected. At the community level, residents must have access to land, housing, jobs, education, and health care. And at the family level, women must be empowered, given opportunities for education and employment, and men must take responsibility for their role in reproduction.

Human survival will ultimately call for that which we are currently successfully avoiding: cooperation among nation-states, rich and poor (Barnet 1981). Neither weaponry nor intrigue will ensure the survival of humanity. Cooperation will. What it will take for this realization to penetrate the thinking and practice of developed nations such as the United States is one of the most profound questions of our day.

Summary

The global context within which the United States functions is not always readily apparent. Yet it contains problems that are reaching crisis proportions and inflicting suffering on hundreds of millions of people. Two phenomena are of particular importance: the dynamics of world population growth and the impact of underdevelopment on most of the world's peoples.

The size of the earth's population is growing relentlessly. The most rapid population growth is taking place in underdeveloped nations—poor societies in which four-fifths of all human beings live. Population growth rates are high in much of Asia, Latin America, and Africa. In contrast, growth rates in the more affluent developed nations, such as the United States and nations in Europe, are quite low.

Life chances are very limited for many residents of the underdeveloped world. Hundreds of millions of people suffer routinely from hunger and chronic malnutrition, while others periodically fall victim to famine- and war-related starvation. Malnutrition contributes to people's vulnerability to illness and disease and ultimately to lower life expectancy. Underdeveloped nations experience particularly high death rates among women, infants, and children.

Conventional wisdom has it that high rates of population growth cause world poverty and the malnutrition and poor health that accompany it. According to this view, if we reduce population growth rates by birth control, the situation will improve. Critics view this logic as simplistic and naive; they point out that food and other resources are adequate to serve the world's growing population. The problem lies with how these resources are utilized and distributed, both among nations and within them. By and large, most members of underdeveloped nations lack control over such resources. Their children become assets, providing extra hands to help make family survival possible. For the critics, poverty produces population growth.

Thus, the solution to world poverty—and the hunger and poor health that typically accompany it—is not simply more effective birth control. In most underdeveloped nations, political, economic, and social changes must occur. Production must be rechanneled and its fruits more equitably spread among low-income groups. With economic security, families will have less reason to produce many children.

Obstacles to such changes abound. Underdevelopment has meant vulnerability and dependency, so that developed nations have been able to exploit formerly colonized peoples. Neocolonialism has been the result, as developed nations such as the United States continue to look to poor nations for cheap labor, inexpensive raw materials and agricultural products, and markets. For example, American multinational corporations have invested billions of dollars for such purposes in underdeveloped Latin American nations. Consequently, movements for fundamental economic and political change that periodically arise in such nations are commonly viewed as dangerous to our national interest.

Conditions in underdeveloped nations, if left unaltered, are likely to produce more and more movements for change. Violence and terrorism will escalate within these nations. The relationships between the underdeveloped world and developed nations such as the United States will become extremely unstable. Human survival ultimately will call for cooperation among nation-states, rich and poor. The conditions under which the need for cooperation will be realized is one of the most profound questions of our day.

Key Terms

Birthrate 99
Death rate 99
Malthusian logic 106
Neocolonialism 116

Population explosion 98
Population growth rate 99
Transnational capitalist class 119

Discussion Questions

1. Think about how underdeveloped, or Third World, nations are portrayed typically in the mass media. What stereotypes might the portrayals help to create or to reinforce? What aspects of life are not communicated?

2. In battlefield jargon, *triage* involves separating incoming casualties into three groups: those whose wounds are not serious, those with quite serious wounds, and those who are almost certain to die even with treatment. When medical resources are limited, primary attention goes to the middle group, not to those who are most in danger of death. Some would argue that triage should be the approach taken to aiding other nations that are in distress. Take a position on this and defend it.

3. Choose an underdeveloped nation and do research into the quality of life of its people before, during, and in the wake of colonization. What conclusions are suggested by your research?

4. Economist Robert L. Heilbroner, in *Inquiry into the Human Prospect,* suggests it is unlikely that we would willingly make sacrifices to improve the well-being of people around the world who at present live in abject poverty. Do you agree with Heilbroner? Why or why not?

5. Many colleges and universities have foreign student or international centers where students from outside the United States often congregate. Visit such a center and talk with students about the differences they see between their own societies and the United States. Report your findings to members of the class.

Suggested Readings

Hartman, Betsy. *Reproductive Rights and Wrongs: The Global Politics of Population Control.* Rev. ed. (Boston: South End Press, 1995).
Provides critical analysis of current population control policies and suggests alternative strategies.

Lappé, Frances Moore, and Joseph Collins. *World Hunger: Twelve Myths* (New York: Grove Press, 1986).
Mobilization of data in support of the position that world hunger is not inevitable or necessary.

Sen, Amartya. *Development as Freedom* (New York: Anchor Books, 2000).
Overview of global development issues and processes, with a focus on individual freedom and human rights. Offers alternative future directions for thinking about and accomplishing development.

Sklair, Leslie. *Sociology of the Global System* (Baltimore: Johns Hopkins University Press, 1991).
Discussion of the globalization of economic, political, and cultural relations that transcend national boundaries.

United Nations Children's Fund. *The State of the World's Children 2002* (New York: Oxford University Press, 2002).
Annual publication on the health and well-being of children, with special focus on problems in underdeveloped nations.

Worldwatch Institute. *State of the World 2002* (New York: W. W. Norton, 2002).
Annual review of worldwide environmental and population developments, underscoring emergent trends.

chapter 5

Environmental Abuse

Resources should be devoted to the preservation and conservation of the natural environment, and technological decisions must take into account the well-being of future generations.

People in the United States have long been abusing the environment. We have poured gaseous and solid wastes into the air and water, poisoned and otherwise misused the land, and consumed irreplaceable commodities. We are all aware of environmental abuse—and we all contribute to it. When we drive our cars, discard trash, or set thermostats high in winter and low in summer, we are helping abuse the environment. Billboards blocking the view, airplanes roaring overhead, and trucks crowding our highways are some of the kinds of environmental abuse we take for granted.

The term *ecology* is used to refer to "the intricate web of relationships between living organisms and their living and nonliving surroundings" (Council on Environmental Quality 1970:6). Every action we take within our environment—indeed our very presence—has some impact on the earth. Our environment is not "out there" and apart from humanity. We and our societal institutions are a part of it, whether we think in such terms or not.

The nature of the relationship between human beings and the environment is brought out in the following basic principles of ecology (see Bock 1972:21–25):

1. Living organisms (including people) and their surroundings are mutually interdependent. The earth is one big **ecosystem** in which each part—including human institutions—serves functions that have a bearing on the system as a whole. In turn, the well-being of the whole has implications for the various parts.

2. Every living organism is part of this global ecosystem. All life is, however indirectly and distantly, interconnected.

3. Each species of life carries out its activities in its own environmental niche. Some species have proved to be much more adaptable to changes in their surroundings than others. Adaptability contributes to ecosystem stability.

4. The more species there are, the more stable the ecosystem is likely to be. This is because of the increased probability that some species will take over an important system function if another cannot.

5. Species tend to be dependent on one another and to be interconnected through chains or cycles. For example, we live by inhaling oxygen from the air and exhaling carbon dioxide. Plants, in effect, do the reverse. Thus, people and plants need one another. Likewise, just about every species of life uses another as food and in turn serves as nourishment for an additional species.

6. It is impossible to throw anything away in the global ecosystem. Everything must go somewhere. When something is disposed of, there is an impact on the part of the system from which it is removed and on the part into which it is discarded.

7. No part of the ecosystem is "free." Whenever we use or deplete some part of the system, this affects the functioning of the ecosystem as a whole.

8. People and the institutions people create are only one part of the global ecosystem, and perhaps not even the most important part. We are far more dependent on other living species than they are on us. The ecosystem could probably easily survive without humanity.

These principles make it clear that polluting the air, land, and water; spreading radioactivity into the atmosphere; generating increasing levels of noise; creating numerous wastes; and consuming irreplaceable resources change or otherwise affect the global ecosystem. Since human beings are part of the ecosystem, we too are affected by these activities. The term *ecocatastrophe* is an apt description of the overall effect such harmful human activities seem to be having. While obviously not all human activities are ecologically harmful, those cited appear to be undoing millions of years of nature's complex work.

In some cases the damage being done to the air, water, and land and the life they sustain poses a threat to human survival. Since all people are participants in the global ecosystem, this threat goes beyond the political boundaries of the United States. Many other nations are engaged in environmental abuse. But the United States stands out in terms of its massive contribution to environmental ills. For example, while it possesses only 4.7 percent of the world's population, no other nation consumes so much of the world's nonrenewable resources each year.

In this chapter we look at the macro problem of environmental abuse. We distinguish among a number of types of environmental abuse, indicating their extent and their implications for the future. Finally, we examine the causes of and possible solutions to this basic and far-reaching problem, discussing the institutional and individual obstacles that we must work to overcome.

Nature and Extent of Environmental Abuse

The term **environmental abuse** refers to several varied types of human activities, from dirtying the atmosphere to depleting irreplaceable resources. In this section we look at major types of environmental abuse. We estimate the extent of each type and look at the possible effects on the human condition.

Air Pollution

Most of us take the life-sustaining activity of breathing for granted. But threats to this activity have been a matter of serious concern since the 1960s. Prior to that time, most people saw "dirty air" as a localized phenomenon, not as the national and international threat it is.

The earth's atmosphere contains a finite amount of air—5 to 6 quadrillion tons of it. Under ordinary circumstances, this air is constantly being recycled and cleansed of contaminants through a complex process involving wind, rain, and changes in temperature. Air pollution occurs when so many contaminants are released into the atmosphere that the recycling and cleansing functions begin to break down.

Although U.S. environmental laws and regulations (e.g., governing industrial and motor vehicle emissions) have helped to lower levels of most types of air pollution since 1970 (U.S. Environmental Protection Agency 1991), such pollution remains a critical problem. An estimated 208.4 million metric tons of pollutants are still being released into the air each year in the United States (U.S. Bureau of the Census 2004:233). This tonnage may seem insignificant in relation to the amount of air in the earth's atmosphere, but it is not really the weight of pollutants that counts. More important is the fact that pollution is concentrated in particular geographical areas—most notably in large cities and their suburbs. Since most U.S. residents live in and around cities, air pollution directly affects most members of our society. Of course, pollutants from cities migrate into rural areas.

There are several common classes of air pollutants (Wagner 1994). *Carbon monoxide* is a colorless, odorless, poisonous gas that constitutes 58 percent of air pollution tonnage. Almost 62 percent of this gas comes from motor vehicle engines. *Particulate matter*—that is, solid and liquid substances that may or may not be visible to the naked eye—makes up 15 percent of pollution tonnage. Particulates are emitted during industrial operations and the combustion of fuels in stationary sources (e.g., electric power plants). *Sulfur oxides* enter the air as a by-product of the use of sulfur-containing fuels (coal and oil). Industry and generators of electric power are the biggest users. The oxides are released in the form of poisonous, corrosive gases and constitute 7.6 percent of our annual pollution output (U.S. Bureau of the Census 2004). *Nitrogen oxides* represent 10.7 percent of our pollution tonnage. They are a major component of what is commonly called *smog*. The major contributors are power plants and transportation vehicles. *Volatile Organic Compounds (VOCs)* also play a role in smog formation. These compounds of carbon make up another 8.6 percent of pollution tonnage. VOCs are primarily emitted by automobiles, gasoline, and manufacturers and users of chemicals and solvents. In the formation of smog, hydrocarbons and nitrogen oxides react in sunlight to form ozone (smog's principal constituent). Finally, *lead* is a pollutant that, though low in tonnage (about 1.2 percent of total air pollutants), is highly toxic. It largely stems from lead gasoline additives, metal smelters, and battery manufacturers.

Researchers do not agree about the effects of particular pollutants on the human body, but it is certain that some or all of them do have negative effects. For example, medical researchers have found a correspondence between air pollution and coughing, colds, and other respiratory diseases, lung cancer, cardiovascular diseases, infant mortality rates, death rates among the elderly, and the speed of recovery from illness (Briggs 2003; Christiani 1993).

Investigators believe that persons living in or near urban centers are especially subject to health risks posed by air pollution. One group of researchers has noted:

Environmental issues are an important dimension of urban policy. With 75 percent of the nation's population, metropolitan areas are major sources of environmental pollution. Aside from sheer volume of pollutants generated, density and other physical features of cities contribute to the severity of urban pollution problems. To the extent that urban environments are degraded, 75 percent of the nation's population are exposed to or suffer from problems associated with that degradation. (Gillett et al. 1992: 377–78)

People living in air-polluted urban areas are subject to higher rates of such illnesses as emphysema, bronchitis, and lung cancer than experienced by their rural counterparts.

According to the Council of Environmental Quality, the United States now spends approximately $30 billion on air pollution control efforts annually (Wagner 1994). Even with the progress made in fighting air pollution over the last three decades, largely under the impetus of the federal Clean Air Act passed in 1970, much more needs to be done. (See Table 5.1.) Effects of the pollution that is not yet controlled continue to cost many billions of dollars per year.

These costs stem from treatment of unnecessary health problems, damage to residential property, extra cleaning expenses, and harm to vegetation (including crops) and materials (e.g., steel, rubber, marble). No real dollar value can be assigned to the ways air pollution hastens the death of living things—including people.

The "Greenhouse Effect"

For some years now, scientists have been warning that air pollution could create a **greenhouse effect** that would produce increased temperatures all over the world. Although scientists

Table 5.1	National Air Pollutant Emissions: 1970 to 2001						
Year	PM-10	PM-10, fugitive dust*	Sulfur dioxide	Nitrogen dioxide	Volatile organic compounds	Carbon monoxide	Lead
1970	12,838	(NA)	31,096	20,625	30,646	128,079	219,471
1980	6,928	(NA)	25,813	23,281	25,893	115,625	74,956
1983	5,849	(NA)	22,471	22,364	24,607	115,334	49,232
1984	6,126	(NA)	23,396	23,172	25,572	114,262	42,217
1985	3,676	44,701	23,148	22,853	25,417	112,072	20,124
1986	3,679	49,940	22,361	22,409	24,826	108,070	7,296
1987	3,630	42,131	22,085	22,386	24,338	105,117	6,840
1988	3,697	59,975	22,535	23,221	24,961	106,100	6,464
1989	3,661	53,323	22,653	23,250	23,731	100,806	6,099
1990	4,229	44,929	22,261	23,192	24,276	103,753	5,635
1991	3,902	49,127	22,149	22,977	23,508	99,898	5,020
1992	3,676	44,953	21,592	22,991	23,020	96,368	4,741
1993	3,688	41,801	21,888	23,402	23,312	97,208	4,885
1995	8,807	17,012	18,619	24,956	22,041	126,777	3,929
2001	9,442	14,662	15,790	22,349	17,963	120,759	NA

[In thousands of tons. PM-10 = Particulate matter of less than 10 microns.] NA Not available.

*Sources such as agricultural tilling, construction, mining and quarrying, paved roads, unpaved roads, and wind erosion.

Source: U.S. Department of Commerce, Bureau of the Census, *Statistical Abstract of the United States, 1995* (Washington, DC: U.S. Government Printing Office, 1995), p. 233; U.S. Department of Commerce, Bureau of the Census, *Statistical Abstract of the United States, 2003* (Washington, DC: U.S. Government Printing Office, 2004), p. 233.

remain cautious in their statements about this issue, many argue that the greenhouse effect is now upon us and that it will have a tremendous impact in the not-too-distant future (World Resources Institute 2004).

We can start with the fact that the earth and its surrounding atmosphere function naturally much as a greenhouse. Sunlight, on which we depend and which we generally enjoy, strikes the earth. The earth then radiates heat in the form of infrared rays. Some of these warming rays escape through the earth's atmosphere and into space, yet the carbon dioxide (CO_2) in this atmosphere captures some of the warmth. Without this natural process, the planet would be afflicted with subfreezing temperatures. Human activities, scientists have warned, are undoing the delicate balance of sun, earth, and atmosphere.

What actually is happening? The level of concentration of CO_2, which traps heat and thus warms the earth, has been increasing in the atmosphere. Scientists blame this development on the increased burning of fossil fuels, such as oil and coal. Systematic measurements begun in 1958 indicate the CO_2 level in the atmosphere has gone up 25 percent since that time. The United States leads the world in CO_2 releases and it, along with China, is responsible for one-third of all nations' CO_2 emissions. The Russian Federation, Japan, India, and Germany are other major contributors (World Resources Institute 2004:258–59).

But other factors are responsible for the CO_2 buildup as well. In many underdeveloped nations large landholders have been cutting down tropical forests at an unprecedented rate, both for the wood and to expand open land for agriculture. Some 78 million acres of forest are lost each year, or 2.4 acres each second. At the current rate of tropical forest destruction, they will all be gone by 2030 (Rainforest Action Network, available at www.ran.org).

Latin American nations like Brazil are leaders in this regard. In Brazil tropical forests have been cut down for the lumber; for roads, highways, and various development projects; and for massive cattle ranches that produce beef products for export to rich developed nations (see Chapter 4). But the trees cut down are no longer available to naturally absorb CO_2 from the air, and new CO_2 is released from the cut-down trees and the earth disturbed by the cutting process. *Deforestation,* as this process of forest elimination is called, makes a direct contribution to the greenhouse effect.

Scientists estimate that the CO_2 buildup accounts for about half of the warming associated

Scientists suspect that the increase in carbon dioxide in the atmosphere is prompting changes in the earth's temperatures and climatic patterns. Widespread destruction of forests, such as is pictured here, are believed to be contributing to the problem.

with the greenhouse effect. Other pollutants help produce the rest. Methane is one such pollutant, resulting from wood burning, the raising of farm animals such as cattle, and similar activities. Nitrous oxide, a common component of power plant and motor vehicle emissions, is another pollutant. Finally, there are chlorofluorocarbons (CFCs), chemicals that are commonly used as refrigeration and air conditioner coolants as well as in foam products and solvents. CFCs are held to be the principal cause of the growing destruction of the earth's ozone layer, to be discussed in the next section.

As the pollutants—from CO_2 to CFCs—concentrate in the earth's atmosphere, more and more heat is trapped and the earth's temperature rises. Scientists speculate that the temperature could rise on average anywhere from 2 to 9 degrees Fahrenheit by the year 2050. The increases are unlikely to be spread evenly around the earth: Temperature increases near the equator could be small, whereas the upper latitudes could have increases that are twice the global average.

Such a warming trend will affect climates, although no one is sure precisely how. Here is one projection:

A warming is likely to change rainfall patterns, prevailing winds, and ocean currents, which might lead to more severe storms as the temperature differential between the equatorial region and the higher latitudes widens. Higher temperatures in some areas would also bring an overall increase in evaporation and rainfall, but the changes would not be evenly distributed. Some regions would become wetter; others drier. (Brown and Flavin 1988:16)

Such climatic transformations have enormous implications for agricultural activity. Farming goes on where it does, and takes on the form that it does, in response to a history of relatively constant climatic conditions. Change these conditions and world food production could be

seriously affected. Nations' entire economies could be placed under disruptive stresses.

But there is more. Because of the greenhouse effect, the level of the world's oceans is expected to rise dramatically in coming decades—a process scientists say is now under way. As temperatures increase, water warms and expands. Beyond this, warming reduces the water now held within polar ice caps and glaciers; a melting process adds to the oceans' waters. Predictions are that the global sea level may rise by 8 inches in the next 40 years, and almost 1.5 feet within the next 100 years (since 1900 the oceans have risen 4 inches) (*Science Daily,* Feb. 20, 2002; available at www.sciencedaily.com).

Areas of the world where a great deal of food production takes place in low-lying flood plains and river deltas—such as Asia with its rice crops—could be decimated. Some island nations, the Maldives and Seychelles, for example, might become submerged. The vast populations living in cities and towns along coastal areas around the world may have to abandon their places of work and residence. In the United States, for example, more than half the population resides near the Atlantic or Pacific Ocean, the Gulf of Mexico, or the Great Lakes. The costs and dislocations associated with coastal flooding would be without precedent. All continents would be affected.

Biological species other than humans would also face many new demands as a result of the greenhouse effect. Many species of plants and animals that had adapted to past climatic features may not be able to survive the new temperatures and seasons, particularly given the rapidity with which these changes could occur. The biological diversity of, and natural balance among, species will change in ways that cannot be predicted.

A former chairman of the President's Council on Environmental Quality, Gus Speth, provided this warning to the U.S. Senate way back in 1980: "The insidious nature of the CO_2 problem is that if a response is postponed until significant and harmful climate changes are actually observed or until scientific uncertainties are largely resolved, it may be too late to avoid even more severe climate changes" (cf. Regenstein 1982:203).

In 1992 over 150 nations signed the United Nations Framework Convention on Climate Change, agreeing to take steps to slow down emissions of pollutants thought to be producing the greenhouse effect. But largely at the insistence of the U.S. government, individual nations' efforts to address these emissions were left voluntary. U.S. officials refused to accept the need for mandatory actions unless justified by more definitive scientific data on the greenhouse effect and its causes. Yet many scientists believe we have enough data and that nations must act in concert before it is too late. It is estimated that a 50 percent reduction in current global emissions must occur just to keep concentrations of CO_2 and other gases in the atmosphere from getting worse (Intergovernmental Panel on Climate Change 2001).

Ideas as to what nations can do abound. Slow down fossil fuel consumption and look to alternative energy sources such as solar, wind, geothermal, or even nuclear power. Eliminate totally the use of such chemicals as CFCs, introducing environmentally acceptable substitutes. Develop new crops that can adapt to heat and drought and resist predatory insects. Encourage economic growth and population settlement away from endangered coastal areas, and build protective seawalls where possible for areas at risk of flooding. Be ready to undertake massive investments in irrigation and drainage projects in geographic areas that become favorable to agricultural production.

Such ideas are alive among scientists and environmental activists in many nations, and most national leaders are willing to acknowledge the need to do something. But when it comes right down to it, in most nations these kinds of ideas are often either considered of low priority, too complex or expensive to consider implementing, unfeasible because of the sacrifices they would require from the population, or contrary to the vested interests of powerful economic and political elites (Christie 1992; Smil 1990). Thus, the concerted worldwide action that is needed to reverse the greenhouse trends is lacking, at least right now.

Ozone Layer Depletion

In the previous section we alluded in passing to yet another case of major environmental damage for which humans can take responsibility: destruction of the ozone layer that is in the earth's upper atmosphere. Like the greenhouse effect, the implications of this ozone depletion are far-reaching (World Resources Institute 2004).

About 15 miles above the earth's surface there is a paper-thin layer of ozone (a modified form of oxygen). This ozone layer serves important protective functions for all forms of life. While scientists have been theorizing about this since the early 1970s, it was not until 1985 that firm evidence of ozone depletion became available. A few scientists found a way to actually measure ozone levels and discovered that atmospheric ozone over Antarctica was in decline. Further inquiries revealed that the process of ozone depletion had been going on for some time and increasing steadily each year, and it was occurring not only over Antarctica but over much of the rest of the world as well.

Why is ozone depletion occurring? In 1930 researchers discovered a new group of chemical compounds—chlorofluorocarbons, or CFCs. As mentioned in the previous section of this chapter, CFCs are widely used in refrigeration and air-conditioning units. They are used in various products, including foam building insulation and solvents. They have been used as a propellant in aerosol spray cans. Until reductions in their production and use began in the 1990s, sales of CFCs in the United States were estimated at $750 million each year, and they have been used in products that have sales of many billions more.

Although CFCs are useful, some of their properties present dangers we have only recently begun to recognize (Cagin and Dray 1993). Products in which they are used release the CFCs into the air, whereupon they float up into the upper atmosphere. Under complex conditions that scientists are trying to understand, the CFCs eat away at the ozone. As more CFCs are introduced into the environment, the process of ozone depletion continues. Other ozone-depleting agents include halons (used in fire extinguishers), methyl chloroform and carbon tetrachloride (industrial solvents), and methyl bromide (a pesticide used on produce). The most attention, however, has been focused on the dangers of CFCs because they pose the greatest threat to the ozone layer.

The ozone layer is critical to maintain, for it shields life on earth from the damaging effects of ultraviolet radiation from the sun. This radiation, unless blocked, can do many things. It can disrupt the oceans' food chains, upon which many forms of life (including human) depend. As the ozone layer is depleted, the ultraviolet radiation will increase the incidence of skin cancers and cataracts of the eye. This radiation can damage our immune systems, leaving us helpless to fight off a variety of infectious diseases. Construction materials, particularly plastics, will more quickly deteriorate. And damage to crops could be monumental (DeGruijl 1995, available at www.gcrio.org; McKee 1994).

In 1987 the United States joined with many other nations in the United Nations' Montreal Protocol on Substances That Deplete the Ozone Layer. Signatory nations agreed to restrict CFC use and substantially cut production and sales by the end of the century. A few years later, this accord was tightened to encourage a complete phaseout of the use of CFCs, a process that is now under way in a number of nations. The largest reductions will have to be by industrial nations such as the United States, which pro-

duce and use most of the CFCs and thus make the largest contribution to the problem. This international accord helped to further the belief that increasingly our environmental problems do not recognize national boundaries and that solutions require all nations' cooperation.

Despite the progress made, however, the damage continues. For example, as people discard unwanted refrigeration units, home and auto air conditioners, and so on, the CFCs within will join those already in the atmosphere. While in the United States and some other industrial nations efforts have been under way to capture and control the discard of CFCs from such sources, such practices do not exist everywhere. Illegal production and sales of CFCs go on, even in the United States. And many underdeveloped nations, which depend on meager refrigeration facilities to help reduce food spoilage that would exacerbate existing shortages, find it difficult and expensive to make a transition away from CFCs (Edson 1994).

Some of the substitutes for CFCs to which manufacturers are switching still contribute, albeit at a much reduced rate, to ozone depletion and may also contribute to the greenhouse effect. Harmless alternatives to CFCs and other ozone-depleting products must be developed and used, for the ozone depletion process cannot quickly and easily be reversed. In the words of one scientist, "The only way to return things to the way they were is to stop using chlorofluorocarbons completely and then wait a couple of centuries" (*U.S. News and World Report,* March 28, 1988:10).

Acid Rain

In recent years a new airborne pollutant—acid rain—has come to be recognized as a serious problem in a number of nations in the Northern Hemisphere, including the United States, Canada, Japan, and some European nations (Forster 1993; Wellburn 1994). Acid rain is sometimes referred to as acid precipitation or acid deposition. It too is an outcome of burning fossil fuels (particularly coal and, to a much lesser degree, oil and natural gas). Coal-burning power plants and industrial processors are the heaviest contributors to acid rain.

The sulfur dioxide and nitrogen oxides that are produced by burning coal, for example, rise up into the air, where they combine with water to form acid droplets. Eventually acidic precipitation comes back down to earth in the form of rain, snow, sleet, and hail or attached to particles of dust. In effect, the land and water are being sprinkled with dilute forms of nitric and sulfuric acids—the dangers of which are familiar to anyone who has been exposed to a chemistry course.

Acid rain has come to be seen by some as a serious problem for different reasons (U.S. Environmental Protection Agency 2004, available at www.epa.gov/airmarkets/acidrain). It enters lakes and streams and destroys plant and aquatic life. Runoffs and sudden snow melts endanger the safe use of reservoirs that are major public water supplies. Acid rain is a menace to crops as well as to forests, and it eats away at buildings and historical monuments. Moreover, it is thought to contribute to respiratory and cardiovascular disease as well as to cancer. Its destructive potential is enormous if it goes unchecked.

At present the U.S. emission of sulfur into the atmosphere is over 22 million metric tons a year. Emission of nitrogen is also over 20 million metric tons. Much of this flows out of smokestacks in the industrial Midwest, coming down as acid rain hundreds, even thousands, of miles away. It is possible that three-fourths of the acid rain that falls in Canada originates with U.S.-based emissions. Aquatic life in lakes in both Canada and the United States has been adversely affected. For example, in the U.S. Adirondack region of New York, 10 percent of the lakes have become too acidic to support fish (Wagner 1994). Canada and the United States have had difficulty agreeing on solutions, but

each nation has taken some steps to restrict its respective contribution to the acid rain problem. The United States faces a much greater task since it is—as with other forms of environmental abuse—the principal contributor.

Water Pollution

Travelers to underdeveloped nations are often warned against drinking anything but sterilized liquids sealed in bottles. Contaminated water is a major problem in the United States as well. Over the years, we managed to pollute virtually every major body of water in the nation. Rivers, streams, lakes, harbors, and bays have been fouled with organic and inorganic chemical wastes. Public water supplies and even private wells have been found to contain substances linked with cancer. Federal laws have sought since the 1970s to regulate the most obvious and repugnant pollutants—indeed, many lakes, streams, and waterways are now more swimmable and fishable than they have been in years. Yet water pollution remains a form of environmental abuse that continues to cry out for attention.

Water, like air, is a prerequisite of life. We drink it, bathe in it, use it for recreational purposes, eat many of the creatures that live in it, and rely on it for use at home and in our economy. Each day the United States uses 467 billion gallons of freshwater, more than 1,800 gallons per person. Slightly more than 10 percent is used for public tap water, 10 percent for industry, 41 percent for agriculture, and 40 percent for cooling electric power-generating plants. The United States has a higher rate of freshwater consumption than any other industrialized society (Brown 1999, available at www.fs.fed.us; World Resources Institute 2004). Water pollution thus constitutes a threat that is just as serious as the abuse of the earth's air. There is a distinct possibility that we could run short of usable water, not only because of pollution but also because the demand for freshwater is subject to increase.

Many pollutants have been found in our water, and there is good reason to believe that many others have not yet been discovered. How these pollutants affect one another is unknown. Some water pollutants come from "point sources," that is, identifiable sites where the sources of the pollution can be controlled. Federal laws on water pollution have been most successful in limiting point source pollution, although it has by no means been eliminated.

One of the major point source contaminants is *industrial waste*. Often, factories discharge water containing wastes, many of which are known to be toxic. Most such wastes have come from the paper, organic chemicals, steel, and petroleum industries.

Thermal pollution is another serious type of point source pollution. It is principally generated by the electric power industry. Power plants use great amounts of water for coolant purposes, then pour the used water back into rivers, streams, and lakes, raising their temperature and adversely affecting aquatic life.

Municipal wastes are also a point source contributor to water pollution. The treatment of the enormous wastes generated by homes, commercial establishments, and industry is often inadequate in urban areas. Much of the nation's population lacks access to safe means of sewage disposal.

"Non-point-source" water pollutants, on the other hand, are those that cannot be easily traced to a single site and that are thus much more difficult to control than point source pollutants. For example, *agricultural wastes* include animal and chemical wastes. Each year animals produce the same amount of organic wastes as do 2 billion people. Agricultural animals are often reared in centralized feedlots, where their wastes become highly concentrated and are impervious to natural decomposition. Elements of these wastes then seep into underground water channels and surface waters. A similar process occurs as a consequence of the heavy use of chemical fertilizers and pesticides, not only in

farm areas but in suburbs where people cultivate their lawns.

Other forms of non-point-source pollution abound. Our waters are subject to contamination by land erosion and sediments. Landfills containing household and other wastes leach pollutants into groundwater. Oils and other hazardous substances from motor vehicles are washed off roads and highways, or spilled—by accident or on purpose—into waterways. Fuels and other pollutants are often discharged or dumped from boats. Mine drainage (particularly from strip mining) fills streams and rivers with toxic metals and acids. And acid rain, as we have seen, can threaten the ability of bodies of still water to sustain plant and aquatic life. While important inroads have been made into the reduction of point source pollution, serious threats to the nation's water from non-point-source contamination remain (Wagner 1994).

Noticeable changes have been taking place in the oceans. For years it was assumed that the oceans could readily dilute and absorb whatever we decided to dump into them. The results of this assault are finally being felt (Goldberg 1976; Johnston 1977). Since toxic wastes are absorbed by fish and other forms of sea life, the chemicals dumped into the oceans often appear on our dinner plates. In many areas, beaches have been spoiled and recreational activities disrupted. Oil and other substances dumped are thought to have implications for our climate. Solid wastes, sludge from sewage, industrial and hospital wastes, explosives, radioactive wastes, and dredge spoils (e.g., from harbor construction) threaten to turn the oceans into huge cesspools (Bingham 1994).

Toxic Substances

Only in the last couple of decades have we begun to understand the full implications of the unsafe disposal of humanly created toxic substances. The U.S. Environmental Protection Agency estimates that there are anywhere from

Environmental catastrophe occurred in northern Spain in 2002, when an oil tanker loaded with 77,000 tons of fuel oil sank and spilled tens of thousands of tons of oil into the sea. Here, a bird struggles to flap its oil-soaked wings on the polluted beach.

32,000 to 50,000 sites in the United States where hazardous wastes have been disposed. Anywhere from 1,200 to 2,000 pose highly significant health risks to people and other living things. Table 5.2 indicates states with the most known hazardous sites. As recently as 1980, some 200 new chemical waste sites were being discovered each month (Regenstein 1982). Take Times Beach, Missouri, for example. In 1982 the U.S. Environmental Protection Agency took the dramatic step of closing the entire town and shutting down all roads into one of the nation's most contaminated areas. The town had spent many years controlling dust on its streets and parking lots by spraying waste oil on them. Unfortunately, the manufacturing processes for which the oil was originally used produced the highly toxic chemical dioxin, contaminating the oil that was now being sprayed liberally all over town. The EPA had to permanently relocate more than 2,000 residents and destroy every home and business in the town. It took 15 years to clean 265,000 tons of contaminated soil (www.epa.gov). The town is no longer a residential area; it has been turned into a state park.

Dramatic Incidents, such as Times Beach and Love Canal (to be discussed), are really only manifestations of a much larger problem: How are we to prevent many of the 70,000 chemicals manufactured each year from being used and/or disposed of in such a way that they endanger health and lives? Why are we not looking at the health dangers that may accompany the 500 to 1,000 new chemical compounds that

Table 5.2	Hazardous Waste Sites on the National Priority List, by State: 2002				
State	Total sites	Rank	Percent distribution	Federal	Nonfederal
Total	1,291	(X)	(X)	164	1,127
United States	**1,278**	**(X)**	**100.0**	**163**	**1,115**
Alabama	15	24	1.2	3	12
Alaska	6	44	0.5	5	1
Arizona	9	41	0.7	2	7
Arkansas	12	32	0.9	—	12
California	98	2	7.7	24	74
Colorado	17	22	1.3	3	14
Connecticut	16	23	1.3	1	15
Delaware	15	24	1.2	1	14
District of Columbia	1	(X)	0.1	1	—
Florida	52	6	4.1	6	46
Georgia	15	24	1.2	2	13
Hawaii	3	46	0.2	2	1
Idaho	10	40	0.8	2	8
Illinois	45	8	3.5	5	40
Indiana	29	14	2.3	—	29
Iowa	14	29	1.1	1	13
Kansas	12	32	0.9	2	10
Kentucky	14	29	1.1	1	13
Louisiana	15	24	1.2	1	14
Maine	12	32	0.8	3	9
Maryland	19	20	1.5	9	10
Massachusetts	32	12	2.5	7	25
Michigan	69	5	5.4	1	68
Minnesota	24	17	1.9	2	22
Mississippi	4	45	0.4	—	4
Missouri	23	18	1.8	3	20
Montana	15	24	1.2	—	15
Nebraska	11	38	0.9	1	10
Nevada	1	49	0.1	—	1
New Hampshire	19	20	1.5	1	18
New Jersey	115	1	9.0	8	107

State	Total sites	Rank	Percent distribution	Federal	Nonfederal
New Mexico	12	32	0.9	1	11
New York	91	4	7.1	4	87
North Carolina	28	15	2.2	2	26
North Dakota	—	50	—	—	—
Ohio	33	11	2.6	5	28
Oklahoma	11	38	0.9	1	10
Oregon	12	32	0.9	2	10
Pennsylvania	96	3	7.5	6	90
Rhode Island	12	32	0.9	2	10
South Carolina	25	16	2.0	2	23
South Dakota	2	47	0.2	1	1
Tennessee	13	31	1.0	4	9
Texas	43	9	3.4	4	39
Utah	21	19	1.6	4	17
Vermont	9	41	0.7	—	9
Virginia	30	13	2.3	11	19
Washington	47	7	3.7	14	33
West Virginia	9	41	0.7	2	7
Wisconsin	40	10	3.1	—	40
Wyoming	2	47	0.2	1	1
Guam	2	(X)	(X)	1	1
Puerto Rico	9	(X)	(X)	1	9
Virgin Islands	2	(X)	(X)	—	2

[Includes both proposed and final sites listed on the National Priorities List for the Superfund program as authorized by the Comprehensive Environmental Response, Compensation, and Liability Act of 1980 and the Superfund Amendments and Reauthorization Act of 1986.]

—*Represents zero. X Not applicable.*

Source: U.S. Department of Commerce, Bureau of the Census, *Statistical Abstract of the United States, 2003* (Washington, DC: U.S. Government Printing Office, 2004), p. 237.

manufacturers introduce into the environment annually? Only now are we starting to feel the full danger of the mindless poisoning of our land and water with highly toxic substances (Epstein, Brown, and Pope 1982).

The story of Love Canal, a small suburb of Niagara Falls, New York, was and is terrifying (Brown 1980). In 1978, 240 families were forced to evacuate their homes in Love Canal. These families, ordered from their homes by the state government, all lived within two blocks of an abandoned canal that was used as a landfill. Substances known to be toxic, and in some cases known to cause cancer, were discovered in the soil, groundwater, and air around these homes. Later, in 1980, an additional 710 families were forced to evacuate. Authorities fenced in the area to keep people out, purchased homes from the residents, tore down those homes closest to the canal, and built a clay cover over the landfill area to stop leaks of toxic substances.

The story is not a pretty one. Investigations revealed that dozens of chemicals, including such known carcinogens as benzene and toluene, had seeped into the soil and contaminated water underground. Since 1942 the Hooker Chemical Company had been dumping millions of pounds of waste chemicals, including some of the most dangerous known to modern science. Several hundred pounds of one chemical were found, of which less than three ounces are sufficient to lethally poison millions of people.

In 1953 Hooker Chemical, knowing what it had deposited on the site of Love Canal, nonetheless agreed to sell the land and surrounding property to the school board and the city of Niagara Falls. The corporation's price was $1.00, and the property was sold with the understanding that Hooker Chemical would henceforth not be liable for any injuries or damages resulting from the property's contents. With the dangers of what lay beneath the surface left unrevealed, the city built an elementary school on the site. New homes were erected.

Love Canal residents appear to have been victimized by much higher than expected rates of diseases such as cancer as well as miscarriages and birth defects. In 1990 government authorities declared some Love Canal neighborhoods safe for habitation, and many new families proceeded to purchase homes and move in. But to this day no one is sure just how dangerous Love Canal still is, what the full range of health outcomes ultimately may be for those who were living there, or how long one may safely reside there now without being at risk (Hoffman 1995).

More recently, in a case made famous by the popular movie *Erin Brockovich*, Pacific Gas & Electric Company (PG&E) discharged vast amounts of chromium 6, a highly carcinogenic chemical, which seeped into the groundwater of Barstow, California. PG&E did not notify the community of the dangers, although the firm knew about the extreme toxicity of the chemical as early as 1965. As a result, people in the community drank, bathed, swam, and cooked with the contaminated water; the all-volunteer fire department used the contaminated water in its service to the community (Ascenzi 2000; available at www.fumento.com/buspress.html). By 1996 severe clusters of cancer, birth defects, and miscarriages began surfacing in the small town, and subsequent lawsuits established that the company's practice of disposing of its hazardous waste had indeed been the cause.

In newspapers across the nation, news stories regularly depict new discoveries of situations that parallel the Love Canal poisoning, although not necessarily on the same scale. The U.S. Environmental Protection Agency (EPA) has issued statements that imply our entire society has become a big Love Canal. For example, the EPA has estimated that 440 million pounds of PCBs (polychlorinated biphenyls)—among the most toxic substances ever synthesized—are present in the environment (Regenstein 1982). Millions of gallons of PCB-contaminated liquids were found in 1995, for example, to have been leaking unnoticed for over a decade from a landfill in Toledo, Ohio (Ferner 1995). The health outcomes of exposure to PCBs let loose in the environment may be subtle, but they are very real. Researchers have found, for example, that children exposed to PCBs prenatally have cognitive deficits that can adversely affect their learning ability (*Psychology Today* 1992).

The dangers of toxic substances in our environment led a former EPA administrator, Douglas Costle, to state:

We look back on the Middle Ages and we say, "No wonder they had bubonic plague—they used to throw their garbage in the streets." Now I just hope that in the year 2025 my grandchildren don't look back on this generation and say, "No wonder they had problems—look at all the chemicals just carelessly introduced into the environment, uncontrolled." (quoted in Newsweek, *August 21, 1978:28)*

Nor should we be sanguine about the possibility of large-scale accidents in which literally hundreds of thousands of men, women, and children become victims of exposure to toxic substances. Consider, for example, the enormous tragedy in Bhopal, India. On December 3, 1984, a toxic gas used in the production of pesticides—methyl isocyanate—leaked from a plant owned by Union Carbide, a U.S. firm. The result was the largest number of casualties from an industrial accident in history. An estimated 2,500 people died in the first week, and the death toll now may be as high as 14,000 as people still continue to succumb to effects of exposure to the gas. As many as 500,000 people were injured by the leak, many of them permanently disabled with everything from breathing difficulties to impaired vision. Children born to persons poisoned in the 1984 tragedy also suffer serious health problems and many of them too have died (Crossette 1994; Moore 1994). The possibility of a Bhopal in the United States—a nightmare to even consider—is real.

Nuclear Radiation

▲ The Fallout from Nuclear Weaponry

Almost 50 years ago, a group of U.S. scientists and technicians participated in the secret, federally sponsored Manhattan Project. This wartime effort resulted in the first atomic bombs, which were used in the war against Japan. The explosion of atomic bombs in Hiroshima and Nagasaki in 1945 produced death, injury, and property destruction on a scale never before seen. Scientists throughout the world began working with nuclear power, not only for military uses but also for peacetime needs, particularly to meet growing energy demands.

It was not until the 1950s that some serious dangers of nuclear power began to be discerned (Commoner 1974; Wasserman and Solomon

1982). The United States, Great Britain, and the Soviet Union were detonating atomic explosions in remote areas for test purposes. Suddenly, scientists found that the tests were producing radioactive debris that was literally showering down on the earth far away from the test sites. Radioactivity was appearing everywhere—in water, soil, plants, animals. One component of the *nuclear fallout*—strontium 90—was a possible cancer-causing agent. Other radioactive elements were associated with genetic defects. For the first time, atomic radiation began to be seriously appreciated for what it is: a major threat to life. While such atmospheric testing has since been sharply curtailed, radioactivity from the original tests is still around and will be for many years. Persons who lived in the United States during the 1950s and 1960s may not know it, but they are members of an "atomic generation."

More recently, people in the United States have become aware of many heretofore hidden dangers associated with weapons-testing sites and manufacturing plants that have been used over the years to build nuclear weapons (Shulman 1992; see also National Center for Environmental Health Radiation Studies, available at www.cdc .gov/nceh/radiation/fallout). Careless practices, screened from view by the high level of secrecy surrounding the U.S. Department of Energy's operation of these facilities, have introduced huge amounts of highly dangerous radioactivity into the environment. Enormous quantities of radioactive plutonium and other nuclear wastes have been put into the air, soil, and water of a dozen states stretching from Washington to Florida, increasing the risks of cancer, brain tumors, and birth defects for persons living in the vicinity of the contamination. Even now many wastes are sitting in "interim" storage at DOE nuclear weapons facilities, waiting to be permanently disposed of if and when safe ways to do so can be found (World Resources Institute 2004).

Cleaning up this nuclear mess will take at least 30 years and will cost an estimated

$200 billion. And since plutonium has a half-life of 24,000 years—the time required for half its quantity to decay—this threat will plague the country for centuries (Peart 1994:21).

▲ The Risks from Nuclear Power Plants

Even the peacetime uses of atomic energy have become a source of major concern. The United States joined other nations in the 1960s and early 1970s in an expanding program of nuclear power plant construction. However, by the late 1970s and early 1980s the nuclear power industry began to unravel through a combination of factors (Deudney and Flavin 1983). Costs of construction were beginning to be exorbitant, well outpacing original estimates, and members of the public began to awake to some of the real and potential dangers associated with nuclear power.

As a consequence, construction has been curtailed. More than 140 of the 170 new plants expected to be in operation by the year 2000 have been canceled or deferred. In 2002 some 103 nuclear power plants were operating in the United States, supplying 20 percent of the nation's total electrical energy needs (Nuclear Energy Institute, available at www.nei.org). But the dangers, expenses, and some frightening accidents (to be discussed in the following paragraphs) have cast a shadow over the future of nuclear power for electricity generation in this country. Although a number of countries have sought to slow or reverse their reliance on nuclear power, still others—including some underdeveloped nations—continue to view nuclear power as a viable option.

Several dangers are inherent in the production of nuclear power (Gyorgy 1979). Nuclear power plants require enormous amounts of freshwater and produce far more thermal pollution than do conventional power generators. They emit radioactive effluents as well, such as krypton 85 and tritium. Although only small amounts are involved, a progressive buildup of these elements in the atmosphere could create a serious health hazard.

Nuclear power plants also produce extremely dangerous radioactive wastes that must be handled carefully. These wastes must be isolated from humanity for many, many years. High-level radioactive wastes are classified as either nuclear fission products or by-products. Strontium 90 and cesium 137, the most abundant fission products, have half-lives of 300 years. Thus, these fission products will remain dangerously radioactive for 600 to 1,000 years. Plutonium 239, a fission by-product, has a 24,000-year half-life; it must be kept away from humanity for almost 50,000 years.

At present, wastes from nuclear power plants are primarily stored on the site of the plants. This can only be a temporary measure. On-site storage facilities are filling up rapidly, but there is *no* method of permanent storage yet devised that scientists agree is safe. Even worse, very few ideas exist on how to deal with plants as they wear out and/or permanently break down.

There is also the constant danger of accidental radiation leakage from power plants. On March 28, 1979, water pumps broke down at the Three Mile Island nuclear power plant near Harrisburg, Pennsylvania. When the plant's cooling system failed, the plant overheated and began a core meltdown, leaking radiation into the surrounding environment. State authorities asked for the evacuation of all children and pregnant women living within five miles of the plant.

By the time matters were under control, the partial meltdown of the core of the reactor had destroyed it. The damaged reactor was shut down, and it took 14 years and a cost of $1 billion to clean up the radioactive wastes that remained in the reactor building (*New York Times* 1993). What was the primary cause of all this? Human error.

A much more severe accident in the former Soviet Union reinforced concern over nuclear power plant safety. On April 26, 1986, a nuclear reactor at the Chernobyl Nuclear Power Station in the Ukraine accidentally overheated and subsequently released the largest amount of radioactivity into the atmosphere that has ever been recorded. The radioactivity released "was equivalent to the fallout from several dozen Hiroshima bombs" (Hohenemser and Renn 1988:5). Once in the atmosphere, it traveled throughout the Northern Hemisphere, although its principal impact was on the western Soviet Union and parts of Europe.

The Chernobyl accident, said to be the result of nuclear reactor design flaws and errors by plant managers, killed 31 people at the time and caused numerous cases of radiation-induced illnesses that have since led to many more deaths. Deaths also occurred among the workers sent in to clean up the highly radioactive accident site. Children born subsequent to their parents' exposure to radiation leaked by Chernobyl have suffered high rates of birth defects.

Approximately 115,000 people had to be evacuated from Chernobyl and its surrounding area (Read 1993). The community was turned into a ghost town. Even today many people have been unable to return to their homes and places of work in the area. Still others remain dependent on food being transported in from outside the Chernobyl region, since land around Chernobyl is considered too radioactively contaminated to produce crops safe to eat (United Nations, UNDP/UNICEF 2002 Report, available at www.chernobyl.info; see also U.S. Congress, Senate 1992).

All told, almost 3 billion people in the Northern Hemisphere received some radiation from the Chernobyl accident; 26 percent of these, or about 800 million, received enough to be statistically at risk to a greater degree from cancer (Anspaugh, Catlin, and Goldman 1988). The increased risk is small, particularly for those residing outside the general area in which the nuclear plant is located, and deaths are expected to be statistically indistinguishable from cancer deaths occurring from other causes. Nonetheless, Chernobyl-like incidents understandably

are feared and condemned as intolerable. While as of this writing no nuclear accident of this magnitude has occurred in the United States, it is within the realm of possibility.

Nuclear power plants are also susceptible to sabotage and military attack—even a war with conventional weapons could unleash radiation. Unforeseeable accidents or such natural disasters as earthquakes could lead to similar results. Finally, with the increased use, production, and transport of radioactive materials around the country, the possibility of theft increases. It may be possible for an individual or group to use stolen materials to construct a nuclear weapon.

At present, all of us are subject to some degree of exposure to radiation. Natural radiation regularly enters the atmosphere from outer space. Radioactive elements can be found in water and mineral deposits. We are often exposed to radiation from X-rays, luminous watch dials, color television sets, microwave ovens, and radar. Some workers are routinely bombarded at their place of employment. Scientists seem to agree that all radiation is harmful, but there is little consensus on the amount we can safely tolerate. The continued manufacture, testing, and possible use of nuclear weapons and/or the use of nuclear power plants to generate electricity could provide a tragic answer to the question of tolerance (Lichtenstein and Helfand 1993).

Radon: An Indoor Threat

The various environmental hazards described in this chapter may make people yearn to remain in the safety and security of their homes. The discovery of a deadly indoor pollutant—radon gas—makes one wonder whether homes are necessarily sanctuaries (*Science* 1988; *Newsweek* 1988).

The formation of the earth some 4.5 billion years ago left us with deposits of uranium, a highly radioactive element. Left alone, uranium undergoes a natural process of decay and becomes harmless. Perhaps half of the earth's uranium has undergone this decay process. Out of this process comes various by-products, including radioactive radon gas. The gas is invisible and cannot be detected by taste or smell. Wherever uranium deposits are found, radon gas silently seeps out of rock deposits, sediments, and soil. It may enter the air we breathe.

Scientists have known for over 30 years that radon gas may be life-threatening, noting that rates of lung cancer are extremely high among those who work in uranium mines. But it was not until 1984 that evidence revealed radon gas was to be found in dangerous concentrations in people's homes.

Radon gas typically enters homes through cracks and holes in basement floors or foundation walls. Then, attached to particles in the air, it is carried throughout the house. After years of breathing this radioactive indoor pollution, people are likely to succumb to lung cancer (U.S. Environmental Protection Agency 1992). Officials at the federal Environmental Protection Agency believe that anywhere from 5,000 to 20,000 deaths per year are attributable to radon gas. As one scientist has put it,

Hundreds of thousands of Americans living in homes that have high radon levels receive as large an exposure of radiation yearly as those people living in the vicinity of the Chernobyl nuclear power plant did in 1986. (cf. Science, April 29, 1988:607)

Consequently, people are as likely to die from long-term exposure to radon gas as they are from at-home falls or fires.

No one knows for sure the extent of the threat. While more definitive research results are being sought, a survey by the EPA suggests that growing public concern is well placed. The EPA estimated that 1 out of every 15 households across the country may have radon concentrations at a level high enough to suggest occupants take actions to protect their health and safety. In actuality, there is no "safe" radon level: Its pres-

ence in any amount may carry potential health risks (www.epa.gov/radon; U.S. Environmental Protection Agency 1993).

The threat posed by radon gas is natural rather than humanly constructed, which sets it apart from many other environmental hazards we are discussing. Yet steps can be taken to minimize the threat. Since there seems to be a synergistic effect between smoking and exposure to radon gas—that is, lung cancer is much more likely to occur when both are present—cessation of smoking must be a major part of any solution. In addition, radon gas levels may be substantially reduced where it is possible to use pipes and vents to route the gas from beneath foundations into the outside air.

In 1988 the EPA and the Office of the Surgeon General advised that every home and every apartment up to a building's second floor be tested for radon gas. Inexpensive test kits for "do-it-yourselfers" have since become widely available and there are signs that many people are taking this environmental threat seriously. Significantly, it is now common for potential home buyers to request radon test results. Pressures may grow on builders to adopt new construction standards to combat what some are now calling the deadliest air pollutant.

Solid Wastes

A key indicator of the United States' material affluence is its volume of junk, garbage, and other forms of solid waste. Most of it is in the form of agricultural, mineral, and industrial waste (Brown 1980).

Agricultural and mineral wastes generally go unnoticed, for they are concentrated in nonurban settings. Industrial waste is far more noticeable, since it often contributes to the waste disposal problems facing highly populated areas. Fly ash from electric utility companies, scrap metals, rags, and bales and drums of industrial by-products must all be thrown away somewhere.

Our output of junk is almost mind-boggling. (See Table 5.3.) In 1960 U.S. municipalities

| Table 5.3 | Municipal Solid Waste Generation, Recovery, and Disposal: 1960 to 2001 |

Item and material	1960	1970	1980	1990	2001
Waste generated	87.8	121.9	151.5	198.0	229.2
Per person per day (lb.)	2.7	3.3	3.7	4.3	4.4
Materials recovered	5.9	8.6	14.5	32.9	68.0
Per person per day (lb.)	0.18	0.23	0.35	0.7	1.3
Combustion for energy recovery	(NA)	0.4	2.7	29.7	33.6
Per person per day (lb.)	(NA)	0.02	0.06	0.7	0.7
Combustion without energy recovery	27.0	24.7	11.0	2.2	NA
Per person per day (lb.)	0.82	0.66	0.27	0.05	NA
Landfill, other disposal	54.9	88.2	123.3	133.2	127.6
Per person per day (lb.)	1.67	2.37	2.97	2.9	2.5
Percent distribution of generation:					
Paper and paperboard	34.1	36.3	36.1	36.7	35.7
Glass	7.6	10.4	9.9	6.7	5.5
Metals	12.0	11.6	9.6	8.3	7.9
Plastics	0.5	2.5	5.2	8.5	11.1
Rubber and leather	2.3	2.6	2.8	3.0	2.8
Textiles	1.9	1.6	1.7	3.3	4.3
Wood	3.4	3.3	4.4	6.2	5.7
Food wastes	13.9	10.5	8.7	6.7	11.4
Yard wastes	22.8	19.0	18.2	17.7	12.2
Other wastes	1.6	2.2	3.4	3.1	3.4

[In millions of tons, except as indicated. Covers postconsumer residential and commercial solid wastes, which comprise the major portion of typical municipal collections. Excludes mining, agricultural and industrial processing, demolition and construction wastes, sewage sludge, and junked autos and obsolete equipment wastes. Based on material-flows estimating procedure and wet weight as generated.]

NA Not available.

Source: U.S. Department of Commerce, Bureau of the Census, *Statistical Abstract of the United States, 1995* (Washington, DC: U.S. Government Printing Office, 1995), p. 236; Department of Commerce, Bureau of the Census, *Statistical Abstract of the United States, 2003* (Washington, DC: U.S. Government Printing Office, 2004), p. 234.

accumulated 87.8 million metric tons of waste from residential, commercial, and institutional disposers. This figure more than doubled to 195.7 million metric tons in 1990. In that year, municipalities accumulated 4.3 pounds of waste per person per day. Paper, glass, and plastics account for over half of the waste generated. Although recycling efforts have been on the increase since the 1980s, less than one-third of municipal waste is recovered for recycling (U.S. Bureau of the Census 2004:235).

Where does it all go? The solid waste collected in most municipalities is simply hauled away to open dumps. Only a small percentage gets buried in sanitary landfills or burned in incinerators. Dumping exhausts land space that could be more fruitfully used; it also poses possible health hazards. Incineration (along with fires caused by spontaneous combustion in open dumps) contributes to pollution of the air.

To underscore the problems involved, let us look at some examples. By weight, paper and paper products are a major type of refuse. In recent years paper consumption has increased to the point that the average person in the United States now uses several hundred pounds annually. Much of this is associated with the use of heavily packaged products. Most paper fails to be recycled in the United States—70 percent is simply dumped or burned. While paper and paper products are bulky and take up space, fortunately they do eventually decompose. When burned, however, they contribute to air pollution.

Plastics are a different matter. The production and use of plastics have grown enormously in recent years. Modern plastics are substances with high durability and resistance to biological decomposition. Plastics thus are being used in the place of wood, metals, and cloth for many products. It is their very properties that render plastics an ecological problem. Since they do not decompose, they simply pile up permanently. If burned, plastics are likely to melt and foul up incinerator operations, while emitting gaseous pollutants that are often poisonous. It

Part of the millions of tons of solid wastes people in the United States dispose of simply ends up littering our cities. Junk and garbage create health and safety hazards and also make an area look unpleasant and unlivable.

has been claimed that plastics pollute the air even in garbage dumps, because of solar heat and the heat processes that lead to spontaneous combustion.

Metal cans and glass bottles are another solid waste problem. Cans decompose too slowly to disappear before even more cans are dumped. Glass is rather invulnerable to natural decomposition. Bottles, along with some plastic products and metals used in cans, can be reclaimed for use, and progress has been made along such lines. Corporate producers could help reduce waste volume. Instead many still sell throwaway containers, which often end up littering our roadways and recreational areas. The throwaway trend may be convenient for consumers, but it is not a sign of ecological sanity. Though states have begun to restrict the use of disposable bottles and encourage recycling, the waste problem overall continues to grow.

Automobiles, besides being a major source of air pollution, tend to be a rather conspicuous form of solid waste. There are over 120 million vehicles registered for use in the United States, and 11 million go permanently out of service annually. Of these, perhaps a million are simply abandoned. The rest wind up in our 33,000 auto junkyards. Only a small percentage are recycled for scrap; most, having been cannibalized for usable parts, are left in piles where the metal rusts and the plastic parts remain. Between 2.5 and 4.5 million abandoned autos, of little value to junk firms, lie along city streets, in vacant lots, and in rural settings. The millions of auto tires tossed out each year are bulky and difficult to get rid of. When they are burned, tires pollute the air.

Noise and Visual Pollution

We tend to take the sounds of our surroundings for granted and to consider the noise level as somehow inevitable. The sounds of home appliances, traffic, factory and office machinery, aircraft, boats, lawn mowers, construction projects, and sirens affect people in the United States daily. Urban dwellers in particular are bombarded by a constant, almost unremitting din.

The effects of noise on people have been found to vary, for not all individuals are equally sensitive to sounds. Nevertheless, there is reason for concern about the dangers to human hearing. According to the U.S. Environmental Protection Agency, some 20 million people in the United States are victimized by levels of noise that can impair their hearing permanently. Eighteen million already have hearing

loss as a consequence of excess noise, often connected with the workplace (Kavaler 1978). Excess levels of noise are known to have a bearing on physiological functioning. In experiments, noise has caused the constriction of arteries, increased pulse and respiration rates, involuntary muscle reactions, and abnormal fatigue. In addition, noise is often simply distracting and annoying. Extremely loud noises, such as the sonic booms created by jet aircraft, fit into this description (Aftandilian 1999, available at www.consciouschoice.com; Bronzaft 1993). (Sonic booms have also been known to cause physical damage to buildings and other structures.)

We rarely think about visual pollution, except when we are confronted with its most extreme manifestations. One type of visual pollution actually prevents people from seeing their surroundings. Photochemical smog, for example, is more than a health hazard. For drivers and pilots it can be a safety hazard as well. It can also be an aesthetic nuisance, blocking out views that are visually pleasing.

There are aspects of our surroundings that many persons, when given a choice, would just as soon not see. This second type of visual pollution is, one might argue, really a matter of taste. Billboards and signs dot the countryside and proliferate in metropolitan areas. Attention-seeking architecture surrounds us, often in the form of neon-lit commercial "strips." Buildings are often put up with no attention to the views they block. Roads and highways tear up neighborhoods and areas of scenic beauty. Polluted rivers and lakes not only smell bad, but are ugly. Mining operations denude the countryside in many areas, as soil and timber are stripped away to expose coal seams. Public dumps and auto junkyards are not known for their aesthetic appeal. Despite rather expensive efforts to cope with it, litter continues to assault the eyes. In so many ways, human activities continually alter the color, shape, and context of parts of the ecosystem without regard to taste and sensibility.

Land Misuse

Many of the examples of visual pollution relate to the impact of human activities on U.S. land. But the environmental abuses associated with land use go far beyond aesthetics and taste. In 1970 the President's Council on Environmental Quality concluded that "Misuse of the land is now one of the most serious and difficult challenges to environmental quality, because it is the most out-of-hand, and irreversible" (Council on Environmental Quality 1970:165). Decades later, this form of environmental abuse remains most serious.

The casual way this nation's 2.3 billion acres of land have been used is indicative of what Gene Marine has called the "engineering mentality." Marine says that the engineering mentality is displayed when public or private landowners tamper with land resources without regard to the well-being of the ecosystem as a whole. Their focus is limited to the financial costs and technical feasibility of projects intended to meet immediate, narrowly defined objectives (Marine 1969). As with other mindless assaults on the ecosystem, the cumulative effects of land misuse are coming back to haunt us. Here we shall consider some major examples (Little 1992).

People in the United States seem to assume that this nation has an unlimited abundance of land for unhindered development and exploitation. But our supply of open land is finite, and shortages are beginning to appear. Among the reasons are urban development and suburban sprawl; the linking of major cities by strips of densely populated, developed land; airport and highway construction; and the creation of reservoirs and large-scale flood control projects. Each year approximately a million acres of rural land are gobbled up. Farmlands are turned over to other uses. Irreplaceable marshes and wetlands—the environmental niches in which many species breed and survive—disappear permanently. Such land misuse spreads pollution of all types and eliminates areas that previously had recreational value.

The construction of dams, canals, and waterways also alters land-use patterns. Dredging, draining, filling, and changing the natural routes of streams and rivers have all been done without concern for the environmental consequences. As a result, the habitats of fish and animals have been destroyed, land has been taken away from other uses, and water pollution has occurred.

In recent years we have become aware of the impact of mining practices on U.S. land. Surface or strip mining, which has blighted the coal-rich Appalachian region and has spread into a number of western states, involves ripping the natural covering off the land (including hills and mountainsides) in order to get at the mineral seams. This is followed by blasting and gouging so that the seams can be fully exposed for removal. The result is often total destruction of natural land contours. Vegetation and wildlife are uprooted, their niches in the ecosystem destroyed. Drainage from such mining areas, containing acids and sediments, contaminates inland waters to the detriment of aquatic life (Johnson 1992).

Exploitation of the nation's public and private forest lands is having similar adverse consequences. Commercial operations in timber reserves have increasingly taken the form of **clearcutting,** in which large areas are stripped of all trees, leaving behind nothing but short stumps. Logging roads to remote sections bisect otherwise unblemished wilderness. Clearcutting also negatively alters soil conditions, since removal of forest covering exposes soil to the weather, weakening its nutrient properties. Land erosion increases, and streams become choked with debris and sediments. Again, vegetation and wildlife habitats are despoiled (Devall 1995; see also www.powerlink.net/fen/clearbib.htm).

A major controversy over the use of public lands arose in the early 1980s. The administration of President Ronald Reagan sought to open millions of acres of federal (i.e., taxpayer-owned) rangeland, forest, and wilderness and much of the ocean-covered Outer Continental Shelf to commercial exploitation. Rights to accelerate development of property previously untouched and kept guarded out of concern for conservation were to be granted to interested large corporations. In other cases property would be sold outright to the highest corporate bidder. In effect, government officials were preparing to abandon conservation in favor of improving the profitability of firms that would be given inexpensive access to important reserves of timber, oil, natural gas, coal, uranium, and other minable materials. The outcry of concerned members of the public, along with unprecedented political activity on the part of conservation and environmental organizations, slowed the government's efforts (Friends of the Earth 1982). Still, corporate interests pose a continual threat to public control over land and water that is not yet exploited for profit and despoiled (Rosenbaum 2001).

Resource Depletion

Our discussion has for the most part focused on what U.S. society puts *into* the ecosystem, rather than what we take *from* it. Obviously, these two matters are interrelated, given the basic ecological principle that what we throw away had to be first removed from somewhere. In this section we shall deal with the United States' need for minerals and other materials. Nothing in the ecosystem is really free for the taking. As we shall see, the costs of **resource depletion** promise to be extremely high.

▲ The Exhaustion of Irreplaceable Commodities

Not too long ago U.S. society's gross national product—the sum value of all the goods and services produced each year—rose to $7 trillion. The GNP is a rough indicator of a nation's overall economic activity, and that of the United States is the largest in world history. Such un-

precedented economic activity is dependent on, among other things, access to mineral supplies, including those that provide energy. This is not a profound observation, but it is one that few people in the United States had to think about until the 1970s. The point was most dramatically brought home during the nationwide energy crisis that jarred us in 1973–1974, when shortages and increased costs of oil, gasoline, and natural gas forced many people to turn down thermostats, turn off lights, drive less, and pay higher prices for virtually all goods and services.

With 4.7 percent of the world's total population, the United States consumes 50 percent of the world's nonrenewable resources. Moreover, we are voracious users of energy. If annual U.S. energy consumption is converted to its coal equivalent (a standard measure), it equaled 98.8 billion metric tons in 2000. In that same year the entire world consumed the equivalent of 397.4 billion tons (U.S. Bureau of the Census 2004:847).

Though most of the minerals and other materials we consume are available domestically, the insatiable demands of the U.S. economy are beginning to endanger our supplies. We are already dependent on imports in a number of crucial areas. (See Table 5.4.) From 90 to 100 percent of such commodities as asbestos, columbium, graphite, manganese, thallium, and bauxite must be sought outside the United States. We import from 50 to 90 percent of our antimony, cobalt, tin, nickel, chromium, and tungsten. At present, the United States imports almost as much crude oil as it produces. Over time the United States has moved from being a resource-rich nation to one that cannot grow economically—or even sustain itself as is—without purchasing key resources from other nations.

This situation raises some extremely important issues. The resources necessary for our high GNP—and, indeed, our lifestyles—are finite. All of them are probably subject to depletion at some point (Council on Environmental Quality and Department of State 1980). At present, the United

Table 5.4	**Net U.S. Imports of Selected Minerals and Metals as Percentage of Apparent Consumption, 1980 to 2002, and by Major Foreign Sources**		

Mineral	1980	1990	2002
Columbium	100	100	100
Manganese	98	100	100
Mica (sheet)	100	100	100
Strontium	100	100	100
Bauxite*	94	98	100
Asbestos	78	90	NA
Platinum group	87	88	NA
Tantalum	90	86	80
Cobalt	93	84	75
Chromium	91	71	63
Tungsten	53	81	70
Nickel	76	64	43
Tin	79	71	79
Barite	44	71	76
Potash	65	68	80
Antimony	47	51	NA
Cadmium	55	46	0
Selenium	59	46	NA
Zinc	60	†41	60
Gypsum	35	36	25
Iron ore	25	21	11
Iron and steel	13	13	14
Sulfur	14	15	15
Copper	16	3	37
Aluminum	(¶)	(¶)	39
Silver	7	(NA)	61
Mercury	27	(D)	NA
Titanium	32	(¶)	80
Vanadium	35	(D)	100

[Percentage, based on net imports which equal the difference between imports and exports plus or minus government stockpile and industry stock changes.]

D Withheld to avoid disclosure.

NA Not available.

*Includes alumina.

†Effect of sharp rise in exports of concentrates. If calculated on a refined zinc-only basis, reliance would be about the same as pre-1990 level; 1990, 64%; 1991, 61%; and 1992, 64%.

¶ Net exports.

Source: U.S. Department of Commerce, Bureau of the Census, *Statistical Abstract of the United States, 1995* (Washington, DC: U.S. Government Printing Office, 1995), p. 715; Department of Commerce, Bureau of the Census, *Statistical Abstract of the United States, 2003* (Washington, DC: U.S. Government Printing Office, 2004), p. 571.

States, the consumer society par excellence, is making the greatest single contribution to the exhaustion of irreplaceable commodities. We and other consumer societies then restore these resources to the global ecosystem in the form of wastes and other pollutants.

▲ Resource Depletion and the Underdeveloped World

The threat of resource depletion is real. But the timetable is unclear because of a number of unpredictable factors: the possibility of new discoveries, the costs of extraction and processing, changes in technology, and the degree to which more readily available commodities can be substituted for scarcer ones. The depletion issue is also related to the fact that many of the minerals and materials on which our economy is dependent, and which we increasingly must import, are located in poor, underdeveloped nations. As we saw in Chapter 3, "Militarism, War, and Terrorism," this society's economic dominance rests on its ability to exploit underdeveloped nations' raw material cheaply (Magdoff 1969). The gap between rich nations and poor nations promises to be the main political challenge confronting our foreign policymakers in the twenty-first century (Heilbroner 1996). In the area of resources, the stakes are great.

Underdeveloped nations cannot develop economically or socially without expanded resource consumption opportunities. In practical terms, the advance of these poor nations—within which four-fifths of the world's population lives—can take place in one of two ways. Resources could be distributed away from the United States and other rich nations to underdeveloped nations, which seems highly unlikely. Or poor nations could increase their resource consumption by engaging in more intense exploitation of existing commodity supplies for their own use. Under current conditions, this second scenario also seems unlikely, as powerful developed nations continue to be successful in maneuvers to retain access to the resources they need for themselves, even if this means that poor nations will stay poor (Chatterjee and Finger 1994).

Our growing dependence on key imports from underdeveloped nations has produced another issue, one revealed through oil-producing nations' embargo on petroleum shipments and the subsequent price increases. The poor but resource-rich countries, by cooperating with one another and forming cartels to control commodity production and prices, may be able to force important concessions from the developed world. What would happen if such nations collectively decided to improve their well-being by forcing a redistribution of consumption opportunities away from the rich nations and to the poor?

Should such a stranglehold be placed upon U.S. society (and/or other rich nations in which U.S. corporations have substantial economic interests), it could well generate a military response. For example, in the aftermath of the 1970s Arab oil embargo, as Middle East petroleum prices continued to rise because of cartel action, U.S. officials and the mass media discussed and/or hinted at the desirability of military action. Military action was taken, of course, when Iraq tried to expand its control over Middle East oil resources and sparked the Persian Gulf War.

The world is now facing a tension-filled dilemma. Irreplaceable resources are being depleted. The United States must bear a large amount of the responsibility for this attack on the global ecosystem. If we try to maintain the status quo, the depletion rate will continue—but so will the misery and political hostility of the poor nations. Cartels and efforts to squeeze greater rewards in return for declining resource supplies may be the order of the day, perhaps calling forth a military solution. If, on the other hand, we attempt to maintain our present growth rates while offering to help poor nations increase theirs, serious conflict may be avoided. But resource depletion rates will escalate, and conflicts are bound to emerge once serious scarcities begin to be felt.

Searching for Causes

The changes now occurring in the global ecosystem are obviously the consequence of human activities. Our environment is not polluting and depleting itself. But there is little agreement about just what it is about people and their actions that is causing the current ecocatastrophe. A consensus on causes is a crucial first step toward ending environmental abuse. Here we shall highlight some of the different views, indicating which ones make the most sense.

Human Nature

Now and again observers claim that environmental abuse is a result of human nature. People, it is alleged, are basically dirty. Unlike other forms of animal life, we are prone to "fouling our own nests" (Commoner 1974:122–23). This being the case, there is really no way to stop the destruction of the environment short of eliminating people from the global ecosystem.

This view is very seductive because of its simplicity. But there is no evidence that it is correct. Other animals are "clean" only because they return what they remove from the ecosystem in forms useful to those parts of the system on which they are dependent. They do not violate the chains and cycles on which their survival is based. There is no evidence to suggest that people cannot do the same, even if we cannot match the efficiency of other animal species. Human beings are capable of making conscious, rational choices as to how they wish to relate to the rest of the ecosystem. Over time our choices have been ecologically disastrous. But our awareness of environmental deterioration offers the possibility of our choosing to end it— assuming that we can figure out how, that we are willing to bear the costs, and that it is not too late. If we accept the human nature argument, we can only sit back and wait for the Big Collapse or hasten the collapse through an orgy of environmental abuse.

Population and Affluence

An alternative view stresses the significance of the growth in population that is taking place in the United States and around the world. Environmental deterioration, it is alleged, is an inevitable outcome of loading the earth with too many people. The more people there are, the greater the impact they make on the ecosystem as a whole. Increased world population means increased demands on finite resources, along with more waste disposal problems, land misuse, pollution, and so on (see Lappé and Collins [1981] for a critique of this position). The solution to environmental abuse, in this view, is to limit or even decrease the world's population— particularly in the many poor countries where a "population explosion" is well under way.

This view is also attractively simple: Increase the effectiveness of birth control and the ecocatastrophe will go away. As we saw in Chapter 4, a high rate of population expansion is a serious problem primarily in nations where food is scarce and/or the productive resources are held by and benefit a small elite. The major perpetrators of environmental deterioration are *not* these poorer societies. Rather, the economically developed nations, such as the United States, which are not experiencing severe population explosions, are contributing most to the ecocatastrophe.

Developed nations consume most of the world's irreplaceable resources while dumping the largest volume of wastes and harmful contaminants back into the global ecosystem. Moreover, countries like the United States have been exporting products to underdeveloped nations that are known to be damaging to the environment and that cannot be sold at home (Clapp 2001), as well as exploiting these poor nations by paying them to accept shipments of toxic wastes that would be difficult or expensive to process domestically (www.hrw.org; Alston 1990; Cohen 1990). Underdeveloped nations are thus used as dumping sites for developed nations' toxic products and wastes.

This is not to say that underdeveloped nations when left alone live in harmony with the ecosystem or that future developments will not see them playing a more important role in environmental deterioration. Such nations tend to have weakly enforced environmental protection laws, to the degree to which they have such laws at all, and suffer from problems ranging from urban air and water pollution to deforestation and despoilment of land. But the present-day level of global environmental crisis is primarily an outcome of actions by the developed world, not simply a matter of underdeveloped nations' population changes.

Even if we limit ourselves to the United States, it is hard to find a direct correspondence between population expansion and rates of environmental deterioration. For example, while our population grew between the end of World War II and the consciousness-raising celebration of the first Earth Day in 1970, changes in U.S. population growth rates came nowhere near matching the increases in pollution during that 25-year period (Commoner 1974). Something more than numbers of people is involved here.

Moreover, all people in the United States do not pollute equally. As noted in Chapter 6, "Economic Inequality and Poverty," the affluent are more able to consume due to the unequal distribution of wealth and income. Just as rich nations consume and pollute at far higher rates than poorer ones, the affluent minority in this country makes a greater contribution to environmental deterioration than its numbers would indicate. Moreover, the affluent are the ones who own and control the businesses and industries that are major environmental abusers.

In the United States researchers have found evidence that people of color and poor people are more likely than other citizens to reside in communities chosen as sites for toxic waste facilities and where the health hazards from pollution of the air, land, and water are high. In recent years there has been a great deal of protest on the part of community grassroots organizations around issues of "environmental justice" and **environmental racism** (Bryant and Mohai 1992; Bullard 1993; Maher 1998). The more privileged members of U.S. society are able to avoid residing in such communities and have the political clout to keep toxic waste facilities from invading their living situations.

Obviously, population growth and size have something to do with the demands being made on the ecosystem. But population alone does not explain the problem.

Science and Technology

Many who reject the population argument blame environmental deterioration on modern science and technology. Somehow, it is alleged, modern science and technology have taken on a life of their own. We are now at the mercy of our own cultural ingenuity; the tools that originally were developed to conquer nature have begun to run wild. We have lost control of these tools and are being forced to bow to their imperatives, and environmental deterioration is the result (Heilbroner 1996).

According to this view, we cannot solve the problem with more technology. People must retreat to the "golden years" of the past when small groups of families lived simply, spartanly, and communally in the woods or on the prairies. Life in those days may have been short and brutish, but at least the entire global ecosystem was not threatened by scientific and technological change. You could breathe the air, drink the water, eat plants and animals, admire the untouched scenery, and enjoy quiet.

As with population expansion, it would be erroneous to say that science and technology have nothing to do with environmental deterioration. On the other hand, neither is it true that these areas of human activity have a life of their own or have created a set of imperatives to which we must bow. Science and technology are tools, and tools can be used in many different ways. How or whether we use them is a matter of *choice*. We can use science and technology to help us live in harmony with the rest of the ecosystem or to hasten its collapse.

Economic Organization

When we look at science and technology as causes of the ecocatastrophe, we must also consider the societal contexts in which such tools are employed. This realization has led some analysts to contrast environmental policies in capitalist and socialist societies, the idea being that the political and economic priorities of a society ultimately dictate the uses to which science and technology are put. Michael Parenti (1995: 115–16) comments on capitalism and the environment:

Profits are higher when corporations can plunder our natural resources at will, dump their diseconomies onto the public, and get us to consume at unusually high and wasteful levels. . . . Capitalism's modus operandi is to produce and sell an ever expanding supply of goods and services for ever greater profits. But the earth is finite. So is its ability to absorb wastes and toxins. . . . An ever expanding capitalism and a fragile, finite ecology appear to be on a calamitous collision course.

In this view, the ecocatastrophe is a result of a system of economic organization that benefits only a tiny percentage of the world's peoples. The benefits—great wealth, power, and prestige—may prove to be hollow for the few that enjoy them.

In capitalist societies such as the United States, economic and political priorities often place profits before people. Environmental abuse is an inevitable by-product of the private pursuit of money. Pollution, land misuse, and resource depletion are "costs" that are being passed on to the population in return for an enlarged gross national product. A large GNP means jobs and consumer goods. Eliminate

capitalism and its quest for unlimited growth as a way of organizing and operating our productive system, say proponents of this view, and you undercut the coming ecological collapse.

It does seem to be true that the activities of business and industry frequently run counter to environmental sanity. Go back and think about who, or whose products, are intimately tied to the forms of environmental abuse reviewed earlier in this chapter. Then check Chapter 2, "Concentration of Political and Economic Power," for some ideas about why so much of the abuse is only being monitored, regulated, measured, and studied rather than totally eliminated.

Earlier we noted that in the United States pollution rates have well outstripped population growth. Environmental researcher Barry Commoner has pointed out that after World War II U.S. corporations began to draw upon advances in science and technology to produce new products in new ways, with ecologically devastating results. Why? Commoner strongly believes that the answer lies with short-term profit interest (Commoner 1974). Since 1946 the GNP has grown enormously, while the ecosystem has been assaulted.

A few examples of developments that have taken place only since World War II will make the point. Plastics are cheaper to produce than many of the materials they have displaced, but while the plastics industry has grown so have the plastic products we cannot get rid of. Synthetic fibers require less labor to produce than wool or cotton and are hence very profitable. They are about as impervious to destruction as plastics. Rearing agricultural animals on feedlots, rather than grazing them in pastures, produces a lot of meat quickly and inexpensively. But the animal wastes pose a monumental disposal problem and may foul water sources. Cars built in most years of the post–World War II era have been bigger and heavier, with more powerful engines than cars built earlier. They contribute to fuel depletion, but have proven a boon to oil, steel, chromium, plastic, glass, and rubber firms. While fuel supplies have been pressed to keep up with demand, until recently utility companies encouraged electric heating, the use of air conditioners and freezers, plenty of lighting, and more. Even while open land is being depleted, land speculators and developers encourage us to "spread out" without regard to the ecological implications. This, of course, means that we must have more roads and highways—a requirement that does not go unnoticed by automobile and oil concerns.

In recounting such post-1946 changes, in which business and industry leaders have been key decision makers, Commoner (1974:298–99) concludes:

Human beings have broken out of the circle of life, driven not by biological need, but by the social organization which they have devised to "conquer" nature: means of gaining wealth that are governed by requirements conflicting with those which govern nature. The end result is the environmental crisis, a crisis of survival. Once more, to survive, we must close the circle.

Capitalism plus science and technology equals environmental deterioration. In other words, the organization and operation of our society, ecologically speaking, harm living things—including people.

Yet environmental abuse has also been of great concern in noncapitalist societies like the former Soviet Union and the People's Republic of China (Stewart 1992; www.loc.gov/rr/ scitech/ tracer-bullets/sovietvtb.html; www.eia.doe.gov /emeu/cabs/chinaenv.html). While the United States is far ahead of any other nation—capitalist or socialist—in its contribution to environmental deterioration, it is not possible to determine the exact reason. Is it because of our corporate capitalist economy? Or is it a result of our advanced levels of consumption and "dirty" production techniques? The socialist societies to

which the United States is usually compared tend to be less advanced in terms of industrialization, to utilize lesser amounts of the earth's resources, and to produce fewer consumer goods on a per capita basis.

In theory, socialist economies are not geared toward satisfying the profit interests of a handful of large private owners, but instead try to meet the all-around needs of members of society as a whole. They thus should find it easier to rationalize the costs of environmentally sane operations. In capitalist societies, where business and industry are privately owned, corporate elites do not want to absorb costs that cut into the maximization of profits. They can only pass on some of the costs of pollution control to consumers in the form of higher prices or lower-quality goods and to workers in the form of restricted wages. In socialist societies, however, state-run enterprises provide the bulk of goods and services. The decision to institute environmentally sound economic operations can be made centrally by the government and the costs can be balanced against the well-being of the citizenry.

So at least in theory it should be much easier to make environmentally sound decisions in socialist societies. But in reality such societies also place strong emphasis on economic growth and expansion, and in many cases they have tended to mimic some of capitalism's environmental abuses. In the 1990s major socialist nations began to undergo significant internal changes, transforming important parts of their economies so that they are subject to capitalist operating principles. The implications of these changes for environmental practices are worrisome, given the track record of capitalist nations such as the United States.

Searching for Solutions

Why don't we do something about environmental abuse? In this section we will see how our lack of knowledge about the relationship between human beings and the environment has slowed down attempts to correct environmental abuse. We will then look at some of the things we can do to protect the environment.

Problems in Combating Environmental Abuse

It is only in the last three decades that awareness of ecological matters has existed on a nationwide basis. International interest is even more recent. Some observers believe that national concern began in 1970, with the celebration of the first Earth Day. Since that time agencies of government and private industry have started to curb environmental abuse—frequently in response to public discontent and aggressive legal actions by citizens' organizations.

Ignorance is a serious problem. We must work toward a fuller understanding of the ways in which human activities affect the ecosystem. Until quite recently, scientists were not particularly interested in such practical knowledge, a viewpoint that reinforced public perceptions of just how serious environmental concerns are. As recently as 2004, only one-third of the respondents in a survey considered global warming to be a very serious issue requiring major changes in lifestyles (Public Interest Project April 5–8, 2004), and only 16 percent in a *U.S. News & World Report* Survey (March 16–April 4, 2004) thought that combating global warming and other environmental threats was "extremely important" for U.S. foreign policy. Thus, much environmental damage has been done almost inadvertently. It is growing increasingly true that a process of production or a product thought to be harmless today is suddenly seen as calamitous as its effects become felt.

Nor does there seem to be any consensus about the causes of environmental deterioration. Is environmental abuse an inevitable outcome of population growth? Is it caused by the excesses of capitalism? Or is it a result of lack of foresight in the use of technology, resources, and industrial

capabilities? As we have seen, agreement on causes will have a great deal to do with solutions. We must work toward a consensus in this area.

Besides our ignorance about the impact of human activities on the global ecosystem and our disagreements about the causes of environmental deterioration, solutions are being held up by other difficulties. Cultural drives, apathy, economic considerations, and political hurdles seem to work against the total elimination—as opposed to the slowdown—of environmental abuse. The initial sense of crisis of the early 1970s has given way to a process of monitoring and regulating the production and distribution of damage (Weisberg 1971). In other words, now that our efforts to *conquer* our surroundings have failed, we are trying to *manage* the ecosystem. Given the basic ecological principles outlined earlier, this is akin to expecting the tail to wag the dog. We are no longer even asking whether the managerial approach (setting "standards" and "tolerance levels," minimizing "impact," balancing "priorities," etc.) is the wisest course to take, given our past track record.

Some of the resistance to making difficult choices in the interest of preserving the environment derives from the belief that natural resources are somehow unlimited or that nature can take care of itself. One survey discovered that almost half of the respondents believed that "a growing population will not be a major problem because we will find a way to stretch our natural resources" (Pew Research Center, April 6–May 6, 1999). Worse yet, some of the resistance to curbing a lifestyle of unbridled consumption of resources and a destruction of the environment is reinforced by political power. The George W. Bush administration stands alone in the international community in its refusal to sign the Kyoto Accords, an environmental treaty designed to address global warming and environmental degradation by establishing international environmental regulations. The administration has determined that such treaties invite the global community to interfere with

U.S. sovereignty in governing its own lifestyles and economy. Moreover, the Bush administration has worked very hard to roll back environmental laws and regulations, on the grounds that these cut too far into corporate profits and thus damage the economy.

The financial costs and economic dislocations that may ultimately be required to bring human activities into harmony with the rest of the ecosystem are difficult to estimate. The question of who should be made to bear these costs has yet to be seriously addressed. For example, are we willing to shut down dirty production facilities if it means some will lose their jobs? At present we appear to be looking for the cheapest way out of the ecocatastrophe. Moreover, a significant number of people continue to insist on maintaining their current lifestyles. Forty-four percent of the respondents in a 1999 survey indicated that they "would be willing to accept some health risk from exposure to chemicals in exchange for modern products and a convenient lifestyle" (Wirthlin Worldwide, June 2–7, 1999). A 2001 Gallup survey in the United States found that almost one-third of the respondents believed it was possible to solve the nation's energy problems and still retain their current lifestyles (Gallup Organization, May 18–20, 2001). Another survey found that 56 percent of the respondents considered "building new power plants to meet electricity demand" to be a high priority as a way to meet energy goals, more than cutting back on the use of energy (Nuclear Energy Institute, March 20–22, 2001). Ultimately, unbridled consumption must be ended no matter what the costs, if we are to provide for the survival of future generations.

At least one writer doubts that we care about the well-being of future waves of humanity. In the words of economist Robert L. Heilbroner (1996:169):

When men can generally acquiesce in, even relish, the destruction of their living contemporaries, when they can regard with indifference or irritation the fate of those who live in slums, rot in prison, or starve in lands that have meaning only insofar as they are vacation resorts, why should they be expected to take the painful actions to prevent the destruction of future generations whose faces they will never live to see?

Changing Institutions and Activities

What are you willing to give up? In return for what? How serious are you about this? Really? The answers to such questions will determine whether people will find a niche in the ecosystem to enjoy after you are gone. From chlorofluorocarbons to billboards, from radiation to plastics, from climatic modification to toxic chemicals—this particular macro problem is all around us.

Can we end, not just slow down, the United States' current contribution to ecosystem collapse? We can, but it will not be easy or occur overnight.

Strict controls must be imposed over what is produced in our economy and how. At present, political and economic policymakers are much more concerned with increasing the GNP than they are with the environmental impact of the economic activities it represents. We must turn away from a fixation with the dollar value of this society's productive efforts and begin considering the ecological value.

A start in this direction has already been made by the federal government. In recent years, states and localities have been required to assess the environmental impact of proposed projects and programs prior to receiving federal funding. Although this procedure is far from perfect, it has helped promote environmental consciousness in the public sector of the economy.

In the private sector, however, business and industry pour out goods and services that require no environmental assessment or are restricted only after extreme damage has been done. The private sector must be made responsible and accountable for its actions, for example, through the federal chartering of firms. Federal chartering means that firms would be required to obtain a license from the federal government in order to operate. To receive this license or charter, the firms would be required to assess and publicly report on the environmental impact of their operations and products. They would also have to agree to be subject to nationwide regulations, tailored to particular types of business and industry, designed to minimize or eliminate negative environmental practices. Any business that failed to abide by the conditions of its charter could either be shut down or placed under public ownership and control—in effect, put under federal receivership—until it met the conditions. Such "infringement" on the freedom of the private sector seems to be unavoidable so long as short-range profit interests continue to override ecological sanity.

Furthermore, we must be willing to alter our own lifestyles. Basically, this means directing our consumption patterns into ecologically sane pathways. What is needed is a profound cultural shift wherein the "good life" is no longer defined in terms of the possession of things that are of danger to the environment. Our use of energy and energy-using products could easily be cut down. We could demand increased production of goods made of recyclable materials. A change in lifestyle also seems to be unavoidable if we have any interest in the world we are leaving future generations. As consumers, we must allow the demands of the ecosystem to begin to manage us as individuals as well as the economic institutions to which we look to meet our basic needs.

Summary

Environmental abuse occurs as humans violate basic principles of ecology. Polluting the air and water, spreading radioactivity into the atmosphere, increasing levels of noise, creating numerous wastes, and consuming irreplaceable resources—all affect the global ecosystem. Since human beings are part of the ecosystem, we too are affected by these activities.

There are a number of major types of environmental abuse. Air pollution is known to have harmful effects on health and property and contributes to highly damaging acid precipitation. Pollution of water brings the threat of disease, shortages of clean water, and destruction of plant and aquatic life. Toxic substances pose serious threats to public health. Nuclear power and production of nuclear weapons pose dangers of radioactive contamination. Solid wastes, many of which are not biologically decomposable, accumulate. Noise and visual pollution are on the increase, the former affecting health and both harming the appeal of our environment. Land is being lost to misuse, often to the detriment of vegetation and wildlife. Finally, irreplaceable resources (e.g., energy-producing fuels and ores crucial to manufacturing) are facing rapid depletion. Conflict over scarce resources, many of which are located primarily in poor underdeveloped countries, promises to emerge in the future.

There are different views on why environmental abuse is taking place. Some feel it is a result of human nature. Blame has also been placed on population growth, as well as on a loss of control over science and technology. Finally, the profit-seeking and unlimited growth orientation of capitalism has been blamed. There is little consensus on causes.

Many obstacles stand in the way of eliminating environmental abuse. Ignorance is a serious problem. Cultural drives, apathy, economic considerations, and political hurdles seem to work against the elimination—as opposed to the slowdown—of environmental abuse. Possible solutions include imposing strict controls over what is produced in our economy and how. We must alter our lifestyles by directing our consumption patterns into ecologically sane pathways.

Key Terms

Clearcutting 148
Ecosystem 127
Environmental abuse 128

Environmental racism 153
Greenhouse effect 130
Resource depletion 149

Discussion Questions

1. Go into a supermarket and record the ingredients from the labels of commonly used bottled, canned, and boxed products. Discuss what you do and do not know about the ingredients and their effects on your health.

2. Take an inventory of all the things you own. How many of these items are made to be disposable or to have a limited useful life? How many are biologically decomposable? How many are cheaper to repair than to dispose of and replace?

3. List the aspects of your everyday activities and lifestyle that are directly affected by a concern for the ecosystem. List the aspects that are not. Compare your lists with those of others, and discuss the impact you are having on the environment.

4. Is the American Dream of material affluence and luxurious consumption compatible with the basic principles of ecology outlined in this chapter? Why or why not? If we must adapt our lifestyles to the demands of the ecosystem, what are the implications for the American Dream?

5. Most people would probably be outraged if someone sprayed them with poisonous air or fed them dangerous chemicals. In effect, this is what industrial polluters and many of their products are doing. Why, then, are people not outraged?

6. You have magically acquired the power to totally eliminate any one type of environmental abuse. Which would you choose and why? What vested interests would your action most adversely affect?

Suggested Readings

Nadakavukaren, Anne. *Our Global Environment: A Health Perspective.* 5th ed. (Long Grove, IL: Waveland Press, 2000).
An extensive analysis of the damage to human health being brought about by pollutants and toxic wastes, global warming, and environmental degradation.

Schnaiberg, Allan, and Kenneth Alan Gould. *Environment & Society: The Enduring Conflict* (Caldwell, NJ: The Blackburn Press, 2000). Social causes of environmental abuse and obstacles to its elimination that must be overcome.

Strydom, Piet. *Risk, Environment, and Society: Ongoing Debates, Current Issues, and Future Prospects* (Berkshire, England: Open University Press, 2002).
An analysis of risks to humans and the ecology posed by nuclear threats and global environmental degradation.

United Nations Environmental Program. *Global Biodiversity Assessment* (New York: Cambridge University Press, 1995).
The first worldwide examination of the threatened extinction of many of the earth's plants and animals and the deleterious effects of reduced biodiversity.

Wagner, Travis. *In Our Backyard* (New York: Van Nostrand Reinhold, 1994).
Highly readable summary and overview of the ways in which production processes and consumer products are polluting our environment.

World Resources Institute. *World Resources, 2002–2004* (New York: Oxford University Press, 2004).
Analysis of global environmental problems; includes detailed tables.

part II

Group Problems

chapter 6
Economic Inequality and Poverty

Gross differences in personal wealth and income should be greatly reduced, so that the life chances of all U.S. citizens are relatively equal and so that all share more equitably in the goods and services being produced.

The Reality of Economic Inequality
Concentration of Wealth and Ownership
Unequal Distribution of Income
Growing Economic Disparities
People of Color and Economic Inequality
Perpetuation of Economic Inequality
Wealth Begets Wealth
The Unequal Burden of Taxation
Ideological Supports for Inequality
Poverty amidst Affluence
What Is Poverty?
Who Are the Poor?
Why Are They Poor?
The Effects of Economic Inequality
Inequality and Life Chances
Homelessness
Hunger and Malnutrition
The Need for Government Intervention
Summary
Key Terms
Discussion Questions
Suggested Readings

Since the 1980s tens of millions of U.S. men, women, and children have experienced economic insecurity, deprivation, and stress at a level not seen in many years. Largely because of unemployment, changes in the occupational structure, and an increase in female-headed families, rates of poverty have risen to where they were in the 1960s, when the situation was considered very severe. Early in that decade the federal government declared a "War on Poverty." Clearly, the war has not been won.

Yet many of us may feel that poverty does not really affect us, and we may find it hard to identify with the people it does affect. At least part of our complacence stems from the knowledge that we are members of one of the most affluent societies in the world. The United States' material abundance stands in stark contrast to the scarcity experienced by most of the world's peoples. And our sense of national well-being is reinforced and supported in many ways. Political leaders periodically conjure up visions of our society's historical progress and international economic leadership. Economic problems are usually portrayed as temporary situations that can be righted. Our gross national product, one measure of our nation's economic vitality and growth, is measured in the trillions of dollars. Stores and shops are filled with an amazing array of items awaiting consumption. Time- and labor-saving devices for the home and workshop abound. Indeed, we cannot flip through a magazine or newspaper without being reminded of the wide diversity of goods and services available for our use and enjoyment.

Yet while our society enjoys tremendous productive capacity, not all share equally in the goods and services produced. The poor and near-poor—nearly one in five people in the United States—receive very little at all (May 1994). But while many suffer economic deprivation quietly, virtually invisible to more affluent citizens, the most desperate have grown increasingly noticeable in their numbers and needs.

Thus, in the 1980s and 1990s we began to see more and more people, including whole families, who had no permanent shelter. Their numbers are estimated at up to 600,000 people nationwide on any one night, with 7.2 million people at risk for homelessness over any 3-year period (*Society* 1994a). Homeless persons and others of the nation's poverty-stricken population have also become more visible as they desperately search for ways to cope with hunger (Shapiro 1994).

In this chapter we look at evidence of the greatly unequal distribution of wealth and income and the prevalence of poverty and near poverty in our society. As we shall see, gross economic inequality is an integral feature of life in the United States. Such inequality is not in the process of disappearing, and its continuance poses consequences that each of us should be willing to confront.

Literally millions of people in the United States have suffered homelessness in recent years. Not only individuals but, increasingly, families are among the homeless. Homeless people like this family seeking assistance from passing motorists have become common sights in U.S. cities and towns.

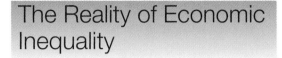

The Reality of Economic Inequality

The economic status of an individual or a family is based on the possession of wealth and income. **Income** is money received in the form of hourly wages or annual salaries, or government benefits, or return on investments. **Wealth** is the value of the assets or property that one owns. The difference between income and wealth is that income is a relatively immediate payment that does not accumulate over time; once a worker or a government benefit recipient dies, the income stream stops. In contrast, wealth does accumulate value over time and can be passed from generation to generation. This difference between income and wealth matters: Those with access to significant sources of wealth may enhance their access (and that of their children) to other resources that will affect their opportunities and life chances. Access to income sources may enable one to purchase the more immediate needs of survival, but does not necessarily enhance opportunity access for future generations. In this section we examine data indicating that both wealth and income are disproportionately concentrated in the hands of a few. Moreover, we will see that people of color are particularly disadvantaged in terms of sharing the wealth and income that are available.

Concentration of Wealth and Ownership

Any consideration of economic inequality in the United States must recognize that ours is basically a **capitalist economy.** In such an economic arrangement, the key institutions that constitute the economy—business and industry—are privately owned. Production of the goods and services consumed is done through the cooperative efforts of workers who are paid by the owners of the means of production. But workers are not paid the full value of the wealth they produce; instead, owners of the means of production pay the workers whatever wages they wish or that they can negotiate in exchange for the workers' labor. Owners then keep the wealth produced by workers' collective labor. Workers, then, get an income out of their own labor; owners get wealth from others' labor. Ownership of the largest, most economically significant businesses takes the form of shares of corporate stock. These shares increase or decrease in dollar value in rough accordance with the economic success and profitability of the corporation.

Corporate stock is, and has long been, one of the principal forms of wealth available to members of this society. Income is derived from stock ownership in two ways. First, the directors of the corporation may pay shareholders an annual dividend for each share held—a significant form of income for those who hold many shares. Second, owners of shares may buy and sell holdings in such a way as to realize substantial monetary gains. The distribution of stock ownership can tell us a lot about economic inequality in the United States.

Stock ownership is concentrated in the hands of an extremely small percentage of the population. In 2001 only 21.3 percent of U.S. families directly owned shares of stock (Kennickell 2003). The vast majority of residents of the United States lack the surplus cash to lay out for the purchase of stock and thus own no shares at all. The ownership of a share of stock gives an individual a vote on corporate policy. This franchise is monopolized by a highly privileged few.

The concentration of stock ownership is not a new and unique phenomenon. Ownership has been concentrated for many decades. Stock is often passed from one generation to the next through gifts and inheritance. Intermarriage among members of the minuscule ownership class has also contributed to continued concentration of stock holdings by individuals and family groupings.

Among the most significant members of the ownership class are the top managers and directors of business and industry and their heirs. High-level executives not only receive large salaries, annual bonuses, expense accounts, and other benefits of rank but are also typically granted options to purchase stock in their own companies at attractive rates. The rationale behind granting stock options is that they provide an added incentive for executives to push for increased profitability, since this enhances the value of their own holdings.

Wealth other than corporate stock is also generally concentrated in the hands of a few, and in recent years we have watched the rich get even richer. Economist Edward N. Wolff calculated that between 1983 and 1989 the nation's net worth increased from $13.5 trillion to $20.2 trillion. Over half of the increase, $3.9 trillion, went to the top one-half of 1 percent of U.S. households. This one-half of 1 percent of U.S. households now owns more than half of all assets. The top 10 percent of households owns more than 86 percent. (See Figure 6.1.) This concentration of wealth in a small proportion of households is greater than that of any other industrialized nation (Kennickell 2003; Wolff 1995).

One consequence of this concentration is that a small number of wealthy people—among

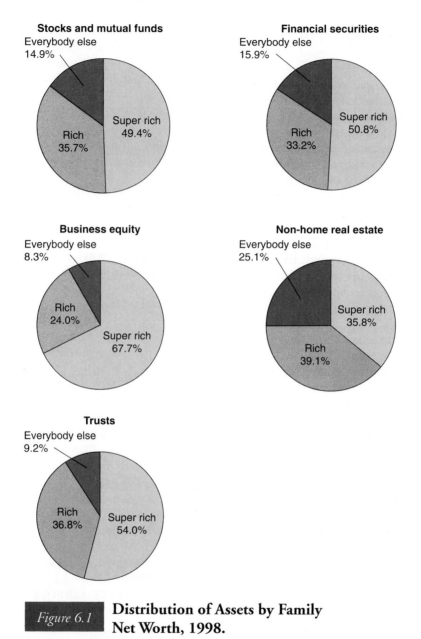

Stocks and mutual funds
Everybody else
14.9%
Rich
35.7%
Super rich
49.4%

Financial securities
Everybody else
15.9%
Rich
33.2%
Super rich
50.8%

Business equity
Everybody else
8.3%
Rich
24.0%
Super rich
67.7%

Non-home real estate
Everybody else
25.1%
Rich
39.1%
Super rich
35.8%

Trusts
Everybody else
9.2%
Rich
36.8%
Super rich
54.0%

Figure 6.1   **Distribution of Assets by Family Net Worth, 1998.**

Families are classified into wealth class on the basis of their net worth. In the top 1 percent of the wealth distribution (the *super rich*) are families with a net worth of $3,352,100 or more in 1998; in the next 9 percent (the *rich*) are families with a net worth greater than or equal to $475,600 but less than $3,352,100; in the bottom 90 percent (*everybody else*) are families with a net worth less than $475,600.

Source: 1998 Survey of Consumer Finances. Federal Reserve Board of Washington, DC.

whom are the directors and managers of our largest economic institutions—possess an inordinate degree of economic power. This economic power includes more than the ability to spend and consume; it also includes the ability to influence decisions that bear on the direction in which our society will go. (See Chapter 2.)

Thus far we have concentrated on the holdings of a small ownership class. What about the distribution of wealth within the U.S. population as a whole? Table 6.1 reveals that as family income goes up, so does net worth. The 17.6 percent of families with the lowest incomes (less than $10,000) have a mean net worth of $44,300. In contrast, the 7.3 percent of families with the highest incomes ($100,000 and more) have a mean net worth of $1,324,200 (Aizcorbe, Kennickell, and Moore 2003).

The average U.S. household falls short of any real affluence. One way of comprehending the meaning of the concentration of wealth is to imagine how long the majority of family units could survive on their "wealth" if they had to live only on the sale of what they owned, and to contrast this with the highest net worth class, where survival would not be anywhere near a problem.

In order for the nation's total wealth to be more equitably distributed among the people of the United States, property holdings worth hundreds of billions of dollars would have to be removed from the ownership class and reallocated among tens of millions of households. At present this is an unlikely event. There is a definite relationship between the ability to command great economic power and the ability to exercise influence over political questions of national significance, as we saw in Chapter 2.

Unequal Distribution of Income

The members of the ownership class derive most of their annual incomes from their property holdings (dividends, capital gains, interest, rents, and so on), not their jobs. Most residents of the United States are not so fortunate. Instead, they are forced to base their economic well-being on the sale of their labor to others (only 7.1 percent of the U.S. labor force is independently self-employed) (U.S. Bureau of the Census 2004:385, 394). In return for the sale of their labor, members of the workforce receive annual salaries or hourly wages, and their earned income rests on their **marketability**— the demand for their labor on the part of public and private employers. Those people who cannot work—because of age, disabilities, or the lack of anyone who wants to buy their labor— must depend on alternative sources of income, such as retirement benefits, pensions, social security payments, veterans' benefits, welfare payments, and unemployment compensation.

Like wealth, income is not distributed equally among members of the U.S. population. In fact, the unequal distribution of income grew worse in the 1980s and 1990s (Peterson 1994; Thurow 1987).

Figure 6.2 shows how the distribution of income in the United States is highly imbalanced. In this figure the total number of U.S. families is divided into five equally sized groups, ranked from high to low in order of annual family income. The top fifth, consisting of the 20 percent of families having the highest annual incomes, received 47.7 percent of the total family income in 2001. The bottom fifth, the 20 percent of families having the lowest annual incomes, received only 4.2 percent of the total. If income were equally distributed among families, each group would receive 20 percent of the total—no more and no less.

To carry this a bit further, the top two-fifths, or most affluent 40 percent of families, received over 70 percent of total family income, while the bottom three-fifths—the majority of families in the United States—had to make do with less than 30 percent. It seems clear that a minority of family units appropriates the majority of income and consequently possesses superior access to the

Table 6.1	Mean and Median Net Worth, by Selected Family Characteristics, 2001

Characteristic	Percentage of families	Net worth in thousands	
		Mean	Median
All families	**100**	**395.5**	**86.1**
Income quintiles			
Lowest quintile		52.6	7.9
Second quintile		114.3	37.2
Third quintile		160.9	62.5
Fourth quintile		292.1	141.5
Highest quintile		1357.5	548.4
Age of head (years)			
Less than 35		90.7	11.6
35–44		259.5	77.6
45–54		485.6	132.0
55–64		727.0	181.5
65–74		673.8	176.3
75 and more		465.9	151.4
Education of head			
No high school diploma		103.0	25.5
High school diploma		180.7	58.1
Some college		284.7	71.6
College degree		793.7	213.3
Race or ethnicity of head			
White non-Latino/a		482.9	120.9
Nonwhite or Latino/a		115.3	17.1
Current work status of head			
Working for someone else		225.3	65.0
Self-employed		1,257.9	352.3
Retired		450.1	113.7
Other not working		179.2	9.0
Housing status			
Owner		558.1	171.7
Renter or other		55.0	4.8

Source: Ana M. Aizcorbe, Arthur B. Kennickell, and Kevin B. Moore, "Recent Changes in U.S. Family Finances: Evidence from the 1998 and 2001 Survey of Consumer Finances," *Federal Reserve Bulletin* 89 (January 2003): 1–32.

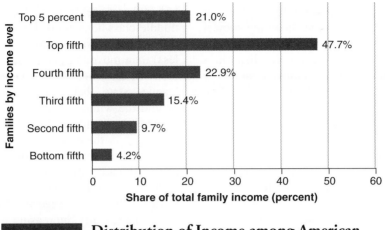

Source: U.S. Department of Commerce, Bureau of the Census, *Statistical Abstract of the U.S., 2003* (Washington, DC: Government Printing Office, 2004), p. 459. Available at www.census.gov.

Figure 6.2   **Distribution of Income among American Families, 2001**

goods and services of the affluent society. After the ownership class and other high-income earners take out their share, the remaining economic resources are divided among the many.

The economic well-being of the majority of people living in the United States would be even more tenuous were it not possible for them to charge consumer purchases on credit cards and take out loans for major expenditures. By buying on the promise of future income—in effect, by going into planned debt—many members of the workforce are able to gain an additional share of the goods and services they help produce. For example, while in the 1980s wages remained for the most part stagnant, consumer debt increased by 140 percent (Milbank 1991) and the typical U.S. household carried close to $9,000 in non-mortgage personal debt (Granfield 1991). By 2003 U.S. consumer debt soared to $1.98 trillion from credit cards and car loans (and excluding mortgages). This averages out to $18,700 of debt for every U.S. household (Laurier 2004). It is on this rather shaky basis that the supposed "middle classness" of the U.S. population rests.

With inflation periodically eating away at the purchasing power of the dollar, and with constant increases in the prices of essential goods and services, the income stability of the average household in the United States has been under attack in recent years. Lacking funds to invest as a hedge against inflation—a luxury taken for granted by members of the ownership class and others with surplus income—many members of the labor force find themselves running in place. Income gains are quickly eaten up by the rising costs of living. Old debts must be paid off, and new ones seem to constantly emerge. Increasingly, families can remain in the middle class only by accumulating new debts, increasing the number of family members who work outside the home, or increasing the number of jobs held by employed members of the household.

Growing Economic Disparities

The data in the previous section illustrate the vast gap in income shares received by families at the very top and at the very bottom of our class structure. But these data cover only a single year and thus mask a trend that has been the subject of a great deal of comment and speculation. The trend involves growing economic disparities between the majority of U.S. families, including those of the middle class, and the families of the affluent minority.

Some significant facts emerge when examining income changes between 1980 and 2001. First, the poorest families in the United States were on average worse off in 2001 than in 1980: The poor literally have grown poorer. Second, families at middle-income levels experienced a good deal of income stagnation if not net income loss. Finally, the highest income families—especially the extremely affluent—were far better off in 2001 than they were in 1980. In effect, the trend has been for economic power to slowly seep upward, leaving the poor ravaged and the middle-income strata struggling to hold their own. As we shall see, there is a definite relationship between the worsening of conditions for low-income families and, for example, the spread of homelessness and hunger in the United States.

As these changes in family income distribution have occurred, the implications for the future of the middle class in the United States have become the subject of much debate (Horrigan and Haugen 1988; Lerman and Salzman 1988). In the 1980s some argued that the middle class may be in danger of disappearing, turning the United States into a two-tier society, "leaving the country torn, like many third-world [sic] societies, between an affluent minority and a horde of the desperately poor" (Ehrenreich 1986:44). Such a development would reflect "an occupational structure characterized by a polarization between highly paid professional and technical workers on the one hand and poorly paid, unorganized, lower level workers on the other" (Harrington and Levinson 1985:426).

Researchers have shown that during the 1980s fewer people moved into the middle class (defined as households with after-tax income of $55,000 or more) from the lower class, and more middle-class households fell into the lower class (households with after-tax income of $18,500 or less) than moved up, confirming the earlier predictions. Researcher Greg Duncan and his colleagues state that "the biggest single factor behind the withering of the middle class is the growing inequality in the distribution of men's earnings . . . the economic rewards of a college degree increased dramatically, while less-educated adults often saw the real value of their earnings decline" (Duncan, Smeeding, and Rodgers 1992:34–38; see also Johnson 1994).

Consequently, increasing numbers of families in the United States have found it much more difficult to meet the constantly rising costs of their children's college attendance and virtually impossible to send them to expensive private institutions. This situation has been exacerbated by federal cutbacks in student aid that middle-income families had grown to rely on. And the children themselves—even those fortunate enough to go on to pursue a college education—increasingly find themselves wondering how they will be able to afford to purchase a home and lifestyle similar to that of their family (Newman 1993; Rubin 1994). Meanwhile, reflecting the top end of the income spectrum and its growing affluence, sales of imported luxury motor vehicles, boats, second and third homes, jewelry, furs, and art objects all continue to boom. At the bottom end of the spectrum are people without any homes at all, without the money to purchase sufficient food.

People of Color and Economic Inequality

Economic well-being depends to a large extent on whether one is a person of color. In 2001 the median income for white households was $44,517. (See Table 6.2.) In that same year, the median income for African American households was $29,470. Or, using the government poverty-level figure of $18,104 for a family of four, we

| Table 6.2 | Money Income of Households—Percent Distribution of Money Income Level in Constant (2001) Dollars, by Race and Latino/a Origin of Householder, 1980–2001 |

Year	Number of house-holds (1,000)	Under $15,000	$15,000– $24,999	$25,000– $34,999	$35,000– $49,999	$50,000– $74,999	$75,000– $99,999	$100,000 and Over	Median Income (dollars)
All Households									
1980	82,368	19.7	15.2	13.9	18.4	19.4	7.8	5.6	36,035
1990	94,312	17.9	13.9	13.3	17.3	18.9	9.4	9.2	39,324
1995	99,627	17.8	14.5	12.9	16.3	18.4	9.8	10.3	39,306
2001	109,297	15.9	13.3	12.4	15.4	18.4	10.8	13.8	42,228
White									
1980	71,872	17.6	14.8	14.0	18.9	20.4	8.3	6.1	36,017
1990	80,968	15.7	13.8	13.4	17.8	19.7	10.0	9.9	41,016
1995	84,511	15.8	14.2	12.8	16.6	19.1	10.2	11.1	41,255
2001	90,682	14.3	13.0	12.2	15.5	18.8	11.4	14.8	44,517
African American									
1980	8,847	36.9	18.9	13.8	14.2	11.0	3.7	1.5	21,902
1990	10,671	35.1	15.7	13.4	14.6	13.1	4.8	3.4	24,527
1995	11,577	31.6	17.3	14.2	14.2	12.9	6.4	3.4	25,830
2001	13,315	26.4	16.5	14.3	14.9	15.4	6.8	5.6	29,470
Latino/a*									
1980	3,906	25.4	20.1	16.2	16.5	14.9	4.4	2.5	27,776
1990	6,220	25.5	18.2	15.1	17.3	14.3	5.5	4.0	29,326
1995	7,939	28.1	19.6	15.1	14.8	13.3	4.9	4.1	26,368
2001	10,499	18.9	17.5	15.4	17.3	16.5	7.5	7.0	33,565
Asian and Pacific Islander**									
1990	1,958	13.5	11.00	9.9	15.0	21.0	13.9	15.7	50,496
1995	2,777	15.8	10.7	10.8	15.9	19.6	12.0	15.1	46,847
2001	4,071	12.3	10.0	9.9	14.3	19.0	12.5	21.9	53,635

*Latinos/as may be of any race.
**No data were reported out for Asian and Pacific Islander prior to 1990.
Source: U.S. Department of Commerce, Bureau of the Census, *Statistical Abstract of the United States, 2003* (Washington, D.C.: U.S. Government Printing Office, 2004), p. 456. Available at www.census.gov.

find that in 2001 some 9.9 percent of the white population was poor, while 22.7 percent of African Americans fell into this category. Other people of color have not been faring much better. For example, 21.4 percent of Latinos/as were living in poverty in 2001, the highest rate since data were first collected in 1973 (U.S. Bureau of the Census 2004:456, 466).

We do not need elaborate tables to realize that people of color are dramatically underrepresented in the upper-income ranges and grossly overrepresented in the lower ranges. Moreover, we may be sure that the United States' ownership class is almost wholly "lily-white." It is also clear that only a massive reallocation of economic resources can change the distribution of wealth and income between whites and people of color. These economic resources have to come from somewhere.

Thus it becomes easier to understand the uneasiness displayed by many of tens of millions of white workers who are running in place or losing ground, and who feel threatened by the realization that some people of color are successfully competing for an increased share of the economic pie. In the absence of any reallocation of income and wealth, most whites are forced to compete with people of color for the relatively small amount left over after the affluent have taken their bite. Expressions of racism and intergroup hostilities may be increased under the prevailing competition for scarce resources—in this case job slots at higher income levels.

Contrary to stereotypes held by many white people in the United States, the income differential between whites and people of color has not disappeared in recent years. (See Table 6.2.) It has not even undergone a dramatic decline. It is true that the household income of African Americans, for example, has risen substantially since World War II. But so has the income of whites, and African American income has not risen appreciably *relative* to that of the racial majority. African Americans must make even greater

annual percentage gains than whites just to keep the already wide income gap from widening further.

Perpetuation of Economic Inequality

As we have seen, income and wealth are far from equally distributed among individuals and families in the United States. The net worth of most households is minimal, a reflection of what little property people have been able to collect on the basis of the sale of their own labor to employers. Real wealth, on the other hand, is monopolized by a small ownership class. In this section we will look at the reasons why inequality remains such a permanent part of our economic life.

Wealth Begets Wealth

What does the ownership class *do* with all its money? Enormous wealth makes possible a great deal of luxurious consumption. Wealth can be used to obtain the best available goods and services. Yet while members of the ownership class are capable of material acquisition far beyond the level of most people in the United States, such spending can be managed without making much of a dent in their overall holdings.

More important, wealth is used to accumulate more wealth. With professional financial and legal assistance, members of the ownership class are able to keep their wealth active. Their money managers advise them on buying and selling holdings and guide them to investments in profitable income-producing properties that will further enhance or protect their net worth. Through such activities, wealth re-creates itself, and the increased wealth re-creates itself. The problem facing the very rich is one of deciding how best to increase their affluence in the face of a host of opportunities, not how to hold on to it. As wealth begets wealth, the

The financial resources of members of the ownership class enable them to purchase and consume luxurious goods and services without imperiling their financial standing. The very rich can afford the most expensive leisure-time pursuits and material things—vacations in exclusive resorts, opening nights at the opera or ballet, elaborate dinner parties and balls, sprawling homes and private jets— and still have plenty of money left over for investment. This photograph shows affluent potential buyers examining a well-equipped private jet at a Paris air show.

economic gap between the ownership class and the majority of people in the United States is maintained over time.

On the other hand, even if the majority of people could afford to pay for financial and legal assistance, they would have little money to invest. They certainly would not have assets of the magnitude to get involved in the most profitable large-scale investments open to the ownership class. Thus, one might also say that nonaffluence begets nonaffluence. The economic condition of most people in the United States is one of relative stagnation and almost total dependence

on the sale of their labor and/or various modest to meager government benefits for continued economic maintenance. If you have wealth, it is easy to parlay it into more; if you have little or none, then that is likely to remain the case.

The Unequal Burden of Taxation

Many people view the various taxes levied at different governmental levels as means of decreasing economic inequality, particularly income inequality. But is the existing tax structure really a progressive force, a mechanism of income leveling and income redistribution, or does it simply support economic inequality? When we examine the tax structure and the ways in which the burden of taxation is distributed, we must conclude that the outcome is to perpetuate economic inequality (Parenti 2001; Phillips 1993).

Many citizens of the United States believe that more affluent people bear a heavier tax burden than those who are less well off. But the affluent, with the financial and legal talent only they can afford to employ, are able to seek out and take advantage of various tax loopholes that effectively reduce their tax burden to a minimum.

For example, the 1986 Tax Reform Act was passed with the claim that it would cut taxes to the poorest—and it did by 13 percent for individuals and families with incomes under $15,000 in 1991. But for those with incomes above a half-million dollars, taxes were cut at a rate nearly three times the rate for the poor—38 percent—saving the average upper-income family over $300,000, compared to the savings of $73 for the poorer taxpayer. Those in the middle-income range, between $20,000 and $50,000, received a 15 percent tax cut for a savings of $586 (Barlett and Steele 1994). Tax cuts instituted in 2001 will intensify this inequality and the rewards to the wealthiest compared to the poor and middle class: The wealthiest 5 percent of the population are scheduled to reap $587 billion in tax cuts between 2001 and 2010, and most of this ($477 billion) will accrue to the wealthiest 1 percent, or those averaging more than $1 million in income (Sklar 2002).

One way the affluent invest surplus cash is by purchasing tax-exempt state or local bonds. Such bonds are sold to help finance many worthwhile public projects. The interest received from these bonds is tax-free. This is quite unlike the interest the average person receives on a bank or credit union savings account, on which taxes must be paid. In effect, it is a form of welfare, a reward or subsidy for being wealthy enough to buy such bonds.

Certain common taxes affect the average worker more than they do the affluent. We are all familiar with the sales tax, levied by states and localities around the country. Most families must spend a substantial percentage of their annual incomes on essentials; what is left over may go toward some luxury items. This means that a large amount of their income is spent on items subject to the sales tax. The more affluent do not spend most or all of their income in this manner. Instead, they save or invest surplus income, and the returns on these investments offset much of the burden stemming from sales tax on their consumer expenditures. Hence, the burden of sales tax weighs most heavily on the average family, who can neither avoid nor offset the tax. Lower-income families, who must spend literally all of their income, feel the burden of this type of tax more than anyone else. Thus, the sales tax, rather than being a progressive form of taxation that decreases economic inequality, is actually a regressive tax that penalizes the nonaffluent.

A similar situation prevails with regard to Social Security taxation. As this tax is set up, workers pay a certain percentage of their annual wages or salaries to the government up to a specified dollar cutoff point. In 2005, for example, workers earning up to $90,000 were taxed at a rate of 7.65 percent. Since the vast majority of workers earn less than this, the average worker's entire income tends to be subject to this form of taxation. In the case of the affluent, however, salary income over $90,000 is not subject to this tax, as it is above the official cutoff point. Moreover, most of their income is from investments, not job earnings subject to this tax.

The Social Security tax hits hardest at the nonaffluent majority, while the economically privileged generally escape its impact. By contrast, 669,000 individuals and families with incomes over $100,000 took tax deductions on investment interest expenses in 1990 totaling

$9.4 billion. This is the interest paid on money borrowed to speculate in gold futures or to buy shares on Wall Street (Sklar 2002).

As these examples indicate, the majority of working people in the United States bear the brunt of taxation out of all proportion to their ability to pay. The tax structure, rather than reducing economic inequality, permits such inequality to continue unabated.

Ideological Supports for Inequality

Thus far we have considered two primary reasons why extreme economic inequality is such an integral feature of U.S. society. Wealth begets wealth in a cumulative process that favors the propertied few. Moreover, the overall tax structure is organized so that economic inequalities go virtually unaffected. A third reason economic inequalities persist is that our own culture favors these inequalities. That is, values and beliefs held by many people in the United States support the economic status quo and hinder criticism of it (Huber and Form 1973; Lewis 1978).

An important component of this value system is a belief in what might be called **competitive individualism.** From the time we are children, we are taught that nobody gets or deserves a free ride in U.S. society and that hard work, a willingness to strive, and winning out in competition against others will result in success. Appropriate attitudes toward work and economic rewards are typically instilled in the home as a part of childhood socialization. The schools also drill children in competitive individualism (Cummings and Del Taebel 1978). In both school and the labor market, individuals are encouraged to believe that they are fully responsible for their own economic fates.

In any truly competitive situation there will be both winners and losers. Not all can win in the competition for economic success—for high incomes and accumulation of wealth. Some will do much better than others. So we are

encouraged to believe that economic success, or the lack of it, is almost totally an outcome of individual effort and competitive capabilities. The value system does not take into account the fact that the race may be rigged—that some start out just in front of the finish line, while others run the race wearing concrete boots.

When we internalize the belief in competitive individualism, we are simultaneously adopting an explanation of why economic rewards are unequally distributed. The affluent, we logically conclude, must deserve their privileged economic status or else they would not have it. And the nonaffluent must equally deserve their plight. In a 2003 survey 70 percent agreed that it is "still possible to start out poor in this country, work hard, and become rich" (CBS News/*New York Times Poll,* July 13–27, 2003). In another survey, 72 percent of respondents agreed that, "Most people who want to get ahead can make it if they're willing to work hard" (Children's Research and Education Institute, Child Tax Credit Survey, January 8–13, 2003).

Obviously, this explanation of economic inequality leaves much to be desired. It simplistically ignores some factors that result in affluence for a few, hard-earned subsistence for most, and economic deprivation for all too many. We have already seen how, for example, inheritance and the tax structure help perpetuate the concentration of wealth and disparities in income over time. In the next section, additional inadequacies of our taken-for-granted beliefs are suggested.

If we really believe that achieving economic well-being is like running a race, that the race is open and equally fair to all, and that people get what they deserve, then we have no reason to be critical of the economic inequality that prevails in U.S. society. Those at the very top, in the middle, and at the very bottom deserve their economic status. Possession of wealth and income becomes a measure of personal worth. If we believe all this, then we will not question inequality. But who benefits the most from our failure to engage in such questioning? Obviously, it is the ownership class, the most affluent—for so long as most members of U.S. society accept economic inequality as natural and proper, the economic position of the most privileged is not threatened.

Poverty amidst Affluence

According to the system of values and beliefs in the United States, the poor are the losers in fair competition for economic rewards. So it is not surprising that most citizens, even while recognizing that obstacles to economic well-being do exist, believe that poverty is a result of supposed faults of the poor themselves. Among these supposed faults are individual character deficiencies, lack of motivation to achieve, and unwillingness to strive to better their position. For example, a 2001 survey on poverty conducted by NPR/Kaiser/Kennedy School found that 54 percent of respondents believed that "too many jobs being part time or low wage" was an important explanation for poverty. Yet, at the same time, 48 percent believed that "people are not doing enough to help themselves out of poverty," and 41 percent thought that a shortage of jobs was only a minor cause of poverty (NPR/Kaiser/Kennedy School 2001).

Some claim that the poor possess a unique set of cultural values that places little or no emphasis on hard work and economic success, that is, they embrace a **culture of poverty** that differs from middle-class values (Billings and Blee 2000; Lewis 1959). According to this argument, the circumstances of being poor shape people's adaptive strategies so that they come to value instant gratification, shun formal education, disrespect law and order, and adopt cynical attitudes about the value of hard work and effort (Banfield 1974). They are likely to pass these values along to their children and thus ensure a replication of poverty handed down from one generation to another. The analysis suggests that once one is poor, one is permanently deprived of any motivation to escape poverty. The poor consciously embrace the culture of poverty and that, in turn, reduces their ability to break the cycle of poverty. Such was the ideological underpinning of welfare reforms of the 1990s in the United States. Since work was assumed to be the antidote to poverty, the poor would be coerced out of poverty by being cut off from welfare benefits and forced to support themselves through work outside the home. Not only do such policies ignore the work ethic possessed by most poor people. The culture of poverty thesis does not consider the larger structural constraints that are important factors in producing poverty. For example, can valuing hard work and education ensure upward mobility for individuals if there are not enough jobs paying living wages for all the people who want and need them? Many adults who are poor work full-time, year-round.

Public opinion polls regarding economic success issues suggest the powerful appeal of the culture of poverty thesis, even when people understand the institutional factors that produce economic inequality. In a 2002 survey by Pew Research Center, 61 percent of the respondents believed that individual failures were major factors for poverty. Yet 61 percent of these respondents recognized that most people who are poor work but can't earn enough money to avoid poverty, suggesting that poverty is beyond the control of individuals (http://roperweb.ropercenter.uconn.edu). Apparently, even when a majority of people recognize the role that the economy and society play in generating poverty, most still believe that the poor are themselves to blame because of deficient personal characteristics. This contradiction indicates that the twin ideologies of culture of poverty and competitive individualism are powerful, pervasive, and tenacious, even in the face of contradictory information.

These ideologies inhibit critical thinking that might challenge notions like the culture of poverty. For example, is it appropriate or accurate to consider economic achievement in terms of a competition that has winners and losers? Does each generation of contestants begin the competition on a level playing field regardless of their parents' or previous generations' economic positions? Might such a competition, in fact, be rigged at the outset, with some beginning with greater advantages to support success and others carrying heavy institutional hindrances throughout? Is individual effort the most important factor in determining economic success? Are there institutional arrangements and practices in the economy and the state that might shape opportunity structures, making individual effort less important?

Beyond all this, the word *poverty* is often a synonym or code name for people of color. When someone says "the poor," many unknowledgeable persons immediately think of African Americans, Puerto Ricans, Native Americans, or Chicanos. The typical poor person is often inappropriately envisioned as a young, able-bodied person of color, living willingly (even happily) at the lowest income levels. Some people mindlessly suggest that the poor are really rather affluent in their poverty, living quite well on the welfare rolls. Many in ignorance think that the typical poor person chooses not to work, preferring public welfare benefits to employment.

This view of poverty, while fitting well with our system of values and beliefs about economic inequality, is out of step with reality. Poverty is a matter of economic deprivation, not character deficiency. Whatever the deficiencies of the poor, they do not include happy acquiescence in being poor. Sixty-seven percent of the people who are poor in the United States are white. Rather than being able-bodied and available for employment, most members of the poverty population cannot hold full-time jobs because they are too old, too young, or disabled, or because they are mothers who cannot readily leave their children. Only 1 in 25 welfare recipient families has an able-bodied father in the house. Eligibility for welfare is quite restricted, and only 42 percent of all poor households receive cash welfare benefits. Those who are on welfare find that it provides a bare basis for survival as opposed to a life of comfort: Recipients tend to feel humiliated and degraded by their reliance on it.

In this section, we examine poverty and the plight of the poor. We shall see that, just as there are mechanisms at work to ensure affluence and continued economic well-being for a privileged few, there are also mechanisms to provoke and perpetuate poverty for many millions.

What Is Poverty?

Poverty is first and foremost an economic state. Being poor means, essentially, lacking a means of subsistence capable of providing what—in this society and at this time—could be considered a secure and adequate standard of living. On the one hand, poverty is an absolute state: By any objective measure the poor are materially deprived to the point where survival often becomes an issue. And, on the other hand, poverty is a relative state: The poor are materially deprived in comparison with the majority of the population (Goldstein and Sachs 1983).

For the purposes of discussion we will be using federal statistics on poverty. These statistics define poverty in a particular way. Since the 1960s the federal government has been measuring the extent of poverty in the population in accordance with the "thrifty food plan." This involves estimating the costs of a basic subsistence diet and then multiplying it by 3, under the assumption that poor people spend about a third of their incomes on food. The dollar amount calculated is considered the official poverty line; persons whose incomes fall below this dollar amount are considered poor. The dollar figure is adjusted for family size, and it is adjusted annually for changes in the costs of living. In 1964

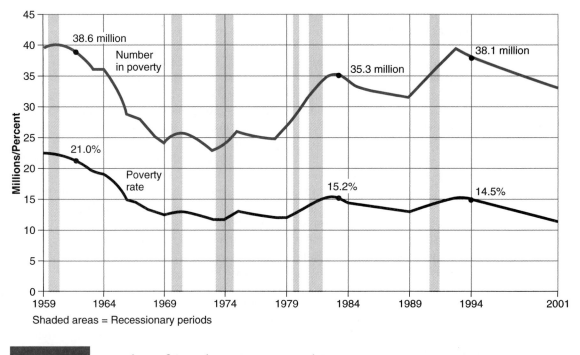

Figure 6.3   **Number of People in Poverty and Poverty Rate, 1959–2001**

Source: U.S. Department of Commerce, Bureau of the Census, *Income, Poverty, and Valuation of Noncash Benefits: 1994* (Washington, DC: U.S. Government Printing Office, 1995), p. xv; U.S. Department of Commerce, Bureau of the Census, *Poverty in the United States: 2001*, p. 2, available at www.census.gov.

the official poverty line for a family of four was about $3,000. In 2001 the line was drawn at $18,104. (See Figure 6.3.)

Critics have pointed out, and the federal government has admitted, that poor people typically must spend more than a third of their income to maintain a bare subsistence diet. An official poverty line that assumes otherwise is drawn too low and minimizes the extent to which there are people living in states of serious economic deprivation. Some would argue that poverty-level income should be considered to be that which falls more than 50 percent below the nation's income median. Such a statistic would add many more millions of people to the official poverty population.

Persons living in poverty typically have *some* means of subsistence. For some poor

families it is public welfare, while most others who are poor or near-poor receive either a primary or partial source of subsistence from employment. For the employed poor, including those who work year-round and full-time, the income derived from working is too low to provide a secure and adequate standard of living. Thus, even though an individual may be eager to work, no one may want to employ him or her, or the wages offered may be below the level necessary to move out of poverty. Being poor does not necessarily mean that the person is unwilling to embrace the notion of competitive individualism, but rather that the person's labor is not marketable or is poorly rewarded.

Likewise, a person who is too old or too young to sell his or her labor, who is too disabled to go to work, or who must place the responsibilities of child care ahead of full-time employment may effectively be cut off from a secure and adequate standard of living. Apparently, unless one can contribute to the U.S. economy as a worker, one is useless to it, no matter what the underlying reasons. Uselessness is underscored by according nonworkers the most negligible share of the nation's economic resources. Consequently, many persons are also rendered useless as consumers.

The poor, in essence, are the tens of millions of people who are economically obsolete—those men, women, and children whose contribution to production and consumption is considered peripheral to the ongoing operation of the United States' economic system. Unable to produce or unable to demand sufficient rewards for their contributions to production, and thus unable to consume, tens of millions of people in the United States live in a state of economic deprivation. The promises of the consumer society remain well beyond their reach.

Who Are the Poor?

While the poor constitute a numerical minority within the United States, this minority is by no means an insignificant one. Census data for 2001, in which only the most destitute were considered poor, revealed that almost 33 million persons were living in a state of poverty—more than 1 out of 10 people. These 33 million poor people included almost 7 million families and an additional 9.2 million unrelated individuals (see Table 6.3).

The official definition of poverty used by the U.S. Bureau of the Census varies for different categories of people; for example, a family of four was considered poor if its annual income was under $18,104. But in all cases the dollar definition of poverty encompassed those who were worst off both in absolute and in relative terms. It is estimated, however, that there are an additional 26 million people who had incomes that placed them in the category of *near-poor;* that is, their incomes were so low that any slight drop (as a consequence of job loss, layoffs, serious illness, or disability) would place them below the official poverty line (Schwarz and Volgy 1992, 1993). If we were to include this group with the official poor, it would mean that one out of four people in the United States is living in or close to poverty!

If we break down the poverty figures further, we get a better idea of which groups constitute the poverty population. Census data show that almost 36 percent of the poor are under 18 years of age and that more than 10 percent are 65 and older. Thus, almost half of the poor are very young, school-age children and youth, and the elderly. To this we can add another 27 percent of the poor—females who are heads of families and unattached females. In other words, three-fourths of the poor fall outside the category of persons we usually think of as traditional breadwinners.

Though more than two-thirds of poor persons in the United States are white, people of color are poor out of all proportion to their representation in the total population. African Americans constitute 12 percent of the population but are 25 percent of the poor. The prevalence of poverty among families of color contributes substantially to the income differential between whites and people of color discussed earlier.

Data on the numbers of persons who are poor, collected annually by the U.S. Bureau of the Census, are somewhat misleading. Such annual data mask the full extent to which poverty is experienced by people in the United States. When researchers examined a representative sample of families whose economic status was followed over a 10-year period, they found that a *quarter* of all people in the United States experienced poverty at one time or another during the 1970s. That is, there is substantial turnover among the poverty population, as people's economic fortunes change for better or worse (Duncan et al. 1984).

Table 6.3	**Persons and Families Below Poverty Level by Selected Characteristics, 2001**		
		2001	
Characteristic	Number		Percent
Persons			
Total	32,907		11.7
White	22,739		9.9
Not of Latino origin	15,271		7.8
African American	8,136		22.7
Asian and Pacific Islander	1,275		10.2
Latino origin*	7,997		21.4
Family Status			
In families	23,215		9.9
Householder	6,813		9.2
Related children under 18	11,175		15.8
Related children under 6	4,188		18.2
In unrelated subfamilies	466		39.8
Children under 18	292		44.6
Unrelated individual	9,226		19.9
Male	3,833		17.3
Female	5,393		22.3
Age			
Under 18 years	11,733		16.3
18 to 64 years	17,760		10.1
65 years and over	3,414		10.1
Families			
Total	6,813		9.2
White	4,579		7.4
Not of Latino origin	3,051		5.7
African American	1,829		20.7
Asian and Pacific Islander	234		7.8
Latino origin*	1,649		19.4
Type of Family			
Married-couple	2,760		4.9
White	2,242		4.5
African American	328		7.8
Latino origin*	799		13.8
Female householder, no husband present	3,470		26.4
White	1,939		22.4
African American	1,351		35.2
Latino origin*	711		50.0

Persons of Latino origin may be of any race.

Source: U.S. Department of Commerce, Bureau of the Census, Current Population Reports, P60-219, *Poverty in the United States, 2001* (Washington, DC: U.S. Government Printing Office, 2002), p. 3.

Why Are They Poor?

As we saw earlier, poverty is very often considered the fault of the poor themselves. Our system of values and beliefs suggests that we must blame the victim for lack of economic success (Ryan 1976). But poverty is an economic state. People are poor because they lack money. And they lack money because they are unable to sell their labor or because they are paid only very small incomes. In other words, the cause of poverty is not the victim but is instead the nature of the political economic system in the United States and the ways it deals with people (Kerbo 2003).

▲ Business Practices Contributing to Poverty

Among the forces contributing to poverty has been the **structural transformation of the economy** from goods production to service work. From the turn of the twentieth century until shortly after World War II, workers in the United States were increasingly employed in goods production: manufacturing, mining, and construction. These jobs have been the stronghold of the unionization movement and thus were increasingly better paid, and carried better benefits, than employment in agriculture or in the service industry. Since the end of World War II, however, workers in goods production have seen their jobs increasingly disappear, as employers **outsource** their jobs to poverty-stricken and highly exploitable labor forces in underdeveloped countries, where labor can be paid a fraction of the wages paid to U.S. workers. Many of the largest corporations have become international operations with plants around the world. To increase profits and thus reward stockholders, corporate executives have been channeling resources into other nations. Many products that were once made by U.S. workers are now being made elsewhere. In effect this has meant the export of jobs, increasing the competition for employment in this country and contributing to the high rates of unemployment that so often prevail.

Meanwhile, employment in the service sector has exploded, such that three-fourths of the workforce in the United States is now employed in that sector. This shift in employment pattern matters, because jobs in the service sector are commonly nonunionized, and consequently they tend to be low-wage, with few or no health and retirement benefits, and are often seasonal or part-time. When workers are paid minimum wage, even if they work full-time and year-round, their wages will fall below the poverty line. And that is before taxes are deducted from their wages and they pay for health care. Part-time workers are guaranteed poverty.

Workers also found increasing insecurity in their employment in the 1980s and into the new century, as employers increasingly **downsized** their workforce in pursuit of streamlining and becoming more competitive with international employers. Moreover, mergers between giant corporations typically meant massive layoffs of middle-management and technological and engineering employees, in an effort to reduce duplication of jobs between the merged firms. Suddenly, workers with good jobs found themselves forced to accept lower-paying jobs with few if any benefits and little security, sharing the experiences of low-wage workers. Many of them became the **new poor,** people who were highly educated and used to a strong income stream suddenly thrust into poverty because their employers sought to enhance the firms' profit margins. Still other workers found themselves thrust into a growing **contingency workforce** who are hired to do projects or consulting work, only to be unemployed as soon as the project is completed. These contingency jobs pay less than the more secure managerial, professional, and technical jobs once did, and they commonly provide no benefits.

The pay scales of business and industry also contribute to poverty. Some workers have a certain amount of job security, higher wages, retirement pensions, and other worker benefits as a result of union membership. Yet in 2002 only 9.3 percent of private-sector wage and salary workers were unionized (down from almost 19 percent in 1983) (U.S. Bureau of the Census 2004:431). For some of those tens of millions of U.S. workers who do not belong to unions, wages received for working full-time are so low as to place them near (if not in) a poverty situation. Although federal and state governments have established minimum wages for a variety of occupational areas, the minimum wage is generally set so low that it does not provide families with a secure and adequate standard of living. Moreover, periodic upward revisions in the minimum wage have not been sufficient to offset cumulative effects of inflation and increases in the cost of living.

We will explore these changes more carefully in Chapter 11, "The Changing Structure of Work," but this brief description indicates the contribution of employers' corporate decisions to poverty.

Technological change has also contributed to poverty. Decisions by executives in business and industry to automate or increase mechanization of their operations—in order to increase efficiency and profits—have resulted in the displacement of many workers and have closed opportunities for new entrants into the labor force. Those most affected by technological change are unskilled and semiskilled workers. Thrown out of jobs or denied them in the first place, such persons have difficulty finding any work, not to mention work that pays enough to provide a secure and adequate standard of living.

Worker displacement is not limited to large industrial centers. Over the decades, the nation's farms have become large mechanized corporations, requiring fewer and fewer people to produce food for the population. Today less than 3 percent of the U.S. workforce feeds us all. As mechanization of agriculture has spread and intensified, millions of farm workers who lack the training and skills required to compete successfully in the urban labor market have found themselves economically obsolete. Displaced farm workers have contributed substantially to the size of the poverty population as a consequence of decisions over which they had no control.

▲ Government Benefits

Many members of the workforce—particularly those in unskilled and semiskilled positions—are subject to periodic unemployment. Layoffs and seasonal unemployment most affect those with marginal skills. Contrary to popular belief, the **unemployment compensation** provided by government agencies for these and other workers does not necessarily prevent poverty. Unemployment compensation is not available to all members of the labor force, pays only a percentage of the wage formerly earned by the unemployed, and is cut off after a given period of time. Unless a worker can find a new job or get the old one back, welfare may be the next resort.

The rules concerning eligibility for welfare differ from state to state, as do the type and amount of benefits available. In no state does welfare provide more than a basis for subsistence well *below* the official poverty line (Abramovitz 2000; Piven and Cloward 1993). Potential recipients are subjected to a degrading screening process in which the state probes into virtually every area of their personal lives. Benefits are given grudgingly, and recipients are continually rechecked for eligibility and to make sure they do not have other sources of income (Rank 1995). While welfare cheats have been found, only a tiny percentage of recipients cheat the system (despite the publicity accorded them) (Physician Task Force on Hunger in America 1985). Yet far more people in the United States have negative feelings about welfare recipients than about the "welfare benefits" the affluent routinely collect under the tax laws.

Congress responded to the negative public attitudes toward welfare and welfare recipients and ardently pursued **welfare reform** through the 1996 Personal Responsibility Act. Benefit amounts and allowable length of time of benefits for welfare recipients were sharply reduced. Recipients would be permitted to collect welfare benefits only for a lifetime federal limit of 5 years; 22 states have since instituted far more stringent time restrictions. Recipients must find paid employment to continue to be eligible for assistance (Beaulieu 1998). These reforms were based on the stereotype of the lazy **welfare queen** who continued to live off the public dole indefinitely, refusing to work, having more children in order to increase her benefits, and acting as a financial drain on public resources (Sidel 2000). That stereotype, however, never matched the reality: Relatively few recipients ever actually remained very long on welfare (over 70 percent received welfare assistance for less than 2 years, and only 8 percent remained on welfare for over 8 years); the average family size of welfare recipients, at two children, was no larger than the average middle-class family size, and more than 75 percent of welfare recipients had three children or fewer; and most welfare recipients are not lazy people who refuse to work, but instead are women who have lost jobs or who work at low-wage jobs that fail to provide income above the poverty level (Seccombe 1999; U.S. Dept. of Commerce and Census Bureau 1999). These facts did not dissuade those in Congress who were intent on further dismantling social welfare programs.

When welfare reform was implemented, the number of people on public assistance or welfare dropped sharply. The assumption has been that this decline indicates the success of the program of weaning those who have grown dependent on the state by forcing them to get jobs. But the question remains: Where did these former welfare recipients go? Are they off the welfare rolls because they are now gainfully employed? Has welfare reform thus served to significantly reduce poverty? The answer to the last two questions apparently is no. Many former recipients have simply run out of benefits but have been without an opportunity to complete education or training programs to secure decent jobs. Others have jobs, but these are minimum wage or low-paying jobs that often carry few or no benefits (Abramovitz 2000; Casey 1998). The Urban Institute found, for example, that 61 percent of welfare recipients had jobs after leaving welfare, but they were earning a median wage of $6.61 per hour, and fewer than one-fourth of them had medical benefits from their jobs (Gault and Um'rani 2000).

Evidence from individual states confirms the finding that welfare reform is not reducing poverty, even if it is reducing the number of people receiving welfare assistance. The Wisconsin Works (W-2) program reduced welfare rolls by half in three years, but most participants have remained in poverty: One-fourth of those who left welfare returned for cash assistance, and half of those who found jobs are earning so little they remain below the poverty line (www.legis. state.wi.us/lab/reports/01-7full.pdf). A mother of two working full-time, year-round at a minimum-wage job simply does not have enough income to move her family above the poverty line, and the loss of benefits such as medical care compounds the poverty. Other former recipients have simply disappeared out of the system, sometimes to the streets among the homeless.

Among the hardest hit by welfare reform have been women of color and their children. This is partly because Latinas and African American women "are more vulnerable to poverty than white women," having higher rates of both poverty and unemployment. Researchers attribute this racial disparity to educational disadvantages and both gender and racial discrimination by employers (Gault and Um'rani 2000). Many states have compounded the likelihood of continued poverty among former welfare recipients, particularly among women of color and their children: In their enthusiasm for welfare reform, they have failed to inform recipients and the working poor who leave welfare that they or their children are still eligible for programs like

Food Stamps, Medicaid, housing assistance, and the like (Houppert 1999).

Evidence strongly indicates that welfare reform and the significant cuts in antipoverty programs under the "New Federalism" approach of shifting responsibility for social programs to the state and local governments have served to intensify poverty, particularly among women, children, people of color, and people with disabilities (Schram and Beer 1999). Programs such as welfare reform and the New Federalism are based on the assumption that the capitalist economy has the ability to solve social problems like poverty. However, an economy that increasingly offers minimum-wage service work with no benefits as the only real option to the poor, and which does not seriously address discrimination in employment and education opportunities, is in no position to reduce structured economic inequality (Blau 1999; Eitzen and Baca Zinn 2000; Huber and Kosser 1999).

▲ Gender and Poverty

As the previous discussion indicates, vulnerability to poverty is related to gender. Although women's share of jobs in the labor force increased during the 1980s and 1990s, their poverty rates rose significantly. This was because work in and of itself is insufficient to prevent poverty. Most of the newly created jobs have been minimum-wage, part-time service-sector jobs with no benefits (Ehrenreich 2001). Working part-time might provide women who are also single mothers with more time and flexibility to raise their children (a goal vigorously embraced by conservative lawmakers), but it ensures that women (and their children) will also be entrenched in poverty and hunger, and quite possibly homelessness. Single-parent families increased from 13 percent of the total number of families in 1970 to 23.7 percent in 2002, and most of these were female headed. While the median family income of married couples increased almost 2 percent between 2000 and 2001, the median income of female-headed households actually declined by 2 percent (U.S. Bureau of the Census 2004:460). Although the overall rate of poverty in the United States in 2001 was 11.7 percent, the rate of poverty among female-headed families was an astounding 26.4 percent (compared with a rate of 4.9 percent for married-couple families) (U.S. Bureau of the Census 2004). And when women, and single mothers in particular, are impoverished, so are children. In 2001, 16.3 percent of children under 18 were poor, and an alarming 44.6 percent of children under 18 in unrelated subfamilies were poverty-stricken. One might be able to argue that adults may stave off poverty by getting a job, but children are not able to do so.

Many observers use the term **feminization of poverty** to refer to the disproportionate number of women who are poor (Roschelle 1999). However, that term suggests that women have either chosen to be poor (because they have decided to remain on welfare to stay at home to raise their children, for example) or have somehow brought poverty on themselves (by leaving their marriages, for instance). Other observers prefer to term the problem one of the **pauperization of motherhood,** a concept that explicitly identifies the institutional forces (particularly market and state policies and practices) that have impoverished women and children (Amott 1993; Folbre 1985). The term *feminization of poverty* also focuses public attention on women and their life choices and distracts attention away from the gendering of economic inequality. While women are substantially more vulnerable to poverty than men, men are also more likely to be affluent. In fact, the majority of the most affluent individuals in the United States are men, a social fact reflected in the notion of the **masculinization of wealth.** Although economic inequality is gendered, however, some scholars have noted that not all men are affluent. The most affluent men in the United States are predominantly *white*. Men of color confront a glass ceiling against rising to the most prestigious, powerful, and lucrative positions much like the ceiling faced by women. And women of color faced a double-paned glass ceiling of racism and sexism as they struggle to shatter both (U.S. Department of Labor 1991). Poverty, like wealth, is not only gendered but is also a matter of racism: Single mothers of color are the most vulnerable to poverty, owing to a combination of racism and sexism in both the labor market and the state's welfare policies (Neubeck and Cazenave 2001).

▲ Other Economic and Social Factors

As we have seen, *age* is closely linked to poverty. Many adults reach retirement age only to find that their savings and other economic resources are inadequate and that poverty is their future state. Senior citizens on fixed incomes (e.g., income from many insurance programs and pension plans, which does not increase with inflation) find that they cannot keep up with annual increases in the costs of living. Food costs, medical costs, rent, and utilities escalate, but incomes do not keep pace. For many, welfare is the only answer—and not much of an answer at that. Ten percent of people in the United States who are 65 or older are poor, and many more are near-poor. Age, of course, works against finding or holding employment.

Like the aged, the young are confronted with the societal rule that people will be permitted to consume in accordance with their output (marketability), not in accordance with their requirements. Of the 40 percent of the poor under 18 years of age, most are too young to work at all (even if jobs were available) and must depend on others to provide for them. A large proportion of those old enough to work are of school age, and sacrificing schooling for work typically means employment in the most low-paying, dead-end occupations. In general, the young are powerless to overcome poverty completely on their own volition; their situation is quite similar to that of the elderly poor.

Sex and *marital status* are also linked to the probability that one will be poor and will find it difficult to extricate oneself from poverty. As mentioned, we are seeing the slow feminization of poverty as more women with young children are affected by it. Over time there has been an increase in the percentage of families in the United States headed by women, and today slightly over half of all poor families fall into this category. Employed women earn less than men, on the average. This is partly a result of sex discrimination in hiring, which limits the types of jobs available to women. But even when women perform the same jobs as men, the women are often paid less. The woman who heads a household faces many problems, not the least of which is finding a job that will keep her family out of poverty. The serious shortage of reliable and inexpensive child-care facilities makes it even more difficult for female heads of households to avoid poverty.

To this add *racism*. As we have mentioned, most poor people are white. But African Americans, for example, are disproportionately represented among the low-income and poverty populations. For African Americans, a vicious cycle seems to be operating involving educational discrimination and the failure of public schools to equip African Americans to compete on an equal basis with whites for decent jobs; discrimination by employers, who hire whites over African Americans and/or pay African American workers less than whites for the same jobs; exclusion of African American workers from union membership in the better-paying skilled trades; and frequent unemployment, a reflection of the fact that the African American worker is most likely to be in a job that is insecure and subject to either periodic layoffs or disappearance through mechanization. The unemployment rate among African Americans is normally twice that of whites. Finding that they cannot keep a job or earn enough while working to support a family, African American men, like similarly situated white men, often define themselves as failures. Their sense of economic obsolescence, felt as personal worthlessness, often creates tensions in the home that contribute to family breakup (Stack 1974). We then have a female-headed household, which, as we have seen, is quite likely to be poor or near-poor.

As was implied previously, another factor that contributes to the creation and perpetuation of poverty is *education.* It is clear that without the kind and degree of education or training that will make one marketable, a decent paying job is beyond one's reach. While it is questionable whether many jobs today really require the amount of schooling employers demand, a high school or college diploma is a necessity for marketability. But the dropout rates in schools serving poor children are high, and many children of the poor emerge from years of schooling as functional illiterates. Insofar as public schools fail to provide an adequate education or skills for children of the poor, the probability is increased that such children will replicate their parents' low-income position.

However, we should emphasize here that increasing the educational achievements of the poor and near-poor will not alone guarantee an end to poverty. The U.S. economy must be capable of providing job opportunities for all—and at levels of remuneration above the poverty level—in order for increased education to be put to use. Even people with education and skills can find it difficult to obtain secure, well-paying jobs today, and many such persons are increasingly found among the ranks of "contingent workers" who hold part-time or temporary full-time employment. Without major expansion of employment opportunities, the reduction of poverty through education is bound to be thwarted.

▲ The Structural Basis of Poverty

To answer the question "Why are they poor?" we must look well beyond the alleged personality characteristics, values, and genetic makeup of the poor. The organization of the economy and its machinations; the profit-oriented decisions made by top executives in business and industry; governmental policy; discrimination on the basis of age, sex, race, and ethnicity—all bear on the poor and tend to be outside their immediate control. The propensity to blame the victims of poverty for the economic deprivation under which they labor, while consistent with dominant values and beliefs regarding inequality, ignores all too many realities. Under the existing structure of our society, any of us could be poor if deprived of adequate means of subsistence by virtue of forces and decisions originating outside our control.

Just as our economic system perpetuates the privilege of the ownership class, so does it perpetuate the life situation of the poor. Many members of the ownership class earn more in one year than poor persons can reasonably expect to accumulate in a lifetime—a stark reflection of the extremes of economic inequality in the United States.

The Effects of Economic Inequality

Economic inequality is not simply an abstract intellectual concept. And the previous brief assessment of some of its dimensions and underlying causes barely begins to cover the topic. But at this point we turn away to suggest some of the consequences of economic inequality for U.S. society. We then consider potential solutions.

Inequality and Life Chances

We live in a society in which wealth and income have an undeniable bearing on a citizen's life chances. To some extent, at least, we must "buy" life just as we purchase any other commodity. Our economic situation will determine whether we eat and whether we can afford nutritious foods. It will determine whether we are safely and comfortably housed and whether we can afford to pay for quality health care (or any health care at all). Our economic situation will determine the area in which we can afford to live and the quality of educational opportunities available to our children. It will determine whether we have leisure time, how much we have, and how we can use it. It will determine whether our children live through birth, as well as the future life expectancy for us and them. Our economic situation will be inextricably linked to our sense of security, personal well-being, and self-worth. To the degree to which economic resources— wealth and income—are unequally distributed, life chances are also unequally distributed. By accident of birth and little more, a child born into the ownership class will be able to "buy" a life that is both longer and qualitatively different from that of a child born into poverty. While we all may have unalienable rights to "life, liberty, and the pursuit of happiness," economic inequality—with its impact on life chances— obviously stands in the way of the exercise of these rights.

Economic inequality also means that U.S. society is incapable of harnessing and utilizing the potential talents and abilities of all its members. For example, educational opportunities closely correspond to economic position. It is the children of the affluent minority who most frequently go to private schools and academies, receive special tutoring, are "broadened" by travel, and are sent to elite colleges and universities. These advantages are conferred not because the children of the affluent deserve them more than anyone else, but because their parents can easily afford them. The children of the poor and of the average working family, on the other hand, must be happy with what little educational opportunity they receive in return for their parents' tax payments. Education, like the automobile, is a commodity; basically, you get what you pay for.

The denial of educational advantages means that much human talent remains hidden and repressed. Talent that goes unrecognized and insufficiently cultivated is not going to be utilized. The shortage of imaginative teachers, inventive medical practitioners, participants in the creative arts, and sensitive administrators and politicians is an arbitrary shortage. We have no real way of knowing how much potential talent goes to waste annually because millions of families lack the economic resources to ensure their children an opportunity to cultivate and demonstrate it. As a consequence, the whole society is poorer both culturally and materially.

Furthermore, economic inequality is becoming increasingly costly. How much does the United States devote to welfare relief, to unemployment compensation, and to paying the salaries of the armies of bureaucrats and workers who administer relief funds? How much do we devote to cleaning up the physical and mental damage done to those persons whose economic situation exerts a negative influence on their bodies and minds? How much do we devote to processing through the legal, judicial, and penal systems those who steal in order to secure temporary increases in their disposable incomes? The expenditures are enormous, and they are a result of the pervasiveness of economic inequality and poverty. In the absence of a shift in the distribution of wealth, income, and opportunity, the costs of maintaining the status quo can only be expected to continue to grow.

Some mention must also be made of the psychic costs of economic inequality. The competition for scarce economic resources, and thus life chances, leaves no one untouched. The thought of being a loser, of being or becoming economically obsolete, is a permanent nightmare for members of U.S. society (Henry 1965). Competition separates people from one another and contributes to intergroup jealousies and hatreds, periodic conflicts, and tragic episodes of personal and collective strife. It means that the only people who are honored or revered are the winners—the affluent minority. And the anxieties, tensions, and frustrations economic inequality and competition generate may well be a contributing factor to many expressions of individual "deviance"—ranging from criminal behavior to mental illness. All these costs, though difficult to measure, are felt in real ways.

Homelessness

Among the most visible outcomes of economic inequality in the United States in recent years have been the growing numbers of men, women, children, and youth who have no homes. Homeless people have become an increasingly common sight as they seek shelter on the nation's streets, in bus and train stations, in parks and plazas, as well as in and around public buildings. The fastest-growing segment of the homeless population consists of families, most often mothers and their children. There has been a dramatic decrease in the average age of the homeless, such that it is now reckoned to be in the mid-30s. Shelters for the homeless cannot keep up with the demands placed on them; in extreme weather the homeless outside shelters sometimes die.

The mobility and transience of many of the homeless, along with the fact that people are continually entering or leaving this group, make estimating their numbers difficult. Although observers agree that homelessness has been on the increase through the 1980s and into the 1990s, precise statistics remain a matter of dispute (Rossi 1988; Rossi et al. 1987). On a March night in 1990, the U.S. Bureau of the Census attempted to count the homeless by sending 15,000 workers out to shelters, bus stations, parks, vacant lots, and shantytowns. The Bureau came up with a count of 228,821 but, at the same time, discredited the figure as not large enough (*Society* 1994a). A 2000 study by the Urban Institute is thought to provide a more accurate count. On the basis of its survey of 27 cities, the Urban Institute estimated that approximately 3.5 million people are homeless at any given time; 1.35 million—that is, 39 percent—of these homeless people are children. One-third of the 3.5 million are "hard-core" homeless, while the rest of the homeless population may change in composition every few months. Over any 3-year period, it is estimated that 7.2 million people are at risk for homelessness (National Coalition for the Homeless 2002).

The U.S. Conference of Mayors, concerned about the increasing numbers of homeless and the growing costs localities face in helping them, initiated a study covering 25 major cities. Its research helped to shed light on the characteristics of the homeless population. They found that in 2001, 41 percent of the homeless in these cities were single men. Another 41 percent were families with children. The remaining were single women and youths unaccompanied by families. Almost a quarter of the homeless were found to be employed. Within the homeless population are people who have serious physical and mental disabilities, illness, and disease, as well as persons caught up in addictive substance abuse. All of the homeless need homes. Many need extensive care and services in addition to permanent shelter (United States Conference of Mayors 2002).

It would be an error, obviously, to view the homeless as an undifferentiated mass. Examined closely, the homeless are quite heterogeneous. In response to the question "Who are the homeless?" Leanne G. Rivlin (1986:4) answers:

Single men and women and poor elderly who have lost their marginal housing, ex-offenders, single-parent households, runaway youths, "throwaway" youths (abandoned by their families or victims of family abuse), young people who have moved out of foster care, women escaping from domestic violence, undocumented and illegal immigrants, Native Americans leaving the reservation after Federal cutbacks and unemployment, alcoholics and drug abusers, ex-psychiatric patients, and the so-called "new poor" who are victims of unemployment and changes in the job market.

These very different types of people have one thing in common, though. Either they lack a source of income, or their incomes are so low—even if they are employed—that they cannot find affordable housing.

A major shift in housing costs that has been under way since the 1970s has made low-cost housing for families and individuals increasingly scarce. Between 1970 and 1983 rents tripled while renters' incomes only doubled. As this trend has continued, more and more people have been finding their incomes eaten up by the costs of shelter. By the beginning of the 1990s an estimated 11 million families had to spend over a third of their incomes on rent; 5 million actually spent more than *one-half* of their incomes in this way (Applebaum 1989; Shinn and Gillespie 1994). As rents have risen relative to incomes, the cost of purchasing a home has risen astronomically. The Economic Policy Institute estimates that in the early 1990s, *90 percent* of the nation's renters could not afford to make a down payment on a medium-priced house ($79,000) (Peterson 1994). Thus, many young people are unable to purchase their first homes and remain in competition for available rentals. This competition, along with altogether insufficient rates of new construction of low- to moderate-income rental housing, helps to drive rents up faster than incomes can increase.

Housing that people with low incomes can afford has also been disappearing at a dramatic rate. Urban redevelopment projects have displaced low-income people from properties that have been converted into offices or condominium housing for the well-to-do. Urban renewal projects in and around the downtown areas of cities have frequently meant the destruction of single-room-occupancy hotels and rooming houses sheltering low-income individuals. Developers find it much more profitable to build office towers and luxury apartment buildings for the upscale lifestyle of high-income people than to address the housing needs of the economically deprived.

In New York City, for example, single-room-occupancy units declined from 170,000 in 1971 to 14,000 in the 1980s. Between 1978 and 1984 New York City suffered a loss of some 715,000 units renting at or below $300 per month (Applebaum 1989). The poverty rate in New York City rose from 15 percent in 1975 to 24 percent in 1992, at precisely the same time as affordable housing for the poor was rapidly diminishing (United Way of New York City 1995). These trends help us understand why there are so many poor and homeless people visible on the streets of this city of 7.3 million inhabitants. As such trends have repeated themselves across the nation, homeless people have literally been "manufactured" into existence.

In the meantime, publicly owned and government-subsidized housing, the last resort for low-income people who cannot compete in the private housing market, has been in decline (see Applebaum 1989). About 2 percent of all housing units (or 1.4 million) are publicly owned. Each year 75,000 units are demolished; many more are in a state of dilapidation and terminal deterioration. Few new units are being built. The federal government all but abandoned its commitment to subsidized housing for low-income people during the Reagan and Bush administrations (1980 to 1992). Expenditures for such housing went from $32 billion to $6 billion between 1981 and 1989. To suggest the priorities of those who govern, in 1981 federal officials spent $7 on defense for every dollar they spent on housing. By 1989 the ratio had changed to $46 on defense for each housing dollar. Government failure to support publicly owned and subsidized housing in the face of substantial and growing demand has contributed to homelessness. In most major cities there are waiting lists of up to two years for such housing; for the most part these waiting lists are closed.

In sum, costs of shelter in the private housing market have been outracing the ability of low-income individuals and families to pay. Housing costs have been going up dramatically at the same time. As we saw earlier in the chapter, the income of the poor has actually been declining and that of many other people has been stagnating. Low- to moderate-income housing is not being built to even remotely approach existing needs. Publicly owned and government-subsidized housing no longer provides a safety net for the desperate.

In one study done for the U.S. Congress, researchers predicted that by the year 2003 "the gap between the total low-rent housing supply (subsidized and unsubsidized) and households needing such housing is expected to grow to 7.8 million units" (MIT professor Philip Clay, cf. Applebaum 1989). This would mean that nationwide nearly 19 million people would be at risk for homelessness. Little has occurred since this prediction was made to improve the situation, and the dire scenario the study warned against was hardly an exaggeration. The incredible suffering already documented (Liebow 1993; Snow 1993) would appear to have been hellishly magnified, particularly in the wake of natural disasters like the devastation of New Orleans and Biloxi, Mississippi, in the wake of Hurricane Katrina in 2005.

Hunger and Malnutrition

We learned that it is not uncommon for elderly people, living alone in apartments with no cooking facilities, to consume an evening meal of a tin of cat food and a raw egg. (Physician Task Force on Hunger in America 1985:79)

This quote, from a task force based at the Harvard School of Public Health, is an expression of yet another tragic consequence of economic inequality. Even as we function as one of the world's principal producers of grain and other foodstuffs, exporting to other nations and maintaining massive warehouses of surplus at home, a record 27.4 million people in the United States in 1993—or about 10 percent of the nation's

population—were receiving food stamps, up by 9 million since 1989. Over half of all food stamp recipients were children. It is estimated that there are 20 million additional U.S. citizens who are economically eligible for food stamps but are currently not receiving them (Clarke 1993; *New York Times* 1994). Simply put, the economic circumstances of tens of millions of people are such that the amount and types of food they are able to consume put them at risk of being "chronically short of the nutrients necessary for growth and good health" (Brown 1987:37).

In the decade of the 1970s the United States successfully fought to minimize hunger and malnutrition within the population. A public shocked by the discovery of the extent of such problems during the 1960s (Board of Inquiry into Hunger and Malnutrition 1968) pressured the federal government to act. As a consequence, the food stamp program, intended to permit low-income households to obtain a more nutritious diet, was expanded to cover many more needy people. New programs were set up and existing ones expanded to address needs of the isolated elderly, schoolchildren, pregnant women, and mothers and their infants. By the end of the 1970s the nutritional needs of low-income people were thought to have been pretty much taken care of.

Then, in the 1980s and 1990s, hunger began to appear in the U.S. population much as did homelessness. The changing distribution of income, described earlier, meant that the real income of those in poverty went into decline. Poverty rates rose from where they had been in the 1970s. The purchasing power of cash benefits from welfare—benefits received by only a minority of those living under the official poverty line—fell by 36 percent between 1970 and 1990. In effect, the poor began to become poorer and found it increasingly difficult to afford adequate food. But does one have to be in poverty to be hungry? Second Harvest, a nationwide network of food banks, has chronicled the growth of a group it calls the "new hungry"— those whose incomes are too high to qualify for

Hunger, malnutrition, and life-threatening poverty are not restricted to underdeveloped nations. Chronic poverty threatens the life chances of millions of people in wealthy nations like the U.S., too. When Hurricane Katrina devastated New Orleans in 2005, tens of thousands of people who were too poor to get transportation to flee the city as the storm approached became trapped and stranded without food, water, shelter, or protection for many days. More than a thousand people died, and many more seriously injured. Here, thousands of those finally rescued were temporarily evacuated to the Houston Astrodome.

food stamps. They are among the individuals and families most recently seen using emergency food bank programs. A study by the United States Conference of Mayors estimated that over a third of adults requesting food assistance had jobs (U.S. Conference of Mayors 2002).

While economic adversity has grown among those at the bottom levels of the United States' class structure, federally supported food assistance and nutrition programs have failed to keep pace with the magnitude of people's needs. Federal budget cuts aimed at restricting the rate

of growth of such programs demonstrate the same lack of commitment to addressing problems of hunger and poor nutrition as has become evident in the government's failure to help provide low-income people with opportunities for affordable housing. The result? An epidemic of hunger and increased demand on the 50,000 private food banks and pantries throughout the United States.

Hunger is not always readily visible to the casual observer of everyday life. But since the early 1990s social service agencies and religious organizations have been beset by those in need of food, and physicians and hospital staffs have seen health problems associated with hunger and malnutrition. These problems included anemia, tuberculosis, and osteoporosis, as well as diseases ordinarily found only in underdeveloped nations where malnutrition is most advanced (e.g., kwashiorkor and marasmus). The inability of millions of people in the United States to get enough to eat has become a major public health problem.

The consequences of nutrition-related problems tend to be most severe within certain groups. Pregnant women must eat well to avoid debilitating illnesses such as anemia and toxemia. Poor nutrition during pregnancy threatens the health and future prospects of the fetus, drastically increasing the likelihood of premature births and low-birth-weight babies. The latter have a higher than normal probability of mental retardation and developmental disabilities. Low birth weight is directly linked with infant mortality, the rates of which are very high in the United States. Malnutrition in infancy affects brain development and learning potential. And malnourished children are highly susceptible to infections and disease and are unlikely to function effectively in school and in social relationships. Inadequate nutrition in old age leaves elders vulnerable not only to chronic health problems but also to life-threatening ailments. In sum, women, children, and the elderly are at greatest risk when faced with hunger. In this respect the situation in the United States is not unlike that of the poorest nations of the world.

Most people do not choose to be hungry, any more than they choose to be homeless. It is a tragedy that befalls people for no other reason than lack of money. An elderly person on a fixed income may have to pay a rent increase or a large fuel bill, thus cutting back on money available for food. A mother may be faced with unexpected medical debts, thus forcing her to skip meals so that her children may eat. An undocumented worker may be unable to seek emergency food assistance for his children out of fear of being reported to immigration authorities and deported. An infant may find her formula watered down, as her jobless parents seek to find ways to stretch their last dollars. Such people "choose" to be hungry only in the most narrowly constricted sense.

In a society such as ours, hunger and malnutrition are not only an embarrassment but also unnecessary. The Physician Task Force on Hunger in America (1985) stated that we could virtually eliminate the situation by increasing federal expenditures on food programs annually by the amount of money we spend on two nuclear attack carriers. The question to seriously ponder is why we don't.

The Need for Government Intervention

Economic inequality is a deeply rooted but by no means inevitable feature of U.S. society. It is possible to reduce differences in personal wealth and income, thus making the life chances of all more nearly equal and enabling all to share more equitably in the goods and services being produced.

One of the first steps involves a change in attitudes toward economic inequality and poverty. U.S. citizens must become more familiar with the facts about inequality and the harm stemming from it. Members of this society must also begin to reject the notion that extensive economic inequality is part of the natural order of things and that, therefore, nothing meaningful can be done about it. Other developed nations do not have the magnitude of wealth and income inequality that exists in the United States, and their governments are much more concerned with the general welfare of their populations. Gross inequalities and their effects can be attacked, but only if concerned people are willing to collectively press this issue in the national political arena.

The next major step is to work out precise mechanisms to redistribute wealth and income. The goal should be to provide a decent standard of living for all persons, while placing some restrictions on the senseless accumulation of wealth by a few. In recent years, various ideas on how to reduce inequality have been put forth by individual scholars and a few legislators. It is time that such proposals become a matter of public debate, so that members of this society can decide which show the most promise.

For example, one proposal involves providing a guaranteed minimum income through the **negative income tax** (NIT). Essentially, the NIT would be based on a periodic report of income, which each person or family would file with the federal government. If the income reported was above a set minimum amount, taxes would be paid on the excess above the minimum, with tax rates set low on earnings just above the minimum. If, on the other hand, the income reported was below the minimum, the federal government would issue a direct cash payment to make up the difference. The minimum must obviously be set high enough to move people out of poverty. The NIT would provide an income floor for the most needy individuals and families. Its primary beneficiaries would be members of low-income groups, who would no longer have to struggle along on poverty-level wages or plead for welfare assistance. The present welfare system could be reduced in scope, at a substantial savings to taxpayers, and reoriented toward providing human services to anyone in need.

Mechanisms to eliminate poverty and enhance the standard of living of low-income groups must be accompanied by major changes in the United States' tax structure. In particular, income taxes must be made much more progressive in reality as well as in theory, so that those who have higher incomes are made to pay their fair share. Recent (2004) tax reforms reinforce a tax structure that is tilted toward preserving the advantages of the rich at the expense of the average citizen. In general, all the loopholes that provide a form of welfare for the rich must be closed, and the tax structure should place some reasonable limit on the maximum levels of income and wealth that can legally be accumulated by an individual or family.

Ways must also be investigated to redistribute wealth and increase the net worths of the millions of U.S. citizens who own little or nothing. The federal government could, for example, place a **net worth tax** on millionaire families, of whom there are currently several hundred thousand. This tax would provide the federal government with sufficient revenue to permit special tax reductions for less affluent families who have put a certain amount of money into savings (thus accumulating an estate). The net result would be a gradual reduction in the concentration of wealth among the rich and greater economic independence for large numbers of people in the United States.

No matter which mechanisms are adopted to reduce inequality, any surplus tax funds that are generated must be used to expand the supply of *free or low-cost services* available to all members of this society. Such services include education and job training, child- and elder-care facilities, efficient networks of public transportation, and health care. The purpose of attacking economic inequality is not simply to redistribute money but also to improve the quality of living for all. Basic services should be readily available to all people of the United States by right, no matter what their economic circumstance.

The reduction of economic inequality will involve costs—but primarily for the most affluent, who will be most adversely affected by tax reforms aimed at the redistribution of income and wealth. To the degree to which redistribution fosters increased equality in material terms, the economically derived status differences between the affluent and everyone else will be diminished. Such costs seem minor in comparison with the costs accompanying maintenance of the status quo, in which tens of millions are being forced to suffer.

As we have seen, the problem of economic inequality cannot be solved unless it is pressed in the national political arena. In Chapter 2 we analyzed the national political system and some of the political obstacles that must be overcome in dealing with inequality.

Summary

In this chapter we have seen that the United States is a class-divided society. Wealth is heavily concentrated in a small ownership class, and a minority of family units receive the majority of the total annual family income. Gross economic inequality is perpetuated as wealth begets wealth, the taxation structure leaves inequalities largely untouched, and dominant cultural values provide a rationale for viewing such inequalities as natural and proper.

Those worst off within this class-divided society are the tens of millions of poor and near-poor people. While the vast majority are white, the poverty rate among people of color is far out of proportion to their numbers in the population. Contrary to myth, most poor people are very young, very old, disabled, and females who are heads of families. They are poor not because of individual deficiencies but because they are victims of decisions and circumstances outside of their immediate control. Just as social mechanisms help the rich maintain their affluence, there are economic, political, and social factors that render it difficult for people to escape poverty.

In a society in which one's opportunities and lifestyle are closely linked to having money, economic inequality translates into unequal life chances. As millions suffer in poverty, the potential talents and abilities of such persons go untapped: The entire society is poorer culturally and materially. The costs of poverty are also felt in our welfare, health care, and penal systems. More generally, the competition for scarce resources leaves no one untouched and is a source of individual anxiety and intergroup conflicts.

Gross economic inequality is not inevitable. It can be altered through government intervention. Mechanisms to change the distribution of wealth and income exist; for example, the negative income tax and net worth tax. Such measures can be implemented. People must press the issue of economic inequality in the national political arena, or else the senseless suppression of talent and ability will simply continue.

Key Terms

Capitalist economy 165
Competitive individualism 175
Contingency workforce 181
Culture of poverty 176
Downsizing 181
Feminization of poverty 184
Income 164
Marketability 167
Masculinization of wealth 184
Negative income tax 193
Net worth tax 193

New poor 181
Outsourcing 181
Pauperization of motherhood 184
Poverty 177
Structural transportation of the economy 181
Technological change 182
Unemployment compensation 182
Wealth 164
Welfare queen 183
Welfare reform 182

Discussion Questions

1. What is the probability that you or your children will ever become part of the ownership class (roughly the richest 2 percent of all U.S. families)? What factors stand in the way?

2. Is it true that *anyone* can be economically successful if he or she really tries? Why?

3. What are your feelings about economic inequality? Should poverty be eliminated? If so, how should the costs of this be shared?

4. It is commonly held that any serious move toward the equalization of wealth and income will reduce people's incentive to work. What are the arguments for and against this view?

5. If you were a member of the ownership class, what arguments would you make against tax reforms that would take away much of your money to help eliminate poverty? If you were a member of the poverty population, what arguments would you make in favor of such tax reforms?

6. If economic growth in the United States seriously falters in the coming decades, job opportunities—even for college graduates—may undergo a marked decline. Moreover, opportunities for upward mobility may be restricted so that most workers are locked in place. Under such circumstances, what arguments might be made for the redistribution of wealth and income?

Suggested Readings

Kozol, Jonathan. *Amazing Grace: The Lives of Children and the Conscience of a Nation* (New York: Crown, 1995).
A moving chronicle of children living in the South Bronx, the poorest congressional district in the nation.

Lavelle, Robert, ed. *America's New War on Poverty: A Reader for Action* (San Francisco: KQED Books, 1994).
Compelling accounts of poverty throughout the United States as well as profiles of social action programs that address the causes.

Lyson, Thomas A., and William W. Falk, eds. *Forgotten Places: Uneven Development in Rural America* (Lawrence: University Press of Kansas, 1993).
An examination of poverty in depressed rural regions that have seen little if any economic development or social welfare benefits.

Rank, Mark Robert. *Living on the Edge: The Realities of Welfare in America* (New York: Columbia University Press, 1995).
Myths surrounding the welfare system and its recipients are dispelled through the accounts of individuals and families who receive welfare assistance.

Seltser, Barry Jay, and Donald E. Miller. *Homeless Families: The Struggle for Dignity* (Urbana: University of Illinois Press, 1993).
Presenting the new faces of homelessness—families—with their experiences and possible solutions.

Wolff, Edward N. *Top Heavy: A Study of the Increasing Inequality of Wealth in America* (New York: The Twentieth Century Fund Press, 1995).
Linkages between the widening gap in household wealth and income, how the U.S. compares to Europe, and how our tax system influences the growth of disparity.

chapter 7

Racism

There should be no personal and institutional discrimination against individuals on the basis of race and ethnicity.

"The very concept of 'race' is inherently racist." So observed Audrey Smedley, who argued that race is an ideology asserting that different groups are inherently unequal and thus can be ranked in a hierarchy of superiority and inferiority. This is quite a provocative statement, particularly in a society like the United States where many people are highly uncomfortable talking about race and racism but where race appears to be at the heart of so many social patterns and relations. What did Smedley mean by this statement, and why did she make it? Her comment strikes at the very heart of the sociological meaning of race.

Race is often treated in popular culture and in widespread usage as if it were a matter of biology. In the United States, race is commonly understood to be a matter of skin color: black and white. But Latinos are frequently accorded similar treatment as African Americans, and Latinos may be light- or dark-skinned. What they have in common is not skin color, but perhaps language, and we know that language is learned, not genetically inherited. And Asians, who are also commonly pooled together as a race, speak dozens of different languages and, like Latinos, may be either light- or dark-skinned. What they share is a common continent of heritage, and that is a matter of geography rather than genetics. Native Americans share a heritage of residence in the Americas and of genocide at the hands of Europeans, but little else.

This discussion suggests that "race" is not so much a matter of biology and genetically inherited sets of characteristics but more one of social constructions of categories that presumably have some underlying significance. These categories are defined and shaped by dominants in society, as illustrated by the fact that the courts have historically determined the racial categorization of groups. Indeed, it is not unusual for people to use the term *race* to refer to a particular ethnic group. An **ethnic group** refers to people who share a common culture, which may be defined by a common heritage, language or dialect, religion, geographic ancestry, norms, and customs. Notably, over time some of these ethnic groups that were previously defined as a separate race, such as Irish and Italian immigrants and Jews in the early twentieth century, became more socially accepted and assimilated into the dominant culture, and legally redefined by U.S. federal courts as "white" (Haney Lopez 1996). Indeed, the Census Bureau continues to struggle with how to define the population racially. It finally included a category of "two or more races" in the 2000 census, a move that indicated the agency's recognition of the problematic assumption of "pure" races. That dominants in society have the power to decide the categories and to redefine these at will legally or as a matter of practice is a strong indicator that race is not a biological concept, but a social construction.

Race is a category assigned to people based on the social meaning and significance accorded to physical or cultural characteristics of members of a society's population. Although it is often used as a way to categorize people, race is a meaningless concept in biology (Gould 1996). All people, regardless of skin color or heritage, belong to a single human species. While people with a common geographic ancestry may share similar physical characteristics, variations in physical characteristics have no biological significance in terms of the heritability of things like intelligence, strength, temperament, agility, ability, or athletic prowess. Neither do language, religious belief, or cultural customs.

Because the term *race* is so commonly used and carries a strong assumption of biological significance, sociologists Michael Omi and Howard Winant (1994:55) suggest the term *racial formation* to highlight the notion that race is a social construction. **Racial formation** is "the sociohistorical process by which racial categories are created, inhabited, transformed, and destroyed." The designation of a group of people as a race may be the first step in a process that singles them out for discrimination. Differential treatment is often justified on the assumption that their presumed inferiority is genetic and thus will not change regardless of increased

opportunities and advantages. The extreme outcome of this assumption can be, and at times has been, **genocide,** the systematic extermination of a group of people by dominants in society who consider themselves to be racially superior, as in the case of the near-extermination of Native Americans in seventeenth- to nineteenth-century United States, and Jews in Nazi Germany.

Since race is not a meaningful biological term, a society in which the "race" of people carries assumptions of significance is likely to be racist, as Smedley's provocative observation suggests. There is no other reason for variations in appearance, cultural ancestry, religion, or language to be of any particular concern other than to single groups out for discrimination. Systems of racial inequality, or **racism,** are socially constructed on the basis of the false assumption that these variations are linked biologically to how people will behave and thus their social worth.

From the time the Plymouth settlement was founded by English colonists, the United States has been run by and in the interests of white people—and consciously so. Though men and women with a variety of other "racial" and cultural backgrounds have been major participants in the shaping of U.S. history, most whites know little and care less about their roles. Alternately used, abused, and ignored by the white majority, Native Americans, African Americans, Latino Americans, Asian Americans, and other minority groups have had a history of racial oppression in U.S. society. When we use the term *minority*, we are not referring necessarily to numbers. People of color make up most of humanity and thus are not a "minority" in numbers. In the context of this chapter, the term **minority** or **minority group** refers to people who are marginalized or oppressed by a system of white domination. In some cases a minority group constitutes a numerical majority within society (e.g., blacks who lived under South Africa's system of apartheid). Thus, the notion of minority and majority relations is one of power. In the United States this is manifested in differential opportunities and life chances based on one's race: not only have the rights to "life, liberty, and the pursuit of happiness" historically been distributed along color lines, but to a large extent, this is still the situation today (Aguirre and Turner 2004; Doob 1993; Wellman 1993).

Today, for example, there are almost 2.8 million Native Americans (U.S. Bureau of the Census 2004). This group has suffered enormous injustice. Shortly after the European settlers arrived on this continent, they found it expedient to clear out the indigenous groups whose nations stood in the way of territorial conquest and colonial expansion. The firm belief of whites in their own racial and cultural superiority (a belief without any real foundation) provided a ready rationale for their vicious treatment of the native peoples. Native Americans were subjected to a continuing series of attacks: the takeover of ancestral lands, racially inspired killings, confinement on white-controlled reservations, bureaucratic manipulation by governmental agencies, and so on. Now, after generations of white domination, Native Americans are among the poorest and most oppressed minority groups in the United States. Their traditional patterns of living have been largely destroyed, and their life chances are almost completely subject to the whims of white-controlled institutions (James 1992; Thornton 1987). They were, and are, victims of racism.

The immediate territorial expansion of white European American society involved pushing indigenous peoples back, aside, and under. And its early economic development to a large extent revolved around the wholesale purchase of human beings, their enslavement, and the use of their forced labor. Kidnapped and transported from the African continent, black men and women were forced to become a part of a white-run U.S. society. Bought and sold, assaulted and bred, black slaves were worked relentlessly under a system of subjugation that was based on the assumption that they were not really human. When slavery in a society with democratic ideals began to present irreconcilable moral dilemmas (and, more important,

when slavery became politically and economically questionable to maintain), it was cast aside as one outcome of a bloody Civil War. Yet the ingrained belief of whites in their own racial and cultural superiority did not significantly wither. Formal enslavement of black people was replaced by conscious racial segregation and other forms of discrimination that have functioned to keep African Americans "in their place." More than a century after the abolition of slavery, imposed inequalities continue to weigh upon many of the more than 33 million African Americans living in the United States (Ashmore 1982; Franklin and Massis 2000; Staples 1986).

Westward expansion was carried out at great cost to another group that was also made a part of the United States against its will. Prior to 1848 the southwestern portion of the United States was a part of Mexico. The people of Spanish and Native American ancestry occupying the territory had been there long before the colonists landed near Plymouth Rock. When white settlers began to migrate to the western frontier, the government of the United States precipitated a war against Mexico to "liberate" the rich agricultural lands and natural resources of the southwest. Upon winning the war, the United States proceeded to annex half of Mexico's sovereign territory. Natives of Mexico who had occupied the lands for many generations were considered to have been conquered, and most landholdings were subsequently transferred into the hands of the victorious "Anglos." Once again the belief of whites in their own racial and cultural superiority came into play, conditioning the treatment of persons of Mexican ancestry. Today 14 million Mexican Americans, most of whom reside in the south and west, continue to struggle under Anglo control and domination (Acuña 1988; Shorris 2001).

The U.S. government's historical willingness to pursue territorial acquisition through conquest was responsible for pulling yet another group into this society's collection of minorities. Not too long after the annexation of the southwest, the United States initiated a war against

Spain—ostensibly to end Spanish colonial excesses in Cuba. After winning the war, the United States went on to claim the small Caribbean island of Puerto Rico. Spain ceded Puerto Rico to the United States, whereupon it fell—and remains today—under this society's political and economic control. Particularly in the years since World War II, Puerto Ricans—people whose ancestry includes mixtures of Spanish, African, and Taino Indian—have taken advantage of their U.S. citizenship to migrate from the poverty-ridden island. Members of this group have settled primarily in the cities of the Northeast, especially in New York City. Mainland businesses, seeking cheap unskilled or semiskilled labor, have encouraged this migration. Once on the U.S. mainland, Puerto Ricans are just another racial minority so far as the dominant white population is concerned. The socioeconomic status of the almost 3 million Puerto Ricans on the mainland is severely depressed, and many are the victims of poverty and unemployment. Movement to and from the mainland is constant, as members of this group struggle for ways to deal with their difficult situation (Fernandez 1994; Fitzpatrick 1987).

The Latino American population has been growing five times as fast as the rest of the country, according to census data. While people of Mexican origin constitute the numerically largest Latino group in the United States, for more than 20 years the fastest-growing sector of the U.S. Latino population has been of Central and South American origin. They now number some 3 million people. Many Central and South American immigrants are in the United States after unsuccessful attempts to overcome crushing poverty conditions and harsh political repression by authoritarian governments. Often these regimes are financially and politically supported by the United States, as is the case with Guatemala and El Salvador. Such recent patterns of immigration, together with new births among Latinos residing in the United States, have helped to establish Latino Americans as the

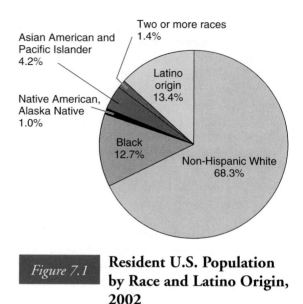

Figure 7.1   **Resident U.S. Population by Race and Latino Origin, 2002**

Source: U.S. Bureau of the Census, *Statistical Abstract of the United States, 2003* (Washington, DC: Government Printing Office, 2004), Table 13.

largest minority group in this country, now totaling some 39 million people (see Figure 7.1).

It is important to note that Latino Americans often view themselves as white. For example, 50.6 percent of Mexican Americans identified themselves in this way in the 1990 U.S. Census. Nonetheless, we categorize all Latino Americans as members of a minority group, including those who identify as white, because Latinos have been and still are discriminated against in the United States, based on the dominant white Anglo population's belief in their alleged inferiority.

Most of the groups mentioned to this point originally came within the domain of the United States and its white Anglo majority involuntarily. Native Americans were forcibly conquered and their homelands taken away. African Americans were captured, transported to the United States, and enslaved. Mexican Americans and Puerto Ricans occupied areas taken over by the U.S. government as spoils of war.

In contrast to the involuntary nature of these groups' original entry into this society, Asian Americans have typically been voluntary immigrants from abroad (Kitano and Daniels 2000; Okirhiro 2004). Nonetheless, the historical record shows that Asian Americans, living in the United States for well over 100 years, have suffered from racism. Subject to exploitation, violence, strict immigration quotas, and even mass imprisonment (in the case of 90 percent of all Japanese Americans during World War II), Asian Americans have struggled against values of white supremacy. Today they comprise some 10 million people and are thought to be the fastest-growing minority group, principally as a consequence of the liberalization of immigration laws. It is a diverse group, largely made up of persons of Chinese, Filipino, Japanese, Asian Indian, Korean, Vietnamese, Cambodian, Thai, and Pacific Islander ancestry. All face barriers erected by racism, notable exceptions notwithstanding.

Legal as well as illegal immigration, along with natural population growth, are rapidly changing the color composition of the United States. The U.S. population consists of some 288 million people, including millions of immigrants who have arrived in recent years (see Table 7.1). At present, minority group members—African Americans, Latino Americans, Asian Americans, and Native Americans—together make up about 33 percent of the U.S. population. By the year 2050, roughly 40 percent of U.S. residents will be minority group members (U.S. Bureau of the Census 2004:15). The multiracial character of the United States is becoming markedly more apparent every day and will continue to do so.

Some locales are undergoing transformation more rapidly than others. California, for example, has substantial numbers of Latino and Asian Americans, as well as other minority groups. It is estimated that by the year 2020, white (Anglo) residents may make up only 40 percent of California's population. Even now most schoolchildren in the state are members of minority groups. But many other states or parts of states are showing signs of rapid change as well.

Minority group members are often openly proud of their ancestry, identify strongly with their particular group, and seek to hold on to aspects of their cultural heritage rather than "assimilate" into the majority. Such assimilation is problematic in any event, given the distinguishing physical characteristics that often set minority group members apart from most whites, and to which whites react. The United States more and more resembles a pluralistic "salad bowl" of different and distinct peoples, rather than a "melting pot" wherein people tend toward homogeneity in looks and behavior.

Critics see contemporary immigration and the resultant changes in population composition as a crisis situation, arguing that it undermines needed cultural unity, exacerbates competition for jobs, and inflicts unnecessary education and social welfare costs on U.S. society (Brimelow 1995). These arguments about the downside of immigration, made in the United States since the nineteenth century, tend to ignore the fact that almost all people in the United States are immigrants or their ancestors were. Many immigrants have arrived poor, illiterate, or unable to speak English. Nations like the United States, Canada, Australia, and others whose histories show significant waves of immigration have grown prosperous in part by drawing on the energies and wide range of contributions—in virtually every sphere of life—of their new arrivals.

We often think of living and working with people who are different from us as a challenge, whether we are native-born or newly arrived. However, the diversity of people in U.S. society offers rich opportunities to learn and appreciate not only how we differ from others but how very much we are all alike. Unfortunately, the existence of racism diminishes the exercise of these opportunities while producing intergroup hostilities and conflicts that are harmful to society as a whole. Racism within a society whose

Table 7.1	Immigrants, by Country of Birth: 1971 to 2001 (in Thousands)				
Country of birth	1971–80, Total	1981–90, Total	1991–2000, Total	2000	2001
All countries	**4,493.3**	**7,338.1**	**9,095.4**	**849.8**	**1,064.3**
Europe*	**801.3**	**705.6**	**1,311.4**	**132.5**	**175.4**
France	17.8	23.1	27.5	3.5	4.6
Germany	66.0	70.1	67.7	7.6	9.9
Greece	93.7	29.1	13.6	1.0	1.2
Ireland	14.1	32.8	59.0	1.3	1.5
Italy	130.1	32.9	22.6	3.1	3.1
Poland	43.6	97.4	169.6	11.8	11.8
Portugal	104.5	40.0	22.8	1.4	1.7
Romania	17.5	38.9	57.5	6.9	6.6
Soviet Union, former†	43.2	84.0	103.9	3.3	2.7
Armenia	(NA)	(NA)	26.6	1.3	1.8
Azerbaijan	(NA)	(NA)	12.1	(NA)	0.5
Belarus	(NA)	(NA)	29.0	2.2	2.9
Moldova	(NA)	(NA)	11.7	(NA)	1.3
Russia	(NA)	(NA)	128.0	17.1	20.4
Ukraine	(NA)	(NA)	141.3	15.8	21.0
Uzbekistan	(NA)	(NA)	19.5	(NA)	1.1
Spain	30.0	15.8	(NA)	(NA)	(NA)
United Kingdom	123.5	142.1	135.8	13.4	18.4
Yugoslavia	42.1	19.2	25.9	2.8	6.2
Asia*	**1,633.8**	**2,817.4**	**2,892.2**	**265.4**	**349.8**
Afghanistan	(NA)	26.6	17.4	1.0	1.2
Bangladesh	(NA)	15.2	66.0	7.2	7.2
Cambodia	8.4	116.6	18.5	2.1	2.5
China	†202.5	‡388.8	424.6	45.7	56.4
Taiwan	(‡)	(‡)	106.4	9.0	12.2
Hong Kong	47.5	63.0	74.0	5.4	8.3
India	176.8	261.9	383.3	42.0	70.3
Iran	46.2	154.8	112.6	8.5	10.5
Iraq	23.4	19.6	40.7	5.1	5.0
Israel	26.6	36.3	32.0	2.8	3.8
Japan	47.9	43.2	61.5	7.1	9.6
Jordan	29.6	32.6	39.7	3.9	4.6
Korea	272.0	338.8	171.3	15.8	20.7
Laos	22.6	145.6	43.6	1.4	1.4
Lebanon	33.8	41.6	43.5	3.7	4.6
Pakistan	31.2	61.3	124.6	14.5	16.4
Philippines	360.2	495.3	505.6	42.5	53.2

Country of birth	1971–80, Total	1981–90, Total	1991–2000, Total	2000	2001
Syria	13.3	20.6	26.1	2.4	3.4
Thailand	44.1	64.4	48.4	3.8	4.3
Turkey	18.6	20.9	26.3	2.6	3.2
Vietnam	179.7	401.4	421.1	26.7	35.5
North America*	**1,645.0**	**3,125.0**	**3,917.4**	**344.8**	**407.9**
Canada	114.8	119.2	137.6	16.2	21.9
Mexico	637.2	1,653.3	2,251.4	173.9	206.4
Caribbean*	759.8	892.7	996.1	88.2	103.5
Barbados	20.9	17.4	(NA)	(NA)	NA
Cuba	276.8	159.2	180.9	20.8	27.7
Dominican Republic	148.0	251.8	340.9	17.5	21.3
Haiti	58.7	140.2	181.8	22.4	27.1
Jamaica	142.0	213.8	173.5	16.0	15.4
Trinidad and Tobago	61.8	39.5	63.3	6.7	6.7
Central America*	132.4	458.7	531.8	66.4	75.9
El Salvador	34.4	214.6	217.4	22.6	31.3
Guatemala	25.6	87.9	103.1	10.0	13.6
Honduras	17.2	49.5	66.8	5.9	6.6
Nicaragua	13.0	44.1	97.7	24.0	19.9
Panama	22.7	29.0	24.0	1.8	1.9
South America*	**284.4**	**455.9**	**539.9**	**56.1**	**68.9**
Argentina	25.1	25.7	24.3	2.3	3.3
Brazil	13.7	23.7	52.3	7.0	9.5
Chile	17.6	23.4	16.9	1.7	1.9
Colombia	77.6	124.4	131.0	14.5	16.7
Ecuador	50.2	56.0	76.4	7.7	9.7
Guyana	47.5	95.4	73.9	5.7	8.3
Peru	29.1	64.4	105.7	9.6	11.1
Venezuela	(NA)	17.9	29.9	4.7	5.2
Africa*	**91.5**	**192.3**	**383.0**	**44.7**	**53.9**
Egypt	25.5	31.4	46.7	4.5	5.2
Ethiopia	(NA)	27.2	49.3	4.1	5.1
Ghana	(NA)	14.9	35.6	4.3	4.0
Nigeria	8.8	35.3	67.3	7.9	8.3
South Africa	(NA)	15.7	22.6	2.8	4.1
Other countries§	**37.3**	**41.9**	**48.0**	**5.1**	**6.1**

NA Not available.
Includes countries not shown separately.
†*Includes other republics and unknown republics, not shown separately.*
‡*Data for Taiwan included with China.*
§*Includes Australia, New Zealand, and unknown countries.*

Source: U.S. Department of Commerce, Bureau of the Census, *Statistical Abstract of the United States, 1995* (Washington, DC: U.S. Government Printing Office, 1995), p. 11; U.S. Department of Commerce, Bureau of the Census, *Statistical Abstract of the United States, 2003* (Washington, DC: U.S. Government Printing Office, 2004), p. 11.

composition is so rapidly changing creates an environment that is socially explosive.

In this chapter we examine the major manifestations of racism that minority groups face, to one degree or another, in U.S. society today. We point to reasons why racism exists, and we look at the mechanisms by which the white majority systematically subordinates minorities. Finally, we spell out some of the consequences of this macro problem and point to the need for change.

The Meaning of Racism

The term *racism* is more than an abstract concept. It refers primarily to practices that harm people. Sociologist Robert Blauner (1972:84) provides us with the following definition: "Racism is a principle of social domination by which a group seen as inferior or different in alleged biological characteristics is exploited, controlled, and oppressed socially and psychically by a superordinate group."

Additional facets of racism are reflected in a definition offered by sociologists Joe R. Feagin and Hernan Vera (1995:7), who define white racism as the "socially organized set of attitudes, ideas and practices that deny African Americans and other people of color the dignity, opportunities, freedoms, and rewards that this nation offers white Americans."

Racism may serve a variety of functions. It may provide individuals with a reference group with whom to compare themselves favorably. It is often a means of limiting competition for scarce resources in society (e.g., desirable jobs, entrance into educational programs, preferable housing), and it may provide profit for some, at the expense of others, as when minority group members are paid less than whites for the same work. It may also serve a **scapegoating** function: When members of society are frustrated by crises, they may blame some group as racially responsible, a response that can become an important and dangerous step toward violence and genocide. For example, Jews in Nazi Germany were scapegoated as an inferior race responsible for the collapse of the economy and the degeneration of the culture. Since their inferior genetic contributions were deemed the root of the nation's crises, exterminating them became the "final solution." In post–September 11, 2001, United States, people of Middle Eastern descent, particularly Arabs and Muslims, are profiled and scapegoated as the cause of heightened insecurity and terrorism, as if simply sharing a geographic or religious ancestry somehow genetically predisposes such individuals to threaten the lives of U.S. citizens. Thus, the frustrations and fears of people in the United States have turned to scapegoating Arabs and Muslims as deserving of discriminatory treatment in the name of increased national security.

There are two different types of racism (Hamilton and Carmichael 1967; Knowles and Prewitt 1969). The first type is **personal racism.** Individuals (or small groups) express negative feelings, by word and/or action, toward people of color. The second type is **institutional racism,** wherein the routine operations of such large-scale institutions as business and the political system work to the disadvantage of minority groups generally. While we may examine them separately, these two types may actually be closely intertwined (Essed 1991; Feagin and Feagin 2005). We examine both types of racism in the next section. However, much of the remainder of this chapter focuses on institutional racism.

Personal Racism

Personal racism occurs when individuals (or small groups of individuals) hold attitudes of prejudice and/or engage in discriminatory or similar behavior. Among the manifestations of personal racism are stereotyping individuals on the basis of alleged racial differences, the use of derogatory names and references, discriminatory treatment during the course of interpersonal contacts, and threats and acts of violence against members of a minority group that is alleged to be racially inferior.

The violence occasioned by a court-ordered school busing program in Boston during the mid-1970s demonstrates the extremes that expressions of personal racism can attain. Ironically, people who express personal racism often make use of the very symbols (the American flag, the U.S. Constitution) of the equality they are attempting to deny members of minority groups.
Credit: Stanley J. Forman, Pulitzer Prize, 1977.

Much controversy today surrounds the use—even innocently—of words, phrases, and symbols that members of minority groups (and others) often find offensive. The controversy extends from the utterance of words like *chink* and *spic,* to use of phrases like *colored people* or *those people,* to display of "White Power" bumper stickers or the southern Confederate flag. Some whites dismiss the concerns people of color have over such behaviors. They attack and ridicule demands that such behavior cease as a call for "political correctness" and portray the latter as an infringement on their rights to free speech. Many people do not make the effort to understand just why some forms of expression are offensive. What some whites may label and criticize as political correctness is usually no more than

behavior that is respectful of or sensitive to others' feelings. Those who rail most loudly against political correctness often do not fully appreciate how important speech and other forms of expression can be in subtly reinforcing the notion of white superiority in a society in which racial inequalities prevail (Moore 1995). Personal racism goes well beyond the use of offensive speech and other forms of expression, however. The following are some additional examples:

1. A personnel officer hires people of color only for low-level, low-paying jobs, based on stereotypes about their abilities or fear that placing people of color in supervisory positions will bring about negative reactions from white workers.

2. A teacher assumes that children in the class who are not members of the white majority cannot learn and therefore deserve little attention.

3. A real estate agent shows people of color only homes for sale in minority or mixed neighborhoods under the belief that people should live "with their own kind."

4. A store clerk in an all-white neighborhood follows after the occasional minority group member who comes to shop and makes it clear the person is being watched, under the rationale that such shoppers are probably there to steal.

5. A parole official denies parole to prisoners of color more frequently than to whites imprisoned for the same crimes, believing that minority group members are more dangerous or unreliable.

6. The driver of an automobile stopped at a red light, noticing that several youths of color are about to approach the crosswalk, quickly locks the car doors under the presumption that the youths may intend harm (Cose 1993; Feagin 1991; Feagin and Sikes 1994).

Personal racism involves acts by individuals. Such acts may, or they may not, be approved by others in the organization, community, or other setting in which they take place, and may be so subtle that they go unnoticed.

On the other hand, personal racism may also take the form of overt acts of racial hatred. These often earn media attention, particularly when the acts are life-threatening or otherwise carry implications of violence. In recent years vicious "hate crimes" or "bias crimes" against people of color (as well as against Jewish people, gay males and lesbians, and others) have resulted in serious injuries and deaths, inspiring some states to pass hate crime laws aimed at deterrence (Levin and McDevitt 1993).

Personal racism may involve isolated individual acts or actions by small groups. One such

group is the Ku Klux Klan—a white supremacist organization with a long history of terrorist violence (MacLean 1994). Largely muted in its activities after the passage of historic civil rights legislation in the 1960s, KKK rallies, marches, and recruiting efforts became highly visible once again in the 1980s and early 1990s (Ridgeway 1991; Southern Poverty Law Center 1991). Participation in such a group enables individual whites to communicate dramatically the contempt they have for people of color and thus to act out their personal racism in the company of like-minded individuals.

By the mid-1990s the Ku Klux Klan had slid into a trajectory of decline as a result of internal disputes and lawsuits against it, but meanwhile other white supremacist groups were growing in size and levels of activity. According to the Southern Poverty Law Center (1995), which tracks hate groups, the neo-Nazi, Idaho-based Aryan Nations, founded in the mid-1970s, underwent explosive growth in 1994, spreading into 15 new states from the 3 in which it had been operating. Aryan Nations predicted it would expand to 30 states.

The Southern Poverty Law Center (1995a:1) has characterized Aryan Nations as follows:

Aryan Nations' notorious reputation for violence and other criminal activity has given it legendary status in the white supremacist world. Since 1984, at least 40 Aryan Nations followers have been charged with major felonies ranging from weapons violations to murder.

The broader white supremacist movement, of which Aryan Nations is but a part, "has been linked to at least several dozen murders since 1980" (Hochschild 1994:55). The Skinheads, said by the Southern Poverty Law Center to be in decline, is another particularly violent, racist group (Hamm 1993; Moore 1993). White supremacists not only operate their own organized groups, in which there are an estimated 25,000 hard-core activists, but they are believed to have flocked to join volunteer militia groups and states rights groups, which tend to be all-white. Such groups' existence attracted wide mass media attention following the 1995 bombing of a federal office building in Oklahoma City (see Chapter 2).

Clearly, personal racism may range broadly in intensity and visibility, but the purpose is always the same: to denigrate persons on the basis of their group membership. It is not surprising that some people of color fight back on a similar level. Racial stereotyping, use of derogatory names and references, acts of interpersonal discrimination, and threats and acts of violence are at times aimed at members of the white majority. Indeed, one of the costs of being white in the United States is to be seen as a member of the group that has historically engaged in oppression and exploitation of minorities.

However, as the numerical majority (three-quarters of the U.S. population) and as the group that monopolizes positions of political power in U.S. society, whites are far freer than minority individuals to express personal racism without undue fear of retribution. There are certainly people of color who engage in acts of personal racism, but they are far fewer in number and at far greater risk when doing so than members of the white majority.

When we think of racism, often it is only personal racism—and its most visible forms at that—that comes to mind. But the damage that is done by personal racism, as tragic and painful as it may be, in no way has the same broad impact as institutional racism. It is to this second form that we now turn.

Institutional Racism

Institutional racism is our major concern in this chapter. The term **institution,** as used here, refers to an organizational structure created to perform certain services or tasks within a society. Business and industry, unions, the political system, education, the mass media, the legal system—all may be thought of as institutions.

Ideally, such organizational structures can be made to function so as to take the interests of all social groups into account. In reality, of course, they can be made to perform so as to provide advantages or benefits to some groups over and above others. We have already seen in earlier chapters how a few of these institutions operate to the distinct advantage of the economically affluent and to the disadvantage of those who lack economic power. Institutional racism involves the treatment accorded specifically to minority peoples at the hands of such institutions.

The term *institutional racism* draws attention to the fact that groups such as Native Americans, African Americans, Latino Americans, and Asian Americans—by virtue of their historical exclusion from key institutional policymaking and decision-making roles—frequently find themselves victimized by the routine workings of such organizational structures. Institutional racism does not necessarily require conscious, individual prejudice; it is, rather, a form of discrimination that is supported by institutional structures and practices that produce and reproduce inequality based on racially defined group membership. Unlike some forms of personal racism, the racism that occurs through the day-to-day and year-to-year operation of large-scale institutions is often difficult to detect without careful investigation. It is a form of racism that derives from the very institutional structures themselves that have historically been embedded with racist practices. Whites have historically dominated and filled, and continue to fill, the command positions in key social institutions, and thus white advantage continues, with or without conscious, deliberate, and observable prejudice.

Let us look at some examples:

1. Seniority rules are applied to jobs for which only whites historically had been hired. This now makes recently hired minorities more subject to layoffs than whites (i.e., "last hired, first fired").

2. Standardized tests or academic credentials are routinely used to screen potential employees when such tests or credentials are not relevant indicators of future job performance and are geared to knowledge and experience most likely to be possessed by members of the white middle class.

3. Credit policies of banks and other financial institutions are implemented in ways that make it difficult to obtain mortgages or loans for home improvements in minority neighborhoods, thus promoting housing decline where people of color reside.

4. Preference in law and medical school admissions is given to the offspring of influential and wealthy alumni, the latter of whom are almost always white because of past discriminatory admissions practices.

5. Major family restaurant chains maintain an unwritten policy of discouraging minority group customers with poor or hostile service, hiring people of color only for poorly paid backroom jobs, and selling chain franchises only to whites.

6. Police and other law-enforcement officials routinely stop, search, and arrest people of color based on stereotypes of likely criminals rather than on actual observed behaviors of individuals.

7. Sites of commercial hazardous waste disposal and processing facilities, sources of pollutants harmful to health, are disproportionately located in communities with a high proportion of minority group members (Bowser, Auletta, and Jones 1993; Maher 1998; Massey and Denton 1998; Ross and Yinger 2002; Schauer 2003; Squires 1994; Turner et al. 1991).

As can be seen from the preceding examples, institutional racism may, but need not always, involve acts or policies that directly or intentionally discriminate against people of color. Institutional operations may in some cases be neutral or "color-blind" on the surface,

and appear justifiable or even "fair." But they are forms of institutional racism if they have the ultimate effect of systematically placing minorities at a disadvantage vis-à-vis whites:

Whatever the motivation behind such organizational acts, a process is occurring, the common denominator of which is the denial of equality of opportunity to large numbers of minorities. . . . When unequal outcomes are repeated over time and in numerous societal and geographical areas, it is a clear signal that a discriminatory process is at work. (U.S. Commission on Civil Rights 1981:11)

Institutional racism is a societal phenomenon that whites are in a position to set in motion and sustain. The key element is *power* over organizational structures and their operations. Since people of color generally lack access to positions of power in the key institutions that affect them, they are incapable of discriminating against whites at this level. One can talk, for example, about incidents of "black racism" at the personal level. But it should be remembered that minorities have never had, and do not have today, the means to practice racism on the same institutional scale and thus with the same broad effects as whites.

The Myth of Innate Racial Inferiority

As we mentioned earlier, majority white domination over Native Americans, African Americans, Latino Americans, and Asian Americans has long been accompanied by beliefs in the racial and cultural superiority of whites (Gossett 1965). Such beliefs have frequently taken the form of so-called scientific theories that postulate the innate inferiority of racial minorities as a result of genetic factors. Such theories not only have purported to explain why minorities, on the whole, lag behind whites in terms of educational achievement and economic success but have also served to justify *actions* against people of color by whites. Thus, theories of genetic inferiority are more than abstract systems of ideas or academic exercises. They provide an intellectual rationale for the perpetuation of personal and institutional racism.

A few psychologists and other academicians have rekindled the long-standing controversy over the bases of human intelligence: the "nature versus nurture" debate (Fraser 1995; Herrnstein and Murray 1994). The theories they have put forth rest on the claim that intelligence is determined primarily by genes rather than by environmental influences on learning. These theorists have based many of their conclusions on the results of IQ tests, which they consider devices capable of measuring intelligence. Since, in terms of group averages, some minority groups lag behind whites on test results, the theorists suggest that the genetic characteristics of members of these groups limit their learning potential. Innate genetic differences, it is alleged, interfere with achievement in schooling. The obvious implication of such theories is that the money spent on the education of minorities is wasted. To the degree to which these kinds of ideas receive acceptance by the whites who are in charge of political and educational institutions, the stage is set for cutbacks in the already inadequate educational opportunities provided minority children.

Such theories are based on faulty logic, are not borne out by scientific evidence, and are subtly racist. Theories of innate racial inferiority have been around for many years in one or another form, and are one of the mainstays of thinking among groups like the Ku Klux Klan and Aryan Nations. They are ideologies that support inequalities along color lines as natural and, therefore, inevitable. That such theories are based on unproven assumptions and faulty premises renders them even more distasteful.

The claim that human intelligence is determined primarily by genes is just that—a claim, not a fact (Fraser 1995; Lewontin, Rose, and Kamin 1984). Most geneticists will readily admit that little is known about the relationship between genes and human behavior, and that there is no scientific evidence that genes play the major role in determining intelligence. In fact, there is not even agreement today about what the concept *intelligence* really means. Thus, there is no consensus on how to measure it validly. If there is any explanation for the economic, political, and educational subordination of people of color in U.S. society, it does not rest with genes. Subordination is imposed by racism.

Economic Deprivation and Exploitation

In Chapter 6, "Economic Inequality and Poverty," we saw that the United States is a class society, divided along economic lines. Political and economic power and the privileges of material affluence are closely tied to property ownership and high income. Native Americans, African Americans, and Latino Americans, for example, are unlikely to own income-producing property. Only a small percentage of each of these groups has been able to gain entry into occupations and professions that pay well. These facts, along with the disproportionate presence of people of color in the poverty and low-income sectors of the U.S. population, can best be explained by institutional racism.

Employment and Income

Asian Americans are often stereotyped as a **model minority** that has high educational attainment and is economically successful. This stereotype is often used as "evidence" that there is no racism in the United States, and that any patterns of poverty among other minority groups is rooted in their lack of motivation or work ethic. In fact, however, there is significant variation in education and economic status among Asian Americans (e.g., between Japanese and Vietnamese), including differences between those born in the United States and those recently arrived (Kitano and Daniels 2000). Unemployment and poverty rates are higher for

| Table 7.2 | Unemployment Rates, by Educational Attainment and Race: 1970 to 2002 (in Percent, as of March, for the Civilian Noninstitutional Population, 25 to 64 Years of Age) |

Item	1970	1975	1980	1984	1985	1986	1987	1988	1989	1990	2002
Total	**3.3**	**6.9**	**5.0**	**6.6**	**6.1**	**6.1**	**5.7**	**4.7**	**4.4**	**4.5**	**4.6**
Less than 4 years of high school*	4.6	10.7	8.4	12.1	11.4	11.6	11.1	9.4	8.9	9.6	8.4
4 years of high school, only	2.9	6.9	5.1	7.2	6.9	6.9	6.3	5.4	4.8	4.9	5.3
College: 1–3 years	2.9	5.5	4.3	5.3	4.7	4.7	4.5	3.7	3.4	3.7	4.5
4 years or more	1.3	2.5	1.9	2.7	2.4	2.3	2.3	1.7	2.2	1.9	2.9
White: Total	3.1	6.5	4.4	5.7	5.3	5.5	5.0	4.0	3.8	4.0	4.2
Less than 4 years of high school*	4.5	10.1	7.8	10.9	10.6	10.9	10.2	8.3	7.7	8.3	7.6
4 years of high school, only	2.7	6.5	4.6	6.4	6.1	6.2	5.5	4.6	4.2	4.4	4.6
College: 1–3 years	2.8	5.1	3.9	4.6	3.9	4.2	4.1	3.2	3.0	3.3	4.1
4 years or more	1.3	2.4	1.8	2.4	2.1	2.2	2.2	1.5	2.0	1.8	2.7
Black: Total†	4.7	10.9	9.6	13.3	12.0	10.7	10.6	10.0	9.2	8.6	7.7
Less than 4 years of high school*	5.2	13.5	11.7	17.4	15.3	15.3	14.8	14.6	14.6	15.9	13.3
4 years of high school, only	5.2	10.7	9.5	14.5	13.0	11.7	11.7	11.2	9.2	8.6	8.8
College: 1–3 years	3.5	9.8	9.0	9.7	10.6	8.7	7.6	7.4	6.9	6.5	6.7
4 years or more	0.9	3.9	4.0	6.2	5.4	3.2	4.2	3.3	4.7	1.9	4.2

*Includes persons reporting no school years completed.
†For 1970 and 1975, data refer to black and other workers.

Source: U.S. Department of Commerce, Bureau of the Census, *Statistical Abstract of the United States, 1995* (Washington, DC: U.S. Government Printing Office, 1995), p. 422; U.S. Department of Commerce, Bureau of the Census, *Statistical Abstract of the United States, 2003* (Washington, DC: U.S. Government Printing Office, 2004), p. 409.

parts of the Asian American population, such as the Hmong, than for whites. Native Americans, African Americans, Latino Americans, and members of some Asian American groups are far more likely to be unemployed or sporadically employed than members of the white majority. (See, for example, Table 7.2.) They also are far more likely to be underemployed—that is, to be overqualified for the jobs they hold. And they are far more likely to occupy positions with the lowest income, benefits, security, and status (Tomaskovic-Devey 1993; Turner et al. 1991). How does one explain the marginal occupa-

tional situation of racial minorities as compared to the general white population? Though there are many reasons, institutional racism plays a key role.

The handicap of inadequate schooling must be examined. Census data show that dominant group–minority group differentials in years of education completed have been narrowing. African Americans especially have made some notable gains, and members of some Asian American groups have on average outperformed whites. Latino Americans and Native Americans, along with other Asian Americans, lag behind. Aggregate statistics on years of school completed do not say anything about the *quality* of educational experiences to which many children and teenagers of color continue to be subjected (Kozol 2005). Some limited insight may be gained by examining performance on nationwide achievement tests (in reading, mathematics, etc.). Scores on such tests continue to indicate that whites, on the average, are being taught more than people of color.

Achievement or "aptitude" tests are often used as screening devices by public and private employers. The failure of educational systems to prepare many students of color—even high school graduates—to compete on an equal basis with whites on such tests directly limits their occupational opportunities. The use of such tests especially affects groups whose native language is not English—for example, Puerto Ricans and Mexican Americans. Employers have claimed that the use of such tests is fair and nondiscriminatory (although there are obviously cases in which the tests have little to do with the work to be done). Yet insofar as such screening devices function to the direct disadvantage of minorities, the tendency toward discrimination along color lines is institutionalized (Feagin and Feagin 1986:58–60).

Nor does high performance on tests necessarily guarantee employment and occupational mobility for people of color. White employers often react negatively to distinguishing physical features, dress, accent, and other characteristics associated with minority background and culture. They prefer employees who will "fit in." In a predominantly white establishment, this renders being a person of color a deficit in and of itself (Feagin and Sikes 1994).

Direct discrimination means that even objectively qualified people of color have often needed far more in the way of educational credentials than whites in order to get the same kinds of jobs. If statistics on employment can be believed, many employers routinely pay minorities less than whites for similar work and block

the advancement of minority group members (with the exception of "token success models") (Feagin and Sikes 1994; Hacker 1992).

In business and in government, white monopolization of positions with the highest pay and the most authority remains largely unchallenged. Moreover, many of the very top institutional positions in the public and private sectors (e.g., boards of directors, cabinet and agency heads, judgeships) are typically gained through appointment. Those in a position to do the appointing are likely to be white men, and they tend to choose persons like themselves. Thus, for example, while U.S.-born Asian Americans are more likely than members of the general population to be college graduates, and many hold managerial or professional positions, such Asian Americans typically hit a "glass ceiling" wherein they are blocked from upward mobility to top positions they see opening up.

People of color who aspire to move upward have also found that denial of their cultural backgrounds—that is, becoming operationally "white" on the job—may be a prerequisite to employment security and success. The conflict between "selling out" and freely maintaining and expressing consciousness of minority identity is a forced one. It stems primarily from the need to please white superiors in order to gain acceptance and get ahead in majority-dominated institutions (Benjamin 1991; Cose 1993).

In the labor market as a whole, according to social scientists, there is a division along racial lines (Tomaskovic-Devey 1993). The *primary labor market* consists of the higher-paying, more secure, and most desirable occupations for which employers recruit white workers. For example, white-collar jobs are predominantly filled by white workers. The *secondary labor market* consists of the lower-paying, least secure, and most undesirable jobs. It is within this secondary market that most people of color are likely to find work. For example, within the blue-collar job market, African Americans are mostly found as nonfarm laborers and operatives. They also make up a high percentage of service workers. A competitive threat occurs when minority groups attempt to move up and out of the sector of the labor market in which they have long been believed to "belong"—a threat felt whenever equal treatment is demanded in employment practices. To the degree to which Native Americans, African Americans, Latino Americans, and Asian Americans fall or are pushed aside in the competition for primary labor market positions, whites have an open field.

People of color have made their greatest gains in the U.S. occupational structure when there has been a labor shortage, as during periods of war. When there is work to be done, when there is no other way to get it done, employers have dropped some of their normal procedures for screening, hiring, and promoting employees—a situation that provides opportunities otherwise unavailable. On the other hand, during a period of labor surplus—for example, an economic recession and slowdown—minority group members tend to be the hardest hit. In many sectors of the economy, layoffs are carried out on the basis of seniority; the last to arrive leave first. And those with the most seniority are the first to be rehired. This process at least partially accounts for the extraordinary unemployment rates among minorities during economic slumps.

In recent years, some people of color have been permitted to move upward in the occupational structure as pressures have increased and laws have been passed against blatant discrimination. These individuals tend to be highly visible, giving the impression that great gains are being made. But in *group* terms, most of this society's minorities have tended to remain "in place," a situation verified by continuing lags in income (Hacker 1992). In the 1990s efforts by corporations to "downsize," "rightsize," and "resize" their workforces—by cutting both blue-collar and white-collar employees—have had a more negative effect on people of color than whites. African Americans have been particularly hard-hit (Clarke 1994).

Other factors also influence the occupational situation of many minority group members. People of color have become residentially concentrated in central city areas, while business and industry have been migrating out of large cities to suburbs and smaller towns that offer attractive tax rates and white labor pools. Locked into central city areas by housing segregation, the expense of alternative housing, and the inadequacy or cost of transportation to outlying jobs, urban-dwelling minorities have found it increasingly difficult to find satisfactory employment (Wilson 1987). The "white flight" of business and industry, while not necessarily intended to work to the disadvantage of minorities, effectively does so.

Technological changes, which have altered the makeup of parts of the occupational structure, also work against minority employment. In recent years, new job areas calling for training and skills of an extensive and often esoteric nature have been created. Since educational resources and opportunities are disproportionately available to whites, some whites are in a privileged position to compete for such jobs. At the same time technological advances have enabled employers to cut back on or even eliminate certain positions, typically those that require limited skills. One sociologist has argued that automation, for example, will render much of the labor performed by unskilled African Americans obsolete and exacerbate their employment problems (Willhelm 1983).

Just as neither business nor government has seen fit to eliminate the employment difficulties facing minorities, so has organized labor served as an impediment (Gould 1977). In 2002, 13.3 percent of all U.S. wage and salary workers belonged to unions (U.S. Bureau of the Census 2004:431). Yet union membership and long apprenticeships are requirements for entry into the higher-paying skilled crafts and trades. People of color often have been—and still are—denied membership in many white-dominated unions. Discrimination in this area has meant that minority group members, even if they possess the skills, are locked out of contractual opportunities that would enable them to demand as much for their time and labor as unionized whites.

For example, African American contractors and subcontractors play a rather marginal role in the nation's construction industry, a very important sector of the U.S. economy. In 2001 new construction was valued at more than $842 billion, or over 14 percent of the U.S. gross national product. Yet only 609,000 African Americans were working in construction out of the industry's 9.7 million employees, and many were in unskilled jobs (U.S. Bureau of the Census 2004:404, 585). Racial discrimination in unions, combined with whites' maintenance of a "good old boys" network in contracting and hiring of subcontractors, poses significant obstacles to African Americans' employment opportunities in construction (Brimmer 1992).

Union resistance to minority enrollment is by no means total. In fact, a higher percentage of African American workers (16.9 percent) than white workers (12.8 percent) belongs to unions today, perhaps a reflection of African Americans' employment in the public sector, which has many unionized jobs. The figure for Latinos is like that for whites (11.1 percent) (U.S. Bureau of the Census 2004:431). But for the better-paying, more highly skilled jobs in the private sector, exclusionary practices by organized labor are another form of institutional racism.

The United States has a labor force of 130 million people. As one moves down the occupational and professional hierarchy, the percentage of persons with dark skin increases. As one moves up, it decreases. If we look only at the very top positions in business and government, we could hardly think that ours is a multiracial society. Through institutional racism, minorities are effectively kept at and toward the bottom of the employment ladder.

Many persons in the United States are under the erroneous impression that people of color have made great gains upward in the world of work in the last few decades as a consequence of government affirmative action employment policies. Many individuals have been helped, as those who had previously been excluded from particular workplaces have learned of opportunities and successfully competed for jobs (Lemann 1995). But voluminous data on employment and income also show that, whatever affirmative action policies have done for many individuals, the policies have not come close to equalizing the employment and income status of most people of color and whites in group terms (Bloch 1995; Hacker 1992). This is reflected in Table 7.3.

In 1995 the Federal Glass Ceiling Commission noted that while white males make up only 43 percent of the U.S. labor force, they constitute 95 percent of senior management at industrial and service companies. In the Fortune 1,000 largest industrial corporations, 97 percent of senior managers are white men (Federal Glass Ceiling Commission 1995; Killian 1995; U.S. Department of Labor 1991). Although there are white males who feel that they somehow face impenetrable barriers to employment and job mobility because of reverse discrimination based on their race and sex, and express anger over this, researchers have been able to find little evidence that such barriers actually exist (*New York Times* 1995b). Females continue to face unequal treatment in the labor market (see Chapter 8). Yet Chairwoman Mary Frances Berry of the U.S. Commission on Civil Rights, an independent federal watchdog agency on discrimination issues, readily acknowledged a fact that too often goes ignored: The principal beneficiaries of affirmative action policies have been white women (*Jet* 1995).

People of color, especially men of color, have a long way to go toward achieving employment equality with whites, and affirmative action has not proved to be a panacea. This situation should not be surprising, particularly given that the federal government largely abandoned active

Table 7.3	Family Income and Poverty Status, by Race/Ethnicity, 2001[*]			
	Distribution			
Family income	White	African American	Latino American	Asian American
Less than $15,000	8.0%	20.9%	16.8%	7.6%
$15,000 to $24,999	10.5	16.5	17.7	9.8
$25,000 to $34,999	11.6	14.0	16.2	9.6
$35,000 to $49,999	15.8	15.2	17.3	13.8
$50,000 to $74,999	21.4	17.4	16.8	19.7
$75,000 to $99,999	13.8	8.7	8.1	13.9
$100,000 or more	18.9	7.2	7.3	25.6
Below poverty level				
Families	7.4%	20.7%	26.2%	13.5%
Persons	9.9	22.7	22.6	12.6

[*]Data for Latino Americans are for 1993.

Source: U.S. Department of Commerce, Bureau of the Census, *Statistical Abstract of the United States, 2003* (Washington, DC: U.S. Government Printing Office, 2004), pp. 43, 458.

enforcement of its own affirmative action policies during the Reagan and Bush administrations (1980–1992) (Edsall and Edsall 1992). Since that time many white politicians have been exploiting public stereotypes about and fanning hostility toward affirmative action, crying "reverse discrimination" and even calling for its abolition. They usually do not, however, offer alternative approaches or solutions to continuing patterns of job discrimination (Kirschenman and Neckerman 1991).

Business Ownership

As a result of white domination of high-level positions, the concentration of people of color at the bottom of the economic ladder, and the reluctance of white employers to hire them, there has been much interest in encouraging minority-owned businesses as a means of improving the

economic situations of minority groups. After all, one way to make money and to struggle toward an improved economic position is through the ownership of a business. Minority business owners, so the theory goes, could hire persons in their own communities and thus improve the situation of their entire group.

But despite the interest in and excitement about minority-owned business, business ownership has not resulted in *group* improvement. When we examine business ownership in the United States, it quickly becomes evident that whites overwhelmingly prevail. Surveys by the U.S. Department of Commerce, conducted periodically since the late 1960s, continue to substantiate the same facts (U.S. Bureau of the Census 1971; see also U.S. Bureau of the Census 2004). In terms of their percentage representation in the population, people of color own few businesses. Moreover, minority-owned enterprises are likely to be small and to employ few people. Many are operated by the owner alone, while others also employ unpaid members of the owner's family. All minority-owned enterprises taken together account for only a tiny percentage of the nation's total annual business income.

A number of rationales have been offered to explain the small numbers of minority entrepreneurs and the economic insignificance of most of the firms owned by minorities. Some blame the victim, suggesting that people of color lack the interest and motivation necessary to succeed in the competitive world of profit making. Such explanations are clearly inadequate. It is not minority inability but rather institutional racism that has been responsible for the low rates of minority business ownership.

Starting a new business or expanding an ongoing one requires cash and credit. Unless an individual has a very substantial income and a large amount of savings, it becomes necessary to deal with banks. In the U.S. economy, the financial sector has always been overwhelmingly controlled and staffed by whites. The aspiring minority entrepreneur may be faced with direct rejection by unsympathetic banking officials, simply on the basis of group membership. But institutional policies—which are said to be totally unrelated to discrimination against minorities—often result in the same kind of negative outcome.

Banks and other lending institutions have a plentiful supply of competing white and minority applicants. They are most likely to extend loans to individuals whose economic success in the past renders them excellent credit risks, to those to whom money and credit have successfully been extended before, to those who possess property that can be put up as collateral against loans, and to those who can most easily demonstrate the probable profitability of their business project. On the average, these criteria are met more readily by whites than by minorities.

Thus, while half of white small-business owners are forced to completely finance estab-

lishment of their businesses with money of their own, the figure is 71 percent for African American entrepreneurs, 67 percent for Latinos, and 58 percent for Asian Americans. One study found that almost 60 percent of African American entrepreneurs believe they experienced bias when seeking loans (*Black Enterprise* 1993).

The federal government's Small Business Administration (SBA) has worked with members of the corporate and banking communities to aid minority entrepreneurs. The government has also made limited attempts to purchase more products and services from minority businesses and has urged its large corporate suppliers to do so as well. But these forms of aid, while receiving a great deal of publicity, have not resulted in any dramatic change in the magnitude of minority business ownership.

Indeed, SBA loans, despite the serious economic problems existing within minority communities, have remained modest in amount. One study by the Federal Reserve System indicates a substantial difference in small business loan denials to minority-owned businesses compared to white-owned businesses; the researchers noted that these differences remained regardless of several other variables, including personal wealth, and concluded that their results made it difficult to dismiss racial discrimination as a crucial factor (Cavalluzzo and Wolken 2002). Moreover, federal programs setting aside loan and contract moneys specifically for minority group members underwent sustained attacks by conservative politicians in the 1990s. These attacks were reinforced by a 1995 U.S. Supreme Court ruling placing restrictions on the government policy of giving preference to federal contractors who include minority subcontractors on their jobs (Greenhouse 1995). Thus the courts have begun to engineer an environment making it even more difficult for minority entrepreneurs to obtain assistance in building their businesses.

In the absence of a first chance to become involved in the business world, people of color are likely to remain shut out. It is like being turned down for a job because of lack of formal experience when one can gain such experience only by getting the job. The effect is that one goes nowhere, an experience many minority group members have grown to anticipate in dealing with white-owned economic institutions.

Political Powerlessness

In Chapter 2, "Concentration of Political and Economic Power," we stressed the close relationship between economic power and political clout on the national level. As we have seen, people of color are economically disadvantaged in comparison with the overall white population. Even more than most whites, they are light-years away from competing with the economic and political power wielded by the ownership class—the small segment of the population among whom wealth and income are concentrated. If, as we saw in Chapter 2, many members of the white majority feel powerless to affect national decision making, people of color must feel even more helpless. Minority groups are almost totally dependent on white power-holders for the initiation and enforcement of policies that might improve their life chances. To varying degrees, this situation of political powerlessness prevails right down to the state and local levels of government.

Government Employment

At the national level, African Americans and members of some other minority groups are currently well represented in terms of government employment. But whether we are speaking of the executive, legislative, or judicial branch of the federal government, this representation lies primarily in the lower-paying, nonpolicymaking positions.

Periodically, the U.S. Commission on Civil Rights has castigated various bodies of the federal government for discrimination in the operation of their programs and in their hiring and promotion practices. One of the commission's targets has been the White House itself. Over 1,000 presidential appointments may be made during a president's term in office. These include cabinet-level secretaries, undersecretaries, and assistant secretaries; other executive branch agency heads; U.S. attorneys; judges; and ambassadors. As recently as the 1980s the commission noted that few people of color "have been included in these top Federal Government policymaking positions during this Nation's history" (U.S. Commission on Civil Rights 1983).

During President Ronald Reagan's administration (1980–1988), for example, African Americans were chosen for fewer than 5 percent of the top-level presidential appointments in the executive branch (Pear 1987). Other people of color have fared far worse. As recently as 1992, the end of President George H. W. Bush's administration, only a handful of African Americans had been appointed to the presidential cabinet. (Bush, whose record of making few appointments of people of color rivaled Reagan's, made the controversial appointment of conservative African American jurist Clarence Thomas to the U.S. Supreme Court.) Presidential appointments of minority group members improved overall during President Bill Clinton's administration, and Clinton made two top-level appointments to presidential cabinet posts never before occupied by people of color (McCoy 1994). The visibility of minorities (if not the overall numbers) in high-level positions continued when President George W. Bush appointed Colin Powell as the first African American secretary of state in 2000, replacing him in 2004 with Condoleeza Rice as the first African American woman to hold that position. What is notable is that minorities remain so few in number in such positions that those who do hold these are conspicuous and identifiable by name.

Minorities are also underrepresented in key elected positions at all levels of government

Table 7.4	African American Elected Officials, by Office, 1970 to 2001				
	Total	U.S. and state legislatures*	City and county offices†	Law enforcement‡	Education§
1970 (Feb.)	1,469	179	715	213	362
1980 (July)	4,890	326	2,832	526	1,206
1985 (Jan.)	6,016	407	3,517	661	1,431
1990 (Jan.)	7,335	436	4,485	769	1,645
1991 (Jan.)	7,445	473	4,496	847	1,629
1992 (Jan.)	7,517	499	4,557	847	1,614
1993 (Jan.)	7,984	561	4,819	922	1,682
2001 (Jan.)	9,061	633	5,456	1,044	1,928

*Includes elected state administrators.
†County commissioners and councilmen, mayors, vice mayors, aldermen, regional officials, and other.
‡Judges, magistrates, constables, marshals, sheriffs, justices of the peace, and other.
§Members of state education agencies, college boards, school boards, and other.

Source: U.S. Department of Commerce, Bureau of the Census, *Statistical Abstract of the United States, 2003* (Washington, DC: U.S. Government Printing Office, 2004), p. 268.

(for example, see Table 7.4). While African American leader Jesse Jackson sought to break the pattern in 1984 and 1988, all U.S. presidents have been white, and the white-dominated major political parties have persistently avoided any attempts to alter that trend.

Only four African Americans have ever served in the U.S. Senate, and only one of those four has been a woman, Illinois senator Carol Mosely Braun, who served from 1993–1999. As of 2005, 42 African Americans were serving in the U.S. House of Representatives, a high point in representation. Only one African American was in the Senate: Barack Obama of Illinois who took office in 2005. Many representatives were from states that had not had an African American congressperson since post–Civil War Reconstruction! Although Latino American representation in Congress stood at a record in 2005 with 29 serving, that number is still small relative to the proportion of Latinos and Latinas in the United States. Eight members of Congress

were Asian or Pacific Islander, and only one was Native American (serving in the House of Representatives) (CRS Report for Congress, available at www.senate.gov/reference/resources/pdf/RS22007.pdf).

People of color who manage to get to Congress find that their numbers are far too few to allow them to wield much influence in the face of an overwhelmingly white majority of lawmakers. Although often expected to represent minority concerns, they can do little without the support of their white colleagues.

The situation is similar on the state level. The first African American state governor, L. Douglas Wilder, entered office in 1990. In 2001 the number of African American U.S. and state elected officials totaled only 633. Latino state elected officials numbered a third of that. Most state officials were from large metropolitan areas or resided in states where Latinos or African Americans constitute a significant proportion of the population (U.S. Bureau of the

Census 2004:263, 268). The situation facing other, smaller minority groups—for example, Native Americans and Asian Americans—is even worse.

In the last couple of decades, more than 30 cities with populations of 50,000 or more—including major cities such as Los Angeles, Minneapolis, Detroit, Chicago, New York, Philadelphia, and Atlanta—have voted African American mayors into office. To some this is evidence of the existence of growing minority political power. In actuality it reflects one outcome of the changing color of U.S. central cities, where many members of minority groups reside. Yet the signs of political arrival of groups long out of power must be placed in their full context.

African American mayors have been arriving in office in an era when very few resources are available from state and federal governments to help deal with city problems. Moreover, mayors, no matter what their color, must often confront the reality of an existing urban or metropolitan area power structure that acts as a "hidden government." This urban power structure is typically composed of whites who hold command positions in local (or locally headquartered) corporations and financial institutions such as banks. City governments are often highly dependent on this urban power structure to get anything substantial done, and such dependency limits the ability of mayors and other elected city officials to be responsive

People of color have yet to achieve significant representation in those governmental positions where important decisions affecting racial minority groups are made. The U.S. Congress, for example, whose members are shown here being sworn into office, remains a largely white legislative body.

to minority concerns and needs (Cummings 1988; Glasberg 1989).

This brief overview suggests the kinds of problems people of color confront in getting their concerns expressed and dealt with through our political system. Yet we have left aside the whole question of the *quality* of the representation minorities have achieved. As in the area of employment generally, at least some of those who manage to make their way into key political positions progressively lose identification with their minority constituencies.

Fearing that failure to adapt to majority views or practices will result in the loss of newly achieved power and prestige, they often let themselves become co-opted by or assimilated into the white-dominated political and governmental system. People of color who hold office may find themselves forced to mute their race-related concerns in the interests of accommodation and compromise with more powerful representatives of the white majority. If they press minority concerns too vigorously and are too unyielding, they may see their overall political effectiveness jeopardized. This too contributes to the dilution of minority political power.

Minority political representation has been further complicated by the electoral success of a small number of politicians of color who do receive white support and who are avowedly conservative on matters of particular concern to many minority group members, such as affirmative action, enforcement of antidiscrimination laws in employment and housing, public school desegregation, and elimination of bias in the criminal justice system and application of the death penalty. In the contemporary political environment, many white politicians are successful in gaining or retaining elected office while paying lip service, feigning indifference, or even expressing open hostility to minority concerns (Edsall and Edsall 1992; Rose 1992). The alliances they form with conservative representatives of color further diminish the likelihood that these concerns will be addressed.

It is important to point out as well that not all members of U.S. minority groups are in lockstep in terms of their political views. While, for example, public opinion polls on such issues as affirmative action or the death penalty often show sharp cleavages between African Americans and whites, there are African Americans who share the view of those whites who believe that affirmative action policies cause harm and that the death penalty should be imposed with greater ease and more frequently.

Likewise, in California, which we noted has a large Latino American and Asian American population, many members of these minority groups joined with the majority of whites to vote for Proposition 187, a controversial state referendum item restricting access to state-financed health care and education to legal immigrants and their families only. This proposition, rejected by the courts as unlawful would have cut off services from undocumented immigrants who have often been living, working, and paying taxes in the United States for many years, or who came seeking asylum from political repression and terrorist persecution in their home countries. Splits and divisions within (or between) minority groups may further dilute these groups' power vis-à-vis whites, as when minority group members' votes are directed to opposing positions in referenda and elections.

Voter Participation

The forces generating political powerlessness also include the lack of voter participation. For years exercise of the franchise by people of color lagged behind that considered normal for whites, a situation slowly undergoing change. Yet, as recently as 2000, 65.6 percent of eligible whites reported they were registered to vote; while the proportion of African Americans registered to vote was only slightly lower than that of whites (at 63.6 percent), only 35 percent of Latino and Latina Americans said they were registered. Even smaller percentages of each group reported having voted in 2000, a presidential election year (U.S. Bureau of the Census 2004:269).

A common explanation of lower minority voter registration and voting again blames the victim. Persons of low socioeconomic status and limited formal education—members of minority groups or not—tend to have little desire and energy to get involved in institutionalized political activity, especially because they believe that it is dominated by the more affluent and highly educated. This common phenomenon is exacerbated in the case of minority groups, whose members disproportionately fall in the lower depths of the class structure.

More to the point is the fact that many people of color in the United States have historically been faced with extraordinary resistance to their participation in the political system at any level—including voting. African Americans and other minorities have faced white-controlled election laws and rules designed to impede voter registration and the exercise of the franchise. Among these rules has been insistence that Native Americans and Latino Americans take literacy tests in English and the imposition of poll taxes on poor people who could not afford to pay them. Those who objected or sought to vote anyway were often subject to threats and acts of economic reprisal such as job loss. Gerrymandering has also been common; that is, white decision makers have altered district boundaries to keep minority group members from making up a majority of voters and thus influencing the outcome of elections.

In 1965 the U.S. Congress, appalled by flagrant violations of constitutionally guaranteed voting rights and under pressure from a militant civil rights movement, passed the Voting Rights Act. The act prohibits various procedures and devices intended to discourage registration and voting, provides for examiners and observers to keep an eye on local voting processes, and sets up channels through which citizens of color may seek redress when their rights are violated. The Voting Rights Act as passed in 1965 was primarily intended to protect the rights of southern African Americans. The act was extended to cover Latino Americans in 1975 and then amended to cover the entire nation in 1982. It has helped to eliminate many discriminatory practices, although Mexican Americans and other Latino/as have faced somewhat different problems in gaining political power than African Americans despite the Voting Rights Act (Skerry 1993).

Unfortunately, the presidential election in 2000 served to reinforce cynicism that the structure of politics was more inclusive and open now than in the previous decades. The election of George W. Bush as president was tainted by charges of racially motivated practices, particularly in Florida, that denied many people of color the chance to exercise their right to vote. Ultimately, the United States Supreme Court discontinued the inspection of votes cast as well as votes denied and pronounced Bush as the winner of Florida's electoral votes, a decision that decided the full outcome of the presidential election.

Many people of color were left feeling disenfranchised and disregarded by a political system that had institutionalized their oppression. Indeed, the 2000 presidential election underscored the need for greater diversity in Congress. The Senate had no African American members that election year and the House of Representatives had barely over three dozen. A Senate rejection of the Supreme Court's assertion of the Florida results would have required a single senator requesting a congressional investigation into that state's electoral process. One after the other, African American members of the House brought petitions from their constituents beseeching the Senate to launch such an investigation, but not one senator stood up to honor that request. It is difficult to ignore that an overwhelmingly white Senate ignored these pleas for a simple reassurance that the Supreme Court did not deny thousands of African Americans the constitutional right for their votes to count.

As a consequence of discriminatory practices and white domination of the voting population, people of color have long viewed elections with cynicism. Only relatively recently have representatives of numerically large groups—such as African Americans and Mexican Americans concentrated in urban areas or certain states—been successful in getting more minority candidates into elected office. And it has only been relatively recently that agencies of the federal government have provided protections and guarantees of the right to vote for those who had been manipulated or harassed out of the franchise for many years.

In sum, important decisions affecting the life chances of minorities are made for them, not by them. One outcome of institutional racism in the political structure is the continuing, sporadic outburst of militant protests directed against the abuses of the white power structure. Such outbursts can be seen as indications of the failure of this structure to incorporate or adequately respond to minority concerns.

Minorities and the Law

Existing laws, and provisions for the enforcement of these laws, have all been created by representatives of the white majority. In the past, law has actually been used to deprive minorities of rights taken for granted by white citizens. Discriminatory practices have continued even as such laws have slowly been repealed, and it has taken years of struggle by minorities and their allies to get new laws guaranteeing protection of their rights passed. The struggle to get such laws enforced is still going on in such areas as education, employment, and housing discrimination. It is no wonder, then, that many people of color have little confidence in law as a facilitator of their interests.

Minority discontent has been especially noteworthy in the area of criminal law and its enforcement. In part this discontent reflects minority treatment by police forces that are overwhelmingly controlled by whites. Discrimination in police recruitment, hiring, and promotion has been rampant, not only at the state and local level but even in federal law enforcement agencies such as the Federal Bureau of Investigation. This situation has undergone some change as minority group members have filed complaints and initiated lawsuits to demand enforcement of antidiscrimination laws.

Furthermore, people of color have long felt themselves to be the prime victims of police misconduct and brutality. Most police forces are not under the supervision of civilian review boards through which allegations of misconduct and brutality could be investigated by concerned citizens. The police investigate themselves when charges are levied, and in most cases this accomplishes little. Hence, predominantly white police forces have the freedom to exercise power over minorities—including the indiscriminate use of force—without a great deal of accountability (Cashmore and McLaughlin 1991).

Discriminatory treatment of people of color by white police officers may involve both personal and institutional racism. Personal contact with police in ghettos, barrios, and reservations has led to widespread hostility and distrust on the part of minorities. For example, in the aftermath of the urban rebellions of the 1960s, a presidentially appointed commission found that the major grievance voiced by ghetto residents was police brutality and harassment (National Advisory Commission on Civil Disorders 1968).

This brutality and harassment has been manifest in many locales to the point where it can be viewed as the expression of unwritten institutional policy, at times generating the kinds of responses seen in the 1960s. Between 1980 and 1991 the city of Miami experienced four major racial rebellions, the first of which resulted in 10 deaths, some 400 injuries, and property damage of $100 million. In each case

African American residents of Miami battled police officers in the streets. In three of the four rebellions the street violence was sparked by police killing or being acquitted for killing African Americans.

Then, in 1992, the United States experienced one of the most damaging urban rebellions in its history. It followed a suburban Los Angeles jury's decision to acquit four police officers who had been videotaped beating Rodney King, an African American man who was stopped for speeding. While the rebellion in south-central Los Angeles involved African Americans, Latino Americans, and people from other groups, most of those arrested were Latinos; 51 people were killed and 2,300 were injured, while the value of property damaged, plundered, or destroyed was $1 billion (Lacey 1992). Violence simultaneously occurred in other U.S. cities as well.

The problem is not limited to the actions and attitudes of individual police officers. Racism in the administration of justice, as elsewhere, is an institutionalized process. Prosecutors, judges, juries, prison personnel, members of parole boards—all tend to be white. Minority group members are commonly stopped and searched as a result of the criminal justice system's practice of racial profiling, accused of crimes, placed under arrest, denied bail or given higher bail, detained in jail before trial, forced to rely on public defenders for legal assistance, prosecuted, found guilty, given severe sentences (including the death penalty), and denied early parole more than whites (American Civil Liberties Union 2000–present Human Rights Watch 2000; Schauer 2003; Tonry 1995). While in prison minorities may be subject to racial denigration by guards and other staff, as well as by prisoners organized into white supremacist groups. Once out of prison, they are handicapped not only by an arrest record (and in many states the permanent loss of their right to vote) but also by the extra burden of discrimination in the labor market that even those people of color who have never been arrested must face.

All of this is made possible by minority political powerlessness and the continued exclusion of minorities from institutional positions from which more just and equitable policies could be fashioned.

Educational Deprivation

Formal education is not a guarantee of employment or security in our competitive, hierarchical society. But the lack of quality formal education, coupled with experiences of denigration and school failure, is likely to leave an individual in an untenable economic position. This is true for both whites and members of minority groups, but more so for the latter, given discrimination in the world of work. The burden of school failure disproportionately falls on children of color. Political powerlessness also means that many minority group parents have little or no control over how, what, and how much their children are encouraged or permitted to learn in school.

In considering institutional racism in education, we again come back to the question of power. Who holds the command positions through which decisions about education are made and resources allocated? In general, at the federal, state, and local levels, decisions regarding education are made by representatives of the white majority. Minorities thus find it enormously difficult to pressure educational systems to make them provide learning experiences commensurate with their children's needs. School segregation, limited educational programs and teaching resources, alienating curricula, and racist practices by school personnel contribute to the poor education of millions of children of color.

The Battle against Segregation

Not long ago, racially segregated public schools were maintained by whites with support from the society's legal system (U.S. Commission on Civil Rights 1981b). Tens of millions of minority group children passed through "their own" schools, while whites went elsewhere. Typically, fewer resources were allocated to the schools that served children of color, since it was not expected that they would go on to higher education or get jobs that required education. North and south, east and west, rural and urban, inequalities in school expenditures operated in the interests of children of the white majority, particularly the more affluent whites.

In 1954, after decades of legal battling by people of color and their white allies, the nation's courts were persuaded to address the question of whether school segregation was a denial of equal rights under the law. Court decisions such as *Brown v. Board of Education of Topeka* called for an end to dual school systems. They were followed up by civil rights legislation in the 1960s. The focus was primarily on educational systems in the southern and border states. Since then, white children and children of color have slowly been brought together under the same school roofs.

At first, court decisions and antisegregation legislation had little impact in the northern and western states. Only later did the courts begin to move against segregation in these regions, and less progress has been made than in the South. Where dual school systems have been found to exist, particularly in urban areas, white school officials have blamed this on uncontrollable population shifts and the movement of minorities into racially homogeneous ghettos and barrios. In most central city school systems of northern and western states, segregation has noticeably *increased* since 1954. Urban minority populations have grown, many whites have fled to the residentially segregated suburbs, and city "neighborhood school" policies have continued to perpetuate the racial isolation of minorities. Cities in the southern and border states have begun to develop in similar directions, even while denying intentional segregation practices.

Obstacles to Equal Education

Segregation is an important concern not only because it separates white children and children of color into two different worlds. The real problem regarding segregation involves the quality of education received by minorities as compared with whites. Public school systems rely heavily on local property taxes for their money. The flight of affluent families to the largely segregated white suburbs, the failure of government to take steps to control urban blight, and the movement of business and industry out of central city areas have all contributed to school fiscal crises. Educational costs—like everything else in recent years—have steadily gone up, and the revenues needed to meet these costs have failed to keep pace. Thus the city schools that serve many minority children often find that they cannot afford the kinds of programs and services commonly available in affluent white suburbs. Instead, they must make do with outdated physical plants and equipment, overcrowded classrooms, and limited curricular offerings (Kozol 1991).

Despite the increasing minority enrollment in central city schools, whites predominate in the running of most schools. From the school board, to superintendent, to principals, and often on down to teachers and counselors, minorities are underrepresented, and procedures for input from people of color are the exception rather than the rule. Members of the dominant white majority administer education to children whose backgrounds, cultures, and everyday life experiences in racially isolated communities are too often little understood and viewed as alien. Learning is unlikely to take place when understanding and respect are lacking (Irvine 1991).

Until quite recently, textbooks and other curricular materials were produced primarily for the children of the white Anglo majority and did not reflect the multiracial character of U.S. society and of the world population generally. Social studies texts either ignored the history and present status of minorities or implied that such topics were unimportant by their brevity of coverage. The implication was that only whites have said or done anything worth learning about. This encouraged and reinforced minority feelings of racial isolation and even of inferiority. Shortcomings in curricula have also extended to the ways in which peoples who live outside the white Western world are treated. The history and cultures of peoples of color in underdeveloped nations, for example, are still rarely dealt with fully and equitably, thereby again suggesting the notion of white superiority (Apple and Christian-Smith 1991; McCarthy and Crichlow 1993).

The commonly used IQ tests favor those students who have best mastered the vocabulary common in middle-class homes. Yet children of color are often channeled into one or another school program on the basis of their performance on such tests. Testing is used to place children in ability groups. On the average, minority group children tend to perform less well on the tests than those for whom they were originally designed, so they are generally shunted into groups set up for students with low measured ability.

Marian Wright Edelman has noted that African American children, for example, are disproportionately routed into public school classes for the "educable mentally retarded," or "EMR." As many as 1 in 30 African American children are in such classes. According to Edelman (1988:154), "A white child is twice as likely to be placed in a class for gifted students as in an EMR class; a black child is almost three times as likely to be placed in an EMR class as in a class for gifted students."

Ability groups are no secret to the children placed in them. Children of color are likely to take their placement seriously and doubt their own potential and intelligence. School personnel also tend to view children in low-ability groups as inferior. Such a view may be expressed through attitudes toward the children or through the use of curricular materials that demand very little of them. The result is a self-fulfilling prophecy, as white school personnel demand little from minority group children, teach little, and find that their students learn little (Losen and Orfield, 2002; *New York Times* 1990; Oakes 1985).

Institutional racism in education fosters failure. The performance of children of color, on the average, tends to be below grade level when compared with children of the white majority. Minority group children have higher suspension, expulsion, and dropout rates than their white counterparts. Proportionately fewer students of color go on to higher education. The inadequate educational preparation many receive along with family financial problems contributes to lower rates of college completion for those who do manage to go on. All these outcomes, in turn, intensify the economic disadvantage that people of color face in the labor market, and the circle closes.

Although the Supreme Court's 1954 *Brown v. Board of Education* decision determined that racially segregated schools were inherently unequal, the reality of segregation continues today. In Connecticut, for example, the case of *Scheff v. O'Neill* argued that Hartford's largely African American and Latino/a schools were denying students an education equal to that of students in overwhelmingly white suburban schools. The case highlighted an even more fundamental problem that reproduced racial discrimination: Discriminatory housing practices and patterns in effect resulted in two Connecticuts—one poor and minority, clustered in the state's urban areas; the other white and middle class and affluent in the suburban communities. Decades of banks' practice of redlining the cities for mortgages and real estate practices of steering people of color away from suburban developments meant that local school populations were highly unlikely to be racially diverse, and that urban schools were unlikely to have strong enough budgets to provide adequate educations to their students. The courts ruled that the state was required to seek remedies to this unacceptable situation, prompting a program of specialized magnet schools to attract white students into the cities. Yet, as of 2004, the state had not sought remedies to the problem of housing discrimination and the magnet schools' ability to diversify the local schools was mediocre. Much work obviously remains to correct the problem of segregation and institutional educational and housing discrimination.

Notably, education may be an important element for upward mobility and opportunity, but it is not enough. Even those who do attain higher levels of education are not necessarily guaranteed an equal economic return to their education. Although everyone enjoys the greater likelihood of higher average incomes from higher levels of educational attainment regardless of race, whites clearly gain a greater benefit than African Americans and Latino/as (see Figure 7.2). This suggests that access to educational opportunity is important for people of

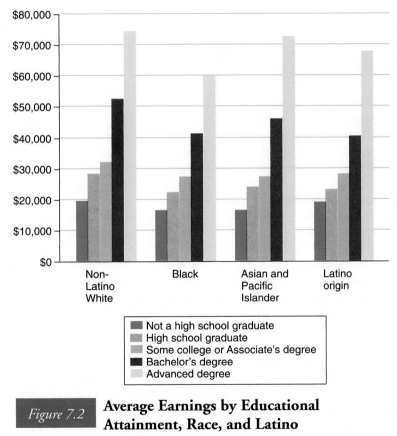

| Not a high school graduate
| High school graduate
| Some college or Associate's degree
| Bachelor's degree
| Advanced degree

Figure 7.2 **Average Earnings by Educational Attainment, Race, and Latino Origin, 2002***

*Data are for all workers, 18 years and older.

Source: U.S. Department of Commerce, Bureau of the Census, *Educational Attainment in the United States, 2003.* Current Population Reports P20–550, (Washington, DC: Government Printing Office, June, 2004), p. 7.

color to be able to access better employment and income opportunities; but educational attainment is not sufficient to explain the gap in average annual income between whites on one hand and African Americans and Latinos/as on the other. Institutional racism continues to affect this gap, despite individual efforts and investments in their own educations.

When discrimination is so embedded in institutions because of centuries of institutional practice and structures, how can these be interrupted and changed? One way that the U.S. policymakers have sought to do so is through affirmative action. Let's look at what that means, and doesn't mean, and how it has worked.

Affirmative Action

In 1961 President John F. Kennedy issued an executive order requiring that companies receiving federal funds take positive steps to rid their employment practices of racial bias. This order, known as **affirmative action,** was later expanded by the federal government to include discrimination based on gender, in both employment and educational opportunity. Affirmative action was to be a temporary mechanism for "leveling the playing field" by ensuring that prospective employers and educational institutions engaged in a good faith effort to identify qualified applicants, particularly among those groups who were previously underrepresented or absent among their employees or students. That effort included not just identification of already qualified candidates, but also enactment of steps to make those qualifications more accessible to underrepresented groups. The policy also mandated that employers and educational institutions develop goals and timetables to correct past racial gender imbalances.

If the intent was to wipe away discrimination, why institute a policy that appeared to some to institute a new form of preference? President Johnson pointedly addressed this in a graduation speech at Howard University in 1965:

You do not wipe away the scars of centuries by saying: "now, you are free to go where you want, do as you desire, and choose the leaders you please." You do not take a man [sic] who for years has been hobbled by chains, liberate him, bring him to the starting line of a race, saying, "you are free to compete with all the others," and still justly believe you have been completely fair. . . . We seek not just freedom but opportunity—not just legal equity but human ability—not just equality as a right and a theory, but equality as a fact and as a result. (www.infoplease.com)

While some may have lauded affirmative action as a measure to level the playing field and ensure equal opportunity, others saw it as a form of **reverse discrimination** giving unfair preference to less qualified candidates of color because of past discrimination, and penalizing more qualified whites (and often males) for past practices that they felt had nothing to do with them. By 1978 Alan Bakke sought help from the Supreme Court to strike down affirmative action as discriminatory against whites. Bakke had been rejected twice from the University of California's Medical School at Davis, and he argued that the school's practice of reserving 16 of its 100 places in the incoming class for minority and economically disadvantaged applicants discriminated against him on the basis of his race. His claim was effectively one of reverse discrimination. The case became a landmark challenge to affirmative action. The Supreme Court determined that race was a valid factor to be considered in the admissions process, but that the school's use of a finite quota was not constitutional. The case established that while affirmative action remained a legitimate strategy for interrupting past patterns of institutional discrimination, quotas were not. The challenge has become one of balancing the need to redress past discrimination while avoiding the imposition of quotas. Indeed, the use of quotas actually held the potential to limit the success of affirmative action by allowing employers and educational institutions to define how few people of color they would have to accept in order to comply with the letter of the law if not the intent. Once that quota was filled, they would no longer have to make good faith efforts. Thus, although opponents of affirmative action had hoped the *Regents of the University of California v. Bakke* case would end affirmative action and what they saw as reverse discrimination, the case ironically helped to define more carefully how the measure was to operate.

Affirmative action continues to be challenged by court cases. In 1995 four white applicants to the University of Texas Law School repeated the claim of reverse discrimination when they were rejected. They asserted that they were rejected in favor of less qualified minority applicants. The complainants in the *Hopwood v. University of Texas Law School* case challenged the legitimacy of the school's position that its affirmative action program served a "compelling interest" in establishing a diverse student body. The Supreme Court upheld a lower court's determination that the school's admission policy goal of a diverse student body was not a legitimate or compelling state interest, thus ending the use of race as a factor in admissions processes in Texas.

Although critics of affirmative action saw the *Hopwood* case as a major victory, the victory was short-lived. By 2003 the Supreme Court once again was confronted with a challenge in the *Grutter v. Bollinger* case against the University of Michigan's Law School admissions policies. Once again, the legitimacy of the goal of a diverse student body was at issue. This time, however, the Supreme Court ruled that race

could indeed be included among a whole range of factors considered in producing a diverse student body, a goal the Court deemed "compelling." What the Court did not find acceptable, however, was the university's practice of awarding additional point values to individual minority applicants. The Court thus reaffirmed the validity of affirmative action to redress past patterns of group discrimination while identifying individualized practices that were unacceptable in reaching the goal of diversity and equal opportunity.

Clearly, affirmative action is a lightning rod in debates about racism in the United States. It raises questions concerning the very meaning of a "color-blind" society, and whether such a thing is possible without federal policies to alter past practices of discrimination that are now embedded in institutions. It raises the question of the meaning of a "temporary" legislative solution and the definition of success and therefore the end of the policy: Are we there yet? Is affirmative action no longer necessary? And it raises the question of the very meaning of discrimination and reverse discrimination: Is it possible for there to be reverse discrimination unless those previously denied opportunity are actually in control of the institutions and resources that matter? Considering that there is no shortage to the challenges to affirmative action that continue to work their way through the judicial system to the Supreme Court, these questions have yet to be resolved.

Racism and Society

The economic deprivation, political powerlessness, and educational inequality fostered by institutional racism have consequences for the society as a whole as well as for members of racial minorities. In this section we spell out some of the costs white people in the United

States pay for the institutionalization of racism. We then look at minority responses to racism and their effect on U.S. society. Finally, we consider some proposals for change.

The Costs of Racism

It is obvious that institutional racism makes it extremely difficult for members of racial minorities to achieve in economic, political, and educational spheres. But racism also has negative consequences for *whites,* whether they are active practitioners of or allegedly innocent bystanders to minority subordination (Bowser and Hunt 1981).

Because of institutional racism, minorities have been regularly denied resources and excluded from opportunities through which they could more fully develop and display their human capabilities. That is, racism arbitrarily restricts the development and utilization of vast amounts of human talent. This talent could be mobilized in the interests of society as a whole, and its restriction means a loss to us all.

Racism ultimately translates into monetary costs as well. Taxes paid by both whites and people of color must be diverted to deal with conditions that institutional racism has helped create and perpetuate. Since unequal educational opportunities, employment discrimination, and the movement of business and industry out of central cities have meant high levels of joblessness and depressed wages for minorities, tax money must be diverted to pay for family income assistance and other forms of aid. The ghettoization of poor minorities and the abandonment of central city areas by affluent whites are components of what has been called the urban crisis. A great deal of tax money must go into central cities just to keep them functioning. Despite their flight, whites cannot escape paying for the urban stagnation afflicting cities across the country.

Then there are the unmeasurable psychic costs to whites. Historians of slavery have commented that the slaveholder's own sense of security and freedom was circumscribed so long as he restricted the freedom of others. Knowing that rebellion and acts of retribution were constant possibilities, he always had to look over his shoulder and remain ready to protect himself or his property. More than a century after the formal abolition of slavery, majority-minority relations in this society still give rise to white anxiety and fear. Racial conflict—and the possibility of further racial conflict—has led to massive investments in police forces and other instruments of social control.

Racism divides our society. It provides a channel through which members of the white majority can release their frustrations. Minority groups have been said to play the role of lightning rods for the dissatisfactions that whites feel they must somehow express. Since minorities are disadvantaged in terms of ability to fight back freely, they provide a relatively easy target. But the problems that frustrate many members of the white majority—economic difficulties, political powerlessness, and so on—are similar to those people of color face. Racism prevents whites from seeing how much they have in common with minorities; it obscures the fact that all might gain by cooperating and uniting. Intergroup conflict and distrust along racial lines mean that the dissatisfactions of many whites are expressed downward—toward powerless groups that are not responsible for the problems. In the meantime, the handful of whites who hold economic and political power and who make decisions affecting all those below them benefit from racial disunity. Through a conscious or unconscious divide-and-conquer strategy, societal elites can subtly use racism to the disadvantage of everyone else.

As sociologists Joe R. Feagin and Hernan Vera (1995:9) have noted, racism is a form of societal waste: "Americans should see white racism for what it actually is: a tremendously wasteful set of practices, legitimated by deeply embedded myths, that deprives its victims, its perpetrators, and U.S. society as a whole of much valuable human talent and energy and many social, economic, and political resources."

Although institutional structures that reinforce racism are formidable, they are not unchangeable. Social movements have resisted and challenged these structures and the social practices and cultural repertoires they inspire. It is to this question of resistance and change that we now turn.

The Inspiration of Minority Responses

People in the United States have long believed that "white is beautiful." People who neither look nor act as if they are full-fledged members of the dominant white majority have continuously been kept aware of their "disability." To be permanently stigmatized by virtue of color and culture, to be dealt with as inferior and systematically subordinated, may easily cause individuals to doubt their own self-worth. If such doubts are internalized, they lend support to white dominance by making people of color believe that they deserve inequitable treatment (Pettigrew 1964).

In the past some social science literature has portrayed minority peoples as mentally crushed by racism (Grier and Cobbs 1968). In many individual cases, this is no doubt true. But the portrayal of such peoples as mentally or spiritually crushed is a distortion of reality when applied to members of minority groups generally. It is another version of blaming the victim—of considering racially oppressed groups as incapable and thus responsible for their continuing economic, political, and social disadvantage vis-à-vis whites.

In fact, of course, we can hardly help but be inspired by the emotional and spiritual health of people of color in the face of racism. Millions of men, women, and children have revealed the extraordinary ability of human beings to endure imposed hardships. Though many individuals have been crushed by these hardships, overall, Native Americans, African Americans, Latino Americans, and Asian Americans have survived generations of subordination, denigration, and material disadvantage and have organized and struggled to assert their worth. Despite all that has been done to them historically, such groups have continued to battle for even the smallest gains toward equality with whites (Medoff and Sklar 1994).

Ironically, one rarely considered consequence of racism in the United States has been the development of social movements that continue to inspire many persons who seek social change, no matter what their color. The contemporary feminist movement, gay rights movement, and disability rights movement, for example, have drawn inspiration from struggles by African Americans, Latino Americans, Asian Americans, and Native Americans for civil rights.

The Civil Rights Movement

The most famous struggle by people of color against racial discrimination is the African American civil rights movement of the 1950s and 1960s (Ashmore 1982; Franklin and Massis 2000). In 1954 the efforts of such groups as the National Association for the Advancement of Colored People (NAACP) culminated in a Supreme Court decision outlawing segregated public schooling. Although it would be years before the decision would begin having any substantial impact on the education of racial minorities, it did signal a new era in U.S. race relations. Once the Supreme Court ruled that segregated schools denied African Americans their constitutional rights, it was obvious that discriminatory voting laws and segregated public facilities, housing, transportation systems, and workplaces had to go.

One day in 1955, in Montgomery, Alabama, an African American seamstress named Mrs. Rosa Parks refused to give up her seat in the front of section on a segregated city bus so that a white man could sit. Inspired by her arrest, over 50,000 African Americans soon joined a boycott of segregated public transportation in that city; and after a yearlong struggle, the buses were desegregated. This protest demonstrated that segregation could be fought by grassroots collective action. And it turned a leader of the Montgomery protest, Dr. Martin Luther King, Jr., into a national civil rights figure.

Inspired by the success in Montgomery, groups of African Americans and their supporters slowly began to test other resistances to desegregation both in the South and in the North. By the early 1960s, this testing had begun to take on the characteristics of a national social movement, led by such groups as the NAACP, the Congress of Racial Equality (CORE), the Student Nonviolent Coordinating Committee (SNCC), and Dr. King's Southern Christian Leadership Conference (SCLC). Peaceful marches, boycotts, and sit-ins against segre-

gationist practices captured public attention nationwide. The response to civil rights demonstrations was frequently violent. Incidents of harassment and terrorism were directed at both African American and white civil rights advocates, in some cases resulting in tragic deaths. Many people in the United States were outraged, and the incidents thus resulted in increased public support for civil rights.

In 1963 over a quarter million supporters of the civil rights movement staged a dramatic march in Washington, D.C. There, movement leaders such as Dr. King called on the public and federal officials to support new legal measures that would force an end to segregation. The immediate outcome was the passage of new federal civil rights legislation—most notably the Civil Rights Act of 1964 and the previously discussed Voting Rights Act of 1965. African Americans and other people of color could now appeal to the law when faced with racial discrimination.

Civil rights demonstrations in the late 1950s and 1960s resulted in considerable public support for legislation to protect the rights of minorities in the United States.

Unfortunately, the new legislation did little for African Americans who resided in the nation's urban ghettos. If anything, the sense of isolation and hopelessness among many ghettoized African Americans was inflamed. It had become clear to many that outlawing discrimination was not the same as upgrading ghetto schools, eliminating poverty and inferior housing, reducing police brutality, and providing decent employment opportunities. In the mid-1960s African American ghetto communities began to erupt in rebellion from coast to coast, largely sparked by incidents of white police brutality and then, in 1968, by the assassination of Dr. Martin Luther King. The United States' "race problem" took yet another turn as the civil rights movement began to splinter.

Groups that had long battled for desegregation and integration, such as the NAACP, maintained their commitment to such goals and continued to solicit white support. CORE and SNCC, on the other hand, began to reject white participation in their activities and called for "Black Power" (Allen 1969; Hamilton and Carmichael 1967). Basically, this meant that African Americans should collectively strive to take over those white-dominated institutions that directly affected their lives. It meant community control of schools, local political apparatus, police departments, economic endeavors, and social services. As CORE and SNCC began to mobilize support for Black Power, more militant African American organizations began to emerge in ghetto areas. The most well known was the Black Panther Party. To the Panthers, racism was the immediate enemy, but its roots were to be found in the capitalist makeup of U.S. society. The ultimate goal to be pursued was not desegregation or even community control. The goal was the abolition of capitalism and the creation of a socialist alternative (Foner 1970).

The ghetto rebellions that rocked the nation each year from 1965 to 1968 and the growing political militancy of segments of the civil rights movement alienated many whites. At the same time, the more moderate elements of the movement lost the one charismatic leader with white support, Dr. Martin Luther King. In the wake of his death, the already segmented civil rights movement began to founder.

Between the mid- and late 1960s, the federal government used a carrot-and-stick approach to ghetto discontent. Limited funds were poured into new federal programs, like the War on Poverty and the Model Cities Program, that were designed to foster the impression that ghetto problems were being addressed in concrete ways. Simultaneously, federal agencies such as the FBI—along with local police departments—began to systematically harass and disrupt both the militant and the moderate civil rights groups (Blackstock 1976; Garrow 1983).

By the early 1970s the civil rights movement was in a state of disarray. Many members of the white majority lost interest in the continuing plight of racial minorities. Other national issues, such as military involvement in Southeast Asia and economic recession, overshadowed racism. The gains of the civil rights movement were substantial—especially when measured against the harsh treatment of the recent past. But since the early 1970s little has been done to further improve the life chances of people of color, largely as a consequence of a white backlash against their efforts and demands for change (Neubeck and Cazenave 2001; Quadagno 1994).

In the last decade or so, civil rights organizations that remain committed to desegregation have concentrated on two key issues, neither of which has drawn a great deal of support from whites. Attacks on employment discrimination through legal efforts to bring about affirmative action in hiring have proved threatening to many whites and an anathema to most white politicians. Attacks on urban school segregation have also aroused white concern, if not outright resistance.

Most recently, the civil rights movement has begun to turn its attention to issues of economic justice, including the pursuit of controversial *reparations*. Proponents of reparations argue that slavery stole untold millions and perhaps billions of dollars of resources generated by slave labor and redistributed these to white slave owners. Over the course of many generations, this has meant a widening wealth gap between whites and blacks as the original unearned wealth of whites grew and the undeserved deprivation of African Americans deepened. Meanwhile, the segregation of African Americans from white schools compounded the loss by denying generations of blacks the skills and education necessary for upward mobility. The reparations movement seeks to redress this deprivation and denial by investing federal money in support of better educational, housing, and employment opportunities for African Americans (Robinson 2001).

After an era of conflict and minority advance, African American–white relations seem to have settled into an uneasy holding pattern. The subordinate position of the African American population—as well as that of Latino Americans, Asian Americans, and Native Americans—has only been eased by the successes of the civil rights movement, not eliminated.

Toward a More Equal Society

The elimination of personal and institutional racism will benefit not only people of color, but also the white majority. Racism and its consequences ultimately harm everyone.

Attacks against racism must take place on two levels. First, racist ideas must be attacked and discredited. Ideas alleging the inferiority of people of color, no matter how subtly they are stated, are inevitably used to justify their denigration or to rationalize minority disadvantage.

Second, attacks must also be made on practices that—whether intended to do so or not—contribute to the subordinate status of minorities. This means fighting discrimination and exploitation wherever they appear and pushing for affirmative institutional practices that will upgrade and enhance equal opportunities for people of color. Movements to end school and housing segregation and to put an end to discrimination

in employment must once again become as energized as the 1960s civil rights movement. More people must join or create collective efforts against racism, if only out of a self-interested desire to avoid sharing in its costs.

We must not lose sight of the fact that many of the problems facing people of color are matters afflicting tens of millions of white people as well. Poverty, hunger, substandard schooling, unemployment, and poor housing or homelessness are not solely or even primarily minority problems. As we saw in Chapter 6, the vast majority of poor people in the United States are white. By pushing for societal changes, such as a reduction in economic inequality and the expansion of free or low-cost services, the plight of many whites as well as people of color can be measurably improved. Cutbacks in spending on welfare, education, health, and other social programs that are pushed by political conservatives, at times motivated by or intended to play upon racist sentiments, in actuality impose substantial harm on whites as well.

Under the prevailing order, improvement in the social, economic, and political position of minority groups is often portrayed as a threat to whites. The assumption is that whites will sustain losses if minorities make gains in employment, education, and politics. This will continue to be a problem so long as we believe that competition for existing resources and opportunities is part of the "natural order." We need to begin ignoring the color line, so that people with common wants and needs can develop strategies for change through which all can gain. This means white people and people of color must cooperate with one another and form coalitions across group lines. The only losers should be those whose inordinate power and privilege depend on maintaining racial antagonisms and preserving the status quo.

Summary

The multiracial character of U.S. society grows more apparent every day as a result of immigration and natural population increases. By the year 2050, an estimated 40 percent of the U.S. population may be members of minority groups. Racist practices currently engaged in or tolerated by members of the white majority and white-controlled institutions, if allowed to continue, place U.S. society on an explosive course.

Native Americans, African Americans, Latino Americans, and Asian Americans are among the minorities that have been subjected to harm by the dominant white majority. Members of such groups have experienced personal racism, as expressed by individual or small groups of whites, ranging from social slurs to white supremacist terrorism. And they have been victimized by institutional racism. The routine operations of white-dominated institutions continue to function to minority disadvantage. This treatment of people of color has often been rationalized by so-called scientific theories that allege they are genetically inferior. Such theories have no basis in fact, but they provide an intellectual climate for the perpetuation of personal and institutional racism.

Institutional racism operates in the area of employment. Hiring and promotion practices are often subtly discriminatory—for example, the use of criteria that favor whites as a result of the superior educational and economic advantages they often enjoy. Those who hire or appoint people to key positions are usually white men, and they tend to choose people who are like themselves and who will "fit in." Consequently the labor market is divided along racial (and gender) lines. The primary labor market, consisting of the more desirable occupations, is largely populated by whites. The secondary labor market, where wages are low and jobs less secure, is the one in which people of color are most likely to find work.

As antidiscrimination laws, including affirmative action, have brought the most blatant discrimination to an end, many individual minority group members have been permitted to move upward in the job hierarchy. But in *group* terms, Native Americans, African Americans, Latino Americans, and members of some Asian American groups have not made significant gains. Factors other than those mentioned help account for this. The white flight of business and industry out of central cities has made it increasingly difficult for ghettoized minorities to find satisfactory employment. Technological changes threaten the existence of unskilled and semiskilled jobs in which many people of color are concentrated, while opening up jobs requiring specialized skills for which whites are disproportionately prepared. Exclusionary practices by white-dominated unions have helped keep people of color out of the better-paying skilled crafts and trades. Finally, minorities who want to open their own businesses have been subjected to discrimination by banks and other financial institutions. The limited efforts to aid minority entrepreneurs in recent years have not resulted in any dramatic improvement in minority business ownership, and even these efforts are increasingly under fire by those who demand an end to "racial preferences."

Institutional racism also operates in the political sphere. Minority employment in government is primarily in the lower-paying, non-policymaking positions. At the national level, few people of color have been appointed to public office, and few hold elected office. Minority political officials find themselves outnumbered and pressured to limit expression of race-related concerns. Some progressively lose identification with their minority constituencies, thus further diluting the political power of people of color. Until quite recently, minority group members were even discouraged from voting by racist practices. Now that voting rights are protected by law, minority voter activity has been on the increase and more people of color hold office. But important decisions affecting the life chances of minorities continue to be made *for* them, not *by* them.

In comparison to the dominant white majority, with some notable exceptions minorities are educationally deprived. Segregated schooling continues, and urban fiscal crises exacerbate the problem of financing education for the ghettoized on a level with that of white suburbs. Whites continue to dominate in the administration of educational programs at the federal, state, and local levels. Within educational systems, children of color are often taught by persons who have little understanding of or respect for their culture and experiences. Curricular materials have suggested white superiority by their failure to reflect the multiracial character of society, a situation only recently undergoing some change. Testing practices that favor the environmental advantages experienced by many whites are still used to assign minorities to low-ability classes. Once there, differential treatment leads to differential learning and performance. School failure intensifies the disadvantages that people of color face in the labor market.

Institutional racism harms people of color, and it hurts whites as well. Racism restricts the pool of talent from which society as a whole could benefit. It forces tax expenditures to rise in order to counter the human outcome of unequal educational opportunities, unemployment, and poverty: crime, drug abuse, family discord. Racism leaves whites with anxiety and fear in relating to people of color and stirs the possibility of racial conflicts against which investment in police forces and other forms of social control must be made. Finally, racism divides our society. The common problems both whites and people of color face tend to be obscured. Those whites who hold economic and political power benefit from racial disunity, consciously or unconsciously using a divide-and-conquer strategy to the disadvantage of everyone else.

Despite the harm done them, minority groups have not been mentally or spiritually crushed. Indeed, their historic struggles for survival and equality with whites have revealed the extraordinary ability of human beings to endure imposed hardships. One consequence of racism has been the development of social movements—for example, the civil rights movement of the 1950s and 1960s—that have inspired many persons who seek to bring about changes in U.S. society. The gains of the civil rights movement were substantial when measured against the past, but much more effort is needed to eliminate the subordination of people of color.

Attacks must be made against racist ideas, as these are inevitably used to justify the denigration of minority groups or to rationalize their situations of disadvantage. Moreover, attacks must be made on personal and institutional practices that—intended or not—subordinate minorities. Many of the problems facing people of color are faced by tens of millions of whites as well. Efforts to deal with poverty, hunger, substandard schooling, unemployment, homelessness, and poor housing will relieve the plight of many whites—not just people of color. The only whites who stand to lose from attacks against racism are those whose power and privilege depend on maintaining racial antagonisms and preserving the status quo.

Key Terms

Affirmative action 226
Ethnic group 197
Genocide 198
Institution 207
Institutional racism 204
Minority or minority group 198
Model minority 209

Personal racism 204
Race 198
Racial formation 198
Racism 198
Reverse discrimination 226
Scapegoating 204

Discussion Questions

1. A childless white couple wishes to adopt a child. The demand for healthy white infants has outstripped the supply, but several children of color are available. What arguments could be made for and against the adoption of a minority group child by whites?

2. Two applicants—one white and one a person of color—are equally qualified for a professional job opening. What arguments could be made for and against giving preference to the minority applicant? If preference is not given, how will the under-representation of people of color in the professions ever be altered?

3. If you are white, discuss your feelings about being in a social situation in which you are the only white person present. If you are a person of color, discuss your feelings about being in a social situation that is wholly white. In both cases, discuss the sources of your feelings.

4. At predominantly white campuses across the country, it is common to see students of color gathered in peer clusters. For example, all–African American tables in cafeterias are not uncommon. How does one account for this informal segregation? Is it desirable or undesirable? How so?

5. Some years ago, a movie depicted changes in the life of a white man who woke up one morning and found he had turned black. If you are white and this were to happen to you, what would your reactions be? If you are a person of color and you were to wake up white, what would your reactions be? In both cases, discuss the change in life chances and opportunities that your color alteration could entail.

6. If, as we noted in this chapter, racism harms whites, why don't more whites see the struggle against personal and institutional racism as in their self-interest? Under what conditions could this situation change?

Suggested Readings

Bowen, William G., and Derek Bok. *The Shape of the River: Long-Term Consequences of Considering Race in College University Admissions* (Princeton, NJ: Princeton University Press, 2000).
A myth-shattering empirical analysis of the effects of affirmative action and race-sensitive admissions policies.

Chideya, Farai. *Don't Believe the Hype: Fighting Cultural Misinformation about African Americans* (New York: Plume, 1995).
A question/answer guide addressing misconceptions and racial stereotypes that are often reinforced by the mass media.

Feagin, Joe R., and Melvin Sikes. *Living with Racism* (Boston: Beacon Press, 1994).
Documents the significance of racism in the everyday lives of African Americans who occupy positions in the middle class.

Feagin, Joe R., and Hernan Vera. *White Racism* (New York: Routledge, 1995).
Case studies and interviews focusing on the dynamics of racism in U.S. society today.

Kivel, Paul. *Uprooting Racism: How White People Can Work for Racial Justice* (Philadelphia: New Society Publishers, 1996).
Insights and practical advice for whites who oppose racism and wish to take actions to combat it.

Massey, Douglas, and Nancy Denton. *American Apartheid* (Cambridge, MA: Harvard University Press, 1993).
Sources and consequences of the racial segregation and ghettoization of people of color that characterize U.S. central cities.

Ross, Stephen L., and John Yinger. *The Color of Credit: Mortgage Discrimination, Research Methodology, and Fair-Lending Enforcement* (Cambridge, MA: MIT Press, 2002).
Empirical analysis of racial disparities in mortgage lending and the implications this has for wealth inequality.

Schauer, Frederick. *Profiles, Probabilities, and Stereotypes* (Cambridge, MA: Belknap Press, 2003).
Explores the meaning and consequences of racial profiling in criminal justice.

There should be no personal and institutional discrimination against individuals on the basis of sex.

In earlier chapters we examined several distinct patterns of inequality, each of which is an integral feature of the overall structure of this society. We saw that the unequal distribution of wealth, income, and educational opportunity divides people in the United States into separate classes. Political power is concentrated in the hands of a few, and decisions about the nature and course of U.S. society generally serve the interests of the dominant economic class. Institutional racism creates further cleavages within the population, subordinating people of color and obscuring the problems many different groups have in common. Such macro problems adversely affect the life chances of millions of persons, young and old.

Yet another pattern of inequality limits life chances—the pattern of sex inequality. Women are a majority in numbers, constituting slightly over 50 percent of the U.S. population; but they are a minority group in treatment, in that they are socially, economically, and politically disadvantaged in comparison to men. The fact that women are collectively disadvantaged and are thus a minority group is still not fully accepted (see Hacker 1951). Many men and some women greet this idea with derision, even while acknowledging that there are certain costs associated with being born female.

In this chapter we look at the minority status of women in the United States. We first consider the phenomenon of sexism and the myths that back it up. The chapter then goes into the economic and political effects of sexism—for both women and men. Finally, we consider the goals, gains, and future hopes of the feminist movement as it attempts to alter women's subordinate status in all spheres, public and private.

The Meaning of Sexism

Sexism is the systematic subordination of persons on the basis of their sex. In the United States, sexism limits females to very circumscribed roles, based on the belief that **biology is destiny.** The notion that biology is destiny

239

suggests that women's and men's different reproductive roles and hormones predetermine things like intelligence, strength, temperament, size, leadership abilities, emotions, and the like (Amneus 1979; Fausto-Sterling 1985; Goldberg 1973). This belief has been perpetuated and instilled in women through everyday socialization practices, and the subordination it calls for has been carried out in male-dominated institutions.

Male Chauvinism versus Institutional Sexism

In Chapter 7, we drew a distinction between personal and institutional racism. A somewhat parallel distinction can be drawn between male chauvinism and institutional sexism. **Male chauvinism** is exhibited at the level of interpersonal relationships. The term refers to attitudes and actions through which individual males display their sense of superiority over women. For example, by using such slang terms as *chick, fox,* and *bitch,* men place women metaphorically on the level of animals. Other terms, such as *broad* for *woman,* refer to things, or properties, rather than human beings. Statements such as the male-to-male query "Are you getting any?" segment human relations into genital relations, a process more directly expressed when women are entertained (or paid) for the sole purpose of sexual exploitation.

Within the home, male chauvinism is expressed in other ways. Many men refuse to perform routine housekeeping tasks, such as cooking and cleaning. After all, they worked hard all day (the implication is that their wives or partners did not), and besides, such activities are women's work. Women who work outside the home commonly find that they are expected to work a "double day" and bear the burdens of housework as well (Hochschild and Machung 1997). It is also not uncommon for a man to insist that a woman bear full responsibility for contraception, or that she be at her mate's beck and call to satisfy his sexual whims. In our culture, "a man's home is his castle," and since few households have paid servants, the "little woman" must often suffice. Women who work outside the home are often expected to be cheerful coffee-brewers and desk-top straighteners for busy men. Working women may have to put up with being eyed and ogled or subjected to pats and chucks under the chin by friendly males (Schroedel and Steinberg 1985). At annual office holiday parties, the real reason behind the year's paternal or playful pats is sometimes expressed more directly. To refuse to play along, or to get upset, can put a woman's job in jeopardy, even with established policies against such actions in place. Men may dismiss a woman's outbursts of fury and resentment over being subjected to these indignities (which few men would silently endure) with comments such as "Where's your sense of humor?" or "It must be that time of the month." Women who aggressively challenge expressions of male chauvinism are likely to be accused of being sexually frustrated, frigid, or lesbians.

Chauvinist attitudes and actions reduce women to objects or to servants catering to the self-defined physical and emotional needs of men. Not all men are chauvinists. Some chauvinists do not recognize themselves as such. Others freely admit their chauvinism but seem not to understand that their attitudes and actions degrade women as people. On the other hand, not all women chafe under the separate and unequal role into which chauvinists place them. The definition of male chauvinism as sexist (and, indeed, the term itself) is a relatively recent phenomenon. It is attributable largely to the consciousness-raising effects of feminism, wherein women sensitive to sexism have encouraged such sensitivity among others.

As annoying and difficult as male chauvinism is, **institutional sexism**—the subordination of women built into societal institutions—has far greater implications. Institutional sexism has proved to be just as pervasive as male chauvinism, if not more so. While male chauvinism operates at the level of interpersonal relations, institutional sexism is more on the level of ongoing organizational routine. In the economy, in politics, and in education, women are systematically treated in a manner that institutionalizes and increases their disadvantage vis-à-vis men. As we shall see later in the chapter, the outcome of institutional sexism for women is lower pay, occupational segregation, political underrepresentation, and public policies that fail to adequately protect or serve the interests of women. However, institutional sexism is often quite subtle and is less amenable to direct confrontation and attack than chauvinism.

Is Biology Destiny?

Both male chauvinism and institutional sexism are based on and justified by the ideology that biology is destiny. According to this ideology, basic biological and psychological differences exist between the sexes. These differences require each sex to play a separate role in social life. Women are the weaker sex—both physically and emotionally. Thus, they are naturally suited, much more so than men, to the performance of domestic duties. A woman's place, under normal circumstances, is within the protective environment of the home. There biologically determined physical limitations and emotional sensitivity are not deficits. Nature has decreed that women play nurturant, caretaker roles such as wife and mother, homemaker and confidante. On the other hand, men are best suited to go out into the competitive world of work and politics, where serious responsibilities must be borne. Men are to be the providers; women and children are "dependents" (Parsons 1955).

This view assumes that men will work and support women and children who remain in the home, a view that some sociologists call the **domestic code** (Amott and Matthaei 1996; Kessler-Harris 1980). It makes no provision for single, widowed, divorced, or abandoned women and their families. The ideology ignores the reality of role demands faced by millions of such women, not to mention all those married women whose husbands' earnings are so low as to force wives' participation in the labor force.

The ideology also holds that women who wish to or must venture outside the household should naturally fill those jobs that are in line with the special capabilities of their sex. It is thus appropriate for women, not men, to be employed as nurses, social workers, elementary school teachers, household helpers, and clerks and secretaries. These positions are simply an extension of women's domestic role as a supportive adjunct to men and their labor. Informal distinctions between "women's work" and "men's work" in the labor force, according to the ideology, are simply a functional reflection of the basic biological differences between the sexes. If women venture outside these working roles into male-dominated occupations and professions, they are often under pressure to renounce wifely and motherly opportunities.

The ideology suggests that nature works in another significant way. For the human species to survive over time, its members must regularly reproduce. Sexual attraction between potential mates is the first step in this necessary process. Thus, women must strive to fill the role of sex object to men. Whether at home or in the labor force, women must make the most of their physical appearance. The role of sex object (and, ultimately, full-time mother) is biologically allocated to women and cannot be lightly dismissed.

Finally, the ideology ignores the possibilities of homosexuality and assumes a fully heterosexual world. It sidesteps the reality that in our own society an estimated 1 in 10 persons is homosexual, while irrationally implying that homosexuals are violators of nature. It is such views that help to encourage and perpetuate homophobia, that is, fear of homosexuals and homosexuality (see Chapter 9).

Sex versus Gender

It is, of course, not true that basic biological and psychological differences between the sexes require each to play such sex-delineated roles in social life. Here it is appropriate to make a distinction between two concepts: **sex** and **gender.** When social scientists refer to sex, they mean the genetic and physical characteristics of persons that identify them as either male or female. Gender, in contrast, is a socially constructed concept referring to the culturally accepted behaviors and ways of relating to others expected of the two sexes. Gender is learned, whereas sex is biologically given. There is ample evidence that male and female gender roles vary from society to society, and those role differences that do exist are largely learned (Lorber 1994; Martin and Voorhies 1975; West and Zimmerman 1987). Since this is the case, they can be changed.

Empirical research, for example, calls into serious question the notion that biology is destiny. Anthropologist Margaret Mead (1935/1963) found evidence that the traits traditionally assumed to be determined by one's sex did not necessarily occur everywhere. She found three tribes in New Guinea where the behavior of men and women did not conform to expectations based on their sex. In two tribes, no sex-typed contrasts existed between men and women. In the Arapesh tribe, both men and women displayed the characteristics and behaviors commonly defined as feminine or maternal: concerned for the welfare of others, unaggressive, and cooperative. Contrast this to the Mundugumor tribe, where both men and women displayed characteristics commonly assumed as masculine: highly aggressive, ruthlessly competitive, and violent. And among the Tchambuli tribe, the characteristics of men and women were the reversal of common expectations: Women were dominant and responsible, taking the leadership role in managing family relations, while men were more passive, nurturing, dependent,

and emotional (Mead 1935/1963). If biology dictated men's and women's respective temperaments and abilities, even these departures would be unlikely in whole societies.

Historical evidence also refutes the assumption of women's abilities as limited by their reproductive biology. Research documents the crucial role of women as pioneers and homesteaders in colonial United States and its western expansion during the eighteenth and nineteenth centuries (Stratton 1982) and in prestate Israel in the twentieth century (Bernstein 1992), as farmers from the sixteenth to the twentieth century (Inhetveen 1998), as organizers and activists in the American labor movement (Dollinger and Dollinger 2000; Kingsolver 1989), and as industrial production workers during World War II (the icon of Rosie the Riveter) (Mandel and Sinclair 2002). Today, highly accomplished athletes like track and field icons Florence Joyner and Jackie Kersee, tennis champion Martina Navratilova, soccer stars Mia Hamm and Brandy Champlain, basketball champions Lisa Leslie, Cheryl Swoopes, and Rebecca Lobo, and figure skating Olympians Kristie Yamaguchi and Katarina Witt are simply the more notable among thousands of a growing number of athletes who happen to be women. The Olympics have witnessed a surge in worldwide interest in the accomplished athleticism among women, even in competitive sports where women were previously thought not to be strong or aggressive enough to participate, such as ice hockey. These varied, demanding, and dominant roles of women in key roles, making significant contributions to history and competing powerfully and successfully in athletics clearly challenge any assumption of women's limited abilities owing to their biology. That these roles could change over the course of history from ones of passivity and subordination to ones of dominance and substance also indicates that gender is a social construction.

Indeed, some researchers specifically talk about a conceptual line between the natural or biological aspects of gender that are unchangeable because they are rooted in biology and the artificial or political aspects that can be changed (Peattie and Rein 1983). Gender becomes defined through a political **claims process** in which the line between these aspects moves more in one direction or another. As such, when women organized and demanded the right to vote, the right to control over the reproductive process, or the right to equal pay for comparable worth, they were struggling to move the line toward recognition of the artificial constructions of gender that can be changed. That this line can be moved at all is evidence of the real limitation of biology as the defining and circumscribing factor affecting women's and men's experiences.

But to the degree people actually believe that biology is destiny and that nature intended for men and women to make different contributions to society, rigid sex-delineated gender roles will be seen as totally acceptable. Expecting women to remain in their place in the home, to limit their aspirations to "women's work" in the labor force, and to preoccupy themselves with sexual attractiveness to men will not be seen as oppression. Instead, such matters will be viewed as part of nature's grand design. Women who question their biological fate—who demand freedom from the roles that are prescribed for them on the basis of sex—are likely to be seen as deviants (Schur 1983).

If gender is a social construction, how is it that people learn how they are expected to behave based on their sex? How do we learn to do gender?

Socialization and Self-Concept

Women make up a numerical majority in U.S. society. Why have they, in general, accepted sexist treatment and allowed its ideology to be perpetuated? One answer lies in everyday patterns of socialization.

Early personality development hinges largely on experiences in one's family, and the meaning attached to sex group membership—both for men and women—begins in the home. At birth, children typically are dressed in either pink or blue—the initial uniform that sets girls and boys apart. Although infants cannot discern the message of these colors, adults can, and it is at this point that gender role differentiation begins. Parents actively impart their own learned and observed sense of what it means to be male or female to their children, thereby *creating* many personality and behavioral differences that would not otherwise exist. As one observer noted, "Girls are raised to 'keep the home fires burning.' Boys are raised to do battle" (Abbott 1998:1; see also Eccles, Jacobs, and Harold 1990). These differences, as they receive subsequent reinforcement through school and exposure to the mass media, help both men and women define their "place" in adult society.

Even such mundane aspects of the child's world as toys and games promote separate gender roles. Girls usually receive dolls (which they can "mother"), cooking and tea sets (to practice "housework"), and cast-off handbags and cosmetic kits (to practice being a "sex object"). Most parents encourage their daughters to develop traits associated with femininity. Aggressive behavior and fighting are discouraged; crying is acceptable. It is all right to be cute, coy, and flirtatious—an operational definition of what it means to be "daddy's little girl."

Conversely, boys are typically given tool kits and building equipment (to practice "work") and sports paraphernalia (so that they might develop masculine "toughness"). So-called feminine traits, such as emotional sensitivity, are discouraged. Aggressiveness, competitiveness, and a drive to excel are prized. The worst insult to a little boy is to say that he acts, sounds, looks, or smells like a girl. Most boys (and girls, for that matter) find it easier to live up to their parents' gender role expectations than to question or resist them. Fortunately, many parents are themselves becoming conscious of the negative impact of gender role stereotyping.

Parental influence is quickly supplemented by the experience of schooling. It is in school that children will have their first in-depth exposure to segregated toilet facilities and single-sex team sports (softball for girls, hardball for boys) (Thorne 1993). In many schools, girls get lessons in home economics while boys take shop. In the upper grades, girls wave pom-poms in support of the team; the boys bear the responsibility of fighting for athletic glory.

Throughout the schooling experience, curricular materials remind children of gender role differentiation (Lips 1989). Numerous studies of sex stereotyping in children's books and school texts have found women portrayed as mothers and housewives to such an extent that one would never guess that there are well over 67 million women currently employed in the labor force. History tends to be about men's accomplishments; social studies, the story of how men govern; and English, the literature and poetry of men (Boulding 1976). Girls cannot help but get the impression that women are not very important, at least not outside of the home, often with negative effects on their educational performance and aspirations (Sadker and Sadker 1994).

By adolescence, girls—having been sensitized to their gender identity by their parents and their school experiences—begin to have their first fears of human obsolescence (Henry 1965). They begin to ask "Will/do/why don't boys like me?" The drive for social acceptability, popularity, and recognition is constantly tempered by concern with what boys will think. Looks attract. But competitive accomplishments—physical or intellectual—can be interpreted as masculine and are likely to repel. It seems safest just to be a woman, a member of the "weaker sex"—a sexually attractive, sensitive, nurturant, supportive companion. Girls thus slip into "woman's place" as defined by the biology-is-destiny ideology. Since successful performance of the female gender role requires them to avoid competing with men, they can see themselves only as something less than men (American Association of University Women 1992; Orenstein 1994).

The Economic Effects of Sexism

The biology-is-destiny ideology might view the ideal woman in the United States as an industrious, happy housewife concerned only with laundry, dishes, children's snacks, and personal cleanliness. But this "ideal" is far from reality. Over the last several decades an ever increasing percentage of the adult female population has been taking on part-time or full-time employment outside the home. By 2002 more than 67 million women were in the U.S. labor force—almost 60 percent of all women over 16 (U.S. Bureau of the Census 2004; see also Reskin and Padavic 1994). Many of the women working part-time were doing so because of an absence of full-time employment opportunities.

For the most part, women work outside the home because of *economic necessity*. In 2002, 61 percent of all married women were in the labor force. Among women who were divorced from their mates or widowed, or whose spouse was absent, as many as 83 percent were in the labor force. Most of them had no choice but to become breadwinners for themselves and their families (Holden and Smock 1991). Finally, more than 67 percent of all single women were in the labor force; they needed means of self-support or had to contribute to their families' earnings.

The belief that women in the United States are not serious participants in the labor force, and that their earnings are merely supplemental, has been challenged by data demonstrating that 55 percent of working women provide *half or more* of their household income (Walters 1995). Additionally, women are not working at just one paid job, but often two and sometimes three.

Figure 8.1   **Civilian Labor Force Participation Rates of Married Women, by Age of Children, 1950–2002**

Source: U.S. Department of Labor, *Time of Change; 1983 Handbook on Women Workers* (Washington, DC: Government Printing Office, 1984), p. 21; U.S. Department of Commerce, Bureau of the Census, *Statistical Abstract of the United States, 1985* (Washington, DC: Government Printing Office, 1986), p. 399; U.S. Department of Labor, Bureau of Labor Statistics, *News,* September 7, 1988; U.S. Department of Labor, Bureau of Labor Statistics, unpublished tabulations from the *Current Population Survey,* March 1994; and U.S. Bureau of the Census, *Statistical Abstract of the United States, 2003,* p. 391, available at www.census.gov

Many of these women are building up their own businesses with income from another job (Hartmann 1994). The labor performed by women outside the household makes a significant contribution to our capitalist economy.

Nor has having children blocked millions of women from seeking work, despite the responsibilities of motherhood. (See Figure 8.1.) Most working mothers have families still living at home. In 2002 some 77 percent of married women with children under 18 and 61 percent of those with children under 6 were in the labor force. It seems silly to argue about whether mothers should be in the labor force—for they are there. The number of mothers employed would probably be higher if many women did not feel guilty about leaving the home (often because they have internalized the biology-is-destiny ideology), if there were more decent-paying employment opportunities for women, and if adequate and affordable child-care facilities were more widely available. The latter two factors particularly hamper women who are heads of households, and make it difficult for low-income mothers to escape poverty (Rank 1995).

A number of forces promise to propel more and more women into the search for employment in future years. Women are marrying later, so it seems likely that a higher percentage of single women will be looking for means of support. More effective means of contraception and a trend toward smaller family size mean that a higher percentage of married women will find it possible to break away from home and/or extend their stay in the labor force. Since divorce and separation rates have been very high in recent years, and since women, on the average, outlive men, an increasing percentage of women will find themselves living without a mate at some period during adult life. Many will require employment to sustain themselves and perhaps their children, and to earn rights to a minimum income when they reach old age. In sum, women's involvement in the U.S. labor force not only is here to stay but can be expected to grow—despite the ideology that woman's place is in the home.

Earnings and Job Opportunities

By 2002 over 144 million persons were in the civilian labor force in the United States; some 47 percent of them were women. What do women receive in return for their labor? By all indications, they get much less in return than men.

We can, for example, examine the median weekly incomes of full-time, year-round workers. When workers' incomes are broken down according to sex, we find that women, on the average, earned $511 a week to men's $672 a week in 2001. This gap between the median earnings of full-time male and female workers has been in existence for decades and shows little sign of dramatic change. What change has been evidenced has come as women's slight increases have met men's decreases in earnings. Thus, at the same time that women's participation in the labor force has been on the increase (primarily out of economic necessity), their economic standing has remained severely disadvantaged.

A further indication of the continuing discrepancy between the earnings of the sexes arises if we group the median weekly earnings of full-time workers by occupation and sex. In 2001 female managers and professionals earned only $732 per week compared with their male counterparts' $1,038 (see Table 8.1). Females in technical, sales, and administrative (including clerical) positions received $473, whereas males received $667. Women work, but they get comparatively little in return for their labor. Research also shows that the gender gap in wages grows even wider among higher-paying jobs than among the lowest-paying positions (Boessenkool 2004).

For the most part the low incomes of women are a result of the *types* of positions women hold. U.S. Labor Department statistics regularly show that men and women work in essentially separate markets, what sociologists call a **dual labor market** of male-dominated jobs (i.e., jobs in which the vast majority of workers are men) in one market and female-dominated jobs (where the substantial majority of workers are women) in the other. Women are grossly overrepresented in low-status, low-paying jobs—for example, clerical work and service occupations. In 2002, for instance, 53 percent of all working women were in jobs with the lowest median earnings (clerical, service, and sales). Conversely, women are underrepresented in the better-paying occupations. In 2002 only 19 percent of employed women held technical and professional jobs, and only 15 percent were in managerial, executive, or administrative positions.

Within occupational categories, the earnings of women are adversely affected by patterns of less work experience than men and less time in the position held than men. Nonetheless, it has been estimated that discrimination probably accounts for *over half* of the male-female pay differences (Blau and Winkler 1989). Despite four decades of affirmative action, upward mobility for women within the workplace is blocked by what is known as the **glass ceiling.** Women may rise through corporate or organizational ranks to an extent, but rarely rise to the highest ranks. White men, while only 29 percent of the workforce, hold about 95 of every 100 senior management positions, and the principal

Table 8.1	Median Weekly Earnings of Full-Time Wage and Salary Workers by Occupation and Sex, 2001

Occupation	Median weekly earnings	
	Men	Women
Managerial and professional specialty	$1,038	$732
Executive, administrative, and managerial	1,060	706
Professional specialty	1,021	749
Technical, sales, and administrative support	667	473
Technicians and related support	783	580
Sales occupations	692	429
Administrative support, including clerical	576	469
Service occupations	438	335
Private household	*	255
Protective service	658	509
Service, except private household and protective	374	332
Precision production, craft, and repair	648	479
Mechanics and repairers	670	594
Construction trades	613	437
Operators, fabricators, and laborers	501	368
Machine operators, assemblers, and inspectors	512	369
Transportation and material moving occupations	587	439
Handlers, equipment cleaners, helpers, and laborers	401	342
Farming, forestry, and fishing	366	308

*Not calculated. Number of persons in category is not significant.

Source: U.S. Bureau of the Census, *Statistical Abstract of the United States, 2003* (Washington, DC: Government Printing Office, 2004), p. 403.

reason for the barrier preventing women and racial minorities from advancing is "the fears and prejudices of white male executives on the lower rungs of the corporate ladder," who fear their own loss of power and opportunity (Kilborn 1995a).

The high concentration of women workers in low-paying and often menial positions and the gap between their earnings and those of men

holding similar jobs are not consequences of female biology. Clearly, not all women in the United States perform menial work at discriminatory wages. And in other nations women are far better represented in so-called men's occupations. Nor can these matters simply be attributed to differences in the educational attainments of women compared with men. For it seems that women in the labor force have, as a group,

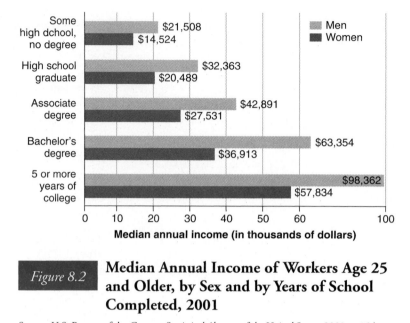

	Men	Women
Some high dchool, no degree	$21,508	$14,524
High school graduate	$32,363	$20,489
Associate degree	$42,891	$27,531
Bachelor's degree	$63,354	$36,913
5 or more years of college	$98,362	$57,834

Median annual income (in thousands of dollars)

Figure 8.2 **Median Annual Income of Workers Age 25 and Older, by Sex and by Years of School Completed, 2001**

Source: U.S. Bureau of the Census, *Statistical Abstract of the United States, 2003*, p. 154, available at www.census.gov.

completed approximately the same number of years of schooling as men. Women's investment in education does not pay off as much as men's. (See Figure 8.2.)

The disadvantaged position of women workers can be explained only in terms of institutional sexism. Women are the losers in a labor market that is segregated along sex lines (Tomaskovic-Devey 1993). Employers—for the most part men—have taken advantage of the biology-is-destiny ideology, treating women differently from men. Direct discrimination in employment, promotion, and pay works to keep women down, often despite their capabilities.

Forces Favoring Economic Subordination

The inferior economic position of women workers is obviously not to their advantage. On first glance, however, it appears to work to the advantage of men in the labor force. The direct employment discrimination that channels women into low-status, low-paying jobs and/or restricts their job mobility also lessens the competition men face for the better positions. In the absence of unlimited occupational opportunities (an absence exacerbated in periods of economic slowdown), there simply is not enough room for all at the top.

But it is more likely that men are hurt by institutional sexism in the world of work (Ehrenreich 1983). For example, discrimination against married women with children reduces family income potential and sustains the pressures on men to achieve economically. In this situation, men are certainly not benefiting from the continuation of sexist employment practices. Neither do they benefit when they must pay their divorced wives child support and/or alimony because the wives cannot earn enough to support themselves and their children. Such payments are a source of economic hardship for many men.

The presence of a large pool of low-paid women who could replace men for cheaper wages acts as a depressant on men's wages. Male workers are aware that they are not totally indispensable; if they are threatened with displacement by women who—out of financial need—are willing to work for less, they must temper their own wage demands. In addition, men who enter occupations currently dominated by women—for example, nursing, secretarial work, elementary school teaching—are likely to find their salaries depressed by the going rates for women's work. Thus, while on one level men generally enjoy benefits from restricted job competition and the subordination of women within the labor market, on another level they must pay the price for sexist practices.

But some men do benefit in this situation. By channeling women into certain types of jobs, restricting their mobility, and keeping their pay

Because existing laws and court orders have made it possible for some women to enter "men's jobs," many people believe that occupational discrimination against women has pretty much become history. But the presence of a small number of female firefighters, police officers, corporate executives, and jet pilots does not change the fact that sexist employment practices are still the norm in many fields and work settings.

low, employers can keep their labor costs down. Insofar as the cost of labor can be kept down, profits are enhanced. Since profit is the key objective requirement of economic institutions operating within the U.S. capitalist economy, the exploitation of women's labor (like that of other minorities) cannot simply be ended without disrupting many businesses and industries. Employers thus have a positive incentive—aside from whatever feelings they may have about women—to perpetuate sexist practices.

The fact that so many women work out of necessity also plays into the hands of employers. In the absence of full-time work opportunities and/or because they must care for their children, millions of women must take part-time jobs. This means being dependent on periodic, temporary, and often seasonal jobs, for which it is too costly to maintain a ready reserve of full-

time workers. In hiring women on a part-time basis, employers save money on such employee benefits as vacation pay, sick pay, and pension plans that full-time, year-round workers expect almost as a matter of right. They are thus able to exploit the fact that women constitute a large reserve labor pool, to be drawn upon at will and sent home when not needed.

In sum, institutional sexism in the labor market is an important force sustaining the success of our economy. As we have seen in past chapters, the benefits of this economy are appropriated to a disproportionate degree by the dominant economic class—primarily those who own and control business and industry. Sexism, then, harms women and has dubious advantages if not adverse consequences for male workers. But it is profitable to the dominant few, who are an important obstacle to its elimination.

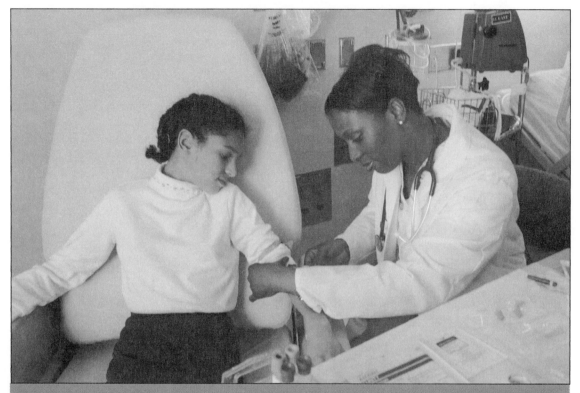

Though the occupation of registered nurse requires considerable training and skill, and though it has a great deal of importance to our society, nursing carries relatively low wages and relatively little prestige. This is a result of the belief that nursing is "women's work." Women have generally been forced to compete against one another in the handful of job categories open to them and wages for these occupations have generally remained low.

The Issue of Comparable Worth

While women and men receive different returns for their labor outside the home, under federal law persons who do the same work must receive the same pay regardless of their sex. This principle, established by the Equal Pay Act of 1963, has resulted in a number of lawsuits against employers and back pay to women employees. Between 1965 and 1976 over $135 million is said by the U.S. Equal Employment Opportunity Commission to have been owed to women who were underpaid in comparison with their male coworkers. However, because of lax enforcement, less than a quarter of this amount was restored to the women during that period (Greenberger 1980). Since then the Equal Pay Act has heightened awareness of discrimination against women in the area of pay, but, although a number of noteworthy settlements have been made, the government has continued to be lax in its willingness to pursue cases (Reskin and Padavic 1994).

As we have seen, the major obstacle to equal pay for women in the workforce is segregation into low-paying positions. These positions are "sex-typed," in that few men are employed in them. The U.S. Census Bureau maintains a list of over 500 occupational classifications.

| Table 8.2 | Women as a Percentage of Workers in Selected Occupations, 1975, 1984, 1992, and 2002 |

	Women as a percentage of total employed*			
Occupations	1975	1984	1992	2002
Airplane pilots and navigators	—	2.1	2.3	4.2
Architects	4.3	10.8	15.3	20.1
Auto mechanics	0.5	0.8	0.8	1.4
Carpenters	0.6	1.3	1.0	1.8
Child-care workers in private households†	98.4	97.4	97.1	97.6
Computer programmers	25.6	35.4	33.0	25.6
Data entry keyers	92.8	91.3	84.9	81.8
Data processing equipment repairers	1.8	9.4	10.4	16.7
Dental assistants	100.0	98.2	98.6	98.0
Dentists	1.8	6.2	8.5	19.4
Economists	13.1	39.6	43.3	55.0
Editors and reporters	44.6	46.2	49.7	48.5
Lawyers and judges	7.1	16.2	21.4	29.3
Librarians	81.1	85.9	87.6	81.7
Mail carriers	8.7	17.1	27.8	29.9
Physicians	13.0	16.0	20.4	30.6
Registered nurses	97.0	96.0	94.3	92.9
Social workers	60.8	64.1	68.9	74.0
Teachers, college and university	31.1	36.6	40.9	42.7
Teachers, elementary school	85.4	84.6	85.4	83.0
Telephone installers and repairers	4.8	8.2	10.4	15.9
Waiters and waitresses	91.1	86.3	79.6	74.9

*Employed civilians age 16 and over.
†Employment and Earnings, January 1993, lists two additional classifications of child care workers: "family child care providers" (98.7 percent female) and "early childhood teachers' assistants" (95.9 percent female).

Source: U.S. Department of Labor, Handbook of Labor Statistics, 1989 (Washington DC: U.S. Government Printing Office, 1989), Table 18; U.S. Department of Labor, Employment and Earnings, 23 (January 1976): Table 2; Employment and Earnings, 40 (January 1993): Table 2; U.S. Bureau of the Census, Statistical Abstract of the United States, 2003 (Washington, DC: Government Printing Office, 2004), pp. 399–401.

In data from the 2003 census, almost one-third of women workers are clustered in just *20* of 503 occupations with secretary, elementary school teacher, and cashier topping the list. Only 11 percent of women work in occupations that are 75 percent male. Table 8.2 provides an indication of the types of jobs women hold.

A single and simple measure of the level of sex segregation in occupations is the **index of segregation.** This index tells us what it would take to achieve an equal distribution of female and male workers throughout the occupational classifications. In 1990 the level was 53, meaning that 53 percent of women workers would have to move to predominantly male occupations in order to have full occupational integration (Reskin and Hartmann 1986; Reskin and Padavic 1994; Tomaskovic-Devey 1993)! Although analyses have not yet produced this index for the more recent 2000 census, the small movement on this gendered distribution of occupational categories suggests that this figure is not likely to improve substantially.

Those who would seek to improve the pay of women in sex-typed positions have come to argue that women's work is underpaid in comparison with men's work by any neutral standard. In 1981 the U.S. Supreme Court acknowledged the legal validity of a theory stating that "pay be equal not just for the same job but, for any given employer, for all jobs that call for comparable skills, effort and responsibility" (Hershey 1983). In other words, jobs that have **comparable worth** must be paid the same.

It is important to emphasize that comparable worth means much more than simply equal pay for equal work, such that men and women in identical jobs would be paid equally. This is already the law of the land, as stated earlier.

Comparable worth rests on the additional assumption that the work traditionally labeled "women's work" or associated with supposed special talents of women ought to be valued equally with those labors traditionally associated with men. For example, caretaking jobs, such as day-care workers, teachers, and nurses, ought to earn at least as much as jobs requiring the lifting of heavy objects or handling of machinery, such as digging ditches, driving trucks, and hauling garbage (Kelly and Bayes 1988:4; see also England 1992).

In effect, comparable worth or pay equity means raising the wages for those positions into which women have traditionally been channeled and segregated. Jobs that are comparable in terms of skill, effort, and responsibility would be paid the same whether men or women filled them. Under comparable worth, employers would have to develop job classifications free of gender bias and rank order them in terms of their worth and appropriate pay.

To date most of the work being done on pay equity issues has been occurring at the state government level. Women working for Washington, Minnesota, Connecticut, Iowa, New York, Massachusetts, Wisconsin, and other states have been the beneficiaries of progressive policies (see, e.g., Chi 1988). Both the federal government and the private sector have successfully ignored or resisted pressures to address comparable worth in their own workforces. Often it is believed that the pay gap dividing women from men is decreasing. It is. But at the current rate, equity in pay will not be achieved until the latter part of the century.

Given existing trends in women's employment opportunities and earnings, the U.S. poverty population may be made up almost wholly of women and children in the future. The failure of the U.S. political system to effectively combat the sources of sex segregation and pay inequities in the workplace not only helps to generate poverty but also ensures that many women will find it extremely difficult—much more so than need be—to climb out of poverty circumstances through gainful employment. Widely implemented comparable worth policies will not eliminate poverty, but they will help those women who are able to work outside the home and who are able to find jobs.

Laboring in the Home

As more married women entered the labor force and provided economically for the family, it was anticipated that men would increase their household responsibilities, but this has not been the case. A significant reason is that housework has always been regarded as "women's work" and men can draw on this belief in order to avoid or limit their participation in the household labor (Gerson 1993; Hood 1993). For the 24 million or 39 percent of married women who do remain at home, being "just a housewife" carries contradictory meanings that hide and devalue household labor.

We are all familiar with the daytime television version of being a housewife. TV commercials typically show young, fresh-faced, fashionably dressed starlets exuding enthusiasm over a product that has perfected the already immaculate state of their beautifully decorated homes. Mothers are shown in total control of their well-behaved, healthy children, blissfully enjoying their biological mission and accomplishing light tasks with playful ease (and the occasional help of a quick-acting drug). The imagery tells us that work is really something that takes place outside the home.

What this imagery ignores is the labor entailed in housework and its unrecognized value to the U.S. economy (Crittenden 2001; Ferree 1983). We can get a good idea of what is involved by imagining how much a husband would have to pay persons to perform the tasks that a wife and mother—in the paid labor force or not—does for free. He would probably have to hire a cook, a cleaning person, a chauffeur, and a baby-sitter or other child-care worker, or hire someone to manage the provisions of these services by others. He might require the services of a nurse, a psychologist, or an accountant. This husband would quickly find that his take-home wages were rapidly depleted when payday came for all his employees. He would have to conclude that his wife's work in the home has monetary value when someone other than a wife does it.

Domestic and child-care workers get paid very little for such tasks because, contrary to television imagery, they are perceived both as drudgery and as a trait that comes "naturally" to women. Most persons do not dream of being domestics—and for good reason. In the labor market, household workers are of low social status and receive the minimal economic rewards associated with the performance of "dirty work" (Romero 1992). Those who are child-care workers, even with undergraduate degrees in child development, are seen to do little more than babysitting and are rewarded accordingly.

Husbands who do not think of housework as a form of labor usually change their minds when, for some unexpected reason, they must temporarily or permanently take over the woman's role (Lamphere et al. 1993; O'Connell 1993). For it is not that housewives do not work. Rather, they labor *outside* the mainstream economy within which work is defined as an activity you are paid to do. Women who call themselves "just a housewife" implicitly recognize the secondary importance attributed to their labor.

In essence, housewives are contributing unpaid labor to the economy. This unpaid labor is a boon to employers. In its absence, husbands would be forced to demand far higher wages than they currently receive in order to pay for housekeeping and child-care services. They would have to take more time off from work, and they would be unable to work overtime. They would be less able to travel frequently, if their jobs demanded travel. So long as wives perform household and child-care tasks for free, employers directly benefit. By maintaining that housewives do not really perform useful work, and certainly not work that deserves wages, employers effectively get *two* employees for the price of one. Should housewives demand wages for the work that allows business and industry to have their husbands each day, the pursuit of profit would be seriously undercut. Again, success for members of the dominant economic class is sustained by women's separate and unequal status, a status celebrated by the biology-is-destiny ideology.

This same argument carries over to women who must work in a job outside the home for pay and then come home to a full-time job of unpaid household responsibilities in a **double** or **triple shift** (if they happen to hold two paying jobs). Because the burden of household labor (or the management of others who must be hired to do it) falls primarily on women, their own jobs and career paths are often constrained, to say nothing of their leisure time (Moen 1992; Women's E-News 2002). Businesses often punish women who try to balance motherhood and a career by channeling them into a **mommy track** that allows only limited upward mobility, while women struggle to maintain the day care and household backup they need to keep their careers in motion.

The Consumer Role

It has been estimated that women are responsible for 75 percent of consumer expenditures annually. Business and industry recognize this and gear billions of dollars in investments toward the production of commodities it is hoped women will buy. Commercial advertising is used to stimulate and elicit consumption, to convince women that they and/or their households simply cannot do without "product Z." Whether women really need these commodities, or are being manipulated into wanting them, is not a concern of business and industry. No matter what the reason, business and industry profit when commodities sell (Ewen 1976).

Sales appeals to women take place on two levels: subtle attacks on their sense of personal adequacy and messages designed to suggest ways to relieve the burdens of housework, further adorn the home, and demonstrate love and nurturance with the acquisition of desired objects for family members. The appeals tend to be written by men and play upon the roles allocated to women by the biology-is-destiny ideology.

Attacks on women's sense of personal adequacy revolve around the idealization of the role

The use of females as sex objects to capture the attention of consumers is a mainstay of advertising. In this photograph a woman is posed with a seductive wink while she suggestively sucks on a lollypop in an ad for a clothing line, although we can hardly see what she is wearing.

of sex object. Advertisers encourage women to worry about their skin, eyes, lips, hair, weight, shape, clothing, and odor. Commercial appeals both create and exploit women's doubts and fears regarding loss of sexual attractiveness. Simultaneously, manufacturers and advertisers provide solutions to the anxieties to which they contribute: Purchase more beauty aids and appliances, clothing, rejuvenating drugs, diet foods, and exercise machines. Immense profits ride on the comparisons women make between themselves and other women. For the woman who sees herself as "just a housewife" or who is functioning as a near robot in the labor force, consumption promises a way to gain a sense of self-worth and identity: At least she can try to emulate commercial standards of sexual attractiveness (Barthel 1988; Wolf 1991). If women were to discard such concerns and ignore commercial appeals, a whole sector of the economy would be disrupted.

The dissatisfactions caused by the burdens of housework provide another basis for consumption in the interests of private profit. By promoting doubts about the adequacy and efficiency of products and appliances currently in use and by singing the glories of new home commodities, advertisers take advantage of the wish to reduce housekeeping time and effort. They also push the idea that "other people do not live like you do" ("Whose wash is whiter?"), suggesting that women can gain self-esteem or raise their social status through improved performance of household labor or the purchase of home adornments that everyone supposedly has.

Advertising does not itself create roles for women. Rather, it serves to reinforce conventional gender roles and to then take advantage of them. Women are not the only targets of sexist advertising. The "macho" appeals to purchase "men's products" both promote and exploit male chauvinism. Such products are often sold by using women as sex objects to capture attention, implying to men that they can overcome doubts about their gender role performance through acts of consumption. Additionally, advertisers convey the promise that women can fulfill the emotional needs of family members for whom women are responsible through the purchase and use of the products and services featured. Thus social relations in the family themselves become commodities, adding another dimension to the sense of inadequacy women are encouraged to obsess over and on which profit interests ride.

The Political Effects of Sexism

The exploitation of women at work and at home, wherein they are cast into separate and unequal gender roles, is closely linked with women's collective exclusion from political power. We have seen in past chapters that political power is associated with wealth and economic influence and with being white. Political power is also associated with being male, and women's rights suffer as a result.

Women's Rights and the Law

The legal system in the United States only peripherally recognizes women's economic plight and their rights as citizens. A case in point is the Civil Rights Act of 1964. This piece of federal legislation was introduced into Congress to put the approval of the national government behind efforts to end discrimination against persons on the basis of race. Before the act was passed, a congressman who hoped to sabotage the bill jokingly added the word *sex* (Bird 1969). His effort to defeat the bill by making it ludicrous failed, and the provision against discrimination on the basis of sex became law. That a bill pertaining to civil rights should almost *accidentally* include women is an indication of how little lawmakers cared about the status of women even as late as the mid-1960s.

The difficulties women face in gaining legal recognition of their rights through the political system are most obvious in the efforts to add the Equal Rights Amendment (ERA) to the U.S. Constitution. This amendment would state: "Equality of rights under the law shall not be denied or abridged by the United States or by any state on the basis of sex." The Fourteenth Amendment to the Constitution has long guaranteed all U.S. citizens—regardless of race, creed, or color—equal rights under the law (the extension of these rights in practice is another question). But the Constitution does not protect persons who are treated differently under the law just because of their sex group membership. After 50 years of effort by women's rights groups, the ERA was finally proposed by Congress in 1972. To become law, it had to be ratified by 38 states. Organized resistance to the ERA has been widespread, and ratification by the required number of states has not occurred. Quite a few women are against the ERA, fearing that it means an end to alimony and the start of drafting women in times of war. As of this writing, the U.S. Constitution guarantees equal rights under the law to all U.S. citizens, so long as they are male (Mansbridge 1986).

Laws that specify different treatment for men and women remain in force in states and localities across the country. Many of these laws deal with employment and allegedly exist as forms of protective legislation; for example, there are laws restricting the hours and working conditions for women. Such laws contribute to the economic subordination of women discussed in the previous section, for they are used as excuses to keep women out of better-paying jobs and job opportunities.

In recent years the need to further women's legal rights has drawn ever increasing concern. Take, for example, the rights of rape victims. Rape involves the infliction of physical and psychological damage on the female victims—ranging in age from infants to the elderly—as men seek to demonstrate power over them in the rawest terms (Brownmiller 1975). Legal obstacles with sexist overtones can make it difficult for many women to prove they were raped, particularly in cases where men are free to interpret women's behavior so as to claim the victim invited and/or willingly participated in the sex acts in question. An estimated 1 to 5 percent of all rape cases actually reach the courtroom. Once there, it is often the rape victim who is put on trial, as defense lawyers use everything from a victim's use of contraceptive pills to her having a history of suffering abuse in an effort to

make the rape charge suspect (LaFree 1989; www.rainn.org).

The phenomenon of **date rape** or acquaintance rape has drawn attention to the fact that it is very common for rapists and victims to know one another. Studies on college campuses, for example, reveal that rape is more common than one could imagine. In one study of 600 students, 15 percent of the women and 7 percent of the men reported being on a date where sexual relations took place against the woman's will (Ehrhart and Sandler 1985; *Psychology Today* 1987). Few of these date rapes are ever reported and prosecuted, so there is little to deter the rapists from breaking the law again. Women students victimized by such sexual violence may even drop out of school.

Another women's rights issue is sexual harassment. Most research and efforts at intervention have focused on the harassment of women workers as well as women students. One definition is as follows:

Sexual harassment includes unwelcome sexual advances, requests for sexual favors, and other verbal or physical conduct of a sexual nature when submission to or rejection of this conduct explicitly or implicitly affects an individual's employment, unreasonably interferes with an individual's work performance, or creates an intimidating, hostile, or offensive work environment. (Conway, Ahern, and Steuernagel 1995:70)

Although declared a form of sex discrimination and thus illegal by the courts and the U.S. Equal Employment Opportunity Commission (EEOC), such harassment is extremely widespread. Following the 1991 confirmation hearings of Supreme Court Justice Clarence Thomas, in which his former employee Anita Hill testified to being sexually harassed by him, cases brought to the EEOC alone doubled over the next 2 years. But enforcement of laws and policies against sexual harassment remains weak and incredibly slow, punishment of those engaged in harassment is rare on average, and women must cope with fears of reprisal should they attempt to secure their right to be left alone. Many women waiting for their cases to be heard wind up jobless, in a lesser job, and generally despondent (Mayer and Abramson 1994; Megan 1994; Morrison 1992).

Thus, once again, even when legislation and court rulings are on the side of women, these may not be sufficient to deter sexist practices, and women may be deterred from seeking justice. However, in the case of Anita Hill, and the women who came forward to testify against Senator Robert Packwood of Oregon, women showed willingness to take a stand, even against members of the U.S. government.

A further issue bearing on women's rights involves prostitution. In cities and towns across the United States and around the world, women who are "in the life" must confront the threats of sexually transmitted disease (including AIDS), violence, and arrest (Monto 2004). Prostitution is a job, but one with some of the most hazardous and degrading working conditions. Key to the violence women face in prostitution are attitudes of male dominance and privilege and female inferiority, as well as perceptions of male power and control (Busch et al. 2002). Most women who become prostitutes are forced to do so because of financial desperation, drug addiction, and/or coercion by sexually domineering and economically exploitative males (Shifman et al. 2003). And it is an alienating job, one of any number of service occupations that women hold requiring them to feign pleasure with male customers for whom they may actually feel contempt. Yet even here women's rights are secondary to those of men. Women are arrested for prostitution; their male clients are likely to go free without charge. Women's suffering is the price of men's enjoyment, courtesy of the law (see Haynes 2004).

The multibillion-dollar industry of pornography provides an additional arena in which women's rights must be considered. Within this industry women are exploited by men for profit, as crass economic greed is harnessed to the gender role of women as sex objects. In many cases what would otherwise pass as erotica includes an emphasis on violence against women, thus suggesting to consumers that there is something sexy or arousing about physically mistreating females (Milburn, Mather, and Conrad 2000). Pornography, protected by law, helps to contribute to an overall societal environment in which all women must live in fear of assault (Gordon and Riger 1988).

Finally, there is the particularly controversial issue of women's reproductive rights under the law (Luker 1984). The right to have an abortion anywhere in the United States was granted by the U.S. Supreme Court in the 1973 *Roe v. Wade* decision. Women who choose to do so not only have been able to end unwanted pregnancies but, through abortion, have protected themselves from serious threats to their health and even their lives. Shortly after the *Roe v. Wade* decision, the nation's maternal mortality rate (deaths of mothers from pregnancy or from giving birth) dropped dramatically and has remained low. But in recent years women's reproductive rights have been under direct attack, particularly by those who share the biology-as-destiny ideology pertaining to women's "proper" gender roles (Klatch 1988). The loss of reproductive rights would have massive ramifications for women and their life chances, as well as for male-female relations in this society. Abortion represents an arena in which women may lose rights only recently won, as opposed to those areas we have mentioned in which women's rights under the law are in need of sensitive revision.

The trend toward restriction of women's access to legal abortions is being facilitated by the U.S. Supreme Court, a majority of whose members no longer consider this access a fundamental constitutional right. In 1989 the Court ruled in *Webster v. Reproductive Health Services* to allow each state to determine its own restrictions when it came to abortion policy. While falling short of overturning *Roe v. Wade,* the 1989 decision represented a fundamental shift in Court thinking about women's reproductive rights (Greenhouse 1989). There have also been increasing incidents of "domestic terrorism" at clinics, including shootings, bombings, and the stalking of clinic workers and others (*Ms.* 1995). Thus, women who wish to terminate unwanted pregnancies are finding it more difficult to do so. Already in some parts of the country women must travel hundreds of miles to obtain an abortion. Women who are ill or poverty-stricken are most likely to find the practical and legal barriers to abortion difficult to overcome. But all women are now finding their freedom to make choices about abortion undergoing restrictions. The ban on "partial birth" abortions in 2004 was seen by many as a major setback to the security of women's reproductive rights and likely to remain the focus of extended court battles in the next several years.

In an environment in which women's access to abortion is significantly restricted by law, those who cannot end unwanted pregnancies will find it more difficult to pursue needed education and training as well as work opportunities. The shortage of quality, affordable child care, the monetary costs associated with child rearing, and conscription into an undesired parental role will weigh heavily on many more women than now. Single women, including teenagers, will be at the greatest disadvantage in facing the competing demands of parenting while attempting to be economically self-supporting. Fewer married women will be able to work outside the home and more will be forced into part-time employment when full-time work actually is needed. The economic power of many women will be lowered, and they will be thrust into greater reliance on welfare assistance or husbands' earnings. As women are weakened economically, the gains they have made in recent years toward more independence and autonomy—particularly in breaking away from traditional biology-is-destiny gender roles—are likely to erode. Thus the barriers being erected to abortion are not simply a challenge to women's reproductive rights, but to women's human rights more generally.

Political Participation

The failure of this society's legal system to protect women's rights fully is due to institutional sexism in the political system (Hoff-Wilson 1987). We need only examine the composition of key political institutions to see one reason why the momentum of sexism continues.

On the federal level women fare poorly in terms of representation in those institutional positions through which the collective interests of women could be pursued. There has never been a woman president, nor have the Democratic and Republican parties ever seriously considered a female candidate. The vice presidency has also steadfastly remained a male post, although the choice of Geraldine Ferraro as the Democratic vice presidential candidate in 1984 was an unprecedented lowering of the sex barrier. Throughout U.S. history, and as of 2004, only 16 women have been appointed to White House cabinet-level positions. Two women have served on the U.S. Supreme Court.

In the House and Senate women are grossly underrepresented in terms of their proportion of the U.S. population. In 2005 there were 14 women senators and only 70 women representatives. All together, women constitute only 15.7 percent of Congress. The few women who manage to get elected to Congress find themselves handicapped by the informal "male locker room" nature of legislative wheeling and dealing, from which they are easily excluded. Most women in Congress have served relatively short terms (many temporarily replacing husbands who died in office); their lack of seniority has limited their ability to attain such powerful positions as chairs of important committees.

At the lower levels of the federal government, the picture remains similar to that of racial minorities. Both in appointed offices and in high-level career civil service posts, women are most notable for their absence. As might be expected, they are more than fully represented in the lowest employment positions, for example, as clerks and secretaries (Berheide 1992).

One cannot expect a male-dominated federal government—which *itself* appoints, hires, and advances men over women—to be deeply concerned about women's social and economic position in the society at large. The exclusion of women from central positions in the national political system renders them the weaker sex when it comes to having their concerns taken seriously and acted on.

The conspicuous absence of women continues on the state level. Only 25 women have ever been governors. Today women hold less important elective and appointed posts in state executive branches, but nowhere near their representation in the population. The same can be said with regard to state legislatures and judicial bodies. In 2004 women made up only 22.4 percent of state legislators (www.gendergap. com). But when there is typing to be done, there are plenty of women in evidence.

Finally, on the local level, the political presence of women improves somewhat. While, as of 2001, only 20 percent of the nation's mayors and municipal council members were female, some posts have been "reserved" for women (www.gendergap.com). For the most part, these are the poorly paid or volunteer positions on local boards deemed "appropriate" for women and found unattractive by many men.

But women do vote; the right was extended to them in 1920, after a long battle. Unfortunately, women are still not using the franchise to the fullest possible degree. Indeed, it was only in 1980 that the percentage of eligible women voting became similar to that of men.

Racial minorities and the poor tend to view politics as being dominated by the white and affluent (a realistic assessment); thus many have

avoided political activity, including voting. In a somewhat parallel vein, women have been encouraged to view politics as part of men's world, and many have restricted or narrowed the range of their involvement in it. But given the fact that women make up 52 percent of the voting population, the possibility of their making some impact through electoral power far exceeds that of other minority groups. It remains to be seen whether women can successfully mobilize this power by putting forth and electing candidates for office who will be more responsive to women's needs—particularly at the national level.

The Feminist Movement

With the development of the **feminist movement,** women's economic and political subordination has come under attack. Earlier in this chapter, we saw some of the reasons why this attack has been so long in coming. Women have tended to see themselves as separate and unequal. Attainment of economic and political equality with men requires the mobilization of personality traits and behaviors that females have been taught are unwomanly. Women have, in effect, been participants in their own oppression. But in the last four decades, under the stimulus of feminism, gender role differentials have been questioned by increasing numbers of women.

The Development of the Feminist Movement

Viewed historically, there have really been two feminist movements in the United States (Cott 1987; Flexner 1973; Friedan 1981). The first movement essentially entailed a 70-year struggle for the right of women to vote, culminating in 1920 with the passage of the Nineteenth Amendment to the Constitution. The women who led that protracted struggle often differed over other issues concerning women's place in a male-dominated society, including the treatment of women within the institution of marriage and within the world of employment. The one issue they were able to coalesce around and agree on was the desirability of women's suffrage. Once the vote was won, this first manifestation of collective political activism among women died off, leaving a period of quietude that lasted all the way up to the mid-1960s. The contemporary feminist movement, of which we shall take note here, took up an agenda of issues that had been left unresolved in the past.

Analyses of the contemporary feminist movement often start by pointing to the stresses that educated, white middle-class women had begun to experience by the 1960s. Increasing numbers of women had been going on for higher education in the post–World War II period but ended up either becoming housewives or taking low-level positions because they were barred from access to men's jobs. Whether at home or at work, women found themselves limited by male dominance—a situation they were expected to endure (Friedan 1984).

Events in the 1960s helped transform the generalized discontent of many women into overt forms of political expression. In the opening years of the decade, female college students became involved in the civil rights movement, the anti–Vietnam War movement, and other political change activities. In spite of their energetic contributions, female political activists found themselves routinely relegated to subordinate roles in male-dominated organizations. By the mid-1960s, many of these women had been struck by the irony: Here they were participating in struggles for minority civil rights and societal changes that were intended to better the life chances of others, while the conditions under which women in the United States were forced to suffer were being ignored. Female activists bridled under the gap between the progressive political rhetoric espoused by their male cohorts and the indifference of these men to their own sexism (Evans 1980). The resentments of politically active women were given impetus by the emergence of a new organization,

one primarily aimed at advancing the interests of educated, middle-class professionals. The National Organization for Women (NOW), founded in 1966, became instrumental in focusing nationwide attention on the subject of sex discrimination. NOW became, if not the voice of a feminist movement, a key consciousness-raiser of political issues with which women could easily identify.

From the mid-1960s onward, the feminist movement has consisted of a wide assortment of groups, ranging from NOW to entirely localized women's organizations and expanding to include women of color. All share common concerns with regard to the treatment of women in U.S. society. But beyond this, such groups reflect a wide spectrum of political perspectives as to just what women should be seeking.

Issues and Goals

In some ways, the term *feminist movement* is a misnomer, for there is not really one unified movement: Rather, there are several (Andersen 2003; Ferree and Hess 2000; Freeman 1973). Just as other minorities who have struggled in recent years to fashion goals and strategies for change have often split into different factions, so it is with women.

There is, first, the liberal feminist faction, perhaps best represented by such groups as the National Organization for Women. NOW is a predominantly white, middle-class group whose goals revolve around increasing the participation of all women in economic and political life. The focus is on integrating women into existing institutions and opening up more opportunities in education and employment. The liberal feminist faction accepts the prevailing societal order but seeks an end to discrimination against women within it. The strategists of NOW, for example, have concentrated their resources on political lobbying, legal battles against discrimination, and educational campaigns to awaken women's and men's consciousness and gain public support.

There are also additional, but much smaller, factions within feminism. Here one may identify two other distinct groups that see the need for far-reaching changes. The first group, the **radical feminists,** consists of women who define men as a collective "enemy" and seek liberation from all roles associated with male dominance. Marriage is considered a particularly oppressive social arrangement for women, placing debilitating restrictions on their potential for human self-realization. Thus, one goal of many radical feminists is the redefinition of the meaning of "family," making it possible for women to enter into relationships with other adults and children on their own terms. The emphasis is on the conscious creation of new roles by and for women—rather than acquiescence to those imposed by and in the interests of men.

A second group, Marxist or **socialist feminists,** sees capitalism, not men, as the enemy to be fought. Both women and men are viewed as victims of an economic system that exploits the labor of both sexes and that serves only the interests of the ownership class. From this perspective, to seek integration into the prevailing order is to accept and strengthen an economic system that deserves to be abolished; to see men alone as the enemy is to divert energies in the wrong direction. Thus, the goal of this group is to call the entire capitalist political economy into question, exposing its faults and encouraging men and women to join in the struggle for a socialist alternative. This goal flows out of the belief that sexism is an integral part of capitalism—in other words, that sexism is a requirement of a society in which those holding power put profit interests before the needs of people. This being the case, sexism cannot be abolished within the prevailing order nor can women truly be liberated within its confines.

The very existence of these factions within feminism points out a number of deeply felt concerns among a growing proportion of the U.S. female population (Ferree and Hess 2000; Jaggar 1983). Women are reacting to a sense of economic, political, legal, and social exclusion. (For women of color these issues intertwine with racial exclusion.) Many are highly dissatis-fied with present male-female and family relationships, within which women have been made to play separate and unequal roles. And there is a concern with the direction of U.S. society as a whole, a society to which both sexes contribute but from which neither seems to receive full human satisfaction. All told, the feminist movement has raised issues that bear on the future roles and well-being of all adults and children—male and female.

The Gains of the Movement

Institutional sexism—the systematic subordination of persons on the basis of their sex—simultaneously has been sustained by and has helped sustain the ideology that biology is destiny. The social, economic, and political disadvantages women face in comparison to men have begun to be addressed, however, and the ideology has begun to lose its power.

Feminism has made some notable gains. It has succeeded in making millions of people conscious of sexist ideas and practices. More and more women have become sensitized to the harm done to them in a sexist society and have been objecting to the gender-delineated roles in which they have traditionally been placed. Partly as a consequence, male-female relations—both outside of and within marriage—have begun to change. To some extent, socialization practices in the home and in school have begun to reflect this new consciousness of sexism. Finally, feminism has produced an ongoing struggle against sexism in the world of work and in the mass media (Ferree and Martin 1995).

But the forces that continue to promote sexism are impressive, and there is some question as to just how much change the existing feminist movement can bring about. This question is particularly relevant with regard to the position of women in the economy, within which sexist practices thrive under the incentive of the pursuit of profit. Insofar as concentrated economic power is crucial to the exercise of political power at the national level, the subordinate position of women in the economy is a major political handicap—just as it is for people of color.

In response to the feminist movement, women may well have gained increased verbal support of their rights. But this is not the same as granting an end to their collective subordination. Again, the struggle of racial minorities is instructive: Laws and constitutional amendments have done little more than legitimate their right to struggle for improved life chances; they have not granted such groups control *over* their life chances. And the gains made can be precarious and subject to erosion or reversal without continued vigilance and even further struggle.

Once more we return to the variable of power. Insofar as economic and political power continues to be concentrated in the hands of a few, insofar as women's separate and unequal position serves, for example, profit interests, and insofar as women are unable to wring concessions from those who benefit from their disadvantage, the movement to eliminate sexism from U.S. society is unlikely to go very much further than it now has.

But unlike the civil rights movement, feminism has not yet withered away, even though its limited successes are far outweighed by the continuing presence of institutional sexism and male chauvinism. Since women constitute over half the U.S. population, a large pool of uninitiated recruits remains available to become future movement activists. And because the feminist movement embraces a lengthy agenda of issues and permits a wide range of styles of expression, it offers a means of pursuing grievances by both women as well as many male allies from all walks of life.

The Question of Men's Liberation

Criticisms of male chauvinism and institutional sexism have also brought a number of men to question their own gender roles (Kimmel 1989, 1992). According to the biology-is-destiny ideology, men are supposed to be aggressive,

competitive, achievement-oriented, and decisive. They are expected to hide their emotions in favor of an impression of strength and toughness. As we have seen, socialization in the family and in school tends to encourage the development of personality traits and behavioral orientations appropriate to the male gender role.

But despite the opportunities and benefits that accrue to men in a sexist society, the role playing expected of them can be highly demanding. Not all men are equally capable of fulfilling the demands; not all men feel comfortable when playing the role. The responsibilities associated with "manhood" can be a source of stress, and many men feel doubts about their adequacy as lovers and providers. The requirement that they bottle up their fears, anxieties, and emotionality means that the tensions accompanying the male gender role may be difficult to dissipate.

Hence, while some men may find themselves threatened by the changing consciousness and more positive self-concepts being promoted by feminism, others would no doubt be relieved to give up acting out the pretense of male superiority. In recent years over 300 college courses in men's studies have emerged, focusing on issues men face, and there are several identifiable factions of what may be called a men's movement (Brooks 1991). More equalitarian interpersonal relationships, in which both sexes share in confronting the problems of living in the United States, should ideally *reduce* the burdens of being a man—not increase them (Kimmel and Messner 2003).

Hopes for the Future

Any approach to the elimination of sexism in the United States must be multifaceted. Not only must more women get involved in attacking sexism, but more men must also join the battle, if only to reduce the costs that sexism exacts from them.

The economic disadvantages suffered by women still remain to be aggressively

Women continue to perform much of the household and child-care labor in the family regardless of their employment outside the home. However, there are signs that in some families this is beginning to change. Here, a woman kisses her young children good-bye as she leaves for her paid job while her husband remains at home as the full-time homemaker and parent.

imperative. Expanding job opportunities would also mean a reduction of men's fear of competition as more and more women enter the workplace.

Accompanying these expanded opportunities must be an expansion of the availability of low-cost child-care facilities. Critics have argued that access to such facilities would contribute to family breakup by encouraging women to abdicate their motherly responsibilities. This is nonsense. Family well-being is more likely to be threatened by the inability of women to make use of child-care facilities so that they can help relieve economic burdens facing their families or so that they can escape the monotony of housework. Moreover, the shortage of child-care facilities places an enormous burden on women who are already heads of households and who must work outside the home.

The contribution of those women who must or wish to remain in the home must be recognized—in a more material way than simply celebrating Mother's Day once a year. It would not be unreasonable to alter the tax structure to provide annual family allowances to women, based perhaps on the full-time versus part-time nature of their household responsibilities and the number of persons being cared for. It has been proposed that we recognize housework as an occupation in order to bring women who are laboring in the home into the social security system. This alone would be a major step toward recognizing housewives' economic contributions. It would also help women of advanced age who were married but who cannot live on the benefits accrued by their husbands.

Expanding job opportunities and child-care facilities will not automatically end discrimination against women in the labor force. As with other minorities, a much more aggressive attack on discrimination and exploitation is required. At the national level, the U.S. Equal Employment Opportunity Commission has the responsibility for handling complaints from around the country

addressed. Women, along with racial minorities, have historically made their greatest gains in the workforce during periods of labor shortage (unfortunately, this has tended to be during times of war). Revamping the U.S. economy through governmental strategies to expand nonhousehold job opportunities is from women and other minorities. The resources allocated to this commission are so meager that aggrieved persons may have to wait *10 years* before any actions are taken (*Washington Post* 1995). There are also heavy backlogs of cases in state equal employment commissions. There is no point in having antidiscrimination laws if they are not going to be enforced quickly and effectively. The current situation ultimately discourages women, since those suffering from discrimination may assume that little good is likely to come from complaining about it.

The foregoing economic questions are clearly political ones as well, and it is thus important for more women and men to press for greater representation of women in political institutions. For starters, pressure must be placed on federal and state governments to practice what they preach and to ensure that women are appointed to top-level decision-making positions. More tax money (increasingly provided through women's labor force participation) must be allocated to programs for the improvement of the status of women. Over half the U.S.

population is female, and women's collective disadvantage is surely significant enough to justify the allocation of such resources.

The relatively few women who run for public office at the state and national levels often seem hesitant to stress the issue of sexism in their campaigns. Thus, an important opportunity to generate discussion and further educate the public is being missed. In the long run, underplaying what must be done by and for women contributes to the maintenance of institutional sexism. More discussion of the issue of sexism could also help persuade male candidates and incumbent politicians to take a more positive stand on women's rights.

Schools and colleges in the United States are an important source of knowledge about and attitudes toward sexism. Though more and more children and youth are being taught that biology is not destiny, students are not being taught how to confront and combat sexism. Schools could be part of the feminist movement, but they are not. Striving to make them so will, at the very least, rejuvenate and stimulate discussion of sexism—a prerequisite to change.

Summary

While women are a majority in numbers, they are a minority group because of their social, economic, and political disadvantage in comparison to men. Women are victims of *sexism*—the systematic subordination of persons on the basis of their sex. Sexism is displayed on one level through *male chauvinism*. This term refers to attitudes and actions through which males display their sense of superiority over women. On another level there is *institutional sexism,* wherein the subordination of women is built into societal institutions. Institutional sexism involves ongoing organizational routine in such areas as the economy, politics, and education.

Male chauvinism and institutional sexism are justified by the ideology that biology is destiny. This ideology holds that there are basic biological and psychological differences between the sexes requiring that men and women play quite different roles in social life. Women, allegedly the weaker sex, belong in the home or should perform only women's work in the labor force. In order for the human species to reproduce, they must strive to fulfill the role of sex object. Despite the claims of this ideology, it is not true that differences between men and women require each to play such sex-delineated roles in social life. Gender roles vary from society to society, and role differences are largely learned rather than biologically based.

Women's acceptance of unequal treatment and the biology-is-destiny ideology has primarily been due to everyday socialization practices. From birth, girls and boys are treated differently in the family as parents impart their own sense of what it means to be male or female. Gender role differentiation by parents helps create personality and behavioral differences that would not otherwise exist. Parental influence is supplemented by the experience of schooling. From sports activities to curricula and textbooks, children are reminded of gender role differences. In the classroom and in dating relationships, girls are likely to find that successful performance of the female role requires them to avoid competing with men and to see themselves as something less than men.

Institutional sexism has economic effects. More and more women have been entering the labor force. Many are married; some have children at home; others are widowed, divorced, separated, or single. Despite their labor force participation, women earn substantially less than men. They are overrepresented in low-status, low-paying jobs. Even when they are in more desirable professional and technical positions, women earn less than men on the average. The labor market is divided along sex lines as employers take advantage of the biology-is-destiny ideology and treat women differently from men. The main beneficiaries of sexism in this case are employers, who are able to profit by keeping labor costs down. The drive toward pay on the basis of comparable worth could greatly improve women's status in the labor market.

Millions of women remain homemakers. The economic value of their labor goes largely unrecognized. In the absence of their unpaid labor, men would be forced to demand far higher wages to pay for housekeeping and child-care services and would be more restricted in their hours and work-related travel. Employers benefit from this unpaid labor, for in essence they get two workers for the price of one. Meanwhile, business and industry appeal to the spending ability of housewives (and women working outside the home as well) by stressing consumption. Sales appeals attack women's sense of personal adequacy and play on dissatisfactions imposed by the burdens of housework. Advertising reinforces stereotyped sex roles and seeks to take advantage of these roles. While such activities may be profitable, they contribute to the biology-is-destiny ideology.

Institutional sexism operates in the political system, where women are collectively excluded from positions of power. The U.S. legal system only peripherally recognizes the economic plight of women and their rights as citizens. The composition of the political system helps account for this. At the federal level, women are grossly underrepresented in key policymaking positions—from the White House, to Congress, to the courts. The situation is similar at the state and local levels. The exclusion of women from central positions in politics renders them the weaker sex when it comes to having their concerns taken seriously and acted on.

Under the impetus of the feminist movement that began in the mid-1960s, women's economic and political subordination and sexual exploitation have come under attack. The feminist movement has consisted of a variety of groups and factions, all concerned with the treatment of women but reflecting a range of political perspectives. The liberal feminist faction has sought increased participation of all women in economic and political life. The radical feminists see men as the oppressors and are concerned with liberating women from roles associated with male dominance—for example, within marriage. Socialist feminists hold that sexism stems from and is crucial to the operation of capitalism; they argue that men and women must struggle together for a socialist alternative.

The feminist movement as a whole has made many gains, particularly in raising people's consciousness of sexism and encouraging women to struggle against social, economic, and political domination. However, its gains are still outweighed by the continuing presence of male chauvinism and institutional sexism. In recent years a number of men have also begun to question their sex-delineated roles. These roles can be highly demanding, despite the opportunities and benefits that often accrue to men in a sexist society. The responsibilities of manhood can be a source of stress. More equalitarian interpersonal relationships, in which both sexes share in confronting problems, should ideally reduce the burdens of being a man.

Both men and women stand to benefit from joining in the battle against sexism. Women's economic disadvantage must be addressed by expanding job opportunities and child-care facilities. The economic contributions of homemakers must be recognized in material terms. Employment discrimination must be more directly and aggressively attacked, and antidiscrimination laws more quickly and efficiently enforced. Pressure must be put on government to employ and appoint more women to top positions, while women and men should do more to make sexism an issue in election campaigns. Finally, schools and colleges have an important role to play. Though more and more children are being taught that biology is not destiny, they are not being taught how to oppose sexism. It is worth making schools part of the feminist movement.

Key Terms

Biology is destiny 239
Claims process 243
Comparable worth 252
Date rape 256
Domestic code 241
Double or triple shift 254
Dual labor market 246
Feminist movement 259
Gender 242

Glass ceiling 246
Index of segregation 252
Institutional sexism 240
Male chauvinism 240
Mommy track 254
Radical feminists 261
Sex 242
Socialist feminists 261

Discussion Questions

1. In your experience, what are the most common ways in which male chauvinism is expressed? How do you feel about being subjected to or witnessing expressions of male chauvinism?

2. Make a list of all the advantages of being male that you can think of. Make a list of all the advantages of being female. Which list is longer? Discuss your lists and compare them with those of your classmates.

3. Two applicants—one male and one female—are equally qualified for a professional job opening. What arguments could be made for and against giving preference to the female applicant? If preference is not given, how will female underrepresentation in the professions ever be altered?

4. Should women be paid for the work they do as housewives? Why? If you think they should be paid, who should pay them, and how should the value of their labor be determined?

5. Obtain a selection of men's, women's, and general circulation magazines from your home, dorm, or library. Examine the advertisements—photographs and texts— and discuss the attitudes they project toward male and female gender roles.

6. If sexism has dubious benefits for, and may even harm, many men, why don't more men see the struggle against sexism as in their self-interest? Under what conditions could this situation change?

Suggested Readings

Andersen, Margaret. *Thinking about Women*. 6th ed. (New York: Allyn & Bacon, 2003).
Sociological examination of the position of women in a range of institutional settings and movements for change.

Baca Zinn, Maxine, and Bonnie Thornton Dill, eds. *Women of Color in U.S. Society* (Philadelphia: Temple University Press, 1993).
Examination of the diversity of women's experiences based on the intersection of race, class, and gender.

Costello, Cynthia, and Anne J. Stone, eds. *The American Woman, 2003–2004: Where We Stand* (New York: W. W. Norton, 2004).
Highly regarded biannual series with a focus in this volume on the status of young women in the United States now; also includes current issues affecting women and a comprehensive statistical portrait of women's lives.

Faludi, Susan. *Backlash: The Undeclared War against Women* (New York: Crown, 1991).
Documentation of the assault on women's rights and the inroads women have made at work, in politics, and in their own development.

Ferree, Myra Marx, and Beth B. Hess. *Controversy and Coalition: The New Feminist Movement*. Rev. ed. (New York: Routledge, 2000).
An overview of women's struggles to respond to sexist policies and practices.

Reskin, Barbara, and Irene Padavic. *Women and Men at Work* (Thousand Oaks, CA: Pine Forge Press, 1994).
Comparison of women's and men's work status that incorporates racial and ethnic differences and offers theoretical explanations for inequality in the labor market.

Rhode, Deborah L. *Speaking of Sex: The Denial of Gender Inequality* (Cambridge, MA: Harvard University Press, 1999).
Exploration of the progress toward gender equality in the last several decades, with incisive analysis of how much more remains to be done.

chapter 9

Heterosexism

There should be no personal and institutional discrimination against individuals on the basis of sexual orientation.

In the United States some 5,000 young people kill themselves each year. The suicide rate among youth has been on the increase, and suicide is now the third-leading cause of death for adolescents (*Morbidity and Mortality Weekly Report* 1995). What is rarely acknowledged or talked about, however, is that gay males and lesbians may make up as many as 30 percent of these unnecessary and tragic deaths (Gibson 1989). Their high rate of completed suicide reflects the fact that young gays are two to three times more likely to attempt to kill themselves than heterosexual youth. Why? What forces move so many gay male and lesbian young people, many of them teenagers, to pursue death and not life?

In this chapter we point to features of U.S. society that create enormous problems in living for anyone whose sexual orientation departs from the dominant and heavily enforced norm of heterosexuality. Young people who come to understand and confirm to themselves that their sexual orientation is not mainstream, but is different from that of most of their peers, face the specter of condemnation and prejudicial treatment—from verbal harassment and physical abuse to terrorist violence or "queerbashing"—if and when this truth becomes known (www.hrw.org/reports/2001/uslgbt/; Savin-Williams 1995). Too often gay youth find themselves dealing with this reality in isolation and without support from family or friends. All too many conclude they cannot handle it, and they take their own lives.

Gay males and lesbians are faced with the prospects of a lifetime of discrimination by heterosexual individuals and the institutions heterosexuals dominate, not for *who* they are, but for *what* they are or are perceived to be. People who are gay can be considered members of a minority group who, like members of other minority groups in U.S. society, have been systematically denied fundamental rights and protections that other people are able to rely on (Hunter, Michaelson, and Stoddard 2004; Mohr 1994). Much like women and racial minority group members in the United States, many gays have joined together to struggle against and resist such discriminatory treatment.

The Meaning of Heterosexism

In our chapters on racism and sexism, we emphasized that negative treatment of persons on the basis of their skin color and sex can be thought of as operating at two different levels, the interpersonal and the institutional. This is also the case with regard to the ways in which gay males and lesbians are treated in U.S. society. Most cultures around the world are characterized by **heteronormativity,** a social construction that privileges heterosexuality as the norm governing the treatment of individuals and their status and participation in society. Heteronormativity is predicated on the assumption that there are only two genders, one based on maleness and the other on femaleness. The treatment and inclusion or exclusion of individuals in society become affected by how well they conform to the norms establishing these two genders. However, some researchers have pointed out that there is actually a continuum of many genders, including gays, lesbians, bisexuals, and transgenders (Lorber 1996). Heteronormativity, then, is a limited social construction that narrows people's perspectives so as to define other genders and sexual orientations as nonnormative or even abnormal, and thus deserving of exclusion, denial of privileges accorded to heterosexuals, or punishment.

On the interpersonal level the term **homophobia** is frequently used to describe the reactions that many members of U.S. society who define themselves as heterosexual have to gay males and lesbians. A phobia is a fear, and homophobia refers to fear of homosexuals and homosexuality. A phobia often involves a fear that is irrational, such as fear of a danger to oneself or others that does not really exist. Mental health practitioners tend to view phobias as expressions of underlying anxieties and stand ready to treat them as mental disorders. But many cases of phobia, including most cases of homophobia, probably do not require professional treatment so much as adoption of a more open-minded and fact-based assessment of reality.

Fear of gay males and lesbians may be sustained by any combination of factors. These factors include lack of contact with persons whose sexual orientation is known to be different from one's own; acceptance of myths and stereotypes about people who are gay, for example, that they are desirous and capable of turning heterosexuals into homosexuals; and underlying questions about one's sexual identity and commitment in a society in which anyone even known to be harboring such thoughts is likely to be considered abnormal and subject to denunciation.

Homophobia is often expressed by distancing oneself from homosexuals. Homophobes may avoid or minimize interpersonal contact whenever possible with anyone who they think might be gay. Myths and stereotypes about gays that depict them as fundamentally perverse and "not like you and me" are embraced uncritically and without questioning by homophobes, a situation facilitated by lack of contact. Homophobes are also likely to avoid self-examination of their own sexual identity and commitment to it, and certainly do not make known any impulses they may have to do so, knowing that others are almost certain to disapprove.

Although homophobia seems to be relatively common in the United States, we really do not know how common. And there is reason to believe that homophobia may be in a state of decline. Many heterosexuals today not only know but acknowledge that they know people who are gay: They are our classmates, coworkers, family members, service providers in stores and restaurants, members of our religious congregations, and so forth. Myths and stereotypes are increasingly being recognized as such and are subject to erosion through knowledge gained from both interacting with people who are gay and learning about the existence and contributions of people from all walks of life who are "out of the closet" (openly gay). And sexual orientation in all its complexity is increasingly being deemed appropriate for discussion in books and the mass media, thus reducing at least some of the anxiety and sense of being unique that people may have who are thinking about their own sexuality.

For a small segment of the U.S. population, reactions to homosexuality go well beyond homophobia. Some express, while others openly or tacitly condone, **homohatred.** As gay rights advocates Marshall Kirk and Hunter Madsen (1989:xxv) put it, "Let's reserve the term 'homophobia' for the psychiatric cases to which it really applies, and find a more honest label for the attitudes, words, and acts of hatred that are, in any event, our real problem." Homohatred occurs when members of the heterosexual majority display prejudicial attitudes and engage in discriminatory actions that demonstrate their dislike of and contempt for persons who are gay. Homohatred can take many forms, including name-calling ("faggot," "fairy," "bull dyke"), intentional interpersonal slights and social ostracism, and physical assaults that extend from beatings to, in some cases, murder (Dunlap 1994; Heredia 2001). The intensity of homophobic violence became nationally personified in the horrific murder of Matthew Shepard in Idaho. He was brutally beaten by men he met in a bar who were enraged by the fact that he was gay, and he was left to die tied to a fence in an isolated area.

Analyses by the U.S. Department of Justice show that people who are gay are probably the most frequent victims of "hate crimes" involving violence (Herek and Berrill 1992). Most avowedly gay males and lesbians, when surveyed, report having been subject to verbal abuse or physical assault—often by their peers and even by family members. Many gay students report being harassed or attacked in junior high, high school, or college by other students (www.hrw.org/reports/2001/uslgbt/).

The San Francisco–based antiviolence advocacy group Community United Against Violence surveyed 26 antiviolence organizations nationwide and found that in 2000 almost 2,500 people were victims of hate crimes against people who are gay; 215 of these antigay attacks resulted in serious injury. The group also found 16 cases of murder motivated by homophobia. The vast majority of hate crimes against gays both on and off campus go unreported to authorities (Heredia 2001). This is often because the victims do not want family members, peers, employers, or others to find out that they are homosexual or because their previous treatment as gay persons by the police has been highly negative (Comstock 1991).

In recent years, acts of homohatred have occurred with such frequency that in 1990 President George H. W. Bush signed the National Hate Crimes Statistics Act into law. The act requires the U.S. Department of Justice to gather data for the first time on crimes committed against people on the basis of their sexual orientation (as well as on crimes committed on the basis of a person's race, religion, or ethnic background). Since the data must be gathered from local police departments, proponents of the act hoped it would encourage more police to take crimes against gays seriously, a recognition of the fact that police forces have often acted in ways that reflect homophobia or even homohatred.

Homohatred is most frequently and intensely expressed by heterosexual males. Most incidents of harassment and hate crimes against gay males and lesbians, for example, are perpetrated by such males. Those who express homohatred are often fearful and angry that gays are rejecting aspects of the existing system of gender inequality upon which male power and privilege rest. Their desire to uphold the existing system of gender inequality, and their own advantageous position in it, may help to explain the antigay sentiments held by many heterosexual males. But antigay sentiments seem to be most strongly maintained by those individuals who are obsessed with confirming their own "masculinity" in the eyes of others, and who are most rigid in their demands that males and females conform to conventional gender roles in which men are dominant. Such males are likely to be as intolerant of the feminist movement as they are of gay rights groups, since both seem to be threatening to break down these roles (Pharr 1995).

In our chapter on sexism, we referred to the fact that the feminist movement has struggled against keeping women in very circumscribed gender roles based on the belief that "biology is destiny." This struggle has helped many women escape an assigned place in the arbitrary division between "men's work" and "women's work." The belief that men and women are so innately different that they should occupy distinct gender roles is also violated by lesbians and gay males who, in some of their behaviors, move outside conventional role boundaries.

For example, some heterosexual males condemn lesbians for not being attached or subject to, economically dependent on, or even interested in establishing sexual relationships with male partners. Lesbians' rejection of male partners violates role expectations that such men have for women. Some heterosexual males also condemn their gay counterparts for not engaging in actions that are supposedly integral to the gender roles of "real men": sexual conquest of and dominance over female partners. Gay males may be considered especially threatening by some heterosexual males for this reason, since they are in effect "traitors" to male unity. This view, of course, ignores the fact that many gay males are—like heterosexual males—sexist in their attitudes toward and treatment of women,

regardless of their sexual orientation. Gay males and lesbians have been at odds over this.

Condemnation of gay males and lesbians for their failure to conform to conventional gender roles is a way of reaffirming the importance of such roles, roles that are central to the system of gender inequality from which men draw disproportionate benefits. Since homosexuality tends to be perceived in terms of gender nonconformity, heterosexual men (and women) who hold strong antigay sentiments often distance themselves from the possibility they might be thought to be gay by emphasizing or exaggerating conventional gender roles and relationships. Acting out antigay sentiments in this way helps to keep society's gender inequalities intact (Pharr 1995).

Homophobia and homohatred operate at the level of interpersonal relations between members of the heterosexual majority and people who are gay. Individuals' fear of homosexuals and homosexuality, their prejudicial attitudes toward gays, and their discriminatory treatment of gay males and lesbians are energized and reinforced by a prevailing ideology in U.S. society we refer to as **heterosexism.** This ideology holds that homosexuality is unnatural and immoral, and that heterosexuality is the only acceptable and viable life option for society's members (Blumenfeld and Raymond 1993).

Heterosexism not only influences interpersonal relations, to the detriment of gays, it is a set of ideas that are deeply embedded in the norms and practices of key societal institutions. We shall discuss ways in which heterosexism is expressed in such institutional settings later. Our intent here is to emphasize just how ubiquitous and all-encompassing heterosexism is in U.S. society. Gay males and lesbians are made to feel marginal and unwanted in a society whose every institution is dominated by a heterosexual majority, many of whose members are often insistent on, and in some cases obsessed with, promoting and defending the ideology of heterosexism.

Sexual Orientation

Our sexual orientation is one of the most important aspects of our lives. We may find ourselves sexually attracted to members of the opposite sex, the same sex, or both sexes. We may be decisive or indecisive about our orientation. Our sexual orientation may change over time, or vacillate back and forth unpredictably and without apparent reason. Such diversity and variability have led scholars to question whether it makes sense to talk of sexual orientation as if it were a fixed trait.

Surprisingly, no one really knows for sure just why sexual orientation per se exists, nor have scientists directed much energy toward finding out. Similarly, no serious research has been conducted into why so many people are attracted toward persons of the opposite sex since, technically speaking, reproduction does not require this. It would seem that the existence of sexual orientation, and more specifically heterosexuality, has been taken for granted by scientists as a phenomenon not in need of inquiry.

The fact that the phenomenon of homosexuality has, in contrast, been subject to sustained investigation may well reflect the influence of the ideology of heterosexism on the institution of science itself. Scientists, in treating homosexuality as a problem to be explored, implicitly accept the notion that there is a heterosexual norm to which everyone should measure up. Indeed, for many years a handful of scientists have struggled to figure out not only why homosexuality exists but how homosexuals could be "fixed" and turned into heterosexuals.

Contemporary research has revealed that both men and women occupy positions on a broad continuum or spectrum with regard to their sexual orientation (Kinsey, Pomeroy, and Martin 1948; Kinsey et al. 1953; Lorber 1996). Figure 9.1 illustrates this spectrum. The diversity and variability in whom people find sexually attractive suggest that the dualistic categories of "homosexual" and "heterosexual" are really rather inadequate, masking more than elucidating existing reality. Even the term **bisexual,** commonly used to refer to persons who find themselves sexually attracted to members of

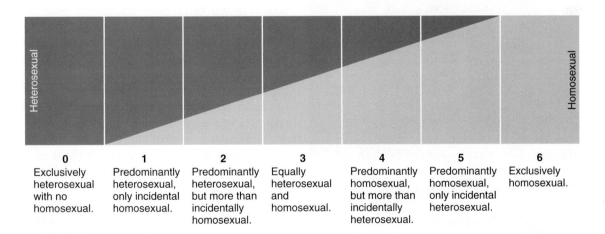

0	1	2	3	4	5	6
Exclusively heterosexual with no homosexual.	Predominantly heterosexual, only incidental homosexual.	Predominantly heterosexual, but more than incidentally homosexual.	Equally heterosexual and homosexual.	Predominantly homosexual, but more than incidentally heterosexual.	Predominantly homosexual, only incidental heterosexual.	Exclusively homosexual.

Figure 9.1   **Range of Human Sexual Orientations**

Source: Adapted from Warren J. Blumenfeld and Diane Raymond, *Looking at Gay and Lesbian Life,* expanded ed. (Boston: Beacon Press, 1993) p. 80.

both sexes, is problematic. Bisexuals may be attracted to members of one sex more frequently or intensively than the other, may do no more than experiment with same-sex sexuality, may use bisexuality as a default position because they are not sure of their orientation or don't see why they need to make a choice, or may be in transition toward homosexuality or heterosexuality on

Not all persons who are attracted to or engage in sexual relations with members of the same sex view themselves as homosexuals. One's sense of identity is an important element of sexual orientation. These young women display their lesbian identity publicly and proudly as they walk with their arms intimately around each other on a street.

a permanent basis (Garber 1995; Rust 1992; Weinberg, Williams, and Pryor 1994).

Most experts today agree that an adequate definition of sexual orientation must go beyond the element of to whom one is attracted—males, females, or members of both sexes. There is also the element of *behavior*. For example, a young woman may find herself strongly attracted to other females and have ambivalent or no sexual feelings toward men. But given the pervasive influence heterosexism has on our choice of socially acceptable partners, and the prejudicial attitudes toward and discriminatory treatment of lesbians, many such women have had to hide their true feelings. Many remain uninvolved with men and never marry. But others have gone ahead and married, borne children, and lived to all appearances as cohabiting heterosexuals.

There are an estimated 1.7 million gay men and lesbians who were once married or remain married (Buxton 1994; Gabriel 1995). When marriages in which one spouse is gay dissolve, as half of all marriages that occur in the United States eventually do, those formerly married persons who subsequently enter into same-sex partnerships and behavior consistent with their actual sexual orientation commonly generate confusion and are met with dismay. Thus behavior can be an important element of any definition of sexual orientation.

Yet another constituent element of sexual orientation is *identity*. An individual may engage in casual sexual relations with partners of the same sex or even maintain a sexual relationship with one such individual over time, but not necessarily view him- or herself as a homosexual. For example, people who must live for a length of time in single-sex environments—such as prisons, boarding schools, residential religious retreats like monasteries and convents, military outposts, or remote work sites—may have homosexual experiences. But, if and when it comes to light, most such persons are likely to vehemently reject the notion that their behavior means they *are* homosexuals. Experimental, occasional, or (in the example here) "situational" homosexuality in terms of behavior is not uncommon among persons whose professed identity is heterosexual.

Thus, when we take these three elements of sexual orientation into account (to whom one is attracted, sexual behavior, and identity), and when we consider the range of variability within the U.S. population around these elements and the changes that occur in many individuals over time, it appears that those who are exclusively lifelong heterosexuals or homosexuals occupy the extremes of the sexual orientation continuum. Yet most people tend to cling to the heterosexual versus homosexual dualism as if sexual orientation were a simple matter of either/or.

Social historians have discovered that this dualism is a relatively recent creation and has not always existed. It was not until the late eighteenth and early nineteenth centuries that the category of "homosexual" emerged and began to be used in Europe and the United States (Greenberg 1988). Individuals who engaged in sexual relations with others of the same sex were, at least up until then, not viewed as members of a separate and unique category of humanity. Moreover, there was a great deal of variability across time and place in the degree to which such behavior was tolerated or condemned, both informally and under the law.

The category of homosexual was created largely by members of the medical profession of the time, who used their claim to scientific expertise to argue that homosexual behavior was abnormal and pathological and only engaged in by persons who were a different human type from everyone else. Despite a lack of empirical evidence, such allegations were powerful, coming as they did from members of a profession who were anxious to solidify their position in Western society and whose status was on the rise. Their ideas were also given credence because they were compatible with the antihomosexual dogma that was held to by major Western religious denominations.

Two hundred years later we still have no evidence that homosexuals form a distinct human type, even while we hold on to the category as if it were real. No one has been able to definitively identify any biological or psychological traits (apart from sexual orientation) that allow us to differentiate homosexuals from everyone else. Research that purports to have located biological markers distinguishing homosexuals, while provocative, is still inconclusive (Small 1993; Wheeler 1993). Moreover, such research is premised on the assumption that the dualistic categories of "homosexual" and "heterosexual" are scientifically valid. This assumption virtually ignores the complex elements and issues that must be taken into account in defining sexual orientation.

Theories as to Why Homosexuality Exists

The creation and acceptance of the notion that "homosexuals" are a different and distinct category of humanity were accompanied by scientific efforts to identify the causes or origins of homosexuality. These efforts have largely been based on the premise that homosexuality is worthy of scientific concern because it represents a deviation from the norm and is thus a "problem" that deserves to be analyzed. This premise is not universally held. Sexual practices we might associate with homosexuality have been found to exist in many cultures that do not categorize particular people as "homosexuals" or such behaviors as a problem (Blackwood 1986). Let us look at some of the efforts to explain why homosexuality exists.

Psychological Theories

The notion that psychological malfunctioning explains homosexuality has a long history. Indeed, it was not until 1973 that the American Psychiatric Association removed homosexuality from the mental troubles listed in its *Diagnostic and Statistical Manual of Mental Disorders,* despite the lack of empirical justification for inclusion of homosexuality and the absence of evidence showing that being gay could be equated with being mentally ill (Kirk and Kutchins 1992).

Psychological theorizing about homosexuality has been heavily influenced by the work of Sigmund Freud (1856–1939), considered the founder of psychoanalytic theory. Freud was extremely interested in the human sex drive. He saw this as a very strong species drive that has to be channeled, repressed, or sublimated in the interests of regulating reproductive practices and encouraging family stability. Freud viewed cultural norms as crucial in this regard, for their dynamics encouraged most people toward heterosexuality as a sexual orientation.

But, Freud held, while cultural norms exist to guide and shape outward expressions of the sex drive toward heterosexuality, thus enhancing societal functioning, not everyone responds to the frustration of their sex drive by these norms in the same way. For any of a variety of reasons, some individuals come to manifest styles of thinking and behavior that depart from cultural norms of heterosexuality, and Freud believed that homosexuality should be viewed in this light. Thus Freud himself did not view homosexuality as unnatural or immoral, nor did he express the view that there was one particular cause. He believed that variation in human sexual development is to be expected and that there is "a very considerable measure of latent or unconscious homosexuality . . . in all normal people" (Freud 1963:158; cf. Blumenfeld and Raymond 1993:135–36).

Freud himself did not view homosexuality as indicative of a mental illness. But many mental health professionals who have been influenced by Freud's psychoanalytic theories have been of a different mind-set and have defined homosexuality as unnatural, as abnormal, and as a mental disorder that needs to be "cured"

(Miller 1995); hence, the inclusion of homosexuality in the American Psychiatric Association's manual of disorders. Mental health practitioners have varied in their explanations of homosexuality. But typically it has been seen as either a problem of disturbed sexual development, an aberrant sexual fixation or obsession, a form of same-sex narcissism, a fear of the opposite sex, or some other deep-seated pathology situated in the realms of the unconscious. Over the years many gays have been encouraged, persuaded, or coerced into treatment for mental illness under the rationale that it was in their own best interests. Attempted "cures" have been notably unsuccessful in turning homosexuals into heterosexuals.

Theories that view homosexuality as a psychological problem founder in the face of the fact that the vast majority of people who are gay are apparently as psychologically healthy as most heterosexuals (Strickland 1995). Many are avowedly happy being gay. While it is true that some gays have more psychological difficulties than others in coping with the treatment handed them in a society in which heterosexism prevails to the point of homohatred, this is an entirely separate issue from the idea that psychological problems cause homosexuality. No one has yet established the existence of underlying psychological problems that distinguish homosexuals from everyone else, although, as we have seen, many mental health practitioners have operated with the notion that such problems must exist.

Social Contagion Theories

Is homosexuality contagious? Can one be turned into a homosexual by associating with gay people or learning about homosexuality in school? Are heterosexual children vulnerable to "recruitment" into the sexual orientation of gay older persons, such as gay teachers, counselors, or family members? Does having a sexual experience with a member of the same sex mean that one will probably turn out to be gay? The answer to each of these questions is no. Homosexuality is not "catching," like a cold.

When considering the significance some would attach to social contagion theories, it is instructive to ponder what role parents or parent substitutes play in this process. We normally think of parents as being highly influential in the lives of those they rear. Yet most people who are gay are born into and raised within heterosexual households. Moreover, the children of gays who become biological or adoptive parents are no more likely to be gay than the children of heterosexual parents, suggesting a similar lack of parental influence over sexual orientation. If years of interaction and emotional involvement with either heterosexual or homosexual parents have no obvious correlation with being gay, how important can social contagion be?

Some have argued that the sexual orientation of parents is less important than the nature of parent-child interaction within heterosexual families. For example, it has been theorized that males who are gay tend to have had fathers who engaged in little interaction with them or were altogether absent, but also had socially dominant mothers. Gay males, in this theory, develop their sexual orientation in response to the absence of a paternal "masculinizing" influence and the presence of a maternal "feminizing" influence.

Such a theory may fit well with the erroneous stereotype that gay males all possess feminine mannerisms and other female characteristics, yet there are some loose ends that must be explained. For example, how would one account for the fact that many males who experience such upbringings are lifelong heterosexuals? How is it possible that brothers in such family settings can end up with different sexual orientations? How do we explain all the gay males who grow up in homes in which they have a great deal of interaction with masculine fathers and nondominant mothers? No one has been able to compile convincing evidence that a particular type of family or style of family interaction causes homosexuality. It appears that gay males and lesbians come from just as wide a range of family situations as heterosexual males and females.

In contemplating the role of social contagion it is also important to examine temporal sequences and the logic surrounding them. If a young person plays on a sports team whose coach is gay, and subsequently defines herself as a lesbian, how do we know the coach had anything at all to do with causing her to be gay? Is it possible that the young woman, inspired by the positive role model provided by the coach, finally worked up the courage to acknowledge and accept her own sexual orientation? If a young man has a pleasurable sexual experience with a male peer while a young teen, and much later comes out to others as gay, is it safe to conclude that this sexual experience turned him away from heterosexuality? Or was the experience pursued and found to be pleasurable because, while he may not have begun to come to grips with the possibility at that age, he was in fact gay?

In short, social contagion theories are undermined by a lack of empirical evidence that would support them. Despite the often highly vocal assertions of members of anti-gay-rights groups, there is no credible evidence that homosexuality is caused by social contact with gays, by exposure to information in school curricula about homosexuality, or even by casual same-sex experimentation. The failure of researchers to find such evidence has pushed interest in possible biological causes of homosexuality to the fore.

Biological Theories

Is there a physical cause for homosexuality? Scientists who believe this is the case usually accept the notion that an individual's social environment plays some role, even if it remains undetermined. But proponents of biological theories treat physical factors as primary.

The notion that there must be a physical basis for homosexuality has been a premise in sociobiology, an interdisciplinary field holding that all universally recognized patterns of human behavior are biologically based and a product of natural selection processes that have occurred over a great expanse of time within the human species. From a sociobiological perspective, homosexuality is one of nature's ways of regulating human population growth, since by definition sexual relations between people of the same sex do not result in reproduction. While homosexuals are not programmed by nature to fulfill reproductive functions and rear the resultant young, they are, according to some sociobiologists, programmed by nature to be altruistic. They make important social contributions by providing caretaking and other necessary services to others in society (Wilson 1979).

Unfortunately, the notion that homosexuals are somehow intended to play a role as regulators of excess population cannot be proved or disproved. Moreover, we know that most persons—regardless of their sexual orientation—may biologically parent, and that many gay males and lesbians in the United States are doing so. Although some gay parenting situations involve adoption, an estimated 6 to 14 million children in the United States have a gay or lesbian parent and in most cases they are biological parents (American Civil Liberties Union 1999).

In addition, no concrete evidence exists to support the idea that homosexuals are any more or less altruistic than anyone else, as reflected in their everyday lives or occupational leanings. Nor is there evidence that people's impulses toward altruism, however that is defined, are fundamentally nature's doing. Were it to be the case that people who are gay are disproportionately present in certain caretaking or service occupations, one would have to eliminate an enormous range of alternative explanations before concluding that this was the outcome of nature.

Investigators have tried to determine if heredity is involved as a cause of homosexuality, often by studying the frequency with which homosexuals are present within families. One problem with such studies is that family members usually are exposed to similar or common social environments and it is thus difficult to sort out the independent effects of heredity. Some researchers have sought to address this problem by focusing on children who have been adopted and comparing their sexual orientations with those of their biological parents. However, it has proved difficult to develop representative samples of adoptees and adoptive parents from whom to generalize and hard to obtain reliable information about their sexual orientations as well. Moreover, there is no way to sort out the influence of social environment in adoptive homes on sexual orientation. Studies of homosexuality in generations of families have yielded inconclusive and often conflicting findings.

Still others have theorized that there are hormonal differences between homosexuals and heterosexuals. For example, it has been postulated that deficiencies in testosterone, a hormone produced by the testes, account for homosexuality in males. But such investigations comparing heterosexuals and homosexuals have not produced any definitive results. Even if differences were conclusively detected, the findings would not prove that hormones cause homosexuality, but only that certain hormonal characteristics are more likely to be associated with one population as opposed to another. Some researchers, for example, have found that stress lowers testosterone levels. If lower levels were to be found in homosexuals, would this best be interpreted as a "cause" of their sexual orientation or a biological reaction to stress stemming from the negative ways they are treated? Finding a correlation is not the same thing as finding a cause.

The latter point is important to keep in mind in assessing periodic news reports of research findings that suggest there are unique biological "markers" in a small percentage of homosexuals. Despite the difficulties in distinguishing causation from correlation, research in this area is increasingly being taken seriously. In 1995, for example, researchers claimed that a minority of male homosexuals have newly discovered genetic material attached to their X chromosome (one of two sex-related chromosomes). From this the researchers postulated that the genetic material may influence the probability of homosexuality in males. (No such finding was discovered for females or for most of the male homosexuals in the researchers' study.) The scientists were going on to try to determine which gene or genes were involved and just what role the genetic material might play in producing homosexuality. Theirs is quite a formidable research task, since no one yet has found a definitive link between any particular genetic trait and any specific form of human behavior (BBC News 1999; Suplee 1995). Yet many scientists today view this line of research as extremely promising, and it is of great interest to many members of the gay population.

Political Implications of Discovery of a "Gay Gene"

Given the limitations and inadequacies of the psychological and social contagion theories of homosexuality we have briefly described, and the scientific community's enthusiasm over the possibility there may be physical causes of homosexuality, many believe that explanations for it will ultimately be based heavily on biological findings. Success in finding a "gay gene" would not preclude continued consideration of the possible role of nonbiological factors in explaining homosexuality. But such a biological finding could have a good deal of *political* significance.

Many persons who condemn homosexuality believe that gay males and lesbians freely choose their sexual orientation and that this orientation is "against nature." Anti-gay-rights groups use such arguments to justify their refusal to acknowledge gays as members of a minority whose rights deserve protection under the law. Often they argue that people who are gay are simply self-serving sexual deviates who are demanding illegitimate "special rights," and in doing so they dismiss gays' protests that people have the right not to be discriminated against in the workplace and elsewhere simply because they have a different sexual orientation.

Persons who are gay typically say that being gay was never a matter of choice for them, and heterosexuals say the same thing with regard to their sexual orientation. Evidence of a biological cause for homosexuality would add credence to such statements as well as to the notion that variation in sexual orientation is as natural as such other human biological differences as sex or skin color. Gays' claim to minority group status and the right to be protected against discrimination might be more compelling to some were it to be scientifically proved that the existence of homosexuality is part of the natural order of things.

On the other hand, there are potential dangers to be addressed should biological causes for homosexuality be definitively established. Modern science is constantly opening up new ways to test for different fetal traits, and women may use test information in deciding whether or not to go through with births. Genetic research advances may also make it possible to clone or "breed" desired traits in human offspring and even to alter the genetic makeup of those already born. In a society in which the ideology of heterosexism prevails, some may wish to use this new knowledge to abort fetuses possessing biological markers associated with homosexuality, or strive to genetically engineer the sexual orientation of offspring either before or after birth to produce heterosexuality. The political implications of such "species cleansing" by heterosexuals—elimination of homosexuals because they are deemed socially undesirable—are chilling to contemplate. Consider that elimination of homosexuals was central to official policies of genocide in Nazi Germany (Grau 1995; Plant 1986).

How Many Homosexuals Are There in the United States?

The pioneering studies of male and female homosexuality, conducted by sex researcher Alfred Kinsey and his associates after World War II, estimated that people who are more or less exclusively homosexual in their behavior constitute approximately 10 percent of the population, although many more people have some same-sex contact to the point of orgasm (Kinsey, Pomeroy, and Martin 1948; Kinsey et al. 1953). Using the 10 percent figure, the number of gays in the United States would total almost 29 million today. Yet there has been controversy over numbers since the Kinsey studies, while conducted by professional sex researchers doing in-depth interviews, did not use modern statistical sampling techniques and focused only on behavior. Attempts to count how many people are homosexual are also challenged by the willingness of individuals to identify themselves as such to enumerators. Nonetheless, estimates suggest that there are some 15 million gays and lesbians in the United States (www.theinfoshop.com). Thus, while some people argue that the 10 percent figure is too low, others assert that the number is too high (Billy et al. 1993; Laumann et al. 1994).

Determining just how many homosexuals there are in the United States is difficult. Some people, no matter what their sexual orientation, view research on this topic as an unwanted invasion of privacy and will not cooperate with it. Gay males and lesbians may choose not to be truthful about their sexual orientation in responding to surveys, especially those who live in fear of anyone ever finding out. The stigma of being gay may lead to gross underreporting by survey respondents; overreporting is highly unlikely.

Moreover, such research is complicated by the need to avoid reifying the dual categories of homosexual and heterosexual; that is, regarding them as fixed and concrete. Questions must be framed in ways that take into account the variety and variability of people's sexual experiences, behaviors, and identities. The number of homosexuals found depends in part on how homosexuality gets defined and the research methods used (Schmalz 1993; Singer and Deschamps 1994).

Limitations of much of the research that has been conducted have left survey findings on the size of the homosexual population open to criticism, and the cumulative results of these studies are considered by many to be inconclusive. But limits on research conducted to date notwithstanding, most experts think the number of people who are gay in U.S. society is substantial, whether the "true" total is 10 million or 40 million.

Does it really matter how many gay males and lesbians there are in the United States? It depends. Those who hold the most negative attitudes toward gays or who prefer to deny their existence may gain some solace from believing there are low numbers, particularly since low numbers can be used to statistically buttress their more general belief in the abnormality of homosexuality. Low numbers can also be used by those negatively disposed toward people who are gay to dismiss the need for protective rights legislation, under the argument that so few people are involved that such legislation is not really necessary. Gay rights advocates, on the other hand, while denying that numbers are relevant to what is "normal" in the sense of being natural, view higher estimates of the number of gays as helping to buttress the assertion that gay people are present throughout U.S. society and that many millions of people are in need of having their rights protected.

The number of people who are gay in the United States is important to other societal actors as well. For example, more and more large corporations are acknowledging the economic significance of the "gay market" in their advertising and corporate sponsorship practices, acting on market researchers' estimates of a gay market containing anywhere from 5 to 20 million people, many of whom are upscale consumers (Baker, Strub, and Henning 1995). And some politicians are now courting blocs of gay voters by acknowledging and at times acting on gay rights issues. Such voters (who are, by definition, age 18 and over) are estimated to number more than 9 million (Clift 1992).

Thus it appears that the size of the gay population is important to different groups for different reasons, most of which have little to do with the contributions to scientific knowledge more precise population data might make.

Myths and Stereotypes about People Who Are Gay

Ignorance about homosexuality and misperceptions of what it means to be a gay male or lesbian are rather widespread in U.S. society. Many people lack knowledge. There are also those who do not wish to know more because they find these topics rather frightening or disturbing. Myths and stereotypes about people who are gay remain common, although we have begun to see the appearance of books directed at popular audiences that marshal facts to dispel them (Marcus 1993). In this section we briefly address some of these myths and stereotypes.

"Homosexuals Are Easy to Identify"

This myth would have it that gays can all be spotted with ease. One poll of adults found that 31 percent believed that people who are gay can be identified simply by their appearance or gestures (Roper 1990). In urban areas with identifiable gay-dominated neighborhoods—as in New York City, Washington, D.C., or San Francisco—some residents participate in local cultures that may include appearance norms (fashions in dress, hairstyles, and so on). But even in those neighborhoods one can never be certain that all individuals with a similar outward appearance are gay. We cannot discern a person's sexual orientation merely by observing his or her appearance or gestures. This is why, for example, the friends and family members of gays who "come out" (announce that they are gay) typically react with great surprise.

"Homosexuals Lead Unproductive, Dissolute Lives"

Those who believe there is "something wrong" with people who are gay are likely to assume that they have difficulty being "normal" in other aspects of their lives. For example, such persons may believe that gays tend to be unproductive and obsessed with the pursuit of lifestyles in which they can be indifferent to moral restraints.

Yet we know there are homosexuals in virtually all occupations, professions, and callings, a fact brought home each time yet another person we know or hear about comes out. As more and more notables in the fields of medicine, the arts, business, the clergy, science, sports, politics, education, the military, and entertainment refuse to hide their sexual orientation, the productivity and contributions of people who are gay will become even more apparent than they are now. (On this point, see Figure 9.2.) Note too that while there are probably plenty of nonproductive, dissolute heterosexuals, no one thinks to blame these traits on their sexual orientation. Why would we do so in the case of gays?

- Julius Caesar, Roman statesman
- Truman Capote, U.S. writer
- Willa Cather, U.S. novelist
- John Cheever, U.S. writer
- Sir Winston Churchill, British statesman
- Craig Claiborne, U.S. chef
- Montgomery Clift, U.S. actor
- Jean Cocteau, French artist
- Aaron Copland, U.S. composer
- Sir Noel Coward, British playwright
- Hart Crane, U.S. poet
- George Cukor, U.S. film director
- Countee Cullen, U.S. poet

Figure 9.2

Source: *The Alyson Almanac: The Fact Book of the Lesbian and Gay Community, 1994–95 Edition,* 3rd ed. (Boston: Alyson Publications, Inc., 1993), pp. 119–142. These names were selected from only those famous persons listed whose last names begin with A, B, or C.

"There Is a Gay Lifestyle"

The term *gay lifestyle* is often used by gay rights opponents as they rhetorically paint all gays with a broad brush of disapproval, although others use the phrase unthinkingly. Yet just as heterosexuals' sexual urges do not define and dictate every single one of the major activities they engage in during their waking hours, gays' sexual orientation does not dominate most of the daily activities in which they engage.

People who are gay are just as diverse in their lifestyles as members of the rest of the population. Like their heterosexual counterparts, gay people differ in their lifestyles in accordance with such variables as age, gender, partnership and parenting status, place of residence, educational level, occupational activity, and income.

Besides these variables, and unlike heterosexuals, people who are gay also differ in terms of whether they are in or out of the closet, a factor affecting how free they feel to make certain lifestyle choices such as living with a partner. Thus there is no such thing as a single "gay lifestyle" any more than there is such a thing as a single "heterosexual lifestyle."

"Homosexuals Are Sexually Obsessed and Promiscuous"

The imagery posed by this stereotype suggests that people who are gay either have stronger sex drives than heterosexuals, are less able to control their sex drives, or both. (It is worth noting that one never hears claims that the heterosexual population is by nature oversexed and loose, even though the topic of its sexuality so heavily infuses today's films, novels, television programming, X-rated video selections, and advertising.) There is simply no evidence to back up the assertion that people who are gay are sexually obsessed or promiscuous or are more so than heterosexuals. However, some issues are worth mentioning that bear upon this stereotype.

Heterosexism in U.S. society bars the sanctioning of gay unions through marriage and often forces gay males and lesbians into furtive relationships from which it is difficult to build stable, lasting partnerships. Gays are not promiscuous by virtue of their sexual orientation per se, yet some end up having many partners because the heterosexual majority has put up all kinds of barriers to permanent unions to which they can be faithful.

Moreover, the absence of marriage, which unites heterosexual partners under the law and often consecrates their union with religious ceremonies, means that permanent gay partnerships lack the institutional underpinnings that help keep many heterosexuals together. The fact that so many gays form and maintain stable and long-lasting partnerships, even in the face of such challenges and difficulties, speaks to the

Contrary to stereotypes held by some people, one cannot tell who is gay simply by looking at outward appearances. For example, there is no evidence to conclude, other than the fact that they appear in this chapter, that the men enjoying drinks together at the outdoor café in this photograph are gay.

commonly ignored fact that being gay is not just about sex, but about entering into loving and fulfilling relationships with other people.

The stereotype of gay promiscuity may be reinforced because those persons on whom many heterosexuals base their generalizations are members of a select group. They tend to be young adult males, who are largely clustered in college towns and gay communities within urban areas where they feel comfortable being visible. These younger gay males are at that stage of the life cycle when dating, sex, and the search for a permanent partner are at an enthusiastic pitch for heterosexuals as well. While heterosexuals accept open expressions of sexuality and the search for partners as natural on the part

of other heterosexuals, male and female (witness the many popular TV sitcoms and soap operas on this theme), many interpret these matters differently when they involve gays. Just as one cannot conclude that heterosexuality is characterized by an obsession with sex and promiscuity simply by watching the behavior of young heterosexuals, the same can be said about homosexuality.

Although gays depart from conventional gender roles in terms of their sexual orientation, in other ways they are often similar to their heterosexual counterparts. For example, gay males living in our male-dominated society are pressured to occupy gender roles that call for men to appear masculine and to engage in stereotypical male leisure activities, while lesbians are pressured to meet role expectations placed on women to appear feminine and engage in feminine pursuits. Regarding sexuality, gay males—simply because they are males—are expected to be and are much more sexually active and have experience with more partners than women, regardless of whether the latter are straight or gay. Gender is an important organizing principle of social life as well as a lens through which we view and relate to others (Connell 1992). This is true for gays and heterosexuals alike.

"Homosexuals Are Sexual Predators and Child Molesters"

Perhaps one of the most erroneous, yet harmful, stereotypes in terms of the fears it generates is that gays are dangerous predators who are out to sexually exploit unsuspecting heterosexuals, including children. This is a stereotype more often applied to gay men than lesbians. But again we have a view for which there is no empirical evidence.

Heterosexuals, with the exception of some who are mentally troubled, do not walk around in a state of urgent and uncontrollable sexual desire that must be acted on. Nor do gays. Just like heterosexuals, gay males and lesbians often find others around them attractive. But while gays differ from heterosexuals in terms of who is likely to attract them, such feelings are not attached to a compulsive need for sex. Thus people who are gay, like those who are not, typically respond graciously to "Thanks, but not interested" from potential partners.

Like heterosexuals, gay males and lesbians do not enjoy the experience of rejection. But within a society that is dominated by heterosexism, there can be serious social penalties for gays who mistakenly approach those who do not share their sexual orientation. Thus, gays typically feel secure inviting relationships with members of the same sex only when the likelihood is high that this is socially appropriate and that those in whom they express interest may respond positively. For this reason, gays may actually be *less* prone than heterosexuals to approach others they find sexually attractive.

Avoiding rejection, social embarrassment, and possibly something worse is one reason gay bars and clubs have historically played a critical role as meeting places (other reasons being the need for secrecy and safety). Today, however—primarily in urban areas—people may choose from a wide range of gay-oriented organizations, services, and activities in which it is possible to meet others. There is, in essence, a highly diverse and lively gay community in which gay males and lesbians are able to interact freely and openly with people who happen to share the same sexual orientation. Moreover, gays are increasingly introduced to one another by heterosexual friends and family members, as more and more people come out and are met with support. In short, there is absolutely nothing in their sexual orientation that would make gays want to "prey" on heterosexuals, and there are serious risks for any who would attempt to do so.

There is also no evidence for the charge that homosexuality leads gay males (or lesbians, for that matter) to sexually exploit children. Indeed, those persons who do so are almost always *heterosexual* in orientation. As we shall see in a subsequent chapter on family-related problems, child sexual abuse and other forms of violence against children occur in U.S. society with surprising frequency. Ordinarily child sexual abuse involves adult family members and family acquaintances, and in just about all cases the adults are heterosexual. Both girls and boys are sexually abused, most often by fathers, stepfathers, other male relatives, or male family friends.

Some cases of child sexual abuse involve pedophilia, a mental disorder identified by the

American Psychiatric Association that involves intense sexual urges and fantasies, and sexual activities by adults with children. As with other forms of child sexual abuse, pedophilia usually involves adult males, and the children can be either boys or girls. In recent years pedophilia has been in the news in connection with criminal charges against members of the religious clergy, teachers, scout leaders, day-care workers, and others who spend a great deal of time with children and youth. Most of those charged are men, and although some are unmarried, others are married and have families. Pedophilia may also be the motivation for some of the adult involvement with child pornography and utilization of child prostitutes. The latter are typically runaway or homeless boys and girls who are exploited by adults—usually men—taking advantage of their desperate need for money and affection.

Although pedophilia may at times involve adult sexual exploitation of children of the same sex, it has nothing in common with being gay. Pedophilia is the manifestation of a serious mental disturbance, one that in some cases can be successfully treated by mental health professionals.

"Homosexuals Give You AIDS"

We discuss the topic of acquired immune deficiency syndrome (AIDS), who has it and why, and how AIDS is transmitted in our chapters on health care and substance abuse. Thus we shall not go into detail on such matters here. Suffice it to say that being homosexual should not be equated with being a carrier of the human immunodeficiency virus (HIV) by which AIDS is spread or with having AIDS. The vast majority of people who are gay are perfectly healthy and HIV-free. Moreover, the AIDS rate is growing most rapidly today in the heterosexual population.

Nonetheless, in one poll of adults, 35 percent said fear of AIDS motivated them to avoid homosexuals and persons they think are gay or lesbian, as well as places where homosexuals meet (Harris Poll, April 21, 1991). It is, of course, not possible to contract AIDS through casual contact, with either homosexuals or heterosexuals. Such people need to let go of the linkage they are maintaining between those who are gay and the risks of contracting AIDS. Such stereotypical thinking about AIDS and homosexuality promotes a societal climate in which a serious epidemic can be mistakenly viewed as the result of a particular sexual orientation, rather than caused by a virus that is at large in the general population (Cochrane 2003). This thinking increases the likelihood that AIDS will spread even further simply because of ignorance, thus unnecessarily escalating the numbers of those who will die.

Arenas of Struggle against Heterosexism

Earlier we referred to the ideology of heterosexism as ubiquitous and all-encompassing, permeating virtually every institutional setting and marginalizing people who are gay. In this section we comment on some of the ways in which heterosexism is expressed and just what gays are struggling against.

Religion

In the United States, religious denominations have been experiencing conflicts about homosexuality, and there is disagreement between and even within denominations over how to deal with it. Such disagreements often revolve around differences in beliefs regarding whether homosexuality is moral or immoral, natural or unnatural, and frequently reflect widely varying interpretations of the Bible and other key religious documents.

The Episcopal denomination, for example, does not view homosexuality as a sin. Indeed, the Episcopalian House of Bishops confirmed Reverend Gene Robinson as bishop of New Hampshire, the first openly gay bishop in the history of the church. Yet while some Episcopalian churches have ordained openly gay persons as ministers, many are against this. The confirmation of Reverend Robinson in 2003 caused some members to leave the church. This controversy surrounding homosexuals serving as clergy occurs in other denominations as well. The Baptists officially consider homosexuality a sin, but there are splits and divisions among Baptists around this doctrine, and Baptist ministers have participated in church ceremonies celebrating gay unions. Protestant evangelical denominations tend to aggressively condemn homosexuality. In contrast, the Religious Society of Friends (Quakers) and the United Church of Christ strongly assert the need for acceptance of gays and their sexual orientation. While Roman Catholicism views the practice of homosexuality as sinful, it is accepting of celibate homosexuals and has been forced to acknowledge that there are gay Catholic priests. Orthodox Jewish congregations generally condemn homosexuality, yet Reform congregations are very open to people who are gay and some synagogues have openly gay rabbis.

Thus there is a great deal of diversity on the issue of homosexuality between and within religious denominations. Moreover, people who are gay—along with their friends and families—can be found in virtually all denominations, including those that officially condemn homosexuality. This fact, along with the ongoing debates over gay rights in the secular world, helps to feed and energize conflicts around heterosexist religious dogma. But despite exceptions, frequent gaps between doctrine and practice, and pressures for change from within, many religious institutions continue to adhere to an ideology of heterosexism in their doctrines. For this reason religion has become a common rallying point for many anti-gay-rights activists.

Government Policy and the Church/State Separation

In the United States, religious beliefs are held to be a very personal matter. Each individual has the right to hold whatever beliefs he or she wishes. This situation is reflected in and assisted greatly by the constitutionally mandated separation between church and state in U.S. society, put there so that government cannot allow the protected religious beliefs of some to deny the constitutional rights of others who do not share these same beliefs.

Advocates of gay rights argue that a movement is afoot to break down this historic church/state separation, and that some anti-gay-rights organizations are attempting to resolve matters in the political arena that cannot be resolved among religious groups. As with other issues, such as abortion, religion has become an important element in setting the terms of debate over government policies toward homosexuality.

For example, Protestant evangelical-based organizations like the 1.7-million-member Christian Coalition have urged their followers to enter the political arena and demand that elected officials restrict, deny, or roll back legal protections for gays. Religious doctrines condemning homosexuality generally allow no compromise. Those who hold to such doctrines, believing them to be divinely ordained and thus morally superior to other views, have been insisting that their religious convictions regarding homosexuality be translated into law.

Their critics argue that the separation between church and state must be maintained. Permitting certain people's religious doctrines to determine government policies toward homosexuals is fraught with dangers. Critics suggest, for instance, that it opens the door for politically influential religious groups in the United States to dictate policies bearing on the rights of individuals on many other issues as well (Blumenfeld 1992; Nava and Dawidoff 1994).

For example, members of anti-gay-rights organizations often also count on members of sympathetic religious groups to campaign for government policies that would limit women's reproductive choices, ban what they define as morally offensive books and music, and keep certain subjects out of public school curricula, such as sex education. Allowing government policies in these and other areas to be dictated by certain groups' religious convictions would deny the rights of others who believe differently. Thus, it is argued, religious beliefs must not be the standard against which the acceptability of laws protecting gay people from discrimination is judged.

Marriage and Family

Often, those who subscribe to the ideology of heterosexism and view homosexuality as unnatural and immoral argue that it undermines the institution of the family. The family to which such persons are typically alluding is heterosexual and comprises a husband, a wife, and their offspring. Those who condemn homosexuality do not see a role for gays in family formation; gay partnerships and parenting by gays violate their definition of what families are supposed to be about. Yet literally millions of gays in the United States are participants in family units that depart from this definition, and by and large such family constellations work exceedingly well for those involved (Bernstein 2003; Drucker

2001; Garner 2004; Howey et al. 2000). Researchers have concluded, for example, that the overall emotional well-being of children raised by gay male or lesbian parents is as healthy as that of children raised by heterosexual parents (Strickland 1995). Many people who are gay feel, however, that their partnerships and parenting activities would be facilitated in important ways were they not denied the right to marry.

In 2001 the Netherlands legalized marriage between members of the same sex, becoming the first nation in the world to do so. Since then thousands of couples have wed, and married gay couples there no longer generate much attention now. Same-sex marriages are now also legal in Belgium, Spain, Canada, and South Africa. In the United States there is an increase in support for civil unions and same-sex marriage: Public opinion polls show that 51 percent of respondents support legal

Although gay male and lesbian couples may not legally marry in most states in the United States, governments of some localities now give official recognition to gay domestic partnerships. These couples are celebrating their marriages after being issued marriage licenses in 2004 in Sandoval County, New Mexico.

recognition of gay and lesbian relationships (Fox News/Opinion Dynamics Poll, May 18–19, 2004; *Newsweek* Poll, May 13–14, 2004). Massachusetts courts legalized same-sex marriages in 2004; that same year San Francisco's City Hall performed scores of gay and lesbian marriages, as did the mayor of New Paltz, New York. Over two dozen municipalities now allow gay male and lesbian couples to file at City Hall for certificates providing recognition of "domestic partnerships" between members of the same sex, and a growing number of churches and synagogues perform "commitment ceremonies" to honor gay unions. Several of the nation's newspapers have abandoned their wedding and engagement pages in favor of "celebration" pages to allow public announcement of such events.

In 1993 Hawaii's state supreme court found prohibition of same-sex marriages to be a form of sex discrimination and unconstitutional unless there is a "compelling state interest" in their prohibition. The legal issues have not been resolved by the Hawaiian government as of this writing, but legalization of gay marriages has forced the issue of their legitimacy to be confronted across U.S. society, since currently every state recognizes marriages performed in all other states (Findlen 1995; Koppleman 1995). As of 2004, 43 states had specifically banned same-sex marriages, and most had no provision recognizing same-sex marriages performed elsewhere. Massachusetts stands alone so far in allowing same-sex marriages, and although New York bans them, it still recognizes same-sex marriages performed in other jurisdictions. Vermont bans same-sex marriages but allows civil unions, as do California and several other states (see the Human Rights Campaign at www.hrc.org).

The issue of gay marriage has become central in recent years to those involved in the struggle for gay rights (Sherman 1992). Why is this an issue for gays? Why do many gay couples wish to marry? The answer lies in part with the desire to have many of the same legal protections and financial benefits that marriage provides to heterosexual couples (Eskridge 1996; Mohr 1994). For example, absence of the right to marry means that only one parent in a same-sex partnership can have legal custody of a child they are rearing together. Ordinarily the second parent is not legally permitted to adopt that same child. In the event that the couple's partnership should end, the second parent cannot pursue custody rights or visitation privileges.

In addition, many gays wish to have legal protections for their decisions involving the inheritance of property, the distribution of assets should their partnership end, the determination of proper medical and nursing home care should a partner grow incapacitated and incapable of making decisions, and the choice of funeral and burial arrangements. Since same-sex couples cannot legally marry and lack the legal protections granted to a married couple, their immediate kin usually have the courts on their side when they seek to intervene on such matters.

Beyond legal protections afforded heterosexual couples, financial benefits from marriage are unavailable to gay partners. For example, employers often provide benefits to employees that extend to their spouses, such as health-care coverage and the ability to share in retirement and death benefits. Although a growing number of government and corporate employers now extend health care and other benefits to same-sex domestic partners of their employees, this is the exception rather than the rule. Nor are gay partners able to benefit from the same kinds of income tax deductions and exemptions as married couples, such as the advantage of filing joint returns. Surviving partners are ineligible for Social Security benefits in the event of the other's death.

Thus, in answer to the question "Why do many gay couples wish to marry?" it is in part because there are many important and practical benefits to be gained. And we have mentioned that marriage would provide the kinds of institutional underpinnings to gay couples that help to stabilize heterosexual marital partnerships and facilitate parenting. But beyond this, gay males and lesbians view the acceptance of gay marriage as necessary to legitimating and sanctioning the loving and fulfilling relationships they enter into with others, and they are no different from heterosexuals in this regard.

The Workplace

A great deal of media and public attention has been devoted to the issue of discrimination against gays employed as members of the U.S. military. Gays have long served in the U.S. military and have been treated with both acceptance and repression (Belkin and Bateman 2003; Rimmerman 1996; Shilts 1993). The Clinton administration initiated a controversial policy lifting in part the official ban on gays serving in the armed forces. (See Figure 9.3.) Under this policy, members of the armed forces will not be asked if they are homosexual and are not required to reveal their sexual orientation. Those who do reveal that they are gay are subject to dismissal, as are persons who engage in any form of homosexual conduct. The antigay discrimination that is obviously contained in this policy reform is being challenged in the courts.

However, far less attention has been given to discrimination in the civilian sector, where most people work. In 1995 Bill Clinton became the first U.S. president to endorse federal legislation outlawing job discrimination in the civilian sector against people who are gay (Holmes 1995). There, gay males and lesbians can be and are refused employment, passed over for transfers or promotions, denied raises and other forms of compensation, or simply fired by employers because of their sexual orientation. These things, of course, may occur no matter how qualified, hardworking, and productive an individual is. Only 13 states and 150 or so localities provide legal protection from job

"Sexual orientation is a personal and private matter. Officials of the Armed Forces will not ask and service members will not be required to reveal their sexual orientation.

"Homosexual orientation alone is not a bar to service entry or continued service unless manifested by homosexual conduct.

"Homosexual conduct includes a homosexual act, a statement by the member that demonstrates a propensity or intent to engage in homosexual acts, or a homosexual marriage or attempted marriage. When a member engages in homosexual conduct, he or she is subject to administrative separation.

"A statement by a member that demonstrates a propensity or intent to engage in **homosexual acts**—such as a statement by the member that he or she is a homosexual—is grounds for separation not because it reflects the member's sexual orientation, but because the statement indicates a likelihood that the member engages in or will engage in homosexual acts."

Figure 9.3   **U.S. Armed Forces Policy on Gay Troops**

Source: Directive issued by U.S. Secretary of Defense Les Aspin on December 22, 1993, U.S. Department of Defense, Washington, DC. The policy took effect on February 28, 1994.

discrimination against gays, and 8 more provide protection from sexual orientation discrimination in public workplaces only; federal laws provide no protections at all (U.S. Congress, Senate 1994; see also www.nolo .com/lawcenter). In 2004, President George W. Bush's Office of Special Counsel ruled that federal employees who are gay could be fired simply for their sexual orientation with no recourse. Immediately following that ruling, the White House began to remove information concerning discrimination based on sexual orientation from federal Web sites (*Federal Times* 2004; *Washington Post* 2004, available at http://daily.misleader.org).

Having little or no legal recourse against such discrimination, people who are gay are frequently forced to hide their sexual orientation from employers and fellow workers, often going to great lengths to do so. Although some work environments are open and accepting of their gay employees, and a growing number of large corporations have developed their own antidiscrimination policies and educational programs to address bias against gays by supervisors and coworkers, the problems that often arise from being "out" in the workplace are such that many gays feel they must strive to keep their sexual orientation a secret (Winfield and Spielman 2001; Woog 2001). Indeed, anticipation and fear of discrimination have even been found to influence career decisions by some people who are gay (Baker et al. 1995; Woods 1993).

Trying to hide the fact that one is gay from people in the workplace can be extremely trying and stressful, particularly given the risks of making a mistake. It means you may not feel free to display photos or other symbols of your relationship with a partner lest questions be asked. It means being unable to talk about persons who are extremely important in your life, while others do so routinely. It means not being able to introduce others to your partner, or bring her or him to employee social affairs. It means censoring one's conversation so as not to reveal anything about dating or romantic interests, being in settings such as gay bars or gay-oriented events, or having an interest in political issues such as gay rights. One may even be forced to look the other way, nod in agreement, or join in when others make statements that express homophobia or homohatred.

Not all of the problems and risks involved in being out in the workplace can be solved by legislation against discrimination, but similar legislation has greatly assisted white women and people of color in their quest for fair treatment. Since all gays are asking for is the opportunity to be judged on their ability to do work, just like other employees, antidiscrimination laws do not involve granting gays special treatment.

Although the majority of adults polled say they support laws protecting people against job discrimination based on sexual orientation, the federal government has been very slow to act. Many members of Congress are either skittish about or hostile to siding with any kind of gay rights legislation. Many fear or agree with vocal cadres of constituents who have been activated by organizations fighting in the political arena to keep such bills off the legislative agenda. Others prefer to avoid, if at all possible, taking positions on issues around which opponents could foster controversy at election time. In the meantime discrimination in the workplace against persons who are gay continues daily, and its victims have relatively little legal clout that would impede it.

Education

The ideology of heterosexism also permeates our educational systems, where young people who are gay must often deal with verbal abuse and physical harassment with little or no protection or support from school authorities, others are without guidance in handling difficult questions of sexual identity, and the formal curriculum ignores or devalues homosexuality (Unks 1995; Woog 1995). Hostile school environments are thought to contribute to the appalling rate of suicide among gay youth mentioned at the opening of this chapter.

The first comprehensive survey of sexual harassment experiences among students in grades 8 to 11 found that such harassment was surprisingly widespread (Barringer 1993). Usually we stereotypically think of sexual harassment as mistreatment of heterosexual females by heterosexual males, and this survey's findings suggested there is plenty of that. But it also revealed that male and female students are victims of abuse and harassment because they are gay, are thought to be gay, or are perceived as acting like gays. For example, in the survey cited, almost 25 percent of boys and 10 percent of girls report having been subject to antihomosexual epithets by others in school. While in some cases school personnel may be quick to act assertively on behalf of victims of abuse and harassment, others choose to ignore it and some even engage in it themselves.

Given the treatment they receive, it is understandable that gay students, or students who suspect they are gay, often keep their sexual identity secret and are frequently terrified that it may somehow be revealed. The stresses and anxieties students must contend with are not unlike those faced by employees who fear exposure of their sexual orientation in the workplace. The difference is that students are usually less mature and less experienced in dealing with such difficult challenges, and, unlike most adults, students often do not have others with whom to share their troubles and receive needed support. Keeping such a secret can be an enormous burden to carry around. Many gay youth feel a sense of relief from being "out" (Heron 1995).

Yet whereas revealing one's sexual orientation may reduce the burden of secrecy, it exposes many students to new burdens that may become overwhelming to handle and that may even lead them to abandon school. A Massachusetts Governor's Commission on Gay and Lesbian Youth Report (1993:6–7) on the treatment of gay males and lesbians in schools had this to say:

Parents, family, peers and teachers are generally ignorant of what it means to be gay or lesbian. Gay and lesbian youth have little chance of talking with a knowledgeable or understanding person concerning his or her gay or lesbian identity. . . . Both adults and peers often reject gay and lesbian youths. This often takes the form of physical violence and verbal harassment, leading 28% of gay and lesbian youth to drop out of high school, according to the U.S. Department of Health and Human Services. The
primary effect of society's hostility and lack of acceptance are feelings of isolation, extreme low self-esteem, and consequent attempts at self-destructive behavior.

The sense of isolation and low self-esteem can only be reinforced by the failure of the typical school curricula to acknowledge homosexuality or to treat it in ways that promote understanding of and respect for people who are gay. The fact that many prominent figures whose accomplishments are studied in school were gay is rarely acknowledged. History and social studies courses virtually ignore the gay rights movement and contemporary gay issues. Sex education courses proceed as if homosexuality were never part of anyone's sexual experiences, or they associate it with the risk of acquiring AIDS. The word *gay* or *homosexual* is rarely found in books assigned to students. And many parents want it this way, fearing that exposure to information about gay males and lesbians may cause their children to become gay or to become accepting of the "gay lifestyle" about which antigay groups talk.

The situation for gay youth is somewhat better in institutions of higher education, although not much. Many colleges and universities have gay-oriented organizations and support groups in which students who are gay can become involved if they wish, as well as policies prohibiting harassment (Evans and Wall 1991). Yet others refuse to recognize gay groups as legitimate campus organizations and do little to help students with sexual identity and harassment issues. However, even in institutions where school authorities make efforts to recognize the existence of the gay population, many gay students still do not feel comfortable or safe in their college environment (D'Augelli 1989; Herek and Berrill 1992).

Despite the appearance of gay and lesbian studies programs on some campuses, and a few courses pertaining to gays at others, the curricula at most colleges and universities are as silent on the accomplishments of people who are gay and gay rights issues as is the case in high schools. The situation is changing, more so than at the lower levels of education, but with excruciating slowness.

The failure of educational systems at all levels to work on breaking down stereotypes and myths about homosexuality, and their failure to foster zero tolerance for abuse and harassment of gays, contributes to homophobia and homohatred. Too often, ignorance is tolerated, and in too many instances school and college personnel act as if gays are responsible for bringing harassment on themselves. Anti-gay-rights groups dismiss attempts to introduce harassment policies and factual material about homosexuality into school and college curricula as misguided efforts to be "politically correct," ignoring the costs of heterosexism for everyone, not only those who are gay.

Consequences of Heterosexism

The ideology of heterosexism, as expressed through institutional operations and interpersonal relations, clearly harms people who are gay. If you are not gay, try to imagine having to deal daily with hostile social environments in school and the workplace, being cast as unnatural and immoral by one's own religion, experiencing rejection from family members and peers, having the legitimacy of being with one's chosen partner denied, and being constantly vulnerable to violence from homohatred. And to what powers-that-be do you look for help, protection, and an end to this ordeal? In most instances, even the government has little to offer. Indeed, as we have previously discussed, at times the government itself reinforces heterosexism in social institutions, including in health care, where, in Michigan in 2004 the legislature voted to allow health-care providers to refuse to treat gay patients without threat of being sued or disciplined (www.365gay.com).

Self-destructive behavior is understandable within such a context, as is hiding and keeping one's head low. For gays, unlike heterosexuals, the desire for privacy demands a search for secrecy. But rebellion and protest in many different forms are also understandable. Those who view themselves as heterosexual should not be surprised at the vehemence with which gay rights advocates press their positions on issues, given what is at stake for the millions who are gay.

Heterosexism harms people who would never choose to be members of a disdained and oppressed group, but who cannot alter their sexual orientation any more than heterosexuals. Yet this situation produces suffering not only for gays. Families, for example, may carry heavy burdens as well. Just about all parents worry about their children. But parents who are open and accepting of the fact that their child is gay, or who learn to be accepting, cannot help but worry over the unique kinds of problems with which their child will have to contend. In many ways, heterosexism is antifamily, as it can create unnecessary divisions between gay and heterosexual family members and force families to endure stresses that would not otherwise exist.

The organization Parents, Families, and Friends of Lesbians and Gays (P-FLAG), whose local chapters exist across the United States, brings people together for mutual support whose lives are often negatively touched by heterosexism, despite the fact that most such persons are heterosexual (Bernstein 2003). This suggests that heterosexism harms the dominant group as well as gays (Blumenfeld 1992).

Harm to the dominant group comes in the broadest sense from the suppression and loss of human talent from which we could all benefit, and heterosexism thus has parallels in this regard with racism and sexism. If, for example, young gay males and lesbians find high school or college to be hostile environments and leave these settings, never to return, many potential contributions they might make disappear. If energetic, productive people are denied jobs or fired because of their sexual orientation, the fall-out is experienced by all.

Finally, we should reiterate a point made earlier in this chapter. Antigay sentiments, expressed in the form of homophobia or homohatred, tend to call for commitment by all to conventional gender roles and thus maintenance of the existing system of gender inequality in U.S. society. Heterosexism—at both the interpersonal and institutional levels—helps to maintain sexism, and vice versa. As we saw in the previous chapter, sexism harms both women and men.

Supporting Gay Rights

Gay rights is a young movement, patterned in many respects after the civil rights movement and other activities for social change that emerged in the United States in the 1960s (Adam 1987; Miller 1995). The movement seeks to end the discriminatory ways in which people who are gay are treated in order that they may live their lives with the same freedom and dignity as heterosexuals (Stevenson and Cogan 2003). This requires combating the ideology of heterosexism and fighting its various expressions, at both the institutional and interpersonal levels.

Although support for the rights of people who are gay is not new in the United States, advocacy that is widespread, organized, and militant has occurred only over the last 30 or so years. Today's gay rights movement is often said to have been sparked by an event that occurred in 1969 in New York City. There, as in most parts of the country, police raids of places where gays came to meet and socialize were frequent and often accompanied by harassment, if not outright police brutality. Those subject to such treatment were often afraid to complain and received little or no response from police authorities and local elected officials even when they did.

On June 17, 1969, the New York City police performed a routine raid on the Stonewall Inn, a neighborhood bar with a largely gay clientele, many of whom were people of color. Unlike previous occasions when such raids occurred, the 200 or so gays in the bar refused to disperse and met police attempts to force them to do so with a collective counterattack that lasted 45 minutes until police reinforcements were able to end it. The incident electrified the gay community and inspired gays in New York and elsewhere across the country to begin organizing around not only police misconduct but discriminatory treatment and harassment in other areas as well. The message was that gays no longer would be passive victims of homophobia and homohatred.

"Gay liberation" groups, as they were initially often called, formed in many urban centers and on college and university campuses. Their activities drew unexpected degrees of support from sympathetic members of the dominant heterosexual community. The growing visibility of political activities led by gay males and lesbians drew more and more gays out of hiding, and the snowballing effect of local organizing activities began to give local groups the weapon of political clout in many of the nation's cities. As gay political consciousness rose, so did a sense of unity (see Seidman 2004).

This unity was facilitated by the growing concentration of gays in particular neighborhoods and residential areas of major cities, which began in the wake of World War II. Gay-owned and operated businesses emerged in these areas, and as time went on, members of local gay communities were able to frequent gay churches, social service organizations, health and recreational facilities, bars and restaurants, and bookstores and could read newspapers and magazines published by and for gays. These communities were not (and still are not) perfect havens, given that they often contained some of the race, class, and gender biases prevailing in the larger society, but they were of economic, social, and political significance to gays. The number of gay activists emerging out of such communities mushroomed, putting pressure on local political party structures to pay attention to increasingly well organized gay voting blocs and constituencies.

Networking within and between cities allowed politically active gay leaders to develop communications and resources that led to the creation of national-level organizations, such as the National Gay and Lesbian Task Force, which gathers information on gay issues and lobbies in coalition with other groups on gay rights matters. Other organizations such as the AIDS Coalition to Unleash Power (ACT-UP), Lambda Legal Defense and Education Fund, and the Human Rights Campaign are active in Washington, D.C., and throughout the United States on gay rights issues. ACT-UP, for example, is an organization known for its outspoken efforts to get the federal government to acknowledge the seriousness of the AIDS epidemic and to increase funding for

AIDS research. ACT-UP has also pressured the federal government and major drug corporations to move faster on testing and approval of medicines that may help people with AIDS, and it fought to reduce the prices drug manufacturers charge for these highly expensive medications.

The passage of the National Hate Crimes Statistics Act of 1990, the government's response to the AIDS crisis, the partial lifting of the ban on gays in the U.S. military, and the emergence of presidential support for legislation against job discrimination on the basis of sexual orientation would not have been possible without the support behind the gay rights movement from people who are gay and many heterosexuals as well. (See Figure 9.4.) But these and other

Attitude	% Responding	Source
Has a close friend who is gay	23%	1
Has a gay person in the family	15	1
Has a coworker or acquaintance who is gay	48	1
Lives in a community that accepts gays who live there	62	1
Has become more accepting of gays and lesbians	32	2
Are not bothered by being around homosexuals	76	3
Agree there should be laws protecting gays and lesbians against discrimination in job opportunities	76	4
Agree there should be laws protecting gays and lesbians against discrimination in housing	74	4
Agree there should be a change in policy to allow gays and lesbians to serve openly in the military	56	4
Would favor a law that would mandate increased penalties for people who commit hate crimes out of prejudice toward gays and lesbians	73	4

Sources:
1. *Los Angeles Times* Poll, March 27–30, 2004
2. CNN/*USA Today* Survey, July 18–20, 2003
3. Pew Research Center Forum on Religion and Public Life Survey, October 15–19, 2003
4. Henry J. Kaiser Family Foundation Survey, February 7–September 4, 2000

Figure 9.4   **Selected Survey Results on Gays and Gay Rights**

Source: *Los Angeles Times* Poll, March 27–30, 2004; CNN/*USA Today* Survey, July 18–20, 2003; Pew Research Center Forum on Religion and Public Life Survey, October 15–19, 2003; and Henry J. Kaiser Family Foundation Survey, February 7–September 4, 2000.

successes do little more than recognize the plight of people who are gay in U.S. society.

We are a long way from abolishing heterosexism and its expressions. Many issues remain open and unresolved on the gay rights agenda. However, the issues themselves are "out of the closet" and cannot readily be put back in. Their resolution in ways that enhance the human rights of people who are gay can only be in the interests of all members of U.S. society.

Summary

Heterosexism is an ideology holding that homosexuality is unnatural and immoral, and that heterosexuality is the only acceptable and viable life option for society's members. This ideology is manifested at the interpersonal level in the form of homophobia and homohatred, and it is also embedded in the norms and practices of key societal institutions.

People occupy positions on a broad spectrum with regard to their sexual orientation, which may even change over time. Defining sexual orientation is complex, as a definition must address not only the question of to whom people are sexually attracted but also the behaviors in which they engage and their sexual identity.

While much theorizing focuses on possible psychological reasons for homosexuality, others posit social contagion theories. To date, no definitive evidence supports either line of theorizing. Research pointing to biological causes looks promising to many, but is a long way from being definitive. Moreover, there is reason to be concerned over the political implications of the discovery of a "gay gene"; in a society dominated by heterosexism, some might seek to use technology to tamper with sexual orientation if they could.

No one knows just how many homosexuals are in the United States. In part this arises from the difficulty of defining sexual orientation and studying it. There are many myths and stereotypes containing negative and erroneous assertions about the nature of homosexuality and the character of people who are gay. These stand in the way of ending negative treatment of gays and support for gay rights.

Although there are exceptions, many religious institutions adhere to an ideology of heterosexism in their doctrines. Gay rights advocates believe that the traditional separation of church and state is being endangered. They argue that politically influential religious groups are, in pushing antigay legislation, trying to dictate policies that threaten the constitutionally protected rights of individuals.

Many people who are gay believe that the partnerships and parenting activities to which they are committed would be facilitated if they had the legal right to marry. Marriage would provide gay males and lesbians with legal protections and financial advantages granted to heterosexual couples, help to stabilize gay partnerships, and legitimate the loving and fulfilling relationships into which many gay couples enter. But to date, only one state has legalized marriage by same-sex couples.

Discrimination in the workplace and in schooling poses enormous difficulties for people who are gay. There is little legal protection against workplace discrimination, and people must often hide their sexual orientation or face harassment and loss of jobs. Schools and colleges likewise often provide hostile social environments. Abuse, harassment, and violence threaten those known or thought to be gay. Likewise, curricula do not ordinarily treat people who are gay in a positive manner. Education too often contributes to homophobia and homohatred, rather than helping to combat it.

Gays clearly suffer in a society dominated by heterosexism, but others do so as well. For example, the parents and families of people who are gay are burdened knowing the problems in living they face. All members of society are negatively affected by the loss of talent, productivity, and contributions of people whose potential is repressed and opportunities denied on the basis of their sexual orientation. Insofar as heterosexism calls for rigid conformity to conventional gender roles, it is supportive of the gender inequality that exacts costs from both women and men.

An active, militant gay rights movement exists and has successfully brought many of these issues into the public eye. We are a long way from abolishing heterosexism and its expressions, but these issues are themselves "out of the closet" and cannot readily be put back in. Their resolution can only be in the interests of all members of U.S. society.

Key Terms

Bisexual 273
Heteronormativity 270
Heterosexism 272

Homohatred 271
Homophobia 270

Discussion Questions

1. Do you have a relative or friend who is gay? Speak with that person about the kinds of problems with which they have to contend and how they deal with them. Share your findings with other members of the class.

2. Surveys indicate that three-quarters of those polled support prohibiting job discrimination against people who are gay, yet only a third approve of legally sanctioned gay marriages. Why?

3. How does homophobia manifest itself among people you know? What do you think it would take for these persons to overcome their homophobia?

4. Homohatred sometimes takes the form of "queerbashing," in which people thought to be gay are physically attacked. Why do you think such crimes are committed?

5. Some have argued that the vocal expression of antigay sentiments by organized groups in recent years, and agreement with these sentiments by a number of highly visible political figures, is feeding homophobia and homohatred. Do you agree or disagree? Why?

6. Characters who are gay are beginning to appear in movies, television dramas, soap operas, and comedies; and gay rights issues are now occasionally portrayed. Why do you think this is occurring? What effects do you think this has?

Suggested Readings

The Alyson Almanac, 1994–95 Edition: The Fact Book of the Gay and Lesbian Community (Boston: Alyson Publications, 1993).
A reference book about people who are gay, including the history of and significant events in the gay community, and lists of gay social and political organizations.

Heron, Ann, ed. *Two Teenagers in Twenty* (Boston: Alyson Publications, 1994).
A guide to problems and challenges faced by young people who are questioning their sexual identity or dealing with the knowledge that they are gay.

Miller, Neil. *Out of the Past: Gay and Lesbian History from 1869 to the Present* (New York: Vintage Books, 1995).
Traces the mistreatment of gays, and documents the evolution of gay resistance and unity that undergirds the contemporary gay rights movement.

Nava, Michael, and Robert Dawidoff. *Created Equal: Why Gay Rights Matter to America* (New York: St. Martin's Press, 1994).
What the gay rights movement is all about and why failure to protect gay people diminishes and threatens the rights of all.

Seidman, Steven. *Beyond the Closet: The Transformation of Gay and Lesbian Life* (New York: Routledge, 2004).
Examines the cultural changes in which gays and lesbians have become increasingly open in their participation in social and political institutions.

Stryker, Susan, and Stephen Whittle, eds. *The Transgender Reader* (New York: Routledge, 2004).
Selected readings of observations by physicians, psychologists, academics, and transgender individuals themselves examining their experiences in a heteronormative world.

Sutton, Roger. *Hearing Us Out: Voices from the Gay and Lesbian Community* (Boston: Little, Brown, 1994).
Gay persons—differing from one another in age, gender, and color—discuss how they and others have dealt with their sexual orientation.

Weeks, Jeffrey. *Sexuality.* 2d ed. (New York: Routledge, 2003).
A sociological exploration of the social construction of sexualities and its relations to the state and its power to regulate these.

chapter 10

Ageism

There should be no personal and institutional discrimination against individuals on the basis of age.

From the moment of birth each of us is involved in the process of aging. That is one thing we can all count on. As we live on, our bodies inevitably undergo some subtle and often visible changes. Somewhere along the way we are deemed "old," based on popular social definitions held by those who are chronologically younger. Often such social definitions bear little relation to our objective capacities to contribute to and draw enjoyment from the society of which we are a part.

Census statistics show a dramatic increase in the proportion of persons who have entered "old age." (Old age is arbitrarily, but commonly, considered to commence at age 65.) Statistics on life expectancy have led to predictions of further dramatic increases in the number and proportion of the population who will enter old age in the first half of the twenty-first century. The "graying of America" is a development that carries significant social, economic, and political ramifications that we are only beginning to appreciate and confront.

For most persons the fact of aging is not in and of itself an overwhelming problem. Aging is, after all, natural and inevitable. It is instead the treatment one receives that is problematic. Thus, in this chapter we consider elders as members of a "minority group," subject to personal prejudice and institutional discrimination. Myths and stereotypes about those who have entered later life are common and help to contribute to an environment in which **ageism** quietly flourishes and turns many older people in the United States into second-class citizens. Ageism is ideas, practices, and structures that discriminate against and produce negative consequences for persons defined as old. Social science theory, as we shall see, has contributed to this process, suggesting that it is necessary for aging persons to disengage from important life roles for the good of society. In practice a substantial (and growing) segment of the U.S. population is denied or discouraged from participation in a variety of arenas of life, prompting dependency and physical decline often well before they occur as a result of biological processes.

As they are encouraged to disengage, many of our elders are confronted simultaneously with a variety of conditions that may speed their demise. Among these conditions, to be reviewed in this chapter, are involuntary unemployment and permanent loss of economically productive roles; economic strain, often to the point of poverty or near-poverty; lack of adequate assistance in maintaining physical and mental health; inadequate housing and transportation; victimization by criminals; and abuse by caregivers. Such conditions render growing old the worst part of life for millions of people now, and many more millions will be affected similarly in the future.

As you read these lines, you are growing older and are coming closer to joining a "minority group" that, sociologically, should never exist. Since we all will probably belong to this group, we all have a stake in how aging people are treated. If only for this reason we should be more than a little concerned about this macro problem.

Biological and Social Definitions of Aging

Aging is a natural and inevitable biological process, one that begins at birth. With increases in chronological age, people undergo physiological changes—some visible, others hidden—that precede an end to life. Physical appearance undergoes a marked alteration with time, including the loss of skin elasticity, the appearance of wrinkles, the graying of hair (because of pigment loss), and signs of frailty. Hidden changes may affect sight and hearing. The circulatory, respiratory, and other major body systems lose their operating efficiency. Susceptibility to illness and disease increases, and aging persons

may lose their ability to combat sickness as well as when they were younger. "Primary aging" occurs naturally, over time, while "secondary aging" occurs when disabilities due to disease or trauma are added on to the primary aging process (Moody 2002).

The rate of biological aging varies among individuals. Thus, a given chronological age does not automatically dictate when the types of changes involved in aging will occur. As yet poorly understood genetic factors may contribute to variations in the aging process among different persons. Certainly environmental influences play a role. One's lifestyle, dietary and nutritional practices, exercise habits, amount of exposure to physically harmful conditions and substances, access to adequate health-care services, and degree of contact with psychologically stressful experiences are thought to affect the biology of aging. Hence, older persons are in reality a heterogeneous group in physiological terms.

In the face of this heterogeneity and the wide differences in mental and physical capacity associated with it, members of U.S. society understandably lack a common definition of when old age commences (Palmore 1999). Often people use a social definition of old age that is largely chronologically based. But however old age is defined, it is typically accompanied by a set of often erroneous assumptions about persons who are reaching their later years. Old age is commonly thought to commence at age 65. This view has been encouraged by the institutionalization of 65 as the age of eligibility for certain federal social insurance benefits, such as Social Security, and (until very recently) the age of mandatory retirement from employment. While an individual may be no different at age 65 than at age 64, except in chronological years, by social definition this one year arbitrarily signals old age.

Even more arbitrary is the fact that entering old age carries with it certain widespread assumptions about what people 65 and beyond are like. Robert N. Butler (1975:6–7) cogently describes what many persons who are chronologically under 65 seem to believe about their older counterparts:

An older person thinks and moves slowly. He does not think as he used to or as creatively. He is bound to himself and to his past and can no longer change or grow. He can learn neither well nor swiftly and if he could, he would not wish to. . . . He enters a second childhood, caught up in increasing egocentricity. . . . He becomes irritable and cantankerous, yet shallow and enfeebled. . . . Indeed, he is a study in decline, the picture of mental and physical failure.

Although Butler refers to "he," his observation also applies to women. And while this description may well depict some small segment of the older population accurately, it does a grave injustice to the bulk of this population by ignoring the heterogeneity we have discussed. Reaching chronological age 65 does not automatically mean entering into a state of "mental and physical failure," a fact to which we shall return in our discussion of myths and stereotypes about old age.

The social definitions bearing on old age also differ by gender. Whereas gray hair for a man who is aging is likely to give him a "distinguished appearance," for a woman it is a sign of "getting old"; women spend a lot of money and effort to color their hair in order to deny their age and "pass" as younger (Gerike 1990; Rich and Macdonald 2001). Because of our social and cultural emphasis on women's role as a sex object (see Chapter 8), any movement away from the artificial mass-media ideal of youth and feminine beauty is widely considered a step toward old age, as well as a step down. Whole industries (cosmetics, hairstyling, clothing, and footwear) thrive on women's commercially induced fear of age obsolescence. The mass media

do not maintain an artificial ideal of youthful beauty for males with anywhere near the intensity that they do for females.

Socially, women are informally defined as old at an earlier age than men. This dual standard has a variety of ramifications. Older men may freely marry women who are chronologically much younger without drawing social criticism, but older women may not marry younger men with such freedom. Since, as we shall see, the proportion of women in the population is much greater than that of men in advanced age groups, widowed, divorced, or never-married heterosexual older women are at a distinct disadvantage in locating male partners. Older men face far less of a problem in this regard.

The social definition of women as being old chronologically earlier than men also has significance in the sphere of employment. Despite legal strictures against age discrimination, there is widespread subtle discrimination toward the hiring of women whose appearance is within or not far from the artificial mass-media ideal of youthful beauty. This is particularly the case in situations where employed women are expected to have extensive public contact by virtue of the work performed. But it is also the case that many male employers believe it is within their prerogative to include "decorating the office" as one unspoken criterion for who will be hired. Many older women face difficulty in finding employment, and this difficulty is not necessarily related to their job skills or record of work experience. Again, men have an advantage in not being as constrained in employment opportunities by such invisible, discriminatory standards.

The social definitions of *old age* often arbitrarily start at age 65, lump a heterogeneous group of older persons together as "mental and physical failures," and treat women as old at earlier ages than men. These social definitions affect tens of millions of people. In the next section we examine those socially defined as "old," people 65 and older.

The Graying of the U.S. Population

Population Trends and Projections

Census figures for 2002 indicate that almost 36 million people in the United States are 65 or older, a number that represents more than 12.3 percent of the population (U.S. Census 2004). There has been a dramatic increase in the number of older people in the United States since the turn of the century. In 1900 only 3.1 million persons, representing 4.0 percent of the population, were 65 or older. In every decade from the 1930s through the 1960s the number of

elders grew by a third, a trend sometimes referred to as the **graying of America** (Gist and Hetzel 2003; Neubeck and Glasberg 2005). Figure 10.1 illustrates the changing age distribution in the United States.

Until early in this century the percentage of the population that was 65 or older remained low. This was primarily due to high birthrates among families, the relative youth of much of the large incoming immigrant population, and limited life expectancies among the aging. Since then birthrates have gone down and life expectancy has increased, largely because of medical advances and improved health practices. Immigration continues but at nowhere near the rate of earlier years.

Birthrates and changes in life expectancy both will play a role in determining the future

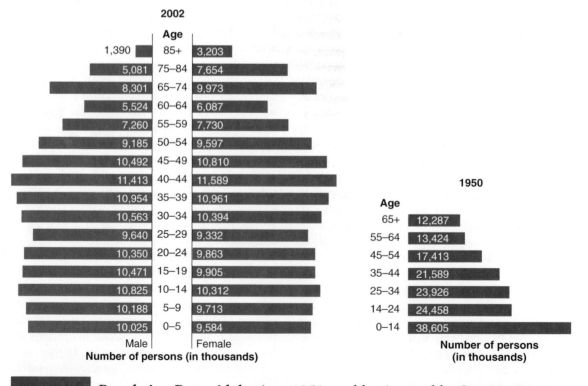

Figure 10.1   **Population Pyramid, by Age, 1950, and by Age and by Sex, 2002**

Source: U.S. Bureau of the Census, *Statistical Abstract of the United States* (Washington, DC: Government Printing Office, 2004), p. 13.

age composition of the U.S. population. Experts currently estimate that the 65-and-older population could increase as follows: by 2015, up to 46.8 million, or 13 percent; by 2025, up to 63.5 million, or 18.2 percent; and by 2050 up to 86.7 million, or 20.7 percent (U.S. Bureau of the Census 2004). A dramatic jump between 2010 and 2025 is forecast because that is the period when the members of the post–World War II "baby boom" will reach 65 and thus "old age." Much of how these predicted trends emerge depends on whether the present low rates of birth continue. Fewer members of the baby boom are still in their childbearing years. A decrease in the birthrate due to reduced childbearing by baby boom members could have the effect of speed-

ing the rate of percentage increase of persons 65 and older in the twenty-first century.

Just as changes in the birthrate could affect current projections, so might increases in average life expectancy. As it now stands, life expectancy is estimated at more than 77 years for those persons born in 2000. (The average life expectancy in 1900 was 49 years.) White females born in 2000 are thought to have an average life expectancy of 80.1 years; for African American females, it is 75.2 years. White males have a shorter average life expectancy of 74.9 years, and African American males lag far behind at 68.3 years (U.S. Bureau of the Census 2004). Figure 10.2 illustrates these differences as well as changes over time.

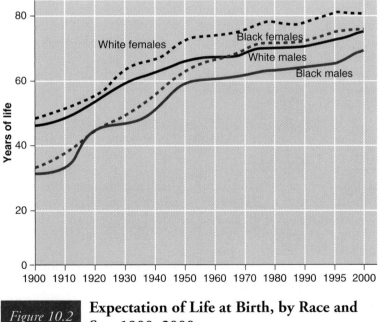

Figure 10.2 **Expectation of Life at Birth, by Race and Sex: 1900–2000**

Source: Cynthia M. Tauber, *America in Transition: An Aging Society,* Bureau of the Census (Washington, DC: Government Printing Office, 1983), p. 5; National Center for Health Statistics, *Monthly Vital Statistics Report* 33 (December 20, 1984): 3; U.S. Department of Health and Human Services, *Health, United States, 1988* (Washington, DC: Government Printing Office, 1989), p. 53; U.S. Department of Commerce, Bureau of the Census, *Statistical Abstract of the United States, 1995* (Washington, DC: Government Printing Office, 1995), p. 86; and U.S. Bureau of the Census, *Statistical Abstract of the United States, 2003* (Washington, DC: Government Printing Office, 2004), p. 85.

Earlier medical advances in this century helped to reduce infant mortality. More modern advances promise to extend old age further in chronological time. The three leading causes of death for those 65 and older are heart disease, cancer, and stroke. Seventy-five percent of deaths in this age category are from these causes. Preventive and curative practices in recent years, as well as innovations and discoveries expected in the future, are likely to increase the average life expectancy beyond what it is today. Indeed, current projections see average life expectancy moving from today's 77 years to almost 79 years by 2010 (U.S. Bureau of the Census 2004).

No one disagrees that the graying of America is taking place and that the proportion of the U.S. population age 65 and over will be substantial in the twenty-first century. Statistical projections are, however, somewhat tentative because of uncertainty over what actual birthrates and life expectancies will be. But all experts agree that the changing age composition of the population will place many new demands on members of U.S. society (Siegel 1993; Zedlewski et al. 1990).

Characteristics of the Elderly

Earlier we noted that the rate of biological aging varies and that this creates a degree of heterogeneity among older people in the United States in terms of their physical and mental capacities. The heterogeneity exists on many other levels as well, making it even more erroneous to refer to "old people" as if they were all the same. In this section we describe further sources of difference.

▲ Financial Status

Many people are under the impression that older people are affluent. It is true that the nation's wealthy, discussed in Chapter 6, tend to be older persons. But the bulk of wealth-holdings among elders is concentrated in a very small segment of this population. The net worth of most elders is not very great, often amounting to no more than equity in an aging home and a small body of savings. Income, likewise, is unevenly distributed among those 65 and older. While 15 percent of elders had total incomes over $50,000 in 2001, 16 percent had incomes between $5,000 and $9,999, and 18 percent had incomes between $10,000 and $14,999; another 5 percent had incomes below $5,000 (U.S. Department of Health and Human Services 2002:11).

Elderly people have long been forced to function under severely strained economic conditions (Fischer 1981). Until fairly recently, the percentage of elderly falling within the federal government's official definition of poverty was very high. In 1960, for example, about 35 percent of those 65 and older lived in poverty. According to James H. Schultz (1980:46), "the economic status of the elderly has changed dramatically in recent years, primarily as a result of rising social security, private pension, and government employees' pension income." Nonetheless, in 2002 over 10 percent of the 65-and-older population, a figure representing 3.6 million people, had poverty-level household incomes. Those who were "near-poor" (with incomes no higher than 125 percent of the official poverty line) constituted another 5.8 million. Thus, in 2002 one in four of those 65 and older was deemed poor or near-poor (Proctor and Dalaker 2003). (We shall return to poverty among elders in a later section.)

▲ Ethnic and Racial Composition

Many older persons in the United States today (10.6 percent) are foreign-born, largely as a consequence of migration from European countries early in the twentieth century until World War I. The majority of persons 65 and older are white (see Table 10.1), but because the life expectancy of people of color is lower than that of the white majority, a smaller percentage reaches old age than would be expected on the basis of their representation in the overall population. In 2002 the

Table 10.1	Persons 65 Years Old and Over by Sex, 2002	
Characteristic	Male	Female
Total (million)	**14.2**	**19.5**
White (million)	8.4	16.1
Black (million)	1.1	1.7
Percent below poverty level	7.7	12.4
Percent distribution		
Marital status:		
Single	4.7	4.3
Married	75.7	42.9
Spouse present	73.1	40.8
Spouse absent	2.6	2.1
Widowed	13.9	45.5
Divorced	6.7	8.0
Family status:		
In families	79.2	57.6
Nonfamily householders	19.3	41.5
Secondary individuals	1.5	1.0
Living arrangements:		
Living in household		
Living alone	19.0	40.0
Spouse present	73.0	50.0
Living with someone else	3.0	3.0
Not in household	0.1	0.2
Years of school completed:		
Eight years or less	16.5	15.2
One to three years of high school	13.7	14.9
Four years of high school	30.2	39.0
One to three years of college	17.6	18.1
Four years or more of college	22.0	12.8
Labor force participation:		
Employed	17.2	9.5
Unemployed	0.6	0.4
Not in labor force	82.1	90.2

Source: U.S. Department of Commerce, Bureau of the Census, *Statistical Abstract of the United States, 2003* (Washington, DC: U.S. Government Printing Office, 2004).

percentage of African Americans who were 65 and older was 8.0; in contrast, 13.5 percent of whites were in this group. For Asian Americans the rate was 8.0, and for Latino and Latina Americans it was only 5.1 percent (U.S. Bureau of the Census 2003:15).

Nonetheless, the proportion of those age 65 and over who are people of color is growing,

Members of U.S. society who are in their "old age" are a very heterogeneous group, contrary to popular stereotypes. It is erroneous to make broad generalizations about older people without keeping many qualifications and exceptions in mind. The runner pictured here helps to remind us that the aging process is not uniform for all.

reflecting the increasing diversity of the U.S. population we discussed in Chapter 7. One U.S. Census projection foresees whites decreasing from almost 88 percent of the 65 and over population in 2002 to 65 percent in 2050. African Americans, Asian Americans, and Native Americans would constitute 20 percent, and Latino Americans 15 percent of elders (Goldstein 1993; U.S. Bureau of the Census 2004).

▲ Sex Composition

The life expectancy differences between men and women noted earlier clearly affect the sex composition of the 65-and-older population. Women in this group outnumbered men in 2002 by over 6 million. In that year the census found 20.8 million older women and 14.8 million older men. As one moves up chronologically in the 65-and-older grouping, the ratio between men and women changes. In the 65 to 74 age category there are 83 men for every 100 women. By ages 75 to 84 this ratio is down to 66 men for every 100 women, and among those 85 and above there are only 43 men for every 100 women (U.S. Bureau of the Census 2003:13).

Since older women infrequently marry younger men, this disparity underscores the high probability that a married woman, reaching old age, will spend a number of years without her spouse. Indeed, only 1.6 percent of men 65 and older live alone, compared with 36.4 percent of women. By age 85, only 1 percent of men are living alone, compared with 47 percent of women (Gist and Hetzel 2004). Women have little opportunity to remarry if they lose their spouse. There are more than three times as many widows as there are widowers among elders, and twice as many widowers marry each year (Palmore 1999; U.S. Bureau of the Census 2004:42).

▲ Educational Attainment

When today's elders were born, completion of a high school education was not yet the norm. Moreover, many were foreign-born and had little contact with U.S. schooling. Thus, the 65-and-older group has, on the average, fewer years of formal education than the general population. Only 33.5 percent of those 65 years of age and older have one or more years of college (Gist and Hetzel 2004). This situation is changing because persons born since World War I, and especially since World War II, have had progressively greater educational opportunities and reasons to pursue them. Hence, persons reaching old age in coming decades will have far greater levels of formal education than many present-day elders. The difference between this group and the general population in this regard will become minimal.

▲ Labor Force Participation

Since the turn of the century the proportion of persons 65 years of age and older who continue to work has dropped markedly. In 1900 two-thirds of all males in this age group worked, as did 1 in 12 females. While the female rate of labor force participation has remained about the same, the male rate has declined. By 1950 less than half of all older males were in the labor force. This number has since dropped to 18.6 percent. Thus, in a relatively short period, retirement from the labor force by age 65 has become the norm. In fact, over a third of those in the sixty to sixty-four age category are no longer working (U.S. Bureau of the Census 2004). In the 65-and-over group, two out of five retirees claim to have left work involuntarily. Those who remain working past 65 are concentrated in low-paying, often part-time positions.

▲ Geographical Distribution

Although early in this century elders were uniformly distributed throughout the United States, this pattern has changed. Since World War II members of this population have become concentrated in relatively few states. About one-third of the 65-and-older population lives in the South. Nine states have more than a million elders: New York, California, Florida, Pennsylvania, Illinois,

Ohio, Michigan, Texas, and New Jersey (U.S. Bureau of the Census 2004). In general, older persons are likely to live either in U.S. central cities or in small rural towns.

▲ Comment on Diversity

Clearly, the 65-and-older population is far from being a homogeneous social entity. While some may be economically comfortable or even affluent, one in four is poor or near-poor. Although predominantly a white population, many are non-native-born, and people of color are an important segment that is increasing in size. Females dominate proportionately and in numbers, and this is progressively true as we look at age categories beyond 65. Thus the older male is much less likely to be living alone without a spouse than his female age counterpart. Most older people in the United States have, on the average, less formal educational attainment than the general population, but this difference is undergoing change. Elders tend to be either small-town or central city residents. Perhaps the one thing most of those 65 and older are coming to share is lack of labor force participation: Only a small percentage are employed.

Yet despite their diversity—both in where they stand in terms of biological aging and in their mixed social and economic characteristics— elders are victims. They are victims of myths and stereotypes, personal prejudice, and institutional discrimination. In short, they are victims of ageism: ideas, practices, and structures that have negative consequences for persons who are socially defined as "old." In the next section these topics are examined in some detail.

Myths and Stereotypes

In the words of Robert N. Butler (1975:2–3),

We have shaped a society which is extremely harsh to live in when old. The tragedy of old age is not the fact that each of us must grow old and die but that the process of doing so has been made unnecessarily and at times excruciatingly painful, humiliating, debilitating and isolating through insensitivity, ignorance and poverty. The potentials for satisfactions and even triumphs in late life are real and vastly unexplored. For the most part, the elderly struggle to exist in an inhospitable world.

Aging does not mean an end to the physical expression of love and affection, something of importance to all human beings. Our elders may be sexually active in the absence of poor health and lack of partners. The discomfort this thought causes many younger persons reflects common stereotypes about growing old.

Part of this inhospitableness is the prevalence of myths and stereotypes, in reality expressions of insensitivity and ignorance, that are inflicted on older people in U.S. society (Palmore 1999; White 1987). Indeed, one study of narrative humor found several common ageist stereotypes, including the impotent (and often vain) male, the unattractive (and often sexually insatiable) female, the forgetful old person, and the infirm old person (Bowd 2003). Let's look at some of the stereotypes of aging.

"Old People Are All the Same"

Older people are as highly differentiated as those of any other age group. After all, they were once young, and people tend to carry their unique personal characteristics with them into their later years. Older people bear the mark of their accumulated personal experiences throughout life and perhaps become more different from one another with age, since the different experiences each has had are more numerous.

Moreover, there are invisible "generational" differences in the life-forming experiences of those 65 and older. For example, today's 65-year-olds had no direct involvement with World War II (1939–1945). This is not the case for today's 85-year olds. They had to respond to sacrifices demanded by the war effort precisely when they were beginning to grapple with major adult work and family responsibilities. In that era today's 65-year-olds were but dependent children. Such generational differences among elders accentuate their diversity.

"Old People Are Unproductive"

With advancing age, people leave the labor force. Their childbearing activities are long over, and there is typically an end to the assumption of any major responsibility for the children raised in their homes. But to view older persons as "unproductive" in such contexts is a form of blaming the victim for his or her personal situation. As we shall see later, older workers have been both ejected involuntarily and economically enticed into retiring. Moreover, change in roles and responsibilities vis-à-vis children in families is a natural outcome of family life cycles; most young people can barely wait to "be on their own."

Most older people are indeed productive. Even if they do not continue to work outside the home, most remain socially active in a wide range of settings, politically involved at a level higher than that of most other age groups (as indicated, for example, by voting practices), engaged in volunteer work, and active as key supporters of and participants in religious and other culture-disseminating institutions (Bass 1995; Essman 2002). If older persons are less engaged in such self-activity than they could be, it is because of younger persons. Older persons are expected to "act their age," meaning that they may be admonished or ridiculed when they strive to continue many of the activities and behaviors arbitrarily reserved for and by those who are chronologically younger.

"Old People Are Senile"

Because some older persons exhibit psychological and behavioral deviations from what is socially defined by those younger as normal, it is often assumed that all do or someday will act in such a manner. In reality, relatively few persons age 65 and older exhibit such deviations, and in many cases "senility" is treatable and reversible (West and Yassuda 2004). To a degree, senility is induced by the treatment accorded older persons in this society.

There are two sources of medically untreatable senility, both involving brain damage. In one case, the arteries to the brain harden. But in recent years much more attention has been directed at what is known as Alzheimer's disease, wherein neurons (nerve cells) in the brain are steadily lost or become degraded. (See Chapter 13.)

Alzheimer's disease currently affects an estimated 4.5 million people in the United States, most of them elderly. Each year over 100,000 people die from its progressive effects. Nationwide concern grew after former president Ronald Reagan died in 2004 of the debilitating disease and his widow and children made an impassioned plea for federal funding of stem cell research to treat the disease. Although Reagan was a highly visible sufferer of Alzheimer's, he was clearly not unique. Some have referred to Alzheimer's disease as an "epidemic," for it is a disease estimated to strike 10 percent of those 65 and older (National Institute on Aging 2003; U.S. Congress, House 1992a). The disease will pose even more of a problem in the future as the median age of those 65 and over increases and the percentage of "old-old" (85 and over), among whom the disease is most prevalent, grows. At present, the old-old population is growing twice as fast as the 65-and-over group. Elders in the 85-and-older category are projected to increase from 4.6 million in 2002 to almost 21 million in the year 2050 (U.S. Bureau of the Census 2004:14–15).

Unfortunately, the cause of Alzheimer's disease is unknown. Correct diagnosis is usually not possible until symptoms are severe and debilitating. These include memory loss and disrupted thought processes, reflections of brain degeneration and shrinkage. There currently is no cure or way to halt the slow death that often results.

Still, it is important to emphasize that much of what is popularly called senility involves expressions of anxiety and depression that have no known physiological causes but are no doubt linked to problems in living faced by many aging people. Misuse of drugs and alcohol can produce similar symptoms. Thus, much so-called senility is not only treatable but avoidable. This fact has only recently been recognized in the health arena and has not yet entered the public mind to counter the senility stereotype.

"Old People Are in a State of Deterioration and Decline"

This myth often is found in a variety of areas. Elders are stereotypically viewed as an extremely unhealthy group, stricken by disabling illnesses and handicaps that force them into a state of dependency. In fact, most older persons are quite healthy until their very final years, and the vast majority live independently in their own homes. At any one time, only 4.4 percent of those 65 and older are to be found in "old age homes" or nursing homes. Of those 65 and older, perhaps 43 percent will spend some portion of their lives in nursing homes (Manheimer 1994; U.S. Bureau of the Census 2004:66).

The notion of deterioration and decline is commonly directed at the intelligence of older persons. "Intelligence" is a slippery concept, but recent studies that have measured the mental traits of individuals repeatedly as they aged have found no significant evidence of decline. Indeed, depending on what trait is being measured, there is evidence that intelligence increases with age. This is the case, for example, for abilities based on accumulated past experience and socialization (West 1985).

Finally, the socially taboo topic of sexual interest and activity on the part of older persons is worthy of mention. There is supposedly a period in life often referred to as the "sexless older years." Although sexual interest and activity do tend to decline among many older persons, the rate at which this takes place, and whether it takes place at all, is highly variable. For the most part, older people do remain sexually active, barring serious physical ailments or the inability to find a sexual partner.

Disengagement versus Activity Theory

Popular myths and stereotypes about old age abound, but social science has certainly not been neutral with regard to the role of those who grow old. For well over 40 years debate has gone on between those who see old age through **disengagement theory** and those who approach old age through **activity theory.**

The debate was touched off by Elaine Cumming and William E. Henry (1961), whose *Growing Old: The Process of Disengagement* continues to generate discussion today. The researchers proposed a theory that was intended to shed light on the withdrawal, or "disengagement," of many aging persons from active roles in society. Cumming and Henry suggested that disengagement was "an inevitable process in which many of the relationships between a person and other members of society are severed and those remaining are altered in quality." While they note that total disengagement occurs with death, "the fully disengaged condition of the living can be considered to exist when only those bonds necessary to sustain life remain." The process of disengagement was said to be a social response to the biological and psychological decline that Cumming and Henry assumed was an intrinsic part of growing old. It was also, in effect, a response by and to the old-ager in anticipation of his or her death.

Cumming and Henry suggested that disengagement behavior was undertaken both by the aging individual and by the larger society. This mutual disengagement was thought to be functional (i.e., to serve certain functions). For example, as older people retired from their work roles (voluntarily or involuntarily), this served the function of opening up occupational opportunities for younger persons. The latter were likely to suffuse their work roles with new energies and talents, to the benefit of society as a whole. Moreover, as older people routinely withdrew from such roles, society avoided the disruption and disharmony that could occur were aging role incumbents always being unpredictably stricken with debilitating disease or death. Finally, disengagement was thought to function in the interests of aging individuals as well. Withdrawal from work and other roles was said to be an appropriate way for such individuals to shed responsibilities and relationships that would be burdensome to persons in a state of biological and psychological decline. Disengagement was thus theorized to be the way to a more comfortable and "successful" old age. In sum, according to Cumming and Henry, growing old necessitated changes in lifestyle and levels of involvement with others.

Disengagement theory has spawned a host of critics and has been the impetus to a good deal of research (Hochschild 1975; Levin and Levin 1980). A typical response to Cumming and Henry's point of view is as follows:

1. Research findings do not support the notion that old age inevitably means decline and that this characteristic causes disengagement. Older persons are often sufficiently healthy and capable of filling important social roles until shortly before death.

2. Disengagement, rather than contributing in a positive way to societal functioning, often has a negative impact. Persons with valuable knowledge and wisdom based on years of experience are often cut off from making contributions, thus depriving society. Lack of concrete roles for older persons to play may provide a basis for prejudiced attitudes and treatment by younger people, thus contributing to differential distribution of self-esteem and unnecessary intergroup tensions within society.

3. While early retirement from work roles may open up opportunities for younger workers, the shortage of such opportunities should

not be blamed on the old, nor should mandatory retirement be considered natural. The availability of work opportunity for younger persons is a function of elite-made economic and political decisions over which aging workers have no control. The main beneficiaries of mandatory retirement policies (largely eliminated under current federal law) have been employers, who usually pay younger workers less in wages and benefits.

4. Aging individuals who are "disengaged," particularly involuntarily (e.g., through mandatory or informally forced retirement), may face many serious problems as a consequence—problems that impose a cost on society. Such problems may include poverty or near-poverty, impaired physical and mental health, isolation, and loneliness. For all too many, disengagement is a route to an uncomfortable and unsuccessful old age.

Opponents of disengagement theory sometimes view it as an ideology justifying the exclusion of older persons from active participation in society. This exclusion actually creates much of the psychic and physical decline. This thinking has been characteristic of those who adhere to an *activity theory* of old age.

Disengagement theory, in viewing old age as a period requiring changes in lifestyles and especially reduced levels of involvement with others, rejected the notion that the activities enjoyed in middle age can be carried on. Activity theory, on the other hand, argues not only that activities enjoyed in middle age can be carried on by most older persons but that they should be. In the words of Jack Levin and William C. Levin (1980:53):

Activity theory suggests that there is a positive relationship between activity and life-satisfaction and that the greater the role loss, the lower the life-satisfaction. Thus, those who wish to enjoy their last years of life should continue to live as they had during their middle years right to the time death or illness stops them.

This, of course, assumes that the middle years were indeed a source of enjoyment. In many cases, persons who faced problems in living in the middle years will continue to face them when older. For example, poor middle-aged persons may well be poor elderly persons. Still, on balance most research tends to support activity theory (Palmore 1999). Indeed, one study found that being subjected to ageist stereotypes tended to significantly depress the walking pace of older people, while positive comments resulted in a brisker gait (Sheridan et al. 2003). This is a finding that supports the notion that stereotypes act as a self-fulfilling prophecy and the argument that encouragement of physical activity serves to improve the quality of life of older individuals.

What kinds of difficulties hinder the ability of the aged to be active participants in society? What kinds of problems plague many older people in the United States, turning the notion of the "golden years" into an absurdity? In the next section some responses to these questions are explored.

Income and Poverty Status

Income is a crucial determinant of how the aged live. The level, the adequacy, and the maintenance of income affects other aspects of the lives of the elderly: the maintenance of physical and mental health, transportation utilization, housing and nutrition adequacy, vulnerability to crime, level of social participation and the general quality of life. (Harris 1978:36)

In light of the preceding quote, it becomes significant that as recently as 2002 over 10 percent of all persons 65 and older, more than 1 in 10, were officially considered poor. Counting those who were "near-poor" (i.e., with incomes no more than 125 percent of the official poverty line), more than 25 percent, or 1 out of 4 persons 65 and older, were living on severely restricted incomes (Proctor and Dalaker 2003).

It is true that the poverty rates for older people in the United States have declined significantly over the years. For example, almost one-third of those 65 and older were considered poor in 1960. This figure dropped to 24.5 percent in 1970, to 15.3 percent in 1975, and to 12 percent in 1993. Indeed, the poverty rate among elders is now substantially lower than it is for children, whose poverty rate is currently nearly 20 percent. Yet while their poverty rate has undergone decline, symptoms of economic deprivation among elders are quite apparent. Nutrition experts estimate that 25 percent of older persons suffer from some form of malnutrition, which increases risks of illness and hinders recovery from injury and disease. Although many elders who are not poor fail to eat well, poverty is a key cause of malnourishment (*New York Times* 1995a).

The 2002 poverty rate of 10 percent (involving 3.6 million persons) is an overall figure, and one that masks the distribution of poverty within the 65-and-older population. For example, in 1999 the rate for whites was 8.2 percent, but for African Americans it was almost three times as high—23.5 percent. There were also significant sex differences, with older women much more likely to be poor than older men, particularly those women who lived alone. While women were almost 59 percent of those 65 and older, they made up more than 70 percent of elders who were poor.

The poverty rate for older women was 12.4 percent in 2002; for older men it was 7.7 percent. Yet these figures do not tell the whole story of the range of distribution. While white men 65 and older had a poverty rate of 5.8 percent, African American women had a rate of 27.4 percent and Latina elders a poverty rate of 23.0 percent (www.agingstats.gov).

Over 90 percent of elders receive Social Security benefits from the federal government, and the majority of persons in this age group depend on government programs as their principal income source (Gist and Hetzel 2004). However, such benefits do not necessarily mean that one lives above the poverty line. This is particularly the case for those older persons whose earlier lives had been conducted at low income levels. Persons who were poor or near-poor before reaching 65 generally continue to be so in old age. Since African Americans and other people of color are disproportionately represented in the overall poverty population (see Chapter 6), it should be no surprise that this holds true in the so-called golden years of life as well (Margolis 1990).

Unfortunately, the limited safety net that Social Security benefits may provide is now at the center of heated debate. As the baby boom generation ages into retirement, some observers fear that there will be far more retired recipients than the number of those in the paid labor market to support them, an observation which itself is widely debated. President George W. Bush has made a commitment to privatizing Social Security by allowing individuals to invest significant proportions of their personal retirement accounts into the stock market and sharply reducing the federal burden of providing for elders. This approach would certainly reduce the fiscal pressures that might confront the Social Security program, but its promise of producing viable income for retirees is hotly contested by critics. Many point to the collapse of Enron Corporation's stock in 2003 and the subsequent evaporation of retirement funds for hundreds of thousands of investors as warning signals that privatizing Social Security will only privatize the retirement benefit crisis rather than resolve it. This debate highlights how fragile is the social contract of Social Security as a financial support for older individuals.

Employment and Retirement

A key factor determining income for all families is the movement of a member into or out of the paid labor force. Most older persons live with a spouse or alone, and the loss of income from employment can have a significant impact on quality of life in the household. Consider that in 1999 the median income of a household whose members were 65 and over was only $27,050 (Gist and Hetzel 2004).

In an earlier section we noted that since 1900 a smaller proportion of the 65-and-over population has remained employed, until today only 18 percent of males and even fewer females in this age group are holding down jobs. Moreover, retirement before 65 is becoming increasingly common. These trends are expected to continue, even while a larger proportion of the U.S. population enters old age.

Withdrawal from the labor force is voluntary for most older people, but for many it is not. For perhaps as many as 40 percent of retirees, involuntary retirement has been a reality. For some it is a matter of responding to episodic or seemingly permanent unemployment. Not only are unemployment rates high for older workers, but durations of unemployment tend to be longer than those for their younger counterparts. They tend to be longest for those 55 to 65 or older. Insofar as permanent withdrawal from the labor force at least renders one eligible for bare survival-level government benefits (usually Social Security), it becomes a reluctant alternative to the stress and humiliation of unemployment.

But it is not only the unemployed worker who involuntarily retires. Employers' rules for mandatory retirement (until fairly recently set at age 65) forced millions of able, willing, and financially vulnerable persons into a limbo of joblessness. While 1986 amendments to the federal Age Discrimination in Employment Act largely outlawed mandatory retirement based on age (partly out of a desire to slow the growing budgetary burden of paying out Social Security benefits), it is likely that much retirement will remain involuntary and continue to take place at 65, if not before. There are several reasons for this (Gregory 2001):

1. Job dissatisfaction, particularly among blue-collar workers, is an incentive to early retirement. Moreover, jobs held by blue-collar workers are often dangerous, physically punishing, or otherwise conducive to ill health, thus forcing persons to retire because of physical disability or the fear of it.

2. Although laws against discrimination in employment on the basis of age exist, such discrimination on the part of employers continues. Subtle informal pressures to retire are difficult and frequently expensive to fight in private legal suits. Government agencies charged with antidiscrimination enforcement are poorly funded, short-staffed, and backlogged with years of complaints.

3. Social and cultural expectations in general support withdrawal from the labor force. Thus, many workers, faced with real or internalized pressures to disengage from their work role, simply do so. They may believe what so many falsely allege: When you reach 65 (or earlier), you are supposed to move over and let someone younger take your place. They are simply fulfilling what they see as others' expectations.

4. Our system of Social Security, begun in 1935 to supplement income but now heavily relied on as a primary source by so many, encourages labor force withdrawal. Since its benefits are linked only to reaching the chronological age of 65, and not to disability or unemployment, persons reaching that magic age are faced with the incentive of retiring to receive Social Security benefits. Private pension plans may offer similar incentives to stop work at 65, or special provisions for retirement even earlier.

Retirement means the acceptance of reduced income on a permanent basis—ordinarily half or less of what one might have earned while employed full-time—but its impact goes beyond income restrictions. The loss of a work role may affect self-esteem and self-image, reduce social contacts and enjoyment gained from peer and friendship groups, and in general lower morale. Involuntary loss of a work role in many cases may help increase vulnerability to mental and physical health problems, as well as self-destructive behavior (from alcoholism or other forms of substance abuse to suicide).

Health and Health Care

Earlier we addressed the stereotype that depicted persons 65 and older as all living in a state of mental and physical failure. Although this is an incorrect depiction of elders, increasing age does bring with it a greater vulnerability to and hence probability of certain health problems. Many variables enter into the determination of health status, including income level, dietary and nutritional practices, behavior known to be associated with health problems (e.g., smoking and alcohol abuse), exercise routines, degree of exposure to dangerous conditions and polluting substances, experiences of psychological and physical stress, and access to (and ability to obtain) adequate health care when needed.

A major reason that our 65-and-over population is growing is the successful eradication of illness and disease that resulted in many people dying in their younger years. Hence, more persons have the opportunity today to be afflicted with health problems long experienced by segments of the aging population. For the most part, when health problems do exist among older people, they are chronic (i.e., of relatively long duration). Examples of such conditions are arthritis and rheumatism, hearing and vision impairment, and high blood pressure. Such health problems may slow people down, but ordinarily

they do not require institutionalization. In summing up physical health care problems, one expert put the situation this way:

With advancing age, the basic health care requirements of the population become greater than those in younger age categories; with advancing age, the basic health requirements become different from those in younger age categories because of their chronic nature. (Harris 1978:111–12)

Despite the preceding situation, health care for elders is widely acknowledged as inadequate (Olson 1982). One survey in 2003 found that 66 percent of respondents chose to continue working after retirement because they needed the health benefits, a finding that suggests the severe limitations of health coverage available for elderly individuals in the United States (AARP 2003). Among the problems is the fact that health in one's later years is so greatly affected by what the individual experiences while younger. If one's environment and environmentally associated behaviors are not health-enhancing all through life—as is particularly the case for so many poor and working-class people—health problems can be expected in one's later years. In essence, health care for elders is a process that should begin before birth and go on from there, and it should include preventive policies that maximize the probability of good health in old age. Needless to say, the U.S. health-care system does not fit this model very well. As we will see in Chapter 13, it is far more attuned to responding to experiences of illness after the fact than it is to helping alter environments that facilitate the development of such illnesses.

But more than the preceding is involved in the inadequacy of health care available to many older people:

1. Few physicians specialize in the health problems of older persons, despite the fact

that such persons are an increasing proportion of the U.S. population.

2. Persons in the medical field often hold common stereotypes about and prejudices toward elderly people. This cannot help but affect their interest and effectiveness in dealing with them. Moreover, chronic health problems are often considered medically uninteresting and routine, in comparison to "acute" illnesses. The latter are often serious, demand urgent attention, and usually can be quickly resolved with proper medical procedures. The rate of acute illness among older persons is very low.

3. For many persons health and related services are simply inaccessible. This can be the case for diverse reasons. There are gaps in government programs that assist older persons in paying for care and services (Medicare and Medicaid), thus making them too expensive for many to afford. In some cases, serious illness results in expenses that propel persons into poverty. Today there are the "new poor" who become so by divesting themselves of assets (such as homes and savings) acquired while members of the working or even the middle class. Rural areas and lower-income urban neighborhoods where many older persons reside have very limited medical services, thus hampering accessibility for those who are not geographically mobile.

4. Many older individuals face an increasing need for expensive prescription medications for chronic diseases at precisely that time in their lives when any prescription drug benefits they may have had through their jobs are discontinued and their income becomes sharply limited. Many elders are now crossing the borders into Mexico and Canada seeking less expensive prescription drugs, or they order less expensive medications over the Internet from abroad. Though this strategy in most cases links elders to high-quality medications, there is no guarantee that this will be the case. Congress attempted to address this problem in 2004 when it passed a confusing and complicated drug prescription program for retirees, with the promise of expanded prescription benefits. Unfortunately, the program remains under serious question, because many are already complaining of difficulty getting the medications they need at a reasonable cost, and others are suggesting that the cost limitations of the program will leave many prescription drugs out of reach. As we noted in Chapter 2, the power of corporations, particularly those in the pharmaceutical industry, has affected the development of federal policy. They have invested a great deal in their struggle against attempts to limit what they may charge for medications.

Housing and Transportation

At first glance older people in the United States appear to be in good shape with regard to housing. More than 80 percent of those 65 and older live in homes they own (U.S. Bureau of the Census 2004). Most housing owned by elders is held without a mortgage. Yet a true picture must go beyond such superficial information.

For most elderly home owners, housing is both the largest and the only significant asset they possess. Yet it is a nonliquid asset; as long as they want to hold on to their property and remain in their homes, the money value of the housing is unavailable for day-to-day living expenses. Yet it is these expenses—property taxes, utilities, energy costs, housing maintenance—that have routinely gone up over the past years. Most older persons face highly restricted and relatively fixed incomes in retirement. One in four of those 65 and older is poor or in near-poverty. Many older persons cannot afford to stay in the houses they own; some find they are forced to cut back on expenditures in such areas as food and medical services in order to pay heating bills.

Those elders who reside in apartments, boardinghouses, and hotels tend to live in even more economically precarious positions than those in owner-occupied housing. Yet they too face increased costs, reflected in high rents and utilities. Since for some years there has been a serious shortage of rental properties to accommodate the housing needs of the population in general, not to mention older persons, demands in the face of shortage allow landlords to charge higher rents than might otherwise be the case. Owners of such properties are increasingly finding it more profitable to either abandon them (when the rising costs outrun the ability of occupants to pay higher rents) or convert them to private condominiums. The sales prices of the latter are ordinarily well beyond the ability of elderly renters to pay; thus, they cannot stay in their homes.

There are other problems as well. Government surveys indicate that 675,000 units of elderly occupied housing have "serious physical problems" with plumbing, heating, electrical systems, and upkeep, and another 885,000 units have "moderate physical problems" (Darnay 1994:438). Much of the housing occupied by elders was built many years ago and thus needs more repair and heat than newer housing in which younger people tend to reside. Many elderly are housed in the nation's central cities, where lower-income neighborhood decline and deterioration are common, and the environment surrounding their housing is often unattractive, unsafe, and a source of stress. In both blighted central city neighborhoods and the rural small towns in which older people also are likely to live, services that are supportive of their particular needs and lifestyles are likely to be lacking. These kinds of difficulties lead Laura K. Olson (1982:164) to conclude: "Given their poor neighborhood conditions, inaccessibility of essential supportive services, higher

maintenance and rental costs relative to income, and other housing-related problems, the vast majority of older persons lack adequate housing."

While the housing situation of many if not most older people could stand significant improvement, the same may be said of transportation. Like many others, elders are dependent on automobile transportation. Yet as this dependency increases, the likelihood that one can afford to keep an automobile, as well as maintain the ability to drive one, decreases. Some 25 percent of households headed by persons 65 and older do not own a car (a rate twice that of younger households). There are numerous reasons for this. The rising costs of car ownership, maintenance and repair, fuel, licensing, and insurance become too much for persons on relatively fixed incomes. Older persons pay more than younger persons for car insurance and may have their insurance policies canceled when a certain age is reached. Finally, for some, health-related disabilities may make driving a private vehicle a risky endeavor if not an impossibility.

This situation would not be so serious if it were not for the paucity of adequate and affordable public transportation. In many cases (e.g., rural areas) such transportation is either very limited or nonexistent. In central city areas the situation is often somewhat better, but rising costs, fear of criminal victimization, and at times intimidating physical demands associated with using public transportation restrict its use. The result is geographic immobility, isolation, and barriers between older persons and the medical, recreational, educational, and social services they frequently must have to sustain a decent way of life.

Criminal Victimization

One would like to think that security against criminal victimization is possible for elders, yet they do not escape the ravages of property crimes and crimes of violence. As we shall see, the impact of criminal victimization may weigh more heavily on the old than on the young.

Crime statistics must always be taken with caution. Official statistics on crimes reported to the police tend to be underestimates of the amount of crime actually taking place (see Chapter 15, "Criminal Behavior"). With respect to the elderly and crime, our knowledge is limited by the fact that until fairly recently data were not collected or organized to provide knowledge about the 65-and-older group.

At the national level, overall criminal victimization rates are lower for the older population than for the younger population for crimes of violence, theft, and household crimes (U.S. Department of Justice 2003:Table 3). There is, of course, underreporting. Federal victimization statistics indicate that less than two-thirds of all crimes of violence against those 65 and over are reported to police, and barely more than a quarter of crimes of theft are reported (U.S. Department of Justice 2003:Table 96). Lower criminal victimization rates for elders may also mean that certain segments of the 65-and-older population successfully isolate themselves from the risk of victimization. Yet looking at particular crimes and at older persons living in particular locales, some have argued that older persons are *more* likely to be crime victims than younger persons. Further inquiry is needed to clarify the question of victimization rates and their relation to old age.

Leaving aside the adequacy of official statistics, it seems accurate to say that older people in the United States are most likely to be victims of property crimes as opposed to crimes of violence. Yet both types of crime are held to have more severe effects on the old than on the young. Robbery on the street, burglary in the home, vehicle theft, and victimization through fraud or confidence games often have a devastating impact on elders. Many older persons live on relatively fixed incomes and cannot afford to lose their meager Social Security or pension payments or small accumulated savings. Since persons 65 and older are unlikely to be working, cars and material possessions often cannot be easily replaced. A property loss that a younger person might angrily shrug off is likely to be a major blow to the more vulnerable elder.

Similarly, while victimization by crimes of violence is far less frequent than by property offenses, older persons are at a disadvantage. As aging may slow down physical agility, so may it slow down rates of recuperation. With advanced age for some comes physical frailty, so that a severe blow or fall can readily result in serious trauma and even death. A third of the 65-and-over victims of crimes of violence are injured (U.S. Department of Justice 2003, Table 75). In the words of Charles S. Harris (1978:260), "The problem of crimes against older Americans must be measured by the effect of crime on the victim rather than by the frequency of assault."

Some social scientists have been surprised that fear of criminal victimization is very high among older people, even while overall statistics suggest that victimization is less frequent than for younger persons. This fear is itself a form of injury. Many older persons, particularly in densely populated central cities, are virtually immobilized by their fear of crime and the likelihood that they will be singled out as easy marks by local predators. As Alan Malinchak (1980:41–42) put it: "Soft-core sentiment and emotions play no part in the hard-core dealings of criminal activity. A criminal cannot afford to be generous. Crime involves the element of risk. It is only natural for the criminal to prey upon the elderly, for there is less risk in being apprehended and suffering the consequences of a prison term."

Such fear may even be a source of some of the disengagement from active participation in social roles and relationships with others of which we spoke earlier. Living in a state of nervous isolation behind locked doors, afraid to venture out on the street, potential victims are denied normal lives in what are supposed to be the "golden years." Crime and fear of crime alter the lifestyles and adversely affect the mobility of the old much more than of younger people.

Elder Abuse

For most elders, the struggle to lead happy lives in a society afflicted with ageism is relatively successful. Yet a significant minority is held hostage to physical and/or mental abuse by members of their own families or households. **Elder abuse** has become what one champion of the aged, the late U.S. representative Claude Pepper, called "a national disgrace." He was responding to figures in a 1985 House subcommittee report estimating that 1.1 million people in the United States over age 65 suffer such abuse annually (*Newsweek* 1985). Reports of elder abuse sharply increased by over 150 percent in just the 10-year period between 1986 and 1996, an increase that far outpaces the 10 percent increase in the older population during that same period (www.aoa.dhhs.gov/Factsheets/abuse).

States' reports on substantiated cases of abuse indicate that almost half take the form of neglect. Another 20 percent of the abuse is physical, while psychological/emotional abuse is involved in 14 percent of the cases. In 17 percent financial/material exploitation occurs. Women are the victims in 68 percent of the cases reported. In 90 percent of the cases where the abuser is known, perpetrators of elder abuse were family members: Two-thirds of these were adult children or spouses of the victims (www.aoa.dhhs.gov/Factsheets/abuse). Almost one-third of the murders of people 65 and older are committed by a family member (www.apa.org), and most of the victims are women with chronic illnesses or disabilities (www.surgeongeneral.gov). Rates of abuse have also been found to rise with age category, with those in their late 80s more likely to be abused than those in their late 60s. With the proportion of the population 65 and over growing, and the proportion that is "old-old" (85 and over) growing most rapidly, the numbers of elders at risk for abuse will continue to escalate.

There appear to be two views or schools of thought on how to account for elder abuse (Pillemer and Finkelhor 1989; Steinmetz 1987). One view emphasizes the stresses and burdens placed on those who care for infirm and incapacitated older people. Caregivers are often adult children or spouses who, it is believed, grow resentful and angry over the dependency of another on them. In response to the demands they must suffer, caregivers may respond with abuse. In effect, this view is suggesting that normally nonabusive people are being driven by circumstances into negative behaviors. The characteristics of the elderly bring on the abuse.

The second school of thought focuses instead on the characteristics of the abusers. It has been suggested that abusers of the elderly are *themselves* likely to be dependent people. The persons for whom they are caring may be supporting them financially in whole or part, responsible for their shelter, health insurance, and so on. Further, abusers—more than nonabusive caretakers of the elderly—are thought to be people with troubles. They are, it is argued, more likely to have mental difficulties, problems with substance abuse, and law violations involving them with the police.

Until recently few data were available to help sort out which of these two views was most likely the case. Now, however, research appears to lend support to the view that it is the dependent, troubled caregiver who abuses. Based on the first large-scale random-sample survey on this question, in this case conducted in the greater Boston area, researchers Karl Pillemer and David Finkelhor (1989:186) concluded:

The picture of maltreatment that emerged . . . [shows] relatively well-functioning elderly who have responsibility for, or are at least required to interact with, ill and socioemotionally unstable relatives. The abuse appears to be a reflection of the abuser's problems and dependency rather than the elderly victim's characteristics. . . . Instead of well-meaning caregivers who are driven to abuse by the demands of an old person, elder abusers appear to be severely troubled individuals with histories of antisocial behavior or instability.

As Pillemer and Finkelhor point out, their findings undermine any tendency we might have to "blame the victim," that is, to suggest that aging people are so stressful and hard to care for that their abuse is understandable if not forgivable. As they argue, just as we have come to understand that rape victims, battered spouses, and victims of incest and child abuse can hardly be viewed as having in some way "asked for it," so also should we understand the victims of elder abuse. Although this research does not put the discussion to rest, and although there may well be other contributing factors to elder abuse (see the discussion of family violence in Chapter 14), the attention such abuse is receiving harbors hope for those who may be at risk.

Old Age and Political Power

With one in eight members of the U.S. population at age 65 or over and an even larger proportion forecast (see Figure 10.3), older people may play a much more significant political role in the future than they do today. As we have seen, there are a variety of areas within which transformations are required to mitigate harmful conditions facing this age group—from economic deprivation to elder abuse. However, few experts agree on just what the political implications are of an aging population (Wallace et al, 1991).

Here are some facts stemming from social science research that may bear on the role of older people in politics as we look into the future:

1. In general, rates of political participation (e.g., voting behavior, expression of opinions on political issues) rise with increased age.

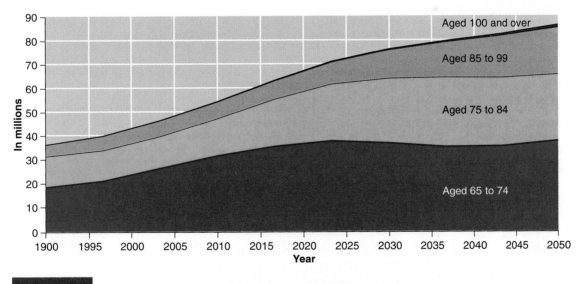

Figure 10.3   **Population of Persons Age 65 and Over, 1990 to 2050**

Source: U.S. Department of Commerce, Bureau of the Census, *Statistical Abstract of the United States, 2003* (Washington, DC: Government Printing Office, 2004), p. 14.

2. The commonly held view that political attitudes grow more conservative with age does not appear to be true; aging per se seems not to systematically affect political outlooks.

3. Too little is known to be able to predict whether in the future elders are likely to become a major political force—whether through acting as an effective voting bloc or through taking part in militant social movement activities revolving around age-related policy issues.

Item 3 relates to the question of whether older people are likely to develop **age consciousness.** That is, will older people come to see themselves as possessing important political and economic interests in common and seek to advance these interests through societywide mobilization? There are different points of view on such questions.

Among the factors that may help to promote age consciousness are an increase in the proportion of the population made up of older people; the trend toward residential segregation, whereupon elders live apart from younger kin (increasingly in "retirement communities"); the presence of government programs and publicly financed services that bring older people together and increase opportunities for group interaction; higher levels of educational attainment and political sophistication among future elders; and possible resistance on the part of persons who are not old to continuing demands for taxation stemming from the growing needs of an aging population. As the numbers of aging persons who find themselves dependent on those younger increase, will the burden become such that the younger rebel? Such generational conflict is frequently portrayed as both a possible cause and a possible outcome of age consciousness.

Yet others are doubtful that such age consciousness is likely to occur to any great degree or that older people will mobilize on a societywide basis. The emphasis in this point of view is on the heterogeneity that will continue into the future. Diversity—whether it be economic, ethnic, racial, geographic, or gender-based— serves to splinter the older population and reduce the probability that it might come to function as a unified political force. Moreover, the 65-and-over population is not static but is undergoing constantly changing membership as new persons enter old age and still others die. Fluctuation in group membership is seen as another force undermining effective political unity.

Still, even with heterogeneity and the transiency of old-age group membership, it is conceivable that attacks on

Many elders are active politically and involved in issues that affect old and young alike. The elders in this 2004 photograph are demonstrating at the Blue Water Bridge linking Canada and the United States to support legalization of importation of cheaper prescription medications from Canada.

the well-being of our elders in the future could galvanize a far-reaching response. Alarmed by the treatment of elders and the economic threat to the nonold that their swelling numbers may pose, Jack Levin and Arnold Arlucke (1983:A31) suggest that our society may be heading toward a "final solution." They state:

A de facto mass extermination may already be taking place. Many elders suffer a social death in which they are removed from the main stream of life. . . . Elders are also the victims of benign neglect: They are deprived of the food, shelter and health care needed to survive. . . . The intellectual justification for a final solution can already be observed in our changing attitudes toward aging and death.

Levin and Arlucke see a subtle movement toward writing off the old, in effect "exterminating" many of them through indifference and negligence—a movement that could escalate in the future.

Surely, we would presume, any such steps will generate a substantial reaction from older persons, and many of their younger counterparts as well. Consider the growing strength of the AARP (formerly the American Association of Retired Persons), a social movement organization of more than 32 million members over the age of 50. It lobbies legislators for better legal protections of the rights of the elderly, and it informs the rest of society of those rights through education, advocacy, and service in the community. The AARP routinely conducts voter registration drives and voter education campaigns and has been a forceful lobbyist for health-care and prescription coverage. And they have become increasingly vocal critics of the plan to privatize Social Security. Its strength in membership is likely to grow as the members of the baby boom generation age and join its ranks. Organizations such as this are likely to increase age consciousness and a growing resistance to any efforts to marginalize, exterminate, or devalue older people.

Summary

In the words of Simone de Beauvoir (1973:131), "By the way in which a society behaves toward its old people it uncovers the naked and often carefully hidden truth about its real principles and aims."

If the preceding words are true, then our treatment (or maltreatment) of those who have served U.S. society longest is a sad commentary on our principles and aims. In the preceding pages we have seen that myths and stereotypes, often quite derogatory and harmful, have been inflicted on those who enter the arbitrarily defined period of "old age." Such myths and stereotypes, along with questionable social science theory that calls for older persons to disengage from life roles for the good of society, promote minority group status for tens of millions in their later years. Such ideas also justify ignoring the numerous problems that elders face, problems that pose direct harm to the quality, if not the length, of their lives. As a consequence, one in four older people in the United States is poor or near-poor. For many, retirement is an involuntary removal from an important work role, or escape from chronic job dissatisfaction and unemployment, rather than a retreat into the "golden years" of life. Economic vulnerability is, as well, linked to problems of physical and mental health. So are the stresses connected with inadequate housing and immobility because of lack of transportation. As if this were not enough, older people silently suffer fear of criminal victimization as well as its reality, and they may be abused by family members.

There is no sign that these problems will go away and that the lives of our elders will be transformed. Yet, as the 65-and-over segment of the population grows, conditions could well become such that old-agers will be a far more potent and unified political force in this society than they are at present. With "age consciousness" could come the mobilization of a rather heterogeneous group to attack ageism. This group could include younger persons as well.

In Irving Rosow's (1976:54) view, "The crucial people are *not* the aged, but the *younger* groups. It is *we* who determine the status and position of the old." As we, through action and inaction, determine the status and position of the old in society, we are determining what *we* shall be allowed to become when we reach "old age."

Key Terms

Activity theory 310
Age consciousness 320
Ageism 299

Disengagement theory 310
Elder abuse 318
Graying of America 302

Discussion Questions

1. Discuss the differences and the similarities between ageism, on the one hand, and racism or sexism, on the other hand.

2. Suppose medical discoveries make it possible for our average life expectancy to go from 77 years (about where it is now) to 100 or more years. Discuss the consequences of such a change for U.S. society.

3. What, typically, are older people doing when you somehow feel they are not "acting their age"? Why are you made uncomfortable by their actions?

4. Older people are often the butt of jokes and the subject of humor. What characteristics of older people are commonly communicated through jokes and humor? To what degree are these characteristics stereotypical and degrading?

5. Make a list of what you are likely to do in the course of a typical day after you turn 65. Compare the lists produced by males in your class with those produced by females. What conclusions may be drawn?

Suggested Readings

Bass, Scott A. *Older and Active: How Americans over 55 Are Contributing to Society* (New Haven, CT: Yale University Press, 1995).
A comprehensive survey of the extent to which older persons are engaged in mainstream activities on into their old age.

Rich, Cynthia, and Barbara Macdonald. *Look Me in the Eye: Old Women, Aging, and Ageism* (Minneapolis: Spinsters Book Company, 2001). Puts a human face on the intersection of gender and ageism as it explores the patterns of age discrimination.

Fischer, David H. *Growing Old in America* (New York: Oxford University Press, 1981).
Traces the treatment of elders historically, suggesting how and why their status has changed.

Friedan, Betty. *The Fountain of Age* (New York: Simon & Schuster, 1993).
An upbeat account of ways in which many elders manage to maintain active roles in society.

Moody, Harry R. *Aging: Concepts and Controversies.* 4th ed. (Thousand Oaks, CA: Pine Forge Press, 2002).
Provides data on aging and identifies key issues in the debate over how to meet the needs of an aging population.

Palmore, Erdman B. *Ageism: Negative and Positive.* 2d ed. (New York: Springer, 1999).
Explores the meaning of ageism, its causes and consequences, and strategies to reduce it.

part III

Institutional Problems

chapter 11
The Changing Structure of Work

Work must be freely available to all. It should be organized cooperatively, with special attention to providing meaning, dignity, satisfaction, and security.

The income most people receive from work is a key resource affecting their life chances. Their ability to survive is thus affected by both their ability to secure a job and the money these jobs pay. Unfortunately, in the last several decades important changes in the structure of work have taken place that make people's chances of finding and keeping gainful employment increasingly problematic.

Most broadly defined, **work** is an "activity that produces something of value for other people" (U.S. Department of Health, Education, and Welfare 1973:2). This definition encompasses a broad range of human behavior. Child care and household tasks are forms of work. Such home labor is socially necessary and economically useful. So is the informal volunteer work performed in the United States. Each year tens of millions of people contribute their time and effort to everything from visiting the hospitalized to assisting in political campaigns. While we recognize that the term *work* means more than paid labor, we limit our attention in this chapter primarily to work activity for which people receive wages or salaries.

Sociologists have been studying work for a long time. In the nineteenth century French sociologist Émile Durkheim (1965) observed that the division of labor in society made people dependent on one another. Durkheim felt that this interdependence contributed to societal stability and integration, both of which he believed to be necessary for human well-being. Another nineteenth-century thinker, Karl Marx, saw labor as the principal means by which the human species sought to fulfill its potential. Marx believed that the industrializing societies of his day were turning work into a degrading, dehumanizing experience for the majority of workers (Bottomore and Rubel 1964). As we shall see, Marx's concerns are still relevant.

Contemporary social scientists have suggested a number of ways in which work is central to our everyday lives (Braude 1975; Pahl 1988). Work is the means by which we are expected to pursue the American Dream—the

327

acquisition of material goods and services and financial security. The pay we receive for our labor helps determine our standard of living and our lifestyle. The jobs we hold are also major determinants of our position in the overall class structure. This is true not only in purely economic terms but also with regard to power and prestige. Thus, the nature of our work often tells other people who we are. We may be treated with deference, accepted as an equal, or dismissed as a nonperson depending on our work status.

Social scientists have found that work has a very personal meaning to people. It can serve as an important source of self-esteem. If we are confronted by challenges at work, and if we overcome them, we gain a sense of accomplishment. Work tasks may give us the chance to feel a sense of mastery over our immediate environment and to display particular talents. Our self-esteem may be further enhanced if our work is valued and rated positively by others, both on and off the job. All in all, work serves as a measure of our social worth and a key source of our personal identity.

Unfortunately, millions of people today are unable to find work or face the prospect of unemployment. Many unemployed men and women, while wanting and needing jobs, have become so discouraged that they have given up looking for them. Others may have jobs, but the wages they receive are so low that they remain poor and struggle for the basics of survival, such as housing, food, fuel, and health care. As we saw in Chapter 6, "Economic Inequality and Poverty," the wages received by the working poor and near-poor are woefully inadequate; they find pursuit of the American Dream by means of work to be impossible. Many workers are trying hard to grasp on to the American Dream by holding down more than one job. Others find themselves moving in and out of the workplace as members of a growing pool of part-time and temporary workers, reflecting the rise in what is called **contingency work.**

College-educated, white-collar members of the middle class have been experiencing the effects of corporate restructuring and downsizing, and they now often face the same sense of job insecurity that many blue-collar workers have long endured. Whereas social scientists in the past have been concerned with studying issues of job satisfaction, in more recent times workers' worries over possibly not keeping their jobs, not whether they are satisfied with them, have begun to receive research interest. Before examining some of these topics in more detail, we look at key historical trends that have helped shape today's work world.

The Changing Structure of Work

Unemployment, job insecurity, and other work-related problems are a result of certain historical trends in the structure of work. In particular, four trends have, since the Industrial Revolution of the nineteenth century, helped create the work world we know today. The first trend is the shift from an agricultural society first to an industrial and more recently to a deindustrialized society. Related to **deindustrialization** is the second trend, the decline of self-employment among workers. The past century has also seen a dramatic increase in the bureaucratization of the workplace. Finally, in recent years we have begun to see a rise in contingency work, reflecting the fact that members of the labor force can no longer count on finding permanent full-time jobs, nor can they expect a guarantee of continued full-time employment in firms to which they pledge their loyalty.

The Deindustrialized Society

Social scientists often divide a society's system of work activity into three sectors: **primary** (agriculture), **secondary** (manufacturing), and **tertiary** (services). Two hundred years ago most members of the labor force in the United States were engaged in the primary sector. There was little industry, and most of that was in the hands of individual craftsmen and artisans. Then, under the impetus of the Industrial Revolution of the nineteenth century, the proportion of the labor force engaged in agriculture underwent a marked decline. Not only were more people needed to fill the growing numbers of new jobs in manufacturing, but advances in agricultural production meant that fewer workers could provide the citizens of the United States with food (Lasley et al. 1995). By the end of the nineteenth century, 30.5 percent of the labor force was involved in the secondary or manufacturing sector of the economy. (See Figure 11.1.)

Now, particularly since World War II, there has been an explosive expansion of the tertiary,

or service, sector. Today about three-fourths of all workers are engaged in providing services in such fields as business, transportation, communications, utilities, education, health, and government. The percentage of the labor force holding manufacturing jobs has seen periods of fluctuation since 1900, but in recent years there has been a steady decline of jobs in this sector, with the current figure being now about 21 percent of the U.S. labor force. The major change has been in agriculture, where only about 2 percent of U.S. workers are now employed (U.S. Bureau of the Census 2004).

Many observers feel that the economy is experiencing what has come to be called deindustrialization (Bluestone and Harrison 1982). For it has become apparent that our long-heralded productivity in manufacturing currently lags far

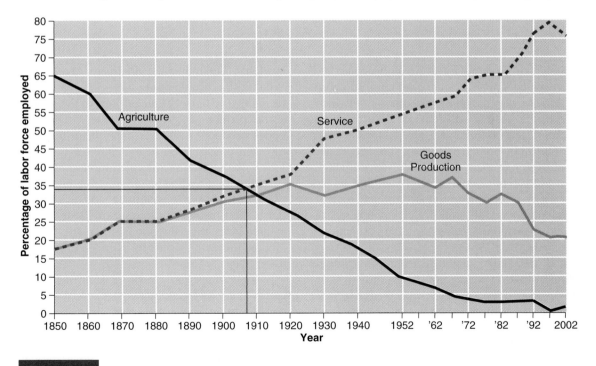

Figure 11.1 **Distribution of Employment by Major Sector, 1850–2002**

Source: U.S. Department of Labor, *Monthly Labor Review* 107 (April 1984): 16; U.S. Department of Labor, *Employment and Earnings* 36 (November 1989): 12, 49; *Employment and Earnings* 42 (January 1995): 222; and U.S. Bureau of the Census, *Statistical Abstract of the United States, 2003* (Washington, DC: Government Printing Office, 2004), p. 404, available at www.census.gov.

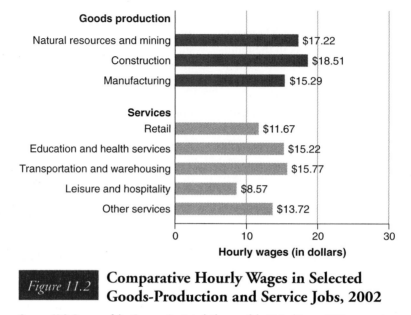

Goods production
Natural resources and mining — $17.22
Construction — $18.51
Manufacturing — $15.29

Services
Retail — $11.67
Education and health services — $15.22
Transportation and warehousing — $15.77
Leisure and hospitality — $8.57
Other services — $13.72

Hourly wages (in dollars)

Figure 11.2 **Comparative Hourly Wages in Selected Goods-Production and Service Jobs, 2002**

Source: U.S. Bureau of the Census, *Statistical Abstract of the United States, 2003* (Washington, DC: Government Printing Office, 2004), p. 420.

behind our productivity in agriculture and that we have been losing rapidly the ability to compete in the world market with other goods-manufacturing nations (Blumberg 1980; Bowles, Gordon, and Weisskopf 1984; Magaziner and Reich 1983). Forty years ago we supplied 98 percent of our own products. Now we are dependent on foreign imports, unable to find buyers for many of our own products abroad (agricultural products and some high technology, including weaponry, being the main exceptions) (*BusinessWeek* 1984).

Some, most notably former presidents Ronald Reagan, George H. W. Bush, Bill Clinton, and now President George W. Bush, have argued that while jobs are indeed disappearing, more new jobs are being created to take their place. And indeed, it is true that there has been a net increase in newly created jobs. Then why does deindustrialization and the shift from manufacturing to service work as the defining characteristics of the U.S. economy matter? The problem is not simply how many jobs are

available, but rather the quality of these jobs: What do the people doing these jobs earn? The fact is that the newly created jobs in the service sector do not pay as well as the lost jobs in goods production such as manufacturing, mining, and construction (see Figure 11.2). Many jobs in the service sector pay minimum wage or very low wages, often insufficient for a full-time worker to rise above poverty, a situation sociologists call **underemployment.** These newly created jobs thus do not compensate for the income lost as jobs shift from goods production to services.

The greatest job growth is occurring in the sector that pays lower wages; the annual average compensation in the shrinking industries is almost $12,000 higher than the wage rate in the expanding industries (U.S. Bureau of the Census 2004). This helps explain why women may show lower rates of unemployment than men, but still suffer substantially higher comparative rates of poverty: The gendered **dual labor markets** in which men and women commonly work has meant that women have traditionally worked in the service sector while men were more likely to be employed in goods production (see Chapter 8). While jobs in goods production pay significantly higher wages, these are precisely the jobs that have been disappearing, producing higher unemployment rates for men, but higher comparative wages for those men who are still employed there. On the other hand, women's work opportunities in the services have been expanding dramatically, even if they do pay much lower wages than jobs in goods production. Thus, women may have an easier time finding employment in the growing service sector than men in the goods-producing sector; but the wages of those women who are employed are likely to be significantly lower than those of men, and for many these wages will not be sufficient to rise above poverty.

The future of the U.S. manufacturing sector is uncertain. Looking beyond the present, some argue that manufacturing will continue to decline and that the number of jobs for workers in high-skilled, knowledge-based service occupations will greatly expand. Robert Reich, a former U.S. secretary of labor, for example, believes this process is well under way and that we are already experiencing a skills shortage among U.S. workers that needs to be remedied through education and training if we are to be able to compete in the world markets (Raymend 2001; Reich 1991, 1994).

In actuality, the future of work in the United States in all three sectors—manufacturing, service, and agriculture—is uncertain. It is likely that in the twenty-first century we may have to totally rethink the meaning of work, for it has become obvious that we live in a global economy fueled not only by a global workforce but by rapid technological advances that have changed and reduced workforce needs and eliminated many time and distance restrictions on the conduct of work (Aronowitz and DiFazio 1994; Rifkin 1995b; Uchitelle and Kleinfield 1996).

The Decline of Self-Employment

Today when we consider joining the labor force, we are likely to think in terms of working for someone. This was not always the case. At the time of the American Revolution, 80 percent of the labor force was self-employed. (In this discussion, we are leaving aside consideration of the sizable slave population.) Most were engaged in family farming. But whatever their role in the division of labor, working people

Farming was once seen as an occupation in which individual farmers were independent owners and managers of their own enterprises. Today, however, most food in the United States is produced by huge corporate farms. This photograph shows a feed lot in Texas that is capable of feeding several thousands of head of cattle simultaneously.

typically owned their own tools and income-producing property. Government was for the most part neither an active overseer of the domestic economy nor a source of employment.

By 1880 the self-employed made up only a third of the labor force, and today they represent less than 10 percent. In the wake of the Industrial Revolution, industry and then agriculture were progressively taken over by large-scale corporate enterprises. With the expansion of productive capability that stemmed from technological advances, the creation of modern transportation and communication networks, and the emergence of regional and national markets for inexpensively produced goods, independent entrepreneurs (small business owners) and family farmers could not compete with heavily capitalized firms. More and more people found that they had to depend on jobs offered by others in order to survive. Today we are a nation of employees, forced to compete with one another for employment opportunities. In the words of one observer, most labor force participants "have virtually no access to income from property or control over the production process. [Their] economic welfare is determined by the vicissitudes of the labor market" (Reich 1978:181). Although Michael Reich made this observation almost 30 years ago, it is still pertinent today.

There has been a slight increase in recent years in self-employment. This increase has occurred largely because persons who have lost their jobs as a result of corporate restructuring and downsizing have been finding work as independent contractors. However, much of this self-employment is actually underemployment. Successfully contracting your skills out requires that they be regularly in demand, and for many self-employed people this is a problem. Many of the newly self-employed are working and earning less compared to when they were on regular payrolls and are often without such important benefits as health coverage (Mishel and Bernstein 2003).

Along with the growth of big business and corporate agriculture has come the expansion of public employment. Today almost 16 percent of the labor force is employed by government in service jobs. The federal government employed 2.8 million civilians in 2002, while state and local governments had 18.7 million employees on their payrolls (U.S. Bureau of the Census 2004:416). We have come a long way from the days when government workers were a rarity.

Given that most members of the labor force lack any means of economic subsistence apart from that provided in return for their labor, workers are in a state of dependence and extreme vulnerability. Economic decisions made by affluent executives, both in and out of government, routinely throw out of work people whose faces the decision makers never see (Eitzen and Baca Zinn 1989; Sklar 1995). The decline of self-employment has also meant a loss of self-determination, for it has rendered most workers subject to the whims of bureaucratic decision makers over whom they have no control.

Bureaucratization of the Workplace

Implicit in the historical decline of self-employment is a third historical trend, the rise of the formal organization, or bureaucracy, as a setting for work activity. The term **bureaucracy** is not used loosely by sociologists. It refers to places in which the following features are normally present:

1. A clear-cut division of labor, within which each worker is formally assigned specialized tasks and duties.

2. A hierarchy of authority, in which every individual has a supervisor or boss whose work-related directives must be obeyed.

3. Organizational rules and regulations that govern work performance, delineate the rights

and responsibilities of each individual, and dictate proper channels of communication.

4. Demands for rationality and efficiency in the performance of work tasks, requiring individuals to set aside their personal feelings when dealing with others.

5. A ladderlike system of material and symbolic rewards based on technical qualifications and the ability to perform specialized work tasks. The rewards are intended to motivate individuals to compete for movement upward in the bureaucracy and to stimulate loyalty to the work organization (Gerth and Mills 1968).

Bureaucratic organization facilitates employers' control over work and workers in the interest of attaining a particular goal (Ritzer 1996). In the corporate world, the goal is generally to maximize profits, while the goal for government is to provide public services dictated by law (e.g., tax collection, defense, law enforcement, aid to the disadvantaged). Work policies, the rules and regulations developed to attain the goal, are decreed by those who hold command positions in a bureaucracy. Workers are expected to obey, even if they do not agree with the policies or the organizational goals. Compliance, or doing what they are told, is a virtue expected of those who wish to remain employed.

This is not to say that those who labor in bureaucratic settings are mindless robots whose every action is controlled. Sociologists have long used the term **informal organization** to underscore the nonofficial behaviors engaged in by workers and their peers (Blau and Meyer 1971). Workers may help a bureaucracy operate more efficiently when they bypass red tape and official channels. On the other hand, informal organization may also enable workers to sabotage superiors' planned use of their labor. In either case, the existence of informal organization indicates that bureaucratic control is by no means total (Edwards 1979).

In some cases workers can count on unions to protect them from abuses of bureaucratic control and to assist them in bargaining with organizational managers over workplace conditions, wages, and benefits. But only a small proportion of workers in the United States belong to unions today, and many unions have grown weak. Organized labor has been adversely affected by the loss of many traditionally unionized industrial jobs and an increasing climate of hostility toward unions on the part of employers. Only 13.3 percent of wage and salary workers are members of unions today, more than a 50 percent drop since the 1950s. Government workers are almost four times as likely to be represented by unions as workers in the private sector (U.S. Bureau of the Census 2004:431). (See Table 11.1. Note wage differentials between union and nonunion workers.)

Despite the substantial decline in unionization in the last several decades, there is evidence of a resurgent interest among service and white-collar workers for unionization. These workers are increasingly recognizing what blue-collar workers understood in the twentieth century: Unionization offers greater bargaining power to workers in their struggles for living wages, decent benefits, better working conditions, and dignity. For example, home-based child-care workers in Rhode Island have been working toward unionization with the Service Employees International Union, and by 2004 the state's Labor Relations Board agreed that they were indeed eligible for the right to collective bargaining (*Providence Journal* 2004). Although the state's governor continues to resist this movement, the home-care workers are not dissuaded in their efforts.

Similarly, graduate students at universities around the country continue to work toward unionization to help them in their struggles against exploitation by their academic employers. Since 1969 graduate students have increasingly been used to teach courses much as faculty do, but for a fraction of the salary that tenured

| Table 11.1 | Union Members, by Selected Characteristics, 2002 (in Thousands) |

Characteristic	Employed wage and salary workers		
	Total	Percent union members*	Percent represented by unions†
Total§	**122,009**	**13.3**	**14.6**
16 to 24 years old	19,258	5.1	5.9
25 to 34 years old	28,253	11.2	12.5
35 to 44 years old	31,296	14.2	15.6
45 to 54 years old	27,086	18.5	20.2
55 to 64 years old	12,982	17.4	19.0
65 years and over	3,133	7.9	9.1
Men	63,384	14.7	16.0
Women	58,625	11.6	13.0
White	**101,082**	**12.8**	**14.1**
Men	53,305	14.4	15.6
Women	47,777	10.9	12.3
Black	**14,127**	**16.9**	**18.7**
Men	6,499	18.2	20.0
Women	7,628	15.7	17.7
Hispanic¶	**15,523**	**10.5**	**11.7**
Men	9,131	11.1	12.2
Women	6,392	9.8	11.1
Full-time workers	100,204	14.6	16.0
Part-time workers	21,573	6.9	7.7
Managerial and professional specialty	36,969	13.0	15.0
Technical sales, and admin. support	35,770	8.9	9.9
Service occupations	17,898	12.6	13.8
Precision, production, craft, and repair	12,413	20.7	21.6
Operators, fabricators, and laborers	16,901	19.1	20.3
Farming, forestry, and fishing	2.058	4.3	5.1
Agricultural wage and salary workers	1,819	2.3	2.8
Private nonagricultural wage and salary workers			
Mining	458	8.5	10.0
Construction	6,883	17.2	17.8
Manufacturing	17,324	14.3	15.1
Transportation and public utilities	7,433	23.0	24.3
Wholesale and retail trade, total	25,475	4.5	4.9
Finance, insurance, and real estate	7,849	1.9	2.5
Services	35,179	5.7	6.7
Government	19,589	37.5	42.0

Annual averages of monthly data. Covers employed wage and salary workers 16 years old and over. Excludes self-employed workers whose businesses are incorporated although they technically qualify as wage and salary workers. Based on Current Population Survey, B Data not shown where base is less than 50,000. NA Not available. X Not applicable.
*Members of a labor union or an employee association similar to a labor union.
†Members of a labor union or an employee association similar to a union as well as workers who report no union affiliation but whose jobs are covered by a union or an employee association contract.*

| Table 11.1 | (*Continued*) |

Median usual weekly earnings[‡] (dollars)			
Total	Union members*	Represented by unions[†]	Not represented by unions
609	**740**	**734**	**587**
381	497	494	374
591	682	670	577
699	759	753	647
707	789	787	675
673	787	784	639
502	592	594	484
680	780	776	652
530	667	662	510
624	763	757	602
702	804	801	674
549	695	688	521
498	615	610	477
523	651	640	502
474	588	588	445
423	623	617	408
449	666	655	422
396	558	569	381
609	740	734	587
(X)	(X)	(X)	(X)
884	890	884	884
550	633	625	536
384	595	585	358
629	821	814	590
482	635	627	445
363	548	524	357
372	(B)	(B)	371
822	(B)	(B)	825
599	845	836	559
624	654	653	619
706	810	805	664
480	552	540	477
676	598	601	681
596	650	645	592
708	770	767	640

[‡]*For full-time employed wage and salary workers.*
[§]*Includes races not shown separately. Includes a small number of multiple jobholders whose full- and/or part-time status cannot be determined for their principal job.*
[¶]*Persons of Hispanic origin may be of any race.*
Source: U.S. Department of Commerce, Bureau of the Census, *Statistical Abstract of the United States, 2003* (Washington, DC: U.S. Government Printing Office, 2004), p. 431.

professors make, and often with few or no health-care benefits. The number of graduate students employed as part-time, expendable faculty has increased by over 35 percent since 1969, and that number is likely to continue to increase, as will more intense interest in unionization among this contingent workforce. Graduate students at such institutions as the University of Wisconsin, the University of California at Berkeley, The State University of New York, Yale University, and New York University have formed unions or have been recognized by the Labor Relations Board as having a right to collective bargaining. Students at several other universities are continuing their insistence on that same right (Cavell 2000).

Beginning with the Industrial Revolution, an ever larger proportion of the labor force in the United States has come to be employed in bureaucratic settings. By the 1980s, 20 percent of our industrial workforce was employed by a mere 16 giant corporations. Earlier we noted that the federal government, as a single employer, carries almost 3 million people on its civilian payroll. Yet in recent years we have begun to see some reversal of this concentration of employment in a relatively small number of bureaucratic organizations, as major corporations such as General Motors, AT&T, IBM, and others have implemented vast layoffs.

At the end of the 1970s, firms began to fundamentally reassess their employment and wage-setting practices. Large integrated (high-wage) firms began to downsize and rely more heavily on low-wage suppliers. Advances in telecommunications and transportation facilitated the relocation of lower-skilled operations to low-wage sites, leaving behind a core of permanent, relatively skilled employees supplemented increasingly by part-time and temporary workers. (Howell 1994:86)

Today, work in the United States most certainly means entering a competitive labor market and seeking to become someone's employee. With increasing frequency, it means taking a job in the growing service sector, particularly as the process of deindustrialization continues. As corporate restructuring and downsizing affect job opportunities, growing numbers of workers are finding that the only jobs available are part-time or temporary. For those who do work full-time within bureaucratic settings, job pressures and demands to work overtime are growing as the workers who remain take over the tasks done by others who are no longer there. Worries over job insecurity permeate many workplaces, as no one knows who may be the next to go.

The Rise of Contingency Work

One of the more ominous changes taking place in the structure of work in the United States, alluded to earlier, has been the rapid rise in the number of "contingent workers" and their increase as a proportion of the total labor force. Although no official definition of contingent workers exists (therefore making it difficult to count them), they are usually defined by the length of time a person expects to be employed or the number of hours a week a person expects to work.

In terms of length of employment, *contingent work* is any job that does not have "an explicit or implicit contract for long-term employment;" and for hours worked it is "any job in which the minimum hours worked vary irregularly" (Thomson 1995:45–48). Thus contingent workers usually include part-time workers, independent contractors who are self-employed, workers hired directly by a company for a temporary period, and workers who get jobs through temporary agencies.

One way to measure the growth of this sector of workers is through the increase in jobs that are controlled by temporary agencies. In a recent 8-year period the proportion of jobs in the labor force obtained through such agencies doubled, and one agency, Manpower Inc., is now said to be the largest private employer in the United States. Workers provided by temporary agencies include not only clerks and word processors but also accountants, engineers, attorneys, technicians, and even managerial executives. The range of people in need of work who are unable to find permanent full-time jobs has enabled one Michigan electronics manufacturer to open a factory staffed totally by temporary workers (Sklar 1995).

Because of the different ways in which contingent workers are sometimes defined, estimates vary as to just how large a segment of the U.S. labor force such workers constitute. Figure 11.3 shows one estimate of the growth in temporary and involuntary part-time employment a situation that shows no signs of improving in the new century. The estimates all suggest that the numbers of contingent workers are significant: It is thought that as many as 30 million workers, representing almost a quarter of U.S. workers, are in this status (Bond 1994; Cook 2000). Their numbers have steadily increased as firms have reduced their full-time workforces. Temp agencies alone provide about one-fourth of all new jobs created since 1984 and now employ almost 3 million workers.

Where part-time and temporary workers once were primarily clerical workers, today they are a substantial part of the labor force in every sector of the economy; they include computer software engineers as well as administrative office workers, janitors, taxicab drivers, adjunct college professors, and home health-care workers (Cook 2000). Even colleges and universities are increasingly adopting this corporate model of the temporary workforce. Many of your college instructors may themselves be temporary or adjunct faculty, hired to teach courses for a fraction of the cost of full-time faculty (Noble 2001).

The benefits of contingent workers for employers begin with the ability to use "temporary help agencies like spigots, bringing temporary workers in when business heats up and pulling the plug on them when it cools" (Kilborn 1995a:A1). Flexibility is also matched in savings on health benefits, social security, pensions, disability insurance, and unemployment compensation. Nor are temporary workers protected by unions that can resist restrictive work rules. Discrimination in job placement on the basis of race, gender, or disability can easily occur under such circumstances, with little recourse on the part of the worker or often even the knowledge that it is taking place.

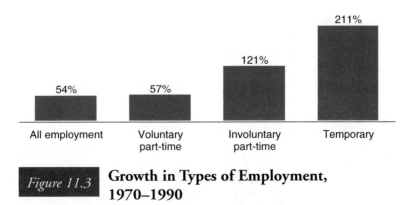

Figure 11.3 **Growth in Types of Employment, 1970–1990**

Source: Nancy Folbre and the Center for Popular Economics, *The New Field Guide to the U.S. Economy* (New York: The New Press, 1995), pp. 2, 4.

A core of the contingent workforce prefers temporary or part-time work. Among this core group are young adults living at home who have not settled on a future career, retirees who want to keep their hand in the workforce, as well as men and women whose marital or live-in partners are earning wages at regular full-time jobs that are enough to support the household. However, increasing numbers of people faced with contingent work do not prefer it. The head of Manpower Inc. estimated that two-thirds of his workers would prefer to be in permanent jobs. The recent growth in part-time employment, from 16.6 percent of jobs in 1973 to 23.8 percent in 2002, is due almost exclusively to *involuntary* part-timers, notably among male workers who earn considerably less than men working full-time (Mishel and Bernstein 2003; U.S. Bureau of the Census 2004:393). Although these workers are not always happy with the jobs they have, they are happy they have a job.

Unemployment

Though most persons who wish to participate in the work world are able to do so, millions of people in the United States have been unable to market their labor. In the early 1980s the United States was in the throes of an economic recession more severe than any since World War II. There was a slowdown in production and hiring, and according to the U.S. Department of Labor, the official rate of **unemployment** reached 10.8 percent in December 1982—the highest rate since the Great Depression of the 1930s. Out of a total labor force of over 100 million people, 12 million were involuntarily out of work. Most of the unemployed either had been dismissed from their last job or were new entrants to the labor force who could not find work (U.S. Department of Labor, available at www.bls.gov).

But it is not only during recessions that millions of people are out of work. In the 1980s the Reagan/Bush administration argued that a 5.5 percent unemployment rate should be considered "full employment." Over time we have come to tacitly accept a permanent pool of jobless people. Between 1983 and 1989, a period that included the longest peacetime expansion in our history, the unemployment rate averaged 7.15 percent or about 8.9 million people (Yates 1994). Although the rate has gone down somewhat in the 1990s and into the twenty-first century, there have been relatively few years since World War II in which the rate has dipped below the 4.5 percent level, and it usually has been much higher (see Table 11.2). Unemployment and job insecurity are now such chronic features of the economy that most workers feel vulnerable. It was no surprise when a 2003 Gallup poll showed 65 percent of respondents indicating they personally worried about unemployment. What do such statistics mean? Why does unemployment seem to be a permanent feature of U.S. society, even during nonrecessionary years? What impact does joblessness have on people?

Extent of Unemployment

Government statistics on unemployment have been severely criticized for *underestimating* the extent of joblessness (National Commission on Employment and Unemployment Statistics 1979). Much of this criticism is directed at the ways in which the U.S. Department of Labor defines the term **labor force.** The civilian labor force is said to consist of people who are 16 years of age or older (with the exception of inmates of institutions). To be counted as a member of the labor force, people must either have a full-time or part-time job or have been actively seeking work in the 4-week period prior to the Labor Department's monthly unemployment survey. People who do not meet these criteria are not considered members of the labor force and hence are not counted as employed or unemployed.

| Table 11.2 | Employment Status of the Civilian Noninstitutional Population 16 Years and Over, 1955 to 2002 (in Thousands) | | | | | | | |

| | | Annual averages | | | | | | |
| | | Civilian labor force | | | | Unemployment rates | | |
Year and month	Civilian noninstitutional population	Total	Percent of population	Employed	Unemployed	Total	Men	Women
1955	109,633	65,023	59.3	62,170	2,852	4.4	4.2	4.9
1960	117,245	69,628	59.4	65,778	3,852	5.5	5.4	5.9
1965	126,513	74,455	58.9	71,088	3,366	4.5	4.0	5.5
1970	137,085	82,771	60.4	78,678	4,093	4.9	4.4	5.9
1975	153,153	93,775	61.2	85,846	7,929	8.5	7.9	9.3
1980	167,745	106,940	63.8	99,303	7,637	7.1	6.9	7.4
1985	178,206	115,461	64.8	107,150	8,312	7.2	7.0	7.4
1990	188,049	124,788	66.4	117,914	6,874	5.5	5.6	5.4
1995	198,584	132,304	66.6	124,900	7,404	5.6	5.6	5.6
2002	217,570	144,863	66.6	136,485	8,378	5.8	5.9	5.6

Source: U.S. Department of Labor, *Employment and Earnings,* 36 (November 1989): 14; *Employment and Earnings* 42 (January 1995): 17; U.S. Bureau of the Census, Statistical Abstract of the United States, 2003 (Washington, DC: Government Printing Office, 2004), p. 386.

If the government's definition of the labor force were not so restricted, say critics, the unemployment rate would be dramatically higher. Many 14- and 15-year-olds are capable of and interested in holding jobs—at least part-time—but their joblessness is ignored. Many older students would prefer a full-time job to school attendance, but they are not considered in labor force statistics. Mothers in the home, many of whom do not look for work because their pay would not offset extra child-care costs, are also excluded. Then there are the individuals who have become discouraged in the search for employment and have simply given up. They just drop out of existence in terms of official unemployment statistics. Meanwhile, workers who are on strike, on vacation, or ill are counted as part of the employed labor force even if they are not receiving wages.

Thus, a more inclusive definition of the U.S. labor force would probably give us an unemployment rate far greater than that now reported by the government. The rate would expand even more if we counted the growing numbers of **involuntary part-time workers** who need and want full-time jobs.

Government unemployment statistics generally do not depict the changes that take place in the pool of people who are jobless. Over a given period, *different* people are constantly becoming employed and unemployed. If the federal government were to give more publicity to the numbers of persons who experience unemployment over, say, a year's time, its full impact would be better revealed. The U.S. Department of Labor has investigated this situation. In 1986 the official unemployment rate averaged 7 percent over the course of the year, or an average of 8.2 million people monthly. Yet when researchers inquired into how many different people experienced unemployment at some point during 1986, the results were quite startling. Sixteen percent of the labor force was touched by joblessness—a total of 20.7 million people (Mellor and Parks 1988)!

The statistics with which the federal government depicts unemployment are chosen for their political neutrality, according to the critics. By making the rate of joblessness seem to be lower than it truly is, the government is able to obscure the extent to which satisfactory work opportunities are absent. As unemployment grows, there has even been discussion of moving the "full employment" rate to 6 percent in order to discourage discussion of the fact that there are just not enough employment opportunities to go around.

Causes of Unemployment

What factors underlie the United States' seeming inability to deliver enough jobs to its people? A quick but erroneous explanation is that millions of people simply do not care to work. There is no evidence that this is the case. (See Table 11.3.) On the contrary, surveys indicate that most persons would choose to work even if their financial situations did not require it (Quinn and Staines 1979). In fact, money is not the primary factor affecting people's reasons for working. One survey found that 72 percent of respondents would prefer a job that provided low pay but offered a high degree of satisfaction (*New York Times* 1999). What is at issue today is whether or not the jobs are there for all the people who want to work. By the end of 1996 IBM, AT&T, General Motors, Sears, and the U.S. Postal Service laid off close to 400,000

workers. For IBM alone the reduction represented a loss of 30 percent of its workforce (Kirk 1995).

To understand the causes of unemployment we must look beyond the millions of jobless individuals to focus on factors that are largely beyond their control. In a previous chapter we saw that there are forces creating and perpetuating poverty. Likewise, there are forces that the unemployed cannot counter or overcome. Moreover, many of the underlying causes of poverty are the same as those that put and keep people out of work.

▲ Automation and Technological Change

One cause of unemployment is the introduction of computers and other "labor-saving" machines into the workplace. Employers install new machinery in order to increase worker productivity and/or cut labor costs. Automation, computerization, introduction of robotics, and other such technological changes often displace workers from existing jobs and also close certain categories of work opportunities for newcomers to the labor force. There are fewer jobs for telephone operators, coal miners, and farm laborers, among others, because of technological displacement. Between 1938 and 1993 the banking industry eliminated 179,000 tellers or 37 percent of its workforce and replaced them with automated teller machines (Rifkin 1995a). Banks now increasingly charge customers for using human tellers instead of automated teller machines, a move that is sure to reinforce the reduction in employment opportunities. The steel and auto industries have found that substituting machines for people can help hold down labor costs. While automation and technological change do create new job categories—for example, computer programmer and skilled machine technician—it seems likely that more jobs are lost than created. Furthermore, technologically displaced workers are likely to find it difficult to qualify for and adjust themselves to the new opportunities that open up (Leontief 1982; U.S. General Accounting Office 1982).

Those hit hardest by technological displacement are unskilled and semiskilled workers, such as clerical employees, laborers, and lower-level blue-collar workers. These workers often do not have the educational attainments and training to qualify for jobs requiring more skills. Until the late 1980s, it was thought that technical and professional workers and white-collar administrative personnel were more likely to be insulated from technological displacement and were more flexible in terms of the work roles they can readily assume. However, the recession of the early 1990s saw the acceleration of worker displacement in every type of white-collar occupation. Since then many of these white-collar displaced workers have had to compete for declining numbers of jobs like those they held, are doing independent consulting or temporary work, or are taking jobs that unskilled and semiskilled workers are also seeking. The types of jobs that are fast growing can be seen in Table 11.4.

The precise impact of automation and technological change on unemployment statistics remains a matter of conjecture. But it is clear that, in selected sectors of the economy, people have been put out of work. Observers disagree about the prospects in store for the future (Vedder 1982). Some downplay the topic of unemployment, suggesting only that changes will be taking place in the nature of work and in the forms of work organization in which people will be employed. Others feel that the growth of new work opportunities will fail to keep up with the natural growth of the labor force and that a steady increase in unemployment will be the result. Still others contend that there will be plenty of work, but that labor force members will have to work fewer hours per week in order to spread job opportunities around. Whatever the future, it is unlikely to be the unemployed who determine its

direction. Such decisions are in the hands of public and private employers—those who hold command positions in bureaucratic work settings.

▲ Job Export and Goods Import

Many of the largest U.S. corporations have been opening plants in other countries, **outsourcing** entire operations or parts of these. This trend is part of the globalization of the economy (see Chapter 4) Foreign operations have made it possible for such firms to take advantage of cheaper foreign labor and gain better accessibility to foreign markets (Barnet and Cavanaugh 1994; Rosen 2002). Wal-Mart, which once proudly asserted that its merchandise was made in the USA, now is one of the largest forces behind outsourcing: Its tremendous size as a retailer gives it the power to demand that its suppliers provide extremely low-priced merchandise or lose its business. The need for suppliers to use Wal-Mart's enormous market reach to sell their products pressures them to seek to pay the lowest wages anywhere they can. Goods sold at Wal-Marts are now primarily manufactured in China, where wages have been driven down to such desperately low levels as to impoverish workers there and to destroy jobs manufacturing these goods in the United States (U.S. Congress, House 2004). According to organized labor, multinational corporations that invest in plants outside this country and/or close down domestic facilities to reopen elsewhere are guilty of exporting jobs.

Some critics decry this globalization trend of searching for the cheapest, most exploitable labor while destroying jobs and living wages in nations like the United States as a **race to the bottom** that depresses everyone's wages worldwide (Brecher, Costello, and Smith 2000). This race to the bottom has encouraged a shocking rise in **sweatshops** all around the world, where workers (including many children) toil in overcrowded, unsafe conditions for below-poverty wages, mandatory but unpaid overtime,

Table 11.3	Unemployed Persons by Reason for Unemployment, Sex, and Race (in Thousands)			
	Total, 16 years and over		Men, 20 years and over	
Reason	2002	2003	2002	2003
Number of unemployed				
Total unemployed	8,378	8,774	3,896	4,209
Job losers and persons who completed temporary jobs	4,607	4,838	2,702	2,899
On temporary layoff	1,124	1,121	701	686
Not on temporary layoff	3,484	3,717	2,000	2,213
Permanent job losers	2,701	2,846	1,537	1,667
Persons who completed temporary jobs	783	871	464	546
Job leavers	866	818	386	376
Reentrants	2,368	2,477	743	846
New entrants	536	641	65	88
Percent distribution				
Total unemployed	100.0	100.0	100.0	100.0
Job losers and persons who completed temporary jobs	55.0	55.1	69.3	68.9
On temporary layoff	13.4	12.8	18.0	16.3
Not on temporary layoff	41.6	42.4	51.3	52.6
Job leavers	10.3	9.3	9.9	8.9
Reentrants	28.3	28.2	19.1	20.1
New entrants	6.4	7.3	1.7	2.1
Unemployed as a percentage of the civilian labor force				
Job losers and persons who completed temporary jobs	3.2	3.3	3.7	3.9
Job leavers	.6	.6	.5	.5
Reentrants	1.6	1.7	1.0	1.1
New entrants	.4	.4	.1	.1

and with few or no protections. These sweatshops produce everything from licensed college T-shirts and sweatshirts to electronics and housewares.

Corporate leaders typically reject this charge, arguing that a substantial percentage of their increased profits flows back into this country. They claim that foreign investments create new jobs in the United States—for example, through the expansion of operations at company headquarters—a claim endorsed by every president, from Ronald Reagan to George W. Bush. However, as in the case of automation and technological change, it is not clear that the numbers

Table 11.3 (*Continued*)

Women, 20 years and over		Both sexes, 16 to 19 years		White		Black	
2002	2003	2002	2003	2002	2003	2002	2003
3,228	3,314	1,253	1,251	6,137	6,311	1,693	1,787
1,708	1,751	197	188	3,491	3,613	840	876
360	367	62	68	921	924	148	138
1,348	1,384	136	120	2,570	2,689	691	738
1,082	1,102	82	77	2,029	2,085	488	530
265	282	54	43	541	604	203	208
389	357	91	85	684	619	135	132
1,028	1,076	597	554	1,619	1,676	576	614
102	130	368	424	342	403	142	165
100.0	100.0	100.0	100.0	100.0	100.0	100.0	100.0
52.9	52.8	15.7	15.0	56.9	57.3	49.6	49.0
11.2	11.1	4.9	5.4	15.0	14.6	8.8	7.7
41.7	41.8	10.8	9.6	41.9	42.6	40.8	41.3
12.1	10.8	7.3	6.8	11.2	9.8	8.0	7.4
31.8	32.5	47.6	44.3	26.4	26.6	34.0	34.4
3.2	3.9	29.4	33.9	5.6	6.4	8.4	9.2
2.7	2.7	2.6	2.6	2.9	3.0	5.1	5.3
.6	.6	1.2	1.2	.6	.5	.8	.8
1.6	1.7	7.9	7.7	1.3	1.4	3.5	3.7
.2	.2	4.9	5.9	.3	.3	.9	1.0

Source: U.S. Department of Labor, *Employment and Earnings,* Household Data Annual Averages, Tables 27 and 28, pp. 238 and 239, available at www.bls.gov.

of jobs being exported are fully offset by the new ones created. Similarly, workers whose jobs disappear because of factory closings are unlikely to qualify for the new and different work opportunities that replaced their old jobs. Thus, we see an increasing frequency of "downward mobility" among workers (e.g., in the auto and steel industries) whose plants have closed and whose jobs have been exported. Formerly able to support their families modestly with factory jobs, many such workers are now eking out a living in low-wage positions—becoming janitors,

Table 11.4	Fastest-Growing Occupations, 2002–2012 (in Thousands)			
	Employment			
Occupation	2002	2012	Numerical change	Percent change
Medical assistants	**365**	**579**	**215**	**59**
Network systems and data communications analysts	186	292	106	57
Physician assistants	63	94	31	49
Social and human service assistants	305	454	149	49
Home health aides	580	859	279	48
Medical records and health information technicians	147	216	69	47
Physical therapist aides	37	54	17	46
Computer software engineers, applications	394	573	179	46
Computer software engineers, systems software	281	409	128	45
Physical therapist assistants	50	73	22	45

Source: U.S. Department of Labor, *News: 2002–2012 Employment Projections.* Released February 11, 2004. Available at www.bls.gov.

fast-food workers, hospital orderlies. These are the types of "service-sector" jobs that many are forced into in the face of deindustrialization (Ehrenreich 2001; Leidner 1993).

Corporate relocation has an effect similar to job export. Corporate relocation occurs when employers move their facilities from one place to another. For example, firms that want low-wage, nonunionized workers have at times found it desirable to relocate to the southern United States or, now with the North American Free Trade Agreement (NAFTA), to Mexico or Canada. In 1994 alone, 60 percent of the workers who lost jobs because of the free trade agreement lost them because U.S. production was shifted out of the country to either Mexico or Canada (*New York Times* 1994a). By 2002, the U.S. Department of Labor had certified that more than a half-million U.S. workers had lost their jobs because of NAFTA (www. citizen.org).

Many workers cannot uproot themselves and their families in order to follow relocated firms and factories across or out of the country. They must hunt for other jobs and often find themselves among the unemployed. Workers are also left behind when companies move their headquarters and plants out of central city areas to distant suburbs or small towns—often to gain tax relief, to obtain inexpensive labor, or to obtain additional space in which to conduct operations. Left behind are those who cannot afford to relocate or commute far beyond city limits. Over the last 40 years, the movement of business and industry out of central city areas has contributed to the erosion of the tax bases on which the services of city governments depend. Services mean jobs—from sanitation work, to public school teaching, to medical care in city hospitals. The financial crises experienced by such large cities as New York, in which thousands of public employees

Modern technology has made it possible for corporations to replace human labor with machines. In this photograph, an automatic teller machine dispenses money, transfers money from one account to another, and accepts deposits. This is a job that once was done by human bank tellers. In the future the use of robots for production and service tasks may have profound effects on the structure of work opportunities.

have lost their jobs, are linked at least in part to corporate relocation.

Earlier we mentioned that the United States has become a goods-importing nation. This has a direct bearing on unemployment. Although foreign-made goods are often cheaper than their domestically produced equivalents, purchase of such goods, again, is akin to exporting jobs. In a rather short time period production of radios, television sets, stereos, bicycles, automobiles, and ships—to mention a few products—has come largely under the control of foreign manufacturers. Semiconductors, solar cells, and videotape recorders were invented in the United States but are now among our imports from elsewhere. Our historic dominance in the manufacture of aircraft, plastics, and drugs is slowly ebbing away. The import of steel from Japan and other nations has helped to undermine employment in an industry that has long been central to our economy. In sum, manufacturing jobs have been and are now being lost, and this is reflected in unemployment.

▲ Government Spending and Taxation

Since the depression of the 1930s the federal government has played an ever more active role in determining the overall course of the economy. In two areas—spending and taxation—federal policies directly affect unemployment rates.

Each year the federal treasury is the recipient of billions of dollars that it turns back into the economy. In fiscal year 2003, for example, government revenues were roughly $1,782 billion. This money came from personal and corporate income taxes, Social Security taxes, excise taxes, and loans from private financial institutions. That year, the government spent some $2,158 billion (or $375 billion more than its revenues) on the defense establishment, grants to states and localities, payments to individuals, loan debts, and general federal operations.

There are legal limitations on how the federal government may use the money in its treasury. For example, each year billions of dollars must go to Social Security recipients and federal retirees. However, some flexibility is often permitted within the law, and new legislation is always being passed and old restrictions modified. Given the huge amounts of money involved, spending priorities directly affect the existing structure and growth of work opportunities. For example, during the 1980s the federal government began to escalate its rate of spending on research, development, and production of weapons systems to be made available to the nation's military forces. A 5-year plan was instituted in which total defense expenditures, including spending in the areas mentioned previously, would total some $1.6 trillion. Those states and communities fortunate enough to be major recipients of defense dollars were able to maintain some semblance of economic stability even as unemployment rates elsewhere reached double-digit figures (e.g., in late 1982). The modest defense cutbacks that occurred in the 1990s, a response to the end of the Cold War and a growing federal budget deficit, increased unemployment in states and communities that benefited from job growth in the previous decade.

At times, as in the 1980s and 1990s, the federal government has tried to restrict annual spending on nondefense programs, both by eliminating them outright and by reducing their funding. This strategy, which is considered a way of fighting inflation and reducing the growing deficit, also increases unemployment across the country. Federal policymakers at times tell us that higher unemployment rates are a cost this society must be willing to bear in order to slow down inflation and the rising costs of living. The idea is that people will then have more money to spend on consumer goods and services, and ultimately the unemployed (or at least some of them) will be called back to work. Unfortunately, many are not called back. They remain unemployed, and many fall out of the labor force statistics altogether. Many of those fortunate enough to find work suffer drops in earning ability because in desperation they must take almost any jobs they can find in order to survive.

Taxation policy also has an impact on unemployment. Of each dollar flowing into the federal treasury, 46 cents comes from individual income taxes and less than 8 cents from corporate income taxes (U.S. Bureau of the Census 2004:325). When individual income tax rates are lowered, consumers have more money to spend on goods and services. Assuming that they choose to spend this money, sales will increase, creating more jobs in business and industry. When corporate taxes are cut, firms may choose to invest in new equipment, expanded operations, or higher wages for employees—all of which help create jobs. On the other hand, lower personal and/or corporate income taxes also may mean less revenue for the federal treasury and pressure to slow down government spending. The negative effect of the latter on unemployment somehow must be balanced against anticipated job growth in the private sector of the economy—a very tricky balancing act indeed.

▲ Discrimination

Discrimination may not directly cause unemployment per se, as much as it determines who will be without a job. Institutional discrimination directly affects the employment opportunities open to people of color and women. Minority group unemployment rates are ordinarily quite high. African Americans, for example, are twice as likely as whites to be out of work and are usually jobless for longer periods of time. The unemployment rates for women are normally higher than those for men. Considering the defects of government unemployment statistics, the true rates of joblessness among people of color and women are no doubt considerably understated.

Discrimination on the basis of age is pervasive in the structure of work. Young persons between the ages of 16 and 19—especially minority group teenagers—have extraordinarily high joblessness rates. Since they are likely to possess few skills and little work experience, it is difficult for them to get a decent start in the labor market. Old age, on the other hand, may mean that education and skills are out of date.

Even where this is not the case, employers whose main concern is to cut labor costs often find it desirable to replace older employees with persons who will work for less.

Until the early 1990s there had been a steady decline in the labor force participation of persons over 65. A good deal of this decline was attributable to the existence of Social Security and pension plans. In 1900 two-thirds of the men aged 65 and over were in the labor force; today the figure is around 19 percent (U.S. Bureau of the Census 2004:385). However, while that figure is substantially lower than a century ago, it is showing signs of climbing upward again. Part of the reason for this new increase is financial need, including the need to maintain health benefits. Although most elders look forward to retirement from work, others do not. Retirees often face financial problems (nearly one person in ten who is 65 or older lives in poverty) and/or difficulties adjusting to the loss of a work role and job-related friendships. Forced retirement of workers in their 60s and younger, despite its often negative impact, has been common and is frequently linked to corporations' desire to downsize their workforce. However, a small but growing number of retirees are beginning to take low-wage service-sector jobs (such as employees in fast-food restaurants and as retail stores' "greeters") in order to supplement insufficient Social Security benefits. One survey found that 68 percent of respondents indicated they expect to work for pay after retirement (American Savings Council 2004).

During the 1970s this society's "senior citizens" (whose presence is increasingly noticeable because of changes in the age composition of the population) became politically active. Their grassroots organizing has been felt at the national level on such issues as mandatory retirement. In 1978 Congress passed legislation that removed the mandatory retirement age from most federal jobs and placed it at 70 years of age for most jobs in the private sector. This action was intended to provide some protection for those who otherwise would automatically be pushed out of work in their early or mid-60s. Nonetheless, many older workers retire involuntarily, with consequent financial difficulties (see Chapter 10).

The Impact of Unemployment

Individuals who find themselves involuntarily unemployed often discover that their lives and the lives of their families have changed for the worse. For example, Michael Aiken and his associates (1968) conducted a study of automobile workers who lost their jobs when their plant was permanently shut down. As their financial resources became depleted, many of the unemployed workers withdrew from contact with friends and relatives because they could not afford to return social favors and obligations. Thus, the unemployed avoided the very persons whose contacts might have been useful in finding new work. Beyond this, the unemployed workers were unhappy over the loss of on-the-job friendships that had helped give meaning to their everyday lives. Not only did they feel a sense of social isolation, but the loss of a work role made them doubt whether they were useful to society. Work was no longer providing personal identity and a sense of social worth. The unemployed had to depend on other family members to bear wage-earning responsibilities, frequently resulting in serious tensions in the home. The economic deprivation stemming from unemployment led many of the persons studied to agree that

> *You sometimes can't help wondering whether life is worth living anymore.*
>
> *These days I get a feeling that I'm just not a part of things.*
>
> *No one is going to care much about what happens to you when you get right down to it. (Aiken, Ferman, and Sheppard 1968:67)*

In *Rusted Dreams,* David Bensman and Roberta Lynch (1987) explored some of the human dilemmas and tragedies attributed to the decline of the steel industry. This is one of several industries in which large numbers of jobs have simply vanished in the deindustrialization process. Bensman and Lynch (1987:98) showed how the unemployment statistics mask these kinds of realities:

> *Skilled workers no one will hire even for unskilled positions because they are thought to be overqualified, too old (even if in their fifties), or judged likely to leave for other jobs;*
>
> *People whose health insurance was in effect only so long as they were employed, now pleading with or even lying about their insurance status to doctors and hospitals in order to receive medical treatment;*
>
> *Workers who have no source of income to support their families and whose unemployment compensation has run out, now finding they are ineligible for welfare or food stamps because they own a car or a home;*
>
> *The offspring and spouses of the unemployed who find themselves victimized by violence and abuse in the home, as the worker vents his or her frustration and anger (often exacerbated by alcohol and other drugs);*
>
> *The children of workers without jobs who engage in juvenile crime out of a sense of aimlessness and hopelessness generated by a deteriorating family situation;*
>
> *The women whose job loss sends their families into economic spirals and those whose husbands are out of work, can no longer deal with marriage, and opt for divorce or simply abandonment of their families; [and]*
>
> *The workers who give up all hope: "I used to work with the kid. After the mill closed he was about to lose his home. He took a gun to his head and blew his brains out."*

The stress, anxiety, tension, and depression found among the jobless testify to the central role work plays for people in this society (Dudley 1994; Pappas 1989; Rosen 1987).

Nor are the distresses associated with unemployment found only among blue-collar workers. In the 1980s more than 1.5 million midlevel management jobs were eliminated, and the 1990s saw increasing numbers of upper-middle-management executives losing their jobs as well. Newman (1999) termed the serious decline in their standard of living and their lost grasp on the American Dream a **fall from grace.**

One study of male white-collar professionals—including engineers, scientists, and technicians—demonstrated that they share similar experiences with blue-collar workers. The unemployed professionals tended to go through several stages, according to researchers Douglas H. Powell and Paul F. Driscoll (1973). Most of the professionals had been anticipating being laid off as they followed the problems being faced by their employers. So their first feeling was relief when the expected occurred. Given their educational credentials and long employment experience in responsible positions, the professionals were confident about finding new work. They tended to put off looking for a position right away; they wanted to enjoy their newly discovered freedom for a while. Family life, in this initial stage, remained normal.

In the second stage the unemployed professionals began to tire of full-time leisure and to get concerned about not having a job. At this point, they launched highly organized efforts to find work. Economic deprivation had not yet been a problem, as most had savings and other resources to carry them along. Family and friends offered encouragement, and the confidence level of the unemployed was high.

For those whose job-seeking efforts yielded no concrete results, the third stage was characterized by doubt and depression. Their psychological moods interfered with the job search, and relationships with friends and family began to fall apart. The jobless professionals, like their blue-collar counterparts, began to doubt their worth. Confronting feelings of obsolescence, they became alternately frustrated, furious, and filled with despair. Family relations were at their lowest ebb. It was in this stage that suicides were most likely to occur.

In the fourth and final stage, malaise and cynicism set in among the jobless. Job-seeking efforts slowed down to a cursory level, and anxieties decreased as the professionals settled unhappily into their assigned roles. Family relations improved with the recognition of an extremely difficult situation. In the words of researchers Powell and Driscoll (1973:26):

The image of competent and energetic men reduced to listless discouragement highlights the personal tragedy and the loss of valuable resources when there is substantial unemployment. . . . Perhaps more significantly, the situation of these middle-class unemployed further dramatizes the plight of the larger numbers of unemployed nonskilled workers whose fate is to deal with unemployment often during their life-time.

More recent researchers have found similar results (Heckscher 1995; Newman 1999).

For workers who fall into the unskilled category, unemployment simply makes the already difficult challenge of being self-sufficient or contributing to family support that much more difficult. Unskilled workers feel worthless and doubt themselves even when they are employed. In his classic study, *Tally's Corner,* social anthropologist Elliot Liebow (1967) examined the lives of a group of men who lived in a poor neighborhood in Washington, D.C. The men either were unemployed or were construction workers, day laborers, and menial workers in retail and service establishments. Given their position in the occupational structure, all these men had experienced or could realistically look forward to bouts of joblessness. Marriages regularly broke down, and some men were reluctant to embark on permanent marital relationships because of their precarious economic situations. According to Liebow (1967:210): "The way in which the man makes a living and the kind of living he makes have important consequences for how the man sees himself and is seen by others." In their search for some source of pride and self-esteem—since neither work nor home provided these—the men turned to one another, hung around on street corners, and tried to forget their economic, social, and personal sense of failure.

Researcher M. Harvey Brenner (1973, 1977) is among those who have examined the relationship between rising unemployment rates and various social costs. Brenner's work indicates that as unemployment rises, there are sharp increases in a variety of problem areas. Summarizing some of Brenner's conclusions, Barry Bluestone and Benjamin Harrison (1982:65) note:

[A] one percent increase in the aggregate unemployment rate sustained over a period of six years has been associated with approximately:

- *37,000 total deaths (including 20,000 cardiovascular deaths)*
- *920 suicides*
- *650 homicides*
- *500 deaths from cirrhosis of the liver*
- *4,000 state mental hospital admissions*
- *3,300 state prison admissions*

As research bearing on unemployment has proceeded, the focus has come to include family members of the unemployed, who are also victims. The stresses that are borne by spouses, children, and other members of the household are often extremely serious. Psychological and physical abuse may accompany more general family discord, leading to family breakup (Liem and Liem 1988; Liem and Rayman 1982). By and large, social service providers, unions, and employers are ill prepared to be of help as these kinds of difficulties arise in so many households.

Job Satisfaction

If asked, each of us could probably come up with a list of attributes to be found in the ideal job. What kinds of things are most important to workers? The most comprehensive attempt to answer this question is a series of University of Michigan studies begun in 1969 (Quinn and Staines 1979; Staines and Quinn 1979). As a part of their research, the investigators conducted lengthy interviews with a carefully selected sample of employed persons. Those interviewed said that the following things were important in a job: work that is interesting; enough help, equipment, information, and authority to get the job done; an opportunity to develop one's special abilities; the opportunity to see the results of one's work; good pay; and job security. In other words, the content of the job, the resources to do it well, and a chance to realize one's talents were of as much importance as the pay.

If these are the things working people consider important, how satisfied are members of the workforce with the jobs they hold? The concept of **job satisfaction** is extremely difficult to measure. Most experts agree that efforts to measure satisfaction and dissatisfaction have been primitive. Thus we must consider any findings as indicative, rather than final and firm.

In some studies workers have simply been asked if their work is satisfying. Over the years, public polling firms such as Gallup have asked this question, and anywhere from 80 to 90 percent of those responding have expressed satisfaction. Critics of such polls assert that this approach does not probe deeply enough into worker attitudes. There is a possibility that most workers answer positively because they have become resigned to their fate. Such criticisms have been supported by the University of Michigan's Quality of Employment Surveys. When the Michigan researchers have probed, many of the respondents who claimed to be satisfied admitted to definite complaints about particular aspects of their jobs—for example, their inability to influence supervisors' decisions and to get responses to suggestions on how their work might be better performed (Staines and Quinn 1979). More recent surveys have similarly found that although 76 percent of respondents indicate it is very important to them that they have influence in deciding how they do their jobs, 56 percent said it was not likely that they would have that influence (Princeton Survey Research 1994).

Another way of measuring job satisfaction has been to ask questions about workers' desire to change jobs, and in a slightly different approach, workers have been asked whether or not they would choose similar jobs again. In general, the data on job satisfaction indicate that the higher the social status of a job, the more satisfied are those who hold it. The status continuum of occupations and professions tends to be correlated with the monetary rewards associated with different categories of work. But just as important, the ranking of jobs in terms of satisfaction appears to fit with the probable presence or absence of those things workers feel are important about a job. The jobs of nonprofessional white-collar workers and blue-collar workers, unlike those of many professionals, are unlikely to be intrinsically interesting or to allow for the development of talents. Other items that workers see as important—from enough resources to get the job done well to job security—are also likely to be associated with the higher status, better paying professional positions.

Survey findings also suggest that people of color and women are much more likely than whites and men to be dissatisfied with their work situations. This is to be expected, given the overrepresentation of such groups in nonprofessional white-collar and blue-collar jobs and the barriers they face in advancement. And, finally, young workers seem to be dissatisfied with much greater frequency than their elders. One study noted "a significant gap between the expectations or values of young workers and what they actually experience on the job"(U.S. Department of Health, Education, and Welfare 1973:37). Since over a third of the labor force is under 35 years of age, the failure of work to live up to the expectations of many youthful workers is by no means a minor problem.

The Blue-Collar Worker

If we were to distinguish between "brain jobs" and "brawn jobs," blue-collar workers would be found performing most of the latter (Levison 1974). Blue-collar jobs encompass a wide variety of skills and skill levels. The unskilled worker is usually employed in a job for which the training requirements are negligible. The required work tasks are so repetitive and routine that they can be learned in a very short time. By contrast, skilled blue-collar work often demands extensive training, ordinarily carried out during a period of apprenticeship. Obviously, the difference between the skill requirements for assembly-line work and cabinetmaking is extreme.

In recent years, however, the distinction between skilled, semiskilled, and unskilled workers has somewhat blurred as technology has increasingly displaced even many skilled workers and forced them to compete with less skilled

workers for jobs that require little or no training. Because of the large pool of unemployed and underemployed labor, many employers can be very specific about job requirements and choosy about whom they will hire, while offering a lower rate of pay than would be the case when there is a labor shortage.

Katherine Newman and Chauncy Lennon (1995) tracked fast-food industry jobs in the low-wage labor market in the Harlem section of New York City, jobs that are usually thought to be easy to land with little or no skill, education, or prior work experience. What they found is that fast-food jobs once held by school dropouts or young people first starting out are being held by people in their 20s who have skills, education, and prior experience. Such persons actively compete with one another for low-wage manual jobs in order to have any work at all, a situation that is becoming increasingly common across the country.

Others have drawn attention to the growing numbers of workers who have immigrated to the United States in the last 10 to 15 years, many of whom have been forced to join the ranks of the unemployed and underemployed. About 800,000 immigrants a year have been entering the United States since 1990. Many of the recent immigrants are from Latin American and Asian nations. They have tended to settle in urban areas on both coasts and have also moved heavily into the Midwest (Lamphere, Stepick, and Grenier 1994). According to the U.S. Bureau of the Census (2004), recent adult immigrants are just as likely as native-born adults to have college degrees (Larson 2004). But almost 33 percent of recent immigrants over 25 have not finished high school, compared with 12.5 percent of those born in the United States. The entry of many less formally educated immigrants into the labor market has at times escalated ethnic and racial tensions, as their quest for work adds to the competition of the native-born for low-wage manual jobs.

Blue-collar workers who have been able to maintain their jobs often face the specter of potential unemployment. In some ways job insecurity can be just as dysfunctional for such workers as joblessness. An increased sense of job insecurity can lead to a lower level of satisfaction with the job, a lower trust of management, a lower level of organizational commitment, and a greater interest in leaving. Psychosomatic symptoms often accompany such a sense of insecurity, as well as experiences of depression (Hartley et al. 1991; Warner 2003). Job security has been found to have a greater impact on self-esteem and physical well-being than job satisfaction, and stress felt from job insecurity has a "spillover" effect on workers' family lives (Burchell et al. 1999; Larson, Wilson, and Beley 1994).

Blue-collar workers tend to suffer from a sense of low social status in comparison to white-collar workers. This is reflected in, and no doubt reinforced by, the treatment accorded blue-collar workers in the mass media. Their activities are rarely considered worthy of news reporters' attention, except when there are strikes, layoffs, or serious accidents. With a few ethnic and regional exceptions, blue-collar workers are not commonly the subject of popular music. Television programs have tended to mock "brawn" workers, portraying them as stupid, closed-minded, bigoted, chauvinistic, and politically conservative—erroneous stereotypes rarely applied to white-collar workers. Federal task force interviews with blue-collar workers have

revealed an almost overwhelming sense of inferiority: the worker cannot talk proudly to his children about his job, and many workers feel they must apologize for their status. Thus the working-class home may be permeated with an atmosphere of failure—even of depressing self-degradation. (U.S. Department of Health, Education, and Welfare 1973:29; see also Sennet and Cobb 1972)

Blue-collar work is also physically punitive and often dangerous (Berman 1978; Brodeur 1974). Each year almost as many persons die in industrial accidents as were being killed at the height of the Vietnam war. In 2001, for example, of the 5,900 work-related fatalities that occurred, 67 percent were due to accidents of various types (including transportation incidents, explosions, falls, collapsing equipment), and 8 percent were due to exposure to harmful substances and environments. But 15 percent of the deaths in the workplace were a result of assaults and violent acts. Another 10.7 million workers suffered occupational injuries and illnesses in 2001. The rate of injury and illness was 8.1 per 100 full-time workers in manufacturing and 7.9 per 100 in construction, compared with 5.7 for the private sector as a whole(U.S. Bureau of the Census 2004:428–29).

Whereas the war in Vietnam called forth protest against human carnage, the daily toll among blue-collar workers generates no such concern. "Brawn" workers are constantly exposed to the possibility of permanent physical impairment and temporary total disability through on-the-job injuries. Occupational diseases—involving everything from respiratory problems to cancer—plague members of the blue-collar sector. We have already noted that blue-collar workers have the highest rates of job dissatisfaction; evidence links job dissatisfaction to longevity: The physical and mental stresses at work actually reduce life expectancy (U.S. Department of Health, Education, and Welfare 1973:62).

Politicians have at times characterized blue-collar workers as the "silent majority" and the "invisible Americans." Research indicates a definite relationship between blue-collar status and political alienation. The sense of inferiority, social isolation, and economic insecurity of many blue-collar workers make them ripe for exploitation by political demagogues who know how to channel the frustrations of blue-collar life into the voting booth, while leaving the objective sources of their discontent intact (Aiken et al. 1968; Sheppard and Herrick 1972). In the words of one worker interviewed by Lillian Rubin (1994:126), who had worked for years for an automobile parts factory and is now employed as a maintenance worker:

Used to be you worked hard, you figured you got someplace. Not anymore. . . . We did everything we were supposed to do—worked hard, saved some money, tried to raise our kids to be decent law-abiding people—and what do we get? The goddamn company goes belly-up and look at me now.

Maintenance, they call it; I'm nothing but a goddamn janitor . . . I worked hard to get where I was, and it's damn hard to go backward.

The frustration and anger that this blue-collar worker and others like him harbor are often exploited by politicians, who inflame voter discontent by blaming widespread job problems on affirmative action, welfare expenditures, and other matters that have little or nothing to do with the failure of the U.S. economy to provide people with adequate employment opportunities (Edsall and Edsall 1992).

The White-Collar Worker

At the turn of the century, the superior wages, social status, and working conditions accorded white-collar workers clearly distinguished them from manual workers. At that time, only 18 percent of the labor force could be counted as white-collar workers. Today the figure is closer to 60 percent (U.S. Bureau of the Census 2004:399–400). With this growth in the proportion of workers wearing white collars, the sharpness of the distinction between white- and blue-collar work has faded. Particularly

affected have been sales and clerical workers. Today there are about as many nonprofessional white-collar workers as there are professional, technical, and managerial personnel. White-collar nonprofessionals confront some, if not most, of the work-related difficulties under which blue-collar workers tend to suffer (Mills 1951; see also Braverman 1974; Clawson 1980).

Like the industrial workplace, large retail establishments and offices are typically highly bureaucratic. In offices, small armies of clerks, typists, secretaries, receptionists, and office assistants perform segmented work tasks under the constant supervision of higher-ranking authorities. In one such company,

long lines of women sit at spartan desks, slitting envelopes, sorting contents and filling out "control cards" that record how many letters they have opened and how long it has taken them. . . . Nearby, other women tap keyboards, keeping pace with a quota that demands 8,500 strokes an hour.

The room is silent. Talking is forbidden. The windows are covered. Coffee mugs, religious pictures, and other adornments are barred from workers' desks. (Horwitz 1994:A9)

The same type of bureaucratic environment typically prevails in retail establishments. The surveillance of white-collar workers in offices and stores—through the use of computer monitoring, phones, or hidden cameras—is creating a work environment in which they feel increasingly pressured, stressed, and paranoid.

Finally, the social status attached to many nonprofessional jobs is low, and in some cases the wages are less than those accorded semiskilled blue-collar workers. It is for such reasons that job dissatisfaction is high among white-collar nonprofessionals, as indicated by the fact that less than half of those surveyed say they would choose similar work again (Kahn 1974).

Blue-collar workers have long confronted job insecurity. Today, corporate "downsizing" and layoffs have cost many white-collar workers their jobs as well, creating a sense of job insecurity among those for whom the possibility of job loss is new. In this photograph, workers who have lost their jobs share their common experience of job insecurity as they line up in the cold at a job fair in New York City.

Nor is the structure of work consistently rosy even for white-collar professionals, despite their generally high performance on measures of job satisfaction and their relatively high income and status and good working conditions. In libraries, public school systems, hospitals, colleges and universities, and social welfare agencies, as well as in law, architecture, and engineering firms, professionals are fighting to maintain their prerogatives and autonomy in the face of control by administrative authorities. Pay and the availability of resources have also become major issues. The institutions just mentioned are all client oriented. Any increase in the number of clients without an attendant increase in professional staff and supportive services is akin to the assembly-line speedup industrial workers are continually battling. Slowly, members of the professional sector are beginning to suffer many of the same work-related problems as lower-level workers.

Another white-collar group facing work difficulties is middle management, bureaucratic authorities who report to the top executives and oversee professional and technical employees as well as lower-level supervisors. Middle managers now represent some 5 percent of the labor force, and the pressures and problems they confront are inevitably felt by those millions who labor below them. Members of this group have complaints about salaries, job insecurity, the threat of being laid off or forced into early retirement, limits to upward mobility, and heavy responsibilities that are combined with constraints on their authority from above (Kay 1974; Medbroadcast 2004).

Workplace conditions for middle managers can be especially dissatisfying when their firms undergo downsizing through layoffs. Many of those let go are long-term employees. Managers who are given the task of dismissing workers are encountering "survivor sickness" among those workers who remain, reflected in the striking increase in the number of disability claims for emotional illnesses, increased rates of absenteeism, and alcoholism. Remaining workers are dissatisfied not only because greater demands are being placed on them as a consequence of workforce reductions. The "survivors often feel guilty because from their perspective it is arbitrary; they are no worthier than those who were fired, only luckier. Under the circumstances, it seems almost immoral to take much joy in work" (Smith 1994:45). Middle managers are finding it difficult to get the levels of productivity their bosses demand out of the troubled and increasingly overworked employees under their supervision.

Sociologists have often restricted the term *working class* to refer only to blue-collar workers. Some sociologists have suggested that a "new working class" exists (Silverman and Yanowitch 1974). The erosion of white-collar privilege, the bureaucratization of virtually all white-collar work, job-related complaints that sound like those factory workers often voice, movements toward white-collar unionization—all suggest that virtually no part of the labor force is immune to job dissatisfaction.

Job Dissatisfaction and the Consumer Society

Members of the U.S. labor force do more than produce something of value for other people in return for monetary rewards. Workers and their families are also consumers, a fact that must not be divorced from a discussion of the significance of work.

According to Paul Baran and Paul Sweezy (1969:128), corporate advertisers are constantly "waging, on behalf of the producers and sellers of consumer goods, a relentless war against saving and in favor of consumption." Psychologist Erich Fromm (1955:123; see also Ewen and Ewen 1982) contended that they have been immensely successful:

Modern man, if he dared to be articulate about his concept of heaven, would suggest a vision which would look like the biggest department store in the world. . . . He would wander open-mouthed in this heaven of gadgets and commodities, provided only that there were ever more and newer things to buy, and perhaps that his neighbors were just a little less privileged than he.

While Fromm's language usage refers to men, his observations are pertinent to women as well: Work provides the financial means—at least for most members of the labor force—of pursuing this visionary heaven here on earth.

One can speculate that spending money on consumer goods is one way dissatisfied workers can temporarily blot out and separate themselves from the lack of fulfillment provided by their jobs. For most members of the labor force, work is strictly segmented from leisure pursuits. A dissatisfying or tension-filled workday can be offset by the hours spent at home tinkering with tools, guns, and cars. In the after-work pursuit of crafts and hobbies, employees who are told what to do all day on the job are transformed into their own bosses. Here they can make up for the lack of opportunities to develop their special abilities, and here they can see the results of their own work (De Graaf 2003; Schor 1991). Status denied workers within a bureaucratic setting can be gained by the conspicuous consumption of commodities—from color televisions to camping trailers—that will be noticed and admired by others. Ironically, play, recreation, and leisure have themselves become commodities as corporate advertisers pitch their campaigns to unfulfilled interests and needs (Ritzer 1996).

The wages and salaries of millions of workers are not high enough to enable them to buy all the commodities they are encouraged to crave (Alderman 1995). Nevertheless, the producers and sellers of consumer products must unload their goods on a regular basis if they are to realize profit goals. Thus, credit has been extended to virtually anyone holding a job. By going into debt—that is, by taking out loans or buying on the installment plan—members of the labor force are able to buy and consume well beyond their immediate means. Producers and sellers prosper. Indeed, easy credit actually means more jobs for workers. But members of the labor force, in order to pay off debts and maintain a credit rating that will allow more debt in the future, must continue to labor. The extension of consumer credit carries with it the subtle effect of forcing workers to stay on the job—even if the job is highly unsatisfying. Workers who would like to quit, to rebel against their bureaucratic superiors, or to take a more satisfying job that pays less must weigh such moves against their debts. Ironically, it would actually harm workers to reject the consumer society, the way the economy is now organized. To reject debt and commodities not only would limit the outlets currently available to the dissatisfied but would throw millions more people out of work (Manning 2000; Ritzer 1995).

Controlling People/ Controlling Work

In the realm of paid labor, people today are forced to function somewhat like objects—subject to economic forces, institutional constraints, and the will of bureaucratic superiors. Becoming employed or unemployed more and more happens *to* people; they have little control over it. Pay, rank, and working conditions are set *for* employees, not by them. Job dissatisfaction is a result of events and conditions that impinge *upon* workers and that cannot easily be altered or escaped.

Work and Other Macro Problems

Many of the macro problems we have or will consider simultaneously express themselves in the structure of work. With the exception of the very rich, for whom property ownership is the major source of income, the economic well-being of most people in the United States depends on the marketing of their labor. The income inequalities that prevail in this society and that help determine people's life chances reflect existing employment opportunities.

Political decisions at the national level have a direct impact on unemployment, wages, and prices. To the degree political power is concentrated in the hands of a few, decisions in these areas will be made for working people rather than by them. The erosion of political democracy is being replicated at the workplace, where many people perform dissatisfying labor within the confines of bureaucratic control from above.

Racism, sexism, and heterosexism, coupled with inequalities in educational opportunity, arbitrarily disqualify millions who are basically capable of filling positions toward the top of the job hierarchy. Since work is linked to one's sense of self-worth, subordination based on race, sex, and sexual orientation creates millions of unhappy, unfulfilled people. They are joined by the aged in their sense of human obsolescence.

The notion of work as an activity that produces something of value for other people is perverted by the dependence of many workers on the "economy of death." While billions of dollars are allocated to upgrade the production of military-related goods, dangerous and disease-producing conditions persist in the underdeveloped, civilian economy. In both the civilian and military sectors, products are developed and by-products discarded that pose an immense threat to the surrounding environment and to people.

To improve the structure of work, we would want to alter unemployment, job dissatisfaction, job security, the stark relationship between work status and life chances, barriers to the full utilization of human talent, and production that leads to the destruction of life, rather than its enhancement. In our concern with work, we are simultaneously confronted with the challenge of dealing with all the macro problems considered in this book.

Improving the Nature of Work

There is a critical need to revise the official definition of *unemployment* so that it reflects more accurately the extent to which our economy fails to provide sufficient work opportunities. Approaches to unemployment that focus only on reducing the official defined rate ignore the work needs of tens of millions.

There is a need for centralized coordination and control over the introduction of new technologies that displace workers and eliminate jobs. Such coordination and control might be handled through the federal chartering of business firms (see Chapter 5 for a discussion of federal chartering). Or it might be handled by a board responsible for national industrial policy and planning.

Control over the degree to which business and industry are permitted to invest money outside this country or to move productive activities elsewhere is also needed. The profit benefits of such activities may well be offset by the human and social welfare costs of domestic unemployment. This trade-off needs to be investigated.

Given the paucity of work opportunities for all who want and need them, federal and state governments should be willing to serve as "employers of last resort." If government is unable to fully stimulate the private sector into providing sufficient work for people to do, it should find ways to organize and allocate its own resources to pick up the slack. Most people in the United States support this notion today. Likewise, training and retraining (for misskilled and/or displaced workers) fall far short of what might be done. As new jobs are created and old ones disappear, workers must be assisted in making transitions, not left to flounder and forced into downward mobility.

It is time to move beyond the assumption that putting all members of the labor force in a job is sufficient in and of itself. Work conditions themselves are in need of drastic change. There are many possibilities here, including federal incentives for business firms to develop comprehensive programs of worker participation and control. What is needed is increased worker involvement in planning and decision making and decreased hierarchy and bureaucratic control from above. Some firms are taking such steps now.

It is also time to begin breaking up concentrated ownership within the private sector, spreading it more widely among the producers of corporate wealth. Federal chartering of business firms, alluded to earlier, might be used to help workers buy some of the firms to which they contribute their labor. This would be another way of democratizing the workplace.

As we saw in Chapter 2, "Concentration of Political and Economic Power," the interests of elites may run counter to change that is in the general interest. Pressure for change must come from organized labor, the unemployed, and all men and women who want to leave their children a better world in which to labor.

Summary

Work, an activity that produces something of value for other people, is central to our everyday lives. We are encouraged to pursue the American Dream of material affluence through work. Work helps determine our class position and lifestyle, and the jobs we do may affect how others treat us. Finally, work is an important source of self-esteem and self-identity.

The structure of work has been changing as a result of four historical trends. The United States has moved from an agricultural society to one in which manufacturing and, more recently, the provision of services occupy most workers. The "deindustrialization" of the United States is under way. Most members of the labor force were self-employed 200 years ago; few are today. Jobholders have increasingly become part of work organizations in which they are subject to bureaucratic authority and control. And more and more people who wish to do so can no longer find full-time permanent employment and instead must enter the steadily growing ranks of contingent workers. Such persons are often underemployed and unable to obtain adequate wages and benefits.

Our labor force totals well over 100 million people, yet millions are unemployed.

Government unemployment statistics, critics charge, underestimate the true extent of joblessness. Various factors underlie unemployment. These include automation and technological changes that displace workers; the movement of corporate plants abroad or out of urban areas in which the need for jobs is great; government taxation and spending policies that affect consumer and corporate activities; and patterns of discrimination that affect who is jobless on the basis of race, sex, and age. The impact of unemployment on many of those affected is highly negative—whether we are talking about white-collar professionals or unskilled, blue-collar workers.

When asked what is important to them in work, people generally mention the content of the job, the resources to do it well, and a chance to realize their talents. These are as important as pay. There are signs that numerous workers are dissatisfied with the jobs they hold (e.g., they would prefer different jobs). Dissatisfaction is greatest among blue-collar workers, followed by white-collar nonprofessionals. White-collar professionals show the least dissatisfaction. The ranking of jobs in terms of satisfaction appears to reflect the presence or absence of those things workers feel are important to them in work. Dissatisfaction is reflected in lowered productivity, high absenteeism and turnover rates, strikes, and sabotage. Changes in the economy have produced growing job insecurity, and people are often faced with laboring in dissatisfying jobs in lieu of having no jobs at all. The insecurity is damaging to those workers subject to it and often spills over and affects employers as workers' commitment to the job and level of productivity decline.

Blue-collar workers perform most of the "brawn jobs," as opposed to the "brain jobs." Wages and job security vary, depending on a worker's skill level. But blue-collar workers in general suffer from low social status. Their work is physically punitive and often dangerous. White-collar nonprofessionals confront many similar work-related difficulties. They often labor in a setting that is as bureaucratic as the industrial workplace. The social status of many nonprofessional jobs is low, as are wages. White-collar professionals express the most job satisfaction, yet even they face difficulties. In many instances, professionals must fight to maintain their prerogatives and autonomy in the face of control by administrative authorities.

U.S. society emphasizes consumption, and this may be one way that dissatisfied workers can blot out and separate themselves from the lack of fulfillment provided by their jobs. Consumption means that many must go into debt through the use of credit and loans. Such debt carries with it the subtle effect of forcing workers to stay on the job—even if the job is highly unsatisfying and insecure.

The structure of work is linked to many of the problems considered in this book, and in altering work we are confronted with the challenge of dealing with those problems. Among the steps to be taken to improve the nature of work are revising the official definition of unemployment to make statistics on joblessness more accurate; coordinating and controlling new technologies that displace workers and eliminate jobs; limiting corporate investments overseas that create more domestic unemployment; using federal and state governments as employers of last resort; expanding training and retraining opportunities; expanding worker participation in planning and decision making; and promoting increased worker ownership of the firms to which they contribute their labor.

Key Terms

Discussion Questions

1. With all the work that needs to be done in this society, how is it that millions of people do not have jobs? Who or what is responsible for their joblessness?

2. Would you rather be self-employed or an employee? Justify your choice. Which are you most likely to be in the future? Why?

3. Think about the work activity for which you most recently received wages or salary. Would you care to perform this work on a permanent basis? Why?

4. If your financial security were guaranteed, would you still want to be a part of the workforce? Why?

5. Most of us agree that some positions in the structure of work are far less desirable than others. What arguments could be made for and against dramatically increasing the pay and benefits associated with the least desirable jobs?

6. What do you see as the advantages and disadvantages of increased worker participation in planning and decision making in the organizations where they work? Who or what are the obstacles to such increased participation?

Suggested Readings

Applebaum, Eileen, Annette Bernhardt, and Richard J. Murnane, eds. *Low-Wage America: How Employers Are Reshaping Opportunity in the Workplace* (New York: Russell Sage Foundation, 2003).
Case studies documenting the effects on workers of corporate responses to economic restructuring.

Baumol, William J., Alan S. Blinder, Edward N. Wolff, and Julian N. May. *Downsizing in America: Reality, Causes, and Consequences* (New York: Russell Sage Foundation, 2003).
Examination of the actual extent of downsizing, the industries most affected, the motivations for this corporate strategy, and the outcomes—for both workers and corporations.

Dudley, Kathryn Marie. *The End of the Line: Lost Jobs, New Lives in Postindustrial America* (Chicago: The University of Chicago Press, 1994).
The impact of the closing of an auto plant on the workers and their community.

Hearn, Frank, ed. *The Transformation of Industrial Organization* (Belmont, CA: Wadsworth, 1988).
Readings tracing the United States' industrial origins to present-day changes toward a service economy facing unprecedented world competition.

Rifkin, Jeremy. *The End of Work: The Decline of the Global Labor Force and the Dawn of the Post-Market Era* (New York: G. P. Putnam's Sons, 1995).

The extraordinary impact that technology, especially computers, is having in the workplace and implications for the future.

Rubin, Lillian B. *Families on the Faultline: America's Working Class Speaks Out about the Family, the Economy, Race, and Ethnicity* (New York: HarperCollins, 1994).
Case studies with working-class families on the impact of economic shifts and social changes on their lives and those of their children.

Simmons, Louise, ed. *Welfare, the Working Poor, and Labor* (Armonk, NY: M. E. Sharpe, 2004).
A collection of readings exploring the role of low-wage jobs in the production of poverty, and discussions of labor's increasing role in resisting the "race to the bottom."

chapter 12

Schooling and Unequal Educational Opportunity

In previous chapters, we examined macro problems that harm millions of people in the United States—such as economic inequality and the concentration of power. As we suggested, part of the reason these problems continue to plague our nation may be found in our educational system.

In this chapter, we examine some of the ideals and beliefs people in the United States hold about the educational system and evaluate their accuracy. We consider the impact of schools on the socialization of children and on inequality in the United States. The chapter concludes with proposals for altering the educational system.

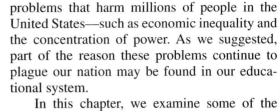

The "Great School Legend"

Societies develop institutions like education to address a variety of survival needs. Schools are supposed to transmit information to new members of society so that they may contribute to the overall ability of society to operate, as well as to ensure their own survival. But institutions do much more than what societies design them to do, and education is no different. As an institution, education performs both manifest and latent functions. Let's look at these.

Manifest Functions of Education

Manifest functions are those tasks an institution is specifically organized to accomplish. The manifest function of education is to make members of society literate, to teach them the skills they will need to be productive members of society, and, in the case of highly heterogeneous societies like the United States, to provide a common cultural base to help new immigrants assimilate into the larger society. Historians of U.S. education have generally provided a positive view of the contributions of the educational system. They claim that education has strengthened the U.S. political system, that it has helped energize our economy, and that it has contributed to lessening class inequalities.

When the United States' system of mass public education was established in the 1800s, the men and women who founded the various local school systems presumably wanted, among other things, to improve the readiness of people to participate in the political system. They felt—as do many today—that only with an educated citizenry could the United States function as a democracy. Since that time the schools have sought to instill common political values in millions of members of our otherwise diverse population. Among these values has been respect for existing political institutions and procedures. U.S. education, in the view of many historians, has contributed to political participation and has helped foster democratic ideals.

Historians have also pointed to the contribution made by our system of education to the economic development of the United States. Mass public education was introduced during a period of rapid industrialization. At that time, literacy and the creation and transmittal of new knowledge became more and more important to continued economic growth. Business and industry had to have people who could fill positions in the increasingly complex world of work. The schools responded by providing literacy and skills training, thus increasing our technological know-how and aiding the efficiency and productivity of the U.S. economic system.

Finally, historians have suggested that mass public education has enhanced the ability of citizens to protect or better their socioeconomic positions. In the public schools, all children compete on the basis of individual merit, rather than on family position. This has made it possible for the poor to change their circumstances. We have, historians point out, moved a long way from the time when education—particularly higher education—was readily accessible only to the children of the affluent. Today almost all youngsters attend school. (See Table 12.1.)

Latent Functions of Education

There is certainly some truth to such historical generalizations. Our system of education has been handed vast responsibilities and has carried many of them out—often with very meager resources. But education has not only acted as a force for change and improvement. It has functioned as a conservative force as well. The positive picture of the contributions of education has been challenged by so-called revisionist historians (Armaline, Farber, and Nelson-Rowe 1994; Aronowitz and Giroux 1993).

While institutions like education perform their manifest functions, they also produce unintended, often overlooked consequences, or **latent functions.** And sometimes these conflict in important ways. For example, schools in the United States have the task of providing education for all, ideally acting as a great equalizer and as the base of a **meritocracy** in which individuals' ability to earn rewards are based entirely on their efforts and merit. But the very manner in which schools are financed generates the latent function of reproducing economic and racial inequality apart from the skills and efforts of individuals. This is because schools' budgets are derived from property tax revenues.

Schools in economically impoverished communities will have meager property tax revenues and therefore very limited school budgets. That means high student-to-teacher ratios, insufficient and often out-of-date textbooks, insufficient or nonexistent facilities such as laboratories and computers, limited curricula offerings, and run-down buildings with broken windows, leaking roofs, and insufficient heat. Teaching and learning in such an environment is likely to be problematic, and that has a great risk of reproducing the poverty of the students who attend these schools because they will have difficulty achieving the academic credentials to get into college.

Contrast this with schools in economically affluent communities, where property tax

Table 12.1	**Percentage of the Population 3 to 34 Years Old Enrolled in School,* by Race/Ethnicity, Sex, and Age: October 2001**			
		Total		
Age	All races	White, non-Latino/a	Black, non-Latino/a	Latino/a origin
Total, 3 to 34 years	56.3	56.3	59.5	51.4
3 and 4 years	52.4	55.2	60.5	39.9
5 and 6 years	95.3	95.3	95.9	93.6
7 to 9 years	98.2	98.5	97.9	97.4
10 to 13 years	98.4	98.8	96.9	98.3
14 and 15 years	98.1	98.2	97.9	97.8
16 and 17 years	93.4	94.6	92.0	88.3
18 and 19 years	61.0	64.0	60.4	45.6
20 and 21 years	46.0	50.7	37.2	28.0
22 to 24 years	25.4	25.6	27.1	15.6
25 to 29 years	11.8	11.7	11.8	7.9
30 to 34 years	6.9	6.4	11.7	4.4

*Includes enrollment in any type of graded public, parochial, or other private schools. Includes nursery schools, kindergartens, elementary schools, high schools, colleges, universities, and professional schools. Attendance may be on either a full-time or part-time basis and during the day or night. Enrollments in "special" schools, such as trade schools, business colleges, or correspondence schools, are not included.

Source: National Center for Education Statistics, *Digest of Education Statistics, 2002* (Washington, DC: U.S. Government Printing Office, 2003), p. 16.

revenues are strong and therefore school budgets are healthy. Their abundant budget resources can support low student-to-teacher ratios, ensuring more individualized attention and instruction; they can also afford up-to-date textbooks, a full range of facilities and curricular offerings (including college preparation and enrichment courses), and state-of-the art building and laboratory facilities. Teaching and learning in this environment is likely to be a rich and rewarding experience: Talent, creativity, and intellectual skill are likely to be nurtured and enriched here, and thus students are more likely to reproduce the affluence that brought them to these schools. Apart from individuals' intellectual capacities,

talent, or hard work, those schooled in impoverished communities will have limited training to escape their poverty, while those schooled in affluent communities will have ample opportunities to remain among the privileged.

In recent years, some scholars have grown dissatisfied with the emphasis placed on education's successes. Revisionist historians have attempted to balance the picture, suggesting that there are aspects of the history of education not deserving of celebration (Lazerson 1973; Ravitch 1978). It is important to look at some critical assessments of the history of education in the United States before considering the functions of education today.

In *The Great School Legend*, Colin Greer (1972) has taken a look at the belief that mass public education was developed in order to democratize the United States. According to Greer, mass public education was an important part of the **assimilation** or "Americanization" movement of the nineteenth century. This movement was aimed at indoctrinating the millions of people who immigrated to the United States, so that they would "fit into" its political order. Wealthy and politically influential people encouraged the development of local school systems and adult education programs during the nineteenth century in the hope that schooling would head off political dissension and conflict.

They felt that if poor and working-class immigrants could be brought to accept the elite-dominated political system and to work within it, class and ethnic grievances could be channeled into manageable directions. Citing historical documents and statements by nineteenth-century elites, Greer (1972:74) suggests that the mission of education "was to maintain and transmit the values considered necessary to prevent political, social, or economic upheaval." In other words, instead of enhancing the democratic process, education was expected to function as a mechanism of social control that would protect the political and economic interests of the governing class.

One of the major goals of mass education in the nineteenth century was to Americanize immigrants—to teach them to fit into the existing political and social order. This goal was met not only by developing curricula for the children of immigrants but also through a system of adult education in which citizenship was taught along with lessons in the English language. Here, workers at a mill in Massachusetts attend such a class after a full day's work.

Revisionist historians have also found documentary evidence suggesting that the role of education in industrialization was not exactly what earlier historians claimed. Nineteenth-century industrialization caused changes in the nature of work. In particular, more and more workers were becoming employees of enterprises owned by others. A way had to be found to smooth the transition into this new world of work. According to Samuel Bowles (1972:43): "An ideal preparation for factory work was found in the social relations of the school, specifically in its emphasis on discipline, punctuality, acceptance of authority outside the family and individual accountability for one's work." By organizing mass public education to resemble the bureaucratic economic organizations of the United States in the nineteenth and early twentieth centuries, schooling was intended to foster a disciplined labor force—one that would not question managerial privileges and authority (Violas 1978).

The claim that U.S. education has made a substantial impact on class inequalities has also been questioned. In a reexamination of the development of mass public education in the nineteenth century, historian Michael Katz (1968, 1971) showed that U.S. public education has always been class biased. Though it was introduced with the intention of opening up opportunities for all, education has both reflected and helped perpetuate class inequalities over time:

It is the children of the well-to-do, not the children of the poor, who have benefited most from public education. That is especially true of the higher levels of schooling, one important function of which has been to secure differential advantage to the children of the affluent. (Katz 1971:109–110)

Furthermore, Katz observed that public schooling has historically functioned to secure such advantage primarily for children from affluent *white* families. Generations of African Americans, for example, were subjected to substandard education in racially segregated public schools—a situation that has been addressed only in the last four decades (Gibson and Ogbu 1991; Ogbu 1978).

Thus the efforts to balance educational historians' celebration of U.S. schooling have led to some critical findings (Carnoy and Levin 1985). If the U.S. system of mass public education performed in the way the revisionist historians claim, what about education today? As we will see, there is evidence to suggest that not too much has really changed. Education still seems organized to foster political acquiescence, to nurture a compliant labor force, and to conserve existing economic inequality (Apple 2004).

Schooling as an Agent of Socialization

Though laws pertaining to school attendance vary from state to state, in all states children are required by law to attend until the age of 16. State governments dictate the number of hours and days per year that children must spend in school; indeed, state financial aid to local schools is often based on average levels of attendance. A local school system may lose money if absenteeism and truancy are high. Truancy is a crime, and parents may not withhold children from school attendance without providing a state-approved substitute.

Because of compulsory attendance, the majority of children in the United States are exposed to schooling for many hours every year, whether they prefer to attend school or not. What are children expected to learn during these many hours? Sociologists of education generally agree that two distinct kinds of lessons are presented in the classroom (Apple 2004; Bennett and LeCompte 1998). First, there are the formal lessons—reading, arithmetic, history, and so forth. Second, certain standardized ways of thinking and behaving are also being encouraged. The second kind of lesson is often called the *hidden curriculum*, because of its subtle nature.

School systems differ from locale to locale, and control over public schools by 50 different states ensures some measure of diversity across the nation (Spring 1997). Still, most school systems are organized bureaucratically. (The structure of elementary and secondary education may be seen in Figure 12.1.) Authority over children is vested in the hands of administrators and teachers, who are in turn responsible to an elected board of education. Students are urged to accommodate themselves to a system of administrative rules and regulations, and school authorities judge and reward students on the basis of how they respond to directions and commands. Such bureaucratic arrangements are said to be necessary in order to process large numbers of children each school day in a relatively impersonal, orderly, and efficient manner (Bennett and LeCompte 1998). The same rationale for bureaucratic organization is often applied to prisons and mental hospitals.

In the late 1960s the Carnegie Corporation of New York sponsored an inquiry into the state of public education across the United States. Charles E. Silberman, a well-known journalist and scholar, spent three years crisscrossing the country before presenting his findings in *Crisis in the Classroom*. His observations of school systems in action led Silberman (1970) to the conclusion that *docility* is being emphasized. Outbursts of spontaneity, originality, and nonconformity are commonly discouraged, while passivity and adherence to routine are stressed.

Silberman's observations are consistent with those of Paulo Freire (1970), a Brazilian educator, whose writings have been highly critical of what he calls the "banking method" of teaching. This is a top-down teaching approach in which the teacher is the sole authority in the classroom; his or her job is to make "deposits" of information in students' minds:

> The teacher teaches and the students are taught.
>
> The teacher knows everything and the students know nothing.

> The teacher thinks and the students are thought about.
>
> The teacher talks and the students listen meekly.
>
> The teacher chooses and enforces a choice, and the students comply.
>
> The teacher is the subject of the learning process, while the pupils are mere objects.

In Freire's view, students learn best by being active contributors to and participants in their own and others' learning, a process that is barred by the banking method of teaching.

A more recent in-depth study of schools by educational researcher John I. Goodlad and his associates seems to suggest that Silberman's observations from the late 1960s continue to be valid. In Goodlad's (1984:109) words,

For the most part, the teachers in our sample of schools controlled rather firmly the central role of deciding what, where, when, and how their students were to learn. . . . When students played a role, it was somewhat peripheral, such as deciding where they sat. . . . The picture that emerges is one of students increasingly conforming, not assuming an increasingly independent decision-making role in their own education.

Silberman and others have argued that compulsory participation in bureaucratic school settings fosters the formation of certain personality traits. Mass public education, it is said, promotes attitudes and habits of behavior that fit well with highly structured settings, those calling for rationality and predictability. Although there has not been definitive research supporting such broad generalizations, several in-depth case studies of schooling do provide some evidence that this is the case.

The "Organization Child"

Sociologist Rosabeth Moss Kanter (1972) spent seven months studying a typical suburban nursery school located in the Midwest. According

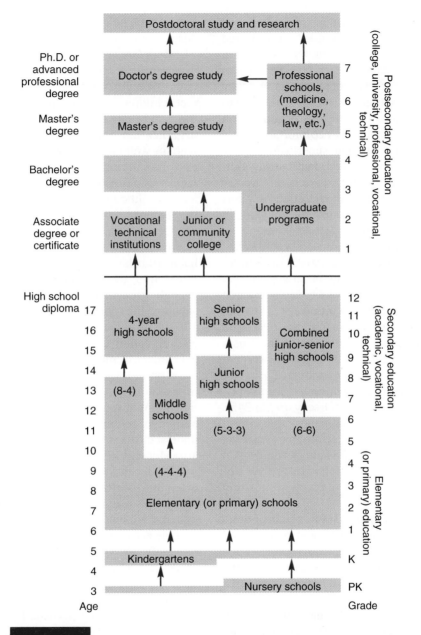

Figure 12.1   **The Structure of Education in the United States**

Note that adult education programs, while not separately delineated above, may provide instruction at the elementary, secondary, or higher education level. Chart reflects typical patterns of progression rather than all possible variations.

Source: National Center for Education Statistics. *Digest of Education Statistics, 2002* (Washington, DC: Government Printing Office, 2003), available at http://nces.ed.gov.

to Kanter, the teachers in this school believed that children who followed orders and exerted self-control were mentally healthy. As a result, the teachers constantly urged the children to adapt to the planned classroom routine, and they set up a round of activities each day conducive to promoting, in Kanter's terms, the **organization child**—the child who is most comfortable when those in authority provide supervision, guidance, and roles to be fulfilled. In requiring children to adapt to such experiences, Kanter concludes, the schools both reflect and support the trend toward bureaucratization of work in U.S. society (see Chapter 11).

Similar conclusions have also been reached by Harry L. Gracey (1972a, 1972b), a sociologist who studied classrooms in an eastern elementary school. One part of Gracey's research focused on kindergarten, which he came to call **academic boot camp.** Kindergarten works to teach the student role to children not previously conditioned to organized schooling. The content of the student role is "the repertoire of behavior and attitudes regarded by educators as appropriate to children in school" (Gracey 1972a:245). Such behaviors include willingness to conform to teacher demands and to perform the "work" at hand without resistance. Educators believe that children who have successfully learned the student role in kindergarten will function smoothly in the later grades.

Gracey found that school administrators best liked the teachers who most quickly and effectively produced order and routine. Such teachers elicited desired responses from the children with no more than a look, a few words, or a simple command signal. Gracey believed that these teachers were grooming the children to respond without question to officialdom and to follow orders without dissent. Even though many of the requests did not seem to make much sense to them, most of the children obeyed. Those who broke away from routines or resisted classroom authority were likely to be treated as "bad children" and to be sent to the

school psychologist for guidance on how to adapt.

Both Gracey and Kanter concluded that the experience of organized schooling fosters certain personality traits. Since, if Silberman is correct, children are urged to conform for hours, days, and years on end, the outcome may be the **organization adult**—the team-oriented person who fits well into nonschool bureaucracies, such as corporations, the military, and the government. As Silberman (1970:141) puts it, "The teacher, although he may disclaim the title, is the students' first 'Boss.'"

Of course, organized schooling is only one of the factors influencing personality traits and habits of behavior. Students—especially as they move into the advanced grades—often find enough strength in peer support to resist and sabotage the routines set up for them (Everhart 1983). In his classic study *The Adolescent Society,* James Coleman (1961) found that the peer values of many young adults ran counter to those promoted by high school teachers and administrators. In his view, the high schools often failed to motivate students into conformity with academic routine because educators did not understand how to counter peer influence (see also McLeod 1995).

In recent years, the matter of school discipline—enforcing school routine—has been a major issue in many city and suburban school systems. Violence and vandalism have plagued schools across the country. An estimated 2 million thefts and violent crimes occur each year on or near school grounds (U.S. Census 2004:156). Teachers have been subject to physical attack and robbery. Many students live with constant fears of victimization (Canada 1995). Such fears have led to increasing numbers of school-age children being found carrying (and occasionally using) weapons—including firearms—in school settings (Riley 1994). The response has been public outcries for greater surveillance and control practices, as schools struggle to maintain authority (National Center for Injury Prevention and Control, 2004; U.S. Congress, Senate 1993, 1999).

Hence, the degree to which bureaucratically organized mass public education actually succeeds in producing adult prototypes of the organization child is open to question. Nonetheless, it seems that organized schooling today, as in the nineteenth century, is oriented toward doing so. "Good children" are presumably the sought-after result.

Learning to Participate in the Economy

Besides attempting to expose students to bureaucratic values, schools are said to promote attitudes and habits of behavior that are unique to a capitalist society. Jules Henry (1965), a social anthropologist, conducted extensive field research on this topic over a period of years. He compiled data for a case study by careful observation of a midwestern elementary school. On the basis of his research, Henry (1965:283) concluded that "school is an institution for drilling children in cultural orientations."

Henry pointed out that public schools are faced with two incompatible tasks. On the one hand, they are expected to transmit dominant cultural values and beliefs; on the other hand, they are charged with liberating the minds of young people. Typically, according to Henry, they resolve this dilemma in favor of the first of the two tasks, keeping creativity—which may involve questioning and rejecting accepted ways of thinking about and doing things—under strict control. Henry's research indicated that the schools direct creative talent into certain channels, such as science and mathematics. Creative children generally are not encouraged to expend their energies on social studies, since this might require analysis and criticism of prevailing social and economic arrangements and conventional political and religious beliefs. Henry suggested that talent is pushed toward areas that serve the United States' technological economy and its ability to conduct sophisticated warfare.

In his research in the elementary grades, Henry was interested in what he came to call *noise,* that is, what children absorb in school aside from the formal subject matter. Noise is similar to the hidden curriculum, mentioned earlier. As part of his research, Henry recorded children's reactions to the games teachers introduced to make learning pleasurable. Whether involved in singing contests or spelling bees, children were constantly being pushed to compete against one another. On occasion, competition revolved around gaining the teacher's attention and winning the rewards only she or he could provide. Children quickly learned that their loss in a competitive arena meant someone else's gain. The winner's elation and excitement were, by definition, at the expense of the loser's depression and unhappiness.

Henry concluded that schooling teaches children (as noise) to be afraid of failure, to dislike themselves when they do fail, and to resent those who succeed at their expense. Children learn to compete at an early age and learn to see competition as natural. This, according to Henry, prepares them to compete with others throughout the course of their school careers and beyond. People learn to be motivated by the fear of failure and to be driven by the specter of personal obsolescence. They find themselves working hard to become a success even if it means pushing others aside.

Children who fail to play competitive games, for whatever reason, are likely to be viewed as out of step with the expectations of school authorities. In the words of Edgar Friedenberg (1965:49), a sociologist who conducted research on the values of high school students: "[The school] helps to see to it that the kinds of people who get ahead are those who will support the social system it represents; while those who might, through intent or merely by their being, subvert it are left behind as a salutary moral lesson."

Again, one may question such broad generalizations, based as they are on very limited empirical evidence. But schools are arenas of competition—whether it be for grades, for dates, or for glory on the playing field. The noise says, in each such instance, "Do not be a loser" (Rich and DeVitis 1992). It seems logical that such attitudes and values continue to guide people's behavior in adult life.

Some evidence has surfaced to indicate that the values of students include an uncritical acceptance of corporate capitalism, which is, after all, only one way to organize an industrial society successfully. Scott Cummings and Del Taebel (1978) surveyed children from grades 3, 6, 9, and 12 in a major urban area of the Southwest. The researchers were interested in assessing the attitudes and understandings held by children toward such topics as the organization of workers into unions, public ownership of large industrial enterprises, and government intervention into economic affairs. An uncritical acceptance of corporate capitalism would involve negative attitudes on each of these topics.

Cummings and Taebel found that while third and sixth graders are nonevaluative toward unions (as well as ignorant of their function), in the higher grades students progressively express attitudes unfavorable to unionization. In the view of twelfth graders, unions are "too big, too powerful, and jeopardize social stability" (Cummings and Taebel 1978:203). This is, of course, the position that has typically been taken by those espousing the cause of big business over and against that made on behalf of working people.

Children were also asked about private versus public ownership of large industrial enterprises. Examples cited to them were oil and steel, two areas where a few major corporations monopolize economic activity. Again, while third graders are neutral, in the remaining grades students become progressively more negative toward the notion of public ownership.

Third and sixth graders, according to Cummings and Taebel, tend to view the state as benevolent and positive in its actions, and helpful in economic affairs (e.g., aid to the poor). Older students, on the other hand, see government intervention as politically disruptive, interfering with the natural laws of the marketplace, and posing the threat of socialism or communism. Sixth and twelfth graders also tended to explain the plight of poor people as resulting from alleged weaknesses in their character as well as lack of motivation, skills, and training. Students thus were insensitive to the possibility that the workings of our capitalist economic system itself may create joblessness or that most of the poor (being children under 18 and adults 60 and older) are unable to work.

In concluding, the researchers suggested that their data show the progressive development, in individual consciousness, of political ideals endorsing and legitimizing some of the more important features of capitalist economic thinking: private ownership of the means of production, individual striving and meritocratic explanations of inequality, and limited state intervention into business affairs. Conversely, children appear to develop explicitly anticollective, antiunion, and antisocialist sentiments (Cummings and Taebel 1978:208). To the degree to which students are armed with such values, they not only find it difficult to understand and appreciate other economic systems but also lack the ability to engage in critical reasoning and judgments about their own. The lack of such an ability is a sign of ideological dominance, not education (Harty 1979; Starr 1998; McGowan 1993).

The Political Impact of Schooling

In the words of Joel Spring (1972:152), contemporary mass public education is an "instrument of power." It prepares the young "for the acceptance of control by dominant elites." To experience schooling is to be exposed to political indoctrination, for schools, whether consciously or unconsciously, make a contribution to the political outlook and behavior of the young.

Studies by political scientists have led them to conclude that public education functions to legitimate existing power relationships in the United States (Gimpel 2003; Ziegler and Peak 1970). We should not be surprised that this is the case. Education in every known society—be it formal schooling or learning from one's parents—involves the transmission of the society's culture. That typically means transmission of the dominant cultural values, including the support of prevailing political arrangements. Or, as Ralph Miliband (1969:239) put it: "Educational institutions at all levels generally fulfill an important conservative role and act, with greater or lesser effectiveness, as legitimating agencies in and for their societies."

Research shows that children develop political consciousness in stages (Banks and Roker 1994). At a very early age they are encouraged to have positive ideas about their society and government. In the first years of schooling, a simple form of patriotism is fostered. Children are taught to respect the symbols of government and political authority—from the U.S. flag to the uniform of the police officer and the soldier.

As children slowly become capable of grasping more abstract political ideas, they are introduced to such concepts as democracy, voting, and civil liberties in their classes. They are taught about local, state, and national government. The political order is depicted largely in terms of political authority that should be respected and accepted in much the same way as children are expected to treat authority in the schools (Moore, Care, and Wagner 1985). Not surprisingly, the political status quo is presented as a given, not as an entity against which people might have valid reasons to struggle.

According to political scientist Jerry Tucker (1974), students are encouraged to celebrate the political status quo as a rather idealized state of affairs. Tucker calls this kind of political education the **tooth fairy approach.** His experience with college students led him to believe that, by and large, public schools teach slogans and rhetoric instead of encouraging substantive inquiry. Too often, children in classrooms not only are sheltered from controversial issues and from the often seamy underside of modern political life but, even worse, are likely to be rendered politically ignorant. This then cripples their ability to function in the political system as adults (Bacon 1988; Macedo 1994).

Research on political socialization reveals that the political knowledge of youth in the United States is extremely limited (Ross 1985). Students from the United States who study abroad are usually quite surprised at the depth of knowledge and enthusiasm with which their foreign counterparts approach political issues in routine conversation.

The tooth fairy approach to political education has also been noted in analyses of commonly used classroom materials:

Textbooks generally present an unrealistic picture of American society and government. . . . In statements about democracy and the good life, textbooks often do not separate prescriptions from descriptions. (Dye and Ziegler 1972:143)

Because they are led to confuse the political system as it should be with the political system as it is, according to Tucker, young people are likely to be bewildered and disillusioned when they run into political facts at variance with what they were taught. One study found that U.S. students have developed a strong sense of cynicism and a dislike for politics, more so than any other category of people in the nation (Matthews 1993).

The daily experience of organized schooling also fails to encourage active political participation. We have noted that mass public education is both compulsory and bureaucratically organized. Students are drafted into school; they cannot choose to stay away: "We forget that children are conscripts. . . . Nowhere else is such a large group of noncriminal individuals forced to remain in an institution for so long" (Bennett and LeCompte 1990:97; see also Ayers, Dohrn, and Ayers 2001). While in school students are subject to rule from above and are likely to be punished if they resist the demands of authority. Much like inmates in a prison or mental institution, people in school are permitted little or no input into policies and decisions that directly affect them. Thus, though children are taught the rhetoric and slogans of democracy, they are simultaneously denied democracy in practice.

Consider, for example, the widespread phenomena of class elections and student governments. These activities are said to have educational merit. Yet, in reality, they are only an artificial exercise in political education, taking place in a vacuum. Elected student officers or representatives are rarely permitted a role in school decision making. At best, they may be invited to advise administrators and teachers. Student governments, ironically, exist only at the discretion and under the supervision of higher authorities. "Democracy" of this kind is an empty activity that does not prepare people to struggle in their own interests.

A similar situation exists with regard to the typical school newspaper. Freedom of the press, one of the principles underlying any truly democratic order, is usually sharply restricted. Censorship rights over student publications are reserved by school authorities. The right of censorship typically extends even to "creative" student publications, such as literary magazines, in which one might reasonably expect to find expressions of political discontent and heretical views. In the larger society, many newspaper publishers and other media groups have fought to maintain the concept of freedom of the press, but students are discouraged from doing so.

The Constitution of the United States guarantees freedom of assembly and speech. Public schools are tax-supported institutions, which means that they are paid for by citizens, including the parents of the students. But the use of school property is subject to approval and control by educational authorities, who alone determine what groups of students may gather and for what purposes. The assembly of large numbers of students, no matter what the official reason, is always carefully monitored (allegedly for safety reasons).

Politics is very much a part of schooling. For one thing, the tooth fairy approach to political education is itself a form of politics. Moreover, politics often directly intrudes into the conduct of public schooling through the actions of elected school boards. The members of such boards hold authority over administrators and teachers and may use this authority to impose their own views about proper educational experiences for children and young people.

In an environment so dominated by authority, it is highly unlikely that citizens' rights and responsibilities and political expertise could be taught. Rather, "our schools teach passivity instead of responsible activism" (Tucker 1974:136). To the degree that the schools are successful in teaching this lesson, they are turning children into candidates for political manipulation. Never having been exposed to real-life political struggle, and armed largely with an unrealistic view of the political order, too many people are rendered impotent in the face of concentrated power. Lack of political education contributes to the high levels of apathy, cynicism, and alienation from the prevailing political structure we saw in Chapter 2.

Once again, we do not wish to overstate the degree to which schools are successful in their intended or unintended socialization practices. Many factors—from peer influence to nonschool environmental forces—may function to undermine the effectiveness of such practices. Our knowledge of the ultimate impact of schooling on attitudes and behavior remains rather limited. Indeed, one of the latent functions of education, when schools nurture critical analysis and debate skills, is the development of independent thinking that may encourage students to question and challenge censorship, inequality, authority, and undemocratic leadership. We suggest, however, that the momentum of schooling lies in the opposite direction: the encouragement of social conformity, fear of personal failure, and political passivity.

Schooling and Inequality

Aside from and related to its role in socializing youngsters, the U.S. educational system also functions as a **gatekeeper.** That is, it operates to guide people from and into one or another level of the class system—or to keep them at the same level. Where one stands in the class structure bears a direct relationship to the type, quality, and amount of formal education one is likely to receive. A person's class position is likely to be reaffirmed by the treatment received in school (Oakes 1985; Oakes and Lipton 1994).

Children from rural and urban poverty areas face a real problem. They are most likely to attend public schools with a limited range of educational resources. Failure and dropout rates tend to be high in schools serving low-income populations. For example, in 2000 the dropout rate among schoolchildren from families in the lowest 20 percent of income was 10.0 percent, compared with rates of 5.2 percent in the middle 60 percent of income and 1.6 percent in the highest 20 percent (U.S. Department of Education 2001). Many poor children, dissatisfied with their school experiences and/or drawn by the need to find employment to help their families, quit when they are legally old enough (Fine 1991; U.S. Department of Education 2001). Some barely wait that long. In 2000 almost 11 percent of children and young adults aged 16 to 24 had not completed high school and were not enrolled in school (U.S. Census 2004). Most came from low-income backgrounds.

Dropouts are most likely to wind up with low-paying blue-collar jobs. They have an unemployment rate almost double that of high school graduates. In 2002 almost 19 percent of recent high school dropouts were unemployed, compared with 13 percent of graduates who were not enrolled in college (U.S. Census 2004:178). Lacking the credentials that would help their marketability in the world of work (see Chapter 11), children from low-income families are likely to find themselves in the same position in the class structure as their parents. The relationship between schooling completed and earnings is illustrated in Figure 12.2. Mass public education, rather than helping low-income children change their class position, often functions to reaffirm their poverty.

By contrast, children who come from more affluent communities tend to have a more positive experience. They are likely to enter public schools with a built-in head start, since their parents are best able to provide the money and other resources to prepare their children for school. It is in affluent homes that expensive educational toys, games, books, computers, musical instruments, and hobby materials are likely to be found. Children may gain experience from travel and preschool enrollment in enriched settings. They then enter schools whose structure and climate are in line with their childhood experiences.

Of equal importance is the fact that the public schools are ready for them. Schools serving middle- and upper-income populations tend to have the best teaching resources, the widest array of educational services, and high expectations for performance. Dropout rates are low, and movement into higher education is common. Thus, with the assistance of quality treatment, children of the affluent are channeled toward positions that replicate their parents' class standing.

A number of outside factors support the gatekeeping process. Expenditures on public education differ from state to state, depending on the state's economic well-being and the priority placed on school spending. Within each state, local per pupil expenditures differ among school systems. Though school systems receive state

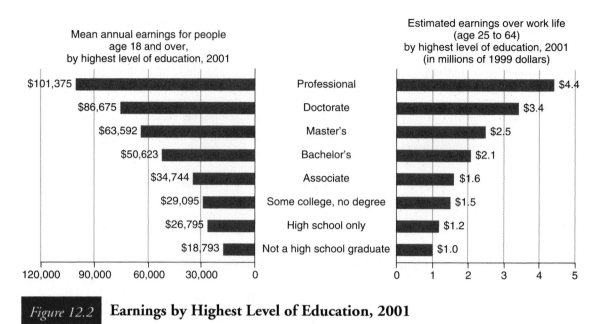

Mean annual earnings for people age 18 and over, by highest level of education, 2001

Estimated earnings over work life (age 25 to 64) by highest level of education, 2001 (in millions of 1999 dollars)

Level of education	Mean annual earnings	Estimated earnings over work life
Professional	$101,375	$4.4
Doctorate	$86,675	$3.4
Master's	$63,592	$2.5
Bachelor's	$50,623	$2.1
Associate	$34,744	$1.6
Some college, no degree	$29,095	$1.5
High school only	$26,795	$1.2
Not a high school graduate	$18,793	$1.0

Figure 12.2   **Earnings by Highest Level of Education, 2001**

Source: U.S. Department of Labor, Bureau of Labor Statistics, *Occupational Outlook Quarterly*, Fall 2002, p. 48, available at www.bls.gov; U.S. Bureau of the Census, *Statistical Abstract of the United States, 2003* (Washington, DC: Government Printing Office, 2004), p. 154, available at www.census.gov.

and federal funds, local school financing is based heavily on property taxes. Consequently, inequities abound.

More affluent communities—in which property values are high—can provide a great deal of money for schooling at low tax rates. In communities in which property values are low, even very high tax rates will generate insufficient money for education. Often, for example, there are significant differences between central cities and their surrounding suburbs in terms of ability to generate the level of funds required to provide children with a quality education (see Chapter 6).

Supreme courts in several states have found their methods of financing public education unconstitutional, and more than half the states have cases pending. Still, a child's education typically reflects the value of the land and buildings in his or her community. Children from low-income families are most likely to be educationally shortchanged, since their parents lack the financial resources that are typically required to locate in affluent communities (Kozol 1991).

Even where expenditures appear to be equal for all children, this may mask the fact that special outlays may be needed to aid children whose families were unable to get them ready for school success. Equal spending does not necessarily mean equal educational outcomes, given the damage that poverty-level living can do to the development of a child. And children from low-income families are often faced with discriminatory treatment when attending school with more affluent children. Teacher expectations, the channeling of children into special groups for instruction, and the use of questionable testing devices are all part of the gatekeeping process.

In the next section we go into more detail about the relationship between education and inequality. We examine the mechanisms and processes through which organized schooling ensures that the class position of less affluent children is not appreciably altered.

Tracking and Testing—An Overview

When mass public education was introduced into the United States in the nineteenth century, increasing numbers of children enrolled in tax-supported school systems. Soon members of the poor and working classes dominated the population of the public schools (Bowles 1974; Bowles and Gintis 1976; Cohen and Lazerson 1972). This was particularly the case when school attendance became compulsory under the law. In general, however, the low-income children left school early to go to work. The higher grades primarily served those from affluent backgrounds.

But by the beginning of the twentieth century, a shift began to take place in the composition of the higher grades. Laws passed to keep children in school longer (and thus reduce the number of children in the labor force) began to be effective. The occupational structure itself was changing, and new employment opportunities existed for people with literacy skills. More people could afford to let their children remain in school, instead of sending them out to find work at the first legal opportunity. Finally, there was a growing belief in education as a route to self-improvement and movement upward in the class system.

The result was that public high schools were faced with an influx of students from poorer families. Educators tried to find a solution to the problem of accommodating these students. They came up with the idea—deemed innovative at the time—of organizing high school curricula around a system of **tracks,** each geared to a different occupational or educational end. The tracks were set up to prepare students for what they would most likely be doing upon graduation. Educators assumed that children

Low-income white and minority students tend to have high dropout rates and thus are often poorly equipped to enter the job market. High school dropouts are likely to be eligible for only those jobs where pay is low and mobility upward very limited, such as entry-level positions in service firms. Performing unskilled work in a fast-food establishment can be a dead end for a dropout as opposed to a wayside stop for a graduate-to-be.

from economically disadvantaged backgrounds were destined for similar futures. Thus a **vocational track** was created for this group. The affluent were steered into an **academic track** on the assumption that they were likely to go on to college or to enter occupations in which academic skills would be useful.

Placement into one of these tracks was based not only on the socioeconomic standing of students' parents. Earlier performance in school was also taken into account. But since performance in academic subjects tended to reflect the environmental advantages associated with class background, the end result was the same. Placement in a vocational or academic track generally reflected class differences.

At the same time, educators were able to argue that all children were receiving an equal opportunity to be educated—that the schools had simply been organized more efficiently in order to take different abilities into account. In the early twentieth century, the notion of efficiency was of particular relevance, for public school systems were under political pressures to demonstrate that they were using tax funds in a businesslike manner (Callahan 1962). The track system was offered as proof that this was being done.

But despite the track system, the quest for efficiency, and other innovations, the dropout and failure rates in public schools were extremely high. By any real standard, mass public education was failing. In an examination of school surveys from a number of big-city school systems, Colin Greer found that, during the early part of the twentieth century, educators were more concerned with how many students were being enrolled than with what happened to them once they were in school. Greer argues that, ironically, the failures of U.S. education were (and still are) signs that it has been succeeding in maintaining the status quo. High dropout rates, for example, have guaranteed a continuous source of labor for low-paying, low-status jobs (Greer 1972).

Shortly after World War I another innovation began to spread through public school systems. Under the impetus of the newly developing science of psychology, special tests were developed that were said to be useful in measuring intelligence and native ability (Gould 1996). Educators quickly grasped these tests. Here,

presumably, were tools with which individual differences could be discovered among students. With testing, children could be guided to those educational programs for which they were most suited—another step toward making schools efficient.

Needless to say, psychological testing fit well with the already accepted concept of tracking. And performance on the tests largely reflected the advantages associated with class background. Students from low-income backgrounds tended to perform poorly on the new tests, enabling school authorities to justify their placement in tracks demanding little in the way of academic work. The reverse tended to hold true for students coming from economically privileged backgrounds. The combined effects of testing and tracking were to further rigidify differential treatment of children on the basis of their class origins.

The logical accompaniment to the testing movement, and one that followed closely on its heels, was the growth of the guidance counselor profession. New experts were required to administer and interpret the results of the tests. Counselors trained in educational psychology and statistics were hired to work with students and parents. Not only did students from different class backgrounds continue to be channeled into different tracks, but now the guidance counselor could show that they "deserved" the placement.

Today testing remains a common method of ascertaining the so-called intelligence and ability of students (Wallace and Graves 1995). Children from low-income families, both white and of color, by and large perform poorly on IQ tests, for the forms of knowledge and the thought processes required by these tests are most likely to be acquired in middle-class homes and schools. But the use of IQ tests to measure intelligence is still widespread despite the generally acknowledged biases of the testing instruments.

Widespread testing of students intensified in 2002 after President George W. Bush signed the

No Child Left Behind Act, designed to hold schools and teachers accountable by annually measuring the performance of all students in reading, math, and science. Schools that failed to meet goals of federally established proficiency levels would be sanctioned with the loss of federal funding and probation or loss of accreditation. Supporters insisted that this tough approach to school performance would force teachers to ensure all students gained important educational skills, and that this would "level" educational inequality. But critics argued that the program further entrenched inequality by instituting tough standards without providing enhanced financial support for economically deprived school systems to help them meet these standards. It forces teachers to "teach to the test" rather than actually stimulate creative and critical thinking in students, and robs schools in economically depressed communities of already limited resources with which to actually teach children (www.nochildleftbehind.gov; Orfield and Kornhaber 2001). In some cases, No Child Left Behind has ironically forced school systems to refuse to accept federal funds in order to avoid the imposition of impossible standards, and it has largely left whole school systems behind.

In most public school systems some kind of tracking or other system of "ability grouping" still exists (Lucas 1999; Wheelock 1994). Guidance counselors continue to play the role of test administrators and help guide students into the appropriate curriculum. In sum, it is hard not to conclude, along with Colin Greer (1972:152), that

the fact of the matter is that American public schools in general, and urban public schools in particular, are a highly successful enterprise. Basic to that success is the high degree of academic failure among students. . . . The schools do the job today they have always done. They select out individuals for opportunities according to a hierarchical schema which runs parallel to existing social class patterns.

If the public schools attempted to ensure academic success for every child, the supply of school- and self-defined losers would rapidly dwindle. In Greer's view, this would mean trouble, since there would be too many academically successful people from low-income backgrounds who would probably be very restive if forced to perform the least desirable jobs.

An Elementary School Case Study

A case study that focuses on a group of children in an urban elementary school dramatically illustrates the impact of tracking and testing (Rist 1970, 1973, 1977). The study was conducted by Ray C. Rist, a student of the late Jules Henry, whose work on noise we discussed earlier. Rist followed the progress of a group of African American children who were attending public school in St. Louis, Missouri. Teachers in the school likewise were African American.

In the school Rist studied, teachers typically knew something about each child before the child began kindergarten. For example, they knew which children came from homes receiving welfare aid, they had met the mothers during preenrollment interviews, and they had heard about the experiences of other teachers with the children's brothers and sisters. None of this information, Rist notes, necessarily had anything to do with the talent or ability of the new kindergartners. But it did help create a certain set of expectations in each teacher's mind before the first day of class.

Rist observed that by the eighth day of kindergarten, the teacher in the class he was following had made permanent seating arrangements for each child. At the table closest to her (Table 1) were the well-dressed children who were not from welfare families, who seemed comfortable with classroom routine, and who spoke "school language" at all times (in other words, they spoke like the teacher). At the two remaining tables, farther away from the teacher's desk, sat children dressed in old, worn clothing. The Table 2 and Table 3 children were from welfare homes, seemed ill at ease in their surroundings, and rarely spoke. When they did speak, they often used a street dialect rather than "standard English."

The children at Table 1 not only were seated closest to the teacher but also received most of her verbal and physical attention. Moreover, they were given special privileges and responsibilities by the teacher. Table 1 children were chosen to recite the Pledge of Allegiance, to read the weather calendar, to pass out class materials, and to take messages to the office.

Noting these seating arrangements and the positive treatment being accorded Table 1 children, Rist asked the teacher what was going on. The teacher told him that "the first table consisted of her 'fast learners' while those at the last two tables 'had no idea what was going on in the classroom'" (Rist 1970:422). Thus, by the eighth day of school, a process of labeling was already under way. On the basis of class bias, the teacher had effectively written off two tables of kindergartners as being uneducable.

Over time, Rist saw indications that the children at Table 1 were adopting the attitudes of their teacher. The so-called fast learners began to ridicule and belittle the Table 2 and Table 3 children. Within a few weeks, the low-income children had begun to sense that both the teacher and their more affluent peers were against them. In response, some of them became withdrawn, and others engaged in verbal and physical outbursts. This behavior confirmed the teacher's view that these children were different, troublesome, and not interested in learning. In reality, as Rist observed, the teacher herself had set the situation in motion, and the children's behavior was simply an outcome of her own.

The process Rist observed has often been called a **self-fulfilling prophecy.** Put simply, if one acts as if a situation is real, the situation may indeed become real. In this case, the teacher acted as if the low-income children could not

learn, and as a consequence they did not learn. By her actions, the teacher's prophecy that the children were uneducable was fulfilled.

Most of the kindergarten children went on to the first grade. The kindergarten teacher had already given a dossier on each child to the first-grade teacher, who used the dossiers to make permanent seating arrangements. Not surprisingly, the seating plan closely resembled that of the kindergarten classroom. In the first grade, Table 1 children made rapid progress in reading: The kindergarten teacher had prepared them well. The first-grade teacher spent a good deal of time trying to teach the Tables 2 and 3 children the basics they should have learned earlier. Differential teacher expectations had become translated into differential academic performance, through no fault of the low-income children.

Almost all the children moved on to the second grade a year later. There, according to Rist, students were assigned seats on the basis of their scores on reading tests. The second-grade teacher thus had a "scientific" basis on which to predict each child's performance in the classroom. Tables 1, 2, and 3 were almost totally reproduced in the second grade, but with a new element added. The best readers were the Tigers, the next best were the Cardinals, and the slowest readers were the Clowns. A number of the Clowns were repeating second grade.

The kinds of distinctions made among these children, the teachers' expectations for them, and their treatment by the teachers all fed into a system of tracking and testing. Academic retardation or failure, for the poorer children, quickly became cumulative. It seems reasonable to assume that when such children reach high school, they will be persuaded that they deserve to enter a nonacademic track—assuming they have retained interest in education at all and do not join the ranks of dropouts (see Figure 12.3). As Rist (1970:447) concluded: "The public school system, I believe, is justifiably responsible for contributing to the present structure of society. . . .

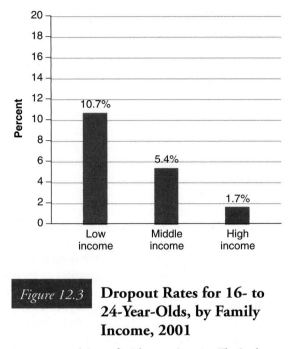

Figure 12.3 **Dropout Rates for 16- to 24-Year-Olds, by Family Income, 2001**

Source: National Center for Education Statistics, *The Condition of Education, 2004* (Washington, DC: Government Printing Office, 2004), p. 8.

The picture that emerges from this study is that the school shares in the complicity of maintaining the organizational perpetuation of poverty and unequal opportunity."

The High School Level

Tracking in other public elementary schools may be more subtle and informal than in the school Rist studied. But by the time a student gets to high school, the process typically becomes quite blatant and rigidified (Goodlad 1984; Page 1991). Walter E. Schafer, Carol Olexa, and Kenneth Polk (1970) studied two typical high schools, located in the Midwest, in an effort to document the impact of tracking in the higher grades. One school was located in a middle-class, academic community; the other in a working-class, industrial area. Both high schools divided their programs into "college prep" and "general" tracks. Students were assigned to one of the tracks upon entering the ninth grade.

The researchers had difficulty determining exactly why a student was assigned to a particular track, though they felt the guidance counselors played a key role. It became clear that "socioeconomic and racial background had an effect on which track a student took, quite apart from either his achievement in junior high or his ability as measured by IQ scores" (Schafer et al. 1970:40). Students attending the high school located in the middle-class community and those from white-collar families in the working-class high school tended to enter the college prep track. Students from blue-collar families, particularly if they were African American, most often entered the general track. For the most part, the decision was permanent; students generally stayed in the same track throughout all 4 years of high school.

Track position was correlated with students' success in school. College prep students had the highest grade average by senior year, and grade differences between this group and the general track students increased between grades 9 and 12. General track students were likely to graduate toward the bottom of their class. The dropout rate was 36 percent for general track students but only 4 percent for those in college prep. Finally, records indicated higher rates of delinquency and violation of school rules for youngsters in the general track than for college prep students.

The problem facing the researchers was one of explaining these differences. Scores on the school achievement and IQ tests the students took in elementary school did not seem to be related to high school performance. The researchers finally reached a conclusion that seems to confirm Rist's findings—that differential academic performance and dropout rates were actually *promoted* by track assignment. That is, being placed in the general track or the college prep track to some extent caused student behavior.

Probing further, Schafer and his colleagues found that students felt stigmatized by not being assigned to college prep. Their placement in the general track negatively affected their self-esteem and eroded their belief in their own abilities. As a result, they did not work hard in school. Furthermore, the teachers and administrators expected little of general track students, and the students tended to respond accordingly. The self-fulfilling prophecy, mentioned earlier, was at work. The teachers felt justified in awarding low grades for the work performed by general track students, no matter how well the work was done. This practice contributed to low student motivation and a lack of commitment to school attendance—factors reflected in high dropout rates. General track students created a peer-group society in opposition to authority, leading to rule violation and delinquent acts in the community. Such phenomena were found in both high schools, despite the fact that they were located in quite different kinds of communities (Oakes 1994).

Once again, the outcome of differential treatment seems clear. Students from more affluent backgrounds, having been given preferential treatment in high school, will typically enter a 4-year college or university. They will most likely get well-paying jobs and occupy a class position much like that of their parents. The students from low-income backgrounds, white and of color, have had their sense of self-worth attacked. They have been told by their track placement, from their treatment by teachers, and by the evaluation of their performance that they are not destined for success. It is unlikely that they will attend college. In such ways, the U.S. system of education produces self-defined losers who, whatever their real talents and abilities, are likely to relive the experiences of their low-income families (Oakes 1993; Wheelock 1992).

Higher Education

As we have seen, the U.S. system of education does a good deal of sifting and sorting. Education also functions as a gatekeeper on the college and university levels. The question of who goes on to higher education is easily answered. If you have money, you go. Ability counts less than dollars. Thus, those from affluent backgrounds tend to have the highest number of years of education completed (see Table 12.2).

Since the end of World War II an increasing percentage of high school graduates have gone on for further years of schooling. An important reason for this is that employers have progressively escalated their requirements for entry-level positions (Berg 1970). Thus, the educational attainment of the labor force has moved steadily upward. Another reason is the failure of the U.S. corporate economy to generate a sufficient number of decent-paying jobs for all who need them.

Table 12.2	Postsecondary Education (PSE) Attainment of 1988 Eighth Graders, by Socioeconomic Status, 2000			
	No PSE	Some PSE but no bachelor's degree	Bachelor's degree	Master's degree or higher
Total	24.3	46.5	25.9	3.4
Socioeconomic status				
Lowest quartile	47.9	44.8	6.9	0.4
Middle two quartiles	23.3	52.7	21.9	2.1
Highest quartile	4.4	36.0	51.0	8.6

Note: Socioeconomic status is based on five equally weighted, standardized components: father's education, mother's education, family income, father's occupation, and mother's occupation. PSE = postsecondary education.

Source: Table 2 in U.S. Department of Education, National Center for Education Statistics, *Coming of Age in the Eighth-Grade Class of 1988, 12 Years Later, NCES 2002-321.* Washington, DC, 2002.

Many young persons have found enrolling in higher education—when they can afford it—preferable to being unemployed. Furthermore, there is more opportunity for students to continue their education, for the number and size of colleges and universities have (until fairly recently) been undergoing substantial growth. Most noteworthy has been the creation of a massive network of 2-year colleges. Today almost 62 percent of high school graduates between the ages of 16 and 24 are enrolled in college, the vast majority of whom are in public higher education institutions (U.S. Census 2004:148, 179).

The gatekeeper function in higher education is seen most clearly in an analysis of which students go on to what kinds of institutions of higher learning. High schools not only channel students to or away from further schooling but also channel students to particular rungs on the status ladder of higher education. Again, class background of a student plays a determining role.

State systems of higher education are ordinarily made up of large universities, 4-year colleges, and 2-year ("community" or "junior") colleges. As one moves from the community college up to the university level—the most

prestigious—the income backgrounds from which most students are drawn increase demonstrably. Since the level at which one enters the labor force is linked with the type of educational credentials one is able to gain, the multitiered system of higher education may be viewed as a part of the tracking process.

Whereas more than 84 percent of all adults aged 25 and over are high school graduates, only 30.4 percent of these graduates have completed 4 or more years of college (U.S. Census 2004:154). Class background influences a student's chances of completing college. Since attendance at any institution of higher education costs money, the least affluent have the most difficult time remaining. Though public institutions tend to cost much less than private ones, and though grant and loan programs help many needy students, costs continue to escalate. Those most likely to drop out completely, or to interrupt their studies for a period of time, come from low-income backgrounds.

Children from economically advantaged families are most likely to enter universities, not community colleges. Many will attend private elite institutions. From there they are likely to go on to graduate or professional schools. Because they, not the low-income students, stay in school longest, attend universities where per pupil costs are high, and go on to even more expensive postbachelor's degree training, the affluent capture a disproportionate amount of the tax funds that go to support higher education. One might say that this is a special "welfare" subsidy available only to the children of upper-income groups, one that helps them remain at the class level of their families.

The Special Role of the Community College

Some 15.4 million students were enrolled in college in 2001—more than three times as many as in 1960. This substantial rate of growth is largely a result of the importance of 2-year colleges. Community college enrollment grew to over 5.9 million in 2001 and constitutes an increasing proportion of overall college enrollment. In 2001 almost 62 percent of those graduating from high school went on to college. While 59 percent of 2000 high school graduates went to 4-year schools, 18 percent went to 2-year colleges (National Center for Educational Statistics 2003).

On the one hand, community colleges are evidence of the democratization of higher education; access to higher education has been made available to ever more people. On the other hand, community colleges have themselves been accused of playing a gatekeeping role (Brint and Karabel 1989; Dougherty 1994). Let us examine how this process works.

Community colleges have taken on two major tasks. First, they offer course work for students wishing to go on to a 4-year degree program at a state college or university. Second, they offer vocational programs for those who wish to (or must) pursue a 2-year terminal degree. Vocational programs range from health services, to data processing, to auto repair.

Admission standards are usually very liberal (a high school diploma or being age 18 or older), and students whose formal educational preparation might be cause for rejection by more exclusive institutions can easily get in. Unlike most 4-year institutions, community colleges use a system of *open enrollment,* which means that they are consciously open to almost all comers.

Costs of community colleges are quite low in comparison to those of 4-year colleges. Increasingly, students with limited financial resources who aspire to a 4-year college degree are choosing to earn their general educational requirements at less expensive community colleges before transferring to the much more expensive 4-year institutions. The lower cost of community colleges also means that their students are more likely to be married, to be over 24 years of age, to live off campus, to attend part-time, and to have parents with at most a high school education (U.S. Department of Education 2002: Tables 174, 178; see also U.S. Department of Education 1998). Community colleges are also more likely than 4-year institutions to enroll women and people of color.

Many of the students who enroll in community colleges aspire to transfer to 4-year schools, but relatively few end up doing so. Community college students are far less likely to complete a 4-year degree than those who begin college in a 4-year institution. In the view of sociologist Kevin Dougherty (1994:83), the fact that aspirants to the bachelor's degree "secure less education and poorer jobs if they enter a community college rather than a four-year college is very troubling. We are talking about something that affects as many as one-third of all community college students (and one-ninth of all college students)."

The reasons students entering community college have problems moving on to obtain a bachelor's degree have been a matter of debate. Dougherty believes that community college students face a series of trials that often undermine their academic survival and make it hard to obtain the baccalaureate:

1. People who enter community colleges experience a higher dropout rate than students in their first 2 years at 4-year colleges, largely because of greater financial aid problems and community colleges' lesser ability to integrate students into an institutional academic and social life.

2. Potential transfers to 4-year institutions face "a difficult move to a new and foreign institution," a move not always encouraged by their home colleges. High costs of enrollment, inadequate financial aid packages, and exclusivity in admissions practices at 4-year colleges pose yet additional barriers.

3. Those who do gain admission as transfers have higher dropout rates than regular 4-year college students in their last 2 years, because of social and academic problems and the failure of the institution to help them, ongoing financial difficulties and the need to work, and inadequate preparation for demanding upper-division studies (Dougherty 1994:84–85).

According to Jerome Karabel (1972:55), "community colleges are, in reality, a vital component of the class-based tracking system." But while those who enroll in 2-year colleges tend to complete fewer years of education and end up in less well paying jobs than those who enroll from the start in 4-year schools, in the absence of such institutions far fewer persons from low-income backgrounds would have the chance of receiving any higher education.

Literacy and Inequality

OVE
RCOM
INGIL
LITE
RACY

So reads the headline of a newspaper article on illiteracy (Foster 1988). The stress and disorientation one feels on being confronted by "words" that do not make any sense are familiar to the illiterate population. Also familiar are feelings of isolation and alienation. We live in a society that is knowledge-driven. The transmission and consumption of information in such forms as text, tables, figures, and maps are central to societal functioning. People who are unable to comprehend such information because of a lack of literacy are more likely than others to endure lives of social, economic, and political marginality.

The definition of **illiteracy** has been the subject of some debate (Kaestle et al. 1991; Kozol 1985). The definition used is crucial, since it has implications for the size of the population about which we should be concerned. One traditional definition is simply the inability to write one's name. By this definition, few adults in the United States could be called illiterate. But when the criteria involve the ability to perform basic everyday tasks requiring reading comprehension or fundamental mathematics, the vast dimensions of illiteracy in the United States stand revealed.

In 1992 the federal government sponsored the National Adult Literacy Survey, the most detailed portrait of adult literacy in the United States to date (*Society* 1994b; U.S. Department of Education 1993). This survey, applicable to this nation's 191 million adults, revealed that as many as 23 percent—some 44 million people—lacked the literacy skills to perform such basic tasks as calculating the total cost of a purchase, locating a particular intersection on a city street map, or entering background information on a simple form.

The study's emphasis on the ability to function in society and perform real-world literacy tasks produced troubling findings. Only the top

While the majority of those disabled by illiteracy are white, members of minority groups are disproportionately represented in the illiterate population. There are volunteer tutorial and other programs for people who need help, no matter what their race or ethnic origins. But these programs are not large enough to help more than a small percentage of those in need.

21 percent, the 40 million adults performing at the highest levels of literacy, "could handle complex documents or bring background knowledge to bear on the tasks given to them" (*Society* 1994b:2).

The survey also confirmed the disturbing results of an earlier study in the mid-1980s that focused on young adults aged 21 to 25. That study found that 5 percent of young adults cannot read at a fourth-grade level of competency and 20 percent cannot read beyond an eighth-grade level (Warner 1986). The findings from such studies suggest that there are very fundamental deficiencies in the knowledge base of adults in the United States, particularly among those tens of millions who constitute what Jonathan Kozol (1985) has come to call "illiterate America."

Who are the illiterate? In contrast to stereotypes held by many, the vast majority are white people born in the United States. The Survey of Adult Literacy did find that low rates of literacy disproportionately exist among native-born African Americans and Latino/a Americans, as well as other native-born U.S. minority groups. Immigrants from outside the United States make up only about a quarter of the adults scoring lowest on literacy in the survey; most of these are adults who are literate in their native language and need only to make the transition to function in English. Overall, persons lacking literacy skills are more likely than other adults to be unemployed or to be in low-paying jobs, and to be poor. The Survey of Adult Literacy found that nearly half of the adults performing at the lowest level of literacy were living in poverty, compared to only 4 to 8 percent of those in the top levels (*Society* 1994b).

The presence of widespread illiteracy among people born in the United States and exposed to its system of educational opportunity should not be cause for surprise. We have seen how this society is divided along class lines and how such practices as tracking in schools often have a negative effect on the education of those from poverty and working-class backgrounds. Illiteracy rates are little more than numerical indicators of the generation of school failures.

As illiterate children grow up and become illiterate adults, they may marry and have families. As parents they live with the constant knowledge that they are unable to help their own children learn how to read. Moreover, illiterate parents are in no position to monitor and appraise their children's school progress (or lack thereof). When such children find themselves in school settings that are subtly inhospitable and/or not responsive to their learning needs, the stage is set for the generation of yet more failures. The phenomena of "social promotion" (promotion from grade to grade without regard to a child's grade-level skills) and of high dropout rates frequently involve illiterates being pushed through and finally out of schooling.

Some argue that the attention illiteracy has been receiving of late is a reflection of concern that the nation can no longer afford such lack of literacy in its labor force (Daniels 1988; National Center on Education and the Economy, 1990). At the same time that the United States is facing sharp competition in world markets and is developing into a service economy based on complex technology and information exchange, it is being discovered that many in the adult population lack the skills to locate the time and place of a meeting on a notice or to calculate the price difference between the costs of two items.

It is estimated that 70 percent of the reading material used in a cross section of the nation's jobs requires comprehension at the ninth-grade level and higher. Some experts predict that abilities at the twelfth grade and beyond will be called for routinely in the new jobs generated in the twenty-first century. As the numbers of people incapable of performing higher than an eighth-grade level of comprehension increase each year, corporate and governmental elites are becoming disturbed over the adequacy of literacy skills in the U.S. labor force. Their concern is less for the problems faced by the illiterate individual than for potential declines in corporate profits and economic growth. Firms unable to depend on a stable supply of workers whose skill levels match job requirements confront inefficiencies and related expenses.

Such practical concerns ignore the crippling costs experienced by the individual who is trapped in a state of illiteracy (Berger 1988). Such persons suffer anxiety, embarrassment, and humiliation in the face of their disability; they may also be paralyzed by feelings of powerlessness and wounded self-esteem. Imagine traveling into unfamiliar places unable to read maps, schedules, or street signs. Daily functioning can be a nightmare of stress when a person cannot comprehend employment applications, newspapers, landlords' leases and notices, labels on foods and medicines, warnings of hazards, restaurant menus, children's homework and teachers' messages, bills and bank notices, telephone directories, recipes, television program schedules, letters from friends and relatives, or even the names of candidates in a voting machine. At the same time as illiterate persons guard against discovery and thus the stigma of being cast as "stupid" by the literate, they are forced to forgo simple pleasures and freedoms that those able to read this textbook take for granted.

Thus, the production of illiterates as a by-product of our system of education in the United States does more than create labor supply problems for employers. It produces men and women engaged in a continual struggle, overwhelmed by a sense of social, economic, and political marginality. Such persons reside in U.S. society but are blocked from full participation in it. Some 60 percent of the people confined in federal and state prisons cannot read above the sixth-grade level (Berger 1988). According to the Survey of Adult Literacy, prisoners are far more likely than other adults to perform at the lowest literacy levels. At the risk of oversimplifying, one suspects that lack of literacy has something to do with the turns many of their lives have taken.

Home Schooling

Some families in the United States have responded to what they saw as inadequacies in the public schools, as well as to the problem of limited parental control over schools' curricula, by resorting to **home schooling:** teaching their children themselves or with a private tutor at home. Homeschooled students' parents may control the political, religious, or cultural content of much of what they add to the standard curriculum, but they are required to comply with individual states' minimal educational guidelines for each grade. Some parents choose home schooling to avoid federal restrictions against a religious-based curriculum, while others may wish to avoid socialization values with which they do not agree (Apple 2000; Riegel 2001; Stevens 2001). By 1999 some 850,000 students were homeschooled. While this represents only 1.7 percent of the total number of students in the United States, there are some noteworthy patterns about home schooling that indicate this is not a viable alternative that anyone may choose (see Table 12.3).

Three-fourths of homeschooled students are white, suggesting that at least some home schooling may be motivated in part by "white flight" from public schools, particularly in cases where the expense of private schools is not an option. Moreover, home schooling requires that at least one parent or guardian must remain at home to teach rather than work in the paid labor market. Such a requirement is clearly more easily accomplished in traditional two-parent families where one (most commonly the mother) remains a full-time homemaker while the other (typically the father) works in the paid labor market. Indeed, the vast majority (more than 80 percent) of homeschooled students live in two-parent households.

In cases where both parents are working in the paid labor force (and more than half of the homeschooled students live in such families), it is likely that home schooling is a function of affluence and that a private tutor is filling the role of home teacher. But notably, almost two-thirds of the homeschooled students in the United States are not from affluent families, but rather from families with annual incomes under $50,000, and almost one-third are from families with annual incomes of $25,000 or less. In households with limited incomes, the concern becomes one of the quality of the resources and materials available to the students.

Another concern is one of students' development of social skills. Though it is true that much bullying and harassment as well as violence may occur in many if not most schools, students do have ample opportunity to learn to navigate the sometimes treacherous terrain of human relationships by encountering many and diverse students in their environment. When students are homeschooled, they are less likely to meet others whose social characteristics dramatically contrast with their own, and therefore they may miss an opportunity to challenge stereotypes. And they are less likely to exchange divergent opinions and worldviews without a daily opportunity to confront such diversity. On the other hand, home schooling may offer an opportunity for individualized attention, curricula tailored to the individual needs and interests of students, and greater parental control over curriculum content.

Altering the Educational System

Organized schooling both reflects and responds to the prevailing economic and political order. By preparing people to enter the adult world, the U.S. system of education plays a socialization role that helps conserve the status quo. Though empirical evidence is scanty, research suggests that the schools fail to liberate children's minds and are as likely to deaden as to enliven human sensibilities. The bureaucratic nature of the school experience, together with the political indoctrination that goes on, may not produce robots. But neither does it produce people who are prepared to critically analyze U.S. society and act collectively to bring about change. Economic inequality and concentrated political power cannot be blamed on public education. But to the degree to which socialization by schools fails to do more than legitimate the prevailing order, the schools cannot escape at least

Table 12.3	Students Who Are Homeschooled by Selected Characteristics, 1999			
Characteristic	Number of students		Percent distribution (of all students)	
	Home-schooled (1,000)	Percent home-schooled	Home-schooled	Non-home-schooled
Race/Ethnicity:				
White, NonLatino	640	2.0	75.3	64.5
Black, NonLatino	84	1.0	9.9	16.1
Latino	77	1.1	9.1	14.1
Other	49	1.9	5.8	5.2
Number of parents in household:				
Two parents	683	2.1	80.4	65.5
One parent	142	0.9	16.7	31.0
Nonparental guardians	25	1.4	2.9	3.5
Parents' participation in labor force:				
2 Parents—1 in labor force	444	4.6	52.2	18.6
2 Parents—both in labor force	237	1.0	27.9	45.9
1 Parent in labor force	98	0.7	11.6	28.0
No parent in labor force	71	1.9	8.3	7.5
Household income:				
$25,000 or less	262	1.6	30.9	33.5
25,001–50,000	278	1.8	32.7	30.3
50,001–75,000	162	1.9	19.1	17.1
75,001 or more	148	1.5	17.4	19.2
Parents' highest educational attainment:				
H.S. diploma or less	160	0.9	18.9	36.8
Voc/Tech degree or some college	287	1.9	33.7	30.2
Bachelor's degree	213	2.6	25.1	16.3
Graduate/Professional school	190	2.3	22.3	16.7

Source: U.S. Department of Commerce, Bureau of the Census, *Statistical Abstract of the United States,* 2004–2005 (Washington, DC: U.S. Government Printing Office, 2005), p. 162.

partial responsibility for the harm done to people within this order.

The gatekeeping function of organized schooling is both more complex and more obvious. On the one hand, the United States' system of education tends to affirm already existing inequalities. On the other hand, one must wonder whether our system of education could bring about a reduction of inequality in the absence of more fundamental changes in the prevailing order. Is education the "weak link" in the chain (Gartner et al. 1973; Illich 1971)? In other words, can the problem of inequality be best attacked by reforming education? Or must economic inequality and the concentration of power be taken care of before we can hope to radically improve the organization and operation of education? In the long run, we agree with Jeannie Oakes (1985:204) that the latter is the case:

Whether school reform can stimulate broad social reconstruction or can only result from such reconstruction, it is clear that if equity is to be attained, educational reform should comprise only one aspect of broader ideological and structural shifts in American society. Ideally, the equalization of the benefits of education for all groups should be a reflection of a movement toward a more equitable social system—one in which racial and ethnic diversity are valued and the access of all groups to political, economic, and social power is ensured.

But in the short run, it is worth pushing the schools, those who run them, and the students who must survive in them toward changes that will minimize the harm being done to millions of children and young adults.

The first, and most basic, change goes to the heart of the U.S. system of education. Whenever it becomes manifestly evident that a school is failing to teach, parents must be able to demand their children's placement in an alternative program of their choice. As it now stands, school attendance is mandatory even when the educational interests of children are not being met. The issue of compulsory attendance would be less critical if all schools were performing in ways that enhanced the development of children's human potential.

Changes are also long overdue in the organization of schools, specifically their bureau-

cratic and hierarchical nature, a situation often exacerbated by large school size. Obviously, rules are required to guide behavior whenever people must function in a group situation, but in many schools rules are used primarily to control and inhibit the freedom of children and youth. Although such rules may serve the interests of the administrators and teachers who create and enforce them, they are not always in the best interests of students. Among the rules that deserve to be revised are those restricting students' freedom of physical movement, use of school facilities during and after school hours, and exercise of the rights of freedom of speech and of the press.

There has been some experimentation by educators seeking to get away from the extreme bureaucratization of the school. Among the innovations tried by some schools are:

1. Open classrooms, which typically allow children freedom to move and talk within the classroom and provide a range of choices of learning tasks during at least part of the school day.

2. Individualized instruction, wherein curricular materials permit each child to work at some learning tasks at his or her own pace and allow teachers to monitor the progress of individual children.

3. Affective education, through which children are encouraged to recognize and understand their own and others' feelings, and their manner of relating to others.

The extensiveness of these innovations remains limited, and their impact remains open to debate. On the face of it, they would seem to be steps in the right direction. However, such classroom programs have often been introduced *within* what remain bureaucratically organized institutions, dominated by educational authorities and subject to a wide array of rules and regulations.

What is needed is the democratization of educational institutions—itself an educational experience for those it would involve. Persons with a stake in school functioning—students, staff, and community representatives—should all freely participate in the formulation of rules. They should also collectively determine the division of labor and responsibilities that are to exist among those who fulfill different roles in the school setting. The point is to activate responsible involvement on the part of children and young people in shaping the decisions that affect them.

The implication is that schools must move toward becoming nonauthoritarian institutions, rather than settings for differential power and prestige. Along with this, schools should also become arenas for cooperation among all participants in the interests of meeting collective goals. The fear of failure is but one way—and a destructive one at that—to motivate young people to learn. Rather than encouraging children to compete, the schools should encourage them to cooperate. Individual learning experiences must be balanced by group efforts, to which all may contribute. Only in this way can the nightmare of personal obsolescence that competitive environments nurture be undercut (Foot, Morgan, and Shute 1990).

Curricular changes that open up classrooms to the outside world must be implemented. Insulation from the world of work, from community problems, and from alternative political views runs counter to the ideal of human development through education. To function intelligently as adults, workers, voters, and taxpayers, students must be directly exposed to situations and issues with which they will have to deal. Rather than only reading about the world of work, students should be out talking to workers, union organizers, managers, professionals, and the under- and unemployed. Besides discussing current events, students should be creating or otherwise participating in political campaigns and social change movements. Volunteer work that provides services to others can be integrated with academic studies in what is known as "service learning." Any chasm between the school and the real world is an artificial one, and there is no reason to permit it to exist.

Thus far we have dwelt on changes in the bureaucratic organization of schools and in the kinds of socialization experiences to which students are exposed. An equally important feature of U.S. education that must be altered is its gatekeeping function. Existing economic inequalities must be neither reflected in nor reinforced by the educational process.

The immediate goal is equality of opportunity for all children to develop their personalities, intellects, and manual skills to their fullest potential. Stark differences in the resources possessed by school systems must be minimized by reducing their financial reliance on local property taxes. Mechanisms to promote equitable funding of all systems through federal and state treasuries should be a top priority.

Within school systems, tracking must be abolished. Increasing numbers of educators are coming to this conclusion (Bellanca and Swartz 1993; Wheelock 1992). More advanced students should routinely help less advanced students. The barriers between academic and vocational learning must also be abolished. All students should be developing interests and experiencing accomplishments that require skill with both head and hands. Testing, if used at all, should be a means to diagnose progress, not a device to channel students away from opportunities.

Educational professionals must be held accountable for their expected contributions to students during their careers in school. Those who are not making a meaningful contribution to school programs should be either retrained or aided in finding some other line of work. While such accountability has been touted as the goal of the No Child Left Behind Act, the policy has had less success in producing effective teaching skills and more success in tying the hands of educators seeking creative solutions to truly stimulate learning.

Funding of schools must also be addressed as a real barrier to education. Reliance on local property tax revenues to fund school budgets institutionalizes and reproduces economic and educational inequality. Some observers suggest the use of school vouchers as a mechanism for aiding economically deprived families to access the high-quality private schools that the wealthy do as a matter of course. Under a voucher system, everyone would be given the same amount of federal funding to apply toward the tuition at any school, private or public, of their choosing. Advocates argue that this program would give the poor the same range of choice as the affluent and would introduce competition between schools for students as paying constituents. That competition would thus presumably force schools to provide a better "product." But critics argue that the affluent have always avoided public schools in favor of private schools anyway, and thus vouchers would simply subsidize what they would pay for in any event. Moreover, the vouchers would never fully cover the cost of private schools, and thus the poor would remain in the impoverished

public schools; meanwhile, the public schools would now be struggling with even fewer resources, as these would be siphoned off to the private schools (Coons and Sugarman 1991; National Education Association 2004). Rather than vouchers, a more effective approach might be to search for new ways to fund public schools so that all students, regardless of their parents' economic abilities, have equal access to educational opportunity.

Finances should also be no barrier to individuals who wish to go beyond high school—no matter at what point in their lives this decision is made. Free or low-cost tuition and flexible admissions policies can make higher education available to more people and can help meet the changing educational needs of people of all ages. Open enrollment must be implemented at all educational institutions that in any way benefit from public tax funds. That way, anyone who meets minimum educational requirements and who shows evidence of motivation will be assured entry into programs of his or her choice.

Rich educational opportunities from cradle to grave can be made available to all—but only if we are willing to press for change rather than moan about the existing system.

Summary

Historians of education have tended to celebrate the positive contributions of the system of mass public education in the United States. They have claimed that education has contributed to political democratization, economic growth, and the minimization of class inequalities. So-called revisionist historians have presented evidence that is somewhat contrary to such positive claims. The revisionists suggest that education has been looked to as a means of political indoctrination and social control, as a device to create a docile and compliant labor force, and as a mechanism to ensure that the children of the affluent will retain their families' privileged class position while the children of the poor go on to fill low-paying, unskilled jobs.

Although we possess only limited knowledge about the impact of schooling on children today, a number of studies suggest that schools are important agents of socialization. Case studies point to the demands for conformity imposed on schoolchildren within bureaucratically organized institutions. It has been suggested that schools foster competition and fear of personal failure. And it is thought that schools function to render children politically unknowledgeable, unprepared for political struggle, and open to manipulation by elites. The success of such socialization remains open to question, but it appears that the momentum of schooling lies in such a direction.

Though mass public education has made schooling possible for everyone, it also performs a gatekeeping function. The resources of the affluent allow them to provide educational opportunities for their children that are qualitatively and quantitatively superior to those available to lower-income groups. Moreover, systems of tracking and testing within school settings operate to place the less affluent in a position of educational disadvantage. A self-fulfilling prophecy operates when nonaffluent children are not expected to learn, are not taught, and thus do not perform at a level with their more affluent peers. Differential treatment in school translates into differential academic outcomes and helps keep class inequalities intact.

The gatekeeping function also operates at the level of higher education. Economically privileged families are best able to ensure that their children will attend college and remain until completion. Children from low-income families are less likely to attend and complete college. Those who do enroll are frequently forced to attend community colleges. Since where one enters the labor force is frequently linked to the type of educational credentials one possesses, children of the affluent have a competitive advantage.

The U.S. system of education can be altered in many ways. Parents must have the right to demand alternative school placement for their children when it is clear they are not being taught. Bureaucratic rules and regulations that are not in children's interests should be abolished, and efforts must be made to democratize educational institutions. Students must have a say in the decisions and policies affecting them. Moreover, schools must be turned into arenas of cooperation instead of competition. They must be opened up to the outside world, so that children can learn about the realities they will confront as adults and how change might be brought about.

All this must be accompanied by the abolition of practices that maintain the gatekeeping function of schools. Educational systems have to be equitably financed, and systems of tracking and testing that perpetuate differential treatment by class origin must be eliminated. The barriers between vocational and academic learning should be dropped, so that all students are able to maximize learning with their heads and hands. Educators must be held responsible for making a meaningful contribution to students throughout their school careers.

Finally, finances should be no obstacle to anyone who wishes to go beyond high school. Institutions of higher education must move toward open-enrollment policies and the reduction of tuition costs. Those who are motivated and possess the basic skills should be assured entry into programs of their choice.

Key Terms

Academic boot camp 370
Academic track 377
Assimilation 366
Gatekeeper 375
Home schooling 387
Illiteracy 385
Latent functions 364
Manifest functions 363

Meritocracy 364
Organization adult 370
Organization child 370
Self-fulfilling prophecy 380
Tooth fairy approach 373
Tracks 377
Vocational track 377

Discussion Questions

1. In what ways has school had an impact on your attitudes and behavior? Give examples.

2. What kinds of in-school behaviors have you engaged in that were in violation of rules and regulations? Looking back, why do you think you engaged in such behavior?

3. What aspects of your school experience involved you in competition with others? How did you feel when winning or losing?

4. To what degree has your schooling provided you with the ability to analyze political issues and take a stand? Give examples.

5. Was there a tracking system in the schools you have attended? How was placement accomplished? How did students in different tracks view one another? What impact did tracking have on you?

6. What alterations would you like to see in the organization and operation of the educational system? Why? Who or what stands in the way of such alterations?

Suggested Readings

Aronowitz, Stanley, and Henry A. Giroux. *Education Still Under Siege.* 2d ed. (Westport, CT: Bergin & Garvey, 1993).

Conservative, liberal, and radical ideas on the functions of schooling.

Bennett de Marrais, Kathleen P., and Margaret LeCompte. *The Way Schools Work.* 3d ed. (New York: Longman, 1998).
Exploration of the subtle, often hidden socialization processes that occur as students are exposed to school.

Hochschild, Jennifer L., and Nathan Scovronick. *The American Dream and the Public Schools* (New York: Oxford University Press, 2003).
An exploration of a variety of public school reform efforts and an assessment of their effectiveness.

Kozol, Jonathan. *Savage Inequalities* (New York: Crown, 1991).
Documents scandalous conditions in poorly financed public schools that deny children educational opportunities.

Massey, Douglas S., Camille Z. Charles, Garvey F. Lundy, and Mary J. Fischer. *The Source of the River: The Social Origins of Freshmen at America's Selective Colleges and Universities* (Princeton, NJ: Princeton University Press, 2003).
An in-depth analysis of the social and economic backgrounds of students entering elite institutions of higher education in the United States.

Oakes, Jeannie. *Keeping Track* (New Haven, CT: Yale University Press, 1985).
Overview of school tracking programs, their history, contemporary examples, and the debate surrounding tracking.

Wheelock, Anne. *Crossing the Tracks* (New York: The New Press, 1992).
Alternatives to ability grouping and tracking in schools, and the benefits to be derived from eliminating such practices.

chapter 13

Health Care

Adequate health care should be a human right and made accessible and affordable to all.

J ust as organizational features of institutions of work and education can affect our individual and collective development as human beings, so too can the health-care system. As we shall see, people in the United States are not necessarily as healthy as persons living in similarly well developed nations. Moreover, major differences in health status by gender, class, and race abound in the United States. Our system of health care tends to be oriented toward responding to people's problems, rather than helping to prevent problems in the first place. Moreover, ready access to health care is not available to everyone. Health-care costs have skyrocketed in recent years, and many persons are unable to afford treatment. And the demands on our already inadequate system are increasing dramatically as we seek to cope with the AIDS epidemic and the chronic health needs of an aging population. These are the matters we consider in this chapter.

The Health Status of People in the United States

A 2005 press release noted that "The United States spends more on health care per capita—$5,700—than any other nation" (www.biz.yahoo.com/prnews/050202). Yet, at the same time a survey found that 60 percent of people in the United States do not believe the nation has the best health-care system in the world, and 64 percent believe most people in the nation lack adequate health care (www.biz.yahoo.com/prnews/050202). How can that be, if the nation is spending more than any other on health care? And is it true that most people lack adequate health care? Let's look first at the health status of people in the United States.

When sociologists assess the health status of a population, they use a variety of measures or indicators. One commonly used indicator is **life expectancy:** How long is the average person born

397

in a given year expected to live? In the case of the United States, by this measure we have grown ever more healthy. A person born in the year 1900 was expected to live about 49 years. In contrast, life expectancy for persons born today is more than 77 (U.S. Bureau of the Census 2004:71).

How does one account for this more than 50 percent increase in life expectancy? To a large extent, it reflects improvements in diet, personal hygiene, housing, and public sanitation (Cockerham 2003; McKeown 1994). Indeed, there is evidence that public health and social change measures have been more responsible for reduced mortality rates in Western nations than modern medical advances (McKinlay and McKinlay 2000). But medical advances in the last century have provided ways to directly combat many infectious diseases and their effects.

In 1900 people regularly died from tuberculosis, pneumonia, and influenza. Children were hard hit by such diseases. With the advent of immunization and the development of antibiotics, many more people were able to live into middle and old age. Thus, the principal causes of death today are noninfectious diseases that are associated with longevity: heart disease and cancer. Relatively few people lived long enough in 1900 to contract the latter.

Another measure of a population's health status is the **infant mortality rate.** This is the number of newborns who die in a given year per 1,000 live births. The statistic encompasses those who die before their first birthday. Again, using this measure, it appears that people in the United States have certainly grown healthier over time. In 1900 the infant mortality rate was 143 per 1,000 newborns. In recent years this has dropped to a little under 10 per 1,000. Improved sanitation and nutrition, the medical advances mentioned, and changes in prenatal, neonatal, and obstetric practices have contributed to this sharp (and welcome) decline in infant deaths.

Since 1957 the federal government has sponsored national surveys in which respondents are asked to assess their own health and that of

family members in their household. In 2004, 67.2 percent made an assessment of "excellent" or "very good," and 23.6 percent said "good." Only 9.2 percent answered "fair" or "poor" (U.S. Department of Health and Human Services 2004). This subjective indicator of the overall health status of people in the United States would seem quite positive.

Yet, although the data mentioned thus far paint a rather positive picture, there is cause for concern. In the next section we dwell at length on the fact that good health is unequally distributed within the U.S. population. Here we wish to note that the United States does not compare particularly well on health-status indicators with other developed nations. Indeed, this is the case despite the fact that we spend more per capita on health than they do.

For example, people born in Japan, Sweden, the Netherlands, Switzerland, Norway, and Canada live longer than those born in the United States. And our infant mortality rate, low compared to what it was in 1900, is worthy of national shame. Over 25 other nations have rates of infant death lower than that in the United States! (See Table 13.1.) Moreover, as one U.S. health-care analyst put it, "The infant mortality rates in several urban regions would qualify the United States as a third-world country" (Kissick 1994:13). Clearly something is very wrong when in this day and age so many tragic and preventable deaths occur.

Class and Health Status

In Chapter 6, "Economic Inequality and Poverty," we saw that the United States is a class-divided society. Data were provided showing that wealth and income are distributed highly unequally, and by all indications this situation has been worsening since the 1980s. Health status is highly correlated with position in the class structure. As one goes down this structure, good health becomes less frequent.

Table 13.1	Infant Mortality Rates: Selected Countries, 1986, 1991, 2000 (Data Are Based on Reporting by Countries)		
	Infant mortality rate*		
Country	1986	1991[†]	2000
Japan	5.24	4.43	3.2
Singapore	9.33	5.44	2.5
Finland	5.85	5.85	3.8
Sweden	5.93	6.13	3.4
Switzerland	6.83	6.23	4.9
Norway	7.96	6.37	3.8
Canada	7.88	6.39	5.3
Netherlands	7.77	6.50	5.1
Hong Kong	7.74	6.64	3.0
Germany[#]	8.87	7.15	4.4
Australia	8.85	7.00	5.2
Scotland	8.89	7.06	5.7
Denmark	8.19	7.24	5.3
France	8.04	7.26	4.6
England and Wales	9.55	7.38	5.6
Northern Ireland	10.16	7.39	5.1
Austria	10.27	7.48	4.8
Ireland	8.69	7.59	6.2
Spain	9.20	7.70	3.9
Belgium	9.60	7.94	4.8
Italy	10.19	8.24	4.5
New Zealand	11.36	8.40	6.3
United States	10.35	8.94	6.9
Greece	12.30	9.03	6.1
Israel	11.44	9.84	5.4
Cuba	13.62	10.74	7.2
Portugal	15.91	10.81	5.5
Czechoslovakia/Czech Republic	13.37	11.45	4.1
Puerto Rico	13.69	13.04	9.9
Costa Rica	17.77	13.83	10.2
Poland	17.51	14.98	8.1

(Continued)

Table 13.1	(Continued)		
	Infant mortality rate*		
Country	1986	1991†	2000
Chile	19.12	15.41	8.9
Hungary	19.05	15.64	9.2
Bulgaria	14.66	16.93	13.3
Russian Federation	—	18.11	15.2
Romania	23.21	22.73	18.6

Number of deaths of infants under 1 year per 1,000 live births.
†*Data for Belgium, Cuba, Federal Republic of Germany, German Democratic Republic, Israel, Italy, and Spain are for 1990.*
#*Data for 1991 and 1986 were calculated by combining information from the Federal Republic of Germany and the German Democratic Republic.*

Source: U.S. Department of Health and Human Services, *Health, United States, 2004* (Washington, DC: U.S. Government Printing Office, 2004), p. 140; U.S. Department of Health and Human Services, *Health, United States, 1994* (Washington, DC: U.S. Government Printing Office, 1995), p. 93.

Let us consider a 1997 federal survey in which people were asked to assess their health and that of family members with whom they live (see Table 13.2). At the highest family income level ($75,000 or more) almost 81 percent of respondents say they are in "excellent" or "very good" health, and less than 3 percent report "fair" or "poor." The corresponding percentages for the lowest family income level (under $20,000) are almost 47 percent "excellent" or "very good" and over 23 percent "fair" or "poor" (Centers for Disease Control and Prevention 2002). Clearly, people assess their health status differentially by economic well-being.

But subjective evaluations aside, there are many objective indicators of the correlation between class and health status (Dutton 1986). Let us return to infant mortality. One of the reasons the United States ranks so shamefully in infant mortality rates is poverty, which is correlated with inadequate nutrition and difficulty in gaining access to medical care. Infant mortality rates are substantially higher among the poor than among the nonpoor. Indeed, death rates for small children in general—not only infants

below the age of one—are higher. Because of this and other factors we shall discuss, the overall life expectancy is less at lower levels of the class structure. To say that poverty kills is no exaggeration.

Infectious diseases, we noted previously, took a major toll on people early in the twentieth century. For the poor today, the toll goes on. For example, cases of pneumonia and influenza, and other infectious diseases such as tuberculosis and diphtheria, are much more routinely diagnosed among the poor than among the more affluent. The principal reason pneumonia and influenza rank sixth among the leading causes of death in the United States (the only infectious diseases among the top 10 causes) is their association with poverty conditions.

Chronic disabling diseases are disproportionately found in lower income groups. These include heart disease, cancer, stroke, and diabetes—all among the leading causes of death in the United States. Impairment of speech, motor skills, and vision is prevalent. Other sources of disability such as arthritis affect the poor more than others.

Table 13.2	Self-Assessment of Health, 1997		
Characteristic	Excellent/very good	Good	Fair/poor
Total	**63.9%**	**24.7%**	**11.5%**
Age			
18–44 years	73.6	20.8	5.6
45–64 years	58.5	26.9	14.6
65–74 years	43.3	33.2	23.5
75 years and older	35.5	35.2	29.3
Family Income			
Less than $20,000	46.9	29.9	23.2
$20,000 or more	70.0	22.7	7.3
$20,000–$34,999	57.9	29.2	12.9
$35,000–$54,999	69.3	23.5	7.3
$55,000–$74,999	76.6	19.0	4.3
$75,000 or more	80.8	16.5	2.7
Poverty status			
Poor	45.7	30.3	24.0
Near poor	51.6	30.1	18.3
Not poor	71.3	21.9	6.9
Sex			
Male	66.1	23.4	10.5
Female	61.8	25.9	12.3
Race/Ethnicity			
White non-Latino	66.0	23.5	10.6
Black non-Latino	54.0	28.2	17.9
Other non-Latino	63.8	27.8	8.4
Latino	59.0	28.8	12.2
Education			
Less than 12 years of school	38.0	34.3	27.7
High school graduate/GED recipient	57.7	29.2	13.1
Some college	68.2	23.7	8.2
Bachelor of arts or sciences/graduate or professional degree	80.6	15.2	4.2

Source: Centers for Disease Control and Prevention, "Summary Health Statistics for U.S. Adults: National Health Interview Survey, 1997," *Vital and Health Statistics*, Series 10, No. 205 (May 2002):53.

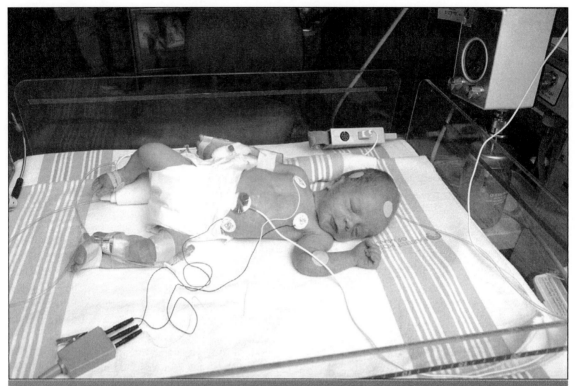

Over 25 other nations have lower rates of infant mortality than does the United States. Many of the infants who die in their first year of life are born premature, such as the baby shown in this photograph who is hospitalized in an intensive care unit. Widespread poverty and lack of access to affordable, quality health care help keep U.S. rates of infant mortality high.

Low-income people are more likely than others to find their daily activities restricted by both chronic (long-lasting) and acute (severe, but not long-lasting) conditions of illness, injury, or impairment. In one federal survey, respondents were asked how many days in 1992 they or members of their household found their activities restricted by such conditions. Those with family incomes under $10,000 reported an average of 29 days of disability in 1992, while those with family incomes of $35,000 or more reported only 10 days of disability on average (U.S. Bureau of the Census 1995:136). Again, such data show a direct correlation between economic well-being and health status.

Diane B. Dutton (1986:37–38) draws our attention to a controversy of some interest:

There has been a longstanding debate about whether the worse health of lower socioeconomic groups should be attributed primarily to the material conditions of poverty and the biological and emotional stresses they create or to aspects of the lifestyle of the disadvantaged (e.g., cultural values and individual behavior).

In other words, are low-income people to be blamed for their ill health, conditions of disability, and premature deaths, or are external factors—largely outside their control—responsible?

Most people in the United States are mentally and physically capable of taking some steps, no matter how minor, to enhance or protect their health status. Indeed, we have witnessed a striking increase of public interest in ways to maintain health and improve fitness (Glassner 1988). The prevalence of cigarette smoking and consumption of hard liquor have gone down. People have been making dietary changes (e.g., eating less red meat and more grains, fruits, and vegetables), a trend reflected in the 2004 revision of the nutrition pyramid published by the U.S. Departments of Agriculture and Health and Human Services. Engagement in exercise such as walking, running, and aerobics has become more frequent. More people are monitoring their blood pressures, cholesterol levels, and weight, as well as avoiding unnecessary exposure to the sun and using sunscreens. Yet despite the publicity we see in the mass media, not everyone is equally involved. Tens of millions of poor and near-poor people in the United States of all ages are largely outside of and unengaged in such activity. Perhaps they should not be, but they are.

However, holding those with low incomes to blame for their health status can easily be a form of "blaming the victim" (Ryan 1976). It implies that they bring their own lower life expectancies and higher rates of infant mortality on themselves; thus, they could be collectively healthier with some simple changes in lifestyle. This would be fine were it not for a growing body of evidence showing the direct link between income level and the nature and quality of the work and living environments to which people are daily exposed. To put it bluntly, the more money you have, the better able you are to avoid exposure to the kinds of hazards and stresses that affect your health negatively. As will become evident, the kinds of lifestyle alterations that have grown popular among more affluent people fail to address the underlying causes of health problems for millions.

Consider the work environment. Those jobs that provide the lowest economic returns tend to be the most physically taxing and hazardous in terms of what workers are exposed to. Imagine going to work in the kinds of jobs where over 14,000 employees die each year, another 100,000 die prematurely, and an additional 400,000 suffer illness from occupationally related diseases. These kinds of tragedies should elicit outrage because they are largely preventable. But neither private-sector employers nor government agencies have seen fit to take the necessary steps toward prevention (McGarity and Shapiro 1993). The results of this negligence are inflicted on low-status, low-wage workers in factories and other work sites across the country.

Low-wage workers are also more likely than others to be in the least secure jobs; for example, seasonal positions and those subject to reductions in force with the shifting economic climate. In Chapter 11, "The Changing Structure of Work," we commented on some of the impacts of unemployment. Not only is the experience of unemployment associated with health problems—from cardiovascular difficulties to ulcers—but the loss of income often has an impact on the unemployed workers' ability to afford adequate health care. As we shall see later, the jobless are among the 45 million people in the United States with no health-care insurance to help pay for treatment (Mills 2001; Weissman and Epstein 1994). But even employment is no guarantee of health-care coverage: 80 percent of those with no health insurance live in families of workers (Geyman 2003).

But it is not only the work setting that is more problematic for the health status of low-income people. Living conditions, too, can be fraught with dangers. Workers exposed to hazardous substances on the job can bring them home on their clothing or bodies, thus endangering others in the household, including children. People living in areas subject to particularly concentrated levels of air pollution (e.g., urban poverty dwellers) are put at high risk for such diseases as lung cancer, emphysema, and bronchitis. The failure of absentee landlords to take an interest in the health and safety aspects of their housing property contributes to lead poisoning from paint chips, the spread of disease by rats and insects, sanitation problems due to inadequate waste disposal, fires, and accidents.

The serious shortage of affordable housing for low-income people not only discourages tenant complaints and household moves but forces many families to double and even triple up so that they can afford shelter (even at the risk of eviction). Overcrowded living conditions contribute to stresses that lower immunity to illness as well as facilitate the spread of infectious diseases.

The abuse of alcohol and other drugs is for some a way to cope with the reality of the kind of living environment we have been describing. It is a way of life that often is also permeated with the threat of criminal victimization. It can be a depressing existence, filled with gray images of dirt, trash, and physical decline. It may be a reality that imposes a sharp sense of social isolation and alienation from the wider society. Substance abuse may offer an escape from all this, but it carries negative ramifications for health. Users' well-being may be endangered. Violence against others in and outside of the home, often but not always associated with the abuse of alcohol and certain illegal drugs (e.g., amphetamines, "crack" cocaine, PCP), is now considered a major public health issue.

Our homes are supposed to be places where we can go to be emotionally replenished, and nutritionally replenished as well. As we saw in Chapter 6, for millions of people in the United States the home provides little in the way of nutritional replenishment. Insufficient food, or the ability to afford only foods that are minimally balanced nutritionally, is a fact of life for too many low-income people. Obesity, a health-threatening condition, often afflicts those whose diets are overloaded with inexpensive starches and carbohydrates. On the other hand, the absence of food in homes has produced the food

insecurity and hunger described in shocking reports in recent years. Most at risk are women (including pregnant women), small children, and the elderly (Schwartz-Nobel 2002; U.S. Congress, House 1992b).

But we also know that not all U.S. residents have homes. And the estimated 2 million to 3 million homeless are beset by serious health problems. Many of these problems stem from malnutrition, stress, fatigue, contact with others' infectious diseases, exposure to unsanitary conditions, and difficulty maintaining personal hygiene. Injury from accidents or others' violent behavior and illness from exposure to the elements are among the environmental threats faced by homeless people. Increasingly the homeless include women and their children. Even people with AIDS—too ill to work, evicted from their dwellings, and shunned by family and friends—are being found on the streets! The failure of this society to provide affordable housing for all its members, and the inability of the homeless to do much about their situation, demonstrates how health problems are organized into existence at the lower levels of the class structure.

People whose home environments, neighborhoods, and work settings are hostile to psychological and physical well-being require more than superficial lifestyle changes if their health status is to improve. The homeless are unlikely to find that jogging or aerobics addresses the sources of their health difficulties. The hungry are unlikely to be concerned with keeping their cholesterol levels down and will understandably eat anything they can get their hands on. While the affluent can afford to take steps to avoid even minor maladies, exercising at health clubs and wearing designer sunglasses, many low-income people are trying to figure out how to survive immediate life-threatening environments. Until such conditions are changed, the sharp class differences in health status will continue unabated.

In addition to the effect that poverty may have on health is the effect of health-care expenses on people's class. Health-care costs rank second among financial worries people indicated in a 2005 Gallup survey, second only to concerns about the overall cost of living (http://feeds.bignewsnetwork.com). People's fears about the cost of health care appear warranted: One study found that medical bills and other related costs of treating illness contributed to more than half of all the bankruptcies in 2001 in the United States (www.theworldforum.org). The staggering cost of caring for one's family and self are clearly daunting: many people fear they are one acute illness or chronic disease away from bankruptcy. This suggests that at least some of the health-care decisions individuals may make are not simply matters of ignorance or poor decision making; it may very well be that many individuals must choose between taking care of themselves or feeding and housing their families. In the short run this is likely to mean eating and sleeping with a roof over one's children overrules a visit to the doctor and all that can cost.

Gender Inequality and Health Care

The structure and organization of health care in the United States remains dominated by men: Physicians, surgeons, researchers, administrators, and executives are primarily male. There are signs, however, that this is changing: Women and men now enter many medical schools in similar proportions, and women are increasingly moving into important positions in health care. Moreover, women who work in health care as well as women who confront the system as patients and clients have been encouraged by the feminist movement to challenge gender bias in patient treatment, medical research, and medical training and practices that might provide inadequate health care to women (Ratcliff 2002).

For example, research on heart disease has traditionally excluded women as subjects, focusing exclusively on men instead, and the conclusions reached by this research have commonly assumed that the findings applied to both women and men alike. However, one-tenth of women between the ages of 45 and 64 have some form of heart disease, and heart disease is the number one cause of death among women. Furthermore, more women than men die from their first heart attack (U.S. Department of Health and Human Services 1998). Some observers note the dangers of gendered bias in research that fails to explore the differential effect of hormones, metabolic rates, and reproduction on diseases and on drug treatments (Cimons 1990).

Not only have women been excluded as subjects from research on illnesses and on drugs that can affect both men and women, but also diseases and concerns that affect women exclusively or far more commonly than men are often left poorly examined or unexplored. More than 25 million older people in the United States suffer from osteoporosis, for example, but twice as many women as men over the age of 65—one out of every three women—develop the disease. Osteoporosis is a disease involving severe loss of bone tissue that leaves its victims vulnerable to fractures, most often of the wrist, hip, and spine. This highly preventable disease is implicated in almost a million and a half fractures a year, resulting in serious physical disability, pain and suffering, and substantial expense. Yet until relatively recently, very little money has supported research and education about this important public health issue affecting far more women than men.

The National Institutes of Health has responded to the criticisms of sexism in health-care research by allocating more research funding to women's health issues. In 1991 NIH began the Women's Health Initiative, the largest federally funded study of women's health. This initiative prompted new research on the causes and treatments of illnesses affecting millions of women, including a variety of types of cancer (such as breast cancer and ovarian cancer), heart disease, and osteoporosis. Although it will be some time before this research is completed, its findings have already begun to produce useful information for women.

Congress also passed legislation in 1993 to require the NIH to ensure an equitable representation of women in its funded research and in its clinical drug trials. However, researchers continue to evidence a gendered imbalance among the participants included in clinical drug trials; even when women participate, researchers engage in very little analysis of their data by sex. One study found that only one-fourth of those participating in published drug trials between 1994 and 1999 were female, and only 14 percent of the published studies analyzed their data by sex (Ramasubbu, Gurm, and Litaker 2001). Clearly, there is still a long way to go before medical research eradicates this gender bias, federal legislation notwithstanding.

In addition to a gendered bias that ignores women's health-care concerns in research and treatment is the issue of gendered inequality in health-care coverage. Chapter 11, "The Changing Structure of Work," outlined women's relatively weaker position than men in the labor market: Women are more likely to be employed, but at significantly lower wages than men, and at contingency, temporary, or part-time jobs. That means women's jobs are less likely to carry important employer-provided benefits, particularly health-care coverage. Indeed, women's jobs are less likely than men's to provide health insurance benefits even when they work full-time. And although one may purchase health-care insurance if the employer does not provide it, that coverage is enormously expensive, often beyond the financial reach of people in low-wage jobs. As such, women who live alone, single mothers, divorcées, widows, and women who are the sole providers for their families are more vulnerable to the precariousness of living without health-care insurance. They are often one serious illness away from financial catastrophe, or worse. They may often have to make decisions between health care or food, rent, and other essentials when illness strikes. Imagine how devastating, then, a serious illness can be.

Moreover, female-headed households are more likely than male-headed households to be poor. Single mothers, then, confront particularly serious and challenging obstacles to gaining access to health care. Many low-income female-headed households must rely on Medicaid, a government-sponsored health-care program serving impoverished people and families. However, Medicaid is not a program providing full services to all who are poor; it is a program that is highly dependent upon the amount of money Congress allots to it, and thus its ability to provide services, regardless of need, becomes restricted by budgetary constraints. Those who rely on Medicaid, then, are chronically underserved.

Racial Inequality and Health Care

People of color in this society are often subject to serious maltreatment and disadvantage, as we saw in Chapter 7, "Racism." As we consider the unequal health status of people in the United States, it is important to note that not only class but race as well is correlated with health status. This is clear if we take one of U.S. society's major racial minority groups, African Americans, as an example.

If U.S. infant mortality rates are higher than they have any reason to be, then the rates for African Americans are most shocking. For whites the rate is 5.7 infant deaths per 1,000 live births. It is more than twice as high for African American infants! Equally saddening and disturbing are data indicating sharp racial differences in life expectancy. Federal statistics estimate that white females born in 2001 can expect to live 80.2 years, compared to 75.5 years for African American females. In contrast to white males' life expectancy of 75 years, African American males can expect only 68.6 years of life. Available data indicate that from 1984 to 1991 the life expectancy of African American males actually went down, rather than up, and only thereafter turned around (U.S. Bureau of the Census 2004:72–73; U.S. Department of Health and Human Services 1998).

The life expectancy rate of African Americans is lowered by their higher rates of infant mortality. But reports provided by the federal government's National Center on Health Statistics reveal that African Americans have higher rates of death than whites from almost all causes. To some degree this may be explained in terms of the disproportionate presence of African Americans in the lowest income levels of the class structure. However, some would argue that treatment of people by race, apart from their class position, exacts an additional toll. One study, for example, found that infant mortality rates among children of African American college-educated parents was twice the rate of children of similarly educated white parents (Schoendorf et al. 1992). Such evidence suggests that something about the social construction of race in the United States is negatively affecting the health status of people of color beyond their class position. Let's explore how racial inequality might result in these health-status differences.

Higher infant mortality rates among African American children may be the result of living in a society characterized by racial inequality and residential segregation. As we saw in Chapter 7, "Racism," people of color are far more likely than whites to live in communities that have become toxic waste dump sites. The presence of toxic waste in the land, water, and air is likely to have a harmful affect on pregnant women and infants, and therefore to contribute to a higher infant mortality rate among African American children (Bullard 1997). Moreover, residential segregation means that even middle-class African Americans are likelier than whites to live in neighborhoods where medical facilities providing high-quality prenatal, postnatal, and pediatric care are limited in number and often understaffed. As such, limited access to adequate

prenatal and infant care can contribute to a higher infant mortality rate among African American children quite apart from their class. Furthermore, college-educated African Americans have lower average annual incomes than similarly educated whites, which can hinder their ability to afford to purchase adequate health-care coverage, contributing to higher infant mortality rates than their white counterparts.

Beyond the differences in health status between whites and African Americans that may be produced by racism in the United States and its economic and social institutions is the question of whether there is racism in the health-care system itself: Do the institutions of health care deliver less adequate care to people of color than to whites simply because of race? The Institute of Medicine found in a 2002 report that people of color on average tend to receive a lower quality of health care than do whites, even when their income level, health insurance, and health conditions are similar (Institute of Medicine 2002). The report cited racial bias, stereotyping, and prejudice toward people of color by health-care providers as key among the contributing factors. And although our discussion in this section focuses on a comparison between whites and African Americans, the report noted that Latinos/as and Asian immigrants faced similar obstacles to adequate health-care access because providers were unresponsive to language and cultural differences.

People of color are also less likely than whites to have access to health-care insurance. In 2000 less than 10 percent of non-Latino whites were without health insurance for the entire year, compared with 18 percent of Asian and Pacific Islanders, 18.5 percent of African Americans, and 32 percent of Latinos/as. White non-Latinos were also more likely to have employer-provided health insurance than people of color; where 69.5 percent of non-Latino whites had employment-based health insurance, only 54.4 percent of African American and 44.6 percent of Latinos/as did. People of color were more likely to depend on Medicaid for health-care coverage: Only 7 percent of non-Latino whites relied on Medicaid, compared with 20.3 percent of African Americans and 18.6 of Latinos/as (Mills 2001). Just as single mothers face inadequate access to quality health care in an underbudgeted, understaffed Medicaid system, so too do people of color.

Similar to the problems women confront in the gendered biases in medical research, people of color often face exclusion in drug testing trials and in access to experimental drugs that could help them in the treatment of disease. For example, AIDS has had a devastating impact on communities of color: Deaths from the disease are substantially higher than they are for whites (National Center for Health Statistics 2001). Yet African Americans and Latinos/as who are infected with the Human Immunodeficiency Virus (HIV) that produces AIDS are only half as likely as whites to be included in clinical trials of promising experimental drugs in the treatment of the disease. It may well be the case that many people of color choose not to participate in the experiments because they do not trust a predominantly white medical establishment. However, exclusion from clinical trials indicates a more systematic racial bias by researchers (Gifford et al. 2002).

Thus, although there is an intersection of race and class in the United States that reinforces inadequate health care and health status for people of color compared to whites, class alone does not fully explain the differences. Racially discriminatory structures in institutions produce unequal access to health care based on race beyond any income or educational differences.

The U.S. Health-Care System

The United States has the most expensive health-care system in the world. It consumes almost 15 percent of our gross national product (GNP), up from 7.4 percent in 1970 (U.S. Bureau of the Census 2004:93). Health care is the United States' next largest industry after aerospace-defense, and health expenditures take up a fifth of the federal budget. No other nation spends as much per capita as does the United States (see, for example, Figure 13.1). Yet, as has been discussed, the health status of people in the United States falls short of what we might expect given these expenditures. This cannot be explained wholly with reference to failings in our lifestyles or even the harsh environmental circumstances endured by many low-income people. We must examine what role the U.S. health-care system itself plays in all this.

Among all highly developed nations in the Western world, only the United States has no comprehensive system of universal health insurance or a national health service providing care for all. Other nations—from Canada to England to West Germany—take the position that health care is a basic human right and provide universal coverage to all their citizens. Only in the United States is the task of securing health care left up to the individual to such an extent. Our system is oriented largely around a "pay-as-you-go" mentality, and health care is considered a commodity that must be purchased if it is to be consumed. Unfortunately, not all people in the United States are in a position to buy (Graig 1999; Navarro 1993).

Almost 70 percent of the U.S. population under age 65, over 160 million people, are covered by some type of private health insurance. (Many others, including persons 65 and over, are eligible for government programs, to be discussed.) Typically, private health insurance is obtained through one's employer, who shares part of the costs. Where this is not the case, the individual must pay the full insurance premium. Insurance costs have gone up significantly in recent years, as health care itself has grown more and more expensive. Employers, faced with inroads on their profit margins due to rising insurance costs, have been successful

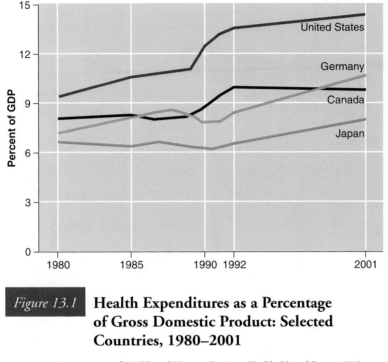

Source: U.S. Department of Health and Human Services, *Health, United States, 1994 Chartbook* (Washington, DC: Government Printing Office, 1995), p. 30; and U.S. Department of Health and Human Services, *Health, United States, 2004 Chartbook* (Washington, DC: Government Printing Office, 2005), p. 325.

Figure 13.1 **Health Expenditures as a Percentage of Gross Domestic Product: Selected Countries, 1980–2001**

in shifting a greater share of the costs to employees. Some employers have even ceased offering coverage, leaving workers on their own to obtain health insurance. The proportion of people with job-related private health plans has been dropping, falling over 9 percent between 1995 and 2002 (National Center for Health Statistics 2004).

It is also the case that most employer insurance plans are very limited in terms of their coverage; for example, some do not cover the children of employees. Nor do such plans cover the full costs of different medical services that may be called for by doctors and hospitals. In all such cases, individuals must pay for part of their expenses out of their pockets. More and more people in the United States are finding it difficult

if not impossible to afford the type and quality of care they need. To pay medical bills, many people have no choice but to exhaust their savings, go heavily into debt, or even sell their homes. In the United States, unlike other developed nations, citizens who suffer from poor health may be allowed to plummet into poverty to pay for care.

Those able to secure employer health insurance are among the fortunate. In 2003 some 45 million people in the United States had no health insurance at all, not even the limited coverage provided certain categories of people under government programs. And the ranks of these uninsured people are growing larger each year. The figure of 45 million uninsured in 2003, for example, represented an increase of over 10 million people since 1990 (see Table 13.3)

Table 13.3	Health Insurance Coverage Status by Selected Characteristics: 1990 to 2002

[Persons as of following year for coverage in the year shown (**248.9 represents 248,900,000**). Government health insurance includes medicare, medicaid, and military plans.]

	Number (mil.)						Percent			
		Covered by private or government health insurance				Not covered by health insurance	Covered by private or government health insurance			Not covered by health insurance
			Private		Government					
Characteristic	Total persons	Total[1]	Total	Group health[2]	Medicare	Medicaid[3]		Total[1]	Private	Medicaid[3]	
1990	248.9	214.2	182.1	150.2	32.3	24.3	34.7	86.1	73.2	9.7	13.9
1995	264.3	223.7	185.9	161.5	34.7	31.9	40.6	84.6	70.3	12.1	15.4
2000[4][5]	279.5	239.7	201.1	177.8	37.7	29.5	39.8	85.8	71.9	10.6	14.2
2001[4][5]	282.1	240.9	199.9	176.6	38.0	31.6	41.2	85.4	70.9	11.2	14.6
2002, total[4][5]	285.9	242.4	199.0	175.3	38.4	33.2	43.6	84.8	69.6	11.6	15.2
Age:											
Under 18 years	73.3	64.8	49.5	46.2	0.5	17.5	8.5	88.4	67.5	23.9	11.6
Under 6 years	23.7	21.1	15.0	14.2	0.2	6.9	2.6	89.1	63.4	29.1	10.9
6 to 11 years	24.3	21.6	16.5	15.6	0.2	5.8	2.7	89.0	68.1	24.0	11.0
12 to 17 years	25.4	22.1	18.0	16.3	0.2	4.8	3.3	87.1	70.7	19.0	12.9
18 to 24 years	27.4	19.3	16.6	13.4	0.2	2.9	8.1	70.4	60.4	10.6	29.6
25 to 34 years	39.2	29.5	26.5	24.8	0.5	2.8	9.8	75.1	67.5	7.1	24.9
35 to 44 years	44.1	36.3	33.2	31.2	0.9	2.7	7.8	82.3	75.4	6.2	17.7
45 to 54 years	40.2	34.6	31.7	29.6	1.4	2.2	5.6	86.1	78.9	5.5	13.9
55 to 64 years	27.4	23.9	20.8	18.5	2.4	1.8	3.5	87.2	75.9	6.5	12.9
65 years and over	34.2	34.0	20.7	11.6	32.6	3.3	0.3	99.3	60.4	9.6	0.8
Sex: Male	139.9	116.5	97.4	87.0	16.6	14.7	23.3	83.3	69.6	10.5	16.7
Female	146.1	125.8	101.6	88.3	21.8	18.6	20.2	86.1	69.6	12.7	13.9
Race: White alone	230.8	198.1	167.2	145.2	33.1	22.2	32.7	85.8	72.4	9.6	14.2
Black alone	35.8	28.6	19.3	18.0	3.8	8.3	7.2	79.8	54.0	23.2	20.2
Asian alone	11.6	9.4	7.9	6.9	1.0	1.2	2.1	81.6	68.7	10.4	18.5
Latino origin[6]	39.4	26.6	18.1	16.7	2.5	7.9	12.8	67.6	46.0	20.2	32.4
Household income:											
Less than $25,000	63.0	48.2	23.7	15.3	18.0	18.7	14.8	76.5	37.7	29.6	23.5
$25,000–$49,999	75.9	61.3	49.8	43.0	11.5	9.2	14.6	80.7	65.6	12.2	19.3

Characteristic	Number (mil.)							Percent			
		Covered by private or government health insurance					Not covered by health insurance	Covered by private or government health insurance			Not covered by health insurance
			Private		Government						
	Total persons	Total[1]	Total	Group health[2]	Medicare	Medicaid[3]		Total[1]	Private	Medicaid[3]	
$50,000–$74,999	58.6	51.7	47.7	44.0	4.5	3.0	6.9	88.2	81.3	5.2	11.8
$75,000 or more	88.4	81.2	77.8	72.9	4.4	2.3	7.3	91.8	88.0	2.6	8.2
Persons below poverty	34.6	24.1	8.7	5.6	5.0	14.0	10.5	69.7	25.3	40.5	30.4

[1] Includes other government insurance, not shown separately. Persons with coverage counted only once in total, even though they may have been covered by more than one type of policy.

[2] Related to employment of self or other family members.

[3] Beginning 1997 persons with no coverage other than access to Indian Health Service are no longer considered covered by health insurance; instead they are considered to be uninsured. The effect of this change on the overall estimates of health insurance coverage is negligible; however, the decrease in the number of people covered by Medicaid may be partially due to this change.

[4] Estimates reflect results of follow-up verification questions.

[5] Implementation of Census 2000 based population controls. Sample expanded by 28,000 households.

[6] Persons of Latino origin may be of any race.

Source: U.S. Department of Commerce, Bureau of the Census, *Statistical Abstract of the United States, 2004–2005* (Washington, DC: Government Printing Office, 2004), p. 103.

(DeNavas-Walt, Proctor, and Mills 2004:15; Summer and Shapiro 1994). The rate has continued to rise annually.

The figures above are for people who reported they were without health insurance for the full year, for example, for all of 2003. Those who lack insurance for only part of a year are not counted by the federal government as uninsured, and thus annual government statistics underestimate the magnitude of the problem. The severity of the situation became clearer when the U.S. Bureau of the Census examined the number of different people who are without insurance during the course of a year. In its last study of this difference, the Census Bureau found that while 11.9 million people lacked insurance for all of 1992–1994, 54 million people—more than a quarter of the entire U.S. population—were without health insurance for at least a month—

long period at some point during that time (Benefield 1996). Such statistics show that while millions of people have no insurance year in and year out, millions more are at risk of being uninsured at any given moment.

Most people without any insurance are workers and their families. Their employers tend to be smaller businesses that do not provide any health benefits. Others are self-employed persons who cannot afford to pay the premiums. Still others have no jobs or are between jobs and have lost their insurance, or they are in part-time or temporary full-time positions that do not carry health-care benefits. The poor, racial minority group members, young adults, and rural dwellers are disproportionately represented among the uninsured. For example, among people who lived in poverty in 2002, 30.4 percent had no health insurance in comparison to less than 16 percent of the nonpoor. Among people of color, 32.4 percent of Latinos and 20.2 percent of African Americans were without any health insurance in 2002, compared with 14.2 percent of whites (U.S. Bureau of the Census 2004:103).

The result of a system that leaves more than one in six people in the United States walking around completely responsible for paying for their health care is predictable. If people cannot afford to pay for care, they will ignore symptoms and likely end up in even greater distress. A study by the Robert Wood Johnson Foundation found that insured people experiencing unexplained chest pain, loss of consciousness, shortness of breath, bleeding, or severe weight loss are likely to seek out medical help. Uninsured people are not (Weissman and Epstein 1994). One can only imagine the results of "toughing it out."

In 1965 the U.S. government agreed to finance a health insurance plan for people aged 65 and older. Known as Medicare, this plan now enrolls some 38.4 million people and has become a major source of income for doctors and hospitals. But as our elders are quite aware, Medicare falls far short of paying the full costs of health care. There are restrictions on just what services will be covered by insurance (e.g., on the length of hospitalization and on long-term care). As a consequence, elderly persons have found themselves squeezed by rising health-care costs just like all other people in the United States. Most must supplement their Medicare coverage with private insurance in a quest for some semblance of protection in their "golden years." For many persons 65 and older, health expenses have become an increasing burden each year.

Also in 1965 the federal government adopted a plan in which it would, in cooperation with the states, jointly fund a program aimed at addressing the health-care needs of the poor. This program is called Medicaid, and it is riddled with serious problems that get in the way of meeting these needs. For example, since by law physicians may not charge poor patients more than Medicaid is willing to pay for services, and since this amount can be low, many doctors refuse to take Medicaid patients! Other problems stem from eligibility criteria, which vary across the individual states. In most states, people can live well below the official poverty line and still not be considered eligible for Medicare. As of 2002 only 40.5 percent of all poor people and only two-thirds of poor children were covered by Medicaid. More than a fifth of all poor children were not covered by any kind of health insurance at all in 2002 (U.S. Census 2004:103; see also Lyter, Sills, and Oh 2002).

Medicaid coverage has been extended automatically to adults and children participating in Temporary Assistance to Needy Families programs, more commonly known as "welfare," and the federal government has called for Medicaid coverage to eventually be expanded to all poor children and pregnant women, including those not on welfare. But currently millions of people below the official poverty line—out of lack of knowledge or ineligibility, and some by choice—lack Medicaid coverage. The net result of all this is that millions of poor people in the United States do not have even the most minimal health-care insurance safety net, while those who participate in Medicaid find it hard to locate physicians willing to treat them.

The pay-as-you-go system of health care, as we have seen, weighs heavily on the backs of individual citizens. And those who suffer the worst health status—persons at the bottom levels of the class structure—are least able to afford care. Economic disadvantage effectively functions as a barrier for access to the existing health-care system. But what of the system itself? In ways we shall address, attributes of the health-care system form barriers to its utilization.

The core of the U.S. health-care system, at least in the last century, has traditionally been the private physician (Starr 1982). Professionally active physicians number over 853,000 today, most functioning in individual and group practice (others work for government or business employers). Most private physicians are affiliated with hospitals that are available to assist them in patient care. This group—1 physician for every 341 people in the United States—on the face of it seems adequate in size to take care of everyone's health needs. Yet there exists what we shall call an "artificial doctor shortage." Let us explain.

With some qualifications, we can say that in general physicians in our pay-as-you-go system of health care are out to make money. If the average incomes they receive are any indicator, they are quite successful in reaching this goal. In 2001 the mean net income of all physicians was almost $206,000. The mean ranged from a low of $137,000 for those in pediatrics to a high of $274,000 for surgeons (U.S. Bureau of the Census 2004:109). To put this in context, only 11 percent of all males and 3 percent of all females in the United States had total money incomes of $75,000 and over in 2001 (U.S. Bureau of the Census 2004:461).

To be economically successful physicians must, like any other businessperson, locate a profitable market for their services. Running a medical practice alone or in concert with others is an expensive undertaking (not to mention the need of new physicians to pay off education debts). Making money means going to those areas where people's income levels are high, where their private insurance plan coverages are broad, and where physician affiliation with a quality hospital or clinic is easily accomplished. As physicians flock to these areas, they in effect create an artificial doctor shortage in other regions. Rural communities, small towns, and inner-city poverty areas suffer the most from this shortage. Much like underdeveloped countries, the United States suffers an internal "brain drain" of medical talent away from areas of need and to areas where physicians prefer to locate.

This brain drain operates in another dimension as well. Particularly since World War II there has been a trend for physicians to become specialized within the medical profession. Today, only a minority function as general practitioners, or "family doctors." (See Table 13.4.) In part this has occurred as a result of the explosion of knowledge and growth of advanced technology available for use in the health field. No one can keep up with everything, and specialization has occurred just as in many other fields (including sociology).

Yet other factors have been at work as well in promoting the specialization trend. The number of professionally active physicians has been on the increase, particularly since the 1980s. We have more than 853,000 today; in 1980 there were only 467,700. Even higher figures are projected into the future. With the growth in numbers of doctors, the threat of competition among them has increased. Specialization is in part a way of sidestepping this threat. Physicians who specialize lay claim to providing unique services for which they are able to command respectable fees. But this skewing of physicians toward "limited practice" involving their technical specialities means that far fewer people in the United States today have access to primary care by physicians interested in their overall well-being.

Victor and Ruth Sidel (1990:175) define a primary care physician as

a physician based in the community rather than in a hospital; a physician people first turn to, who does not regularly see referrals from other physicians; who provides continuing care rather than episodic care; and who serves the function of integrating the work of referral specialists and other community resources in relation to the patients' care.

| Table 13.4 | Physicians by Selected Activity: 1980 to 2002 |

[In thousands (467.7 represents 467,700). As of Dec. 31, except 1990 as of Jan. 1, and as noted. Includes Puerto Rico and island areas]

Activity	1980	1990	1995	1999	2000	2001	2002
Doctors of medicine, total	467.7	615.4	720.3	797.6	813.8	836.2	853.2
Professionally active	435.5	560.0	646.0	720.9	737.5	751.7	768.5
Place of medical education:							
U.S. medical graduates	343.6	437.2	492.2	542.2	554.2	562.3	573.7
Foreign medical graduates[1]	91.8	122.8	153.8	178.7	183.4	189.4	194.8
Sex: Male	386.7	463.9	505.9	544.1	551.7	556.6	564.0
Female	48.7	96.1	140.1	176.7	185.8	195.1	204.5
Active nonfederal	417.7	539.5	624.9	702.8	718.1	731.7	748.3
Patient care	361.9	487.8	564.1	610.7	631.4	652.3	658.1
Office-based practice	271.3	359.9	427.3	473.2	490.4	514.0	516.2
General and family practice	47.8	57.6	59.9	66.2	67.5	70.0	71.7
Cardiovascular diseases	6.7	10.7	13.7	15.6	16.3	17.0	17.0
Dermatology	4.4	6.0	7.0	7.8	8.0	8.2	8.3
Gastroenterology	2.7	5.2	7.3	8.2	8.5	8.9	9.0
Internal medicine	40.5	57.8	72.6	84.6	88.7	94.7	96.5
Pediatrics	17.4	26.5	33.9	40.5	42.2	44.8	46.1
Pulmonary diseases	2.0	3.7	5.0	5.7	6.1	6.6	6.7
General surgery	22.4	24.5	24.1	26.8	24.5	25.6	24.9
Obstetrics and gynecology	19.5	25.5	29.1	31.1	31.7	32.6	32.7
Ophthalmology	10.6	13.1	14.6	15.2	15.6	16.0	16.1
Orthopedic surgery	10.7	14.2	17.1	17.0	17.4	17.8	18.1
Otolaryngology	5.3	6.4	7.1	7.3	7.6	7.9	8.0
Plastic surgery	2.4	3.8	4.6	5.1	5.3	5.5	5.6
Urological surgery	6.2	7.4	8.0	8.2	8.5	8.6	8.6
Anesthesiology	11.3	17.8	23.8	26.6	27.6	28.9	28.7
Diagnostic radiology	4.2	9.8	12.8	14.3	14.6	15.6	15.9
Emergency medicine	(NA)	8.4	11.7	13.9	14.5	15.8	16.9
Neurology	3.2	5.6	7.6	8.1	8.6	9.2	9.0
Pathology, anatomical/clinical	6.0	7.3	9.0	10.1	10.3	10.6	10.1
Psychiatry	15.9	20.0	23.3	24.4	25.0	25.7	25.4
Other specialty	31.9	28.8	35.0	36.4	42.0	44.1	41.0

Activity	1980	1990	1995	1999	2000	2001	2002
Hospital-based practice	90.6	127.9	136.8	137.2	141.0	138.3	141.9
Residents and interns[2]	59.6	89.9	93.7	92.5	95.1	92.9	96.5
Full-time hospital staff	31.0	38.0	43.1	44.8	45.9	45.4	45.3
Other professional activity[3]	35.2	39.0	40.3	41.2	41.6	41.0	41.1
Not classified	20.6	12.7	20.6	50.9	45.1	38.3	49.1
Federal	17.8	20.5	21.1	18.1	19.4	20.0	20.2
Patient care	14.6	16.1	18.1	14.7	16.0	16.6	16.7
Other professional activity[3]	3.2	4.4	3.0	3.4	3.4	3.4	3.5
Inactive/unknown address	32.1	55.4	74.3	76.8	76.3	84.5	84.7
Doctors of osteopathy[4]	18.8	30.9	35.7	43.5	44.9	47.0	49.2

NA Not available. [1]Foreign medical graduates received their medical education in schools outside the United States and Canada. [2]Includes clinical fellows. [3]Includes medical teaching, administration, research, and other. [4]As of June 1. Total DOs. Data from American Osteopathic Association, Chicago, IL.

Source: Except as noted, American Medical Association, Chicago, IL, Physician Characteristics and Distribution in the U.S., annual (copyright). U.S. Department of Commerce, Bureau of the Census, *Statistical Abstract of the United States, 2004–2005* (Washington, DC: Government Printing Office, 2004), p. 107.

Fewer than 9 percent of private physicians are involved in general and family practice (U.S. Bureau of the Census 2004:107). The vast majority of doctors today are not engaged in primary care, but instead are pursuing their specialties. Specialists treat a particular part of the body of those who appear before them, often with the assistance of extremely expensive and complex technology that is more and more likely to be hospital based. This situation simply aggravates the artificial doctor shortage confronted by those whose needs first and foremost lie with primary care.

One consequence is that poor people use the health-care system less than they should, given their actual health needs. Unable to afford to pay private physicians for care, lacking adequate health insurance, and faced with a shortage of doctors oriented toward primary care, those with low incomes often put off contact with physicians until their conditions are seriously disabling. Many have no choice but to use the hospi-

tal emergency department in lieu of any other alternative, enduring long delays, assembly-line treatment by overworked and rushed staff, and lack of follow-up after treatment. The budgets of hospitals that serve the poor are severely strained; for example, voluntary (not-for-profit) hospitals provided an estimated $12 billion in uncompensated care in 1995 alone (Nicholson and Pauly 2001/2002). These "charity" costs are then often passed on to private insurance providers in the form of higher costs for services provided to the insured. The private insurance providers in turn raise their rates. In this way the plight of the poor is passed on to employers and employees who are already beleaguered by rising health-care costs.

Other barriers to quality care facing the poor include corruption. Some medical practitioners of few scruples have chosen to milk government programs like Medicaid for as much money as they can get, no matter what effect this has on their patients. Since physicians customarily

Low-income people often do not have ready access to affordable health care, and in many cases must use hospital emergency departments like the more affluent use their family doctor. There is, of course, likely to be an enormous difference between the quality of the care experiences involved. For many individuals and families there is no choice in the matter.

receive a fee for every service provided to a patient, and since the government pays for every fee submitted, abuse of the system has occurred. Some physicians have made a practice of radically escalating the number of patients they see daily, spending only a few cursory minutes with each. They have insisted on unnecessary return visits, ordered hosts of tests, and written prescriptions that were not needed. In effect, they have exploited the vulnerability and medical powerlessness of the poor for private gain. The tragedy is compounded when one realizes that many such patients have access to the health-care system only through these white-collar criminals.

Should they require hospitalization, those without insurance or with Medicaid and its limited payments to health-care providers face new barriers to decent care. Privately owned hospitals, an increasing percentage of which are turning into for-profit institutions, do not want such patients in their beds (Lindorff 1992). There is pressure within such settings to transfer them—even out of emergency departments—to public hospitals or the teaching hospitals affiliated with university medical schools.

In the case of public hospitals, staffing, facilities, and level of technology are prone to be in need of improvement because of severe financial strains in the face of rising costs. Quite a number of public hospitals have simply had to close down, unable to maintain acceptable standards on the budgets they had to work with. The level of care in public hospitals, then, is likely to be less adequate than in more fiscally prosperous private institutions (Bogdanich 1991; Halvorson 1993).

In the case of university-affiliated hospitals, poor patients frequently are informally segregated and treated by doctors in training, medical school graduates working extraordinarily long hours for little pay simply to gain experience with different types of cases. If a low-income person presents a case that is "interesting" or "unusual," he or she probably will get special attention. Otherwise this may not be the situation. In neither public nor university-affiliated hospitals is the low-income patient likely to receive the personalized care and expressions of concern expected from one's own private doctor by more affluent, appropriately insured people. Moreover, public and teaching hospitals at times do not even have room to treat additional patients. One survey of 277 such hospitals found that 40 percent had turned away ambulances because of overcrowding (Sherrill 1995).

Thus, the economically disadvantaged often must use hospitals (as a result of health conditions grown serious and lack of primary care physicians) that offer an unpleasant experience, to say the least. The world of health care for low-income people is often disjointed, confusing, frustrating, and alienating. Lacking transportation, in need of child care, unable to leave work for erratic medical appointments, and faced with the possibility of second-rate treatment, even people who know they should seek help are discouraged from doing so. The results appear in the sanitized government statistics that are made public each year. In the words of Karen Davis and Diane Rowland (1990:251), "It strains our image as a just and humane society when significant portions of the population endure avoidable pain, suffering, and even death because of an inability to pay for health care."

Ironically, while these avoidable outcomes continue without interruption, the U.S. health-care system has been evolving into what some call a **medical-industrial complex** (Barlett and Steele 2004; Lindorff 1992). Given the enormous amounts of money spent on health in the United States, more than $1.5 trillion in 2002 alone—six times as much as was being spent in 1980—it is understandable that astute businesspeople (including many doctors) would seek new ways to capitalize on this.

The elements of the medical-industrial complex include:

Increases in the number of investor-owned, for-profit private hospitals.

Growth in the size of firms that lease or own hospitals that are run as chains.

Expansion of for-profit operators of health-care plans.

Private investor and corporate expansion into nursing homes, home health services, and local surgical centers and clinics.

Movement by investor-owned hospitals into such areas as private health insurance.

In the United States hospitals originated to serve the health-care needs of the poor. Despite their expansion to serve the needs of others as well, for many years the nation's hospitals were typically nonprofit institutions, often run by local communities, religious groups, or civic organizations. For-profit hospitals had their inception in the 1960s; by the early 1990s a quarter of the 6,000 hospitals in the United States were being run for profit, a trend that continues (Lindorff 1992). This trend means more than the **"McDonaldization" of health care.** There has been a notable move toward concentrated corporate ownership in various sectors of the health-care industry, a trend that parallels what has historically occurred in other U.S. industries such as autos and steel. In 2004 alone the number of hospitals merged into ever-larger health-care organizations grew from 55 to 130, an increase of 136 percent. The amount of money devoted to hospital mergers and acquisitions is considerable: the $9.1 billion spent on such mergers in 2004 represented a quadrupling of the $2.3 billion spent the previous year (Japsen 2005).

For example, in little over a year, one hospital chain, Columbia/HCA Healthcare Corporation, grew from owning 30 hospitals to become the world's largest chain, owning 311 hospitals and 125 outpatient centers in a wide range of locations. This chain possesses half of all for-profit hospital capacity (Sherrill 1995). In another case, a large corporate operator of for-profit health maintenance organizations, or HMOs (an HMO is a type of health-care provider), merged with a major health insurance corporation to become the largest provider of health-care plans in the country. The merger between United Healthcare Corporation and Metrahealth created a company responsible for serving a combined pool of over 14 million health-care plan members across the nation. Many were employees enrolled through benefit packages provided by 40 of the very largest U.S. corporations and tens of thousands of smaller ones (Quint 1995).

Such concentration of control over health-care services by for-profit corporations holds dangers, not only for those whose health needs are already ill served but for many other people as well. Investor-owned health-care corporations like hospital chains and health-care plan operators are not charitable organizations; they are motivated by the same bottom-line profit goals as Ford Motor Company or R. J. Reynolds. Thus, there is a tendency for health-care corporations to avoid involvement in those services that are less profitable than others. For example, owners of for-profit hospitals often close emergency departments, which are relied on by the uninsured and poor, and expand those services that are most in demand in market locations where affluent, insured people are heavily concentrated.

Operators of multiple facilities sometimes simply close down hospitals or clinics they own in a community when they do not like the profit picture, even when such care facilities are desired by community members. Moreover, a Federal Trade Commission lawsuit against at least one merged health-care system alleges that the hospital raised its prices unfairly after its merger. This suggests that increasing hospital mergers mean fewer alternatives and therefore greater power of the existing hospitals to raise prices for higher rates of profit. And that makes health-care access increasingly expensive and inaccessible to more people.

There is no law that says for-profit firms must behave charitably toward the uninsured, the underinsured, or poor people who are dependent on Medicaid. Cost-benefit analyses are being used by operators of health-care plans to determine the kinds of health technology the firms will invest in, with those most likely to generate the most favorable monetary returns preferred. The danger here is that it may come to not matter what people's health needs are: The corporations will go where the money is. This is just the opposite direction from the philosophy of all other highly developed nations. Their health-care systems are aimed at serving the citizenry; people's health misfortunes are not treated as an occasion to enrich the privileged few.

The emergence of the medical-industrial complex has also thrown the traditional power of the medical profession into question. Long in a position of professional dominance and monopoly over medical practice, physicians are now being challenged by the **corporatization of medicine** (Freidson 1970; Starr 1982). More and more doctors have found themselves compelled to affiliate with a for-profit hospital or a corporate hospital chain in order to retain hospital privileges for the patients they treat. Those treating patients admitted to for-profit hospitals or enrolled in for-profit health-care plans often find their diagnostic and treatment decisions subject to cost-efficiency guidelines instituted by corporate management to enhance profit goals, guidelines that may come into conflict with high-quality health care.

One consequence of the corporatization of medicine is **managed care,** a system in which large health insurance companies impose strict limits on the types and amounts of services they will cover. The health insurance industry, which introduced managed care in the 1990s, rationalized this approach as a strategy to contain rising health-care costs. Notably, these costs have continued to skyrocket even under managed care, while insurers' profits have soared (Kleinke 2001). Under managed care, insurance firms make medical decisions based not on health and survival needs but rather on profit generation concerns.

While managed care has clearly helped keep insurance firms profitable, critics argue that it has had a serious negative effect on people's access to critical health care. For example, patients may be denied important diagnostic tests because insurance companies object to their expense. Likewise, patients are often faced with leaving the hospital too soon after treatment, including surgery, because insurance firms strictly limit the number of days they will pay for. Doctors and hospitals must comply with the demands and limits of insurance companies in order to be compensated or reimbursed for the costs they incur for providing care. Doctors who object to what they believe is inadequate medical care imposed by these restrictions often find they have to spend valuable time arguing with—and often losing to—insurance representatives who are not themselves health-care practitioners.

Recently, controversy has arisen in response to policies by operators of health-care plans that require physicians to abide by strict rules for the length of hospital stays. The purpose is to cut unnecessary hospital operating expenses, but many people are ordered home who never should have been released from care. Mothers and their newborn babies—subject to what have been called **drive-through deliveries** as hospitals seek to cut back on use of maternity rooms that cost $1,000 per day to operate—are among the many patients who have had to be readmitted after early release, suffering from sometimes severe complications (Begley 1995).

Dr. Arnold S. Relman of the *New England Journal of Medicine* has described the effects of the corporatization of medicine on doctors:

There's never been a time in the history of American medicine when the independence and autonomy of medical practitioners was as uncertain as it is now. I think that in this process businessmen and their agents will begin to exercise unprecedented control over the allocation of medical resources. (Cf. Eckholm 1994:4, 34)

Dr. Relman may have been speaking in understatement, for it appears that the exercise of unprecedented control over our health care by people who have never attended medical school is well under way. In response, many doctors have sought to hitch a ride on the profit-maximization drive associated with the corporatization of medicine, increasing their own private investments in and ownership ties to the medical-industrial complex. Increasingly, groups of physicians are themselves incorporating and establishing for-profit hospitals and clinics. Whether and how corporatization can bring more equity into the U.S. health-care system remains to be seen. Existing trends are not at all promising in this regard.

AIDS and Health Care

Since 1981, when the first cases were diagnosed, people in the United States and elsewhere around the world have come to fear a new deadly infectious disease: AIDS (acquired immune deficiency syndrome). Although the United States leads all other nations in the number of officially documented cases, AIDS is

Family members visit and assist a man with AIDS who is fortunate to be in a hospice setting devoted to caring for people who are terminally ill. Many other persons dying from AIDS cannot access such specialized treatment because of its costs or the shortage of beds. The AIDS epidemic is serving to underscore some of the fundamental weaknesses and limitations of our system of health care.

(1963–1973). More than seven times as many people have died because of AIDS.

In the United States, AIDS is the ninth-leading cause of death overall and the fifth-leading cause of death for people between ages 25 and 44 (www.kff.org). Unchecked, this epidemic could kill millions in the United States. Outside of this country, the World Health Organization estimates that some 36 million people already have contracted AIDS, over half of whom have died; tens of millions more are likely to die from AIDS as it spreads everywhere across the globe. The deadly disease is now spreading rapidly in Asia, Africa, and Latin America—regions where the majority of the world's population resides. Almost half of all adults living with HIV/AIDS globally are women (www.who.int).

proving to be most devastating to populations in underdeveloped nations (Global AIDS Action Network 2002). From 1981 to 2002, almost 850,000 cases of AIDS were diagnosed in the United States, almost 44,000 in 2002 alone (U.S. Bureau of the Census 2004:121). At the current rate at which new AIDS cases are being reported, by the time this text is in the hands of users, there will likely be over a million known cases in the United States. The spread of AIDS has justifiably been described as epidemic (Hamilton 1995).

The epidemic is a deadly one. From 1943 to 1956 the United States was swept by a polio epidemic that killed 22,000 people. Already, between 1981 and 2000, over 20 times as many people in the United States—more than 448,000 individuals—have died as a consequence of AIDS (www.cdc.gov). Over 58,000 U.S. military personnel were killed in the Vietnam war

As most people in the United States now know, AIDS is spread by the human immunodeficiency virus (HIV) (Auerbach et al. 1994). This virus is readily transmittable from person to person through intimate sexual contact, through the sharing of needles by drug users, and less commonly through blood transfusions. Pregnant women who are infected with HIV may pass it on to the fetus, and there are growing numbers of "AIDS babies" being born in U.S. hospitals. The virus can be carried unknowingly and transmitted to others without any party being aware. The symptoms of AIDS often do not appear until five or more years after HIV is passed on. People with the virus may be perfectly healthy until these symptoms begin to occur. A person with HIV does not have

AIDS, but it is believed that all such persons will eventually develop AIDS and die because of it.

The symptoms of AIDS include chronic fatigue, fevers, unexplained weight loss, diarrhea, enlarged lymph nodes, coughs and sore throat, easy bruising, and unusual skin bumps and blotches. Full-blown cases of AIDS are recognized as such when it becomes apparent that a person's natural ability to fight off disease and infection has broken down. Those with AIDS become susceptible to diseases that most people simply never get. The majority of AIDS patients contract such rare illnesses as *Pneumocystis carinii* pneumonia, a parasitic infection of the lungs, or Kaposi's sarcoma, a type of cancer.

The AIDS virus is currently carried by more than 1.5 million people in the United States and over 36 million in other countries (www.kff.org; www.who.int). In the absence of nationwide programs to screen for HIV infection, these figures are speculative. But the number of new AIDS cases that are appearing each year both in the United States and abroad makes scientists apprehensive that they may be underestimating the number of persons who have become infected with HIV.

As the death toll has grown, the U.S. government has been putting increasing amounts of money into research related to AIDS. Unfortunately, this occurred only after a good deal of foot-dragging and delay on the part of federal officials, who resisted acknowledging there was a serious health problem meriting national concern (Shilts 1987).

Of the 850,000 people in the United States who were diagnosed with AIDS between 1981 and 2002, most are men who have had sexual relations with other men. Primarily these are persons whose sexual orientation is either homosexual or bisexual. The rate of spread of HIV infection has slowed among members of this group, largely because of self-imposed changes in sex practices and safer-sex precautions that have substantially reduced the risk of HIV transmission.

The second major group in which AIDS cases occur with frequency is in need of much more intervention and self-policing. This group is made up of drug users, particularly those users of cocaine and heroin who share needles with one another, and users of crack cocaine who engage in unprotected sex in return for the drug or money to buy it (see Chapter 17, "Substance Abuse"). The vast majority of new cases of HIV infection diagnosed in 2003, after men who had sexual relations with other men, were heterosexual drug users, their sex partners, and their newborn children (www.cdc.gov). Despite a great deal of publicity about the need to engage in safer sex practices, and the street-level needle-exchange programs that now operate in over 40 U.S. cities to help discourage needle sharing, their behaviors keep many drug users at extremely high risk for HIV infection (Des Jarlais and Friedman 1994; U.S. Conference of Mayors 1994).

Previous involvement in drug use and needle sharing helps to account for the exceptionally high rates of HIV infection, AIDS, and deaths resulting from AIDS among both men and women incarcerated in U.S. federal and state prisons. Once in prison, men's risk factor for HIV infection is heightened by the fact that in many prison settings unsanctioned, high-risk, male-to-male sex acts among heterosexual inmates are rampant. In 2001 almost 2 percent of state and federal prisoners were found to be infected with the HIV virus, and of these, almost one-fourth had confirmed AIDS. Of those who died in prison in 2001, 8 percent had AIDS (www.ojp.usdoj.gov). Most people infected with HIV leave prison and return to the general population when their terms are completed, opening up the possibility of further transmissions of the virus.

Some people hold to the stereotype that AIDS is a "gay disease." This view ignores an important reality that should by now be apparent: Heterosexuals are greatly at risk. The rate at which new AIDS cases are being diagnosed among heterosexuals is now identical to the rate for gay people. In most cases the infected heterosexual is an intravenous drug user, has had sexual contact with such a user, or is the child of a user. Families in which someone uses intravenous drugs have been hard hit. Men who patronize drug-using prostitutes are vulnerable to HIV infection, but at even more risk are the prostitutes themselves. Most strikingly, women, particularly women of color, are among the fastest-growing group infected with the HIV virus: By 2003 African American women accounted for 67 percent of all new AIDS diagnoses and Latinas another 16 percent (www.kff.org).

In other instances of heterosexual transmission, no drug use may be involved. For example, almost one-fifth of the nation's 21,000 hemophiliacs are infected with HIV, as are many other people who received blood (e.g., during surgery) before the United States' blood supply began to be screened for HIV in the 1980s. Some of these persons have unknowingly passed on the virus to heterosexual partners or to children to whom they gave birth. In other non-drug-related transmission routes, bisexual males have passed HIV on during contact with female sex partners. The virus has similarly been transmitted during sexual assaults, including date and acquaintance rapes.

Once infected with HIV, persons can unknowingly contribute to expanding the spread of infection within the heterosexual population. Men who patronize prostitutes can unwittingly bring HIV back to their wives, girlfriends, or casual sex partners. Women unknowingly infected through sex with bisexual men, or as a consequence of sexual assaults, can infect male sex partners. In short, HIV is loose in the general population and AIDS is not a "gay disease." When two people have sex today, they literally expose themselves to an HIV risk from every previous sexual encounter their partner has had,

heterosexual or otherwise; hence, the crucial importance of following safer sex practices every time.

The AIDS epidemic has raised significant issues central to our concern with health care. In some cases the issues are dividing the medical community. For example, some doctors are unwilling to work with AIDS patients, thus denying health care to people who desperately need it. This of course is contrary to the professional ethics that we expect physicians to heed (Daniels 1995).

Some 80 to 90 percent of medical education to which physicians are exposed as students is taxpayer financed. Many would ask, "Is not something owed the public in return?" In contrast, those who have chosen to treat and minister to people with AIDS confront the problem of "burnout" from the stress and emotional drain of knowing one's efforts are ultimately useless and watching these predominantly young members of society prematurely die. Both the issue of "freedom not to treat" and that of dealing with burnout are likely to grow ever more central as the number of AIDS patients escalates and the health-care system is put under increasing pressure to respond.

But an even larger concern should be the kind of response people with AIDS often receive from a system organized around the principle of pay as you go. About 40 percent of the persons treated for AIDS have had private health insurance, and another 40 percent have had to seek help under Medicaid. Twenty percent—a much higher proportion than is true of adults in the general population—have been uninsured. Thus, 60 percent of AIDS patients have had limited or no assistance in paying their medical bills, which can be very substantial. Consequently, most have had to rely on the charity of public hospitals. With AIDS cases growing at a rapid rate, particularly among nonaffluent segments of the population such as inner-city drug abusers, the demands on such institutions are bound to grow.

How public hospitals will find the money, staff, and other resources to meet these demands is not known. Unless they receive outside assistance, or other types of hospitals agree to share the burden, public hospitals in areas in which AIDS cases are highly concentrated (New York and California, for instance) will be faced with irresolvable fiscal crises. This is all aside from the issue of the quality of care AIDS patients can reasonably expect in such hard-pressed surroundings.

Private health insurance providers have not been helping the situation. Insurance companies have been avoiding coverage of persons who have AIDS or who are infected with HIV. There is now no way they can avoid covering workers whose employers include them in group insurance policies, but insurance companies have been able to do so in the case of those applying for individual policies. In some cases applicants have had to take tests for the presence of HIV, answer invasive personal questions on applications about their lifestyles and living arrangements, or have a physician produce testimony about their health and likelihood of being at risk. Similarly, employers who "self-insure" their workers—that is, pay their medical bills—may rule out paying for AIDS if they wish. The Americans with Disabilities Act of 1990 may make it more difficult for insurance companies to discriminate against those with HIV or AIDS, but the insurance coverage protections provided by the act remain unclear and subject to contestation by the companies.

Thus, the private sector has tried to get of the health-care system when it comes to AIDS, in sharp contrast to other deadly diseases. Persons who get too sick to work because they are debilitated by AIDS-related diseases lose their health insurance when they leave their jobs. Given the posture of private insurance providers, they find it difficult to purchase individual policies (assuming they can afford them, given unemployment) to help meet their medical expenses. They must then join the ranks of the uninsured or seek eligibility for Medicaid.

(It is possible for AIDS patients to qualify as disabled and obtain assistance under Medicare, but the two-year waiting period for eligibility means they may die first.)

People who want assistance from Medicaid must, as we have seen, be indigent. Given what we have said about the income limits that govern eligibility for Medicaid coverage, an AIDS patient must be almost destitute to take advantage of the program. Many are. Many more will be forced into destitution as they exhaust their savings and assets in response to requests that they pay their bills before they die.

Ironically, it may well be that the tragedy of AIDS will contribute to a crisis in health-care delivery that will cause the needed reassessment of the entire system. The handling of AIDS cases thus far appears to underscore the weaknesses in the system to which we alluded earlier, weaknesses that affect tens of millions of people. Norman Daniels (1995:153), who analyzes the ethics of health care, describes the situation in this way:

HIV patients suffer special forms of discrimination. Nevertheless, the main obstacles to the fair treatment of HIV patients are obstacles any of us might have to overcome because of the way our health care system is designed. All of us potentially face exclusion from insurance because of risk, loss of insurance coverage with job loss or job change, maldistribution of appropriate providers, and inadequate coverage for home care. . . . A system that corrected these and other problems we all risk having to confront would also go a long way toward ensuring fair treatment for HIV patients.

If the need to deal with the AIDS epidemic does not alone force a reassessment of the U.S. health-care system, the reassessment may be pushed along by another growing phenomenon, the "graying of America." The changing age composition of our population, involving an ever increasing percentage of persons age 65 and older, promises to make the inadequacies of the U.S. health-care system even more blatant than at present.

Health Care for Our Elders

In Chapter 10, "Ageism," we dwelt at length with the problems facing many elders in the United States. By and large they are a healthy lot and remain so until their final years. Many do, however, frequently suffer various chronic problems that limit their range of activities. This is particularly true for elderly at the lower income levels. Such chronic problems include heart conditions, arthritis and rheumatism, hypertension, and impairments of the lower extremities and hips. Visual and hearing problems are also common. Treating all these conditions places demands on the U.S. health-care system. These demands are expected to dramatically increase, given the projected growth in the 65-and-older population.

The situation will likely be exacerbated by yet another epidemic, one affecting our elders. This is Alzheimer's disease, now the fourth-leading cause of death in this country after heart disease, cancer, and strokes. As mentioned in Chapter 10, Alzheimer's involves the degeneration of the brain. Brain cells are progressively destroyed, memory loss occurs, personality changes and socially inappropriate behaviors are exhibited, cognitive processes are adversely affected, physical functioning declines, and finally there is death. Over 100,000 people are dying from this epidemic annually at this point, succumbing after anywhere from 3 to 20 years of deterioration and decline. There is no cure for the disease; scientists do not know what causes it.

Recent controversies have erupted over stem-cell research, which many scientists believe holds promising potential for unlocking the mysteries of and treatments for Alzheimer's as well as other as-yet incurable diseases. However, fierce debates over whether or not to allow this research to occur are bound up with abortion politics and bioethical concerns about the use of fetal tissue. Pressures are building from scientists in universities and the families of the afflicted (most notably former President Ronald Reagan's widow, Nancy Reagan) calling for the research to be allowed, and some religious leaders and antiabortion activists arguing against it.

Alzheimer's disease went unrecognized until the 1970s. Until the late 1980s it was thought to affect no more than 1.5 million to 2 million older people in the United States. However, researchers found that some 4 million elders—10 percent of those 65 and older, and 50 percent of those 85 and older—may have Alzheimer's (National Institute on Aging 2003; U.S. Congress, House 1992a). More and more people are reaching and passing age 65, and the size of the 85-and-older population is growing rapidly. Given current projections on the age composition of the U.S. population, it is estimated there will be 16 million Alzheimer's patients to care for in the year 2050 (www.alz.org).

Most people with this disease live and are cared for at home, but perhaps 30 percent must be cared for in hospitals and nursing homes; indeed, "half of all nursing home residents have Alzheimer's disease or a related disorder" (www.alz.org). There is a serious shortage of quality affordable care settings, which is predicted to reach crisis proportions in the future. Indeed, were so many Alzheimer's patients not being cared for by family members, the crisis would be overwhelming right now. As we shall see, one of the reasons families are assuming responsibility to such an extent is not only the shortage of nursing homes but their high cost and the failure of health insurance plans to cover the kind of long-term care that chronic sufferers of the disease require. Nonetheless, the costs of care even today are enormous. More than $100 billion a year is spent to care for persons with Alzheimer's disease, almost 1 in 10 of the health dollars spent in the United States, and the costs are moving higher rapidly (www.alz.org).

Many of those providing care in the home are themselves elderly, and the effort is a source of both physical and emotional strain. It is now believed that stress from caring for Alzheimer's patients actually makes caregivers more vulnerable than usual to infectious diseases. Since these people may not be in the best of health in all cases anyway, their own demise may be hastened. Hence, the growing numbers of elderly in need of long-term care may tragically produce new victims—those who sacrifice to help them. This multiplicative effect puts even more pressure and strain on the U.S. health-care system than would be the case if the caregivers had more in the way of respite and support.

People in the United States age 65 and older are eligible for Medicare, but we have already seen that coverage is restricted and those in need of health care are required to pay for certain services either wholly or in part. Medicare does not cover long-term, chronic-care costs such as those necessary to care for people with Alzheimer's disease in their homes ($18,000 to $20,000 per year) or in nursing home settings ($42,000 to $70,000 per year, on average) (www.alz.org). On the other hand, Medicaid, once again, requires that recipients of assistance be indigent. As in the case of AIDS patients, getting care for the elderly may require that they exhaust all their assets first, then sink into poverty and reliance on public hospitals and nursing homes catering to poor people. Again, the issue of the quality of care becomes pertinent. As is true throughout much of the health-care system, you get what you are able to pay for.

How will we deal with the growing numbers of our elders in need of health care now and in the years ahead? Will older people (including us) be left to struggle within a pay-as-you-go system that allows some people to fall through the cracks altogether and leaves tens of millions dependent on charity care? Or will we reassess our health-care system and bring it more into line with what other developed nations are doing (Binstock 1993)? The outcome of debates around health-care reform will determine the answers to these questions.

Alternatives for the Future

As the limitations of the U.S. health-care system have become ever more evident, and as millions of people's health status and ability to pay for care have become increasingly jeopardized by this system, pressures for change have mounted. Public opinion polls indicate that the vast majority of people in the United States are dissatisfied with the existing system and are willing to support fundamental changes.

There is, however, much confusion over what kinds of changes are desirable and possible. We would do well by more closely studying what other developed nations have done (Graig 1999). They have generally followed one of two alternative models, both with success: either (1) a system of universal health insurance or (2) a national health-care delivery system.

Universal health insurance is the most common route taken by other highly developed nations—from Japan to Canada. Under such a system all of society's members are covered by a comprehensive program of health insurance. The cost of the insurance is typically paid for by some combination of taxes and contributions by employers and employees (for those working). Health-care providers—doctors' offices, clinics, and hospitals—attend to people's needs and then bill the universal health insurance system, which is run by or under the direct supervision of government. Sometimes universal health insurance is called a "single-payer" system, since health-care providers all send their bills to one official authority for payment.

Under universal health insurance all citizens have the charges for needed health care paid on their behalf automatically. There are no uninsured men, women, or children. Coverage is not tied to employment status, income, age, or place of residence. There are no hassles over creditworthiness or past due bills. Nor are there persons whose insurance coverage is more lavish than that of others. Whether you are affluent or poor, young or old, suffering from allergies or AIDS, you are guaranteed the same range of services and quality of treatment from the health-care system. Costly private health insurance plans, such as those currently sold by the United States' 1,500 for-profit health insurance companies to employers and individuals, would become history under a universal health insurance system.

The success of a universal health insurance system not only rests on the extension of equal coverage and services to everyone but also requires aggressive measures by government to keep health-care expenditures (and thus taxes and employer/employee contributions) down. Government has to be vigilant and curb excessive prices and fees, such as those U.S. health-care providers charge patients and insurers to cover purchase and use of equipment, goods, and services.

In the United States, government would have to combat unnecessary duplication, waste, fraud and bill-padding, redundant administrative costs, and price gouging—practices that often arise when uncontrolled private profiteering from government expenditures is allowed to go on, such as we have seen in the aerospace-defense industry. Government would also have to find ways to encourage the expansion of preventive and primary care in order to offset a system that is now too heavily weighted toward waiting for illnesses to occur and use of medical specialists. But with appropriate regulatory controls and incentives in place, the United States could have a health-care system like that of other nations, one that is simultaneously affordable and dramatically more attentive to the health status of the least affluent of its citizens.

A more radical alternative, and perhaps the one that is most alien to our current system, is a national health-care delivery system or **national health service.** As in Great Britain, health-care workers (including doctors) become public employees. Hospitals and clinics are akin to government institutions. In effect, the provision of health-care services is the direct responsibility of government and is not left to the whims of the private economic marketplace and its profit-seeking actors. Medical resources are directed where they are needed, and access to health care for citizens of all socioeconomic classes is guaranteed.

As can be imagined, the idea of a national health service (or "socialized medicine," as some critics call it with derision) draws intense opposition from the medical profession in the United States. Indeed, no sector of the U.S. medical-industrial complex welcomes what would amount to a government takeover of much of the health-care system. Because the other alternative, a universal health insurance system, provides leeway for physicians to remain private entrepreneurs, and for hospitals and other health-care providers to operate for profit, one would think that this is the direction in which the United States is likely to go.

A political struggle over health-care reform erupted full-scale in 1993 when President Bill Clinton's administration presented specific proposals for health-care reform, anticipated since his 1992 presidential campaign (*Newsweek* 1993a, 1993b). The terms of debate rapidly reflected the self-interests of for-profit actors in the medical-industrial complex. People's pressing health-care needs took a backseat in the debate (Weissert and Weissert 2002).

In 1994 the Republican-dominated U.S. Congress essentially rejected the Democratic administration's proposed reforms, which were certainly far more moderate and called for far fewer changes in the status quo than either of the two models just described (Daniels 1995). These reforms called for a system of "managed competition" in which competing health-care providers would vie for the rights to enroll people in each state. States could opt to install single-payer plans that they would administer. Employers and their employees would be required to participate, and people without insurance would be brought into a tax-subsidized basic health-care plan. Government would assume a greater role than it has at present in overseeing health care.

The nation's major health insurance corporations and other powerful business groups both in and outside of the medical-industrial complex helped to shape thinking about the Clinton proposals through a massive advertising and lobbying campaign. In particular, the corporate sector was unwilling to accede powers to government that would allow it to get substantially more involved in controlling costs, regulating health-care delivery policies, or otherwise "interfering" with the free workings of the marketplace when it comes to health care (Barlett and Steele 2004).

The debate over health-care reform has continued, becoming ever more caught up in narrow partisan politics and behind-the-scenes maneuvers by corporate interests seeking to either prevent change or derive special benefits from any departures from the present system. Although some reforms to address the most glaring deficiencies of the existing system are likely to occur, it will take a strong groundswell of nationwide grassroots political activism against entrenched interests if the United States is to ever have a health-care system that is on a par with that provided by other developed nations.

Summary

The U.S. health-care system falls far short of any imaginable ideal. It serves lower-income people and members of racial minorities less well than other segments of the population, as indicated by their second-class health status. When epidemics occur, as in the case of AIDS and Alzheimer's disease, the health-care system is incapable of responding in a way that would provide high-quality, affordable care to all in need. The health-care system is, in short, a feature of the way in which we have organized our society that does the reverse of what we ask it to do: It harms people. Despite the enormous sums we lavish on it each year, it limits people's life chances. Practically no other macro problem cries out so much for change.

Key Terms

Corporatization of medicine 418
Drive-through deliveries 419
Infant mortality rate 398
Life expectancy 397
Managed care 419

"McDonaldization" of health care 417
Medical-industrial complex 417
National health service 426
Universal health insurance 425

Discussion Questions

1. Consider the on-the-job health risks to which office-bound professionals (e.g., business executives, engineers, lawyers, accountants) are likely to be exposed. How do these risks differ from those faced by adults you know who work in blue-collar, manual jobs?

2. Forty-five million people in the United States, including many young people, lack any type of health insurance. Assume you are in this group. Make inquiries to find out how much an insurance company would charge you annually for an individual policy that would provide you with comprehensive medical care and hospitalization coverage.

3. While the U.S. population has many health-care needs, physicians are permitted to choose specialties that leave some needs poorly addressed. What arguments could be made for and against greater public control over (a) the overall supply of physicians and (b) the specialty areas in which they are permitted to practice?

4. Should the United States adopt some form of national health-care plan? If not, why not? If so, what do you think its most prominent features should be?

5. Physicians are pretty much free to choose not to treat certain categories of patients, for example, people with AIDS or chronically ill elders. What arguments might be made on behalf of this situation? What do you think of these arguments?

6. The AIDS virus is currently carried by more than 1.5 million people in the United States. At present there is no national program of screening for HIV infection. Should there be such a program? Should it be mandatory? What should be done with the knowledge when certain individuals test positive for the virus? Why?

Suggested Readings

Barlett, Donald L., and James B. Steele. *Critical Condition: How Health Care in America Became Big Business—and Bad Medicine* (New York: Doubleday, 2004).
A critical assessment with a wide array of research on the U.S. health-care system.

Conrad, Peter, ed. *The Sociology of Health and Illness.* 6th ed. (New York: Worth Publishers, 2000).
Readings on health-care issues from a critical sociological perspective, including the impact of class and racial inequality on health care.

Graig, Laurene A. *Health of Nations: An International Perspective on U.S. Health Care Reform.* 3rd ed. (Washington, DC: Congressional Quarterly Books, 1999).
A comparative analysis of health-care systems in six industrialized nations.

Lee, Phillip R., and Carroll L. Estes, eds. *The Nation's Health.* 7th ed. (Boston: Jones and Bartlett, 2003).
A broad overview of issues and controversies surrounding the U.S. health-care system and recent proposals for reform.

Special attention and support should be freely given to troubled or struggling families and their members, including single-parent households. The bases for violence and abuse within families of all types should be absent.

Sociologists have traditionally viewed the family as a multifunction unit, central to the stability and continuity of human society. Among its functions are economic production, intimacy and nurturance, sexual reproduction, and socialization of the young. Viewed in the abstract, the family may be seen as a social collectivity that protects and aids the individual in confronting the often challenging and sometimes stressful demands of daily life.

In recent decades the nature of the family in the United States has been undergoing change, and a variety of problems related to the family have emerged. There have been significant increases in premarital births and in the numbers of unwed teenage mothers. Rates of marital dissolution also have risen sharply, thus adding to the unprecedented numbers of single-parent households. Researchers have uncovered an unexpectedly high volume of violent behavior within families, most notably in the form of spouse or partner abuse as well as violence and sexual abuse directed at children. One response of children to discord and victimization in the home has been to flee—to become runaways. There are also indications that many children have become "pushouts," being made to leave home.

In this chapter we examine these family-related problems. Our attention focuses on their nature as well as on their extent, causes, and consequences. We begin by looking at premarital births and single teenage mothers.

Premarital Births and Teenage Motherhood

The typical image that comes to mind when we hear the term *family* is likely to be mother, father, and children living together in a household. This image belies the reality of what has been taking place in the United States in recent decades, particularly the surge in the percentage of families living in single-parent households. Although much of the change in family composition has

431

occurred as a consequence of increased rates of divorce (a topic addressed later in this chapter), increasing numbers of families *begin* with a single parent.

In 2002 some 4 million births were recorded in the United States. As Table 14.1 indicates, 34 percent were to unmarried mothers, as compared with 10.7 percent in 1970. The birthrate to unmarried women between 1980 and 1990 alone increased by 50.7 percent, with women in their 20s and 30s accounting for much of the increase (U.S. Bureau of the Census 2004:65). Seventy-eight percent of births to teenaged women occur outside of marriage; teenagers account for almost one-third of all unmarried births (Guttmacher 1999). While that is a substantial decline from 1970, when teenagers accounted for half of all **nonmarital births** in the United States, the number remains very high. But numbers aside, there are many critical issues to consider regarding the overall well-being of teen mothers and their children.

Before assessing these issues we might ask why premarital birthrates are so high, especially among teenagers. A variety of factors seem to be at work. The age of beginning menstruation (and thus susceptibility to becoming pregnant) has been going down over the years, presumably because of overall improvements in the U.S. population's nutrition and health. Thus, the size of the group of young persons at risk for pregnancy has grown.

Perhaps more important is the fact that the percentage of teenagers who are sexually active has risen by more than 60 percent over the past 20 years. The data available suggest that 16 is now the average age for a youth's first experience with sexual intercourse, which means many teens begin even earlier. The likelihood of having intercourse has been increasing at all age levels during the teen years, so that in 1995, 68 percent of teenage males and 65 percent of teenage females had intercourse by the time they turned 18 (Guttmacher 1999). Teens are likely to engage in sexual intercourse based on

the number of "risk factors" in their lives. Risk factors for both females and males include alcohol use, having a boyfriend or girlfriend, poor parental monitoring, and permissive parental sexual values. Other factors associated with early sexual activity include experiences of sexual abuse, poor school performance, and a feeling of limited future economic opportunities (Small and Luster 1994).

Technology has, of course, provided both males and females with means of pregnancy prevention. One would expect unmarried young people to take advantage of birth control measures, a few of which are highly effective, to reduce the risk of premarital pregnancy. Too often, however, they do not do so. As recently as 1995 only 78 percent of sexually active teens were using some form of contraceptive. Teens are at great risk for pregnancy at their first experience with intercourse, when those who do not use birth control are four times more likely to become pregnant than those who do. The Allen Guttmacher Institute (1999) estimates that teens who do not use contraception have a 90 percent chance of becoming pregnant within one year.

If technology to prevent pregnancy is widely available, why is it so underutilized? The reasons are many (Zelnick and Kantner 1979). There is still widespread lack of knowledge and misinformation regarding birth control measures and the conditions under which pregnancy may occur. Much of this ignorance stems from the paucity of education on these matters provided to young people, whether by parents, schools, or religious institutions. Sex education (but particularly education in birth control practices) remains a controversial subject in U.S. society, and among the schools that include it in the curriculum there is great variation in what is taught. Adults who oppose sex education in schools often express fears that young people will be encouraged into premature sexual activity by such information.

Yet data consistently demonstrate that a high percentage of teenagers are already sexually

Table 14.1	Births to Unmarried Women, by Race of Child and Age of Mother, 1970–2002				
Race of child and age of mother	1970	1980	1985	1990	2002
Number (1,000)					
Total live births*	**399**	**666**	**828**	**1,165**	**1,366**
White	175	320	433	647	904
Black	215	326	366	473	405
Under 15 years old	10	9	9	11	7
15 to 19 years old	190	263	271	350	340
20 to 24 years old	127	237	300	404	528
25 to 29 years old	41	100	152	230	268
30 to 34 years old	19	41	67	118	139
35 years old and over	12	16	28	53	83
Percent distribution					
Total*	**100.0**	**100.0**	**100.0**	**100.0**	**100.0**
White	43.9	48.1	52.3	55.6	66.2
Black	54.0	48.9	44.1	40.6	29.6
Under 15 years	2.4	1.4	1.1	0.9	0.5
15 to 19 years	47.8	39.5	32.7	30.0	24.9
20 to 24 years	31.8	35.6	36.3	34.7	38.6
25 to 29 years	10.2	15.0	18.4	19.7	19.7
30 to 34 years	4.8	6.2	8.1	10.1	10.2
35 years and over	3.1	2.4	3.4	4.5	6.1
As percentage of all births in racial groups					
Total*	**10.7**	**18.4**	**22.0**	**28.0**	**34.0**
White	5.7	11.0	14.5	20.1	28.5
Black	37.6	55.2	60.1	65.2	68.2
Birth rate[†]					
Total*[‡]	**26.4**	**29.4**	**32.8**	**43.8**	**43.7**
White[‡]	13.9	17.6	21.8	31.8	38.9
Black[‡]	95.5	82.9	79.0	93.9	66.2
15 to 19 years	22.4	27.6	31.4	42.5	35.4
20 to 24 years	38.4	40.9	46.5	65.1	70.5
25 to 29 years	37.0	34.0	39.9	56.0	61.5
30 to 34 years	27.1	21.1	25.2	37.6	40.8

*Includes other races not shown separately.
[†]Rate per 1,000 unmarried women (never-married, widowed, and divorced) estimated as of July 1.
[‡]Covers women aged 15 to 44 years.

Source: U.S. Department of Commerce, Bureau of the Census, *Statistical Abstract of the United States, 1995* (Washington, DC: U.S. Government Printing Office, 1995), p. 77; U.S. Department of Commerce, Bureau of the Census, *Statistical Abstract of the United States, 2003* (Washington, DC: U.S. Government Printing Office, 2004), p. 65.

active. Failure to combat lack of knowledge and misinformation thus allows the premarital pregnancy rate to remain high. Researchers have found that sex education does not increase the rate of those having intercourse but that it does increase the probability that contraceptives will be used by sexually active teenagers (Grunseit et al. 1997). Yet empirical data along these lines are typically not acknowledged by those who see sex education as contributing to or promoting teenage sexual activity and the pregnancies that so often follow.

Although lack of knowledge and misinformation may contribute to high premarital pregnancy rates, other personal and social factors can get in the way of the utilization of effective birth control measures. Intercourse may occur in an unplanned way, perhaps without original intention. It may also be unplanned in the context of what has been called **acquaintance rape** or **date rape,** wherein the teenage female is sexually coerced or abused, often while under the influence of alcohol or drugs.

As mentioned earlier, harmful life experiences such as sexual abuse are associated with becoming sexually active and at risk for pregnancy while a teenager. In a study of 535 young women who became pregnant as adolescents, researchers found that two-thirds had previously been sexually abused, usually by family members or family friends and acquaintances. Sexually abused teenagers begin engaging in intercourse earlier than other teens, are more likely to use drugs and alcohol, and are less likely to practice birth control (Boyer and Fine 1992).

Teenage boys are not always the ones involved in the sexual activity that produces teen pregnancies. Adult males bear a major responsibility. Recent research indicates that the younger the pregnant teen, the more likely she has been impregnated by someone older, most likely an adult. About one-fifth of the babies born to teenage mothers are fathered by adults who, in many cases, are breaking state laws on statutory rape (Guttmacher 1999). A California study found that two-thirds of the fathers of the 47,000 babies born to high school–age teenagers in that state in 1993 were older than high schoolers (Charen 1995).

Educator with teens discussing sex and reproduction.

Teen pregnancies sometimes occur because persons who are struggling over guilt about becoming sexually active may avoid seeking out birth control measures, thinking that to do so is to make a concrete commitment to future activity. There may be concern, too, over comfort or side effects of some contraceptives. A lack of communication may occur between sexual partners over who is responsible for protection. For some teenagers, obtaining and using contraceptives may appear inconvenient, embarrassing, or dangerous (if parents find out). In addition, some simply cannot afford adequate contraceptive measures (Nathanson 1991).

Finally, some teenagers *want* to get pregnant—in the hope of drawing the father into marriage or of demonstrating maturity and arrival into "adulthood" or out of a need to have someone to love and who will give love in return (Adler and Tschann 1993; Jacobs 1994; Musick 1993).

It is important to note that failure to use contraceptives effectively has implications for the rates of abortion among young females (Torres and Forrest 1988). In 1996 1,365,700 legal abortions were reported to government statistical agencies. (The actual rate of abortion may be 10 to 20 percent higher.) One-fifth of these abortions occurred in the under-20 age group. Most persons having abortions are unmarried (Guttmacher 1999; http://womenissues .about.com).

Thus far we have delayed discussion of the consequences of premarital births and teenage motherhood. Health implications are the first of many concerns. Serious health problems are found among many young mothers and their infants. Young mothers may face complications giving birth. Newborn children of teenage mothers often have low birth weights and a higher than average incidence of serious birth defects. Infant mortality rates are also high among children born to very young mothers. But it is not simply the biological age of young mothers that contributes to health risks. Rather, health problems are exacerbated by the fact that a disproportionate percentage of premarital births occur among teenagers from low-income households.

The lack of adequate or accessible health services for the poor and near-poor (see Chapter 13) means that young people often go without proper prenatal care. Economic deprivation frequently has negative effects on dietary and nutritional practices important to the health of the mother and unborn child. Postnatal and "well-baby" care may also not be readily available or affordable. Low-income youth overall have the least ready access to sex education and effective contraceptive measures and are the least able to afford abortions.

Aside from health problems, teenage pregnancy commonly restricts the life chances of mother and child in other ways. Although public educational institutions cannot refuse to serve pregnant unwed girls of eligible school age, many teenagers have already quit school before they become pregnant. Some leave upon the births of their children as they face the demands of child care and/or the need for some kind of employment. Once they drop out of school, they are unlikely to return and earn their diplomas, thus reducing the likelihood of obtaining jobs that provide adequate pay and security. With this process under way, the probability of living in poverty or near-poverty is very high (Maynard 1996).

Consequently, the children of such unions are likely to suffer the often harsh demands of low-income life. Marriage to a child's father is often not an option for a teenage mother, one reason being that low-income teenage couples typically cannot afford to set up households. Welfare benefits for the children thus become a necessary bare means of survival for the most economically desperate. For the fortunate, family and friends (and, less frequently, the biological father) provide a network of support that enables teenage unwed mothers to manage. The best predictor of an adolescent mother completing high school and/or college is staying in school, living with her parents, receiving welfare during adolescence, and delaying marriage (Testa 1992).

All of these demands and responsibilities of teenage parenthood, it should be emphasized, are being borne by young persons who have not yet reached physical, emotional, or intellectual maturity. Many are barely out of childhood, even while they struggle to be parents and providers. The result can be serious psychological stress in the face of newfound pressures. The frustrations reveal themselves over time in a number of ways, from ill-conceived attempts at marriage and involvements that may incur additional pregnancies to child abuse and self-harmful behaviors.

At this point it may be obvious that practically nothing has been said about the male partner. This is because in many cases of premarital pregnancy and birth among teenagers the male drops out of sight quickly. The likelihood that marriage will occur in such cases has diminished over the years, as the tradition of forced, or "shotgun," marriages has largely broken down. Given the enormous difficulties male teenagers face in supporting a wife and family today and the probability that this means dropping out of school and limiting employment prospects for the foreseeable future, teenage fathers are reluctant to enter into a marital relationship. Moreover, teenage mothers are often unlikely to push them, understanding perhaps that a marriage initiated in such circumstances is unlikely to last (Lerman and Ooms 1993).

The public outcry in the last two decades or so over teenage pregnancy—termed by some an epidemic—appears to focus on two main concerns. First, such pregnancies objectively announce that teenagers are indeed sexually active. This is a fact that many adults would prefer not to know or refuse to tolerate among their own teens (ABC News/*Washington Post* 2003; SADD, Liberty Mutual Group and Atlantic Marketing Research Company 2001).

Second, and perhaps of equal importance, is concern over the costs of teenage pregnancies and their aftermath. This concern is largely voiced in the context of more general antipathy toward impoverished mothers who must call on public assistance for family income support. The increasing proportion over the last 30 years of welfare recipients who are members of female-headed households in which the mother is unmarried seems to be deeply resented. This resentment is expressed not only through moral condemnation of unwed motherhood but also through denunciation of the tax burden posed by welfare recipient families. Ironically, no such resentment is expressed over the massive tax outlays for building and running prisons, whose escalating populations are largely composed of young men from economically disadvantaged backgrounds (Davey 1995).

Indeed, welfare reforms proposed by some members of the U.S. Congress and state legislatures in the 1990s called for ending eligibility for family income assistance altogether for unmarried mothers under 18 and their newborns, arguing that this would sharply deter and reduce teenage pregnancies and thus reduce welfare program costs. Such proposals fail to address the many and complex reasons why teenage girls become pregnant, from inadequate sex education and use of birth control to manipulation and coercion by older males.

Politicians commonly not only fail to address most of the causes of premarital pregnancies but also tend to ignore or downplay the massive problems many teenage mothers face in trying to further the life chances of their children. Condemnation and resentment of unwed mothers apparently have little effect on teenage pregnancy rates or decisions by increasing numbers of young people to be sexually active (Guttmacher 1989).

Marital Dissolution

Marital dissolution is a second major contributor to the growing number of families in which only one parent is present. Most persons whose marriages end in divorce do eventually remarry, but the problems leading to and flowing from family breakup can be harmful to those involved (Cherlin 1992).

The **divorce rate** for the United States can be expressed with different statistics (U.S. Bureau of the Census 2004:88). In 2000 some

Table 14.2	**Marriages and Divorces, 1970–2001**			
	Marriages*		**Divorces and annulments**	
	Rate per 1,000 population		**Rate per 1,000 population**	
Year	Number (1,000)	Total	Number (1,000)	Total
1960	1,667	8.5	393	2.2
1970	2,159	10.6	708	3.5
1975	2,153	10.0	1,036	4.8
1980	2,390	10.6	1,189	5.2
1983	2,446	10.5	1,158	5.0
1984	2,477	10.5	1,169	5.0
1985	2,413	10.1	1,190	5.0
1986	2,407	10.0	1,178	4.9
1987	2,403	9.9	1,166	4.8
1988	2,396	9.7	1,167	4.8
1989	(NA)	(NA)	1,157	4.7
1990	(NA)	(NA)	1,182	4.7
2001	2,345	8.2	NA	4.0

NA Not available.
*Beginning 1980, includes nonlicensed marriages registered in California.
Source: U.S. Department of Commerce, Bureau of the Census, *Statistical Abstract of the United States, 1995* (Washington, DC: U.S. Government Printing Office, 1995), p. 102; U.S. Department of Commerce, Bureau of the Census, *Statistical Abstract of the United States, 2003* (Washington, DC: U.S. Government Printing Office, 2004), p. 72.

2,329,000 couples were married. In that same year 957,200 already existing marriages ended in divorce, for a rate of 411 divorces for every 1,000 marriages. This ratio increased from 258 per 1,000 in 1960 and 328 per 1,000 in 1970. In expressing the divorce rate in this way one must remember that the marriages include persons who were formerly divorced.

A second way to approach the divorce rate is in terms of the number of divorces per 1,000 persons in the population. Viewed in these terms, the rate was 4.0 divorces per 1,000 persons in 2001. The rate was up from 2.2 in 1960 and 3.5 in 1970 (see Table 14.2). This approach must be used cautiously because changes in the age composition of the population affect the numerical divorce rate.

The third and most common way of expressing the divorce rate is to look at the number of divorces per 1,000 married women. In 1970 there were 14.9 divorces per 1,000 married women. This rate rose to a high of 22.6 in 1980 and has since leveled off in 2000 at about 21.9 (U.S. Bureau of the Census 2004:59).

However the divorce rate is expressed, it is clear that marital dissolution has been on a dramatic upswing over the last few decades. Longitudinal statistics show that these recent increases are in reality the extension of a much longer upward trend in divorce rates.

This scene is a familiar one, repeated again and again annually in the United States with varying degrees of ceremony. The probability that heterosexual couples will experience divorce seven years on average after marrying is very high.

Nonetheless, the extent to which this trend has gone up of late is having an impact on millions of people. For example, in the last two decades well over 20 million children have seen their parents enter into a divorce.

Before turning to the consequences of marital dissolution, let us consider some of the factors that may help to account for the more recent acceleration of the divorce rate (Demo and Ganong 1994). Social scientists continue to debate these factors and the weight to be attributed to them.

1.   Laws pertaining to divorce have undergone change. While the upward climb in rates of divorce began well before 1970, prior to that year states would grant a divorce only on such grounds as adultery, cruelty (physical or mental), or desertion. One or the other partner in a marriage had to be found at fault by divorce courts. In 1970 California instituted a no-fault divorce law that allowed couples to dissolve their marriages in court by mutual agreement. Most states have since adopted a similar law or added no-fault grounds to existing laws. Such legal changes are thought to represent and facilitate more permissive attitudes toward divorce among married persons.

2.   The availability of effective means of contraception to married couples is also believed to have had an impact on divorce. Contraception can make extramarital affairs less risky than they otherwise would be: Indeed, infidelity is a major source of breakup in first marriages. Moreover, such contraceptive advances as "the pill" have enabled many couples to exert control over the number of children they wish to have. To the degree to which having children

Table 14.3	Divorces and Annulments—Median Duration of Marriage, Median Age at Divorce, and Children Involved, 1970–1996										
Duration of marriage, age at divorce, and children involved	1970	1975	1980	1983	1984	1985	1986	1987	1988	1989	1996
Median duration of marriage (years)	6.7	6.5	6.8	7.0	6.9	6.8	6.9	7.0	7.1	7.2	7.9
Median age at divorce:											
Men (years)	32.9	32.2	32.7	34.0	34.3	34.4	34.6	34.9	35.1	35.4	30.5
Women (years)	29.8	29.5	30.3	31.5	31.7	31.9	32.1	32.5	32.6	32.9	29.0
Estimated number of children involved in divorce (1,000)	870	1,123	1,174	1,091	1,081	1,091	1,064	1,038	1,044	1,063	1,075
Average number of children per decree	1.22	1.08	0.98	0.94	0.92	0.92	0.90	0.89	0.89	0.91	0.90
Rate per 1,000 children under 18 years of age	12.5	16.7	17.3	17.4	17.2	17.3	16.8	16.3	16.4	16.8	16.8

Source: U.S. Department of Commerce, Bureau of the Census, *Statistical Abstract of the United States, 1995* (Washington, D.C.: U.S. Government Printing Office, 1995), p. 103; Rose M. Kreider and Jason M. Fields, *Number, Timing, and Duration of Marriages and Divorces, 1996,* Current Population Reports P70–80 (Washington, DC: U.S. Bureau of the Census, 2002).

mitigates against marital dissolution, not having them may make divorce a more viable option than it otherwise would be. As indicated in Table 14.3, the average number of children involved in divorce has fallen from 1.22 per divorce in 1970 to 0.90 in recent years. (Yet, as noted earlier, the number of children affected by divorce over the last 20 years is still substantial. More than half of all divorces involve children even now.)

3. Women's participation in the labor force (discussed in Chapter 8) is also a factor to be considered. As women have gained more control over childbearing through contraceptive advances and as they have moved into paid positions outside the home—usually from necessity, but often out of choice—their dependence on the husband as supporter has diminished somewhat. As their roles in the family have undergone change, many women locked into unhappy marriages have looked to their work as a way of escape. It is also possible that men, seeing their wives in a position of being able to pursue economic independence, have become less reluctant to dissolve an unhappy marriage.

4. Stresses faced by today's families are likely to exacerbate everyday problems in living and the normal tensions of family life. For example, since the late 1960s U.S. society has experienced periodic economic downturns that have been accompanied by cycles of high inflation; unemployment and a loss in the value of wages have hit moderate- and low-income groups

especially hard. Official poverty rates have remained quite high. Although economic adversity may bring some families closer, and others may find divorce a financially unsound option, for still other families economic adversity creates a climate in which divorce takes place. The availability of welfare assistance and other forms of government aid to poverty-stricken female-headed households has probably made divorce more thinkable for some men and women. Divorce rates are highest at lower income levels.

5. Changing attitudes toward marriage may help to account for the upsurge in divorce rates. Investigators suggest that marriage is less likely to be viewed as a sacred, permanent institution than it was only a few decades ago. Persons entering marriage are more likely to seek self-fulfillment and personal pleasure out of marriage, as opposed to seeing it as an avenue through which to pursue interpersonal commitment and cooperation in meeting social responsibilities. When self-fulfillment and personal pleasure ebb for one or both partners, there may no longer be much reason to stay married. Nor is there likely to be much public pressure on couples to remain together. The subject of divorce remains the focus of much public hand-wringing, but in reality divorce is usually dismissed as reflecting a relationship that just did not "work out."

6. Finally, divorced people themselves have enumerated the factors that contributed to dissolution of their marriages. Wives report more dissatisfaction with their marriages than husbands. Divorced women cite such problems as their former husbands' authoritarianism, mental cruelty, verbal and physical abuse, excessive drinking, lack of love, neglect of children, emotional and personality problems, and extramarital sex. Men acknowledge that their problems with alcohol, drugs, or physical abuse contribute to divorce. Overall, both women and men share the belief that communication problems, basic unhappiness, and incompatibility contribute to their divorcing (Arendell 1995).

The consequences of marital dissolution are highly variable. Each family member will perceive, define, and experience the pre- and postdivorce process differently. Sharon Price-Bonham, David Wright, and Joe Pittman (1983) have assessed the impact of divorce on adults. They point out that divorce has far-reaching consequences, involving as it does a major life transition. Price-Bonham and her associates found that the time of separation prior to formal divorce is often extremely stressful. Depression and psychosomatic symptoms associated with it (e.g., loss of appetite, sleep problems, increased drinking) are quite common. The separation period may be experienced as especially stressful because of such factors as increased parental responsibilities, sudden economic dislocation, change in familiar habits, and grief over the loss of a love object. Compared with married persons, those who are in the process of divorcing and who are newly divorced have higher rates of mental disturbance, suicide, homicide, accidents, and diseases leading to death.

Adjustment to divorce is a process sometimes described in terms analogous to adjustment to a death. Price-Bonham and her colleagues (1983:131) suggest that adjustment requires a variety of conditions, including "breaking away from the former marriage, accepting new roles, building a new lifestyle, and regenerating one's sense of self concept and trust of others." Other researchers point out that an important predictor of the postdivorce psychological state is the relationship between the marital partners *prior* to the divorce.

For both women and men, better coping and emotional functioning prior to the divorce were associated with more effective coping and less anger and emotional distress following divorce. Preseparation communication and shared decision-making regarding child rearing also were associated with more cooperative involvement between parents after divorce. (Demo and Ganong 1994:204)

The ability to adjust to divorce is influenced by numerous factors. The person who initiated the divorce may experience less stress and readier adjustment, as he or she at least has the advantage of some sense of control over the emerging situation. Economic strain is likely to make adjustment difficult. Having a network of friends and relatives who are supportive in times of need during the pre- and postdivorce period makes adjustment easier. Finally, dating and establishing positive relationships with members of the opposite sex are important to the adjustment process. For most individuals, divorce is a short-term crisis, a period of adjusting to different routines and circumstances, and it should be noted that most persons who divorce also remarry, thereby perhaps signaling an end to the adjustment.

The impact of divorce on children has been much debated. Some social scientists have held that the impact is wholly negative. Others have suggested that children are better off in a single-parent household than in one where the relationship between the parents has obviously fallen apart. Our understanding of the impact on children has been advanced by the research of Judith S. Wallerstein and Joan B. Kelly (1980). These researchers examined a group of 131 children from 60 families who came into contact with a California counseling agency. Meeting with the children at the time of the divorce, 18 months after, and 5 years after, Wallerstein and Kelly gained unique data on the impact of divorce on children over time.

At the time of the divorce between their parents, the children were found to be very upset.

Younger children expressed fright and confusion over the divorce, often seeing themselves as somehow at fault. Older children were found to be angry and concerned over what this situation might mean for them. Five years later, according to the investigators, the psychological effects of the divorce still lingered for most. Although a third of the children were evidently happy and well adjusted, another third showed some signs of unhappiness and the remaining third were seriously dissatisfied. The researchers were able to interview most of the study's children in a series of 10-year follow-up interviews. For all too many, the divorce continued to have a troubling impact (Wallerstein and Blakeslee 1989, 2001).

Andrew J. Cherlin (1992) concluded that all children are likely to be emotionally upset when divorce occurs, but most do adjust. A minority have long-term psychological problems that can be attributed to the dissolution of their parents' marriage. Yet considering that over 20 million children have seen their parents divorce in the last 20 years, the sheer numbers of those who have been emotionally impaired by this process are substantial.

Cherlin noted that the probability of children's successful adjustment to divorce is enhanced by three factors: (1) regular contact with the parent who does not have custody of the children; (2) parental avoidance of involving the children in their differences, so that the latter are not forced to choose sides; and (3) structured, orderly household routine, coupled with an emotionally supportive custodial parent. It should be noted, however, that greater variation in children's psychological well-being is found *within* such family types as two-parent families or single-parent families headed by a divorcée than is found *between* different family types (Demo and Ganong 1994:206).

Perhaps the most difficult task faced by the parent who is left with the major responsibility for child care is economic. Even while all the psychological and social adjustments to the divorce itself are being attempted or made, economic distress may have very negative effects on children of divorce. Indeed, low income and the associated lack of resources—not single parenting per se—are what put children in such households at risk for low levels of school performance, poor attendance, and dropping out (McLanahan and Sandefur 1994). The fact that the **custodial parent** is ordinarily the mother exacerbates household economic distress, given the subordinate and second-class role so many women occupy in the labor force (see Chapter 8).

Divorce almost always has a negative economic impact on the single-parent, female-headed household. The bulk of economic support for the family is typically provided by the husband in intact marriages. When this suddenly disappears or lessens, the standard of living of mothers and children suffers. In most cases of divorce, the father provides little or no **child-support** money.

In 2002, out of the 11.3 million women living with children under 21 with no father present, 7.1 million were expecting to receive court-ordered child-support payments. Only 45.4 percent of these women received full payment. In a quarter of the cases the father simply refused to pay. The amount provided to those receiving payments in 2002 averaged $3,160 annually, hardly a boon to most families who have lost a key wage earner (Grall 2003). The federal government has been using two pieces of legislation to collect delinquent child-support payments: the Federal Child Support Enforcement Act of 1984 and the Family Support Act of 1988. These acts use such strategies as mandatory wage withholding and confiscating federal tax refunds. But in 2002 more than $25 billion was owed to 21.5 million children (Grall 2003).

The economic impact of divorce has been explored in a study by Lenore J. Weitzman (1985). Calculating the incomes of divorced women in relation to their needs in contrast to those of men, Weitzman (1985:339) found: "Just one year after legal divorce, men experience a 42 percent improvement in their postdivorce standard of living, while women experience a 73 percent decline. . . . Divorce is a financial catastrophe for most women."

The women's own words give meaning to Weitzman's statistics.

We ate macaroni and cheese five nights a week. There was a Safeway special for 39 cents a box. We could eat seven dinners for $3.00 a week. . . . I think that's all we ate for months.

I applied for welfare. . . . It was the worst experience of my life. . . . I never dreamed that I, a middle class housewife, would ever be put in a position like that. It was humiliating . . . they make you feel it. . . . But we were desperate, and I had to feed my kids.

You name it, I tried it—food stamps, soup kitchens, shelters. It just about killed me to have the kids live like that. . . . I finally called my parents and said we were coming . . . we couldn't have survived without them.

Sometimes when you are so tense about money you go crazy . . . and you forget what it's like to be twelve years old and to think you can't live without Adidas sneakers . . . and to feel the whole world has deserted you along with your father. (Weitzman 1985:339, 340)

Many divorced mothers are thus forced into the labor market on a full-time basis and/or forced to rely on welfare assistance to provide for their families (Arendell 1987, 1986). Divorce and failure to receive adequate child support have contributed to the so-called feminization of poverty (see Chapter 6). Almost 52 percent of children who are living in households headed by women are poor. The poverty rate for children in single father-headed households is only 5.2 percent (Fields 2003). While there has been considerable debate over the magnitude of Weitzman's data, more recent research supports her more general conclusion that women tend to suffer a substantial erosion in income following divorce (Bartfeld 2000; Hanson, McLanahan, and Thomson 1998; Shelton and Dean 2001). In contrast, divorce tends to improve men's standard of living when they have relied on their partners for less than one-fifth of their married household income (McManus and DiPrete 2001). Since women are far more likely than men to be awarded custody of children, it is likely to plunge children into poverty. In Andrew Cherlin's (1981:81) words, "the most detrimental aspect of the absence of fathers from one-parent families is not the lack of a male presence but the lack of a male income."

Most persons remarry—over 70 percent of all divorced women and an even higher percentage of divorced men. Remarriage usually takes place 3 to 4 years after divorce. It can ease the economic burden carried by divorced mothers; for many of them this is the only viable solution. Yet the divorce rate among the remarried is slightly higher than that for those in their first marriage, a fact that should underscore the fragility of marriage as an institution in contemporary times.

Violence in the Family

Ideally, one's family should always exist as an oasis, a place that is safe and satisfying, where one can seek relief from and aid in dealing with the often stressful demands of the outside world. In too many cases today, however, the family setting is just the opposite; it contains levels of tension, conflict, and violence from which flight might be the only rational response. Many persons now admit to being aware of victims of family violence. The problem is so widespread the U.S. Surgeon General in 2003 termed it a public health issue (www.surgeongeneral.gov). Think about this statement by researchers considered experts in their subject matter:

"Americans run the greatest risk of assault, physical injury, and even murder in their own homes by members of their own families" (Straus, Gelles, and Steinmetz 1980:4; see also Gelles and Loseke 1993). Such statements are based not on alarmist rhetoric but on empirical research that has revealed startling rates of husband and wife abuse, parental abuse of their children, and children's abuse of their parents and one another. By **abuse** we mean acts of physical violence (Gelles 1985).

Prior to research by Murray A. Straus and his colleagues (Straus 1980; Straus et al. 1980), our knowledge of violence in the family was limited. Families in which abuse took place were commonly believed to be abnormal and pathological, their members perhaps victims of mental illness. It was also commonly thought that episodes of violence in the family were almost entirely restricted to the poor. Straus and his associates have systematically destroyed these views as myths.

In a pathbreaking study, the researchers examined 2,143 families who were carefully chosen to be representative of approximately 47 million families in the United States. The families were not known to have any mentally ill members, and they reflected a broad cross section with regard to age, class, race, and region of the country. An adult from each of the 2,143 families was interviewed and asked a variety of questions bearing on violence in the home. The purpose was to establish, for the first time, the "incidence rate" of family violence. (The incidence rate in this case refers to the frequency with which acts of violence occurred in the year prior to the interviews.) Violence was defined as "an act carried out with the intention of, or perceived as having the intention of, physically hurting another person" (Straus 1980:29).

Spouse Abuse

The interviews conducted by Straus and his colleagues revealed that **spouse abuse,** or incidents of violence between husband and wife, had occurred in one in six families in the previous year. While most incidents were relatively minor—involving slapping, shoving, pushing, or throwing things at a person—some were far more serious in terms of real or potential physical harm. In 6 percent of the families, the incidents involved such acts as punching, kicking, biting, hitting with an object, or using a knife or gun.

More recent research has further exposed the extent of the violence. Almost one-third of adult women in the United States suffer at least one physical assault in their lifetime by a partner; about 4 million U.S. women are victims of a serious assault by an intimate partner each year (www.apa.org). And more than 3 million children witness their mothers or female caretakers being abused (www.stopfamilyviolence.org). Although not all of these are incidents of spousal abuse, what this means is that some 3 million families experience serious acts of spouse abuse each year. About 7.5 million experience violence of some sort annually. But only about one-seventh of all domestic violence cases come to the attention of the police (www.stopfamilyviolence.org). It is reasonable to assume, then, that the incidence of spouse abuse is much higher than what is documented.

Domestic violence is a significant factor in homelessness: Many women seek refuge in homeless shelters as they and their children flee the violence in their homes. Fully 57 percent of homeless families identified domestic violence as the primary cause of their homelessness. Ninety-two percent of homeless women have suffered serious physical or sexual violence (www.stopfamilyviolence.org). Notably, welfare reforms of the 1990s may be contributing to a situation in which more women have few options but to tolerate domestic violence. Research finds that poverty-stricken women are increasingly remaining in abusive relationships as the only thing that may stand between them and extreme poverty when their welfare benefits run out under the strict new rules and they struggle to move from welfare to work (Scott, London, and Myers 2002).

Child Abuse

The interviews that Straus and his coworkers conducted revealed rates of **child abuse** that were even higher than those of spouse abuse. Seven out of 10 parents used some form of physical violence on their children in the year prior to the interviews. Again, in most cases this was relatively minor (e.g., spanking). But 14 percent of the children suffered serious attacks. Overall, approximately 6.5 million children in a single year were subject to abuse by being punched, kicked, bitten, hit with an object, beaten up, or attacked with a knife or gun.

These findings are reinforced by more recent research. In 2000 an average of 2,400 children suffered abuse each day, and most of these were victimized in their own homes by their parents. More than 1,400 children died that year of neglect and abuse—nearly four deaths every day (www.surgeongeneral.gov; www.stopfamilyviolence.org).

Child-Initiated Violence

Findings of the research by Straus and colleagues suggest that perhaps one in five children hit a parent the previous year, including a parent who was elderly. One in 10 used a method in which the risk of physical injury was high. Children also attack one another, at rates higher than their physical attacks on anyone else in the family.

Comment on the Findings

Straus and his colleagues have readily admitted that their findings may underestimate the rate of family violence to an unknown degree. There are several reasons for this. Some of those interviewed may not have recalled or may not have chosen to reveal violent incidents. The 2,143

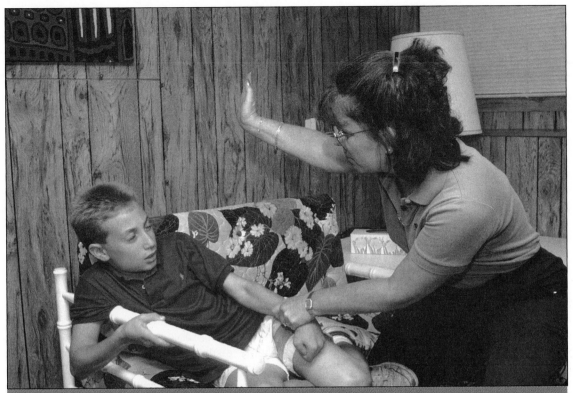

Studies of family violence have revealed that the rate of child abuse is higher than many people realize. Fortunately public awareness has been on the increase and more cases of abuse are being reported. Still, it is difficult to know of all such cases. This mother, shown beating her son, may never have to answer to authorities for her actions.

families studied represent only intact families, thus omitting child abuse data for single-parent households. The research also did not examine violence between parents and their children under age three. Finally, the families studied represented 65 percent of those originally selected. It is conceivable that those who chose not to participate in the study may have functioned in families that were more violent than the families willing to be interviewed.

Nonetheless, the data reveal that violence in the family is widespread, and this fact has been confirmed by subsequent research (Gelles and Straus 1988; Hampton et al. 1993; Tower 1996).

Mental illness does not seem to be a major factor among those involved in violent acts; perhaps no more than 10 percent of the family violence that occurs is linked to psychological problems. Data reveal that although reported incidents of violence occur most frequently in low-income families, such violence is common across all income lines.

The next question is "Why?" How does one account for family violence? If mental illness and the ravages of poverty fail to provide more than partial answers, what are the causes of behavior that can leave adults and children injured and even result in loss of life?

According to Straus and his associates, violence in the family has been around for a long time. Family life may have been even more violent in the past, although this is difficult to ascertain firmly. The reasons underlying family violence cannot be reduced simply to psychological problems; instead they seem to be rooted largely in the nature of the family itself and influenced by other features of U.S. society as a whole. This is not to say that persons who physically abuse other family members are somehow blameless for their actions. But much family violence is thought to be "situational": There are social and cultural influences that may propel persons toward the use of violence, and in many cases this violence is widely tolerated. What are these social and cultural influences?

First, persons may entertain the use of violence in the family setting as an option partially because they themselves were physically abused or because they observed other family members' violence. Thus, the use of violence to solve interpersonal problems becomes part of the outlook on life of clinically "normal" people. The use of violence is also constantly reinforced and subtly sanctioned in books, movies, and television shows, as well as through celebration of the activities of society's military forces, police agencies, and many sports figures. In this sense the types of data being generated on violence in the family reflect both direct and indirect socialization into the larger culture and the behavior it often tolerates.

A second social and cultural influence pertains to social norms. Norms are rules or standards that define what is socially acceptable behavior. Thus, according to Straus and his colleagues, some family violence can be termed **normal violence** in that it is tolerated and accorded legitimacy. As an example of such norms, Straus offers the following: "If someone is doing something wrong and [won't listen to reason,] it is o.k. to hit" (Straus 1980:16). Indeed, it is legal in virtually every state in the United States for parents to "spank, hit, paddle, whip or otherwise inflict punitive pain on a child," so long as the physical punishment does not cross the vague line into state statutes defining abuse (www.childadvocate.org). Courts in Connecticut in 2004 determined that even if the spanking leaves a bruise on the child it is not necessarily abuse, a determination that underscored parents' rights to use normal violence to discipline a child. The United States and Somalia remain the only countries in the United Nations to refuse to ratify the United Nations Convention on the Rights of the Child. All of this indicates a cultural acceptance of normal violence done in the interest of disciplining children.

On the other hand, some violence is seen as socially unacceptable. Termed **abusive violence** by Straus and his coworkers, this usually has the potential for inflicting the most serious physical harm. According to Straus, in some locales police define what is considered abusive violence in accordance with the "stitch rule." The police informally observe a norm holding that unless family disputes result in more than a certain number of stitches, arrests are unlikely to be made. In sum, social norms influence the acceptance or nontolerance of violence within the family.

A third facet of the phenomenon of violence rests with the way in which the family itself is organized. According to Straus and his colleagues, family organization can generate conflict between members that may result in incidents of violence. Conflict may be built into the family setting as a consequence of differences in age and sex of family members or differences in roles to be played (e.g., husband versus wife, parents versus children). Moreover, when differences do arise, they may be felt far more intensely than differences between persons in nonfamily settings, because family members are very involved with one another emotionally.

Family units consider themselves to be collectivities whose business is theirs alone, and others usually share this view. The privacy demanded by and allowed families means that behavior in the home is subject to less public scrutiny and control than behavior in other institutional settings (e.g., a place of employment, worship, schooling).

Families are also subject to a great deal of stress that may help to propel persons into violent behavior. This is particularly the case for low-income families, among whom rates of domestic violence seem to be highest. During their life cycles most families suffer stressful events; at the same time they may be faced with substantial social responsibilities. Husbands and wives, facing stressful life conditions, may include violence in their repertoire of coping mechanisms—hitting out at others who may not even be the cause of the anger they feel. Children, caught up in a situation in which the use of violence has become a norm, may know of no other way of dealing with their own stressful experiences.

In a study sponsored by the U.S. Department of Justice, researchers found that many of the victims of family violence brought to the attention of the courts continue to be victimized for months or even years after the original case is resolved (*New York Times* 1983). The fact that court intervention does not necessarily provide protection for abused family members only serves to underscore the importance of the various social and cultural forces contributing to family violence that social scientists have endeavored to identify.

Sexual Abuse of Children

The attention given to violence in the family in recent years, and particularly to child abuse, has inevitably led to concern with what Florence Rush has called "the best kept secret": sexual abuse of children (Rush 1980). Long considered not a topic to be discussed in polite company, disclosures of sexual abuse by priests in the Catholic Church over the course of several decades brought uncomfortable public scrutiny to the issue. And social scientists have finally begun to explore it. The limited research that has been done indicates that the sexual abuse of children is more widespread than most of us would prefer to believe (Matthews 2004; Peters, Wyatt, and Finkelhor 1986). (Table 14.4 provides data on officially substantiated cases of sexual abuse, as well as other forms of maltreatment of children.)

In one study David Finkelhor (1979) surveyed 796 college students. Of 530 female students, 19 percent admitted to having been sexually victimized during childhood. For males, the percentage was lower—8.6 percent. If the victims' experiences were to be projected to the U.S. population as a whole, this would mean that over 30 million persons will have had a sexual encounter with an adult while in childhood. Although our ability to generalize to the population at large from a survey of college students is doubtful, other research has confirmed the widespread incidence of child sexual abuse.

In a second study, Finkelhor (1984) interviewed parents in 521 Boston families. This carefully selected sample of families had a total of 1,428 children between the ages of 6 and 14. Among the reported findings are these:

1. About 9 percent of the parents said one of their own children had been a victim or attempted victim of sexual abuse. (Finkelhor believes the actual rate could be double the 9 percent, given that children frequently do not report it.)

2. Children from every social class and ethnic and racial background were equally vulnerable to sexual abuse.

3. About 47 percent of the parents knew of a child who was a victim of sexual abuse; in 37 percent of these cases the victim was six years old or younger.

4. About 15 percent of the female parents and 6 percent of the male parents had themselves been sexually abused as children. In only a third of the cases were the abusers strangers; 67 percent of the abusers were relatives, acquaintances, or their own parents.

| Table 14.4 | Child Abuse and Neglect Cases Substantiated, by Victim Characteristics, 1990–2002 |

	1990		1993		2002	
Item	Number	Percent	Number	Percent	Number	Percent
Types of substantiated maltreatment						
Victims, total*	801,143	(X)	1,057,255	(X)	895,569	(X)
Neglect	358,846	44.8	492,211	48.8	523,704	58.5
Physical abuse	205,057	25.6	232,061	23.0	166,920	18.6
Sexual abuse	127,853	16.0	139,326	13.8	88,656	9.9
Emotional maltreatment	47,673	6.0	47,659	4.7	58,022	6.5
Other and unknown	61,714	7.7	145,998	14.5	170,847	19.1
Sex of victim						
Victims, total	775,596	100.0	915,579	100.0	891,671	100.0
Male	360,531	46.5	413,210	45.0	428,815	48.1
Female	409,286	52.8	470,541	51.1	462,856	51.9
Unknown	5,779	0.7	31,828	3.9	Y	Y
Age of victim						
Victims, total	788,338	100.0	915,909	100.0	890,025	100.0
1 year and younger	107,217	13.6	121,689	13.3	142,026	16.0
2 to 5 years old	194,485	24.7	236,925	25.9	167,439	18.8
6 to 9 years old	177,396	22.5	209,227	22.8	207,438	23.3
10 to 13 years old	151,971	19.3	177,537	19.4	188,082	21.1
14 to 17 years old	117,312	14.9	133,852	14.6	134,829	15.1
18 and over	7,184	0.9	6,799	0.7	994	0.1
Unknown	32,773	4.2	29,880	3.3	Y	Y
Race/Ethnic group of victim†						
Victims, total	775,409	100.0	916,185	100.0	715,717	100.0
White	424,470	54.7	497,913	54.3	407,677	57.0
Black	197,400	25.5	229,596	25.1	195,924	27.4

Item	1990		1993		2002	
	Number	Percent	Number	Percent	Number	Percent
Asian and Pacific Islander	6,408	0.8	7,775	0.8	6,486	0.9
American Indian, Eskimo, and Aleut	10,283	1.3	13,657	1.5	13,607	1.9
Other races	11,749	1.5	13,659	1.5	9,407	1.3
Latino origin	73,132	9.4	85,026	9.3	82,616	11.5
Unknown	51,967	6.7	68,559	7.5	Y	Y

X Not applicable.

*More than one type of maltreatment may be substantiated per child.

†Some states were unable to report on the number of Latino victims, thus it is probable that nationwide the percentage of Latino victims is higher.

Source: U.S. Department of Commerce, Bureau of the Census, *Statistical Abstract of the United States, 1995* (Washington, D.C.: U.S. Government Printing Office, 1995), p. 215; U.S. Department of Health and Human Services, Administration for Children and Families factsheets. Available at www.acf.hhs.gov/programs/cb/publications/cm02.

Many of the cases of abuse fail to come to the attention of authorities. In the study of Boston families, only 56 percent of the parents interviewed reported their children's abuse. What is reported thus is no doubt simply the tip of the iceberg. A U.S. Department of Justice study of 11 states and the District of Columbia found that over half of reported rape victims are girls under 18 and about one-fifth are under 12. In the younger group, very few are attacked by strangers (*New York Times* 1994b). Rape, as we shall see in Chapter 15, is one of the most underreported criminal acts.

Cases of sexual abuse are not reported for several reasons, but prevailing explanations focus on parents' reluctance to believe that other adults are capable of such behavior and their failure to believe their own children. Yet despite the underreporting, sexual assault centers and hospitals commonly see children who have been sexually abused, and many children served by youth shelters, runaway services, and juvenile facilities have had such experiences.

Not all cases of child sexual abuse involve such violent acts as rape. Not all come about through the use of force or physical coercion. Nor is sexual intercourse always involved. The bulk of the offenders are thought to be members of the victims' families or family friends. Almost all offenders are male. Faced with demands for sexual activities that many children may not even understand, demands posed by persons who are usually known and trusted, children often simply comply. They may not know that they have the right to refuse, or they may be afraid to do so. Abuse may last for long periods of time, even years.

Florence Rush (1980:2–3) argues that most of the adults who engage in sexual activity with children are not mentally disturbed. They seek out a child for sexual pleasure "because a child, more than a woman, has less sexual experience, less physical strength, is more trusting of and dependent upon adults and therefore can be more easily coerced, seduced, lured, or forced."

Difficulties arise in dealing with child sexual abuse within the circles of family and friends. Adults to whom complaints are made may not believe the victim, or they may even blame the victim. Children may be reluctant to complain in the first place, feeling confused and powerless.

Concerned adults may interpret the incidents as less than serious, often to avoid rupturing interpersonal relationships with the offenders for personal, social, or even economic reasons.

Father or stepfather and daughter incest, found to be the most common form of child sexual abuse in David Finkelhor's study of college students, is a case in point. In many families in which incest takes place, the mother is helpless. Ashamed to reveal what is happening to others, fearful of involving law enforcement officials, often ignorant of other sources of assistance, and dependent on her husband for economic support for herself and other family members, the mother often withdraws and is frequently depressed. As a consequence, most offenders in cases of incest go undetected by outside authorities and are rarely elevated to the status of criminal.

Perhaps one of the most revealing pieces of research on incest and nonfamilial sexual abuse of children is that conducted by Diana Russell (1986) in San Francisco. A carefully selected sample of 930 women residents were interviewed and asked about their experiences as victims of such abuses. The women were first asked if they had ever experienced "incestuous abuse," which "includes any kind of exploitative sexual contact or attempted sexual contact that occurred between relatives, no matter how distant the relationship, before the victim turned eighteen years old" (Russell 1986:59).

Russell found that 16 percent of the women had had at least one experience with incestuous abuse (e.g., sexual propositions, unwanted touching or kissing, forced intercourse) with a relative. In three-fourths of these cases, the incestuous abuse had taken place before the victim was 14 years of age.

Russell also asked whether the women had been victims of sexual abuse apart from that involving relatives (and also omitting unwanted sexual behavior from a partner in the teenage dating years). If we add these cases to those noted in the preceding paragraph, the experiences of abuse are greatly magnified. Russell

found that *38 percent* of the women had had at least one experience with incestuous and/or nonfamilial sexual abuse before reaching age 18. And in two-thirds of all the cases, the abuse was experienced before age 14.

We do not know if Russell's study has produced results that can be safely generalized to the U.S. female population at large. But it seems safe to say that both incestuous and nonfamilial sexual abuse of children and teens are much more common than many of us would like to believe. We can see, however, the impact of the powerlessness and vulnerability of females in our society, in childhood and adulthood.

Amazingly, a few professionals in the mental health field argue that adult sexual encounters with children are in many cases harmless and in some cases even positive (Russell 1986:38–39). That such views are in the minority is largely due to evidence on the often harmful consequences of sexual abuse (Bass and Thornton 1982). These consequences include genital injury, sexually transmitted disease, and pregnancy. Moreover, there are emotional effects. These may be expressed in a variety of ways, including loss of appetite, nightmares, bed-wetting, depression and inability to function, and even suicide. Residues of guilt and anger may last long after the occasions of abuse, but many victims are able to benefit from counseling and therapy (Conte 1993).

While child sexual abuse may be our "best kept secret," in recent years our cultural environment has been one in which children are portrayed in erotic terms. There has been a flowering of attention to child and youth sexuality in films and pornographic materials (so-called kiddie porn) (Finkelhor 1982). Advertisements for consumer items such as clothing have used young girls in adultlike seductive poses to invite attention to the product. Such efforts, motivated by nothing more than a crude quest for profit, may help to legitimate the unspoken and generally unacceptable notion that children can be treated as sex objects. The role of the media in this regard remains speculative, since there is little research on this topic.

Family Violence: A Matter of Power

While much may be made of family stress factors that can contribute to domestic violence, one of the key findings of research is the role of power differentials. It may be true that more generalized cultural acceptance of violence is simply being played out in the home. But it is noteworthy that perpetrators of domestic violence do not ordinarily take their aggression out against authority figures such as the police, their employers, or physically larger or stronger people. Notice, for example, that the typical victims of family violence tend to be those with the least power: women, children, and elders (see Chapter 11). Children and the elderly are often physically less powerful than the abusers and commonly do not possess decision-making power in their families. Likewise, women who are abused often lack decision-making power in their marriages or partnerships (Anderson and Umberson 2001). Gelles and Straus (1988:92) noted that "the risk of intimate violence is greatest when all the decision making in a home is concentrated in the hands of one of the partners. Couples who report the most sharing of decisions report the lowest rates of violence." Gender roles in the family that reinforce male dominance and power in decision making can contribute in important ways, then, to domestic violence (Merry 2002).

Runaways and Homeless Children

One response to neglect or abuse within the family is to flee, even if only temporarily. Since the mid-1970s the federal government has provided limited funds to assist runaways through support of youth shelters and telephone hotlines that encourage children to initiate contact with their families. Yet as more has been learned about the runaways, it has become increasingly apparent that many have not simply fled home but have been made to leave. So-called **pushouts** or **throwaway children,** as they have been termed, are effectively homeless. The pushout phenomenon may be viewed as yet another variant of the overall spectrum of child abuse. Runaways ordinarily can go home; they have a home to return to. Pushouts cannot (U.S. Congress, Senate 1980, 1990).

The National Runaway Switchboard estimates that between 1.3 and 2.8 million children leave home each year, and most of them end up homeless (www.focusas.com). No one really knows how many are pushouts (Finkelhor et al. 1990). But the most frequent reason children give for running away from home is that they have been kicked out (www.homeless.org). At least some of the pushouts are "economic refugees," evicted by parents facing financial crises who find they cannot support their children. Of the millions of children who leave their homes annually, perhaps half have been victims of some form of parental abuse (Stiffman 1989).

Much of what is known about such children is based on surveys of those served by federally funded youth shelters, of which there are currently 343 around the country. Generalizations about the total runaway-pushout population on the basis of shelter surveys must be made with caution. The shelters serve only about 63,000 children annually, or approximately 5 percent of all who leave home. In any event, it is estimated that the average age of this group is 15 and that some 60 percent are female. About 70 percent are white. While perhaps 40 percent are school dropouts, most have never been in any kind of trouble that brought them to the attention of juvenile authorities.

What happens to the children who leave home? Runaways are likely to return, usually within 24 to 48 hours of their disappearance. Of those who do not return in a short period, some will find their way to youth shelters. Others will be picked up by police and placed in jail, either because they must be held for legal disposition as homeless minors or because they have been charged with illegal acts (Sickmund 1990). The latter frequently occur as children away from home struggle to cope with problems of economic survival. Seventy-five percent of runaways who remain on the streets for more than 2 weeks become involved in crime, drugs, and pornography; one-third are drawn into prostitution within 48 hours of running away from home. Survival may be possible only through such acts as theft and prostitution. Prostitution involves boys as well as girls, and it is estimated that 30 percent of homeless children in shelters and 70 percent of those on the streets engage in it. Often prostitution results from coercion by adults to whom the children have turned for assistance and protection (www.focusas.com).

In 2001 police around the nation made 133,300 arrests of children under 18 years of age on the grounds that they were runaways. The characteristics of those arrested may not accurately reflect the runaway population in general, it should be noted. Of those taken into custody, 50,654 or 38 percent were under age 15, while the remainder were 15 to 17 (www.ojjdp.ncjrs.org). The vast majority (77 percent) were white, and most (59 percent) were female (www.ncjrs.org).

Social science research on children who leave home is limited. However, there is evidence to suggest that, at least for runaways, a variety of factors are influential in determining the decision to flee home. First, children who run away are likely to face a lot of stress within their families (Shane 1989). (See Table 14.5.) In the words of Tim Brennan, David Huizinga, and Delbert Elliott (1978:303), which still, sadly, ring true, families of runaways frustrate "important youth needs and satisfactions, such as the need for security and belonging, the need for autonomy, the need for feelings of competence and self-esteem, the need to be understood." The families of runaways are likely to combine displays of power (e.g., physical punishment, denial of privileges) with apparent withdrawal of love and parental remoteness. Often these processes occur simultaneously with family disruption resulting from death, divorce, or job loss. In all, families of runaways provide little in the way of role models for their children.

Brennan and his associates have also found that school experiences typically add to the stresses on children who run away. Runaways are more likely than nonrunaways to experience "negative labeling by teachers, blocked access to rewarding roles, low grades, failure tracks, expulsions, suspensions, being beaten by teachers and so on" (Brennan et al. 1978:303). Thus, bonds to school as well as to family are weakened. Although some children no doubt leave home simply for adventure and a quest for excitement, these cases are clearly in the minority.

As stated earlier, most runaways return home. The situation of pushouts is much more serious, because they are homeless. A U.S. Senate study, commenting on pushouts and throwaway children, warns of the severity of this family-related problem:

There is no reason to doubt the numbers of homeless youth will increase. Certainly the wasted lives and talents of these youngsters represent a tremendous loss of human potential to our society. As the size of the homeless population grows, there will be an even larger underclass of bitter, defeated, or angry people in this country. (U.S. Congress, Senate 1980:83)

Table 14.5	Problems Reported by Youth Seeking Services from Runaway and Homeless Youth Centers, by Type of Problem and by Sex, 1990		
Type of problem	Total	Female	Male
Family problems*	(N = 30,373)	(N = 17,170)	(N = 13,203)
Emotional conflict at home	41%	43%	39%
Parent too strict	21	24	18
Parental physical abuse	20	23	18
Parental neglect	20	19	21
Parent drug or alcohol problems	18	19	17
Family mental health problems	11	12	11
Parental domestic violence	10	10	10
Parental unemployment	9	9	9
Wants to live with other parent	6	7	6
Parental sexual abuse	7	9	2
Physical or sexual abuse by other family member	5	6	3
Physical or sexual abuse by nonfamily member	4	5	2
No parent figure	4	4	5
Parent is homosexual	1	2	1
None of the above	16	13	19
Individual problems*	(N = 30,388)	(N = 17,180)	(N = 13,208)
Poor self-image	49%	51%	46%
Depressed	43	48	36
School attendance or truancy	33	33	33
Bad grades	31	30	33
In trouble with justice system	19	13	27
Drug abuse	15	13	17
Alcohol abuse	13	13	13
Possibly suicidal	12	15	8
Cannot get along with teachers	13	10	17
Learning disability	7	5	10
Custody change	5	5	5
Pregnant or suspects pregnancy	4	7	0
Other health problems or handicap	4	4	4
Homosexual or sexual identity issue	2	2	3
Prostitution	1	2	1
Venereal disease	1	1	0
None of the above	19	19	20

*Because multiple responses are permitted, totals exceed 100 percent.

Source: Kathleen McGuire, Ann L. Pastore, and Timothy J. Flanagan, eds., Sourcebook of Criminal Justice Statistics (Washington, DC: U.S. Government Printing Office, 1993), p. 589.

The Struggle to Juggle Work and Family

One substantial source of stress in families is the increasingly difficult balancing act between the demands of work and those of family life. The strain is particularly acute for women, who have traditionally had to shoulder the full responsibility of domestic labor and child care (Coltrane and Adams 2001; Worley and Vannoy 2001). Mounting family demands, including care of elderly or infirm family members as well as children, commonly fall to women, creating a **sandwich generation** of women caught between the needs of both generations. Forty percent of the 22 million people caring for their elderly parents (or the parents of their partners) are also raising children (Feyerick 1998).

At the same time, women with young children are increasingly also participating in the paid labor market, of necessity as well as by choice. It is increasingly difficult to financially support a family on the income of a single job. More and more two-parent families are discovering the harsh reality of the need for both parents to participate in the paid labor market. The conventional two-parent family in which Mom remains at home as a full-time homemaker and Dad is the breadwinner outside the home describes less than 7 percent of all U.S. families. More than twice as many families consist of two parents, both of whom work outside the home for pay, and their offspring. Another 9 percent are single-parent families (the vast majority of whom are single-mother families), in which all the demands of both work and family must fall to one person. Increasingly, women are finding it highly challenging to be able to afford remaining at home to raise their children: More than two-thirds of the women with children under 6 years old are in the paid labor market (U.S. Bureau of the Census 2004).

There are only 24 hours in a day. One might assume that when women work outside the home their partners must necessarily contribute more time to the household responsibilities. But research suggests otherwise: Women are finding themselves working full-time outside the home for pay, only to come home to confront a **second shift** in the full-time job as homemaker (Hochschild with Machung 1997). The time bind places families in a vise created by the contradicting demands of work and family (Hochschild 1997). Evidence indicates that some men are coming to accept the need for them to contribute more to the division of labor at home (Levine 2000), but that is still far from the practice of most men in the United States. Women continue to struggle to juggle the conflicting demands of work and family.

For some women, the struggle has required a reduction in time spent on the job or the excruciating decision to leave their paid jobs altogether. This has severe consequences on their income as well as their health care and pension benefits, their seniority, and their career paths. And this is a "choice" that men typically are not required to make (Budig and England 2001; Maume 2001).

Clearly, the world of the paid labor market has been slow to recognize that it exists in the context of family life, and institutions supporting families have been just as slow to acknowledge the realities of women and mothers in the labor market. The institutional mismatch between work and family thus contributes greatly to family stresses, particularly for women.

What Is to Be Done?

The picture painted in this chapter is very bleak. One must place these problems in perspective; it is clear that most U.S. families are harmonious and enriching, with children who develop nicely.

With regard to the family-related problem of premarital births and teenage motherhood, some very sensitive issues must be confronted. Youths must be understood as sexual beings, even if they are only in the process of becoming personally, socially, and intellectually mature. As such, many will make the decision to become sexually active and to engage in intercourse. Knowing this, it seems that the only rational response is to seek to reduce the risk of pregnancy (and sexually transmitted diseases, including AIDS). This can be done only by giving teenagers knowledge about contraception and contraceptive devices and seriously promoting birth control as an inviolable prerequisite to premarital sexual behavior. The costs of not doing this—to the unwed mother and child, and to the rest of society—far outweigh the costs of possibly encouraging a small percentage of youths to become sexually active who might not otherwise have done so.

Still, pregnancies will occur. Some teenagers—even when armed with knowledge and with ready access to contraceptive resources—will ignore it all. Accidents will occur. Nor is the technology of contraception 100 percent effective. Abortion will no doubt continue to be a highly charged moral and political issue and an avenue rejected by many pregnant teenagers (as well as adults); in some states abortions have become increasingly difficult to obtain. Some young mothers may opt to place their babies for adoption; many will not.

If nothing else is done for those who do become mothers, current efforts to provide guidance and support in parenting skills, health care, and help in completion of formal education must be greatly expanded. The meager and begrudging help currently offered to unmarried young persons who are locked into the responsibility of mothering young babies is a shocking comment on the level of our concern for human life. With a poverty rate of *53.7 percent* among children under six who live in a female-headed household with no spouse present (http://pubdb3.census.gov), much help is needed.

Marital dissolution cannot be avoided. In many cases divorce is a solution as well as a problem. The two major areas of deepest concern should be those of (1) adjustment to divorce by adults and children, and (2) economic security for those left most vulnerable by family breakup (commonly mothers and their children). The limited steps that are taken to hold fathers to financial responsibility can only be improved. The notion that men who father children have little or no responsibility for the standard of living and life chances of the children after divorce deserves full condemnation.

As for adjustment to divorce, the resources now available to adults—from professional guidance to self-help groups—should be expanded and utilized more fully. The trend toward joint custody, where the divorced parents both play a continual role in parenting, is a positive way of fostering children's emotional adjustment and should be further encouraged. The decline in the number of children on average that are involved in divorce actions is a welcome trend.

Violence in the family seems unstoppable. It is really only in the last 25 years that family violence has been systematically revealed and widely acknowledged as a problem. The same can be said for the sexual abuse of children. It has been argued that such phenomena have long existed in this society and that the widespread attention they are currently receiving represents shifting attitudes that could well be necessary for behavioral change. Concern with the rights of persons within a family setting is perhaps an extension of concern over the rights of other categories of persons whose treatment is often harmful (e.g., people of color, women, elders, gay males and lesbians, people with disabilities).

The identification of hidden and often tolerated acts in family settings as abuse, outside of the realm of socially acceptable behavior, is at least a start. Such a normative shift is likely to mean that situations involving violence and other forms of serious abuse are more likely to be brought to the attention of law enforcement and social service agencies. However, the ability of such agencies to respond and successfully alter the behaviors in question will have to be considerably expanded. At present social service agencies are overwhelmed with "business," and they are—far more than law enforcement agencies—understaffed and precariously funded. None of this, unfortunately, addresses the broader social and cultural determinants of family turmoil and abuse. Attitudinal shifts and increased intervention efforts are thus likely to do little more than stem the tide, barring more radical transformations in the self-concept of the family (and of the organization and operation of U.S. society in general).

So long as families are troubled, children will run away. The runaway phenomenon is best understood as an indicator of the existence of child abuse and/or neglect. Thus, our comments regarding the desirability of attitude shifts and increased intervention to aid families are again applicable. But the pushout phenomenon is something else again. Ideally, there would be reason and opportunity for intervention before parents deny children their homes. Yet it is likely that many children will have no choice but to try and make a life outside their family setting. For most, youth and economic circumstance virtually dictate that they find their way to families and adult caretakers who want to help them. An expansion of foster family care and small-group homes is required to meet the immediate needs of pushouts.

The stressful conflicting demands of work and family require institutional supports. Some changes are beginning to occur in the workplace. For example, a growing number of firms are beginning to accept the concept of **flextime** to enable workers to put in a full day while coming in earlier so they can leave earlier in time to meet children's return home from school. Others are experimenting with allowing workers to work for extended hours each day in order to provide a four-day workweek (Glass and Estes 1997). Such creative rearrangements of the workday to better accommodate the demands of family life are still not the norm, however: Evidence suggests that affluent professionals who have greater autonomy on their jobs are far more likely to use flextime than hourly wage workers who have little power to negotiate such accommodations (Sharp, Hermsen, and Billings 2002).

Some firms have begun to offer **catastrophic leave policy,** which allows workers to donate accumulated vacation, personal, and sick days to an account for use by a fellow employee facing a devastating family crisis (Taylor 2003). This can ease the tension between the conflicting demands of work and family, clearly an advantage for the worker. But the employer also gains the advantage of greater productivity from both the beleaguered worker as well as the rest of the workforce, which now may develop a strong sense of community. And the employer may avoid losing a trained and experienced worker, who can now continue on the job while addressing temporary if catastrophic family needs. Notice, however, that it is fellow workers making the major sacrifices, not the employer.

The state can also help reduce the tensions: Congress passed the Family and Medical Leave Act in 1993 to provide unpaid leave time to parents. This is a step in the right direction, but still leaves the United States behind the progress made in other industrialized democracies. The policy allows both mothers and fathers protection from losing their jobs while they care for newborn or adopted children or other members of their families who fall ill. But, unlike other industrialized nations that provide income supports during family leave, the United States makes no such guarantees. As such, only the most affluent families can afford the lost income during leave time, and very few men take advantage of the policy at all (Levine 2000; Ligos 2000).

Summary

Family-related problems have attracted widespread attention in recent years. The rising rates of premarital pregnancy and teenage unwed motherhood have contributed to an increase in single-parent households. Teenage pregnancies reflect the fact that more teenagers are sexually active than in the past, along with their frequent failure to employ effective contraceptive measures. The role of adult males in manipulating and coercing teenage girls into sexual activity that may lead to pregnancy has only recently been acknowledged. Teenage mothers and their children are at higher than average risk for health-related problems, particularly those who must cope with the demands of poverty and lack of adequate health care, and their life chances are frequently diminished.

Rates of marital dissolution have also been on the increase and have made a contribution to the number of single-parent households. Divorce rates may have gone up because of more permissive divorce laws; contraceptive advances that permit women more control over childbearing; female participation in the labor force and the possibility of economic independence from a husband; stresses faced by families, particularly economic ones; and changing attitudes toward marriage. Divorce, which involves a major life transition, requires difficult emotional adjustments on the part of adults and children. It almost always has a negative economic impact on the single-parent household. The failure of women to receive adequate child support from their former husbands has contributed to the so-called feminization of poverty.

Recent research has also revealed high levels of violence within U.S. families, including spouse abuse, child abuse, and violence by children against their parents and against one another. The reasons for such violence cannot be reduced to individual psychological problems in most cases, but lie more with social and cultural factors. Persons learn by observation that violence is often used to solve interpersonal problems and that it is frequently tolerated or accepted as a norm. Conflict that may escalate into violent acts may be built into family life, because of age, gender, and other differences. Families are permitted a great deal of privacy in handling their own affairs and thus are not subject to much control from without that would impede the expression of violence. Finally, there is the contribution of stress on the family, to which violence may be a response.

As such family-related problems as child abuse have become more widely recognized, the often hidden problem of sexual abuse of children has come to light. Child sexual abuse is more common than we might prefer to believe and usually involves children and adults (almost always male adults) who are either relatives or family acquaintances. For the most part, offenders are thought to be psychologically undisturbed people who take advantage of the vulnerability and trust of children for their own needs. Most cases of abuse fail to come to the attention of law enforcement and social service agencies. While a few mental health professionals have tried to suggest that children's sexual encounters with adults may in many cases be harmless or even positive, reports of harmful physical health and emotional outcomes suggest otherwise. The treatment of children as possible sex objects by the mass media and in pornography may contribute to child sexual abuse.

One response by children to family turmoil, abuse, or neglect is to run away. Not only are runaways likely to have experienced ill treatment by their families, but they—more than nonrunaways—have negative experiences with teachers and schooling as well. Whereas runaways usually return to their homes, many other children have no homes to return to. So-called pushouts, or throwaway children, are made to leave by their families. Pushouts and runaways who remain away from home face problems of economic survival that can propel them into such illegal activities as theft and prostitution.

What is to be done? The family-related problem of premarital births and unwed teenage motherhood makes apparent the need for sex education and encouragement of the use of effective contraceptive measures as a norm for sexually active youth. Greater support in such areas as parenting, health, and completion of formal education for pregnant teenagers who decide to be mothers is imperative.

The two areas of major concern with regard to divorce are adjustment to it and the economic stabilization of the custodial parent (commonly the mother) and children. Ways must be found to hold fathers financially responsible for children involved in divorces. The trend toward joint custody—wherein divorced mothers and fathers continue to share in parenting—is a positive step in the adjustment area. The fact that fewer children on average are involved in divorces (although the number is still substantial) is also a positive trend that may help ease adjustment and economic strains.

As violence in the family and child sexual abuse have become recognized as serious and widespread problems, there has been reduced tolerance of them, which may help bring about behavioral change. At the very least it is becoming more likely that family violence and child sexual abuse will be brought to the attention of law enforcement and social service agencies. More resources that would allow such agencies to respond and successfully alter the behaviors in question are needed.

Such intervention may help to reduce the number of children who flee their homes as runaways; it may also reduce the number of pushouts. The latter, because of their youth and economic circumstances, do need alternative homes where they are wanted. Expanded networks of foster family care and small-group homes are required to meet the immediate needs of such homeless children.

Finally, the strain between conflicting demands of work and family has become increasingly acute, particularly for women. Changes in gendered roles within the family and the domestic division of labor will become increasingly necessary as more and more women enter the paid labor force. But the struggle to juggle and find balance will require creative solutions, not only within individual families and their individual members, but also from institutions. Changes in workplace practices as well as laws governing family leave and the like will be required if balance is to be achieved between the need to address family care pressures such as children and elder care and the need to earn a living to support that family.

Key Terms

Abuse 443
Abusive violence 446
Acquaintance rape/date rape 434
Catastrophic leave policy 456
Child abuse 444
Child support 442
Custodial parent 442
Divorce rate 436
Flextime 456

Marital dissolution 436
Nonmarital births 432
Normal violence 446
Pushouts/throwaway children 451
Sandwich generation 454
Second shift 454
Spouse abuse 443

Discussion Questions

1. Despite the lip service paid to the need for sex education, many parents, religious officials, and politicians continue to protest and resist its implementation in public schools. Simulate a dialogue between those for and those against school sex education.

2. Alarmed by the increasing rate of divorce, some experts have advocated a mandatory trial marriage period. For those who wish to remain together, a permanent license would then be issued and this marriage would be legally very difficult to dissolve. Discuss the pros and cons of such a policy.

3. Children seem to have fewer rights than adults in general, and this lack extends to their ability to avoid or end abuse. What additional rights do you think should be extended to children under the law? What might be the positive and negative outcomes of doing this?

4. As widespread as child and spouse abuse has become, it is time to raise questions about how to better deter it. What further deterrents are there? What are the obstacles to implementing these deterrents?

5. Running away from home is widely treated as a juvenile "status offense" and is punishable by court action. What arguments could be made for and against eliminating treatment of this behavior as a crime?

6. The struggle to achieve balance between the demands of work and family is getting increasingly difficult to achieve. What creative solutions might make that balance easier to achieve? What factors might make it even more difficult, and why? How might these be overcome?

Suggested Readings

Edelman, Marian Wright. *Families in Peril* (Cambridge, MA: Harvard University Press, 1989).
Examination of the impact of family instability and poverty on children.

Loseke, Donileen R., Richard J. Gelles, and Mary M. Cavanaugh, eds. *Current Controversies on Family Violence.* 2d ed. (Newbury Park, CA: Sage, 2004).
Compilation of current theoretical debates on the causes, outcomes, and solutions to family violence.

McLanahan, Sara, and Gary Sandefur. *Growing Up with a Single Parent: What Helps, What Hurts* (Cambridge, MA: Harvard University Press, 1994).
Impact of single parenting on a child's well-being and potential.

Taylor, Ronald L., ed. *Minority Families in the United States: A Multicultural Perspective.* 3d ed. (Englewood Cliffs, NJ: Prentice Hall, 2001).
Provides an insightful overview of the experiences of racial and ethnic families with an emphasis on the structural constraints they face in the United States.

Tower, Cynthia Crosson. *Understanding Child Abuse and Neglect.* 6th ed. (Boston: Allyn & Bacon, 2004).
Comprehensive overview of all aspects of child maltreatment, from the impact of abuse on the child to prevention policies required by families, schools, professionals, and the community.

Weitzman, Lenore J. *The Divorce Revolution: The Unexpected Consequences for Women and Children in America* (New York: The Free Press, 1985).
Groundbreaking study of the legal issues surrounding divorce and child custody and the economic hardships into which women and children are thrust.

part IV

Individual Problems

chapter 15

Criminal Behavior

Members of U.S. society should be at peace with themselves and with one another. The vicarious rewards associated with crime and violence must have no attraction.

Periodically, pollsters ask a representative sample of people in the United States to list and rate the social problems they consider most serious. No list looks exactly like any other, as new issues are added and older ones receive different ratings. But crime shows up in every poll, often near the top of the list.

There is a very realistic basis for our concern with crime. National data reveal that each year crime touches one out of four households. Most are victims of property offenses rather than crimes of violence. In central city areas, particularly in and around low-income neighborhoods, the rates of victimization are even higher.

For the most part, the phrase **crime problem** primarily means larceny, burglary, robbery, auto theft, assault, rape, murder, and arson to people in the United States. These crimes touch people very personally. In several, the victims come face-to-face with the perpetrators. Such experiences are often terrifying, if not dangerous or fatal.

The public is far less concerned about certain other categories of crime, perhaps because these seem rather distant and remote. White-collar crime, which costs many billions of dollars more per year than common theft, arouses little public ire. Organized crime is more frequently a subject of entertainment programs than a threat to public sensibilities. Political crimes—whether engaged in by dissident groups or government officials—seem incomprehensible to many people and are easily ignored. Only the most spectacular incidents or revelations are likely to evoke widespread public concern about these types of crime, and even this is often quite temporary.

Thus, most people in the United States take a narrow view of the crime problem, focusing only on prospects or memories of personal victimization. This lack of concern about other types of crime is also found in the official crime statistics produced by law enforcement agencies. These statistics regularly focus on types of criminal behavior people fear. When publicized by the news media, official crime statistics reaffirm the legitimacy of public concern. The meaning and reliability of these statistics are rarely questioned, except perhaps by sociologists. Nor do most people ordinarily notice that certain categories of crime, such as many white-collar offenses, are absent from official reports.

Because of their concern over the crime problem, people in the United States support policies and expenditures that claim to be able to restore "law and order." Yet we need to understand more about the *causes* of criminal behavior. In the absence of an adequate understanding of the causes, the U.S. system of criminal justice remains only partially effective in curbing the crime problem.

In this chapter we examine crime and criminal behavior in U.S. society today. We try to answer the question "What is crime?" and look at sources of crime statistics and their limitations. With these limitations in mind, we assess the extent and significance of various categories of crime. The chapter then considers some physiological, psychological, and sociological explanations for criminal behavior. Finally, we look at the workings of the criminal justice system.

What Is Crime?

As we have seen, most people in the United States define crime as behavior that turns individuals into victims, posing a direct threat to their personal safety or property. The behaviors that are defined as criminal in this sense are considered evil in and of themselves—**mala in se**—such as murder and burglary. No one should have to live in constant fear of harm or loss of personal belongings. No society could continue to function if its members were free to attack one another or take others' property at will. Such acts are condemned in virtually every society. In short, there is universal agreement that certain offensive behaviors are not to be tolerated: They are "wrong" and thus criminal.

But this popular definition of crime as *mala in se* acts does not account for all types of criminal behavior. To define crime, we must examine the society's system of law. Legally, the concept of crime encompasses many more acts than the average person has in mind when discussing the crime problem. In the United States, the legal definition of **crime** is also very precise, referring to acts that are intentional, inexcusable or indefensible, in violation of an existing law, and punishable by the state.

The popular and legal definitions of crime do not always coincide. People in the United States frequently engage in behaviors that are crimes under the law, but that they do not necessarily think of as crimes. For example, workers often remove supplies or tools from their places of employment without realizing that they are committing property offenses. An estimated 83 million people in the United States age 12 and over say they have tried marijuana (National Institute of Drug Abuse 2004), but most would not describe themselves as drug offenders. Laws against fornication and adultery are broken daily, but the individuals involved are unlikely to see themselves as sex criminals. Not until agencies of law enforcement attempt to confer criminal status on individuals engaging in such acts are most people fully conscious of violating the law. Whether individuals are aware of or agree with the legal definition of crime, it is ultimately the law that makes an activity a crime and allows sanctions to be imposed on violators.

Elements of the Legal Definition

Let us look more closely at the legal definition of crime and the various elements involved in this definition. First, to be defined as a crime, an act must have been *intentional*. Although the concept of intention is somewhat vague, the law assumes that most people are capable of regulating their behavior and avoiding illegal acts.

Hence, those who engaged in law-violating behavior must have intended to do so. While intentions are addressed by prosecutors in court, and accused individuals are given the opportunity to defend themselves, the burden of proving an act to be unintentional is placed squarely on the shoulders of the accused.

The legal definition of crime also involves the idea that the act in question is *inexcusable* or *indefensible.* One of the few excuses is that the individual had no control over the illegal behavior. Thus, individuals are unlikely to be accorded criminal status if they can prove that they were acting under duress, that is, if they were forced by others to violate the law. Likewise, age is considered to be relevant to the issue of control over, and thus responsibility for, criminal behavior. Ordinarily, children under 7 years of age are not held responsible for their actions. Special judicial treatment is accorded individuals between 7 and 16 or 18 years of age, because **juvenile delinquents** are ordinarily considered to be less responsible for their behavior than adults. Finally, individuals may defend their illegal behavior by claiming insanity. In this case, accused persons may claim that they were mentally incapable of avoiding the act in question or incapable of differentiating between right and wrong at the time the law violation took place. (For a discussion of the insanity defense, see Chapter 16.)

Ultimately, however, the key element of the legal definition of crime is the *law* itself. The law enables the state to *punish* those whose acts are considered intentional, inexcusable, and in violation of a law by conferring the status of criminal on them. It is not too much of a truism to say that in the absence of law, criminals would not exist. Without law there is no such thing as crime—at least in the legal sense.

Defining Behavior as Criminal

Why do some acts get defined by law as crime while others do not? There are conflicting answers to this question. According to some, law is formulated in response to the will of the people. Members of society, it is said, share common values. Law is the product of a societal consensus about what forms of behavior are to be allowed and what forms are to be condemned and punished. In this view, we live in a democratic, pluralistic society (see Chapter 2), in which equally powerful interest groups compete to direct and express the public will. The state responds by passing laws that serve the self-defined best interests of society's members. The state itself is neutral. It is not under the sway of any dominant group, for there is no such group in U.S. society.

An alternative view holds that law is formulated in response to the interests of the dominant economic and social class (Greenberg 1993). In a society like ours, wealth, status, and political power are unequally distributed. The dominant class—that which is most advantaged in terms of this distribution—is said to be in the best position to influence actions of the state. This class seeks to protect its economic resources and general well-being through the force of law. In this view, the state is not neutral—either in the formulation of law or in practices of law enforcement. Rather, the state acts in the interests and is an instrument of the dominant class (Lynch 1994; Reiman 2003).

Sociologist William Chambliss (1974; Chambliss and Seidman 1982) has suggested that the real state of affairs lies somewhere in between these two views. According to Chambliss, there is evidence that some laws are indeed expressions of public opinion and are responses to pressure by interest groups. Examples include laws limiting pollution and statutes protecting women and racial minorities against discrimination. Other laws, however, clearly favor the economically advantaged. Examples here are tax loopholes and the absence of severe legal penalties for many white-collar crimes. Thus, says Chambliss, there is evidence that members of the dominant class actively use their political power to influence the formulation of law so as to protect themselves.

Chambliss has proposed a third view of why acts are defined as crimes. He calls this view a **conflict theory of legal change.** This theory begins by recognizing that U.S. society is composed of competing classes and interest groups that seek favors from the state. Since these classes differ in their wealth, power, and prestige, conflicts (e.g., over the control of economic resources) will and do take place. These conflicts ultimately cause acts to be defined as crimes:

It is in the course of working through and living with these inherent conflicts that the law takes its particular content and form. It is out of the conflicts generated by social class divisions that the definition of some acts as criminal or delinquent emerges. (Chambliss 1974:39)

Chambliss notes that the dominant class wins only some of these conflicts. Class-based conflicts are often resolved by the state through compromise legislation or legal decisions that seem fair to most if not all.

Meanwhile, according to Chambliss, a variety of interest groups that are not class-based are also competing for favors from the state. Bureaucracies want their interests protected or advanced. "Moral entrepreneurs"—groups with particular moral concerns that they would like to see translated into law—likewise compete for attention. Again there is winning, losing, and compromise as the state responds.

Chambliss suggests that the formulation of law, and thus the creation of the legal definition of crime, is a dynamic, historical process. This process is not totally democratic; in other words, law does not automatically emerge from and serve the interests of all members of society. Nor is the process totally manipulated by a dominant class. It is, however, a political process:

What gets defined as criminal or delinquent behavior is the result of a political process within which rules are formed which prohibit or require people to behave in certain ways. . . . Nothing is inherently criminal, it is only the response that makes it so. If we are to explain crime, we must first explain the social forces that cause some acts to be defined as criminal while others are not. (Chambliss 1974:39)

Sociologists like Chambliss do research on how laws are formulated and how this leads to the "creation" of crime (see Gibbons 1991). Clearly, the answer to the question "What is crime?" must go beyond a legal definition. The answer must include attention to the societal sources of any such definition.

Crime Statistics

This chapter primarily considers crime as it is legally defined. In the United States, our perception of the crime problem is to a large extent based on official reports, such as the *Uniform Crime Reports* issued annually by the U.S. Department of Justice. Data in this report and from other sources as well must be approached with caution (see Sheley 1999).

Official Statistics

The Justice Department's *Uniform Crime Reports* is a summary of data submitted by more than 16,000 police departments around the country. These agencies of law enforcement are in a position to gather several types of crime statistics, including the number and kinds of crimes reported to or observed by local police, arrest statistics, and statistics on cases in which conviction took place. To assess the amount of crime taking place in the United States, one begins with data on the number of crimes reported to police or otherwise officially detected.

Sociologists have long been aware that the statistics accumulated by police departments and reported by them are of questionable accuracy.

Many crimes simply are not brought to the attention of police and thus do not get counted. Murder is almost always reported; but perhaps several times as many rapes occur as are brought to police attention. Although most people will report the theft of an automobile, far fewer will report the theft of personal property that is worth relatively little. A woman who is beaten up by a stranger on the street is likely to call the police; one who is assaulted by her husband is far less likely to do so.

In some cases, crimes are not reported to law enforcement agencies because the victims know the perpetrator and want to handle the problem informally. This often occurs for minor offenses. In other cases, people may feel that a crime is not worth reporting because it is unlikely that the police will handle it satisfactorily or solve it. In still other cases, the victims may fear retribution or revenge if they report offenses to the police. Finally, some crimes are simply never detected or the illegal acts in question are not defined as crimes by those in a position to do the reporting. Whatever the reasons involved, we know that statistics on crime reported to the police grossly underestimate the extent of crime.

Official crime statistics are also subject to distortion by the actions of police themselves. Police departments differ in their vigilance and in the degree to which they are actively concerned with particular categories of crime. Attention to public complaints and police reaction to observed law violations may vary among police departments at different times. Police departments and individual officers have considerable discretion in making arrests. If they choose to avoid arresting individuals, the amount of crime will look smaller than it actually is. Alternatively, police activism may create the appearance of statistical increases in criminal behavior.

A case in point is the way police handle persons possessing illegal drugs. There has been an upward trend in arrests for possession and sale of illegal drugs in recent decades. Part of this increase can be attributed to the fact that drug use was not considered an important problem during most of the 1960s, so police rarely made arrests, or else concentrated on certain segments of the population, such as the poor, when looking for drugs. From the late 1960s on, however, drug use became both much more widespread and a matter of societal concern, and police became more vigilant. Nonetheless, police today continue to ignore many minor drug offenders: One need only go to a rock concert to see drug laws violated with impunity, often right in front of the police. Such crimes do not find their way into the statistics.

Furthermore, individual police departments have different procedures for collecting and reporting crime statistics. The U.S. Department of Justice has made notable efforts to encourage standardized procedures across the country, but it has not been totally successful. Moreover, as departments change their procedures to conform to federal standards, statistics on incidence may change even if the same amount of crime is occurring. There is also evidence that some police departments do not report all the crimes they know of. For example, in the 1960s the President's Commission on Law Enforcement found that a number of large city police departments kept separate records on crimes that they did not follow up on and those they wanted to keep from the public for political reasons (President's Commission on Law Enforcement and Administration of Justice 1968; Seidman and Conzens 1974).

There is also the question of just what police are counting. A violation may involve one offender or many; it may also involve more than one law. For example, if two teenagers kill someone in a fight, escape by stealing a car after assaulting the driver, and are finally stopped after numerous traffic offenses, who and what is to be counted? When confronted with such dilemmas, police departments are likely to work out their own formulas. They may count crimes by the numbers of victims involved. Or they may count only the most serious crime (for example, in terms of the probable penalty for conviction) committed by each offender. This and other inaccuracies in counting distort official statistics.

If trying to figure out what to make of official statistics is made difficult by such factors, trying to compute crime *rates* is even worse. Crime rates are important for a number of reasons. They make it possible to compare crime in different locales or over periods of time. Many sociologists use comparative crime rates in their search for explanations of crime and criminality. Knowledge of changing rates is also of practical importance to officials interested in evaluating the effectiveness of efforts to prevent or control crime. Members of the public want to know whether the taxes they pay for law enforcement are being used wisely. People also use crime rates as a barometer of the quality of life in their communities.

Crime rates are calculated in terms of the ratio between the number of crimes officially recorded and the size of the population. For example, the murder rate is expressed in terms of the number of known murders per 100,000 people. One would assume that, since most murders become known to police, the murder *rate* is reliable. But there are problems other than the lack of reliability of police statistics. We only count the number of people in the U.S. population every 10 years. Even then, the U.S. Bureau of the Census misses millions. For example, people who are inner-city residents, poor, homeless or transient, or nondocumented immigrants (in the country illegally) are generally undercounted. This means that the population figures so crucial to computing crime rates are estimates. Crime rates can be no more reliable than the statistics that go into them, which means they should be treated with caution.

Another complication involves the changing composition of the U.S. population. What may appear to be a shift in criminality may simply be a reflection of changing population characteristics. For example, young people are responsible for a disproportionate amount of such common crimes as robbery. A decrease in the rates for these crimes may simply be a result of a decreased proportion of young people. Such changes create problems. Do we know all the factors that must be taken into account in order to compare crime rates among locales or over time? How much weight should be given to those factors we do know about in order to interpret rates and compare them?

At best, official crime statistics provide an approximation of the actual amount of crime. Attempts to refine the methods of gathering, reporting, and interpreting such statistics continue, but substantial problems remain. Criminal codes defining what is a crime differ somewhat from state to state. Political considerations in a particular locale will probably always affect police activity and patterns of law enforcement. Individuals will probably never report each and every crime they know about. Although the Justice Department can encourage and demand valid, standardized statistics from law enforcement agencies, it cannot really do anything about such sources of error—except estimate the biases they introduce in crime data.

Victimization Studies

In an attempt to develop more satisfactory data on the extent of crime, some researchers have gone to the real or potential victims. Beginning in 1972, the U.S. Department of Justice began funding the National Crime Victimization Survey (called the National Crime Survey until 1991) in which annual interviews are held with a national sample of people age 12 and over. In these interviews, individuals are asked whether they have been victims of rape, robbery, assault, or larceny in the past year. Data are also collected on burglary, larceny, and motor vehicle theft experienced by households (see Table 15.1).

Table 15.1	Estimated Percent Distribution of Personal and Household Victimizations by Type of Victimization and Reporting to Police, United States, 2003 *

Type of victimization	Number of victimizations	Reported to police[†]
All crimes	23,624,410	
Personal crimes	5,541,610	
Crimes of violence	5,371,570	47.5
Completed	1,704,040	
Attempted	3,667,520	
Rape/Sexual assault	223,290	38.5
Rape	81,310	
Attempted rape	61,060	
Sexual assault	80,910	
Robbery	554,310	60.5
Completed	381,880	
With injury	165,090	
Without injury	216,790	
Attempted	172,440	
With injury	48,160	
Without injury	124,290	
Assault	4,593,970	
Aggravated	1,045,610	59.4
Completed with injury	338,930	
Threatened with weapon	706,680	
Simple	3,548,360	42.1
Completed with minor injury	837,770	
Without injury	2,710,590	
Personal theft	170,050	43.9
Property crimes	18,082,800	31.8
Theft	13,846,520	
Completed	13,379,380	
Less than $50	4,188,440	
$50 or more	7,926,910	
Attempted	539,490	
Household burglary	3,225,670	54.1
Completed	2,703,900	

(*Continued*)

Table 15.1	(Continued)	
Type of victimization	Number of victimizations	Reported to police
Forcible entry	1,016,990	
Unlawful entry without force	1,686,910	
Attempted forcible entry	521,770	
Motor vehicle theft	1,010,610	76.8
Completed	772,070	
Attempted	238,550	

*Subcategories may not sum to total because of rounding.

†Represents the rates at which victimizations were reported to the police, or "police reporting rates."

Source: Shannan N. Catalano, *Sourcebook of Criminal Justice Statistics, 2003* (Washington, DC: U.S. Government Printing Office, 2004), pp. 3, 10.

The National Crime Victimization Survey has shown that many crimes are not reported to police and thus never appear in official police statistics. Further, the reporting of crimes to police varies, depending on the type of crime. For example, in 2003 the survey found that 76.8 percent of motor vehicle thefts, 38.5 percent of rapes, and 43.9 percent of personal theft were reported to police.

Besides the striking evidence of underreported and differentially reported crimes, the National Crime Victimization Surveys also reveal some interesting facts about crime victims. In the case of violent crime, for example, the rates of victimization are highest among those who are under 25, male, African American, divorced or separated or never married, central city residents, and from low-income families (Catalano 2004:7–8).

Victimization surveys can be criticized. The data are best viewed as providing estimates of victimization. One has to assume that the sample of people being interviewed is representative of the population as a whole. One must also assume that those interviewed are providing accurate information—that they are neither consciously distorting nor unintentionally forgetting information. Many crimes are not part of the National Crime Victimization Survey, such as murder, arson, kidnapping, drug abuse, prostitution, drunkenness, as well as consumer fraud, and commercial burglary and robbery. Finally, only one criminal act is counted per incident by the survey; for example, the most serious offense is counted when more than one occurs in an individual's encounter with crime. But even with such possible sources of error and limitations, victimization studies have opened up a whole new way of viewing the extent of crime in the United States. Perhaps the most serious limitation of the National Crime Victimization Survey is its very narrow focus on certain categories of crime to the exclusion of others.

Self-Report Studies

Another way researchers attempt to measure the extent of crime is to ask people to report on their own law-violating behavior. In numerous studies, people have been invited to fill out anonymous questionnaires or submit to confidential interviews. In many cases, researchers have made efforts to validate their interview or questionnaire data against official police records.

The major findings of these self-report studies support common sense. Just about everyone has violated the law at one time or another, committing offenses for which he or she could have been jailed or at least fined. Most of the illegal acts were undetected, at least by law enforcement officials. Most law violators admit to committing only a few minor offenses. A small minority admits to numerous minor offenses and/or some serious crimes.

One of the obvious contributions of self-report studies is that they disprove stereotypes that only certain types of people (e.g., the poor or people of color) or only a small percentage of the population commit most criminal acts. Such studies also suggest that we cannot generalize about the characteristics of those who commit crimes on the basis of knowledge about persons who are arrested or the approximately 1.5 million people who occupy our jails and prisons.

Some argue that the findings of self-report studies on the distribution of criminality by age, sex, race, and class are of doubtful validity. For example, whereas some studies suggest that common crimes are disproportionately committed by lower-class people, other studies throw doubt on such findings. The two most important limitations are that we do not know if the people who answer questionnaires and submit to interviews are providing accurate information and that we cannot trust the validity of the official police records against which the results of such inquiries are at times checked. In addition, self-report studies have frequently been undertaken without much concern over the representativeness of the sample of persons studied, so that the generalizability of their findings is difficult to judge.

More revealing, perhaps, are the occasional self-reports of individuals who are *not* the subjects of research attention. When, for example, an organized crime figure decides to "sing" during a congressional investigation, a whole new world of crime and criminal intrigue may be revealed (Maas 1968). Such dramatic self-reports underscore the shallowness, if not the questionable accuracy, of official crime statistics.

Extent and Distribution of Crime

Criminal behavior, as legally defined, takes a wide variety of forms. In this section we examine a number of different forms of serious crime and look at official statistics on their extent. As we have noted, such statistics are known to underestimate the actual amount of crime in the United States. We also look at "victimless crime," illegal activity people engage in voluntarily, in which allegedly there is no victim. Since certain types of criminal behavior—white-collar, organized, and political crime—do not show up adequately in official statistics, our coverage of these types of crime is descriptive rather than statistical.

Traditional Crime

Despite the problems associated with official crime reports, they are still the best existing source of statistics on common or **traditional crime.** In the vernacular of the U.S. Department of Justice's *Uniform Crime Reports,* we shall address the extent and significance of **index offenses.** Index offenses are serious law violations that, in the view of the Justice Department, indicate the gravity of the United States' crime problem. The eight index offenses are murder and nonnegligent manslaughter, forcible rape, robbery, aggravated assault, burglary (breaking and entering), larceny (theft), motor vehicle theft, and arson. In 2003 a total of 10,661,782 index offenses were reported by police departments, not including cases of arson. On the average, this comes out to one offense every two seconds

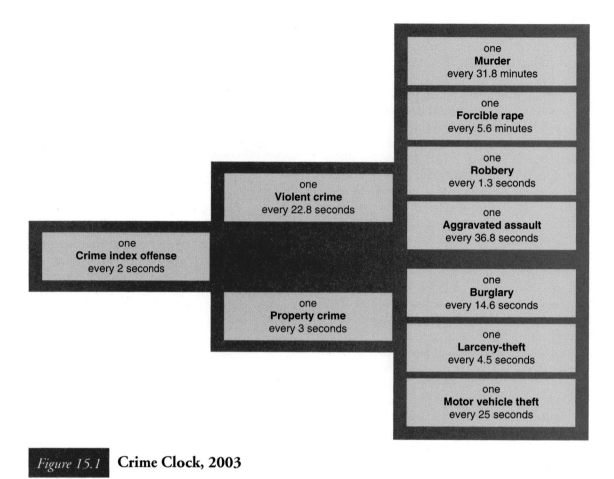

Figure 15.1   **Crime Clock, 2003**

Source: U.S. Department of Justice, *Uniform Crime Reports for the United States, 2003* (Washington, DC: U.S. Government Printing Office, 2004), p. 7.

(see Figure 15.1). Although the overall trend has been upward since 1985, the index offense rate has recently dropped slightly. However, in most crime categories the rate is still higher than a decade ago.

▲ Murder and Nonnegligent Manslaughter

Murder and nonnegligent manslaughter refer to the willful killing of another person, as determined by police investigation. In 2003, 16,503 persons were victims, a 29.3 percent decline from 1994 (see Table 15.2). Almost four-fifths of the victims were males, and almost half were in their 20s or early 30s. Almost half of the victims were African American, meaning that the murder of people of color occurs far more frequently than their percentage representation in the population would lead one to predict. More than three-fourths of the deaths either were within the confines of the family or involved people who knew one another. Such factors render murder a difficult offense to prevent. Nonetheless, almost 43 percent of all known criminal homicides were solved by arrest in 2003—a higher percentage than for any other index crime. Of those arrested, most were males of the same race as the victim, and 44 percent were in the 17 to 34 age group. (There has been a notable trend toward criminal homicide among the young in recent years.) Most of those killed in 2003 died from gunshot wounds: 65 percent of the criminal homicides involved some type of firearms, and in 51 percent of the cases handguns were involved (U.S. Department of Justice 2004).

When people worry about violent crimes, they often think of crimes carried out by strangers. Here, police examine the body of a victim of a drive-by shooting. However, nearly half of all murders in the United States are committed by persons who are family members or acquaintances of the victims.

▲ Aggravated Assault

Serious assaults involve attempts to kill or to inflict severe bodily injury. Police departments reported 857,921 cases of **aggravated assault** in 2003, a decline of almost 23 percent from 1994. In most instances, assault takes place either within the family or between neighbors and acquaintances. Unlike criminal homicide, which mainly involves the use of firearms, the weapons employed in aggravated assaults vary greatly. In 2003, 38.2 percent of the assaults known to the police were solved by arrest. Since the victim, perpetrator, and witnesses are likely to be related to or acquainted with one another, witnesses and victims are often reluctant to testify. According to official statistics, most of those arrested in 2003 were white and 18 or older (U.S. Department of Justice 2004).

▲ Forcible Rape

Rape is one of the most underreported offenses in the United States. Nonetheless, police departments reported 93,433 cases of forcible rape in 2003, a decline of almost 9 percent from 1994.

Like other official crime statistics, those on forcible rape are hard to interpret. The apparent decrease could be partially due to greater reluctance of women to report rape, even though they have been urged to do so by advocates of the feminist movement and by police officials. Rape convictions continue to be difficult to achieve, and victims are often subjected to scorching public scrutiny by defense counsels. Many victims liken the experience to getting raped a second time, and often with little result.

Several widely publicized rape convictions, such as that of Alex Kelly in Connecticut, contradict the perception that a victim cannot gain a conviction of her attacker; and technologies using DNA found on the victims help to identify and convict perpetrators more easily than a decade ago. But that does not necessarily mean that victims are convinced otherwise: DNA evidence can attest that sexual contact has occurred, but it does not establish whether or not the contact was consensual, a limitation that defense attorneys often emphasize. Thus, National

Table 15.2 **Index of Crime, United States, 1984–2003**

Population*	Crime index total[†]	Violent crime[‡]	Property crime[‡]
	Number of offenses		
Population by year:			
1985—238,740,000	12,431,400	1,328,800	11,102,600
1986—241,077,000	13,211,900	1,489,170	11,722,700
1987—243,400,000	13,508,700	1,484,000	12,024,700
1988—245,807,000	13,923,100	1,566,220	12,356,900
1989—248,239,000	14,251,400	1,646,040	12,605,400
1990—248,709,873	14,475,600	1,820,130	12,655,500
1991—252,177,000	14,872,900	1,911,770	12,961,100
1992—255,082,000	14,438,200	1,932,270	12,505,900
1993—257,908,000[§]	14,144,800	1,926,020	12,218,800
1994—260,341,000	13,991,700	1,864,170	12,127,500
2003—290,809,777	11,816,782	1,381,259	10,435,523
Percent change: Number of offenses:			
1994/1993	−1.1	−3.2	−7
1994/1990	−3.3	+2.4	−4.2
1994/1985	+12.6	+40.3	+9.2
2003/1994	−15.5	−25.6	−14.0
	Rate per 100,000 inhabitants		
Year:			
1985	5,207.1	556.6	4,650.5
1986	5,480.4	617.7	4,862.6
1987	5,550.0	609.7	4,940.3
1988	5,664.2	637.2	5,027.1
1989	5,741.0	663.1	5,077.9
1990	5,820.3	731.8	5,088.5
1991	5,897.8	758.1	5,139.7
1992	5,660.2	757.5	4,902.7
1993[§]	5,484.4	746.8	4,737.6
1994	5,374.4	716.0	4,658.3
2003	4,063.4	475.0	3,588.4
Percent change: Rate per 100,000 inhabitants:			
1994/1993	−2.0	−4.1	−1.7
1994/1990	−7.7	−2.2	−8.5
1994/1985	+3.2	+28.6	+.2
2003/1994	−21.4	−33.4	−23.0

Murder and non-negligent manslaughter	Forcible rape	Robbery	Aggravated assault	Burglary	Larceny-theft	Motor vehicle theft
Number of offenses						
18,980	88,670	497,870	723,250	3,073,300	6,926,400	1,102,900
20,610	91,460	542,780	834,320	3,241,400	7,257,200	1,224,100
20,100	91,110	517,700	855,090	3,236,200	7,499,900	1,288,700
20,680	92,490	542,970	910,090	3,218,100	7,705,900	1,432,900
21,500	94,500	578,330	951,710	3,168,200	7,872,400	1,564,800
23,440	102,560	639,270	1,054,860	3,073,900	7,945,700	1,635,900
24,700	106,590	687,730	1,092,740	3,157,200	8,142,200	1,661,700
23,760	109,060	672,480	1,126,970	2,979,900	7,915,200	1,610,800
24,530	106,010	659,870	1,135,610	2,834,800	7,820,900	1,563,100
23,310	102,100	618,820	1,119,950	2,712,200	7,876,300	1,539,100
16,503	93,433	413,402	857,921	2,153,464	7,021,588	1,260,471
−5.0	−3.7	−6.2	−1.4	−4.3	+.7	−1.5
−.6	−.4	−3.2	+6.2	−11.8	−.9	−5.9
+22.8	+15.1	+24.3	+54.8	11.7	+13.7	+39.6
−29.3	−8.6	−33.2	−22.9	−20.6	−10.9	−18.1
Rate per 100,000 inhabitants						
7.9	37.1	208.5	302.9	1,287.3	2,901.2	462.0
8.6	37.9	225.1	346.1	1,344.6	3,010.3	507.8
8.3	37.4	212.7	351.3	1,329.6	3,081.3	529.4
8.4	37.6	220.9	370.2	1,309.2	3,134.9	582.9
8.7	38.1	233.0	383.4	1,276.3	3,171.3	630.4
9.4	41.2	257.0	424.1	1,235.9	3,194.8	657.8
9.8	42.3	272.7	433.3	1,252.0	3,228.8	659.0
9.3	42.8	263.6	441.8	1,168.2	3,103.0	631.5
9.5	41.1	255.9	440.3	1,099.2	3,032.4	606.1
9.0	39.2	237.7	430.2	1,041.8	3,025.4	591.2
5.7	32.1	142.2	295.0	740.5	2,414.5	433.4
−5.3	−4.6	−7.1	−2.3	−5.2	−.2	−2.5
−4.3	−4.9	−7.5	+1.4	−15.7	−5.3	−10.1
+13.9	+5.7	+14.0	+42.0	−19.1	+4.3	+28.0
−36.7	−18.2	−40.2	−31.0	−28.9	−20.2	−26.7

*Populations are Bureau of the Census provisional estimates as of July 1, except 1990, which is the decennial census count.
†Because of rounding, the offenses may not add to totals. ‡Violent crimes are offenses of murder, forcible rape, robbery, and aggravated assault. Property crimes are offenses of burglary, larceny-theft, and motor vehicle theft. Data are not included for the property crime of arson. §The forcible rape, robbery, aggravated assault, and motor vehicle theft categories have been adjusted for 1993.

Source: U.S. Department of Justice, *Uniform Crime Reports for the United States, 1994* (Washington, DC: U.S. Government Printing Office, 1995), p. 58; U.S. Department of Justice, *Uniform Crime Reports for the United States, 2003* (Washington, DC: U.S. Government Printing Office, 2004); available at www.fbi.gov.

Crime Victimization Surveys show only slightly more than one-third of rapes being reported to police, and many would argue that even this is a substantial underestimation of victimization.

Forcible rapes are even less likely to be solved by arrest than aggravated assaults. Only 30.8 percent of those reported resulted in arrests in 2003. These statistics indicate that forcible rape is one of the easiest crimes to get away with, given the low likelihood of ultimate conviction. In 2003, 46 percent of those arrested were under 25 years of age; over two-thirds were white. Contrary to some stereotypes, most forcible rapes take place within racial groups. Victims frequently are acquainted with the rapist, which helps account for the relatively low rates of arrest and prosecution, since it is sometimes difficult for victims to prove that they were indeed assaulted forcibly and against their will. Defense attorneys attempt to put the victims of rape on trial to discredit their accounts. Sexist attitudes on the part of police and prosecutors often work to give accused rapists the benefit of the doubt, although this has been undergoing change (U.S. Department of Justice 2004).

▲ Robbery

Robbery involves stealing, during which force and violence (or the threat of violence) are employed. Police departments reported 413,402 robberies in 2003, a decline of more than 33 percent over 1994. Almost half the robberies known to police were committed on the street; the remainder occurred within households and business establishments. Only 17.5 percent of robberies were solved by arrest. Victims are unlikely to know the law violators, and it is relatively easy to get away with the crime. If we assume that those who are arrested are representative of robbers, young people are very much involved in this index offense. In 2003, 62 percent of those arrested were under 25 years of age. Almost 90 percent of the arrests involved males,

and 54.4 percent of those arrested were African American. According to Justice Department estimates, money and goods valued at $514 million were stolen from robbery victims in 2003 (U.S. Department of Justice 2004).

▲ Burglary

Burglary involves unlawfully breaking into or entering a structure (e.g., a home or business), with the intent of committing theft or some other serious crime. Burglary is a far more common crime than robbery. In 2003 an estimated 2,153,464 burglaries were reported by police departments, down almost 21 percent from 1994. Sixty-six percent involved residences, and 31 percent took place in the daytime. Losses were estimated at $3.5 billion. Despite the volume and costs of burglary, only 9.1 percent of reported burglaries were solved by arrest in 2003. Of those arrested, 63 percent were under 25 years of age, and 29.2 percent were under 18. More than 70 percent of those arrested were white, and almost all were male (U.S. Department of Justice 2004).

▲ Larceny

In 2003, police departments reported 7,021,588 cases of larceny, making it the most frequent of the index offenses. This number represented a decline of almost 11 percent from 1994. Larceny, which does not include motor vehicle theft, involves taking or removing property that belongs to another. In 2003 larceny cost its victims an estimated $4.9 billion. Only 12.8 percent of all cases of larceny known to the police were solved by arrest. Of those arrested, more than 28 percent were under 18 years of age. Significantly, almost one-third of the arrests involved females: They are arrested far more frequently for larceny than for any other single index crime. In 2003 arrests of whites outnumbered arrests of African Americans by more than two to one (U.S. Department of Justice 2004).

▲ Motor Vehicle Theft

In 2003 police reported 1,260,471 cases of motor vehicle theft. This was down over 18 percent from 1994. Although most stolen vehicles were eventually recovered and returned to their owners, only 9.6 percent of such thefts were solved by arrest. Most of those arrested were young; 62.3 percent were under 25, and 29.1 percent were under 18. Most of those arrested were male, and 61.3 percent were white. As with the other index offenses, one can only cautiously assume that those arrested are representative of those who have committed this particular law violation. Stolen vehicles involved losses of some $8.6 billion in 2003 (U.S. Department of Justice 2004).

▲ Arson

Crimes of arson were added to the index crime list at the behest of Congress in 1991. The data provided to the Justice Department are not as complete as those for other index offenses, and trend data are lacking. However, in 2003 more than 64,000 arson offenses were reported. Some 42 percent involved structures (mostly residences), another 33 percent involved mobile property (usually automobiles), and about 25 percent involved other property such as timber or crops. The average monetary value of property damage was $11,942 per incident. While the volume of offenses was highest in large cities and lowest in rural areas, industrial and manufacturing structural fires produced the greatest average monetary losses, averaging $136,644 per offense.

Only 16.7 percent of the arsons were cleared by arrest in 2003. Almost 41 percent of those arrested were under 18, making arson the index offense with the highest juvenile involvement. Most of those arrested were white and male (U.S. Department of Justice 2004).

A Note on Crime and Gender

In reviewing the preceding official crime statistics, little was said about the proportional arrests of males and females. It is clear that the vast majority of arrests for index offenses involve males, and this is particularly true with regard to crimes of violence. Male dominance of arrest figures has been the case since the Justice Department began collecting these data almost 70 years ago.

There has, however, been a visible increase in female arrest rates (Adler, Mueller, and Laufer 2003). In 1960 women accounted for only 11 percent of the nation's total arrests. The rate is now up to almost 22 percent. *Uniform Crime Reports* data covering the period 1994–2003 indicate that the overall arrest rate for men charged with index offenses fell 6.7 percent; for women, the overall arrest rate *increased* 12.3 percent (U.S. Department of Justice 2004). Increased involvement of women in crime has also been discerned in victimization and self-report studies. Finally, women's share of the U.S. prison population has been on the rise, although not as dramatically as the arrest rate, since most arrests of women continue to be for comparatively minor offenses.

There has been a good deal of debate and research bearing on the meaning of such increases (Beirne and Messerschmidt 1995; Price and Sokoloff 2003). Rita James Simon (1975) has argued that the increasing arrest rates for women reflect more involvement on the part of women in criminal activity. Although most of the overall increase that has taken place involves property offenses such as larceny, fraud, and embezzlement as opposed to crimes of violence, to Simon this represents a movement toward sex equality in criminal behavior. Increased labor force participation of women and related breakdowns in traditional sex roles and in patterns of sexist treatment have begun to open up new opportunities for women and to put them under new kinds of pressures as well. As this occurs, Simon argues, we should expect to see changes in the volume of criminal behavior involving women.

A somewhat similar approach to interpreting trends in female criminal behavior has been taken by Freda Adler. She argues that what we are seeing is the rise of "the new woman criminal," a variant of the aggressive, competitive female inspired by the feminist movement. As traditional gender roles blur, as women enter realms of activity always reserved for men and considered "masculine," this shift toward androgyny is carrying over into criminal pursuits. Thus it is argued that

the temptations, challenges, stresses, and strains to which women have been increasingly subjected in recent years cause them to act or react in the same manner in which men have consistently reacted to the same stimuli. In other words, equalization of social and economic roles leads to similar behavior patterns. (Adler, Mueller, and Laufer 1995:42; see also Adler, Mueller, and Laufer 2003)

Critics of the notion of the new woman criminal point out that most of the increase in women's criminal behavior—if overall arrest rates are the indicator—is in property crime, not crimes of violence. This trend can as easily be interpreted as reflecting the continued social and economic subordination of women, as opposed to their stepping into traditional male opportunities and roles. Men still commit the most crimes and dominate in arrests for serious offenses, including the most serious and damaging of property crimes. Critics thus argue that women's economic marginalization into the least secure and least well paying positions in the labor force (which is correlated with their overrepresentation in the poverty and near-poverty population) helps to explain their patterns of crime, in which relatively minor property offenses play the principal role (Beirne and Messerschmidt 1995).

Moreover, the statistical changes in question apparently started early in the 1960s, before the feminist movement began to make its promi-

nent impact and thus could have affected criminal behavior (Steffensmeier and Cobb 1981). Finally, critics have suggested that the rise in both female arrest and imprisonment could simply mean that the police and others who are part of the criminal justice system have had their attitudes altered by the feminist movement. Perhaps women are being treated more equally (and severely) by the system, and chivalry has given way to objectivity (Barak, Flavin, and Leighton 2001; Daly 1994).

Victimless Crime

The eight index offenses are considered by the Justice Department to be the most serious crimes in the United States, in terms of both the damage they inflict and their extensiveness. In its *Uniform Crime Reports,* the Justice Department also presents data on offenses ranging from forgery to loitering. Of the more than 9.5 million arrests made by police departments in 2003, almost 84 percent were for crimes other than index offenses (see Table 15.3). A high percentage of these arrests were for alcohol- and drug-related offenses, gambling, sex offenses and prostitution, pornography offenses, vagrancy, and curfew and loitering violations.

Those crimes, which are entered into voluntarily and do not involve crime victims, are called **victimless crimes.** Victimless crimes are difficult to measure and are a matter of substantial controversy. Though arrest statistics on many victimless crimes are compiled in the Justice Department's *Uniform Crime Reports,* there are no official figures on their extent. Arrest statistics grossly understate the extent of such crimes.

Controversy surrounds victimless crimes for two reasons. First, many people believe that the state has no right to impose its version of morality on certain types of behavior. For example, they argue, if people want to enjoy hardcore pornography, possess and use marijuana, purchase sexual enjoyment, or gamble, they

Table 15.3	Total Estimated Arrests,* United States, 2003
Total[†]	**9,581,423**
Murder and nonnegligent manslaughter	9,119
Forcible rape	18,446
Robbery	75,667
Aggravated assault	315,732
Burglary	204,761
Larceny-theft	817,048
Motor vehicle theft	106,221
Arson	11,330
Violent crime[‡]	418,964
Property crime[§]	1,139,360
Crime index total[¶]	1,558,324
Other assaults	877,105
Forgery and counterfeiting	79,188
Fraud	208,469
Embezzlement	11,986
Stolen property; buying, receiving, possessing	89,560
Vandalism	193,083
Weapons; carrying, possessing, etc.	117,844
Prostitution and commercialized vice	51,686
Sex offenses (except forcible rape and prostitution)	63,759
Drug abuse violations	1,172,222
Gambling	7,414
Offenses against family and children	94,488
Driving under the influence	1,005,777
Liquor laws	431,912
Drunkenness	389,626
Disorderly conduct	453,645
Vagrancy	20,052
All other offenses	2,571,023
Suspicion (not included in totals)	1,812
Curfew and loitering law violations	95,052
Runaways	87,396

*Arrest totals are based on all reporting agencies and estimates for unreported areas. †Because of rounding, figures may not add to totals. ‡Violent crimes are offenses of murder, forcible rape, robbery, and aggravated assault. §Property crimes are offenses of burglary, larceny-theft, motor vehicle theft, and arson. ¶Includes arson.

Source: U.S. Department of Justice, *Uniform Crime Reports for the United States, 2003* (Washington, DC: U.S. Government Printing Office, 2004), p. 280.

should be free to follow their own moral standards without interference by the state. However, others strongly feel that such behaviors should not be permitted under the law.

The second reason victimless crimes are controversial relates to their impact on the criminal justice system. Enough arrests are made for such crimes to clog the system and overwhelm the capacity of the police, courts, and penal institutions. Many experts believe that a new approach to victimless crimes would make the criminal justice system more efficient and less costly. One suggestion is to decrease penalties. In a number of states and localities, for example, possession of a small amount of marijuana for personal use is punishable by a summons (similar to a traffic ticket) and a small fine. This frees the criminal justice system while implicitly recognizing the arguments against unlicensed freedom to use this particular drug.

Some would argue that the term *victimless crime* is a misnomer and that significant costs are involved (Schur and Bedeau 1974). For example, gambling profits often help to sustain the activities of organized crime, as do prostitution, drug sales, and pornography. Prostitution may be an occasion for robbery, crimes of violence, and the spread of sexually transmitted diseases. Drug sales contribute to drug abuse, as well as habitual criminal behavior on the part of some users (e.g., heroin and cocaine addicts in need of funds to support their habits). Both intravenous drug use and prostitution have been implicated in the spread of AIDS. Financial transactions accompanying such offenses are ordinarily hidden from taxation and thus represent a loss to government treasuries. Finally, the inability or failure of the criminal justice system to make headway in the control of such forms of criminal behavior calls the credibility of the system itself into question, thus reducing general citizen respect for it. This is particularly true whenever it is revealed, as it so often is, that some "victimless crimes" go on with police indifference or even cooperation.

We might also mention juvenile "status offenses" as further examples of victimless crime. Status offenses are acts deemed illegal if performed by juveniles but legal if performed by adults. Age status determines the illegality. Examples would include running away from home, sexual promiscuity, being beyond the control of one's parents, or chronic truancy from school. Such offenses may result in juveniles being placed in prisonlike detention centers (Margolis 1988, 1992). Although these victimless crimes may seem quite harmless in comparison with those discussed earlier (e.g., gambling and prostitution), the costs to the juvenile who gets caught up in the criminal justice system can be enormous.

White-Collar and Corporate Crime

The term **white-collar crime** was made popular in the 1940s by criminologist Edwin H. Sutherland (1940). Sutherland believed that researchers were not paying enough attention to criminal practices on the part of business executives and other high-status individuals. In his view, explanations for crime had to encompass the full range of law violations—not just the actions of members of the lower class that come to the attention of local police. To Sutherland (1949:9), white-collar crime was "crime committed by a person of respectability and high social status in the course of his occupation." Note that the beneficiary of the illegal behavior is the offender him- or herself, and that the crimes are commonly the result of opportunities available to individuals in high-power positions.

The narrowness of Sutherland's definition of white-collar crime has come under attack. Scholars have pointed out that individuals other than high-status jobholders also commit acts that are not traditional or common crimes in the course of their occupations. One attempt to expand the definition was proposed by Herbert

Edelhertz (1970), a former official of the U.S. Department of Justice. Edelhertz included as white-collar crimes all illegal acts committed by nonphysical means and by concealment and guile, whose purpose is to obtain money or property, to avoid their loss, or to obtain business or personal advantage. This definition focuses on the crime, rather than on the characteristics of the law violator. It encompasses not only financial fraud by corporate executives but also fraud by such lesser mortals as bank tellers, waitpersons, and cashiers.

In addition, white-collar crimes are distinct from **corporate crimes.** Where white-collar crimes are offenses done by individuals for their own benefit, corporate crimes are violations of the law that are matters of institutional practice or standard operating procedures that largely benefit the corporation or organization. While these offenses are certainly carried out by individuals, often as officers of the firm, they are not designed to benefit the individual but rather the larger organization. In the case of white-collar crime, it is the individual who is the offender; in the case of corporate crime, the organization itself is the criminal. As such, embezzlement, insider trading, and fraud are examples of white-collar crimes, because the individual offender is typically the one benefiting from the violation, often at the expense of the organization itself. In contrast, violations such as toxic waste dumping, stock manipulation, failure to fix known design flaws in products that result in consumer injuries or death, violations of worker health and safety regulations, and accounting fraud are instances of corporate crimes, because it is the firm that benefits, typically financially, from violating the law. Although individual officers in the organization may also benefit, the main motivator in corporate crime is the creation of the image of a healthier financial profile of the firm and its stock values (Rosoff, Pontell, and Tillman 2004).

When Sutherland examined the practices of 70 U.S. corporations over a 45-year period, he found that each corporation had a record of one or more law violations. These included false advertising, restraint of trade, unfair labor practices, and financial fraud. Other researchers have since probed various aspects of white-collar criminality, but in a rather piecemeal fashion (Coleman 2001; Simon 2001). Information is often very difficult to obtain. The offices of executives and professionals are not readily accessible to researchers, and the types of behavior in question are carried out in great secrecy. Often the victims do not know they are being victimized. Moreover, to prove that corporate and white-collar crimes are being committed, researchers may need skills in law, accounting, and economics. Sociologists usually lack this kind of expert knowledge. As a consequence, most of what we know about white-collar crime comes from court cases or occasional government investigations. The information so gained is typically fragmentary and may not be representative in terms of the overall scope of white-collar criminality.

Sociologists still disagree about how to define white-collar and corporate crime and what acts the definitions should encompass. The law is often quite hazy and ambivalent with regard to criminality. For example, during the 1970s a number of large corporations used secret funds to bribe important officials in other countries into doing business with them. These acts were legal until passage of the Federal Corrupt Practices Act in 1977.

Many law violations never reach criminal courts. For example, false advertising and restraint of trade by corporations are often investigated and adjudicated by governmental review boards or other administrative bodies. When it is proved that a company has engaged in false advertising, it may be asked to "cease and desist" its illegal activities. Once it does, the case is closed: There is no "conviction" and no "criminal" insofar as the law is concerned. But has not a white-collar crime been committed?

There is also a fine line between unethical and illegal activity that helps make defining white-collar and corporate crimes complex. In the mid-1990s the U.S. tobacco industry was condemned by consumer advocates and concerned members of Congress for (1) having secretly possessed for many years its own scientific evidence showing ill health effects of smoking and addictive dangers from nicotine, (2) having manipulated levels of nicotine in cigarettes, and (3) denying these activities in response to inquiries from the public and federal officials (Hilts 1995). Manufacturers of tobacco products have spent lavishly on advertising to persuade people in the United States and abroad that smoking is a desirable activity. Young people who might become smokers have been of particular interest to the tobacco industry, and advertisements such as the "Joe Camel" campaign have suggested that smoking is the thing to do. Many people have suffered serious health problems or died from smoking-related illnesses, and continue to do so. Yet the industry claims it is not at fault and has done nothing wrong, and it has fought proposals to declare nicotine a habit-forming drug and thus subject to government regulation. Is the tobacco industry engaged in white-collar crime? In unethical activity? Or just smart business practice?

Difficulties in studying white-collar and corporate criminality and the complexities in defining it hamper attempts to estimate its extensiveness. Moreover, like traditional or common crimes, white-collar and corporate crimes, however defined, are underreported to an unknown degree. Nonetheless, various estimates point to significant economic costs that far outweigh the dollar losses from common property crimes such as burglary, larceny, and robbery. For example, the Judiciary Committee of the U.S. Senate has looked into the costs of corporate activities such as production of faulty goods, monopolistic practices, and other violations. Some 30 years ago, the committee estimated that such activities cost the consumer

from \$174 billion to \$231 billion annually (Clinard and Yeager 1980). The costs are no doubt much higher now. Indeed, the government bailout of the so-called savings and loan crisis of the late 1980s, in which bank executives made decisions that caused banks to fail while they pursued personal profits, may cost taxpayers \$300 billion to \$500 billion by the year 2021 (Calavita and Pontell 1991). Yet such "corporate thievery," costly though it may be, is the subject of little public uproar in comparison to more readily perceived crime in the streets.

Because of the ambiguities surrounding white-collar crime, we can only offer illustrations of the directions it frequently takes. Through media reports in recent years, people in the United States have been made aware of members of Congress accepting bribes while agreeing to influence the letting of government contracts; misrepresentation by doctors about services provided to people in order to get more money from government medical insurance programs; computer-related thefts of money or information; union leaders' use of pension funds for questionable purposes; and environmental crimes involving the illegal dumping of toxic wastes. The list could be expanded indefinitely, even holding to the definitions of white-collar crime offered by Sutherland and Edelhertz. It should be emphasized that the penalties for these white-collar crimes and others are generally far less severe than those for traditional property crimes (Hagan and Parker 1985; Reiman 2003).

Organized Crime

Like white-collar crime, **organized crime** is pervasive in the United States and is believed to be far more costly to the public than traditional crime, although no estimates of its costs are thought to be very reliable (President's Commission on Organized Crime 1986a, 1986b). Research on organized crime in the United States is relatively new, but thanks to government investigators and social science researchers, a great deal has become known in recent years (Kelly et al. 1994).

Organized crime is a cooperative endeavor involving thousands of law violators. Its basic focus is on supplying goods and services illicitly to members of the public. Such goods and services include gambling opportunities, loans, drugs, stolen commodities, pornography, and prostitution. Beyond this, organized crime has successfully infiltrated some legitimate businesses and labor unions. In virtually all facets of its activity, the main objective of organized crime is to make money. Some of this money is used to buy power, including protection from politicians and from agencies of law enforcement.

A major source of income for organized crime is illicit gambling, including numbers games and offtrack betting. Since more money is paid in by gamblers than is paid out to winners, high profits are ensured. Another major source of income is the interest received on loans made to individuals who need funds and cannot get them legally. Organized crime is engaged in loan-sharking, in which loans have much higher interest rates and shorter repayment periods than permitted under the law. Borrowers include individuals with gambling debts, substance abusers and addicts, and even merchants and business executives who find themselves in financial need. Organized crime encourages borrowers to repay loans and interest on time by the threat or use of force—from murder and beatings to property destruction.

The importation and wholesale distribution of illegal drugs is another significant source of profit for organized crime. The international drug market requires far-flung connections and the ability to lay out enormous sums of money for large-scale importation of the drug. In recent years the U.S. government has spent hundreds of millions of dollars in an attempt to reduce the flow of illegal drugs such as heroin, cocaine, and marijuana into the country, with relatively little success (see Chapter 17, "Substance Abuse").

Though relatively little is known about the matter, law enforcement agencies report that organized crime has invested heavily in legitimate businesses. Organized crime figures gain a thin veneer of public respectability and a visible source of legal income through their involvement in such enterprises. Not all business involvement comes about through direct investment. Firms may be secretly acquired in lieu of full repayment of loans or gambling debts or through extortion. Once in business, organized crime figures may use extralegal tactics to ensure high profits. Such tactics range from strong-arming other firms into becoming customers or suppliers to driving competitors out of business. The impact of such business involvement by organized crime remains a matter of speculation. It is often claimed that this involvement has driven up the prices of many goods and services.

Finally, law enforcement authorities have claimed that organized crime has infiltrated and gained control over segments of organized labor. Among the results are the limitation of unionization in certain industries and the negotiation of union contracts favorable to business owners—all in return for financial or other favors. Unions collect a great deal of money from their members, and control over union funds permits organized crime to divert money into its business investments. When organized crime controls a union, companies must look the other way when merchandise is stolen if they wish to gain union cooperation or avoid labor problems. Stolen goods can then be channeled to firms controlled by organized crime or sold to legitimate businesses at an easy profit.

When law enforcement agencies are vigilant and active in investigating organized crime and are intent on prosecuting violations of the law, these activities are more difficult to carry out. So it is to the advantage of organized crime to bribe and threaten politicians and law enforcement officials. No one knows how widespread such corruption is. Its effect is to make interference by agencies of the state less likely. Thus, even when persons complain about known law violations, little may be done. Moreover, complainants never know whether their "tips" to law enforcement agencies may lead to retribution. This helps reduce complaints, and thus the need for corruption.

How extensive is organized crime? No one is certain. In the late 1960s the President's Commission on Law Enforcement surveyed police departments in over 70 major cities. Using the responses of those cities that cooperated along with other sources of information, the commission concluded that organized crime operates in 80 percent of cities with a population of over a million.

The commission also reported that there were 24 groups across the country operating as well-organized "criminal cartels" whose activities were coordinated by a small group of top-level overseers. These groups were said to have a total of at least 5,000 core members, and their activities were assisted by thousands more who were not officially members. Each of the groups was said to be organized in a hierarchical manner, structured like a combination family and business corporation. Policies were made by individual "bosses," and the day-to-day operations were monitored by underlings of different ranks. Those on the very bottom often did not know where orders and directives originated. Group discipline was strictly enforced from within, with systems of internal surveillance used to control members. Membership was restricted, so as to keep out possible informers. The groups were held together by common regional and ethnic ties and by a code of conduct that placed a premium on loyalty and obedience. Collectively, organized crime is popularly referred to as the "Mafia" or "Cosa Nostra," reflecting the stereotype that most members are of Italian-American origin.

Today it is evident that organized crime is not limited to highly structured, hierarchical Italian American groups. In the first place, such crime involves people of many ethnic and racial groups, including African Americans, Latino Americans, Asian Americans, and (recently) Russians. Second, organized crime appears to vary in the degree to which participants formally structure their activities and relationships (Albanese 1994). Finally, by focusing on so-called Mafia groups and their activities, certain highly organized and bureaucratic forms of white-collar crime tend to be ignored. For example, systematic criminality within and between business and government could be viewed as "organized crime."

Because of the extent and effects of organized crime, many would argue that the conclusion rendered by the President's Commission on Law Enforcement almost 40 years ago still holds true today:

In many ways organized crime is the most sinister kind of crime in America. The men who control it have become rich and powerful by encouraging the needy to gamble, by luring the troubled to destroy themselves with drugs, by extorting the profits of honest and hardworking businessmen, by collecting usury from those in financial plight, by maiming or murdering those who oppose them, by bribing those who are sworn to destroy them. (President's Commission on Law Enforcement 1968:485)

Since the late 1970s federal, state, and local law enforcement agencies have allocated much greater resources to the investigation of organized crime (Jacobs et al. 1994). Some major leaders of organized crime and their associates, who long operated with impunity, have been prosecuted for violations of the law and have been imprisoned. But highly publicized trials of a few notwithstanding, organized crime is still a major phenomenon in the United States. Despite the increase in law enforcement efforts in recent years, new organized crime groups and networks have emerged. And participants in organized crime have continued to use legal safeguards of constitutional rights to impede investigations of and prosecution for their highly profitable activities.

Computer Crime and Identity Theft

The rise in the central role that computers play in people's everyday lives has opened the door to new forms of crime: **computer crime** and **identity theft** (see Table 15.4). Unlike many traditional crimes, these crimes do not occur in a face-to-face setting in which the offender confronts the individual. In computer crimes, the very technology that can make life easier becomes the same opportunity for property as well as personal crime. Enterprising computer hackers can break into the programs and databases of

Table 15.4	**Computer-Related Crime Prosecuted by Prosecutors' Offices: 2001 (in percent)**
Type of computer crime prosecuted	Percentage of prosecutors' offices
Any computer-related crime	41.5
Credit card fraud	27.4
Bank card fraud	22.3
Computer sabotage	4.6
Theft of intellectual property	3.2
Transmitting child pornography	30.0
Identity theft	18.2

Source: U.S. Department of Commerce, Bureau of the Census, *Statistical Abstract of the United States, 2004–2005* (Washington, DC: U.S. Government Printing Office, 2005), p. 203.

computer systems located far from that of the offender and introduce the serious havoc of **electronic vandalism** for the victim (Grabosky 2001). For example, an increasing number of viruses have been released worldwide that sabotage the computerized databases of individuals as well as large corporations, universities, hospitals, and even governmental agencies such as the military. Computer viruses can destroy or alter databases, clog systems by replicating themselves until they use up all available memory space, or download important and sensitive information (Wiggins 2002). When viruses strike computer systems, they have the potential to shut down operations of major institutions, damage or destroy individuals' computer systems permanently, interfere with patients' care, and potentially intercede in sensitive intelligence and military operations. Such crimes can be costly financially as well as politically.

In addition to damaging or intercepting databases, computer hackers can actually steal an individual's entire identity. This is because individuals increasingly rely on **electronic transfers** of financial information to bank, shop, and otherwise communicate (Levi 1998; U.S. Congress, Senate 2002). Many people pay all of their monthly bills, including their mortgages, online; still more shop online, posting credit card and bank account or ATM information, and sometimes personal information such as Social Security numbers to make purchases. Although many of the sites people use to make such purchases are secure, not all of them are.

Some creative computer criminals use e-mail to elicit critical information from individuals by posing as a bank or credit card company seeking to confirm customers' information by asking the victim to supply bank account or Social Security numbers. Still others send out fraudulent e-mails claiming to have millions of dollars tied up somewhere that the offender will be happy to share if the victim will help get the money released into the victim's own bank account (which, of course, requires the victim to supply a bank account number).

Computer hackers are thus increasingly able to intercept important information to obtain access to an individual's entire identity in order to illegally obtain goods and financial services, clear out entire bank accounts, and sometimes commit crimes using others' names and identities. This leaves victims with the complicated nightmare of attempting to retrieve and rehabilitate their credit ratings and clear their legal reputations.

Other, more traditional crimes also gain a new ally in computer technology. Increasing reliance on computer-based information technology, particularly in financial services, introduces new opportunities for laundering money garnered from other illegal activities, Internet fraud, forgery, and counterfeiting (Munro 2001; Rider 2001). And rising use of the Internet, especially by children and teenagers, offers the cover of anonymity for predators to conceal their identity as they prowl chat rooms in search of naïve or disaffected youth to target them for cyberstalking, to create or disseminate child pornography, and to solicit unsuspecting children into situations for child sexual abuse (Bocij and McFarlane 2003).

Although the FBI has been getting more sophisticated at locating and prosecuting computer criminals and identity thieves, they are unfortunately still catching up to the creativity and sophistication of the offenders (Bell 2002). Moreover, since these crimes occur in cyberspace, they are in effect **borderless crimes,** and therefore the ability of any one nation to address them will increasingly depend on cooperation between nations (Grabosky 2000).

Political Crime

The term **political crime** refers to illicit acts undertaken with the intention of affecting political policies or the political system as a whole. The term is most often used when the powerless challenge the political status quo. Far less frequently is criminal status bestowed by the state on people who misuse the power they possess, such as high government officials (Beirne and Messerschmidt 1995). In the latter case, the state is prosecuting its own officials, a difficult business.

This is well illustrated by the approach taken by the U.S. Department of Justice to revelations that Central Intelligence Agency operatives had been opening U.S. citizens' mail for 20 years, illegally violating the rights to privacy of tens of thousands of people in the United States. In 1976 the Justice Department recommended that none of those involved be subjected to criminal prosecution, as they were acting on the basis of directives from government officials at higher levels. Yet higher-level government officials remained rather hazy about where such directives came from (Donner 1980).

Probably the most common situation in which criminal status is conferred on people in connection with political activity occurs when citizens engage in protest and dissent. For example, during the 1960s and 1970s, civil rights and antiwar activists were routinely charged with crimes in connection with acts of peaceful civil disobedience. The federal government even passed special laws designed to restrain the leaders of political change organizations. For example, the so-called Rap Brown Law of the 1960s makes it a federal offense to cross state lines for the purpose of inciting a riot. This law was intended to restrict the mobility of popular activists and to make them individually responsible for disruptions involving any assembly of people with whom they might have had the remotest contact.

The threat or reality of prosecution can be a potent weapon against those who want to change the political status quo, even those who use legal channels. There has been reason to believe that government agents have framed dissident individuals to entangle them in legal troubles. In 1972, antiwar priest Father Philip

Political crimes often involve acts by public officials that are spectacular in their audacity and disregard for the law. Connecticut Governor John Rowland, shown here with his wife, Patty, as he announced his resignation in 2004, was forced from office after a scandalous administration marred by abuse of his office and public trust. He was sent to prison for a year and a day.

Berrigan and six others were charged with conspiring to kidnap Henry Kissinger (who at the time was President Richard Nixon's foreign affairs adviser) and to bomb government buildings by sneaking into underground heating pipes (Nelson and Ostrow 1972). The key witness was a paid Federal Bureau of Investigation (FBI) informer. Though the government was unable to prove these charges in court, Father Berrigan was found guilty of smuggling letters out of the federal prison in which he was confined. The person carrying the letters was the FBI informer.

During the 1970s it was revealed that the FBI had been engaging in secret intelligence activities aimed at disrupting protest groups, discrediting dissidents, and generating activities that could lead to arrests. For example, the FBI's COINTELPRO (counterintelligence program) was responsible for hundreds of break-ins and burglaries aimed at political organizations and protest leaders; the spread of **disinformation,** or deliberately inaccurate or false information designed to create divisions within and between protest groups; the use of agents to incite acts of violence; and harassment of individuals through anonymous derogatory letters to spouses and employers of persons involved in political dissent (Blackstock 1976; Garrow 1983). Two FBI officials were finally convicted in 1980 in the wake of investigations into such activities, but they were given light fines and ended up being pardoned by President Ronald Reagan in 1981.

Again in the 1980s "political police" activity on the part of the FBI emerged. A public interest organization, the Center for Constitutional Rights, obtained government documents revealing that the FBI carried out an intensive campaign (from 1981 to 1985) aimed at neutralizing groups and individuals critical of U.S. involvement in Central America. Some 138 groups were targeted, ranging from the American Federation of Teachers to the Southern Christian Leadership Conference (*New York Times* 1988). The FBI used illegal harassment and surveillance techniques that had been widely condemned after revelations of similar activities in the 1970s.

Not all persons who engage in protest and dissent do so nonviolently. The United States has experienced political protest that has ranged from mass uprisings in the nation's ghettos to acts of terrorism by "underground" left- and right-wing groups. While such activities have gone outside the boundaries of the law, in many instances so has the response of the state (Wise 1976). Among the illegal governmental responses have been **police riots** involving the indiscriminate use of force and the extensive violation of constitutional rights during criminal investigations. When government agencies use extralegal means to contain those engaged in extralegal forms of political expression, it is difficult to tell who the political criminals are.

Perhaps one of the most shocking examples of the illegal use of governmental power for political purposes in the 1980s is the "Iran-Contra Affair." U.S. Marine Lieutenant Colonel Oliver North, evidently with the blessing and knowledge of top officials in the White House and Central Intelligence Agency, set up a hidden underground government with its own foreign and military policy. Colonel North proceeded to sell some $25 million worth of military arms to Iran, a nation the U.S. government had publicly denounced (and still does) for involvement in political terrorism (Herman 1987). Still proceeding in secrecy, Colonel North then diverted sales profits to the "Contras," CIA-backed paramilitary units intent on overthrowing the Sandinista government in Nicaragua (Pfost 1987). The reason this deal had to be secret was its illegality: The U.S. Congress had prohibited the use of U.S. funds for such a purpose. Although Colonel North was brought to trial and eventually found guilty of a variety of charges, the roles played by Ronald Reagan, George H. W. Bush, and other high officials remain obscured. Upon appeal, Colonel North was able to reverse most of the guilty verdicts on legal technicalities, and he went on to pursue (unsuccessfully) a seat in the U.S. Senate.

More recently, the Department of Justice and the administration of President George W. Bush have attempted to silence dissidents against the war against Iraq. Among the tactics used have been subpoenas of university records concerning the campus activities of antiwar activists and the arrests, detention, and pepper spraying of antiwar protesters at demonstrations in cities all around the nation. The United States has also been at the center of international outcry for the systematic abuse of Iraqi prisoners at Abu Graib prison and the extended detention of "noncombatant" prisoners of war without charge and without legal representation at Guantanamo Bay in Cuba. Critics argue that both situations represent violations of international law governing war crimes, and at the very least represent an abuse of governmental power in pursuit of a particular political agenda.

Terrorism

In addition to political crimes perpetrated by government officials and high-level political figures are political crimes from those with relatively little power. In particular, **terrorism** involves the use of violence as a strategy to gain political objectives, often used by individuals or groups who have relatively little power otherwise. Because it is a strategy commonly adopted by those with few other avenues of power, social scientists sometimes refer to this as "weapons of the weak" (Scott 1985) or "diplomacy from below" (Kumamoto 1991). Terrorism can be a powerful political weapon because of its capacity to incite tremendous fear and an unsettling sense of vulnerability among a population because of its seemingly random, unpredictable character.

Terrorism often targets important institutions (such as the Pentagon on September 11, 2001), highly visible symbols (such as the World Trade Center on that same day, or the Federal Building in Oklahoma City in 1995), or leaders (such as the assassination of several political leaders in Iraq in 2004–2005). But it can also target "soft targets" such as buses and trains (as occurred in Madrid in 2004), shopping malls, movie theaters, catering halls, tourist attractions, and crowded open markets (as regularly occurs in Israel, Northern Ireland, and elsewhere). Such targets in and of themselves are of no particular political import other than that they are frequently crowded and thus ensure a large and undeniable casualty rate.

Terrorism can also be used to target individuals as representative of whole groups to signal the vulnerability and undesirability of such groups, as often occurred to African Americans at the hands of the Ku Klux Klan. Similarly, rape is often used as a political weapon to terrify or otherwise brutalize whole populations, as has been widely reported in Darfur, Sudan, in 2004–2005.

Perpetrators of terrorism may come from outside the society being targeted, as occurred on September 11, 2001. But they may also be "homegrown," as has been the case with hate groups and militia groups in the United States, exemplified by Timothy McVeigh in the bombing of the Federal Building in Oklahoma City. Regardless of the source of the terrorism, however, the common feature is the use of violence by relatively powerless individuals or groups, whether they use relatively rudimentary weapons such as pipe bombs and fertilizer-fueled explosives, or more sophisticated weapons such as fully fueled hijacked planes aimed at highly populated buildings. Terrorists engage in the calculated use of such weapons as a means to achieve a political objective.

Acts of terrorism characteristically interrupt everyday life and business as usual by altering people's freedom of movement, their sense of security and comfort in their taken-for-granted surroundings, and their confidence that the state and other social institutions and leaders can protect their daily existence. It becomes quite difficult for people to live comfortably without constant fear of the next act of mayhem, to go to work each day, to shop, to travel, to vote, or even to simply open the mail each day without risking the loss of life and limb. Terrorism thus has the capacity to create a **political legitimacy crisis** for the state and its leaders and to destabilize existing governments. The state often has difficulty confronting and responding to terrorism effectively because the perpetrator is not always apparent and thus not likely to be responsive to conventional social control mechanisms such as the police, military repression, and counterviolence.

But while terrorism is often a weapon of the weak, it can also become part of the arsenal of the powerful as a weapon of political violence.

Governments themselves sometimes resort to strategies of terrorism against their own resistant populations to coerce them to submit to the will of the leaders or to eliminate challenges to the existing rule. The military in Argentina and Chile in the 1970s commonly used kidnapping, murder, and torture to purge leftist critics, thousands of whom remain among the "disappeared." In 1999 the president of Yugoslavia ordered or sanctioned the rape, murder, and kidnapping of thousands of citizens in an attempt to "ethnically cleanse" Kosovo of Albanians.

Political crimes reflect the existence of an unequal distribution of power within a society. They are an important indicator of the degree to which a society is meeting the needs of its members, as we discussed in Chapter 2. Despite their significance, neither the public nor the FBI's *Uniform Crime Reports* considers political crimes important enough to categorize them as part of the United States' crime problem.

Violence Deterred? Gun Control and Capital Punishment

In 2001 the rate of homicides using handguns per 100,000 people in the population was higher in the United States than in 25 other industrialized nations (see Table 15. 5). The lowest rate of .03 was in Japan, and the highest rate besides the United States was 3.55 in Northern Ireland. The rate in the United States was 6.24.

▲ Gun Control

Among the forms of criminal behavior most feared by people in the United States, and understandably so, are crimes of violence. Often such crimes involve the use of weapons, principally firearms and knives. Firearms are commonly involved in cases of murder; indeed, almost 67 percent of all cases of murder and nonnegligent manslaughter result from gunshots, most from handguns. Firearms play an

Table 15.5	International Rates of Homicides Using Firearms, 2001	
Country	Households with firearms (%)	Gun homicides (rate per 100,000)
Japan	0.6	0.03
Singapore	0.01	0.07
Taiwan	NA	0.15
Kuwait	NA	0.34
England/Wales	4.0	0.07
Scotland	4.0	0.19
Netherlands	1.9	0.27
Spain	13.1	0.19
Ireland	NA	0.30
Germany	8.9	0.21
Italy	NA	1.16
Sweden	20.0	0.18
Denmark	8.0	0.23
Israel	NA	0.72
New Zealand	20.0	0.22
Australia	16.0	0.56
Belgium	16.6	0.87
Canada	26.0	0.60
Norway	32.0	0.36
Austria	16–18.0	0.42
Northern Ireland	8.4	3.55
France	22.6	0.55
Switzerland	27.2	0.46
Finland	50.0	0.87
U.S.	41.0	6.24

Source: W. Cukor, "Firearms Regulation: Canada in the International Context," *Chronic Diseases in Canada*, April 1998; updated on Web to reflect most recent figures, January 2001. Available at www.guncontrol.ca.

important but less frequent role in other crimes, being involved in about 19 percent of all aggravated assaults, and 42 percent of robberies (U.S. Department of Justice 2004).

The connection between firearms and crime has helped to feed an ongoing debate over the desirability of adopting new policies aimed at **gun control** (Spitzer 1995). This debate periodically intensifies when a crime occurs that is particularly heinous in the public's view. For example, in recent years we have witnessed attempted and successful assassinations of celebrities and important political figures, as well as multiple murders in homes, workplaces, restaurants, and even college and public school grounds. Such crimes involve not only hand-guns but military assault weapons capable of firing over 1,000 rounds per minute.

The United States has the highest rate of gun-related criminal offenses of any Western in-dustrialized nation. Some would argue that this has a great deal to do with the ready, legal access people have to weapons. It has been calculated that a new handgun is manufactured every 20 seconds and the rate of production has been increasing. Nearly half of all the new guns sold are handguns. Today, 41 percent of all U.S. households own one or more firearms. Accord-ing to the National Institute of Justice, although only one-fourth of adults own guns, three-fourths of them owned two or more. More than half of these firearms are stored unlocked, and 16 percent of them are stored unlocked and loaded (www.ojp.usdoj.gov). There are thought to be 200 million firearms in circulation in the United States, about a third of them handguns; if firearms were more equally distributed, the vast majority of men, women, and children in the nation could have one. When surveyed, almost half of handgun owners say their guns are pri-marily for self-protection. Protection is also given as a secondary reason by many other handgun owners, including 40 percent who say they own guns for recreational and sporting ac-tivities, and 20 percent who say their occupa-tions are the principal reason for ownership (www.ncjrs.org).

Although many people say they own hand-guns for self-protection, data from the National Crime Victimization Survey indicate that only a very tiny percentage of crime victims claim to have used a firearm in self-defense against a crime perpetrator, such as an intruder, despite the fact that almost half of all U.S. households own firearms (Cook and Moore 1995). Such data have been disputed by researcher Gary Kleck (1991; Kleck and McElrath 1991), who claims

that guns are used more often in self-defense than in crimes. This controversy has been heated, since the actual facts of the matter have impor-tant implications for debates over gun control.

Besides being readily available from regu-lar retail channels, firearms are available in the underground economy of stolen and bartered goods in which the criminally prone often par-ticipate. In a study of state prisoners, James D. Wright and Peter H. Rossi (1994:xvii) found that only about one in six convicted offenders obtained firearms from legitimate retailers. The findings showed that "criminals almost always obtain guns through private swaps, trades, and purchases with family members, friends, and street sources, or through thefts from private residences." Obtaining a firearm legally or ille-gally, whether a cheap "Saturday-night special" handgun or a high-powered military assault rifle, is a matter accomplished with relative ease in most states and locales.

Proponents of gun control vary in their pol-icy proposals. Some would like to see all owners of firearms required to register their weapons with government authorities and made to report any that are lost or stolen to police. Often regis-tration proposals are accompanied by calls for more stringent screening of the backgrounds of firearms purchasers, as well as tougher restric-tions on weapons transportation, storage, and legal use. But Wright and Rossi's research showed that few of those convicted criminals who bought their guns through legal channels bothered to register them, and the vast majority of felons—who obtained their guns in other ways—certainly were not concerned with legal-ities of gun possession and use.

Those who would go further with gun con-trol thus question whether such policies will have any real impact on the use of guns for crim-inal purposes, suggesting the ante must be in-creased for gun-related crimes. Stiff fines and imprisonment for unauthorized weapon posses-sion or possession of a stolen weapon have been proposed, as have drastic increases in penalties for crimes in which firearms play a role. A few gun control proponents would go even further, calling for a gun-free society. Citizens would be asked to voluntarily surrender their firearms or be subject to their confiscation with penalty.

Although many members of the public (and the police) are sympathetic to one or another gun control measure, the political reality is that relatively little headway has been made in halting the proliferation of weaponry. Powerful lobbying groups such as the National Rifle Association and the firearms industry have managed to block or divert efforts to legislate major changes in law at the federal and state levels. Meanwhile, we are confronted with such facts as these:

- Each day in the United States, 89 people are killed by firearms in homicides, suicides, and accidents, or 1 every 16 minutes (www.vpc.org).

- The presence of a gun in the home raises the risk of suicide fivefold and homicide threefold for household members (www.vpc.org).

- On average, six children and teenagers are killed with guns every day (www.doctorsagainsthandguninjury.org).

- More than 28,000 people suffered firearms deaths in 2002 (www.doctorsagainsthandguninjury.org).

- The leading cause of death for both white and African American teenagers is gunshot wounds (U.S. Department of Justice 2004).

- Almost 500 people died from gunshots while at work in 2003 (www.bls.gov).

- If current trends continue in the United States, annual deaths from firearms will very soon outnumber those from auto accidents.

▲ Capital Punishment

In the United States violent crimes such as murder and forcible rape have frequently exposed offenders to the possibility of the death penalty, or **capital punishment,** which is thought by many citizens to have a deterrent effect. In recent years the death penalty, although infrequently imposed, has become a matter of much controversy. Yet based on available research evidence, many social scientists are skeptical of claims that it has value as a deterrent (Gibbons 1991; Zimring 2004).

Since the earliest colonial days there have been 19,475 executions in this society, insofar as historians have been able to determine (www.ojp.usdoj.gov; Kuntz 1994). The federal government has kept official statistics on capital punishment only since 1930. Between 1930 and 1967, 3,859 people were put to death by civilian authorities. In 1967 challenges to the death penalty led to the blocking of further executions until the Supreme Court could review charges that it was unconstitutional, in violation of the Eighth Amendment stricture against "cruel and unusual punishment" (Costanzo and White 1994).

In a 1972 decision (*Furman v. Georgia*) the Court narrowly ruled that the death penalty itself was not subject to question but that it had been applied to offenders in arbitrary and often discriminatory ways. This ruling had the effect of striking down all state death penalty laws and setting aside the death penalties of the 633 prisoners who were then on **death row.**

The arbitrary and discriminatory application of the death penalty has been well documented by social scientists (Mann 1993). For example, of the 3,859 people executed between 1930 and 1967, 54 percent were African American. Of all those executed, 455 had been convicted of rape; 89 percent of those executed for rape were African American. Whereas African Americans who raped whites were routinely exposed to the death penalty, no known cases exist in which a white man was executed for raping an African American woman. Violent acts by African Americans against whites invite executions; similar acts against African

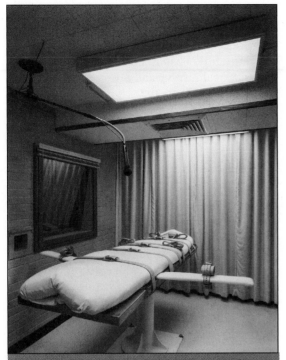

Capital punishment has become a topic of considerable controversy in recent years. While public opinion now leans toward it, some view capital punishment as a form of state-sanctioned murder. The guerny in the lethal injection chamber and witness box await many of those currently confined to "death row."

Americans (whether by other African Americans or by whites) are far less likely to do so.

After the 1972 Supreme Court decision, states rapidly began passing new death penalty statutes designed to avoid the Court's objections to the earlier laws. In the new statutes the jury renders its verdict as to guilt separately from decisions on sentencing. Specific guidelines for judges and juries have been adopted, listing "mitigating" and "aggravating" circumstances to be considered in sentencing decisions.

The Supreme Court upheld such approaches as constitutional in 1976 (e.g., in *Proffitt v.*

Florida), and from 1977 to 2003 some 885 executions were carried out. Thirty-eight states now have a death penalty in place, and as of 2003, 3,374 prisoners were sitting on death row. The fact that death row inmates are disproportionately people of color, and that the latter are still greatly overrepresented among those executed (www.ojp.usdoj.gov), suggests that the question of racial bias in conviction and sentencing continues to deserve serious attention (Tonry 1996). Indeed, DNA testing increasingly suggests that a racial bias has likely affected a rush to judgment in arriving at guilty verdicts and the subsequent assignment of punishments: More than 100 people have been exonerated by DNA testing, most of whom have been people of color (Alter 2000). In the wake of such concerns over the effect of racial inequality on the application of the death penalty, the governor of Illinois called a moratorium in 2003 on all of that state's executions pending an investigation.

Concerns about the constitutionality of the death penalty have also extended to questions about its use against youthful offenders who have been tried for their crimes as adults. Mounting research has begun to indicate that children's thought processes are not fully formed, and in particular are not adequately capable of concretely connecting their immediate actions to future consequences. That research has raised sufficient questions about the ability of children to make considered, deliberate decisions that the Supreme Court in 2005 determined it to be unconstitutional to apply the death penalty to youthful offenders.

What about the deterrent effect of capital punishment (Williams 2001)? Despite widespread public beliefs in the efficacy of the death penalty, researchers have not been able to find evidence supporting capital punishment's alleged deterrent effects (*Journal of Social Issues* 1994). Criminologist Don C. Gibbons has pointed out that homicide rates in adjoining states with similar social and economic characteristics are typically about the same, even when one state has the death penalty and the other does not. Moreover, he notes that when states adopt, abolish, or reintroduce capital punishment, homicide rates do not change in ways that believers in deterrence might expect. Finally, Gibbons observes that killings of police officers are no less frequent in states that have the death penalty than in those that do not. Overall, Gibbons (1991:472) concludes: "One point seems clear enough from the studies of the death penalty and homicide: The deterrent effects, if any, of criminal sanctions are extremely difficult to identify with precision."

But if the death penalty does not have any clear and measurable deterrent effect, what functions does the death penalty serve? Clearly it serves the function of removing convicted offenders permanently from society, including, unfortunately, some who have been erroneously convicted (Harlow et al. 1995; Radelet et al. 1992). In the twentieth century, some 350 people who were later determined to be innocent were convicted for murder or rape, and 139 of them received a death sentence. Twenty-three of the innocent were executed, over 40 percent of whom were African American (Mann 1993:202).

Does capital punishment have other functions? Why is the United States almost the only Western industrial democracy in which the state continues to execute people? Why do we have more people on death row than any other country except Pakistan? David Bruck (1983) argues that the reemergence of the death penalty in the United States in the early 1970s, after a period of waning public support in the 1950s and 1960s, was no accident. The death penalty reemerged in the context of post-1960s economic recession and inflation, U.S. military failure in Southeast Asia, loss of public confidence in government exacerbated by such scandals as Watergate, and the demise of the civil rights movement and other organized initiatives against discrimination and poverty. Bruck points to the fact that the death penalty is most common in societies that use repression to deal with insecurities and lack of direction. Nations like Iran execute criminals; Western democracies have little need to pursue this route to reaffirm national resolve and self-confidence.

The fact that the United States stands practically alone among Western democracies in the implementation of capital punishment is, in Bruck's view, a sign that we have lost our way: The death penalty becomes a "potent social symbol" around which people may rally emotionally—even to the point of throwing tailgate parties outside prisons executing inmates. But it is a symbol that has little or nothing to do with the problem of crime and its deterrence (Ellsworth and Gross 1994).

Bruck's argument is interesting when applied to South Africa. The South African government, once having abolished racial apartheid, moved quickly to abolish capital punishment as well, part of its leaders' announced bid to end a long history of inhumane treatment of citizens by the state and to build a more democratic and egalitarian society. Bruck would no doubt say that capital punishment was no longer "needed" there like it continues to be needed in the United States.

Some have argued that the death penalty plays an important economic function in terms of saving taxpayers' money by avoiding lengthy sentences, perhaps life imprisonment without parole, for offenders. Yet the preparation and conduct of murder trials are extremely expensive, since courts must proceed with a heightened sense of due process when accusations that could lead to the death penalty are at stake. Moreover, once the death penalty has been imposed, those convicted have a variety of opportunities to appeal.

Because the state must pick up the costs of both prosecuting and defending indigent persons accused of capital crimes, as well as all the costs that arise in connection with appeals, and must pay to house and guard individuals through the years the lengthy process from arrest to execution entails, the death penalty actually ends up costing taxpayers much *more* than life imprisonment. For example, researchers studying the North Carolina system calculated that the state spent $2.16 million more for an executed prisoner than for someone sentenced 20 years to life (Verhovek 1995). The extraordinary expenses associated with the death penalty again lead one to wonder whether it continues to exist for reasons other than the common wisdom would provide.

Explanations for Criminal Behavior

As we have seen, many kinds of behavior are considered crimes under the law. Why do people engage in these behaviors? Why do they murder, falsely advertise products, steal, or illicitly repress dissent? *No single explanation can account for all crime.* The factors involved in any type of criminal behavior are extraordinarily complex, and explanations tend to focus on different aspects of crime and criminality. They are often, at best, partial explanations of criminal behavior. In this section we look at some that have been put forth.

Physiological Explanations

Efforts to explain criminal behavior as a result of the physiological traits of criminals have a long history. Since the nineteenth century serious attempts have been made to identify such traits (Shah and Roth 1974). An Italian physician, Cesare Lombroso, conducted research on soldiers and inmates of Italian military prisons in order to show that the propensity for criminal behavior was inborn and that there were physical differences between criminals and law-abiding citizens. Criminals, in his view, were throwbacks to earlier versions of the human species and were often distinguishable by their primitive head shapes, among other stigmatizing features. Lombroso claimed to have found proof for these ideas. His research was harshly criticized for not recognizing that the Italian citizens who were most likely to be involved in criminal activity came from a subsector of Italian society in which such activity was often tolerated for historical and cultural reasons. While members of this subsector—Sicilians—frequently did possess physical features that distinguished them from other Italians, critics observed that these physiological differences could not be accepted as a *cause* of crime since important historical and cultural factors could also be responsible. Lombroso later altered his studies to include such factors.

Lombroso's explanation was further discredited by research conducted in the early twentieth century on English convicts. Charles Goring (1913) compared a group of convicts with a group of Cambridge University students and found no significant physical differences between the two groups. But Goring's research did reveal a high correlation between imprisonment of fathers and imprisonment of sons and a correlation between fathers' and sons' physical characteristics. Thus, he concluded that criminality was inherited. Critics pointed out that Goring had no way of taking into consideration the full range of environmental influences that might have accounted for his findings.

Efforts to demonstrate physiological bases for crime continued. In the 1940s William Sheldon (1949) posited a relationship between body build, personality type, and delinquent behavior. Sheldon classified people into three categories. **Ectomorphs** are thin and fragile, with introverted personalities; **endomorphs** are soft and fat, with submissive personalities; and **mesomorphs** are muscular and tough, with assertive personalities. Sheldon then examined 200 reform school youths. He found that 60 percent of them were mesomorphs. From this he concluded that body build, which has a hereditary basis, was connected with criminality.

Sheldon was roundly criticized for weaknesses in his research design and data. Common sense alone tells us that police officers, athletes, and others with muscular builds are not unusually prone to crime. Subsequent studies have not been able to establish the validity of Sheldon's conclusions without confronting similar criticisms.

More recently, research has focused on a possible relationship between genetics and criminality (Brennan et al. 1995; Herrnstein 1995). For example, researchers have claimed that an unusually large proportion of male prison inmates have an extra Y chromosome and that the presence of this extra Y chromosome causes criminal behavior. (Males generally have one X and one Y chromosome: females generally have two X chromosomes.) This theory has been highly controversial—especially since no one knows what proportion of noninmates (or noncriminals) also possess this extra chromosome. Nor does such an explanation help clarify the causes of female criminal behavior.

Only one conclusion can be drawn about physiological explanations: We have no scientifically acceptable evidence that heredity— either in terms of inherited bodily features or genetic characteristics—plays a significant role in causing criminal behavior. In concentrating on physiological traits, researchers continue to engage in what sociologists call **reductionism.** That is, they are isolating individuals and their behavior from the larger context and are reducing explanations to one very basic variable. There is a sharp parallel between physiological approaches and the explanations for criminal behavior that were popular in the Middle Ages. Then such behavior was commonly attributed to demons or evil spirits afflicting the souls of the unfortunate. Demon theories also ignore the larger context in which people's behavior takes on meaning and is defined in criminal terms. Physiological explanations are almost ludicrous when one recalls that self-report studies typically find that almost everyone admits to having committed some kind of criminal act. Unless we are ready to claim that almost the entire U.S. population is physiologically marred, such explanations must be rejected out of hand.

Psychological and Social-Psychological Explanations

Psychological explanations are those that focus almost entirely on the personality traits of individuals. Social-psychological explanations relate personality traits to the individuals' immediate social environment.

A major psychological approach is the **psychoanalytic explanation,** based on the work of Sigmund Freud (Clinard and Meier 1992). Most psychoanalytic viewpoints see crime as the outcome of unconscious motivations arising within certain troubled individuals (Bromberg 1948). These motivations, in turn, stem from the workings of components of the personality: the id, ego, and superego. Briefly, the **id** represents the drive for pleasure and self-gratification; it is present at birth. The **ego,** which develops later, governs the id's urges, directing the search for pleasure within the limits of surrounding reality. The **superego** is the guardian of right and wrong; its development marks the emergence of a sense of conscience or guilt over violating the wishes of others in the search for pleasure. In psychoanalytic theory, criminal behavior commonly stems from the failure of the ego and the superego to control the urges of the id. Also, the inadequate development of any of the three personality components may result in emotional problems—from neuroses to psychoses. These problems hamper the ability of individuals to function "normally" and render them prone to crime.

While this explanation may seem compelling, one must remember that the id, ego, and superego are theoretical constructs. Even some professional psychoanalysts do not agree that these components exist. Among those who believe they exist, there are disagreements over their functions and their relationship to behavior. Sociologically oriented critics would suggest that psychoanalytic explanations for criminal behavior place too much emphasis on individual personality factors and not enough on factors that are external to the individual. Such critics would also point out that known criminals do not in general appear to be any more psychologically troubled than noncriminals.

A second type of psychological explanation involves the belief that criminal behavior is *learned* (Akers 1973). In this view, people learn to engage in or to avoid such behavior on the basis of **reinforcement**—rewards and punishments. It is assumed that human beings by nature try to seek pleasure and avoid pain. If people are rewarded for criminal behavior, either by other people or by the results of their acts, criminal behavior will have been reinforced as pleasurable. On the other hand, punishment, or the threat of punishment, renders criminal behavior painful and to be avoided.

To an overwhelming degree, this explanation of criminal behavior has been based on experiments with animals, such as pigeons and rats. There are no data on its relevance to actual criminal behavior. One of the major problems lies in the specification and measurement of reinforcers and the meaning of particular reinforcers to different individuals. Moreover, this explanation—like so many others—is always applied after the fact. That is, it is assumed that persons who engage in criminal acts were somehow reinforced into doing so. No one has identified such reinforcers with the precision that would enable predictions of who will commit a crime and under what conditions.

An important social-psychological explanation, one that relates learning more directly to social factors, has been called **differential association theory** (Sutherland and Cressey 1974:75–77). According to this theory, criminal behavior is learned during the course of communication and interaction with criminals or

delinquents. When individuals associate with the criminally prone, they learn the techniques of crime and the motives, attitudes, and rationalizations for criminal behavior. The neophyte criminal then adopts definitions of the legal codes that favor law violation over law-abiding behavior.

Differential association theory has been criticized on a number of counts. It does not explain who is likely to become associated with criminally prone people, or why. Nor does it address the question of exceptions—those whose exposure to criminals leads them to reject criminal behavior. Finally, as with so many other explanations, differential association theory is at best a partial explanation. The individual who cheats on income tax, who secretly patronizes a prostitute, or who murders a family member may have no history of association with criminally prone people.

Another social-psychological explanation that relates psychological characteristics to the social environment is called **containment theory** (Reckless 1961). Containment theory starts with the premise that not all individuals are equally tempted to engage in criminal behavior and asks why this is the case. The answer is that some people are "contained" or controlled and avoid crime because of outer controls and/or inner controls. Outer controls are social pressures that condemn criminal acts, such as community standards. Inner controls are a result of socialization. Family, school, church, and peers may encourage self-control in the face of temptations to engage in crime. Indicators of self-control are said to include a positive self-concept, an orientation to realistic and legitimate goals, the ability to tolerate frustration, and favorable attitudes toward law and law enforcement agencies. On the other hand, those who commit crimes are uncontained and lacking in self-control. Containment theory is extremely broad. We know little about the kinds of social pressures or community standards that help "contain" crime; nor do we fully understand the conditions under which individuals are socialized to develop inner controls.

The preceding explanations all have one common feature. They attempt to infer what goes on in the minds of individuals, and these inferences are then taken to be the causes of criminal behavior. In more general sociological explanations greater attention is given to the features of the larger society and how these might relate to the generation of behavior that comes to be proclaimed criminal.

Sociological Explanations

One of the most famous sociological explanations for criminal behavior is **anomie theory,** developed by Robert Merton (1957; see also Anderson 1998). Merton observed that our culture places a great deal of emphasis on material success and that materialistic values are thus shared by members of this society. But, Merton points out, success in material terms is not readily achievable by all. Opportunities are denied certain groups more than others—for example, racial minorities and the poor. There is, in Merton's terms, a disjunction or gap between cultural success goals and the availability of means to pursue them. This disjunction creates stress, which takes the form of **anomie,** a sense of disorientation or normlessness. Those affected by anomie may respond in one of several ways. They may simply scale down their success goals and go about their daily lives in a ritualistic manner. They may engage in illegal ventures, pursuing goals of material success by illegitimate means. They may simply reject such goals entirely and retreat from participation in the mainstream of society. Or they may rebel and attempt to alter the society whose cultural emphases are unacceptable and unattainable.

Merton's theory is highly suggestive, but it remains rather vague in specifying who is likely to experience anomie and how such persons are likely to respond. Moreover, some crimes appear to have little to do with blocked opportunities for material success. One example that immediately comes to mind is the illegal pursuit of financial advantages by the already rich. Having achieved material success, and with access to legal channels to achieve more, why commit crimes?

Other sociological explanations have focused on particular segments of the U.S. population, suggesting that criminal behavior is more closely linked to certain subcultures than to the dominant societal culture as a whole. Overall, such explanations have limited their attention to crime among low-income groups.

For example, according to sociologist Albert Cohen (1955), lower-class youth possess a distinct subculture within which delinquent behavior has special meaning. Feeling unfairly discriminated against by middle-class society, these youngsters suffer from **status frustration,** which they act out in delinquent forms. Low-income boys engage in delinquent behavior precisely because it is abhorrent to middle-class behavioral standards. Much delinquency takes place among youth gangs, which Cohen sees as collectivities within which such behavior receives support and legitimation.

Richard Cloward and Lloyd Ohlin (1960) have also concerned themselves with lower-class gang behavior, drawing on Merton's ideas to explain it. In their view, the gap between cultural success goals and opportunities to pursue them causes lower-class youths to form delinquent subcultures. Cloward and Ohlin have identified three types of **delinquent subcultures:** *criminal,* wherein property crimes are a main activity; *conflict,* involving a preoccupation with violence; and *retreatist,* where drug use predominates. In their judgment, lower-class communities provide support for one or another of these subcultures. If the adults in a community are involved in property crimes, a criminal subculture will emerge to act as a training ground for delinquent youth. In communities in which such adult models are lacking, youngsters are likely to turn to violence for status. Finally, those who are unable to make it in either of the two other types of subcultures tend to band together in retreatist groups and engage in heavy drug use.

Walter Miller (1958) has posited the existence of an autonomous lower-class culture within which members are socialized into a unique set of values, or "focal concerns." Among these focal concerns are toughness, smartness, trouble, and excitement. The lower-class culture, in Miller's view, automatically brings its adherents into conflict with the law. By contrast, Miller suggests, middle-class subcultural values are more in congruence with behavior required by the legal system.

Such *subcultural explanations* for crime and criminal behavior have limitations. They address such phenomena only among the nonaffluent. Yet we know—if only from self-report studies—that similar behavior takes place outside the lower class and that youth gangs, for example, may be found in well-to-do suburbs (Korem 1994). Moreover, not all sociologists agree on the existence of distinct class subcultures. Among those who do, there is disagreement about whether these subcultural variations *cause* behavior in and of themselves.

Other sociological explanations focus not so much on the groups involved in law violation as on the ways in which people are designated as criminals or delinquents. **Labeling theory** is one such explanation (Lemert 1967). This theory suggests that criminal behavior exists only if and when certain acts are labeled as criminal. It does not address the origins of the acts in question. But in a way, the labeling process may be considered a "cause" of criminal behavior. For example, when the courts identify certain people as criminals, a whole chain of events may be set into motion. Community members, families, and employers may act as if they expect further criminal behavior. In a kind of self-fulfilling prophecy, the newly labeled may be driven toward the behavior expected by others.

A somewhat related explanation is Richard Quinney's (1970) **theory of the social reality of crime.** Like those sociologists who are interested in the labeling process, Quinney has focused on processes of crime definition. In a simple form, his theory is as follows:

1. Crime is a product of law, and law is determined for the most part by legislative action.

2. Legislatures are greatly influenced by the most powerful segments of society.

3. Acts that are in conflict with the interests of the most powerful segments of society are most likely to be addressed under the law.

4. Segments of the society that are not influential in law creation have a high probability of having their behaviors defined as criminal.

5. The behaviors so defined are an outcome of structured opportunities, learning experiences, interpersonal relations, and self-conceptions.

6. Those whose behaviors are defined as crimes come to see themselves as criminals and come to act in response to the expectations that they will fulfill criminal roles.

Thus, Quinney is saying that crime is a social reality that is *constructed:* Behavior that is in conflict with the interests of the powerful is declared unlawful (Greenberg 1993; Taylor 1999). The behavior in question has a variety of underlying causes. In effect, Quinney has not so much come up with a totally new explanation as he has drawn together what he sees as useful parts of other explanations. His theory thus must stand or fall on the strengths of the latter.

The Criminal Justice System

The U.S. system of criminal justice is made up of three interrelated components: the police, the courts, and correctional institutions. As an arm of the state, the main function of this system is to handle those who have violated the law.

Ideally, the criminal justice system operates smoothly and efficiently. The police are supposed to apprehend and arrest those suspected of illegal acts. The accused are to be brought into courts of law, where their guilt or innocence is determined. Those found guilty should be turned over to correctional institutions for supervision and rehabilitation. Needless to say, the system does not always work this way. In this section we look at some of the reasons.

The Police

The presence of police helps deter crime in our communities. Indeed, police spend a good deal of time trying to head off situations in which criminal acts might occur. But an equally important police responsibility is the apprehension and arrest of those suspected of illegal acts. It is at this point that the system first fails to work as it is supposed to.

Of the almost 12 million serious crimes (index offenses) reported by police departments to the Justice Department in 2003, only one-third were solved by arrests (see Figure 15.2).

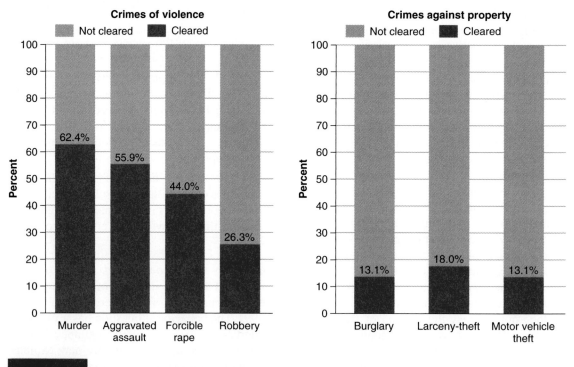

Figure 15.2   **Crimes Cleared by Arrest, 2003**

Source: U.S. Department of Justice, *Uniform Crime Reports for the United States, 2003* (Washington, DC: U.S. Government Printing Office, 2004), p. 256.

Of the 13.64 million arrests made in 2003, most were for relatively minor offenses. For example, one-fifth were for law violations related to alcohol (U.S. Department of Justice 2004). In most large cities, the jails and courts are clogged with persons arrested by police for minor crimes.

There are many reasons that arrest rates for many serious crimes are so low. The sheer volume of crimes known to the police is overwhelming, and there are not enough officers to investigate them all. While many serious offenses are reported to police departments, there is often no way for police to identify the law violators. This is particularly the case with regard to property crimes. Thus, the police generally can apprehend and arrest only persons who violate the law right before their eyes or for whom there is strong suspicion or evidence of criminal behavior.

The whole question of arrest is itself a difficult one for police. On the one hand, police have a great deal of discretion in exercising their arrest powers; at the same time, they are restricted by legal rules in their handling of suspects. Legal restrictions are intended to protect the innocent from the violation of their rights. The police must advise suspects that they have the right to remain silent and to obtain the assistance of an attorney. Police are not allowed to use unnecessary force in making arrests, and they must obtain evidence legally. Although many police officers violate such restrictions, they do so at the risk that those arrested may be set free if the violations become known.

The arrest activity of police is often hampered by corruption among police themselves. In most locales, the police are underpaid. They are expected to do the "dirty work" of society, often at a risk to their own lives. In cities around the country, police have been found engaged in such illegal activities as accepting bribes and payoffs from law violators, selling confiscated drugs, and even engaging in burglaries. Although there is no way to know the extent of such corruption, its existence represents a partial breakdown of the criminal justice system. When even a few police become law violators, the credibility of all police as upholders of the law is diminished. Since the police need the cooperation of the public in apprehending and arresting those suspected of law violations, corruption inhibits police work.

The Courts

After individuals have been arrested, they are ordinarily brought before a prosecutor or other official who draws up the charges that will be presented in court. At this stage, problems frequently crop up, effectively undoing the work of the police. Prosecutors may detect or suspect that arrests were made illegally. They may decide that witnesses and/or evidence would not stand up under examination in court. Many prosecutors are faced with a large backlog of cases, and they generally prefer to draw up charges only when they expect those involved to be found guilty. They thus serve as gatekeepers for the courts.

Prosecutors' decisions place many persons arrested by the police back on the streets—often to police and victims' dismay. The conflicts that arise between prosecutors and police over the handling of those arrested represent a further source of breakdown in the criminal justice system. Police are likely to lose their enthusiasm for arrests when they have to guess at the results that will stem from their efforts.

The courts, especially those in large cities, are faced with far more criminal cases than they can handle. The backlogging of cases has given rise to the routine use of the practice of **plea bargaining,** in which prosecutors offer accused persons the opportunity to plead guilty to a lesser crime. The prosecutor may, for example, offer to reduce a charge of aggravated assault to one of simple assault if the accused will plead guilty. Although plea bargaining is intended to lighten the load of the courts and eliminate the need for time-consuming trials, this practice has some serious side effects. Those who are suspected of serious crimes, in the view of victims and police, too often get off lightly. Those who are innocent of violating the law, but who are faced with possible punishment for crimes they did not commit, may be coerced into accepting criminal status and the stigma that goes with it.

Even when accused individuals have their day in court, the criminal justice system often proves to operate inequitably. When there is a backlog of cases, those arrested frequently have to spend a lengthy period in jail before the trial. Affluent persons often can obtain freedom before their trials by raising money for bail. Low-income people have much more difficulty raising bail money, so it is primarily the poor who populate the jails while awaiting trial. Furthermore, in order to convince a judge to grant release on bail, it helps to have a lawyer who has plenty of time to prepare the case. Again, it is the affluent who are likely to be advantaged in this regard.

The resources available to the accused often affect what happens when cases finally go to court. The nonaffluent usually must rely on attorneys provided to them by the courts. These attorneys often handle so many cases that they can give little attention to preparing a defense for any one individual. To expedite matters, they may advise their clients to take advantage of opportunities for plea bargaining. The affluent, on the other hand, can afford legal talent tailored to their interests and needs.

Judges and trial jurors are typically middle-class people, "respectable" members of the community. Though guilt and innocence are supposed to be determined solely on the basis of the evidence presented rather than on personal prejudices, class, race, and other differences do enter into determinations. Accused individuals who are most "like" the jury members are likeliest to receive gentle treatment. They may be found not guilty, or if found guilty, they may receive light sentences and probation. Guilty verdicts and harsh punishments, consequently,

weigh most heavily on the poor and members of racial minorities. The poor and minorities predominate in jails and prisons across the country, and it is not because they commit the majority of crimes (Reiman 2003).

Corrections

Persons who plead guilty to crimes or who are found guilty by the courts may be handled in a variety of ways. They may be fined, imprisoned, or allowed to remain free during a supervised period of probation. (See Figure 15.3.) We shall deal here with imprisonment, which—aside from the death penalty—is the most severe penalty the state can impose on law violators.

Sending people to jail or prison is supposed to serve several different functions. (Jails hold minor offenders serving short sentences, as well

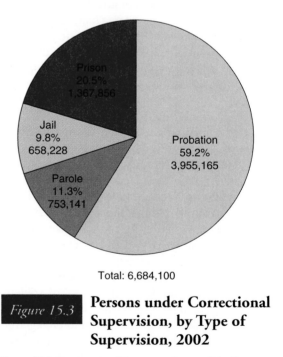

Total: 6,684,100

Figure 15.3   **Persons under Correctional Supervision, by Type of Supervision, 2002**

Source: U.S. Department of Commerce, Bureau of the Census, *Statistical Abstract of the United States, 2004–2005* (Washington, DC: U.S. Government Printing office, 2005), p. 207.

as those awaiting trial. Prisons hold those convicted of more serious offenses and serving longer sentences.) Imprisonment removes law violators from society, thus protecting the public from any further threats they might pose. By taking away freedom, imprisonment serves as a form of punishment and retribution for the offenses committed. The threat of such punishment is intended to serve as a deterrent to anyone tempted to engage in criminal behavior. Finally, imprisonment is intended to place convicted law violators in a controlled environment in order to rehabilitate them.

Prisons are very effective in removing people from society and inflicting punishment. But the threat of imprisonment does not seem to be a major crime deterrent. Given the low likelihood of arrest—even for many serious offenses—criminals have a good chance of avoiding prison. Nor does imprisonment do much to rehabilitate those who experience it. The vast majority of prisoners either have been there before or can be expected to return in the future. The failure of prisons to turn law violators into law-abiding citizens represents the final stage in the breakdown of the criminal justice system.

The basic problem seems to be the contradictory functions imprisonment is supposed to serve. Isolating law violators and taking away their freedom clearly run counter to goals of rehabilitation. On the other hand, the public does not want criminals to be "coddled." Those who violate the law, it is commonly felt, deserve to pay for it. Criminals deserve punishment, not therapy, or else no one would feel any qualms about engaging in criminal acts. In practice, this view prevails in prisons. Only a small percentage of the resources allocated to correctional institutions goes toward anything that could even loosely be called therapy. Most money is spent to maintain security and to keep inmates under careful control.

In response, the inmates develop their own informal society—a subculture with its own set of rules. Prisons have been called schools for crime, as inmates trade knowledge about their techniques of violating the law. Some inmates use physical force or force of personality to exploit others. Crime is rampant inside prisons. Drug use, rape, assault, murder, theft, and extortion are common. From the perspective of most inmates, the prison experience is not only brutal but purposeless. Few come out in better shape than when they went in. Whatever the reasons inmates had for violating the law, these reasons are not eradicated by locking individuals up.

Imprisonment has increasingly been employed in the handling of offenders. Indeed, in mid-2002 the U.S. prison population reached almost one and a half million people, the highest number ever. More than 600,000 more people were in local jails. As one news media report put it,

The increase in prisoners has made the United States second in the world, behind Russia, when it comes to incarceration rates. Counting people both in prisons and those awaiting trial or serving short sentences for misdemeanors in local jails, at the end of [1993], the United States had an incarceration rate more than 4 times that of Canada, more than 5 times that of England, and 14 times that of Japan. (Holmes 1994:A1)

Notably, racial designation appears to be an important factor in whether or not an individual is likely to come under the control of the criminal justice system. African American men are imprisoned almost 10 times more often white men (Human Rights Watch 2000). This suggests that sanctions against criminal behavior are differentially applied so that populations of color are more likely to be socially controlled than whites by correctional institutions.

Because of the sharp rise in incarceration rates, prisons are vastly overcrowded. The imprisoned population cannot be decently housed, and more prisons are being constructed. Conditions within U.S. prisons can only be described as highly dangerous, unhealthy, oppressive, and demoralizing. Given these conditions, prisoner revolts periodically occur.

The policy of placing increasing numbers of people in prisons has been referred to by critics as an **imprisonment binge.** It is a strategy to reduce crime that not only is not working but is draining resources away from other service arenas that are crying out for adequate public support such as public education, job skills training, and drug rehabilitation. The vast majority of people placed in prison are there for nonviolent crimes such as drug possession or technical offenses such as parole violation. The United States is said to be developing a **correctional-industrial complex** or **justice juggernaut** (Gordon 1990; Irwin and Austin 1994), in which various vested interests are benefiting—from politicians who are elected on platforms of "getting tough on crime" to the construction companies and manufacturers that contract to build, equip, and supply the burgeoning prisons. Yet threats of harsh punishment—from the death penalty to imprisonment—do not address the complex reasons the United States experiences so much crime in the first place. The nation seems slow to awaken to this reality.

Summary

People in the United States rate crime as one of the societal problems they consider most serious. Public concern over the crime problem is essentially focused on personal victimization, such as robbery and assault. Less concern is expressed over white-collar, organized, and political crime, perhaps because these seem rather distant or remote.

Crime is linked to a society's system of law. Whether people are aware of or agree with the legal definition of crime, it is ultimately the law that makes an activity a crime. Under the legal definition, a crime is an act that is intentional, inexcusable, in violation of a law, and punishable by the state.

Why do some acts get defined as crimes, while others do not? Some people believe that law is the product of pluralist democracy and consensus on acts that should be outlawed. Others hold that law is formulated in response to the interests of the dominant economic and social class. Somewhere between these views is the conflict theory of legal change, which sees law creation as the product of conflict between classes and among a variety of interest groups that are not class based. Sociologists are just beginning to expand research into how laws are formulated and how this leads to the "creation" of crime.

People's perception of the crime problem is to a large extent based on official reports of crime statistics. Such statistics are known to be inaccurate for a number of reasons. Many crimes are not reported to law enforcement agencies. Police may be either lax or extremely vigilant and aggressive in their handling of certain crimes. The reporting procedures of law enforcement agencies may affect the statistics compiled. Crime rate statistics are also affected by the requirement that they be calculated in conjunction with very accurate population statistics—which we do not possess. At best, official crime statistics, such as those presented in the Justice Department's *Uniform Crime Reports* each year, provide an approximation of the actual amount of crime.

Efforts to develop more satisfactory data on the extent of crime have taken different forms. For example, researchers have carried out victimization studies wherein people are asked if they have recently been crime victims and whether they reported the crimes to police. Data from such studies indicate that official statistics understate the crime problem to a large extent. Researchers have also conducted self-report studies, in which people are asked about their own law-violating behavior. Data disprove the notion that only certain kinds of people commit crimes and suggest that we cannot generalize about criminal characteristics on the basis of those who get caught.

Criminal behavior takes a wide variety of forms. We have official statistics on common or traditional crime, which includes the serious violations the Justice Department calls index offenses: criminal homicide, aggravated assault, forcible rape, robbery, burglary, larceny, motor vehicle theft, and arson. According to official statistics, serious crime recently has leveled off. Most arrests are for less serious offenses, including victimless crimes. These are crimes entered into voluntarily that allegedly do not involve crime victims, like prostitution or gambling as well as status offenses by juveniles. Many people feel that the state should not impose its moral standards on individuals for certain types of behavior. The magnitude of arrests for victimless crimes affects the efficiency of the criminal justice system.

White-collar and corporate crime are both widespread and difficult to define. Along with organized crime and computer crime, they are thought to be far more economically costly to people in the United States than traditional property crimes. Political crimes, like white-collar, corporate, and organized crime, receive little public concern. Political crime and terrorism reflect the existence of an unequal distribution of power within society.

Why do people engage in criminal behavior? No single explanation can account for all crime. Researchers have put forth explanations based on alleged physiological traits of criminals. They have offered explanations referring to alleged personality traits. And they have offered explanations suggesting that certain features of society cause the generation of behavior that comes to be proclaimed criminal. Sociologists continue to seek knowledge about the causes of criminal behavior. In the absence of an adequate understanding of the causes, the U.S. system of criminal justice is hampered in curbing the crime problem.

The criminal justice system is made up of three interrelated elements: the police, the courts, and correctional institutions. The system does not always work smoothly and efficiently, but instead suffers from breakdowns at a number of different points. For example, it catches only a minority of those who break the law; of those it does catch, most will violate the law and probably be caught again.

Key Terms

Discussion Questions

1. Have you ever been the victim of a crime? Why do you think this particular type of crime occurs in the United States? Based on your explanation of why the crime occurs, what do you see as the most appropriate and effective solution?

2. Have you ever knowingly violated the law? Who or what led you to do so? What factors would have had to be present to keep you from violating the law? Based on the importance of such factors, what are solutions to this type of crime?

3. Choose a victimless crime. Develop arguments for and against substantially lowering the penalties for this crime. What arguments could be made for and against making this behavior totally legal?

4. Go to your local police station, courthouse, and jail. Talk with as many people as you can and observe the handling and disposition of those accused of violating the law. What changes in this process do you think are needed? Why?

5. In the United States, people are presumed to be innocent of law violation until proven guilty. If the principle were to be reversed (i.e., guilty until proven innocent), what problems would this give rise to? Which principle is most desirable?

6. If you blew up a bridge, set fire to homes and other buildings, and took lives by the score, you would no doubt be accused of crimes. If you did all these things in time of war, you might be called a hero. What does this tell you about the relation of law and crime "creation"?

Suggested Readings

Barak, Gregg, Jeanne M. Flavin, and Paul S. Leighton. *Class, Race, Gender, and Crime: Social Realities of Justice in America* (Los Angeles: Roxbury Publishing, 2001).
Explores how the main organizing principles of the United States operate in the criminal justice system, both as independent factors and as combining elements.

Coleman, James William. *The Criminal Elite: The Sociology of White Collar Crime.* 5th ed. (New York: St. Martin's Press, 2001).
Cases and analyses of criminal behavior by government and corporate officials.

Gordon, Diana. *The Justice Juggernaut* (New Brunswick, NJ: Rutgers University Press, 1990).
How political and economic policies implemented by elites contribute to high rates of crime, which are then used to justify the expansion of jails and prisons.

Hagan, John. *Crime and Disrepute* (Thousand Oaks, CA: Pine Forge Press, 1994).
A concise overview of contemporary sociological thinking about various forms of criminal behavior.

Kelly, Robert J., Ko-Lin Chin, and Rufus Schatzberg, eds. *Handbook of Organized Crime in the United States* (Westport, CT: Greenwood Press, 1994).
Comprehensive overview of research on the actors, organizations, and activities of those involved in organized crime, and on the effectiveness of efforts to combat it.

Reiman, Jeffrey H. *The Rich Get Rich and the Poor Get Prison.* 7th ed. (New York: Allyn & Bacon, 2003).
Exploration of class bias in the U.S. criminal justice system.

Tonry, Michael. *Malign Neglect: Race, Crime, and Punishment in America* (New York: Oxford University Press, 1996).
Analysis of the forms of discriminatory treatment that members of different racial minority groups have experienced within the U.S. criminal justice system.

Williams, Mary E. *The Death Penalty: Opposing Viewpoints* (Westport, CT: Greenwood Press, 2001).
Examination of contrasting perspectives about the effectiveness and desirability of capital punishment.

chapter 16

Mental Illness

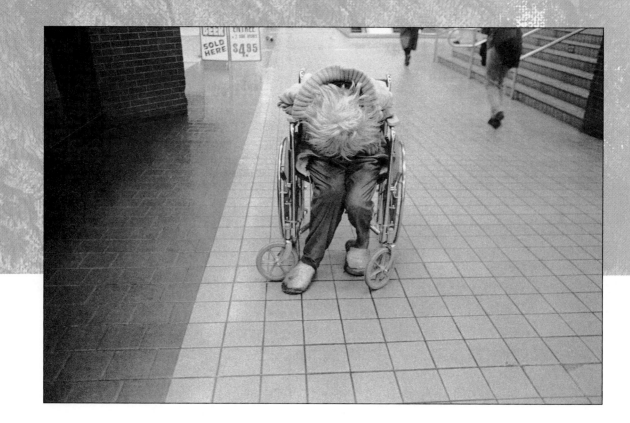

Members of U.S. society should be at peace with themselves and with one another. The social factors that provoke mental troubles should be absent.

During the 1972 presidential campaign, the issue of mental illness was brought before the public in dramatic fashion. Democratic candidate George McGovern's vice presidential running mate, Thomas Eagleton, admitted that he had been hospitalized for nervous exhaustion three times in the 1960s (*Newsweek* 1972; *U.S. News & World Report* 1972). Eagleton had twice undergone electroshock treatments, which were commonly employed during therapy for mental depression.

Though Eagleton and McGovern insisted that this was all in the past and that the vice presidential candidate was in excellent health, the news generated great public concern. If the two men were elected, what would happen if Eagleton had to take over presidential duties? Could the presidency—with its power over domestic, foreign, and military affairs—be entrusted to a person with a history of mental illness? Did the choice of such a running mate reflect badly on McGovern's judgment? As public discussion became increasingly intense, Eagleton withdrew from the campaign. McGovern and his new running mate, Sargent Shriver, lost the 1972 election to the Richard Nixon–Spiro Agnew team, perhaps in part because of the "Eagleton affair."

On one level the Eagleton affair was simply an unfortunate moment in the United States' complex and often fast-paced political history. But on another level, it was extremely revealing about attitudes toward mental illness. The Eagleton affair made it clear that people in the United States harbor deep fears and anxieties about people with mental troubles. Indeed mental illness often generates more negative attitudes than most other forms of disability (Louis Harris and Associates 1991), and at least one opinion poll indicated that 82 percent of respondents in 2002 still believed mental illness carries a lot of **stigma,** or negative social consequences (*Time*/CNN 2002). There was every reason to believe that Eagleton could meet the demands of high executive office. But there was also sufficient public apprehension about his mental state to deny him the opportunity to prove his capabilities. The vice presidential candidate, for all practical purposes, was treated as if he were *still* mentally troubled. This suggests that, even if psychiatrists and other mental health practitioners do not feel that an individual is "ill," he or she may be labeled as such by others (Link et al. 1987; Martin, Pescosolido, and Tuch 2000).

Contrast Eagleton's experience with that of Tipper Gore in 1999, when she announced that she had once been treated for clinical depression but was now recovered. Unlike Eagleton, she herself was not seeking public office; but her husband, Al Gore, was running a difficult campaign for president of the United States, and her announcement ran the risk of repeating Eagleton's devastating experience, damaging any chances Gore's campaign might have had. Instead, her announcement was met with an outpouring of sympathy and admiration for her courage to use her public personae as a springboard to raise awareness about mental health in the United States. She even hosted a White House conference on mental health. Perhaps the fact that she was a candidate's wife rather than the candidate contributed to her more positive public reception than Eagleton received; but perhaps, too, public awareness of mental health issues had to some extent improved in the intervening years.

How common is mental illness in U.S. society? Just what is meant by the term **mental illness?** How does labeling fit into the definition of who is ill? What factors are thought to be associated with, or to cause, mental troubles? What happens to people who are confined in mental institutions? We address such questions in this chapter.

The Extent of Mental Illness

How mentally troubled are people in the United States? Numerous attempts have been made to discover, first, the total number of cases of mental illness existing at any one time and, second, the

number of new cases occurring over time. Findings of both types of research have been inconclusive.

The Prevalence of Mental Illness

Most of the attempts to measure the *prevalence* of mental illness—that is, the total number of cases existing at a given time—have involved surveying a sample of people and then generalizing from the findings. The best known empirical inquiry is the Midtown Manhattan study, conducted by sociologist Leo Srole and his associates (1962). These researchers interviewed a sample of adults in New York City, asking questions bearing on their mental state. The data were then turned over to psychiatric experts, who rated each case on a scale ranging from mentally well to incapacitated. The psychiatrists rated only 18.5 percent of those surveyed as mentally healthy. Almost 25 percent were found to be incapacitated or were said to show severe or marked symptoms of mental impairment. According to the psychiatrists, the remainder of those sampled had moderate or mild symptoms of mental illness. If these findings were valid, it would mean that the majority of New York City residents showed some symptoms of mental illness!

The findings of similar studies conducted in other communities, from Baltimore to Houston, have varied enormously (Kaplan 1972). Prevalence rates have been found that range from 1 percent to 60 percent of those surveyed.

Why is there such variation in estimates of the prevalence of mental illness? The main reason is the lack of agreement among researchers on the appropriate diagnostic measures. Studies have used different criteria for identifying the mentally ill, a variety of survey instruments, and various means for classifying cases. Notions of what constitutes mental illness, and thus what should be counted, reflect social and cultural assumptions on which researchers may differ. This makes comparisons between studies very difficult. Consequently, no one really knows with any precision how prevalent mental illness is among people in the United States. The most commonly quoted figure is around 10 percent, but many would argue that this figure is conservative. One presidential commission concluded that the national rate was closer to 15 percent (President's Commission on Mental Health 1978). Most recently, the National Institute of Mental Health (NIMH) found that in any given 12-month period, 43.3 million people aged 18 and older, or 22.1 percent of the adult population, suffered from some form of mental illness (available at www.nimh.gov) (see Table 16.1).

Table 16.1	**Prevalence of Psychiatric Disorders Experienced within Past 12 Months, 2001**	
	Total	
Disorders	Number (in millions)	Percent
Affective Disorders		
Major depressive episode	9.9	5.0
Manic/bipolar episode	2.3	1.2
Dysthymia	10.9	5.4
Schizophrenia	2.2	1.1
Anxiety Disorders		
Panic disorder	2.4	1.7
Agoraphobia without panic disorder	3.2	2.2
Obsessive-compulsive disorder	3.3	2.3
Post-traumatic stress disorder	5.2	3.6
Social phobia	5.3	3.7
Specific phobia	6.3	4.4
Generalized anxiety disorder	4.0	2.8
Substance Abuse Disorders		
Alcohol abuse without dependence	57.4	19.7
Alcohol dependence	8.2	2.8
Drug abuse without dependence	14.8	5.1
Drug dependence	3.6	1.2
Any substance abuse/dependence	84.0	28.9
Other Disorders		
Antisocial personality	7.3	4.0

Source: National Institute of Mental Health. "The Numbers Count" and "Alcohol, Drug Abuse, Addiction, and Co-occurring Disorders," 2001, available at www.nimh.gov.

The Incidence of Mental Illness

Efforts to identify the *incidence* of mental illness—the number of new cases occurring over time—have primarily been based on statistics concerning treatment. For example, one may examine the number of persons receiving aid through outpatient facilities and the number confined in hospitals.

More than 10 million persons (many of them children) currently receive treatment in mental health facilities each year. Almost one-fourth of them undergo confinement; most are handled as outpatients. The number of people receiving treatment has risen steadily, increasing more than 80 percent over the last 40 years (Manderscheid and Henderson 2001). This might mean that the incidence of mental illness has been on the increase. But it could also mean that people feel more comfortable about seeking help for mental troubles than they did in the past. Or it could be that more people are defining themselves as ill, having no other way to understand or articulate things that are bothering them. We do know that treatment has become more accessible to people in the United States. Since 1970 the total number of mental health organizations providing services to those in need has risen from approximately 3,000 to almost 6,000, with increases occurring in all types of facilities, both inpatient and outpatient (Manderscheid and Henderson 2001; Redick et al. 1992).

The question of incidence is further muddied when other factors bearing on treatment statistics are considered. Obviously, not all persons who are mentally troubled seek out or are brought to clinicians. For example, one national study found that less than 40 percent of the 15- to 54-year-olds who reported having had a mental disorder in their lifetime ever received professional treatment (Regier et al. 1993).

Furthermore, some troubled individuals who seek aid are typically not counted in treatment statistics. This is the case for those who consult religious practitioners or school coun-selors. Still others rely on private psychiatrists, psychologists, psychiatric social workers, or other mental health service providers whose clients generally do not show up in treatment statistics. Family doctors routinely treat patients whose problems are not physical, dispensing advice along with psychoactive drugs ranging from anxiety-reducing tranquilizers such as Valium to antidepressants such as Prozac (Glenmullen 2001; Kramer 1997). Yet such physicians' ministrations to the mentally troubled are not counted. For such reasons, it seems likely that estimates of the incidence of mental illness underreport the number of new cases occurring each year.

Over the last 40 years, there has been a notable drop in the number of persons confined as inpatients in mental hospitals at any given time (a trend that recently has shown some signs of reversing). If we limited our attention to the number confined, we might conclude that mental illness—or at least serious mental illness—has been on the decrease. However, while this drop has been going on, the actual number of new *admissions* to mental hospitals each year has remained high (see Figure 16.1). Though more persons are being admitted, the length of confinement has decreased. One reason is that the extensive use of drugs enables people to function outside of confinement (Gronfein 1985). Second, the increase in nonresidential facilities makes it possible for more individuals to be treated as outpatients. Third, many elderly patients are no longer placed in mental institutions but enter nursing homes or geriatric hospitals. In the past, elderly persons who could not care for themselves were often left to languish in mental institutions. Finally, it costs a great deal to care for the confined. Moving persons out of inpatient facilities more rapidly has been undertaken to help to slow down rising health-care costs (see Chapter 13).

One could argue that the incidence of mental illness is increasing. More people are seeking or being referred for treatment, and the rate of

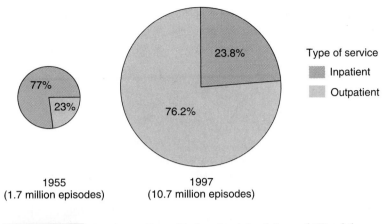

	Type of service
	Inpatient
	Outpatient

23.8%

77%

23%

76.2%

1955
(1.7 million episodes)

1997
(10.7 million episodes)

Figure 16.1 **Patient Care Episodes* in Mental Health Organizations in 1955 and 1997**

Patient care episodes are the number of persons receiving services at the beginning of the year plus the number of patients serviced during the year. It is possible for patients to be counted more than once.

Source: Ronald W. Manderscheid and Mary Anne Sonnenschein, eds., *Mental Health, United States, 1994* (Washington, DC: U.S. Government Printing Office, 1994), p. 83; Ronald W. Manderscheid and Marilyn J. Henderson, *Mental Health, United States, 2000* (Washington, DC: U.S. Government Printing Office, 2001), Table 6.

admission to hospitals is high. But because of the problem of interpreting available statistics, one must advance such an argument with caution. As with prevalence, the incidence of mental illness remains a topic of debate.

Defining Mental Illness

Thus far we have used the term *mental illness* rather freely. After all, everyone seems to know what it means. However, there is some disagreement over whether the term means anything at all. We discuss the problems of definition in this section.

The Medical Model

Only since the nineteenth century have troubled persons been designated as "ill" (Foucault 1965;

Rosen 1968). Prior to that time, they were more likely to be considered "possessed" by spirits, the victims of witchcraft, morally defective, or otherwise afflicted by unknown and unsavory problems. During the nineteenth century, medical practitioners advanced the theory that mental troubles were actually matters of health. They argued that persons exhibiting such troubles should not be harassed and punished or locked up in jails and asylums. Instead, said the doctors, they should be cured and made well.

This approach is usually called the **medical model** or disease model of mental illness (Conrad and Schneider 1992). It is based on the belief that just as one's body is subject to injury or disease, so is one's mind. Unusual forms of behavior and/or signs of psychological disturbances are the warning symptoms of the illness. Psychiatrists and other mental health practitioners (e.g., psychotherapists, psychologists, psychiatric social workers) use the symptoms to diagnose the nature of the illness afflicting the troubled individual. Depending on the diagnosis and on the treatment preferences of the practitioner, a method of cure will be prescribed (Tyrer and Steinberg 1998). The cure may involve the intensive probing of a person's thoughts, drug or electroshock therapy, or group meetings attended by similarly ill people. The mentally ill individual is expected to assume the role of patient and to rely on the expertise and advice of the mental health professional.

The evolution of the medical model has been accompanied by the adoption of a system of diagnostic terms. These terms are used to categorize the various types of mental illness that have been discovered by psychiatrists and to help standardize treatment of individuals exhibiting similar symptoms. In the United States, the American Psychiatric Association (APA) publishes a guide to this diagnostic system called the *Diagnostic and Statistical Manual of Mental Disorders* (American Psychiatric Association 2000).

The APA has issued several editions of its guide (most recently 2000). Each has involved changes in terminology and the addition or subtraction of various forms of behavior, reflecting a changing consensus among psychiatrists of exactly what constitutes mental illness.

The 2000 guide provides the following system of classification (here examples are indicated in parentheses):

1. Disorders usually first evident in infancy, childhood, or adolescence (retardation, autism, learning disabilities)

2. Delirium, dementia, and amnesic and other cognitive disorders (Alzheimer's disease, amnesia)

3. Substance use disorders (abuse of alcohol and other drugs)

4. Schizophrenia and other psychotic disorders (loss of contact with reality, paranoia)

5. Mood disorders (mania, depression)

6. Anxiety disorders (phobias, anxiety, compulsive behavior)

7. Somatoform disorders (hypochondria)

8. Factitious disorders (intentionally produced symptoms of physical or psychological illness)

9. Dissociative disorders (repressed recall, multiple personality)

10. Sexual and gender identity disorders (loss of or inappropriate sexual arousal, discomfort with one's assigned sex)

11. Eating disorders (bulimia, anorexia)

12. Sleep disorders (insomnia, nightmares, sleepwalking)

13. Other disorders of impulse control (pathological gambling, kleptomania)

14. Adjustment disorders (maladaptation to stress)

15. Personality disorders (inflexible and maladaptive traits causing impairment in functioning or distress)

The preceding classification omits a term that has entered into popular usage: neurosis. The category of anxiety disorders encompasses most of what many might more familiarly call neurosis. This older, more familiar term will be employed here as we discuss some serious and not-so-serious forms of mental illness.

▲ Schizophrenia and Other Psychotic Disorders

According to mental health practitioners, the **psychoses** are a very severe form of mental illness. Individuals diagnosed as psychotic frequently have their own versions of reality and thus are often unable to perform the roles expected of them in everyday life. Consequently, treatment of the psychoses often involves voluntary or involuntary confinement.

Psychotics may suffer from hallucinations, deep changes in mood, or an inability to think, speak, or remember. Although psychiatrists have found that some mental disorders accompanied by psychotic symptoms are **organic**—that is, a result of actual physical damage to the brain or of chemical imbalances in a person's system—they claim that most types of psychosis are **functional.** In other words, in most psychoses there is no known or demonstrable physical reason for the symptoms of illness that are displayed. The mind itself is considered unwell and in need of cure.

One of the more common psychoses is called **schizophrenia.** This term is used for people who are extremely withdrawn from their surroundings or who act as if they were living in another world. Schizophrenics' thoughts may appear disorganized and bizarre, their emotions inappropriate for the situation, and their behavior unusual. Various types of schizophrenia have been identified and categorized. For example, persons who exhibit delusions of being persecuted by others are called paranoid schizophrenics. Catatonic schizophrenics act in an excessively excited manner or, alternatively, exist in a mute vegetative state. Disorganized schizophrenics have flat or inappropriate affect and appear to lack organization in their speech and behavior.

In the view of psychiatrists, schizophrenia primarily involves difficulties in thinking. Psychoses may be contrasted with **mood disorders,** which mainly involve changes in emotion. In mood disorders, people may become extremely elated or deeply depressed for no apparent reasons. One type of mood disorder, **seasonal affective disorder (SAD),** is characterized by depression at particular times of the year, often beginning in the fall or winter and ending in the spring. Bi-polar disorders take the form of sudden and severe changes in mood. The person may be gleefully boisterous in the manic state and may seriously contemplate self-destruction in the depressed state. Some psychiatrists believe that severe depression, although not necessarily that associated with bi-polar disorders, is the principal precipitator of suicides.

In everyday language, a person designated as psychotic by a psychiatrist is likely to be considered "mad," "nuts," "cuckoo," or "crazy." These terms are not used by those embracing the medical model. To mental health practitioners, such persons are ill and in need of professional healing (Russell 2000).

▲ Neurosis

Unlike persons with schizophrenia or other forms of psychoses, those suffering from one or another type of **neurosis** are typically capable of functioning in everyday life. Unlike the psychoses, the neuroses generally do not involve distortions of reality. Moreover, neurotics typically know that something is wrong with their thinking or behavior.

The principal symptom of neurosis is evidence of anxiety. In mild cases of neurosis, anxiety may be expressed directly. In some severe cases, a person may appear to be in a state of panic. According to psychiatrists, anxiety may also be expressed indirectly, showing up as a variety of other problems—such as blindness, deafness, exhaustion, inexplicable fear of objects or particular situations, and compulsive activity (e.g., hand washing, obsession with neatness and order).

In most cases, individuals who are suffering from a neurosis do not require hospitalization. In fact, mental health practitioners often find it hard to tell if someone is indeed suffering from an anxiety-produced neurosis—that is, if someone is "ill"—or is merely temporarily responding to pressures that anyone might find distressing. Or perhaps the individual is merely a bit eccentric.

Problems of Classification

Although the APA has come up with an elaborate classification system of mental disorders, many problems continue to be associated with it. For example, application of the various categories, each of which is accompanied by a list of symptoms to guide diagnosis, remains difficult. Psychiatrists often disagree among themselves on the most appropriate diagnostic label to apply, not to mention treatment.

The fact that categories and behaviors identified as disorders change raises questions about the reliability of the system (Kirk and Kutchins 1992). For example, in 1973 members of the APA decided that homosexuality, which had been classified as a mental disorder, should be dropped from the classification scheme. Was homosexuality ever a mental disorder—a form of illness deserving treatment?

There has been a tendency in new editions of the APA guidelines to add various forms of behavior to the list of disorders. Many argue that this contributes to misdiagnosis or overdiagnosis of mental illness, since diagnostic categories are so numerous and broad that *most* people display behaviors that could be construed as indicating *some* type of disorder. Moreover, clinicians often have financial incentives to misdiagnose or overdiagnose, since government programs and private health insurance companies that reimburse them for services are diagnosis based and not all categories of illness qualify for reimbursement (Kirk and Kutchins 1992).

Fundamental questions have been raised, not only about the classification system generally accepted by psychiatrists but about the utility of the medical model itself. It is to this that we now turn.

▲ The Utility of the Medical Model

The problem mental health practitioners have in determining who is ill and who is well has led some critics to question the whole concept of *mental illness*. How accurate and valid are the judgments made by the most prestigious mental health professionals, the psychiatrists? According to David L. Rosenhan (1973:250): "There are a great deal of conflicting data on the reliability, utility, and meaning of such terms as 'sanity,' 'insanity,' 'mental illness,' and 'schizophrenia.'" Prevalence surveys and treatment statistics indicate that many people are mentally troubled. But whether their mental states are best viewed and treated as forms of illness is another issue. Could it be that illness is simply a label routinely applied by believers in the medical model? Are people who are not "ill" subject to misdiagnosis?

Rosenhan set up an ingenious experiment to pursue these questions. He recruited eight people who had no history of mental troubles and were, in the language of the medical model, mentally healthy. At Rosenhan's direction, each of them sought admission to a mental hospital. The staffs of these institutions had no inkling that Rosenhan's associates were "pseudopatients."

Upon arriving at the hospitals, the eight pseudopatients claimed that they had been hearing voices and that they had come to see whether anything was wrong with them. Aside from this deception, they truthfully answered all questions pertaining to their medical backgrounds, lifestyles, and relationships with others. Seven were immediately diagnosed as schizophrenic, and the eighth was judged to be bi-polar. Their deception was not discovered by psychiatrists. Even though they were healthy, they were diagnosed as ill.

Once they were assigned to psychiatric wards, all eight pseudopatients stopped faking the symptoms that had gained them admittance. They behaved in a friendly and cooperative manner and answered questions about their health by saying that they felt fine. But no one—except other patients—doubted that their illnesses were real. After hospitalizations ranging from 7 to 52 days, the eight pseudopatients were released, their illnesses officially diagnosed as in remission. In other words, they were still considered to be mentally ill, but the symptoms of their illnesses were said to have subsided.

To further test the ease with which people are termed ill or well, no matter what their true mental state, Rosenhan carried his experiment one step further. He told the staff of one mental hospital—where his pseudopatient trick had become known—that he would seek to admit more such persons to their wards. In effect, he dared the psychiatric staff to uncover his pseudopatients. Following his dare, the staff screened 193 individuals. Of these, 41 were alleged to be Rosenhan's pseudopatients, and many others were considered suspect. Rosenhan had *not* sent anyone to that hospital!

On the basis of his experiment, Rosenhan (1973:252) concluded that "any diagnostic process that lends itself so readily to massive errors of this sort cannot be a very reliable one." His work helped feed the contemporary controversy over the meaning of mental illness and the utility of the medical model. It lends credence to critics who have urged rejection of the medical model.

Mental Illness as a Myth

The principal critic of the medical model, Thomas Szasz, is himself a psychiatrist. In his writings, Szasz (1984) acknowledges the evidence that links brain damage to certain behavior and/or thinking difficulties. Severe cases of syphilis, the excessive use of alcohol, and physiological changes sometimes accompanying aging, for example, can cause people to behave or think in unusual ways. Szasz also acknowledges the effect of chemical imbalances on mental functioning. In such cases, Szasz tells us, it is correct to state that a person is ill. Moreover, such illnesses are most appropriately handled within a medical context.

But Szasz reminds us that most of the illnesses treated by mental health practitioners are *functional* rather than organic in origin. He contends that these functional disorders are actually individual traits that may deviate from what is considered culturally, socially, ethically, or legally normal. When psychiatrists compare their own standards of what is normal with the traits exhibited by their clients, they are making value judgments about which norms people should follow. They call the people who depart from these norms ill and in need of treatment. Szasz (1991:17) believes that there is a contradiction between judging people as deviant on the one hand and offering them medically oriented diagnoses and treatments on the other: "Since medical interventions are designed to remedy only medical problems, it is logically absurd to expect that they will help solve problems whose very existence have been defined and established on nonmedical grounds."

According to Szasz, the symptoms many psychiatrists associate with mental illness are really no more than styles of communication. People designated as ill are simply saying something, often unacceptable and expressed in unusual terms, about themselves, others, and the world around them (Szasz 1991). These communications are expressed because people find that life is a difficult struggle. Their relations with other people and their contacts with societal institutions are accompanied by a great deal of personal stress and strain. Often their needs, values, and aspirations are going unmet. They are disturbed by the lack of harmony in U.S. society and by unavoidable conflict with others. In Szasz's terms, people face "problems in living." They are not sick or diseased; they are trying to communicate the difficulties with which they are burdened in everyday life.

By calling individuals with problems in living ill, we are implying that something is wrong with them and that they must change. This is why troubled people are encouraged to become patients and to become dependent on professional care (even against their will) (Szasz 1997). The medical model, in Szasz's (1991:5) view, is an ideology that "has succeeded in depriving vast numbers of people—sometimes it seems very nearly everyone—of a vocabulary of their own in which to frame their predicament without paying homage to a psychiatric perspective."

People who face problems in living are encouraged by the medical model to look primarily

In our major cities, there are some men and women whose daily lifestyles may seem unusual, leading people to label them as deviant and sometimes as mentally ill. The man in this photograph does not view himself as homeless, although he has lived on the streets for many years. He views the streets as his home, carrying all his possessions in the shopping cart. On what grounds can we justify calling unusual behavior "sickness" and deserving of medically oriented treatment?

within themselves for the sources of their difficulties. Only if they accept the fact that they are indeed sick and in need of help can they get better. They must adjust and accommodate their thinking and behavior to that considered normal by psychiatrists.

Those who reject the medical model and the treatments flowing from it still must confront the question of what—if anything—might be done for persons who are mentally troubled. Szasz believes that the latter *can* be helped to deal with problems in living without being told that they are sick. In his view, therapists must establish open, humane relationships with such

people. These relationships should be entered into and maintained purely on a voluntary basis and must not place troubled persons in the subordinate role of patient.

Mental Illness as a Sign of Health

Another well-known critic of the medical model, British psychiatrist R. D. Laing, felt that "humanity is estranged from its authentic possibilities." Laing (1967:12) used the term **alienation** to characterize the relations that exist among family members, generations, the sexes, classes, and races: "The 'normally' alienated person, by reason of the fact that he acts more or less like everyone else, is taken to be sane. Other forms of alienation that are out of step with the prevailing state of alienation are those that are labeled by the 'normal' majority as bad or mad." The abnormally alienated are most likely to be noticed, to seek or be brought to treatment, and to be designated as ill under the medical model.

Laing suggested that one of the more severe forms of mental illness, schizophrenia, has nothing to do with disease. Instead, according to Laing (1967:114–15):

The experience and behavior that gets labelled schizophrenia is a special strategy that a person invents in order to live in an unlivable situation. In his life situation the person has come to feel he is in an untenable position. He cannot make a move, or make no move, without being beset by contradictory and paradoxical pressures and demands, pushes and pulls, both internally from himself, and externally from those around him.

Serious disorders, to Laing, are efforts on the part of an individual to escape from alienating societal arrangements. Laing suggested that these efforts to escape existing realities might actually be considered a sign of health. They are certainly a healthier response than living with the problems. "The perfectly adjusted bomber pilot may be a greater threat to species survival than the hospitalized schizophrenic deluded that the Bomb is inside him" (Laing 1967:120).

Likening the schizophrenic experience to an LSD drug "trip" or spiritual journey, Laing felt that psychiatric efforts to cure schizophrenia are more often harmful than helpful. He believed that experienced psychotics should be used to guide those who are in the process of embarking into another level of reality. Needless to say, Laing's ideas—like those of Szasz—are unpopular among those who remain committed to the medical model.

Nonetheless, Laing's observations suggest ways of approaching those who are troubled. His stress on empathy and understanding, implied by the suggestion of using persons who have "been there" to help others, offers an alternative to telling troubled people that there is something wrong with them.

The Labeling Process

Like Rosenhan and Szasz, Laing emphasized that mental illness is a label bestowed on people whose thinking and/or behavior is judged unacceptable. The bestowal of such a label is, according to Laing, a **political event,** in which those with medical, legal, and moral authority are in a position to cast an individual into the role of sick person. This labeling process has been spelled out by sociologist Thomas Scheff (1999). Scheff notes that members of society have handy categories in which to place those who violate commonly accepted rules or norms. Persons who violate the law are "criminals"; those who eat peas with their knives are "ill-mannered." But some forms of behavior are so unusual or unthinkable that they cannot be easily categorized. Such **residual deviance** is likely to be allocated to a catchall category: mentally ill.

Unlike Szasz and Laing, Scheff is not too concerned with pinning down the initial reasons why persons may express unusual thinking and/or behavior. Instead, he simply states that the deviant behaviors called mental illness may arise from diverse sources ranging from the physiological to the socioeconomic.

Scheff contends that the rate of residual deviance is extremely high, and that only a small amount comes to be treated as mental illness. Much deviance is either ignored, unrecognized, or rationalized away. Moreover, much of it is transitory. But at least some is labeled mental illness and is treated. The crucial variable, according to Scheff, is **societal reaction.** The label must be imposed by society for mental illness to exist.

When does society impose the label? Scheff posits that we learn stereotypes of what it means to "act crazy" in early childhood. These stereotypes are then reaffirmed, for example, by the mass media and even in everyday conversations. When residual deviance becomes publicly noticed, such stereotypes are mobilized, and the individual is told that he or she is ill.

An individual who has been labeled mentally ill is encouraged to accept this label and to display the traits stereotypically expected of a sick person. Once this occurs, the illness becomes "stabilized": Mental disorder becomes a social role. The individual impersonates illness by accepting and acting within the diagnostic labels of the medical model.

Scheff observes that persons may actually be rewarded for playing the illness role. Psychiatrists, for example, are pleased when someone accepts their diagnosis and treatments. Conversely, persons may be punished for attempting to shed the role. Once labeled, so-called mentally ill people—even if pronounced cured—may find it difficult to escape discriminatory treatment (as did Thomas Eagleton, whose experiences were discussed at the start of this chapter) (Wahl 1999). Any additional episodes of residual deviance are likely to be interpreted as signs of continued illness. Individuals thus may be caught up in a *career* of being mentally ill, filling this role in response to societal reactions to them.

In sum, there is a controversy over whether most mentally troubled persons are in fact ill. As critics of the medical model contend, such individuals may face problems in living or be alienated from existing societal arrangements. As they respond to their situations with unusual expressions of behavior and/or thinking, they may be labeled as ill and subjected to treatment in a medical context. The critics question the wisdom of such treatment for persons whose troubles are essentially rooted in the societal environment in which they find themselves.

Mental Illness and Criminal Justice

On March 30, 1981, young John W. Hinckley shot President Ronald Reagan and three other persons during an assassination attempt in Washington, D.C. A shocked nation soon learned that Mr. Hinckley, who had been under treatment by a psychiatrist prior to the shooting, was claiming a bizarre motive for his action—the desire to court the favor of Jodie Foster, a movie star. There was no denying his involvement in the assault, as it was recorded on film and widely disseminated on television. A year later, however, Mr. Hinckley's fate was decided: "Not guilty by reason of insanity." He was remanded by the court to a federal mental hospital for treatment and presumably eventual release.

Contrary to most people's beliefs, pleas of not guilty by reason of insanity are actually rare. A National Institute of Mental Health study found that such pleas were involved in no more than 1 percent of all felony cases. These pleas are seldom successful: In the NIMH study two-thirds of those accused of crimes were found guilty despite this defense (Steadman et al. 1993). Moreover, even when successful it is unlikely that persons found not guilty by reason of insanity will find it easy to be set free, as their release must be approved by both clinicians and a judge or jury. For those who committed the most serious crimes, consideration of release is likely to occur in the glare of substantial media attention and be accompanied by negative reactions from members of the public, law enforcement officials, and politicians.

In employing the insanity defense, widely publicized trials such as Hinckley's raise serious issues. **Insanity** is a legal term and involves problematic psychiatric judgments and labeling around which disagreements may occur. Moreover, there is the question of the standard that should be applied to determine when a person should be relieved of responsibility for a criminal act. This question has occupied legal minds for centuries, and to date no resolution has been reached that meets with widespread satisfaction (Robinson 1996; Steadman et al. 1993).

To be found guilty of a serious offense, a defendant ordinarily must be shown to have had criminal intent. The law, in such circumstances, is interested in finding fault and thus establishing individual responsibility. An insanity plea in essence denies individual responsibility. Psychiatric judgments are brought into play by both the prosecution and the defense to provide "expert opinion" to guide decision making by a jury of citizens. Often the judgments of the psychiatrists representing the two sides conflict, as they did in the Hinckley case, thus providing little guidance to a jury. In such cases the rather "inexact science" of psychiatry is highlighted, and its credibility is likely to suffer.

Efforts to establish a standard to determine the criteria for legal insanity have resulted in a couple of major variations (Robinson 1996; Simon and Aaronson 1988). The first, the M'Naghten Rule, resulted from a legal decision in England in 1843 and currently is used in over 20 states. Legal insanity is said to exist if "at the time of the committing of the act, the party accused was laboring under such a defect of reason from disease of the mind as to not know the nature and quality of the act he was doing, or if he did know it, that he did not know he was doing what was wrong" (Kaufman 1982:18). This standard focuses only on the cognitive side of mental illness: What did the defendant know about what he or she was doing? As knowledge of mentally troubled persons has grown, this standard has seemed too narrow to many psychiatrists. It does not give attention to the possibility that the accused may have known what he or she was doing was wrong, but lacked the ability to control the criminal behavior.

Subsequent court decisions have produced an alternative standard of legal insanity that now guides most state and federal courts. "A person is not responsible for criminal conduct if at the time of such conduct as a result of mental

Although a formal plea of insanity occurs only occasionally in the courts, it is common for defendants facing sentencing to argue that stressful life experiences and troubled mental states were responsible for their violent actions. The jury in the highly publicized case of Andrea Yates, a young mother found guilty in 2002 of drowning her five young children, did not accept such arguments. It sentenced her to life in prison.

disease or defect he lacks substantial capacity either to appreciate the wrongfulness of his conduct or to conform his conduct to requirements of law" (Kaufman 1982:18). The problem is one of applying this wider standard—particularly when psychiatric experts give contradictory views of a defendant's mental state. As with the M'Naghten Rule, the burden of proof of legal insanity in almost every jurisdiction is on the defense.

Recent cases have raised complicated and highly charged questions regarding the insanity defense. In 2001 in Texas, Andrea Yates drowned her five young children one by one in a bathtub, laying each of them on a bed after she drowned them. She faced the death penalty for murder. Her attorney pressed an insanity defense, arguing that she had suffered from a severe case of **postpartum depression,** which began after the birth of her first child and deepened after each subsequent birth. She had, in fact, been treated by a psychiatrist for her depression, but it became clear that she was increasingly overwhelmed with caring for the five children and her aging in-laws alone every day (O'Malley 2004). The court apparently agreed that she was not competent to be held accountable for murder, and she remains in prison rather than facing the death penalty. The case touched an emotionally charged nerve in the nation regarding the gendered notion of maternal instinct and the unspeakable possibility of women killing their own children (Meyer et al. 2001). And it raised the question of the validity of postpartum depression and the public's failure to recognize it as a serious and valid mental illness.

Serial killer Michael Ross's defense team also struggled to use an insanity plea to prevent the state of Connecticut from executing him for murdering several young women between 1981 and 1984. Although Ross himself insisted that he was ready to die and did not want his attorneys to appeal his execution, his defenders insisted that he had a diminished capacity to make competent decisions on his own behalf because of his time sitting on death row. They argued that he suffered from **death row syndrome,** in which an extended stay on death row while appeals work their way through the courts reduces prisoners' will to live and can actually convince them of their own guilt even they are innocent. Repeated episodes of reaching the execution date, only to be stayed at the last moment, can intensify the emotional roller coaster that warps defendants' ability to remain sane and defend themselves. By January 2005 Ross's attorneys had successfully pressed the argument, and his scheduled execution was stayed at the last moment. Ross finally was executed on May 13, 2005, after being on death row for 17 years. The case raises a complicated question of whether time on death row in and of itself can damage a defendant's sanity, in which case all capital punishment cases may be subject to an insanity plea. And that raises the issue of whether the death penalty itself is cruel and unusual punishment and indefensible.

In the wake of the verdict of not guilty by reason of insanity in the Hinckley trial, there were calls for an alternative verdict to be made available to juries: "Guilty, but mentally ill." Currently, 12 states have adopted this verdict, most after the Hinckley case. Those found guilty are sentenced as criminals, evaluated for psychiatric treatment needs, and sent for treatment until such time as they are no longer judged "mentally ill." At that point they complete their sentence in a prison setting. The opportunity to render this verdict is being watched to make sure it does not create further confusion for juries and that the party found guilty is indeed provided with adequate treatment. The latter may be most problematic, along with the mental health impact of imprisoning a supposedly "cured" mental patient.

In the words of federal judge Irving R. Kaufman (1982:20), "In the final analysis the key question facing society is this: What should be done with mentally disturbed offenders?" Given the difficulties mental health professionals still face in evaluating, diagnosing, and providing effective treatment to the mentally troubled—including noncriminals—this key question continues to await a humane and wise answer. In the meantime, public dismay and outrage over cases such as that involving John W. Hinckley are not likely to abate (*Annals of the American Academy of Political and Social Science* 1985).

Factors Associated with Mental Illness

Who are the persons whose behaviors are most likely to set the labeling process into motion? Five factors seem to have a lot to do with being defined as mentally ill. These factors are class, economic disruption, racism, sexism, and war and other traumas.

Class

Because of their economic disadvantage, low-income groups face daily problems in living. Thus we should expect many members of such groups to display signs of being mentally troubled. The impact of class on mental functioning has long been recognized. In the 1930s sociologists Robert E. L. Faris and H. Warren Dunham (1939) probed this issue in their research on mental hospitals in Chicago. Faris and Dunham looked at the records of 35,000 persons who had been admitted to the city's private and public mental institutions, checking not only the diagnostic labels that psychiatrists applied to each patient but also the part of the city each came from. They found that the highest rates of hospitalization were for persons residing in unstable low-income areas. Moreover, the most seriously troubled people—those

diagnosed as schizophrenic—tended to come from these same areas.

The study by Faris and Dunham could be criticized for concentrating only on the hospitalized. A more comprehensive inquiry that avoided this pitfall took place during the early 1950s in New Haven, Connecticut (Hollingshead and Redlich 1958; Myers and Bean 1968). This study, which was conducted by August Hollingshead and Fredrick Redlich, covered not only the hospitalized but also persons treated in clinics and by private psychiatrists. Hollingshead and Redlich identified the total population of all persons receiving treatment over a 5-month period. They divided this group into five classes, based on area of residence, occupation, and amount of education. The classes ranged from Class I (business and professional people) down to Class V (unskilled laborers and welfare clients). This division corresponds with differential economic status—Class I being the upper middle class and Class V the poor.

The findings of Hollingshead and Redlich's study were consistent with those of the Chicago study. The severely troubled—those designated as psychotic—most frequently came from Class V. Both the incidence and prevalence of serious mental troubles were highest for this group. Those suffering from less serious problems—that is, the neuroses—were most likely to come from Class I. In fact, Hollingshead and Redlich found that the top four classes contributed fewer patients than one would expect, given their numerical representation in the New Haven population.

Beyond this, Hollingshead and Redlich noted that the *type* of treatment patients received varied in accordance with their class membership. People from the lower classes were most likely to be served by public institutions, most of which provided little more than custodial care. Members of the more affluent classes, particularly Class I, most frequently patronized private psychiatrists; if hospitalization was required, they were likely to enter expensive private institutions. Such differential treatment, it has been suggested, may influence statistics on the high rates of serious disorders among the poor (Miller and Mishler 1959). The prospects for personalized attention and quick release are lower in public, as opposed to private, hospitals. Moreover, the lower classes are more likely to be diagnosed as seriously ill than the more affluent, even when they display the same symptoms—an indication of class bias in the application of psychiatric labels.

Both the Chicago and New Haven studies were limited to persons undergoing treatment, which means that they cannot be generalized to any larger population. However, the Midtown Manhattan study, discussed earlier in this chapter, provides some information about the non-treated sector (Srole et al. 1962). In this study, the cases not only were classified on the basis of the degree of mental impairment but were also ranked in terms of the socioeconomic background of the residents. Almost half of the persons who came from the lowest economic stratum were found to have severe or marked symptoms of impairment, or to be incapacitated. By contrast, little more than 10 percent of those from the highest stratum were judged to be so troubled.

Many other studies have been conducted, and their findings are generally consistent: The highest rates of mental illness, particularly of serious mental difficulties, seem to be found in the lowest economic strata. (Dohrenwend and Dohrenwend 1969)

The affluent may be afflicted with anxieties, which are relatively minor illnesses within the framework of the medical model. But the poor often respond to problems in living by fleeing from reality. Lacking the finances to pursue private, individualized attention from psychiatrists, poor people who are troubled generally must fall back on the tax-supported institutions reserved for them. There, within a medical context, the poor are told that something is the matter with *them*—not with a society whose organization presents them with problems in living (see Rochefort 1997).

Economic Disruption

There is little information about the impact of large-scale societal change on the mental well-being of people in the United States. One of the few studies was conducted by sociologist M. Harvey Brenner. Brenner hypothesized that "mental hospitalization will increase during economic downturns and decrease during upturns" (Brenner 1973). To test this hypothesis, he examined data on hospitalization and economic conditions in New York State, covering a period of nearly 13 decades, from before the Civil War to 1971.

Using sophisticated statistical techniques, Brenner found evidence to support his hypothesis. He discovered that the functional mental illnesses were extremely sensitive to adverse changes in the U.S. economy. Most of the organic illnesses were not sensitive to changes, with the exception of psychoses following excessive alcohol consumption. Evidently, many people try to lose themselves in drink in times of great economic stress. Brenner noted that the people admitted to mental hospitals were typically workers whose occupations were most vulnerable to unemployment or loss of income.

Through his research, Brenner was also able to show that several other factors had nothing to do with changes in hospitalization levels and rates. Among these unrelated factors were the availability of bed space, changing treatment practices, population changes, differences in state treatment facilities, and shifting public and psychiatric definitions of who is ill. By rejecting these alternative explanations, he demonstrated that "the destiny of the individual is to a great extent subject to large-scale changes in the social and economic structure that are in no way under his control" (Brenner 1973).

In discussing the implications of his findings, Brenner questioned the effectiveness and appropriateness of psychiatric treatment. Since many causes of mental illness lie outside the individual, society—not the patient—must be changed in order to reduce mental troubles. Furthermore, he contended: "Hospitalization is not only a psychiatrically inappropriate response to economic stress; it actually compounds the social impact of economic stress enormously. . . . The patient's economic and social careers can be very seriously damaged" (Brenner 1973:228–29). What Brenner was alluding to here is the fact that individuals who have been hospitalized for mental troubles are frequently stigmatized by the hospitalization (Corrigan and Lundin 2001; Fink and Tasman 1992). Their "histories" of mental problems make it difficult for them to find economic security, for they are suspected of still being "sick." This, of course, is akin to Thomas Scheff's concept of mental illness careers.

Beyond this, according to Brenner, mental hospitals are vehicles for social control. They function like prisons in that they remove troubled, and possibly troublesome, people from the population and act as safety valves for the society. Since the systemic sources of mental troubles are rarely acknowledged, the very existence of mental hospitals supports the status quo.

Brenner's empirical findings have been underscored by what happens when the national unemployment rate periodically soars. Staffs at mental health facilities across the country report a rise in the number of individuals and families seeking help. For example, during the serious economic recession of the early 1980s, families in high-unemployment areas experienced "an increased level of severe quarrels, wife beating, child abuse, depression, suicide attempts, excessive alcohol use, insomnia, and fatigue" (Nelson 1983:25). Recent research also suggests that unemployment and underem-

ployment have contributed to an alarming increase in homelessness, and the insecurity, isolation, powerlessness, and deprivation of being homeless itself can contribute to a deterioration of one's mental health (Bhugra 1996; Hartman 2000). Mental and other health troubles are clearly a part of the human toll taken by economic adversity (Liem and Rayman 1982; Perry 1996). And when economic pressures affect the mental health of the primary or only parent, the impact can reach to the mental health of the children in their care as well (Dennis et al. 2003).

Racism

As we saw in Chapter 7, racism is a source of harm for millions of people in the United States. Thus, we would expect to find that racial minority group members experience mental troubles more frequently than whites. However, studies and data relating to race and mental illness are limited and are confused by the impact of class on minorities (see U.S. Surgeon General 2001). People of color are overrepresented in the most economically disadvantaged strata, where mental illness is more prevalent (Kposowa, Tsunokai, and Butler 2002). Moreover, most of the focus of literature on mental health and racism has been on African Americans, although this has begun to change in recent years (Gaw 1993; Martin, Tuch, and Roman 2003; Serafica et al. 1990).

Case studies on the impact of racism are of limited utility. One of the best-known studies was conducted in the early 1950s by Abram Kardiner and Lionel Ovesey (1951). In *The Mark of Oppression,* these researchers concluded that African Americans suffer from extremely low self-esteem and from self-hatred. They reached this conclusion on the basis of interviews with 25 people who were thought to be psychologically disturbed. Though Kardiner and Ovesey's study had an impact on social science thinking about mental troubles of African Americans, it was criticized for stereotyping an entire population on the basis of limited data.

A similar study was published in the late 1960s by two African American psychiatrists, William Grier and Price M. Cobbs (1968). In their book *Black Rage,* Grier and Cobbs suggested that African Americans who live in a predominantly white society develop "cultural paranoia" in response to racism. Every white is an enemy until proved otherwise. In dealing with their minority status, African Americans develop distorted psychological functioning. Behind all this, according to Grier and Cobbs, they are filled with rage. Critics were quick to point out that Grier and Cobbs largely based their claims on contact with psychiatric patients—people having problems functioning in U.S. society. The millions of African Americans—and all other people of color victimized by racism—who do function well were ignored. *Black Rage,* it was noted, failed to shed any light on the mental state of the majority of minority group members. Moreover, as in *The Mark of Oppression*, Grier and Cobbs's emphasis on the alleged pathology of African Americans' mental functioning clearly failed to address the equally important question of strengths that have enabled such groups to survive racial oppression (McCarthy and Yancey 1971; Taylor 1976).

If such case studies fail to shed much light on the mental state of minority group members, investigations of prevalence and incidence are at least as difficult to interpret. Social psychologist Thomas Pettigrew (1964) noted that the overrepresentation of people of color in low-income categories makes it difficult empirically to single out racism as an independent source of mental troubles. Minority group members who suffer from serious disorders often cannot afford to patronize private hospitals. Since they are unlikely to have much faith in white-dominated public facilities, they may avoid seeking help until troubles grow severe. These factors may lead to institutionalization of the most deeply disturbed, inflating statistics on, for example, the frequency of psychoses among racial minorities.

Pettigrew also points out that in some regions of the country, people of color are more likely than whites to be involuntarily committed to institutions. Once in large public hospitals, many of which are informally segregated, a lack of quality care and racist practices may result in prolonged stays. Frequent readmissions may follow. All this is to say that estimates of minority mental troubles based on treatment statistics may be biased by economic and social factors that do not impinge on whites (Ruiz 1990).

Thus, for example, statistics for admissions to mental hospitals indicate that African Americans have higher rates of admission than whites. But such statistics are not easy to interpret. Similarly, the facts that African Americans have higher admission rates for schizophrenia than whites and that first admission rates for anxiety disorders are higher for whites are also hard to interpret. It could be that African Americans simply ignore mental disorders that are not incapacitating, so that only the most seriously troubled are likely to come into contact with treatment agencies.

Furthermore, it is possible that white mental health practitioners may designate people of color as ill more frequently than they apply this label to whites. Not only may there be class bias but there may also be ignorance of minority group members' life pressures and ethnic characteristics (Fernando 1995). Simple things like language barriers may impede understanding the troubles of Spanish-speaking persons (Santiago-Irizarry 2001).

Whatever the facts about the impact of racism on the mental state of minorities and on patterns of treatment, we must remember that the medical model calls for finding fault with the victims. It does not call for fighting the systemic sources of minority mental troubles.

Sexism

Until fairly recently little attention was paid to the mental state of women in the United States. Under the impetus of the feminist movement, sexism and the problems in living to which it gives rise have become more widely discussed. Nonetheless, as psychologist Phyllis Chesler (1971:362–63) once commented: "Contemporary psychiatric and psychological theories and practices both reflect and influence our culture's politically naive understanding and emotionally brutal treatment of women."

Chesler notes that men have long dominated the mental health profession. Though women are well represented among psychiatric social workers, men generally hold the more prestigious positions of psychiatrist, psychoanalyst, and psychologist, and they dominate on faculties that provide professional training. Thus men have determined how women's mental difficulties will be explained and treated. Women with problems in living who seek help from mental health practitioners are likely to be told that they are at fault, "and this by men who have studiously bypassed the objective fact of female oppression" (Chesler 1971:363).

Chesler points to studies indicating that women who exhibit—or wish to exhibit—some of the personality traits of mentally healthy men are likely to be thought ill. That is, women who want to be assertive, independent, and aggressive—traits stereotypically associated with the male gender role—may be seen as abnormal. She suggests that there is a masculine ideology in mental health practice, in which the "healthy" woman is one whose personality does not depart from traditional concepts of femininity (Chesler 1997).

Researchers have found that, when all modes of therapy are taken into account, women undergo treatment for mental troubles far more frequently than men (Russell 2000; Russo 1990; Ussher 1992). Moreover, women have been making up an increasing proportion of those undergoing treatment since the mid-1960s. While there are probably many reasons for this, it seems likely that, as women are growing increasingly aware of and sensitive to their position of subordination, they are searching for ways to cope with the unhappiness they feel. Viewing herself as mentally ill, ironically, may be one of the ways a woman can find someone who will listen to her troubles.

What kinds of symptoms do women undergoing treatment most frequently display? Reviewing literature on female patients, Chesler (1971:371) notes they are often "self-deprecatory, depressed, perplexed, suffering from suicidal thoughts, or making suicide attempts." (Fewer women than men actually commit suicide, however.) These are the kinds of symptoms one would expect among a group that suffers from male chauvinism and institutional sexism, topics we discussed in Chapter 8.

Marriage, long considered to be the proper "place" for women in this society, seems to be a particular source of unhappiness for many. Jessie Bernard (1971:149), in her review of the numerous studies suggesting that wives are less satisfied with their marriages than husbands, underscores the dilemma of many married women. While "their happiness is more dependent upon marriage than men's," women are expected to do the adjusting to their husbands' demands (see also Steil 1989). According to Bernard (1971:149), the psychological costs of such adjustments are often considerable and "may greatly impair mental health."

Many feminists argue that women's mental troubles are linked to their negative treatment within a male-dominated society. Women are often given highly demanding responsibilities and receive little assistance from men in the family setting; are denied the same opportunities and recognition as men receive in other institutional areas, such as the workplace; are made to feel inadequate by male-dominated standards of beauty and sexual desirability; and are far more at risk than men for domestic violence, sexual harassment, and rape (Silverstein 1995; Ussher 1992). Inequality, then, is seen as fostering and precipitating mental disorders, which are often explained away by a male-dominated mental health establishment as due to women's own deficits.

Back in 1892, well-known feminist Charlotte Perkins Gilman (quoted in Ussher 1992:307) stated: "Mental illness . . . for women [is] often a form of logical resistance to a 'kind and benevolent' enemy they are not permitted to openly fight. In a sick society, women who have difficulty fitting in are not ill but demonstrating a healthy positive response."

The feminist movement has given many women a way to redefine the sources of mental troubles they are experiencing and has pointed to broad-based solutions that are possible if women and their male allies work together for social change.

War and Trauma

It is not unusual for soldiers returning from combat to find it difficult to readjust to civilian life. Beyond the mental shift from the regimented daily life of military service to the more individualized routines of civilian life, returning veterans must confront nightmares of violence, some of which they observed, perhaps some they engaged in themselves or to which they were subjected. But it has only been since the conflict in Vietnam that these readjustment problems became recognized as a mental health issue of **post-traumatic stress syndrome** (PTSS). Post-traumatic stress syndrome is suffered by survivors of a whole range of traumas, including sexual abuse, rape, war, terrorism, and other forms of violence such as the shooting of students at Columbine High School in Littleton, Colorado, in 1999 and Red Lake High School in Bemidji, Minnesota, in 2005. Many survivors of the terrorist attacks on September 11, 2001; the tsunami tragedy in South Asia in 2004; and Hurricane Katrina in August 2005, as well as members of rescue and recovery teams, reported symptoms such as nightmares, sleeplessness, depression, anxiety, irritability, relationship difficulties, and guilt at having survived when so many others did not. Returning military veterans of war commonly report similar symptoms, along with the guilt of perhaps having done things in the name of war that they ordinarily would have found abominable (Ursano and Norwood 1996).

People with PTSS often suffer bouts of depression, violence, and suicide, as well as physical illnesses related to the depression and other symptoms. The Veterans Administration, charged with addressing the health-care needs of returning veterans, has had a poor record of diagnosing and treating PTSS effectively, in part because of the immense cost of validating it as a widespread mental health price of battle. Moreover, it is not just the returning veteran or survivor of trauma who suffers: so, too, do the people around them, including their families, coworkers, employers, and neighbors. These "secondary victims" of PTSS often receive even less recognition and care for their mental health needs.

Treating Mental Illness

As we have seen, millions of people in the United States are mentally troubled. Men, women, and children of all races and classes face problems in living that may well be linked to the organization of U.S. society. Some of them respond to these problems by behaving in ways that are labeled mental illnesses.

According to the medical model, which dominates the mental health profession, mentally troubled individuals are sick. Private psychiatric care, community mental health centers, and mental hospitals are used to treat the mentally ill and to foster their adjustment to the societal status quo. Many more are treated with a wide range of drugs. Medical insurance companies urge psychologists and psychiatrists to look to drugs either instead of talk-based therapeutic treatment or as an adjunct to such treatment. This is because the insurance companies believe the drugs encourage quicker recoveries on an outpatient basis, and thus make treatment less costly.

But critics argue that drugs often simply mask the symptoms of illness without treating them at all. And evidence began emerging in 2004 indicating a disquieting trend of administering antidepressant drugs such as Prozac, Paxil, and Zoloft to treat depression and defiant and otherwise disruptive behavior in children, resulting in an increased risk of pediatric suicide. The U.S. Surgeon General has since recommended discontinuing pediatric use of such drugs, or at least more careful monitoring of patients who are taking them.

The push to administer drugs to treat mental illness more quickly than talk-based therapy is clearly related to escalating costs associated with care and treatment. When we include lost productivity due to mental disorders, treatment of mental illness costs tens of billions of dollars each year. One out of three hospital beds in the United States is reserved for the mentally troubled. Figure 16.2 depicts inpatient treatment settings. More money and resources are used for the treatment of mental illness than for the elimination of some of the sources of mental anguish. For example, while government programs in the field of mental health care have expanded in recent years, this has not been the case with programs to eliminate poverty, unemployment, and discrimination.

In the next section we look at one treatment given the seriously mentally ill—confinement in large public institutions. We consider the issue of involuntary confinement and its implications for civil liberties. Finally, we discuss the possibility of alternatives to confinement.

Mental Hospitals as Total Institutions

Many people who are defined as mentally ill and receive treatment are confined in large public institutions. Who are the people most likely to be confined? According to sociologist Robert Perrucci (1974:30):

They are victims of families and communities who can no longer tolerate rule-breaking and problematic behavior. They are victims of poverty, powerlessness, and discrimination and the resulting individual-psychological explanations for their plight as people with a mental illness. They, moreover, are often willing victims insofar as they accept and adopt the roles of madness in order to "solve" the problems of living which they are experiencing. In short, they are not in the hospital because they are mad, but because they have been rejected by society and have no suitable place in it.

In Perrucci's (1974:31) words, mental hospitals function "as a dumping ground for societal rejects."

Large public mental hospitals have a great deal in common with one another. Erving Goffman (1961) calls them **total institutions,** in that eating, sleeping, work, and play all occur within a schedule set up by hospital administrators and staff. Every patient is required to do certain things at certain times, usually in the company of fellow patients, under a system of rules imposed from above. Some, however, might say

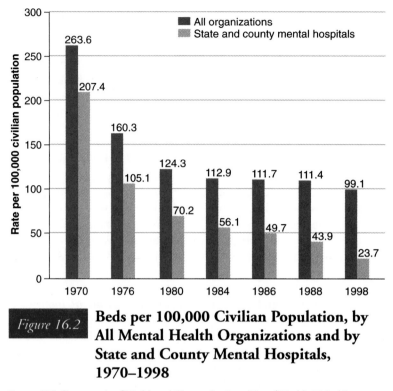

Figure 16.2 **Beds per 100,000 Civilian Population, by All Mental Health Organizations and by State and County Mental Hospitals, 1970–1998**

Source: U.S. Department of Health and Human Services, *Mental Health, United States, 1992* (Washington, DC: U.S. Government Printing Office, 1992), p. 2; Ronald W. Manderscheid and Marilyn J. Henderson, *Mental Health, United States, 2000* (Washington, DC: U.S. Government Printing Office, 2001), Chapter 14, Figure 1.

this is helpful in that patients are relieved of the burden of decision making.

To Goffman the total institution has a great impact on the individual who is confined there. People enter mental hospitals with what Goffman calls a **presenting culture** based on their way of life and the routines they took for granted prior to confinement. They also have a conception of who they are, based on their past participation in social arrangements and interaction with family members, coworkers, friends, and neighbors. According to Goffman, the patients' presenting cultures are ignored in the mental institution; and patients are forced to live in accordance

with the demands of institutional authority. In addition, their self-concepts are attacked and altered.

The attack on patients' self-concepts is done through a process of **mortification.** From the moment they enter the institution, patients are cut off from contact with the outside world. They may be photographed, fingerprinted, weighed, measured, undressed, searched, bathed, and disinfected. Personal belongings and clothing may be taken away, and institutional garments provided. The patient may be labeled with an illness category, assigned an identification number, ordered into required living arrangements, and handed a list of rules and regulations. According to Goffman (1961:16): "In thus being squared away, the new arrival allows himself to be shaped and coded into an object. . . . This object can be fed into the administrative machinery of the establishment, to be worked on smoothly by routine operations."

The staff carefully observes individuals' willingness to accept being "squared away." Patients who resist may be viewed as troublemakers who deserve punishment. Goffman notes that the staff may actually test new arrivals to see how far they can be pushed. By doing this, the staff gets to demonstrate punishments to the newcomers while simultaneously reminding other patients what happens when someone refuses to defer to staff demands.

Goffman felt that the result of the mortification process is to undermine the patient's sense of autonomy and adult self-determination, placing the individual in a position of childlike dependency on the institutional staff. The staff can then more easily maintain order and routine. Furthermore, the mortification process fits well with the medical model, which sees the inmate as sick. As Perrucci (1974:53) puts it: "The self that existed prior to hospitalization is defined as having been in some way the cause of the patient's present condition. Thus, the old self must be destroyed, and a new self incorporated through a resocialization process."

Perrucci tells us that the mortification process occurs in a **world of unfreedom.** Patients have little control over what happens to them in the institution, so they cannot choose to remain unaffected by it. Perrucci found that patients respond to the pressures in various ways. Some "withdraw" from relations with patients and staff but comply with institutional routines. Others engage in "accommodation," trying to be perfect patients. Still others respond with "conversion"—imitating the staff's way of relating to other patients. Finally, some "resist": "Patients operating under this mode are greatly concerned with maintaining their own self-respect and dignity. In this respect, they resist all efforts to place them in the general category of patient" (Perrucci 1974:64).

Novelist Ken Kesey memorialized the resisters—and speculated on their fate—in *One Flew over the Cuckoo's Nest* (Kesey 1962). The novel recounts the experiences of McMurphy, a man who chose confinement in a mental hospital over jail. McMurphy's attempts to humanize his ward by organizing such forbidden activities as gambling and parties run into resistance from a staff member named Big Nurse, who ultimately gains control over McMurphy by forcing him to undergo a frontal lobotomy (a brain operation that can replace assertiveness with meekness). Kesey's fictional depiction of the struggle between institutional authority and a patient who refused to adapt to it was inspired by his observations in an Oregon mental hospital. A similar tale of institutionalization and resistance to confinement, authority, and control was dramatized in the book *Girl, Interrupted* (Kaysen 1994).

There is one more response to confinement. In *Methods of Madness,* psychologist Benjamin Braginsky and his associates (1969) found patients who were content to remain confined. They had been in confinement for so long that they could not even bear to think of leaving the institution. Such patients manipulated the staff by affecting symptoms that would bar their release. Through such **impression management,** they gained some control over their fate.

In Braginsky's view, this behavior was not a result of illness; it was an outcome of the effects of institutionalization itself. Ironically, psychiatrists would likely diagnose such persons as having a condition called **malingering,** considered adaptive and therefore appropriate only in certain circumstances, "for example, feigning illness while a captive of the enemy during wartime" or "in hostage situations" (American Psychiatric Association 2000).

In recent years there have been limited reforms in the administration of large public mental hospitals. And, as we mentioned earlier, the costs of maintaining people in long-term confinement—together with the adoption of drugs that alter the behavior of patients—have decreased the average length of a stay in such institutions. While admission rates have gone up in recent years, so have release rates. Still, the large public mental hospital remains a major focal point for the treatment and mental rearmament of persons who are troubled.

The Politics of Involuntary Confinement

At several points we have alluded to the fact that people may be involuntarily confined to mental institutions. This is true for both adults and children (Armstrong 1993). All states have legal procedures that make it possible to hospitalize individuals who refuse to accept the illness label. These procedures often involve having a judge rule that individuals are a danger to themselves and/or others.

The procedures leading to involuntary confinement raise serious civil liberties issues. Relatives, social welfare agencies, police, or private citizens may start the process, often when they become aware of individuals who communicate their alienation from the status quo in unusual or disruptive ways, or of children or the elderly who do not seem to be able to care for themselves. In other words, the initial judgments about such individuals' mental states are typically made by "accusers" who have no medical or psychiatric training. The judgments are made in terms of value-laden views about what is normal and what is deviant.

In most states, police are empowered to take the "accused" into temporary custody, where he or she may be forced to undergo examination by medical practitioners. Sometimes the examining doctors have no specialized training in psychiatry. Even when they do, as we saw earlier, professional judgments about mental health are

not always accurate. Nevertheless, the examining doctor may recommend that hospitalization take place. Police are not likely to be trained in assessing mental capabilities, and they are likely to routinely accept the judgments of medical personnel. According to sociologist David Mechanic (1969:127), "the commitment process has the form of due process of law but is actually vacuous since the decision tends to be predetermined."

Mental health practitioners tend to assume that a person would never have been brought into commitment proceedings unless something was wrong with him or her. Consequently, many people whose behavior is said to be unacceptable—but who pose no harm to themselves or others—are confined. Even confining those who may be dangerous poses civil liberties issues, since there often is no way to predict such behavior. Hospital administrators generally admit that very few of their patients would harm others if released on the spot.

Further, commitment proceedings assume that hospitalization—even involuntary commitment—will help those who are mentally troubled. We have already seen that the impact of confinement in a total institution may actually be harmful. We have also noted that the stigma of hospitalization may plague persons after release. Moreover, since the sources of problems in living may not necessarily reside within the individual, removal from the community may be a questionable solution.

Can't confinement be replaced by some other type of treatment procedure? David Mechanic (1969:135) does not feel that reforms will lead us in this direction:

Even if we assume adherence to due process in the use of commitment procedures and even if the quality of treatment undergoes impressive improvement, the community will still demand that certain individuals be removed and treated despite no desire on their part for such care. . . . Misfits will always frighten or threaten others, and people will always feel that the interests of the community are best served by placing such deviants in custody. Inevitably what is thought to be in the interests of some is not in the interests of others.

Mechanic's pessimism may cause us to conclude that the tendency to place "misfits" in confinement is traceable to human nature. In reality, not human nature but *power* plays the central role. The label of deviant or "misfit" is forced on individuals who are mentally ill due to physical causes or who may be simply alienated from society. Sociologist Howard Becker (1963:17) has raised and answered the key question: "Who can, in fact, force others to accept their rules and what are the causes of their success? This is, of course, a question of political and economic power."

Parents may exercise their power to have a troublesome child confined. Children may dispose of their aging parents in the same way. Street people and the indigent homeless, whose behavior or simple presence annoys the "solid citizenry," may be taken away or pressured into voluntary surrender to a mental hospital. In such cases, the ability of the accused to resist confinement may be minimal (Szasz 1994). Resistance itself, ironically, may be interpreted as further evidence of illness and may be used to justify confinement. On the other hand, high-status people may most easily avoid the label of mental illness and confinement against their will.

We must not forget that there is much money to be made from the mental health industry, an expanding sector of the economy on which tens of billions of dollars are spent each year. Private psychiatrists often receive $150 or more an hour for their services. Companies profit from the demand for drugs and equipment utilized by the mental health profession. These people have a vested interest in maintaining today's treatment procedures. Were extensive changes to be made, the status and jobs of many such professionals would be jeopardized (Schrag 1978).

The Deinstitutionalization Movement

In the early 1960s the federal government began to provide funds to encourage the creation of community-based treatment centers for the mentally troubled. The intent was that these centers would grow in number and ultimately replace most of the large-scale residential institutions in which so many persons were then confined (Levine 1981).

The **deinstitutionalization** of the mentally troubled was to be facilitated by the availability of new drugs that allowed mental patients to be released into local communities. There they were to obtain treatment and rehabilitation services from the planned network of community mental health centers. Deinstitutionalization in conjunction with community-based treatment was seen as an enlightened and effective way of helping the mentally troubled. Politicians were attracted to this approach by the prospect of cost savings (Scull 1977).

Earlier in this chapter we noted that the total resident populations of mental hospitals have decreased significantly over the last several decades. This is one indicator of the deinstitutionalization process that has gone on. Although perhaps praiseworthy in its intent, the process has been accompanied by severe problems—hundreds of thousands of mentally troubled people have been ill served (Isaac and Armat 1990).

The original federal goal of fostering some 1,600 community mental health centers has long gone unmet. To date, fewer than half this number exist, and many of these suffer from inadequate funding and insufficient staffing. Hence many of those persons who have been deinstitutionalized have failed to link up with community-based treatment or have found inadequate assistance.

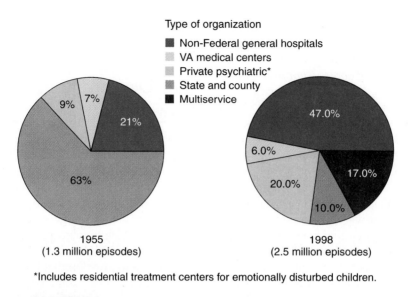

*Includes residential treatment centers for emotionally disturbed children.

| Figure 16.3 | **Inpatient Care Episodes in Mental Health Organizations, 1955 and 1998** |

Source: U.S. Department of Health and Human Services, *Mental Health, United States, 1994* (Washington, DC: U.S. Government Printing Office, 1994), p. 84; Ronald W. Manderscheid and Marilyn J. Henderson, *Mental Health, United States, 2000* (Washington, DC: U.S. Government Printing Office, 2001), Chapter 14, Figure 6.

Too often former mental patients have floundered in the community, only to find themselves reconfined in still-existing residential institutions for repeated durations—a kind of "revolving door" situation (Sheehan 1983; Torrey 1998). The latter is reflected in the fact that while the patient populations in residential institutions have gone down overall, annual new admissions for short-term treatment have gone up (see Figure 16.3). An unknown number of these new admissions are really readmissions of the deinstitutionalized who lack community-based care.

The failure of community-based treatment to grow to meet the needs of released mental patients is painfully evident in towns and cities across the nation. Severely disturbed persons, along with others who are mentally disabled, have come to constitute a new and highly visible minority group in low-income central city areas. There they often settle in single-room-occupancy hotels and rooming houses. Others among this group are part of the nation's estimated 2 million to 3 million homeless persons. Subject to local hostility, fear, and ridicule, and frequently preyed on by criminals, deinstitutionalized persons find their plight made worse by living in a "community" setting (Lamb and Weinberger 2001; Lewis et al. 1991).

The Need for Change

So long as the mentally troubled are automatically defined as being at fault for their plight, the features of U.S. society that provoke problems in living are likely to remain unquestioned. It is far easier to pour money and resources into treating the sick minds of individuals than to confront the prospects of altering society so that humanity is no longer estranged from its authentic possibilities.

But we cannot afford to wait for large-scale societal changes while doing nothing to help the millions who are troubled now. The ideas of Szasz and Laing offer some alternatives to confinement. In fact, Laing's idea of having people who have been troubled help others has become widely accepted. In many cities, people who face common problems in living can join self-help groups and pool their knowledge and experiences to provide one another with mutual support. Those groups that operate outside the medical model, stress voluntary participation, and offer positive, nonalienating relationships can be expected to make an important contribution (Chamberlin 1978).

Moving people out of confinement in public institutions and into the community is an important change. This has been taking place often simply for budgetary reasons because of the rising costs of inpatient care. But the newly released are too frequently set adrift and left to fend for themselves. Many end up isolated and alone and/or suffering from the stigmatization of their confinement. Many are among the homeless and would be helped greatly by more investment in affordable housing. Trained volunteers might be organized to be special friends and companions to such persons in their home environments. Some of the newly released may like to be placed in the homes of persons who would guide them in their transition to full community participation.

Ultimately, however, the societal factors that seem to give rise to problems in living—from poverty to sexism—must be confronted if mental troubles are to be mitigated.

Conditions in many large public mental institutions, where less affluent people are generally confined, are often dismal. Inmates are given tranquilizing drugs and often receive little or no therapy. Confinement in such institutions can be extremely harmful. The men in this photo are whiling away their day in the recreation room of a mental institution with little to do other than stare out the window or doze.

Summary

Millions of people in the United States are mentally troubled. We do not know the exact prevalence of mental illness—that is, the total cases existing at a given time—because of problems of definition and measurement. A rough estimate is that 10 percent of the adult population—over 23 million people—have mental disorders. The number of new cases occurring over time—the incidence of mental illness—appears to be on the increase. But because of the problem of interpreting available data, most of which are based on treatment statistics, one must advance such an argument with caution. Many factors bear on whether or not troubled people seek out and receive treatment.

The dominant approach to the treatment of the mentally troubled is called the medical model. Psychiatrists and other mental health practitioners commonly assume that troubled people are ill and in need of cure. Two major types of illness are psychoses and neuroses. Psychoses are considered very severe forms of illness wherein individuals have their own versions of reality and are often unable to perform expected roles. Neuroses are considered less severe forms of illness and typically involve expressions of underlying anxieties.

The medical model has come under criticism and is a source of controversy. Critics point to problems in classifying mental disorders and symptoms. Questions have been raised as to the accuracy of the judgments made by mental health practitioners in their diagnoses. Critics of the medical model have even questioned the very concept of mental illness. It has been contended that the sometimes unusual forms of behavior and/or thinking of the mentally troubled are actually communications in response to problems in living. So-called mental illness has even been interpreted as a sign of health, a strategy invented by people to allow them to live in an unlivable situation. Finally, it has been pointed out that the mentally troubled are often subject to labeling. Those whose behavior is deemed deviant may be designated as ill, forced to accept the role of patient, and given treatment within the confines of the medical model. Problems in diagnosis and labeling plague the legal arena as well, as experts struggle over definitions of insanity in relation to criminal behavior.

Various factors seem to be associated with what the medical model labels mental illness. The impact of class on mental functioning has long been recognized, as the highest rates of illness—particularly severe disorders—seem to be found in the lowest income strata. Large-scale economic disruption that adversely affects individuals has been found to be related to increased expression of mental troubles and hospitalization rates. Although data are hard to interpret because of the intrusion of class and other factors, there are some indications that racial minorities require treatment for serious illnesses more frequently than whites. Moreover, women undergo treatment for mental illness far more frequently than men.

The treatment of most troubled people is through outpatient facilities, but many enter confinement in mental hospitals. Such hospitals have been called total institutions in recognition of authorities' control over almost every aspect of inmates' living conditions and routine. The mental hospital is said to have a great impact on those confined, attacking their self-concepts and encouraging dependency on institutional staff. People who are confined may respond in any number of ways—from withdrawal to resistance. Some, confined so long that they cannot bear the thought of leaving, manipulate the staff by pretending to be ill.

The process of deinstitutionalization, whereby more and more persons have been released into local communities, has also resulted in problems. Lack of follow-up and community support has left many such persons adrift, even homeless. People may be involuntarily confined to mental hospitals. The procedures involved raise serious civil liberties issues, particularly regarding due process.

There is a need for change. Mental troubles are typically treated as if the individuals are at fault, despite indications that large-scale societal factors have a bearing on such troubles. Ultimately, such societal factors must be confronted. Meanwhile, self-help groups for the troubled, together with affordable housing and community support for persons newly released from confinement, can be useful.

Key Terms

Alienation 518
Death row syndrome 522
Deinstitutionalization 533
Functional psychoses 515
Impression management 531
Insanity 520
Malingering 531
Medical model 513
Mental illness 510
Mental illness as political event 519
Mood disorders 515
Mortification 530
Neurosis 515

Organic psychoses 515
Postpartum depression 522
Post-traumatic stress syndrome 528
Presenting culture 530
Psychoses 514
Residual deviance 519
Schizophrenia 515
Seasonal affective disorder 515
Societal reaction 520
Stigma 509
Total institutions 529
World of unfreedom 531

Discussion Questions

1. Have you ever wondered whether you were mentally ill? Have you ever been convinced of it? What was the basis for your concern? Did you trace the sources of your feelings to something wrong with you or to the life circumstances confronting you?

2. What are the attitudes of your friends and family toward persons who are thought to be mentally troubled? In your view, are their attitudes realistic and appropriate? Why?

3. On most college campuses there are mental health facilities for use by students. What is the general student attitude toward such facilities? What kinds of problems are brought there, and where do such problems originate?

4. According to Jessie Bernard, many studies suggest that women are less satisfied with their marriages than men, and the circumstances of marriage may impair women's mental health. In terms of your own experiences and/or observations, is this often the case? Why?

5. Develop a set of criteria that would allow the courts to determine who among the mentally troubled should be involuntarily confined for examination and possible treatment. Compare your criteria with those of others.

6. Prepare a defense for an adult or child who faces involuntary confinement in a mental hospital because he or she may engage in self-harm or be dangerous to the community, based on your understanding of people's rights under the law.

Suggested Readings

Corrigan, Patrick, and Robert Lundin. *Don't Call Me Nuts: Coping with the Stigma of Mental Illness* (Tinley Park, IL: Recovery Press, 2001). Detailed discussion of the social stigma of being labeled mentally ill, the civil rights of those with mental illness, and strategies of coping and challenging stigma by those labeled.

Goffman, Erving. *Asylums* (New York: Doubleday Anchor Books, 1961). Classic analysis of a large public mental institution, its routines, and its impact on those subject to its demands.

Isaac, Rael Jean, and Virginia C. Armat. *Madness in the Streets: How Psychiatry and the Law Abandoned the Mentally Ill* (New York: Free Press, 1990). Critique of the handling of deinstitutionalization and problems facing the homeless.

Robinson, Daniel N. *Wild Beasts and Idle Humours: The Insanity Defense from Antiquity to the Present* (Cambridge, MA: Harvard University Press, 1996). An overview of the issues and controversies that have surrounded the insanity defense and efforts at reforming its use.

Silverstein, Brett. *Cost of Competence: Why Inequality Causes Depression, Eating Disorders, and Illness in Women* (New York: Oxford University Press, 1995). Suggests a direct link between the U.S. system of gender inequality and problems that come to be defined through the lens of the medical model.

Torrey, E. Fuller. *Out of the Shadows: Confronting America's Mental Illness Crisis* (New York: Wiley, 1998). Provides a critique of the concept of deinstitutionalization and of the treatment of those with mental illness in the United States.

Ursano, Robert J., and Ann E. Norwood, eds. *Emotional Aftermath of the Persian Gulf War: Veterans, Families, Communities, and Nations* (Arlington, VA: American Psychiatric Association, 1996). Analysis of post-traumatic stress syndrome as a consequence of war as a traumatic experience, for the returning veterans as well as their families and communities.

chapter 17

Substance Abuse

Members of U.S. society should be at peace with themselves and with one another. The vicarious rewards associated with the abuse of drugs, including alcohol, should have no attraction.

The widespread use and abuse of drugs have become matters of major public concern during the last several decades. As people—particularly young adults and adolescents—use drugs for nonmedical purposes, moral, medical, legal, and political issues have emerged. Most of these issues revolve around the so-called problem drugs that are readily available through illicit channels. These include marijuana, heroin, cocaine, LSD and other hallucinogens, and amphetamines such as "speed."

Paradoxically, far less controversy and attention surround the abuse of prescription drugs and over-the-counter preparations. Stimulants, barbiturates, and tranquilizers are used often for nonmedical reasons. Sociologist Charlotte Muller (1972) once characterized the United States as an "overmedicated society" in recognition of the degree to which drugs have become an important sought after adjunct to the daily lives of millions of people. Although there has been a notable decrease in the abuse of legal drugs in recent years, it still remains an important problem.

Our emphasis in this chapter is on self-administered drugs. We begin with a discussion of the difficulties involved in defining the term *drug*. We examine the nature and extent of abuse of some illegal and legal drugs, and we look at explanations for drug use and abuse, briefly addressing the problem of the administration of drugs for social control. In schools, mental institutions, nursing homes, and a variety of other settings, drugs are viewed as an appropriate means of controlling potentially disruptive people. They have even been considered as a tool in covert intelligence operations.

One of the most commonly abused drugs is often not thought of as a drug at all: beverage alcohol. Its abuse is so endemic, and the resulting impact on society and its members is so great, that we devote a major part of this chapter to the subject. We describe the general drinking population and consider the distinction between alcohol use and abuse. Then we turn to the phenomenon of alcoholism. We examine definitions of an alcoholic, alternative explanations for alcoholism, the costs of alcoholism and problem drinking, and the various modes of treating alcoholic individuals.

What Is a Drug?

The term **drug** is subject to a wide variety of meanings and uses, each of which includes or excludes certain substances. From a strictly scientific perspective, a drug is typically defined as "any substance other than food which by its chemical nature affects the structure or function of the living organism" (National Commission on Marijuana and Drug Abuse 1973:9). This definition is overwhelmingly broad: Under it, even air and water could qualify as drugs. By contrast, medical practitioners ordinarily use the term to mean substances appropriate for use in treating physical and mental illness or disease. In other words, to doctors drugs are medicines. Finally, from a legal point of view, a drug is any substance that is so defined under the law. Thus, law enforcement personnel may use the term quite differently from scientists and physicians.

Sociologist Erich Goode, an expert on drug use, has asked whether it is possible to arrive at an objective definition that would spell out just what a drug is and is not. In other words, is there any basis on which one could easily distinguish drugs from nondrugs, so that everyone will agree on the meaning of the term? According to Goode (1999:58), there is none: "There is no effect that is common to all substances that are referred to as drugs, that is, at the same time, not by definition a property of those things no one would call drugs." Instead, any and all substances that are designated as drugs are *socially defined* as such. In Goode's (1999:58) words, "Society defines what a drug is, and this social definition shapes our attitudes toward the class of substances so labeled."

What, then, distinguishes the so-called problem drugs from other drugs and from substances that have not been labeled as drugs? The answer is nothing—nothing, that is, except a different and more negative social definition. This social definition does not necessarily have anything to do with hazards or dangers potentially associated with the use and abuse of a substance. For example, there is one drug that "has been massively used for decades; its mechanism of action on the brain and other organs is unknown; it accounts for thousands of deaths and illnesses each year, and it produces not only chromosomal breakage, but actual birth defects in lower animals" (Fort, 1969:5). This sounds like a description of a problem drug, but actually the substance is aspirin—which most people probably do not consider a drug at all. Aspirin is associated with far more known health difficulties than, for example, marijuana.

The importance of social definition is indicated by the results of a poll conducted for the National Commission on Marijuana and Drug Abuse (1973). In a national sampling of adults, 95 percent regarded heroin as a drug, and 80 percent labeled marijuana a drug. Only 39 percent regarded alcohol as a drug, and even fewer adults—27 percent—thought that tobacco products deserved this label. Although there is no objective and meaningful basis for making such distinctions, the social definitions prevailing in the United States have tended to place alcohol and tobacco outside the realm of drug status, and thus not a part of "the drug problem."

Social definitions of problem drugs frequently change over time. Within U.S. society, different groups commonly disagree over such definitions. This has been the case with such addictive narcotic drugs as morphine and heroin (Musto 1999). Morphine first began to be used in the United States in the 1850s. As its pain-relieving qualities became known, its use increased—particularly during and after the Civil War. Physicians enthusiastically endorsed the drug, and medicine companies included morphine in a variety of home remedies. An estimated 2 to 4 percent of the population was addicted by the end of the nineteenth century. Although a number of doctors had grown concerned about morphine addiction by that time, neither the press nor the public saw morphine or addiction to it as a problem.

At the beginning of the twentieth century, heroin was introduced into the United States. Physicians found it to be a stronger pain reliever than morphine, and they believed heroin to be nonaddictive. Use of heroin quickly spread. Like morphine, it could be purchased without a prescription. Before the addictive qualities of heroin became known, the number of drug addicts in the United States further increased. Still, addiction was not viewed in a negative manner by the public.

In the early 1900s, a small group of concerned doctors began pressing for government regulation of addictive drugs. New York passed the first major piece of state legislation in 1904, and other states followed. In 1914 Congress approved the Harrison Narcotic Act. This act regulated the production and distribution of addictive drugs and required users to obtain them by prescription from physicians. Doctors were flooded with prescription seekers and were soon refusing to supply addicts.

As subsequent drug laws further restricted or eliminated legal sources for addictive drugs, a flourishing black market emerged in which organized crime came to play an important role. When morphine and heroin became associated with crime and the underworld, public sentiment shifted against the addict and the drugs that were once available in respectable drugstores. Additional changes in the social definition of heroin may yet occur. The federal government has approved limited experimentation with heroin in the treatment of people who are in terrible pain, such as terminal cancer patients.

Because so many different types of substances can be defined as drugs, it is necessary to limit any discussion of drug use to particular types. In this chapter, we focus on **psychoactive substances,** drugs that may affect the minds of those who consume them.

Illegal Substances

In the 2003 National Household Survey on Drug Abuse, 19.5 million people in the United States admitted to being current users of **illicit drugs,** or drugs that have been formally declared by the government as illegal. "Current use" meant use within the previous 30 days. The highest rates of current users occur among persons under 35 years of age. (See Figure 17.1.)

On the surface it would appear that the United States is in the midst of an unprecedented illegal drug-use epidemic. The figures are indeed very high, indicating that millions of members of U.S. society may be drug-dependent, but trend data show a definite and substantial *decrease* in illegal drug use beginning in the early 1980s and continuing into the 1990s, after a long series of increases in use during the 1960s and 1970s. And though the 2003 survey shows a renewed increase in illicit drug use since 1994, it remains lower than the number 20 years previously. Thus, while more than 19 million people in the United States were using illegal drugs in 2003, this total was down from 24 million in 1979, the peak year for current illicit use. These data, based on surveys of U.S. households, are substantiated by trends uncovered by surveys focusing on drug use by young people. The use of a number of illegal drugs by teenagers has undergone a general decline since the early 1980s, although a slight increase has occurred since 2000 (Johnston et al. 2004a).

This overall downward trend in recent years (see Table 17.1) no doubt reflects a number of factors. Many people have become concerned with issues of health and fitness, and thus more attuned to the risks associated with certain types of drug use. The mass media have exploited the human suffering and criminal activity with

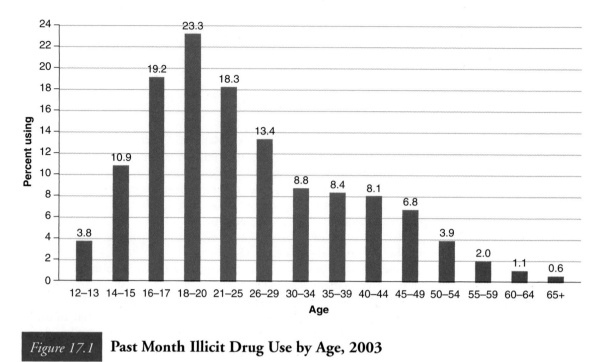

Figure 17.1   **Past Month Illicit Drug Use by Age, 2003**

Source: U.S. Department of Health and Human Services, *Preliminary Estimates for the 2003 National Household Survey on Drug Abuse* (Rockville, MD: Substance Abuse and Mental Health Services Administration, DHHS, September 2004), p. 15.

which illicit drugs have become popularly associated. Celebrities—including popular entertainers and sports figures—have contributed to public discourse as they admit to drug problems and seek treatment, appear in anti-drug-use commercials, or even tragically die. And politicians have made illegal drugs a major focal concern, both appealing to public fears and promising to take steps to alleviate them.

Illegal drug use in the United States is still generally higher than it was in the early 1960s. For example, in 2002, 46 percent of people 12 years old and over admitted to having ever used an illegal drug; marijuana and hashish were the most commonly used illicit drugs, at 40.4 percent. Usage appears to peak among young adults, aged 18 to 25: 20.2 percent admit to being current users of illicit drugs, with marijuana and hashish remaining the most widely

used illegal drug (U.S. Bureau of the Census 2005, Table 186). Moreover, the rate of drug usage among young people in the United States is high compared to that found in other industrialized nations (Johnston et al. 2004b).

In this section we focus on select problem drugs—in other words, illegal substances that are self-administered (knowingly and purposely used). Among the substances around which a great deal of fear and concern have arisen are marijuana, heroin, cocaine, LSD, PCP, "club drugs," and amphetamines.

Marijuana

Marijuana is the most widely used illegal substance in the United States. The source of marijuana is the *Cannabis sativa* plant, and its potency, in terms of its potential effects on

Table 17.1	Drug Use, by Type of Drug and Age Group: 1974 to 2002

	Ever used						Current user					
Age and type of drug	1974	1979	1985	1988	1993	2002	1974	1979	1985	1988	1993	2002
12 to 17 years old												
Marijuana	23.0	30.9	23.2	17.4	11.7	20.6	12.0	16.7	11.9	6.4	4.9	8.2
Cocaine	3.6	5.4	4.8	3.4	1.1	2.7	1.0	1.4	1.4	1.1	0.4	0.6
Inhalants	8.5	9.8	9.6	8.8	5.9	10.5	0.7	2.0	3.7	2.0	1.4	1.2
Hallucinogens	6.0	7.1	3.2	3.5	2.9	5.7	1.3	2.2	1.2	0.8	0.5	1.0
Heroin	1.0	0.5	0.4	0.6	0.2	NA	(B)	(B)	0.1	(B)	0.2	(NA)
Stimulants*	5.0	3.4	5.5	4.2	2.1	NA	1.0	1.2	1.6	1.2	0.5	(NA)
Sedatives*	5.0	3.2	4.1	2.3	1.4	NA	1.0	1.1	1.0	0.6	0.2	(NA)
Tranquilizers*	3.0	4.1	4.9	2.0	1.2	13.7[†]	1.0	0.6	0.6	0.2	0.2	4.0[†]
Analgesics*	(NA)	3.2	6.0	4.1	3.7	NA	(NA)	0.6	1.7	0.9	0.7	(NA)
Alcohol	54.0	70.3	55.4	50.2	41.3	43.4	34.0	37.2	31.0	25.2	18.0	17.6
Cigarettes	52.0	54.1	45.3	42.3	34.5	33.3	25.0	12.1	15.3	11.8	9.6	13.0
18 to 25 years old												
Marijuana	52.7	68.2	59.4	56.4	47.4	53.8	25.2	35.4	21.9	15.5	11.1	17.3
Cocaine	12.7	27.5	24.4	19.7	12.5	15.4	3.1	9.3	7.5	4.5	1.5	2.0
Inhalants	9.2	16.5	13.0	12.5	9.9	15.7	(B)	1.2	0.8	1.7	1.1	0.5
Hallucinogens	16.6	25.1	11.6	13.8	12.5	24.2	2.5	4.4	1.8	1.9	1.3	1.9
Heroin	4.5	3.5	1.3	0.3	0.7	(NA)	(B)	(B)	0.3	(B)	0.4	(NA)
Stimulants*	17.0	18.2	17.5	11.3	6.4	(NA)	3.7	3.5	3.8	2.4	0.9	(NA)
Sedatives*	15.0	17.0	11.8	5.5	2.7	(NA)	1.6	2.8	1.6	0.9	0.6	(NA)
Tranquilizers*	10.0	15.8	12.6	7.8	5.4	27.7[†]	1.2	2.1	1.6	1.0	0.6	5.4[†]
Analgesics*	(NA)	11.8	11.5	9.4	8.7	(NA)	(NA)	1.0	2.0	1.5	1.4	(NA)
Alcohol	81.6	95.3	92.0	90.3	87.1	86.7	69.3	75.9	70.7	65.3	59.3	60.5
Cigarettes	68.8	82.8	75.2	75.0	66.7	71.2	48.8	42.6	36.6	35.2	29.0	40.8
26 years old and over												
Marijuana	9.9	19.6	26.6	30.7	34.3	52.2	2.0	6.0	6.0	3.9	3.0	7.7
Cocaine	0.9	4.3	9.2	9.9	12.5	17.6	(B)	0.9	1.9	0.9	0.5	1.2
Inhalants	1.2	3.9	5.3	3.9	4.3	14.1	(B)	0.5	0.5	0.2	0.2	0.1
Hallucinogens	1.3	4.5	6.0	6.6	8.8	20.6	(B)	(B)	(B)	(B)	(B)	0.5
Heroin	0.5	1.0	1.1	1.1	1.3	(NA)	(B)	(B)	(B)	(B)	(B)	(NA)
Stimulants*	3.0	5.8	7.9	6.6	6.5	(NA)	(B)	0.5	0.7	0.5	0.2	(NA)
Sedatives*	2.0	3.5	5.6	3.3	3.8	(NA)	(B)	(B)	0.6	0.3	0.2	(NA)

(Continued)

Table 17.1	(*Continued*)											
	Ever used						**Current user**					
Age and type of drug	1974	1979	1985	1988	1993	2002	1974	1979	1985	1988	1993	2002
Tranquilizers*	2.0	3.1	7.8	4.5	4.9	24.4[†]	(B)	(B)	1.0	0.6	0.2	3.6[†]
Analgesics*	(NA)	2.7	5.9	4.5	5.5	(NA)	(NA)	(B)	0.9	0.4	0.5	(NA)
Alcohol	73.2	91.5	89.2	88.6	88.7	88.0	54.5	61.3	59.8	54.8	52.1	53.9
Cigarettes	65.4	83.0	80.6	79.6	76.9	73.7	39.1	36.9	32.7	29.8	25.3	25.2

[In percent. Current users are those who used drugs at least once within month prior to this study. Based on national samples of respondents residing in households. Subject to sampling variability.]
B Base too small to meet statistical standards for reliability of a derived figure.
NA Not available.
**Nonmedical use; does not include over-the-counter drugs.*
[†]Includes nonmedical use of any prescription-type pain reliever, tranquilizer, stimulant, or sedative.

Source: U.S. Bureau of the Census, *Statistical Abstract of the United States, 1995* (Washington, DC: U.S. Government Printing Office, 1995), p. 142; U.S. Bureau of the Census, *Statistical Abstract of the United States, 2004–2005* (Washington, DC: U.S. Government Printing Office, 2005), p. 124.

users, stems largely from tetrahydrocannabinol, or THC, an ingredient found in a resin exuded from the plant. Because marijuana can have differing amounts of THC, it is difficult to generalize about the effects of the drug on any particular user. Obviously, the smaller the THC content, the milder the effects of the drug. The THC content of much of the marijuana sold today is substantially higher than was the case when the drug began to gain popularity in the 1960s.

▲ Effects of Marijuana Use

Most marijuana users smoke the leaves, stems, and other parts of the *Cannabis sativa* plant. Some users ingest the drug orally—for example, by mixing it with food. Marijuana often causes

mild euphoria; stimulation of the central nervous system and increased conviviality. The user experiences a pleasant heightening of the senses and relaxed passivity. In moderate doses the substance can cause short lapses of attention and slightly impaired memory and motor functioning. Heavy users have been known to become socially withdrawn and depersonalized and have experienced distortions of the senses. (National Commission on Marijuana and Drug Use in America 1973:158)

Despite the claims often made in the popular media, major scientific reviews of the impact of marijuana on health remain inconclusive. This is largely because widespread use of the drug in the United States is relatively recent, and carefully controlled scientific studies using human subjects are few. Nonetheless, scientists have expressed concern over suspected or potential effects in the following areas: impairment of thinking, learning, and performance of complex tasks; deterioration in lung functioning, leading to cancer or lung disease; reductions in male fertility; deterioration in heart functioning; and decreases in the body's immune response to illness and disease (Goode 1999).

Unlike many other substances, including a large number of drugs that are legal, marijuana is not a lethal drug. There are no documented cases of deaths directly attributable to unadulterated marijuana, which suggests that lethal overdoses are highly unlikely even among the heaviest users. Nor is marijuana physically addictive. Users do not suffer compulsive cravings, and most individuals may at any time cease to employ the drug without suffering physical discomfort. Extremely heavy users may suffer temporary, mild withdrawal symptoms.

The question of whether marijuana is psychologically addictive—or whether users can become psychologically dependent on marijuana use—has been the subject of much debate. In the absence of firm evidence, particularly on the effects of long-term use, the answer seems to be that it is nonaddictive. Those who use the drug regularly do so because they find it to be pleasurable, just as people enjoy regular exercise or reading. Though a minority of marijuana users employ the drug repeatedly, this is no more a sign of addiction than the fact that men seem "addicted" to wearing pants every day.

Unlike some other drugs, including alcohol, marijuana use does not cause people to engage in serious forms of antisocial behavior, including crime. It is not associated with aggressive or violent activity. The only criminality associated with marijuana is a matter of its illegality—the fact that possession, distribution, and sale of marijuana are against the law.

In recent years there has been some exploration of possible uses of marijuana or THC, its key chemical ingredient, in the treatment of medical problems. Researchers believe the drug to be useful in treatment of glaucoma (an eye disease that can lead to blindness), nausea accompanying cancer chemotherapy, asthma, as well as certain types of epileptic seizures and nervous system disorders such as multiple sclerosis. Patients with serious illnesses that are exacerbated by stress and loss of appetite, such as people with AIDS, have sometimes found marijuana helpful. But the federal government has steadfastly maintained heavy restrictions on the conduct of medical research involving THC or marijuana and on its availability for medical purposes (Abadinsky 2004).

▲ Extent of Marijuana Use

According to the 2003 National Household Survey on Drug Abuse, 96.6 million people in the United States age 12 and over have used marijuana at least once, or some 40 percent of that population. The greatest amount of experimentation with this drug has taken place in the past 40 years. Since 1979 national surveys have indicated a sharp overall decrease in marijuana use, although since 1992 numbers of users have risen (see Figure 17.2).

In 2003 the National Household Survey found that 3.1 million persons used marijuana on a daily or almost daily basis over 12 months. About 8 percent of 12- to 17-year-olds, and 17 percent of 18- to 25-year-olds, used marijuana at least once in the previous month. All such figures are estimates. Many users prefer to conceal their participation in what remains illicit activity, even when anonymity is virtually guaranteed. Conversely, others may think that it is "in" to say that they have used the drug even if they haven't.

As was mentioned earlier, marijuana is the most commonly used illegal drug. Arrest rates remain high, and criminal justice agencies have at times become choked with those caught participating in the victimless crime of marijuana possession. In 2003 almost 1.7 million arrests were made for drug abuse violations (manufacture, sale, or possession), most of which involved marijuana (U.S. Department of Justice 2004:270).

Efforts to identify and restrict domestic and foreign sources of marijuana have not been notably successful. Most of the marijuana reaching the U.S. market comes from Colombia and Mexico, with much smaller amounts filtering in

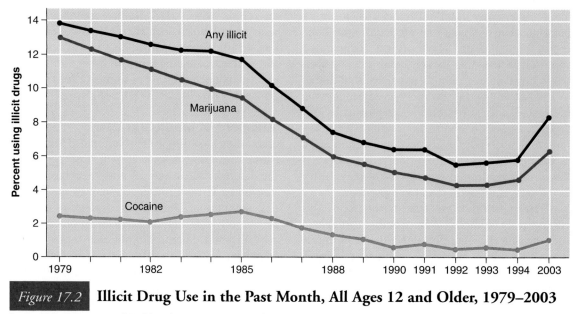

Source: U.S. Department of Health and Human Services, *Preliminary Estimates for the 2003 National Household Survey on Drug Abuse* (Rockville, MD: Substance Abuse and Mental Health Services Administration, DHHS, September 2004).

Figure 17.2   **Illicit Drug Use in the Past Month, All Ages 12 and Older, 1979–2003**

from Jamaica and Southeast Asia (Abadinsky 2004). In recent years the federal government has spent billions of dollars on efforts to interdict incoming shipments and has encouraged eradication programs in exporting nations. The availability of marijuana has not been reduced despite such efforts. Nor has the federal government been able to halt domestic production. Almost half of all marijuana consumed in the United States is domestically grown. Ironically, marijuana may be the most valuable crop cultivated in the United States (Cooper 1988; Hamid 1998).

Around a dozen states have decriminalized possession of small amounts of marijuana, establishing minimal fines and penalties on a level with a traffic offense. Eight states have legalized medical use of marijuana under a physician's prescription (Adams 2002). However, it has not been legalized outright in any community. The prevailing social definition still holds that marijuana is a problem drug.

Heroin

Heroin is a derivative of morphine, which itself is derived from opium, a substance found in the *Papaver somniferum* poppy plant. There are several other opiate (opium-derived) drugs. Most heroin used in the United States originates in Southwest and Southeast Asia and in Mexico. Once imported, the substance is distributed and sold to users under the auspices of organized crime. The distribution network today includes organized crime groups of a variety of ethnic backgrounds, many of whom retain personal and business ties with international producers and exporters in their nations of origin.

▲ Effects of Heroin Use

Much like marijuana, the heroin available to users often varies in potential potency. Before it is sold to individual consumers, heroin is ordinarily "cut" or adulterated with other substances, such as milk sugar, at a number of stages during distribution. The drug is commonly injected into the bloodstream with a needle and syringe (although it may also be sniffed, smoked, or ingested orally), and the variable potency can be a cause of fatal overdoses. Users who unknowingly purchase a unit of heroin that is relatively pure or unadulterated may die immediately upon injecting it because their bodies cannot tolerate the drug's strength. So it is not surprising that the death rate among heroin users is substantially higher than that of nonusers in the same age groups.

The effects of heroin are thought to vary. Nevertheless, most regular users report pleasurable experiences with the drug. Upon injecting it, many users experience a "rush" or wave of sensations somewhat like an intense sexual orgasm. The rush does not last long and is followed by a mild sense of euphoria, the relaxation of tensions, and the disappearance of any physical pains.

Users who take heroin repeatedly develop *tolerance* to it. This means that they must use larger and larger doses to achieve pleasurable effects. Tolerance also means that users must take a greater volume of the drug (or stronger dosages) to ward off discomfort similar to that which occurs when heroin use is suddenly discontinued. Increasing the frequency of use and the amounts used exposes individuals to greater risks of overdose.

Heroin and the other opiates are physically addictive. Heroin addicts who stop using the drug suffer from serious withdrawal symptoms, including cramps, nausea, muscle tremors, diarrhea, chills, and extreme nervousness. Withdrawal symptoms typically begin abating after two or three days and are generally gone within a week. But many addicts make the withdrawal symptoms disappear almost instantaneously by taking more heroin—or even other opiates. Thus some heroin users are literally driven toward continued use of heroin to avoid the pain of withdrawal (although the top priority of all users is to get high, as noted by McAuliffe and

Gordon 1974). Besides being physically addicted, regular heroin users may also be psychologically "hooked" in the sense that every waking hour may be spent planning for and ensuring a dependable drug supply.

In recent years a number of long-held myths concerning heroin and its users have begun to be dispelled. For example, the drug apparently does not cause physiological damage (apart from the tragedy of accidental overdose). Though many heroin users are malnourished, this seems to be due to their lack of interest in any pleasures (including eating) other than those associated with the drug itself. Common diseases among heroin users, such as hepatitis, are a result of the use of unsanitary paraphernalia—as when several persons share the same needles. As will be discussed later, shared needles are also a means by which the HIV virus that causes AIDS is transmitted. Other common illnesses, like pneumonia, are thought to be related to the frenetic lifestyles of addicts, who concentrate on the search for a "fix" and lack concern for health and well-being. This is not to say that heroin use is safe. But taken correctly, heroin does not—so far as we know now—damage the human organism. One need only think of the numerous doctors and nurses who have been addicted to one or another opiate drug for years and who continue to function into old age.

▲ Heroin and Crime

It has long been believed that heroin causes users to engage in criminal acts. This is not the case. Most heroin addicts who run afoul of law enforcement agencies had embarked on criminal activity well before becoming addicted. Nevertheless, though heroin itself does not cause crime, the drive to maintain a constant supply of the drug may require breaking the law. Heroin is expensive, primarily because the criminal elements that supply and market it take advantage of their monopoly position. Users often cannot afford to maintain their drug habits on the wages they could earn on a job. Thus, property crimes such as robbery and burglary may become a way of life. Property crimes committed by heroin addicts are thought to cost victims hundreds of millions of dollars annually.

Heroin does not, in and of itself, make users aggressive or prone to violence. Involvement in, for example, assaults is far more common among users of alcohol. But addicts who are desperate to get money to feed their habit may resort to violence if the victim of, say, a robbery attempt fights back.

▲ Extent of Heroin Use

The National Household Survey on Drug Abuse estimated that in 2003 there were 200,000 heroin addicts in the United States, or 57.4 percent of those who had used heroin in the past year. This is a rough estimate; no one really knows how many there are. In addition to those who are addicted, there are many occasional or so-called weekend users—known as heroin "chippers"—whose existence belies the stereotype that all users are seriously addicted and unable to control their use of the drug. Regular and persistent initial use must precede addiction. Heroin addicts are most likely to be young, male, and residents of large metropolitan areas. Unlike marijuana, whose use until recently has declined, heroin has continued to hold relatively steady appeal; and there are indications that use of purified, potent snortable or sniffable heroin has been on the increase (Sabbag 1994).

Law enforcement efforts have had limited impact on the marketing and consumption of heroin. Domestically, police have tended to concentrate on arresting easily identified users and small dealers. They have not been effective in attacking foreign producers' hold over the heroin market. The people who control the import, distribution, and sale of heroin make so much money that it is well worth it to bribe and corrupt customs inspectors and police. Federal efforts to stem the international traffic in heroin have not yielded significant restrictions in domestic supplies. The poppies that supply opiates are a valuable cash crop for many people in the nations in which they are grown, and government officials in these nations—often mired in drug-related dealings themselves or dependent on financial and political support from those who are—have been generally reluctant to force an end to production (Abadinsky 2004; Hamid 1998).

Cocaine

Cocaine is a drug derived from the leaves of the coca plant, *Erythroxylon coca*. The plant grows in remote areas around the Andes Mountains in South America. Peru, Bolivia, Colombia, and Ecuador are the principal nations in which coca plants are cultivated. Most of the initial processing of the leaves takes place in these nations; however, the task of shipping and smuggling cocaine into the United States has been largely carried out by a small number of criminal cartels in Colombia. These organizations have also been involved in organizing the distribution of cocaine across the United States.

The whole cycle begins with the harvesting and initial processing of the coca leaves. From this processing comes coca paste, a product that may be smoked in marijuana or tobacco cigarettes. Typically, however, the paste is processed further to produce cocaine, which is usually in the form of a white crystalline powder. Light in weight and odorless, it is easily concealed and transported. Although some of the smuggling entails shipment by boat, much comes in the form of delivery by air. Large shipments are broken down and delivered by car and truck across the U.S.–Mexican border.

▲ Effects of Cocaine

Cocaine is a stimulant (as are nicotine, caffeine, and amphetamines). It quickly acts on the central nervous system to produce a sense of euphoria, feelings of power and mastery, replacement of fatigue with limitless energy, and heightened sexual drive. This "high" is experienced as extremely pleasurable, although short-lived (from minutes to an hour or so, depending on how the drug is introduced, the dosage, and other factors). It is followed by an equally steep drop in feelings of psychological and physical well-being. Regular users develop, in many cases, tolerance to the drug. They require larger, more frequent, or more purified dosages to obtain the desirable results and to escape the anxiety and agitation that follow the cocaine high.

Most people who use cocaine inhale the crystalline powder. Other users, seeking more rapid and intense effects, inject themselves intravenously with a cocaine solution. The quickest and most dramatic results are obtained through smoking. By treating cocaine with volatile chemicals such as ether, users create cocaine "freebase." When heated, freebase gives off vapors that can be "smoked" (typically in a water pipe). Cocaine can also be processed with baking soda and water to form a solid known as "crack," which is easily smoked. Crack is less expensive for cocaine users to purchase than the powder.

Cocaine use poses a variety of serious physical dangers. Regular users have been found to suffer from damage to the nasal membranes and lungs, possible neural damage, seizures and previously undiagnosed epilepsy, angina and irregular heartbeat, ruptured blood vessels and strokes, liver damage, and other problems. Overdoses can cause a shutdown of the user's respiratory system, convulsions, and seriously disturbed heart rhythms—all leading to instant death. Some have died after using less of the drug than was their routine on previous occasions.

Hospitals have experienced an influx of so-called crack babies, a term around which controversy exists because it is not clear what role, if any, cocaine itself plays. *Crack baby* is a media-popularized term for infants with severe health and developmental difficulties who are born to women who used cocaine while pregnant. But such women typically are also users of other drugs, especially alcohol and nicotine, which are known to have serious negative effects on fetuses. The women also are frequently from low-income households, do not maintain adequate nutritional practices, suffer from a variety of lifestyle-related diseases and illnesses, and go without crucial prenatal care. Thus it is not possible to ascertain that cocaine per se is a source of the disabilities found among many infants born to cocaine users (Reinerman and Levine 1997).

Because of its relatively low costs and powerful effects, and the compulsive use its properties encourage, a cocaine derivative known as "crack" has achieved a good deal of notoriety in recent years. Initial users often underestimate its potential negative effects. The woman in this photograph, shown smoking crack, not only is engaged in illegal activity but is putting her physical and economic health at risk with continued use.

We do know that AIDS has become endemic among both male and female cocaine users, many of whom share needles for intravenous injection and/or engage in sexual activity with multiple partners in exchange for money and cocaine. We shall address this problem in more detail shortly.

Psychological dependence at a level tantamount to addiction is also common among heavy users: People's lives come to revolve obsessively around the acquisition and use of cocaine much as is the case with those "hooked" on heroin. But there are other negative psychological effects, including depression, anxiety, short-temperedness, irrational suspicion of others, impaired concentration, and loss of interest in work and home responsibilities. Among heavy users, even food and sex may ultimately come to be ignored in favor of pursuit of the cocaine high. For some, a "cocaine psychosis" occurs. Delusions and hallucinations, accompanied by violent behavior directed at imagined persecutors, are among the symptoms. Cocaine's effects can be such that people lose their jobs, rupture relationships with friends and family, sacrifice their homes and other assets—all to gain the transitory pleasure associated with drug taking.

▲ Extent of Cocaine Use

Since its use skyrocketed in the mid-1980s, cocaine use, including use of crack cocaine, had been in decline, until interest resurfaced in the early 1990s. By 1999 almost 10 percent of high school seniors reported having tried cocaine; thereafter, use among high school seniors showed a steady decline until 2004, when once again use began to climb (Johnston et al. 2004a, 2004b). The National Household Survey on Drug Abuse found 2.3 million current users in 2003, down from a peak of 5.3 million in 1985. It is estimated that more than 600,000 are crack users. Most of the decline in cocaine use has involved occasional users or those who use it less often than monthly. But in 2004 over 8 percent of high school seniors said they have tried the drug, an increase in use from the previous year (Johnston et al. 2004a, 2004b).

In contrast to the "business practices" associated with other drugs, those used in the cocaine trade have been extraordinarily violent (Abadinsky 2004; Goode 1999). The criminal cartels based in Colombia have not hesitated to use murder and assassination to protect their interests, both at home and in the United States. From distributors to street-level hawkers of the drug, the use of firearms to capture market areas, enforce deals, or exact revenge has become commonplace. Children and youth enticed into the local drug trade in many central cities go about armed, and they have been losing their lives. Gun battles in cities such as Washington, D.C., have left innocent bystanders wounded or dead. Increasingly, the murder rate in many cities has come to reflect the impact of drug-related warfare.

LSD

LSD, or lysergic acid diethylamide, is derived synthetically from the ergot fungus (a contaminator of rye). It is often referred to as a *hallucinogen* or psychedelic drug in recognition of its special psychoactive qualities, which include its ability to produce experiences akin to hallucinations. Other hallucinogens are mescaline, peyote, and various synthetic substances.

LSD is normally taken orally. It is often sold in the form of square slips of blotter paper that have been immersed in LSD, alcohol, and water; saccharine tablets that are used to absorb liquefied LSD; or small plasticlike squares called "windowpane." Because it is very potent, extremely small dosages are administered. Like many other drugs that are available only from illegal sources, the quality and purity of the LSD obtained by users often vary. It is not unusual for hallucinogens to be adulterated with other substances, unbeknownst to users.

▲ Effects of LSD Use

LSD works slowly, and users may have to wait for half an hour before they begin to feel the drug. The resulting "trip," which lasts from 6 to 12 hours, involves altered consciousness and radical transformations of perceptions, emotions, and thoughts. Interviews with a number of LSD users have indicated that ingestion of the drug often produces:

1. Eidetic imagery. Physical objects are seen to be in motion, often in the form of colorful abstract patterns, when one's eyes are closed.

2. Synthesia. All senses are sharpened and occasionally altered so that music is "seen" and colors are "heard."

3. Perception of a multilevel reality. Objects and ideas may be viewed from a variety of perspectives, often simultaneously.

4. Fluidity. The surrounding environment appears to be in a state of constant flux, with shapes ebbing and flowing.

5. Subjective exaggeration. Unusual and detailed visions may occur wherein objects, events, and moods seem extraordinary and monumental.

6. Emotional lability. Sudden and extreme shifts in emotional states may occur, ranging from ecstasy to despair.

7. Feeling of timelessness. A sense of time, and even the meaning of time, may cease to exist.

8. Irrationalism. The forms of logic through which the world is ordinarily interpreted are replaced by new ways to perceive interrelationships and totalities.

9. Ambivalence. Overwhelming perceptions, thoughts, and emotions may be simultaneously experienced as pleasurable and unsettling (Abadinsky 2004; Goode 1999).

Effects like these have led some observers to label LSD "psychotomimetic"—a drug that causes users to mimic madness or states of psychosis. The only real parallel between LSD trips and psychosis is the loss of touch with reality that characterizes both.

Despite claims that LSD use can cause physical damage, no physiological harm has been found among LSD users that could be traced directly to the drug. Stories of brain damage and genetic harm have not been substantiated by responsible researchers. Nor is the drug physically or psychologically addictive. In fact, those who frequently use LSD often find it difficult to obtain results such as those just described.

Users tend to be able to take LSD or leave it, and most limit themselves to a few trials. But there are dangers associated with LSD use. One fairly common problem is the "bad trip," in which users experience intense fear and anxiety and may actually panic. Ordinarily, bad trips are of short duration, and they often can be handled through the calming influence of individuals who are familiar with such drug effects. In more extreme cases, persons have had to be hospitalized in a state of psychosis. Less frequently, users may experience "flashbacks"; that is, they begin to unexpectedly "trip" again long after the drug has been taken. Finally, because LSD alters perceptions of reality, users have sometimes exposed themselves to physical dangers, and a few have suffered accidental deaths.

▲ Extent of LSD Use

According to the National Commission on Marijuana and Drug Abuse (2004), LSD and other hallucinogens are largely used only for recreational use, and that use has shown an overall decline. Usage among high school seniors has shown a steady decline for almost 10 years; by 2004 researchers found that 4.6 percent of high school seniors have used LSD, down from 13.6 percent in 1997 (Johnston et al., 2004b). Use has declined largely because of fear of dangers associated with it and concerns about the purity of available LSD.

As is the case with marijuana, LSD is not associated with serious antisocial behavior or criminal acts. The only criminality involved concerns the illicit status of the drug. Since LSD is relatively easy to manufacture and to conceal, efforts to dismantle the market within which the drug is distributed and sold have met with limited success.

PCP ("Angel Dust")

PCP (phencyclidine hydrochloride) is a hallucinogen that sharply decreased in popularity between 1996, when 4 percent of high school seniors reported having used it, and 2004, when only 1.6 percent did (Johnston et al. 2004b). This synthetic drug was originally developed for potential use as an anesthetic during surgery. On testing, its anesthetic qualities were found to be satisfactory, but adverse side effects offset this. These side effects included psychological disorientation, agitation and exultation, delirium, and hallucinations.

While rejected for medical purposes (aside from uses by veterinarians), PCP emerged on the illicit drug market in the early 1960s. Users then and since have reported largely unpleasant experiences, and concern over PCP's negative effects has been expressed by medical and mental health practitioners (Landry 1994).

PCP (known by many names, including "angel dust") may be taken orally, snorted, or smoked in a cigarette. Peak effects commence in 30 minutes to an hour. The "high" lasts 4 to 6 hours, and complete cessation of effects can take 24 hours. Users report a change in the sense of their image of their bodies that is discomforting and often feelings of loneliness and isolation. Thought may be disorganized, and users may engage in repetitive motor behavior. Individuals who take large doses may exhibit a loss of control over their emotions, expressing extreme rage. Others may have convulsions.

Poisoning cases have become more frequent because of overdoses, and some deaths have occurred as a result of PCP's pharmacological and behavioral effects. Concern has been expressed about problems that seem to plague many chronic PCP users, such as prolonged psychotic-like symptoms and speech and memory difficulties.

In the past, much PCP use was due to deception; drugs that were offered as LSD or other hallucinogens were sometimes PCP or PCP adulterated. But in more recent years PCP appears to have come into the marketplace under its own identity. As with LSD, the use of PCP remains quite limited; it is hard to see why it would ever be a drug of choice, given the negative effects that have been documented. Nonetheless, according to the 2003 National Household Survey on Drug Abuse, over 9 million people in the United States have tried it.

Club Drugs

One of the most recent categories of illicit drugs to gain prominence is that of **club drugs.** These are substances commonly used by young adults and teenagers, often at dance clubs and bars and all-night dance parties called **raves.** Club drugs include Ecstasy (MDMA), ketamine, and Rohypnol. These drugs tend to be low-cost, and produce trancelike highs. Ecstasy commonly causes a sudden and significant rise in body temperature and interference in metabolism, which can lead to kidney, liver, and heart failure. Chronic use of Ecstasy can alter brain functions and affect memory, aggression, sexual function, sleep patterns, and pain sensitivity (National Institute on Drug Abuse, available at www. nida.nih.gov).

Ketamine (sometimes called Special K or Vitamin K) is largely used as a veterinary anesthetic or tranquilizer: 90 percent of ketamine is legally sold for animal use. Ketamine can produce hallucinations, and high doses can cause delirium, amnesia, sharply high blood pressure, severe depression, and fatal respiratory interference (National Institute on Drug Abuse, available at www.nida.nih.gov).

Rohypnol (sometimes called "roofies" and widely referred to as a date rape drug) is colorless, odorless, and tasteless. When it is mixed with alcohol, even in small doses, it can incapacitate its victims and make it impossible for them to defend themselves against sexual assault. The drug is therefore attractive to sexual predators, who often seek opportunities to drop it into the alcoholic drinks and carbonated beverages of unsuspecting victims. Because of the powerful amnesiac effect of the drug, victims frequently are unable to remember what happened to them while they were under the influence, making it difficult for them to file criminal complaints against their aggressors. Other physical consequences include a drop in blood pressure, dizziness, drowsiness, interference in kidney function, and blurred vision (National Institute on Drug Abuse, available at www.nida.nih.gov).

Some observers note that drugs like Rohypnol become attractive in a rape culture in which women are commonly dehumanized as possessions and objects and thus acceptable targets for violence (Cuklanz 2000; Feltey 2001). In such a cultural context, use of Rohypnol becomes accepted as a means of disabling resistant targets. Unfortunately, since ingestion of Rohypnol is not commonly voluntary, it is difficult to track how widespread its use is.

Because it is commonly difficult to determine the source and chemical purity of club drugs, users are unlikely to be certain of their toxicity, strength, or potential physical consequences. Wider publicity concerning the unpredictable and often deadly consequences of their use has helped to decrease their attractiveness: current users of Ecstasy declined from 676,000 in 2002 to 470,000 in 2003. Similar declines occurred among those who used Ecstasy in the past 12 months, from 3.2 million in 2002 to 2.1 million in 2003 (U.S. Department of Health and Human Services 2004).

Amphetamines

Amphetamines are synthetically derived stimulants that act on the central nervous system. Although stimulants are available legally by means of physicians' prescriptions, perhaps as much as 20 percent of those manufactured are annually diverted into the illicit drug market. Illegal manufacture has also become a serious problem.

Such stimulants as methamphetamine, or "speed," are said to "activate organs and functions of the body, heighten arousal, increase overall behavioral activity, and suppress fatigue" (Goode 1999:270). "Speed freaks" often inject large doses to experience the drug's psychoactive effects. An immediate rush of euphoria is ordinarily followed by a period of dramatic hyperactivity. Users feel compelled to be constantly on the go, often walking and talking incessantly. After repeatedly taking the drug and experiencing its effects for several days, users are likely to reach a state of physical and mental exhaustion. When administration of the drug is halted, they often "crash" or pass out and sleep for 24 hours. Speed freaks take the drug and crash over and over again, often using other drugs to make sleep possible when the effects of the stimulant become too debilitating.

Experts generally agree that this use of stimulants results in both mental and physical harm. Overdoses do occur, and stimulants such as methamphetamine are highly physically addictive. Heavy users may experience withdrawal symptoms, such as fatigue and depression. Health problems—often stemming primarily from the frenetic lifestyles of users and the tendency of stimulants to depress appetite—are not uncommon. Users often become physically weakened and susceptible to disease and illness.

Users of stimulants have been known to become mentally disturbed and to be troubled by psychotic-like states. Among the effects noted have been paranoia, loss of memory, inability to concentrate, extreme emotional surges, fixations and hallucinations, and a tendency toward violent behavior. Such psychological conditions stem directly from the action of the drugs themselves, not simply from the sleepless and hectic lifestyles of heavy users.

The illegal use of speed and other stimulants seems to be largely concentrated among young adults. The popular phrase "speed kills" reflects the fact that the pleasures associated with the use of such drugs may not outweigh the dangers (U.S. Department of Health and Human Services 1989). Even so, in 2004 researchers found that 15 percent of high school seniors had used prescription-type stimulants for nonmedical purposes (Johnston et al. 2004a, 2004b).

Legal Substances

As we mentioned at the beginning of the chapter, people in the United States have expressed far less concern over the consumption of **legal drugs,** prescription and over-the-counter drugs, than over illegal substances. Periodically, attention is turned to the abuse of legal drugs—as when a well-known celebrity commits him- or herself to a clinic that treats addictions to pain killers, tranquilizers, or other prescribed substances. In particular, OxyContin, Percocet, and Vicodin have increasingly been cited among celebrity abuses of legal drugs. But in general, public interest fades as quickly as it forms.

Nature and Extent of Abuse of Legal Drugs

Of those adults surveyed in 2003, some 31 million people aged 12 and older reported they had at some point in their lives engaged in nonmed-ical use of legal drugs. Over 6 million were current users (U.S. Department of Health and Human Services 2004). Such nonmedical use is a form of drug abuse that is clearly widespread. Although the trend for such abuse has been downward since the 1980s, it is high enough to generate continued alarm. Among the legal drugs being abused are pain relievers, stimulants, barbiturates, and tranquilizers. Stimulants, as we saw, act on the central nervous system, producing arousal and intense hyperactivity. Barbiturates and tranquilizers, on the other hand, are *depressants* that act to relax the central nervous system, as do pain relievers.

Medical practitioners often prescribe depressants for medical reasons—both physical and mental. Such substances generally have a quieting and calming effect on users, dispelling anxiety and facilitating rest and sleep. In small or moderate doses, barbiturates and tranquilizers relax users; in larger doses, they may produce loss of consciousness. Large doses of some depressants—particularly barbiturates—may cause death. A significant number of accidental deaths and suicides are linked to overdoses of depressant drugs. Moreover, barbiturates and many types of tranquilizers and pain relievers are physically addictive for regular users. Withdrawal symptoms are often extremely severe. In some cases, withdrawal can bring about a coma or even result in death.

Anabolic Steroids

Anabolic steroids are synthetic drugs that use enhanced doses of the male hormone testosterone to build muscles and enhance athletic performance. The drug can be injected or taken orally. Athletes often take multiple doses of steroids in cycles of specific periods of time (usually several weeks or months just prior to a performance or competition), stopping for a while, and then recycling again. Abuse of steroids can produce liver tumors and cancer, jaundice of the skin, fluid retention, high blood

Steroid abuse among athletes continues to be a problem at both the amateur and professional levels. The problem has gained increasing public attention, particularly when Major League Baseball player Jose Canseco admitted in 2005 in sworn testimony to Congress to his own use of the drug. He also insisted that steroid abuse was widespread among other ball players.

Olympics Association, use is increasing. In 2003, 2.5 percent of high school seniors reported using steroids in the past 12 months, and 1.6 percent reported they were current users; 3.4 percent reported ever using the drugs (Johnston et al. 2004b). The rise in steroid abuse is not surprising, given the cultural context of competitive individualism (Cummings and Taebel 1978; Lipset 1990), millionaire celebrity status, and hypercompetition among athletes. The stakes are quite high: High-performing high school athletes can earn important college scholarships, making college a possibility for students who might otherwise be unable to afford it. Excellence in college athletics can become the entry to enormous professional contracts and salaries unapproachable outside of professional sports. Winners of Olympic gold medals often gain lucrative marketing contracts and professional touring sponsorships. In such a culturally competitive environment, individual athletes are motivated to turn to steroids as a short-term performance-enhancing mechanism.

pressure, severe imbalances in cholesterol (with increases in low-density or bad cholesterol and decreases in high-density or good cholesterol). In men, steroid abuse can cause shrinking of testicles, infertility, baldness, breast development, and prostate cancer. In women, it can cause the growth of facial hair, baldness, interference in the menstrual cycle, and enlargement of the clitoris. Injecting steroids increases the risk of HIV infection and hepatitis. Steroid abusers also run the risk of paranoia, delusions, heightened aggression (sometimes called 'roid rage), and impaired judgment of risk assessment.

Research shows that, despite widespread reports of the damaging effects of steroid abuse, and increased condemnation by schools and athletic associations like the International

It is difficult to envision a significant decline in interest in the drugs among younger athletes, when increasingly professional athletes like Jose Canseco admit to their own steroid abuse at the height of their careers and note that they were not alone by any means in their profession. Such confessions suggest that steroid abuse continues to be widespread, a claim that Congress wants professional sports to seriously address or face legislative action. That debate became very public when several professional baseball superstars came before Congress in 2005 and struggled to deny that they themselves have enhanced Hall of Fame performances using steroids.

Nicotine

Almost 71 million people in the United States, or almost 30 percent of the population aged 12 and older, currently use some form of tobacco product. More than 60 million currently smoke cigarettes, 12.8 million smoke cigars, 7.7 million use smokeless tobacco, and 1.6 million smoke tobacco in pipes. Current smokers in 2003 smoked an average of 13 cigarettes a day, with the average number of cigarettes smoked per day increasing with age. Those who currently smoke cigarettes are more likely to also use other tobacco products, drink alcohol, and use illegal drugs than nonsmokers. Current smokers are also far more likely than nonsmokers to drink excessively or binge drink (more about this later). Males are more likely to use tobacco than females: Almost 36 percent of males aged 12 and older use tobacco products, compared with only 24 percent of females. In particular, males are more than eight times more likely than females to use smokeless tobacco. However, education can affect tobacco use. People with higher levels of education tend to be less likely to smoke cigarettes than people with less education: Whereas more than 35 percent of people who did not complete high school smoke cigarettes, only 14 percent of college graduates do so (U.S. Department of Health and Human Services 2004:33).

Nicotine, one of several thousand chemicals in tobacco smoke, is highly addictive. The U.S. Department of Health and Human Services (2004:40) estimates that almost 36 million cigarette smokers in the United States aged 12 and older are nicotine dependent. That's 59 percent of all cigarette smokers. Dependency increases with age: 38.4 percent of cigarette smokers aged 12–17 were nicotine dependent, compared with more than 70 percent of those aged 50 and older. Those who report the most stubborn dependency in the higher age groups report that they began smoking at a younger age than those who do not report a dependency. It is no surprise, then, to find that tobacco companies increasingly target younger potential smokers with cartoon characters, ads that emphasize how "cool" it is to smoke, and billboards showing glamorous and popular young smokers. If a company can hook a smoker at a very young age, they may hook them for life, not a small goal for an industry worth $50 billion annually. And younger potential smokers are less likely to have achieved higher levels of education that may equip them with information to reject the use of tobacco.

Nicotine produces physical reactions similar to those produced by cocaine and heroin: enhanced stimulation of pleasure centers in the brain, a rush of adrenaline, suppressed insulin production, and increases in blood pressure, heart rate, and respiration (Society for Neuroscience 2002). Because repeated exposure to nicotine raises the body's tolerance to it, users must use higher levels of the drug to achieve the same original effect. Higher tolerance levels produce withdrawal symptoms of slower brain activity, interruptions of sleep patterns, decreased heart rate, and increased anxiety, anger, appetite, and difficulty concentrating (Hughes 1990).

In addition to the more immediate problems of physiological response to withdrawal from nicotine dependence are the long-term health risks, for both the users and the people around them. Smoking produces the most serious effects, including one-third of all cancers. In particular, cigarette smoking has been implicated in 90 percent of cases of lung cancer, the leading cause of disabilities and death (Brody 2001). Smoking also causes increased risk for lung diseases such as chronic bronchitis, emphysema, and asthma, and coronary disease. And smoking affects the lungs and health risks for people who live and work around those who smoke: Almost half a million people die each year from the health hazards produced by secondhand smoke. Children whose parents smoke are three to four times more likely than children whose parents are nonsmokers to develop severe infectious diseases. Infants whose mothers smoked during pregnancy are also more likely to be born with a low birth weight and to suffer lung problems; about 5,600 infants so exposed die each year (Abadinsky 2004).

Certain key segments of U.S. society have contributed to the inappropriate use of legal psychoactive drugs. These segments are the pharmaceutical industry and the medical profession (Hewes and Brewin 1979). As they pursue their own institutional interests, they have helped foster an "overmedicated society," many of whose members are unaware of or confused about the dangers of the drugs to which they are exposed.

Drug Producers, Dispensers, and Users

The U.S. pharmaceutical industry has been undergoing sustained growth since the 1950s. It is currently one of the largest and most profitable sectors of the U.S. corporate economy, with consumers spending $90 billion on prescription drugs (Goode 1999:309). To remain profitable and to keep growing, drug firms constantly seek out new markets for their products and encourage increased use of existing drugs.

Drug firms aim their advertising at the general public and at medical practitioners. Advertising directed at the public is the major means of pushing over-the-counter psychoactive substances, such as nonprescription sleeping aids like Sominex and Nytol. Prescription drugs are now being urged on the public by television ads and are advertised in medical journals for the nation's 516,200 office-based physicians. Drug firms also send traveling sales representatives, who are known as "detail men," to physicians' offices. The sales reps press for the adoption of new drugs and sing the praises of older ones,

leaving behind free samples and advertising brochures. Furthermore, the pharmaceutical industry sponsors displays and programs at medical conventions, where they try to woo physicians and point out or create the need for psychoactive drugs.

The point of the advertising and sales promotion directed at physicians and the general public is to spread the belief that pretty much any personal problem can be viewed in medical terms. If people are anxious, depressed, or lacking in vitality, the solution is medication. Since people in the United States often find it difficult to understand the sources of their discomfort or discontent, many are willing to try such a simple solution.

Medical practitioners are confronted with endless streams of patients, and they want to handle them quickly. But doctors also want to handle their patients effectively; they want to help people feel better, and they don't want to admit that they cannot. Over half of all persons who seek out physicians' services, it is estimated, have no easily diagnosable physical ailment. Physicians find that prescribing psychoactive drugs is a handy way of dealing with these cases. Not only is the patient usually satisfied, but the credibility of the "healing profession" and the doctor's own sense of mastery over his or her craft are sustained.

One outcome is that patients become mystified or confused about their own problems and potential solutions. They are encouraged to feel that psychoactive drugs are the solution to a lack of sense of well-being. But though the emotional pain may be blocked by drugs, as Henry L. Lennard and his associates (1971:24–25) noted:

Drugs do not remedy the unfavorable social and interpersonal arrangements and personal circumstances which generate anxiety or unhappiness. Through the creation of chemical barriers and through the diminishment of gross social deviance, drugs may in fact perpetuate malignant patterns and social arrangements. Were drugs not so readily available, pressure for other solutions and the pursuit of alternative options might be encouraged.

Nonetheless, patients gladly accept drugs, just as the medical profession is pleased to be able to "help" patients with unknown ills. Unfortunately, the prescribed psychoactive substances may be inappropriate for whatever is causing patients' distress. There may also be hazardous side effects, including chronic dependence on and physical addiction to certain routinely prescribed psychoactive drugs. Women have been particularly heavy users of such drugs, and thus have disproportionately suffered their negative effects.

One undesirable social effect accompanying people's reliance on psychoactive drugs pertains to the nature of the role of the medical profession. Doctors who encourage the view that drugs are an acceptable and effective way of dealing with just about any problem in living are likely to be less involved in healing than in drug pushing. Their assumption of this role has facilitated the profit pursuits of the pharmaceutical industry:

It is in the interest of both of these groups to maintain large numbers of persons on drugs. . . . It is, moreover, in the interest of both groups to define more and more problems as medical in order to justify both the medical model and the intervention with drugs. (Lennard et al. 1971:38)

As a result of criticism and greater awareness of their negative effects, physicians' prescriptions of such drugs have undergone significant decline in recent years. Still, women are more likely than men to turn to physicians when they are troubled, and men are much less likely than women to be users of prescribed psychoactive drugs such as tranquilizers and barbiturates (Nellis 1980).

Despite the hazards they pose, prescribed and over-the-counter psychoactive substances do not carry anything resembling the negative social definitions applied to illicit drugs in U.S. society. Thus, they are rarely considered part of the drug problem. As a consequence, millions of people in the United States decry the proliferation of "problem drugs" even while seeking to alter their own states of consciousness.

Explanations for Drug Use and Abuse

Theories about why people turn to psychoactive substances have generally focused on the use of illegal drugs, implying that the abuse of legal drugs is not a matter of concern or is, at least, an entirely different phenomenon. In this section, we look at some of the theories that have been put forth to explain the use of illegal drugs. We then present an explanation that covers both legal and illegal drug use (Goode 1999:91–118). Finally, we analyze a third type of drug use—the involuntary ingestion of psychoactive substances administered for purposes of social control.

Use of Illegal Drugs

One explanation of why people in the United States use illegal drugs focuses on the ready availability of drugs and the interests of those who are in a position to benefit financially from their sale. This so-called peddler or **seller theory** suggests that drug use is a result of the inability of law enforcement agencies to exercise control over supplies of illegal substances and of the ability of sellers to exert wily promotional and sales tactics on innocent nonusers. According to this perspective, users are manipulated and seduced into illegal drug use. But though availability no doubt has something to do with use, and though some persons may be susceptible to "dope peddlers," this explanation is not very persuasive.

Research has shown that most individuals do not embark on the use of illegal drugs as a consequence of contact with sellers.

Another explanation—which has been discredited, at least among sociologists—is an **individualistic, psychological theory,** which holds that individuals use illegal drugs because something is mentally or morally wrong with them. According to this theory, "normal" people are not attracted to such drugs even when they are available. Nor do normal people succumb to the alleged influences exerted by sellers. They simply do not need to alter their minds with psychoactive substances. Thus, say proponents of the theory, those who use illegal drugs must have psychological deficiencies, character disorders, or personal maladjustments. There is no credible evidence to support this theory. Illegal drug use is not reducible to the underlying psychological characteristics of a minority of the population. Research has not discovered psychological characteristics that distinguish users from nonusers. (Of course, the *effects* of some illegal drugs may include undesirable mental reactions.) In sum, an explanation that blames the victim is even more untenable than one that places the blame on the seller.

A more far-reaching explanation for illegal drug use in the United States is a **cultural theory,** which focuses on the place of drugs in the dominant culture. According to Joel Fort (1969:194),

We live in a drug-ridden, drug-saturated society, in which from infancy we have been taught to accept and live the industrial slogan of "Better Living Through Chemistry." We are taught that there is a pill, a drink, or a cigarette for every real or imagined pain, trouble, or problem, and that the more of these substances we use, the better off we will be.

In such a society, according to proponents of this theory, people will use illegal drugs when they have the opportunity to do so.

This explanation has a nice ring to it, but it is overly deterministic. People are not automatons who react to pains, troubles, or problems by taking drugs. Drug use involves a decision: There are, after all, other ways to react to problems. Moreover, this explanation does not address the question of why most people in the United States continue to shun illegal psychoactive substances, even while using many that are legal. On the other hand, those who use such legal drugs as alcohol and nicotine are more likely than nonusers to use illegal substances (Gerstein and Green 1993:15–18; U.S. Department of Health and Human Services 2004). This is not to say that the use of legal substances *causes* illegal drug use. Instead, it merely means that there is a correlation between the two. For example, aspirin users are more likely to smoke marijuana than nonaspirin users. But most aspirin users do not do so.

Some sociological explanations emphasize that illegal drug use is **learned behavior.** Specifically, people learn appropriate attitudes and modes of behavior favorable to drug use through social intercourse. For example, there is evidence that parents exert some influence over their children's attitudes toward drug use (Blum et al. 1972). The main finding to date is that the children of parents who are themselves users of legal or illegal psychoactive substances are more likely to use illegal drugs than the children of drug abstainers (Goode 1999:109). It is believed that friends and peers play a far more important role than parents. Rarely will parents actually introduce their children to the use of illegal drugs; peer associations and influence perform this function (Johnson 1973).

The importance of being inducted into the use of illegal drugs was underscored more than 50 years ago by sociologist Howard Becker, who described the learning process as the product of **differential association** with a subculture of individuals engaged in that behavior. According to Becker (1953), marijuana users (who, at that time, constituted a comparatively small number of persons) provided assurances to potential users that the drug was safe and worthwhile. In other words, those who already smoked the drug helped convert the neophytes to their view of the drug. Moreover, neophyte users had to be taught exactly how to smoke marijuana, what effects they should expect, and how they should perceive and react to these effects. Obviously, people are most likely to embark into such activity with those they know and trust—their friends and peers.

Sociologists generally agree that becoming a user of illegal drugs involves being a member of and identifying with a group of people who are already users. Participation with others in an illegal and, hence, secret activity may also help cement interpersonal relationships. Group members have something in common with one another, and those who do not use illegal drugs may be viewed as "outsiders." Though Becker's work deals primarily with marijuana use, more recent investigations suggest that "peer influences (such as modeling use, providing drugs, and encouraging use) are the most consistent and strongest predictors" of illegal drug use more generally (Normand, Lempert, and O'Brien 1994:33).

But this explanation does not completely get at the heart of the matter. Though it tells us how people learn to become drug users, it does not explain what users of psychoactive substances—both illegal and legal—are really seeking to accomplish. Only by changing our focus from drug users to society in general can we get at an answer to that question.

Drug Abuse and Social Conditions

In the view of sociologist John Clausen (1976:145), both the legal and illegal use of psychoactive drugs may be interpreted as

an aspect or manifestation of a much more general social problem. If substantial numbers of persons find it necessary to use drugs in order to feel comfortable, or if their lives are lacking in meaning and they therefore turn to drugs to provide it, the problem is less in the drugs than in the way of life that has been afforded them.

Clausen's observations suggest that the United States' contemporary concern with drug abuse and the drug problem is misplaced in terms of its focus on the illegal substances of the moment and on the criminalization of users. The important questions are rarely brought up in public debate. What is it about U.S. society that makes so many people seek out and accept the effects of psychoactive substances? What is it about this society and "the way of life that has been afforded" its members that renders the pursuit of altered states of consciousness preferable to non-drugged participation in the prevailing order?

As with mental illness, alcoholism, and suicide, widespread drug use may occur because many people are subjected to harmful social conditions. Drug use may be one of a variety of responses troubled people use to cope with problems in living. In this respect it is noteworthy that the pattern of decline in illegal drug use in recent years has been principally among the more affluent and educated. In contrast, poor and working-class people, particularly persons of color living in U.S. central cities, have been suffering declining opportunities for mobility and loss of hope for improvement in their life chances. Members of this population remain disproportionately involved in the use and abuse of illegal drugs, as well as in the local economy of illegal drug sales and distribution. As a politically powerless and thus highly vulnerable population, its members have been the principal domestic targets in the criminal justice system's "war on drugs" on which government at all levels has been spending tens of billions of dollars annually since the 1980s.

There are now well over 324,000 people imprisoned or jailed for violating drug laws in the United States, almost a third of the unprecedented numbers of those currently serving time. More than 57 percent of federal inmates are serving time for drug offenses; 15 percent of the growth in the prison population since 1995 has been a result of increases in drug offenses (www.ojp.usdoj.gov). Yet the supply of drugs all over the United States remains ample, and purity is high. Despite all law enforcement efforts, the United States still consumes an estimated 60 percent of the world's output of illegal drugs and leads the industrialized world in rates of drug abuse. It is becoming increasingly apparent that the law enforcement approach is incapable of ending the "drug problem." Social scientists have pointed out that the reason for this is policymakers' refusal to address harmful features of society that provoke so many people to be involved with drugs, but thus far this view has received little acceptance from political elites (Currie 1993).

Psychoactive drugs must be available before they can be used. They must be introduced to nonusers—be it by peers, physicians, or peddlers (a category that includes the pharmaceutical industry). But once such substances are available and introduced, many people grasp onto them as palliatives for ills that may really be societal, although experienced as personal.

The tragedy is that drugs are false palliatives, for their use leaves the ultimate sources of people's troubles untouched. In the words of Theodore Roszak (1969:176–77), drug use "is simply another safety valve. If anything, it allows one to bear up under any grim business-as-usual with a bit less anxiety." Psychoactive substances, Roszak observes, function much like the "soma" described in Aldous Huxley's (1970) science fiction novel, *Brave New World*, which helped make otherwise unbearable existences bearable.

Drugs and Social Control

The "brave new world" Huxley described was a politically repressive society of social unequals. Drugs were made available to the populace so that rulers could wield their power without the danger of rebellious disruption. The brave new world was a fictional society, but its use of drugs for social control reflects real-life developments.

In the last few decades the U.S. public has become aware of the uses of psychoactive substances for social control. Controversy erupted in the 1970s regarding physicians' treatment of millions of children said to be suffering from "MBD," or minimal brain dysfunction. Symptoms were said to include hyperactivity, learning disability, and short attention spans. Most of those diagnosed with MBD were boys. The medical response to MBD involved prescribing amphetamines (stimulants), which seemed to allow many children to calm down and focus on the tasks at hand.

Critics decried the catchall label **minimal brain dysfunction** and argued that this diagnosis was being abused. Many parents and teachers were quick to latch on to the diagnostic label and demand that drugs be given to children whose "illness" often seemed to be limited to failure to acquiesce to authority in school or at home. Drugs were seen as being used to medically harness children whose behavior simply did not measure up to adult expectations (Hewes and Brewin 1979).

The public outrage over indiscriminate diagnosis and medicating of schoolchildren resulted in sharp decreases in drug prescription for behaviors associated with MBD. Today, medical literature calls for such children to be tested for a type of impaired brain functioning called **attention deficit hyperactivity disorder** (ADHD) (Guevremont et al. 1992). The diagnostic techniques and criteria for ADHD are much more refined than was the case with

Many nursing homes and other institutions feed drugs to patients to keep them from making demands on staff members' time and attention. Practices like this not only infringe upon the rights of individuals but may also have serious medical consequences.

MBD, and behavior modification therapy may effectively supplement or even substitute for the use of drugs. Nonetheless, the reliability of ADHD diagnosis, risks and dangers from drug side effects, and the use of drugs to control children's behavior justifiably generate controversy even now.

Similar practices are routine in mental hospitals, prisons, and nursing homes. In a report to the Ford Foundation, Patricia M. Wald and Peter Barton Hutt (1972:11) noted the "emerging problem" of the "overprescription of drugs to control the behavior of captive populations" in such settings. For example, Wald and Hutt (1972:11) documented the extensive use of drugs "on elderly patients in nursing homes to keep them from clamoring for the attention of overworked attendants." These researchers predicted that "as the range of behavior-controlling drugs becomes wider, we can anticipate even greater problems in their use in unwarranted situations" (Wald and Hutt 1972:12).

Most studies of drug use in the United States barely mention the ways in which drugs are used for political purposes. The powerless are being subjected to chemical manipulation—students, not teachers; inmates, not guards or caretakers; old people, not those who administer the institutions in which the dying eke out their final days. As Howard Becker (1973:31) observed: "When the one administering the drug has sufficient control over the user, he can safely ignore the other's interests altogether, and his actions can be designed solely to serve his own interests, personal or (more likely) organizational."

Administrators in charge of schools, hospitals, prisons, and nursing homes may find drugs to be a useful tool for the efficient processing of large numbers of people. They are the ones who claim that the best interests of those subject to such chemical pollution are simultaneously being served. The interests of the powerless are being defined from above.

The use of drugs by such U.S. intelligence forces as the Central Intelligence Agency (CIA) borders on the bizarre. To take but one instructive example, investigations by the news media and congressional hearings in 1977 revealed that the CIA had set up a secret drug experimentation program in 1953 (Szulc 1977; *Time* 1977). The purpose of this program, code named MK-Ultra, was to learn how to control the human mind. Presumably this knowledge would be used against foreign enemies. For more than 20 years, using $25 million in tax funds, the CIA paid for projects conducted by researchers in 86 institutions—including colleges and universities, hospitals, prisons, and pharmaceutical companies.

The CIA-sponsored projects included LSD experiments with federal prison inmates and college students, experimentation with tranquilizers and alcohol on inmates and staff of mental hospitals, and the use of a "knockout" drug on unwitting terminally ill cancer patients. The CIA set up special apartments where researchers could observe the effects of LSD and marijuana on unsuspecting men who had been lured to the apartments from bars. A professional magician was employed to write a manual on the use of sleight of hand and how to secretly slip drugs into drinks. No efforts were made to contact the subjects of experiments later to see whether or how their well-being was affected. The U.S. military is known to have conducted similar experiments on members of the armed forces.

Clearly, not all the substances we call drugs are harmful. Many drugs, moreover, are known to have extremely beneficial effects.

One need only consider the many substances that have helped wipe out serious illness and disease and that have helped prolong people's lives. Drugs are tools that may be used either to enhance human well-being or to harm it. As we begin to learn more about the harmful uses to which drugs are being put—and about the *social* implications of such uses—members of U.S. society may begin to react against those forces that have led us to become the "overmedicated society."

Drugs and Public Health: The Case of AIDS

AIDS is, of course, an acronym for acquired immune deficiency syndrome. People with AIDS find that their bodies lose natural immunity against infection and disease. They grow vulnerable to serious illnesses that cannot be overcome. Although there is no known cure for AIDS, some drug treatments have shown promise in slowing the final and inevitable outcome, death.

The source of AIDS is a virus, now carried by more than 1.5 million people in the United States. (No one knows just how many for sure.) Those infected with the virus—called human immunodeficiency virus, or HIV—may have no AIDS symptoms and be unaware they are infected. Scientists believe that all persons carrying HIV will eventually be stricken with AIDS.

The first AIDS cases appeared in the United States in 1981. By 2002 almost 850,000 cases had been diagnosed and about half of those diagnosed had died (U.S. Bureau of the Census 2005:121; www.cdc.gov). While more than two-thirds of those who have died thus far were between 30 and 49 years of age, almost one in five deaths has involved youth and young adults between ages 13 and 29 (National Center for Health Statistics 2001). The data and projections keep changing as new developments affecting the spread of HIV are identified.

The most common way the virus is and has been spread involves sexual contact, and not, as once falsely presumed, only between homosexuals. Beyond sexual contact, however, over one-third of diagnosed AIDS cases are attributed to intravenous drug use (U.S. Bureau of the Census 2005:1221). Out of an estimated 1.3 million intravenous drug users, over 20 percent already are infected with HIV, and the numbers continue to grow. Some three-quarters of newly diagnosed AIDS cases have been among addicts (Kolata 1995).

The spread of the virus is rooted in users' habits of sharing needles and syringes (Goode 1999:337–38). Small amounts of HIV-contaminated blood may remain after use by an infected individual, and this blood is then injected along with the drug by the next needle user. Today the injected drug is most likely to be cocaine, followed by heroin and methamphetamine.

Needle sharing is thought to be simply a matter of convenience, friendship, or ritual among drug users. In a 10-city study of 3,724 intravenous users, none of whom were undergoing any treatment, some 85 percent admitted to needle sharing. Most admitted sharing with two or more persons, and the practice of borrowing others' injection equipment was common. The use of new needles or the cleaning of needles between uses (e.g., with bleach, which kills HIV) was uncommon (National Institute on Drug Abuse 1989).

The growing number of AIDS cases is further enhanced by the sexual practices of intravenous drug users. Since HIV can be spread by sexual contact, it is noteworthy that the previously cited study found that most of the users were sexually active, many had multiple sexual partners, and few took precautions to minimize the risk of HIV infections (e.g., condom use). Consequently, the virus is being transmitted not only to other drug users but to sex partners who do not participate in intravenous drug use at all.

The spread of the virus is most acute among specific segments of the intravenous user population. For example, it is higher among cocaine users than heroin users, in part because the former "shoot up" or inject more frequently. Those men and women who patronize "shooting galleries," back rooms or apartments where drugs and needles are shared (and where money and drugs may be traded for sex acts), are heavily exposed to HIV infection. And since intravenous drug use is disproportionately high among African Americans and Latino Americans, members of these populations are overrepresented among drug-related AIDS cases.

In the 1980s the rate at which AIDS spread was most rapid in the homosexual male population. This is no longer the case. AIDS is now spreading at the same rate among heterosexuals. Indeed, while AIDS/HIV was once stereotyped as a gay men's disease, women now constitute the fastest-growing segment of the population being diagnosed with the virus, largely through sexual contact with partners who have been exposed. This development is directly linked to drug abuse. According to a study by the National Institute on Drug Abuse, 61 percent of U.S.-born heterosexual AIDS patients reported sexual activity with someone who used drugs intravenously (National Institute on Drug Abuse 1988/1989).

Solutions to date include outreach programs encouraging those at risk to avoid sharing injection equipment, to use new or cleaned needles, to cease sexual contact with those whose behaviors raise the possibility of infection, and to practice "safer sex," which includes protective measures. Experiments with the dispensing of free or low-cost needles and syringes to discourage sharing and borrowing have proved successful in slowing the spread of HIV in a number of cities and states. Yet opponents of this practice feel it communicates tolerance or even encouragement of drug abuse. In the meantime, people's pursuit of the alteration of consciousness continues to make a contribution to an incredibly deadly epidemic.

A Postscript: Drug Abuse Warning Network

As we have suggested, the abuse of drugs can cause people to need emergency medical treatment and may result in untimely death. In recent years the federal government's National Institute on Drug Abuse has been trying to monitor the incidence of drug abuse emergencies and fatalities. The Drug Abuse Warning Network (DAWN) gathers systematic data from hospital emergency rooms and medical examiners. Although many nonfatal cases do not reach these settings, those cases that do give us some idea as to problem trends.

According to DAWN, in 1998 hospital emergency rooms handled 542,544 drug abuse episodes (www.dawninfo.samhsa.gov). (An episode is an emergency room admission. Over the course of the year some individuals were admitted more than once.) Males and females each constituted about half of the cases. White patients were 54.5 percent of the cases, African Americans 25 percent, and Latino Americans 10.5 percent (the remainder were unknown or "other"). Emergency drug treatment episode rates were highest for adults below age 35. The most frequently abused drugs for patients were alcohol in combination with other drugs, cocaine, and heroin. Drug overdose was the most common reason for emergency room treatment.

In 1999 DAWN's participating medical examiners reported 11,651 drug abuse–related deaths. Cocaine was the illegal drugs most frequently found in those who died, while heroin and other narcotics followed closely behind, just ahead of alcohol. (Those deceased may have been found using more than one drug.) While most of those who died from use of illegal drugs were 35 years of age and older, many were young adults.

These treatment episodes and deaths are all the more disturbing and tragic because they are preventable. They represent the presence of a great deal of alienation in our midst, the elimination of which will require change in many of the macro problems discussed earlier in this book.

Drinking in the United States

According to the 2003 National Household Survey on Drug Abuse, 119 million people in the United States age 12 and over—about half of those in that population—are current drinkers of alcoholic beverages (U.S. Department of Health and Human Services 2004:25). We should note that among those who drink most heavily, a third also use illegal drugs. For many people, alcohol is a **gateway drug** in the sense that its use typically precedes progression to illegal drugs (Gerstein and Green 1993:15–16).

Over 15 million adults are thought to be alcohol abusers or alcoholics. For reasons to be discussed, the precise number of alcoholics in the United States is not known. While abusers and alcoholics are similar in that their drinking has adverse effects on their health and/or social interactions, alcoholics are said to be distinguished by their physical dependence on alcohol and difficulties regulating consumption (U.S. Department of Health and Human Services 1993).

There is no doubt that alcohol is a drug; pharmaceutically, it is a depressant or tranquilizer. Per capita consumption of this drug (consumption per person) increased steadily in the United States after World War II, primarily because an ever higher percentage of persons became drinkers. Since 1980 consumption has dropped slightly, but it remains high. In 2002 per capita consumption of alcoholic beverages was 21.8 gallons of beer, 1.3 gallons of distilled spirits, and 2.1 gallons of wine. That same year, the average consumer unit spent $376 on alcoholic beverages, $48 more than it spent on dairy products (U.S. Bureau of the Census 2005:132, 438). In this section we look at the private and public interests that benefit from the use of alcohol. We then discuss U.S. drinking practices and patterns of alcohol use and abuse.

Private Profit and Public Income

The term *drug pusher* conjures up an image of a person who loiters around street corners and attempts to lure the innocent into experimentation with heroin or cocaine. Alcohol is "pushed" quite openly by the alcoholic beverage industry, which actively seeks to cut down on the percentage of abstainers in the adult population and to increase annual per capita consumption among those who drink. It was active in past efforts to lower the legal drinking age in locations where people had to be 21 in order to buy alcohol. It has also worked to turn the remaining **dry communities** (where the sale of alcoholic beverages is illegal) into **wet** ones (communities where it is legal) (Jacobson, Hacker, and Atkins 1983).

Though industry advertisements sometimes advise consumers to engage in "responsible drinking," such ads are a recent phenomenon that emerged only after the full dimensions of problem drinking and alcoholism became a matter of public concern. The alcoholic beverage industry still does not publicly acknowledge the fact that it is merchandising a drug. Nor does it advertise the fact that one outcome of the abuse of its product—alcoholism—is the nation's number one health problem.

The industry has a powerful incentive to push alcohol on the public—profit. By maintaining high consumption levels, the industry and its stockholders reap substantial economic rewards. The alcoholic beverage industry claims to provide employment for 131,240 people with

payrolls of $7 billion (U.S. Department of Commerce 2004). Its expenditures on newspaper, magazine, and television advertising—which typically links drinking to youth, sexual pleasure, and relaxation—are measured in the hundreds of millions of dollars a year.

While the industry counts its profits, government capitalizes on the tax revenues that flow from the U.S. population's drinking practices. In 2003 federal, state, and local governments took in $9.1 billion in alcoholic beverage taxes. The federal government alone received $7.9 billion that year (U.S. Bureau of the Census 2005:270, 311). Yet the economic costs of alcohol abuse and alcoholism to U.S. society are typically many times the tax revenues taken in. The U.S. National Institute on Alcohol Abuse and Alcoholism has put the costs at over $184 billion annually (www.niaaa.nih.gov). We shall return to this topic shortly.

U.S. Drinking Practices

Over the last 30 years, sociologists and other social scientists have become increasingly interested in U.S. drinking practices and patterns of alcohol use. As a result of their research, we have gained some solid knowledge about who the drinkers in the United States are.

A landmark nationwide survey of drinking practices was conducted in 1964–1965 (Cahalan, Cisin, and Crossley 1969). This survey studied adults aged 21 and over. (More recent investigations often include teenagers.) The researchers found that 68 percent of U.S. adults drank at least once a year, or enough to be classified as "drinkers," while 32 percent claimed to be abstainers. A third of the abstainers had previously used alcohol. Among the drinkers, 52 percent drank once a month or more; the remaining 48 percent drank less frequently. Of those surveyed, 12 percent were heavy drinkers. Since this survey was released many other studies have been conducted with similar results (U.S. Department of Health and Human Services 1993).

Such surveys, surprisingly consistent over time, do mask one fact that has long gone unemphasized. That is, although most adults in the United States drink, the bulk of the alcohol is consumed by a relatively small segment of the drinking population. According to the National Institute on Alcohol and Alcoholism, "the 10 percent of drinkers (6.5 percent of the total adult population) who drink the most heavily account for fully half of all alcohol consumed" (U.S. Department of Health and Human Services 1987:3).

National surveys of consumption provide statistics that are, at best, rough indicators of the characteristics of the drinking population. As such, they clearly are useful. One difficulty is that the definitions of light, moderate, and heavy drinking have often differed among surveys. As the definitions shift, so may the statistical findings.

Furthermore, survey findings are believed to understate the volume of alcohol consumed, since there is a clear gap between the amount of alcoholic beverages produced and sold and the amount survey respondents claim to drink. Heavy users in particular are unlikely to be completely open about their true consumption.

Patterns of Alcohol Use

Patterns of alcohol use in the United States are believed to be associated with a number of variables. Sex, age, race and ethnicity, and class-related factors all seem to be related to who drinks and how much.

▲ Sex

Drinking has been considered a predominantly male activity. But since World War II the gap between men and women has been narrowing, and women are drinking in generally rising numbers (although in the year between 2002 and 2003 there was a slight drop in the percentage of women who are current drinkers). An estimated 62.4 percent of all men aged 18

and older and 46 percent of all women in that age group are current drinkers.

Men are more likely than women to be moderate or heavier drinkers. There has been speculation that women have been narrowing this gap (Del Boca 1994). In particular, observers have pointed to the increasing numbers of women who are coming into contact with alcoholism treatment agencies as an indication that more women are drinking heavily. However, increased contact with treatment agencies could instead simply mean that individuals who had kept their heavy drinking secret are now seeking help. The fact that well-known women have sought aid for problems with alcohol and other drugs may encourage others to seek treatment.

▲ Age

The use of alcohol is not confined to any one age category. But surveys reveal that a higher percentage of younger people use alcohol than those over 45. Older persons are more likely to be abstainers than the young, and it is believed that most persons taper off or stop drinking with advancing age. Most persons age 65 and older are abstainers (U.S. Department of Health and Human Services 2004). However, this does not mean that heavy drinking does not occur among the elderly. Analyses suggest that it may be undiagnosed and underreported to a significant degree (National Institute on Alcohol Abuse and Alcoholism 1988).

Much attention has been drawn to the drinking practices of school-age youth, particularly in conjunction with automobile accidents and deaths involving alcohol. Most of today's junior and senior high school students have tried alcohol. Among seventh graders, approximately two-thirds of all boys and half of all girls have used alcohol. These percentages shoot up by the twelfth grade to 93 percent for boys and 87 percent for girls. Frequency of drinking and increases in the amounts consumed per occasion also rise steadily by school grade level.

As more research has accumulated concerning the harmful effects of alcohol abuse, alarm has risen over the popularity of drinking among teenage youth. Young people often proceed as if they can handle virtually any dangers associated with drinking; meanwhile, avoidable tragedies accumulate. Here, students on Spring Break consume massive quantities of alcohol as a bartender pours free tequila into a reveler's mouth.

The National Institute on Alcohol Abuse and Alcoholism has reported that while 25 percent of students in the tenth through twelfth grades view themselves as abstainers, at the other extreme 15 percent are self-professed "heavier drinkers." The latter drink at least once a week and in large amounts (five or more drinks) on each occasion. One out of 5 males in grades 10 through 12 is a heavier drinker, while 1 out of 11 females falls into this category. As indicated, rates escalate with grade level. As will be discussed, surveys indicate that the vast majority of college students and young adults use alcohol.

Many continue drinking practices that they developed while in high school.

▲ Race and Ethnicity

Ethnicity has also been found to be correlated with patterns of alcohol use. For some groups, drinking is a part of cultural traditions associated with meals, rituals, or festivities. For other groups, it is not.

Persons whose fathers were born outside the United States are more likely to be drinkers than those with native-born fathers. Among the various ethnic groups in the United States, the

Irish, Italians, Poles, and Russians have a high proportion of drinkers. Persons of English and Scottish origins, on the other hand, are much more likely to be abstainers.

There does not appear to be much difference between African Americans, Latino Americans, and non-Latino whites in terms of alcohol use. A higher percentage of African Americans and Latino Americans are abstainers. But these two populations have a similar proportion of heavy drinkers in comparison to the white majority (U.S. Department of Health and Human Services 2004:28).

Research on racial and ethnic differences in drinking practices is still quite limited. However, it is believed that ethnic groups maintaining cultural norms that limit the use of alcohol have fewer alcohol abusers and alcoholics than groups whose attitudes toward drinking are ambivalent or loose. Nevertheless, though group norms may impede or facilitate drinking, there is within-group variation in alcohol use, and alcoholism is found among virtually all ethnic groups (*Alcohol Health and Research World, II* 1986/1987; U.S. Department of Health and Human Services 2004:28).

▲ Class, Occupation, and Education

As one moves up the class hierarchy, the use of alcohol becomes increasingly common. Low-income people are more likely to be abstainers than more affluent people. Moreover, moderate and heavy drinking also increases as class level rises.

In terms of educational level, the highest percentage of abstainers is found among persons with only an elementary school background. Most college graduates are drinkers. Indeed, college campuses are increasingly noted as centers where concentrations of **binge drinking** (five or more drinks on the same occasion at least once per month) are common and where fraternity and sorority hazing and initiation rites often include excessive and often deadly use of alcohol in short periods of time (Nuwer 2002; Weschsler and Wuethrich 2003).

The findings regarding class membership and educational level are consistent with those on occupational differences. Business executives and professionals, who stand at the top of the occupational structure, are more likely to be drinkers than almost any other occupational group. Contrary to popular stereotypes, people who are unemployed or who are not in the labor force are less likely to be current users of alcohol than the employed; and while those who are unemployed had higher rates of binge or heavy drinking, almost 80 percent of the 51.1 million adult binge drinkers or heavy drinkers were employed (U.S. Department of Health and Human Services 2004:28–30).

Alcohol Abuse

In most of the investigations of alcohol use, an individual who uses alcohol once or more per year is classified as a "drinker." Knowing how many drinkers there are, along with the correlates of drinking behavior (such as sex and age), gives us a sense of the dimensions of use. But most users of alcohol seem to be able to take it or leave it. Their occasional drinking does not pose serious difficulties for themselves or for others.

▲ Correlates of Problem Drinking

When can we say that an individual is using alcohol to the point where he or she might be called a **problem drinker?** Most experts believe that people who exhibit any one of the following symptoms are problem drinkers:

1. Frequent bouts of intoxication, involving heavy alcohol consumption on each occasion.

2. Binge drinking—periodic episodes of intoxication that may last for days at a time.

3. Physical dependence on and loss of control over the use of alcohol.

4. Psychological dependence on drinking in order to relieve depression or escape problems in living.

5. Ruptured relations with family members, friends, and/or neighbors due to drinking behavior.

6. Employment difficulties associated with alcohol use on or off the job.

7. Involvement in accidents and/or contact with law enforcement agencies in connection with alcohol use.

8. Health and/or financial problems due to drinking (Cahalan 1970; Cahalan and Room 1974).

Obviously, the more symptoms that are exhibited, the more serious the negative consequences are for the individual.

For both men and women, **psychological dependence** on drinking to relieve depression or escape problems in living is a very common symptom. Despite the fact that proportionately more of the poor are abstainers than the affluent, problem symptoms are most frequently found among those at the lowest class level. The proportion of drinkers with no problem symptoms is twice as high at the top of the class hierarchy than at the bottom.

The National Institute on Alcohol Abuse and Alcoholism has identified drinking behaviors that reflect alcohol dependence and loss of control. Symptoms include skipping meals when drinking, sneaking drinks, morning drinking, drinking before a party, blackouts, gulping drinks, drinking to get rid of a hangover, being afraid that one is an alcoholic, attempting to cut down or stop drinking but failing to do so, and finding it difficult not to drink to intoxication (U.S. Department of Health and Human Services 1981).

College students, among whom alcohol is widely used despite the fact that it is illegal for most, are at risk for becoming problem drinkers. In a national study of students at 4-year colleges, about 16 percent were found to be nondrinkers. Some 41 percent drank but did not binge drink. But 44 percent of the students surveyed were binge drinkers, and almost a fifth were frequent binge drinkers (they had three or more binge drinking sessions in the previous 2 weeks) and "were deeply involved in a lifestyle characterized by frequent and deliberate intoxication" (Wechsler et al. 1994:1676; see also Wechsler and Wuethrich 2003). While the survey found that most of those who binge do not see themselves as problem drinkers, those who binge drink, and especially those who do so frequently, were far more likely than nonbinge drinkers to be involved in alcohol-related accidents, injuries, violence, high-risk sexual practices, and suicidal behavior.

▲ Correlates of Alcoholism

If we view problem drinking as a continuum, then **alcoholics** are persons who exhibit numerous symptoms of problem drinking. The line between alcohol abuse and alcoholism is not clear-cut. Consequently, experts disagree about what characteristics denote alcoholism (Goode 1999:192–94).

Attempts to define alcoholism have been numerous. The following definitions are typical:

We define alcoholism as a chronic behavioral disorder which is manifested by undue preoccupation with alcohol to the detriment of physical and mental health, by a loss of control when drinking has begun (although it may not be carried to the point of intoxication), and by a self-destructive attitude in dealing with personal relationships and life situations. (National Institute of Mental Health 1972:9)

Alcoholism involves excessive use of the drug to an extent that measurably impairs the person's health, social functioning, or vocational adjustment. (Fort 1973:7)

Alcoholism is a chronic disease, or disorder of behavior, characterized by the repeated drinking of alcoholic beverages to an extent that exceeds customary dietary use or ordinary compliance with the social drinking customs of the community, and which interferes with the drinker's health, interpersonal relations, or economic functioning. (Keller 1958:1)

Given the lack of consensus on how to define alcoholism, no one really knows how many alcoholics there are in the United States. However, the U.S. Department of Health and Human Services estimates that more than 15 million people in the United States suffer serious problems associated with abuse of and/or dependence on alcohol. Within this population, "alcoholics can be distinguished by their physical dependence on alcohol and their impaired ability to control alcohol intake" (U.S. Department of Health and Human Services 1993:xxi). Although there are many female alcoholics, most alcoholics are adult males. The average alcoholic is employed (many others are employable) and lives in a family setting. Alcoholics consume 11 times as much as the average nonalcoholic during the course of a year (U.S. Department of Health, Education, and Welfare 1974:15–16).

Explanations for Alcoholism

How does one explain the presence of what some estimate to be as many as 10 million alcoholics in U.S. society? A number of explanations for alcoholism have been offered, most of which focus on the alcoholic individual (U.S. Department of Health and Human Services 1993). As with the phenomenon of mental illness, the victim is often blamed for his or her own plight.

Physiological Explanations

A great deal of research has been conducted to test the hypothesis that alcoholism is linked to the biological makeup of particular individuals.

Some researchers have hypothesized, for example, that alcoholism is a hereditary condition, related to genetic makeup (Gerstein and Green 1993:52–53). Other studies have tried to determine whether nutritional deficiencies or hormone imbalances cause alcoholism to develop. It has been suggested that alcoholism is a result of allergic reactions to alcohol and/or to the nonalcoholic components of alcoholic beverages. And researchers have tested the idea that alcoholics cannot metabolize (biologically process and eliminate) alcohol as easily as other people can.

Although little support has been found for most such hypotheses, experts do believe that biology plays some role, although how and why have not been determined. For example, a report for the National Research Council notes: "For alcoholism, the heritability of some tendency—heavily modulated by environmental and developmental features—appears reasonably well established" (Gerstein and Green 1993: 52). Much research on this issue still remains to be done, however. While the use of alcohol has physiological effects on people—particularly on alcoholics—physiological causes have not been definitively linked to alcoholism per se.

The limited and slender support for physiological explanations raises questions about the usefulness of viewing alcoholism as a "disease" in medical terms. Yet as with mental illness (see Chapter 16), the medical model is commonly applied to alcoholism (Landry 1994). Publications of the U.S. Department of Health and Human Services routinely use the term disease: "**Alcohol dependence,** often called alcoholism, refers to a disease that is characterized by abnormal alcohol-seeking behavior that leads to impaired control over drinking" (U.S. Department of Health and Human Services 1993:xxi). Alcoholics may incur health problems in connection with drinking, but so far there is insufficient evidence to conclude that such people drink because they are "sick."

Psychological Explanations

Some psychological explanations attribute alcoholism to particular personality traits that only alcoholics presumably possess. Psychological explanations are also frequently framed in terms of the medical model, on the assumption that the alcoholic's mind is "sick" or "disordered."

One influential theory, which incorporates both physiological and psychological causes, was developed by E. M. Jellinek (1960). In his analysis of questionnaires filled out by a group of alcoholics, Jellinek concluded that alcoholism is a disease that proceeds in cycles. An individual first becomes psychologically dependent on the use of alcohol. As the user begins to lose control over drinking, biological dependency occurs. In other words, according to Jellinek, a personality disorder leads to physical addiction to alcohol. Although this explanation certainly sounds logical, no one has been able to demonstrate that alcoholism occurs for such reasons.

Other explanations have proceeded on the psychological level alone. It has been argued that individuals who received insufficient mothering engage in heavy drinking to make up for the oral gratifications they were denied in infancy. Another theory holds that alcoholics are actually latent homosexuals who drink to repress feelings they know to be socially unacceptable. Still another explanation suggests that alcoholics are suicide-prone individuals who drink to satisfy the urge for self-destruction. In each case, alcoholism is explained in terms of a personality or character disorder traceable to defective parent-child relations. None of these explanations has the support of sufficient evidence.

Another explanation focuses on the idea of an **alcoholic personality.** Alcoholics are presumably maladjusted, immature, dependent on others, negative in their views of themselves, suffering from guilt feelings, and incapable of tolerating tension and frustration. However, experts cannot agree on the precise traits characterizing the alcoholic. Nor have researchers been able to develop a list of personality traits that distinguish those who become alcoholics from those who do not.

Finally, it has been suggested that alcoholism is the outcome of a learning process. Certain individuals who are afflicted with deep-seated fears and anxieties learn that drinking can help reduce or eliminate such feelings. It is theorized that alcoholism springs from a basic human instinct to avoid pain and seek pleasure. According to this view, alcohol provides pleasure. However, learning theory does not explain why individuals continue to drink when they begin to suffer from the unpleasant physical, mental, and social effects of alcoholism.

Sociological Explanations

Earlier we mentioned the discovery of a relationship between cultural traditions associated with ethnic group membership and drinking practices. The prevalence of alcoholism is believed to vary among different ethnic populations within the United States, just as it varies among different societies. (For example, rates are high in Russia and low in Israel.)

Researchers who believe that cultural factors are responsible for alcoholism hypothesize that the alcoholism rate will be low among groups with well-established, well-known, and generally accepted drinking customs. In groups with ambivalence about drinking and the absence of group norms and controls pertaining to the use of alcohol, rates of alcoholism are expected to be high (National Institute of Mental Health 1972). This hypothesis, which has not been fully tested, addresses overall differences between groups. But it does not address within-group variance or the question of why particular individuals may come to focus their lives on drinking. Even among groups with well-established drinking customs, alcoholism occurs.

A second major sociological explanation involves the concept of **labeling.** (See Chapter 15 for discussion of the labeling perspective.) In this view alcoholism is no more than a label attached to persons whose drinking habits are defined by others as deviant (Cahn 1970). A number of variables may be involved in determining whether someone will be labeled an alcoholic. These include the quantity, rate, and frequency of drinking; the effects of alcohol consumption on the individual; the reactions of others to the observed effects; the visibility of the drinker to labeling agents (such as police, medical personnel, and employers); the social class position or social status of the drinker; and the effectiveness of formal and informal controls over the individual's drinking behavior.

The labeling approach thus implies that there is no identifiable alcoholic individual whose characteristics may be taken as representative of alcoholics in general. Indeed, we have already noted that experts cannot agree on a definition of alcoholism. It is difficult, for example, to determine when behavior indicative of alcohol abuse is better defined as alcohol dependency. But the labeling approach sidesteps the question of why an individual adopts the drinking behavior that is at issue. What is it that leads people toward patterns of alcohol use that may, under certain conditions, be labeled alcoholism?

Alcoholism and Problems in Living

Most experts seem to agree that heavy users of alcohol are engaged in a retreat from reality. According to the Cooperative Commission on the Study of Alcoholism (1967:130): "Much American drinking is of an 'escapist' nature. That is, alcohol is used as a means of relieving boredom or emptiness, of getting away from authority and restrictions that are considered intolerable, or of overcoming feelings of inadequacy or inferiority." Thus, the abuse of consciousness-altering drugs—in this case, alcohol—may be viewed as a method by which unhappy people attempt to deal with problems in living.

Unfortunately, the use of alcohol for escape is a false haven. The negative effects often associated with heavy drinking may simply exacerbate the problems in living that confront troubled individuals. With nowhere else to turn, and having no other ways to retreat from unendurable realities, the drug becomes everything, and individuals are destroyed.

As we have mentioned, the idea that alcoholism is a disease has become popular. For example, the federal government contends that "alcoholism is a treatable disease, not a failure of character" (U.S. Department of Health and Human Services 1981:ix). This application of the medical model to alcoholism is in some ways progressive. In the past, alcoholics were likely to be treated as moral degenerates, and it is still all too common for down-and-out alcoholics found on the street to be jailed, rather than sympathetically doctored. Since alcoholism is often accompanied by real health problems, some drinkers need medical help to survive.

The problem with conceptualizing alcoholism as a disease is that the medical model implicitly suggests that only the alcoholic needs to be changed. The medical model thereby draws attention away from consideration of societal conditions that may generate problems in living and thus escape through alcohol abuse. It is these conditions that must ultimately be changed if the phenomenon of alcoholism is to be eliminated—or at least seriously reduced.

Effects of Alcohol Abuse

Many costs are associated with alcohol abuse and alcoholism, costs that both drinkers and nondrinkers are forced to bear. In this section we examine the effects of alcoholism on the alcoholic's family and health, on highway safety, and on crime. We also look at some of the monetary costs associated with alcohol abuse.

Personal and Family Relationships

The impact of alcoholism often dramatically affects the alcoholic's relationships with other people, especially family members. Disruptions of family life due to alcohol often end up costing the taxpayer money. Though actual figures are not available, and though many of the costs are nonmonetary, the National Institute on Alcohol Abuse and Alcoholism (U.S. Department of Health, Education, and Welfare, 1974:16) has observed: "Unhappy marriages, broken homes, desertion, divorce, impoverished families, and deprived or displaced children are all parts of the toll. The cost to public and private helping agencies for support of families disabled by alcohol problems amounts to many millions of dollars a year."

When we count family members, it has been estimated that tens of millions of people in U.S. society are caught in "alcohol's web" (Collins, Leonard, and Searles 1990; National Institute of Mental Health 1972:10). This does not take the impact on friends, roommates, neighbors, and acquaintances into account. The personal anguish of many of these millions of people is surely no less tragic than the self-harm alcoholics and other problem drinkers impose on themselves.

Robert J. Ackerman (1978) has drawn attention to the "unseen casualties"—children of alcoholics, most of whom are adolescents and preadolescents. In his words, "Alcoholic behavior in the family can prohibit intimate involvement and clearly impede the development of essential family bonds. When children's emotional needs have been stunted by neglect or destroyed by cruelty, the traditional image of parents as mentors and guides for their offspring becomes a farce" (Ackerman 1978:13).

Since it is estimated that 40 to 60 percent of the children of alcoholics are likely to develop drinking problems themselves, the impact of living in a family setting plagued by alcohol abuse may persist well beyond childhood and young adulthood.

Personal Health

Problem drinkers often pay severe penalties. It has been estimated that alcoholics are likely to die 10 to 12 years sooner than nonalcoholics. Half die before the age of 50, which is one reason there are so few elderly alcoholics. The mortality rate (that is, the number of persons per 100,000 who die each year) among alcoholics is more than two and a half times higher than that of the general population.

Alcoholics often die under violent circumstances; serious accidents, homicide, and suicide are not uncommon. This, together with the physical deterioration accompanying alcoholism, helps explain the limits on life expectancy. In 2002 alone 11,965 people died from alcoholic liver disease (U.S. Bureau of the Census 2005:80). But no one really knows how many deaths are directly attributable to drinking, and all such statistics are estimates. One reason for our limited knowledge is that many physicians do not report alcoholism as the main cause of death out of concern for the feelings of the family of the deceased.

Research on the physiological effects of alcoholism has increased in recent years. Heavy drinking is known to be associated with various types of cancer, particularly among persons who also use tobacco. Alcohol abuse also increases the probability of hypertension, stroke, and coronary heart disease. Cirrhosis of the liver associated with heavy drinking causes that organ to become fatty, scarred, and incapable of functioning normally. In large urban areas, cirrhosis is the fourth most common cause of death among men aged 25 to 45.

Alcohol affects the brain, often permanently damaging the mental functioning of alcoholics. Drinking may reduce the number of living cells in the brain. Since brain cells do not grow back, alcoholics may suffer from organic psychosis (a mental illness traceable to brain damage), loss of memory, and poor physical and mental coordination. One out of four persons admitted to mental hospitals is diagnosed as an alcoholic, and 40 percent of all admissions are alcohol related. Many of the alcoholic inmates are unlikely to recover.

The unborn children of female alcoholics are subject to harm from drinking in what is called **fetal alcohol syndrome.** Because alcohol tends to be a substitute for a balanced diet, alcoholics are often malnourished. Consequently, the newborn children of alcoholic women are likely to be less healthy and less well developed than other babies. Moreover, when a pregnant woman drinks, so (in effect) does her fetus. The children of alcoholic women may die shortly after birth unless they are medically treated for the shock to their systems from suddenly being cut off from alcohol. Furthermore, the impact of alcohol on the woman and her fetus is a major cause of birth defects and organically based mental deficiency among the newborn. The effects of fetal alcohol syndrome on the children of female alcoholics are usually chronic and may be permanently disabling.

Clearly, it is not too much of an exaggeration to say that alcohol kills and maims people. When abused, alcohol is a highly dangerous drug.

Highway and Other Accidents

Each year, street and highway accidents take the lives of many people in the United States. Of the more than 38,000 traffic fatalities that occurred in 2002, 40 percent were known to be alcohol related (www-fars.nhtsa.dot.gov). Some of those killed, it is suspected, are the victims or the perpetrators of alcohol-related suicides, in which the suicidal individual uses the automobile as the death weapon.

In addition to this annual slaughter, roughly 35 percent of crashes producing serious injuries involve drinking drivers (http://alcoholism.about.com). More than a third of the pedestrians who die in traffic accidents each year are heavily under the influence of alcohol (www.druglibrary.org). (Presumably, some of these pedestrians may also be committing suicide.)

No other drug has been found to play such a key role in accidental deaths. Despite warnings by government and public affairs groups not to mix drinking and driving, the deaths continue. (See Table 17.2.) The situation is no doubt exacerbated by the fact that arrests for drunk driving remain so infrequent in comparison with the amount of drunk driving. By one estimate, the probability of being arrested for drunk driving is 1 in 200 (www.dui.com), although recent campaigns against driving under the influence of alcohol have no doubt increased the chances of arrest in many locales.

In addition to motor vehicle–related accidents, drinking is a major cause of death and injuries in many other settings. Of the 5,534 deaths and 10.6 million disabling injuries suffered by workers on the job in 2002, many were alcohol related (http://stats.bls.gov). Noncommercial aviation accidents often involve pilots who have been drinking. Alcohol use is said to be associated with well over half of all drowning deaths and an even higher percentage of deaths and injuries from falls. Most fatalities and nonfatal burns stemming from fire accidents involve alcohol use.

Crime

The use of alcohol is closely tied to certain types of criminal activity and is substantially responsible for the enormous number of arrests made in the United States. Not all alcoholics commit crimes. Not all problem drinkers commit crimes. Of those who do, not all are identified and arrested. Hence, alcohol-related crime statistics—like most other statistics on alcohol users—are rough estimates.

Table 17.2	Licensed Drivers, Fatal Motor Vehicle Accidents, and Alcohol Involvement, by Age of Driver: 2002								
						Age of driver			
Item	Unit	Total	16–20 years	21–24 years	25–34 years	35–44 years	45–64 years	65 years and over
Licensed drivers (estimated)	1,000	193,300	12,765	13,463	33,734	41,040	64,320	27,930
Percent distribution	Percent	100.0	6.6	7.0	17.5	21.2	33.3	14.4
Licensed drivers involved in fatal accidents	Number	52,700	7,400	4,200	10,300	10,300	13,600	6,500
Percent distribution	Percent	100.0	14.0	8.0	19.5	19.5	25.8	12.3
Drinking drivers involved in fatal accidents	Number	57,803	8,082	6,285	11,416	10,896	13,580	6,271
Percent distribution	Percent	100.0	14.0	10.9	19.7	18.9	23.5	10.8

Source: U.S. Department of Commerce, Bureau of the Census, *Statistical Abstract of the United States, 2004/2005* (Washington, DC: U.S. Government Printing Office, 2005), p. 702.

Half of all murders and a third of all suicides involve drinking, and many thousands of people die annually as a result. Physical assaults, child abuse, rape, and other sex crimes are frequently associated with alcohol use. So are acts of vandalism, arson, and other property crimes.

In 2003 some 13.6 million arrests were made in this country. About a quarter were for law violations related to alcohol use: public drunkenness, disorderly conduct, vagrancy, violation of liquor laws, and drunken driving (U.S. Department of Justice 2004:270). To this we may add many other arrests for crimes against people and property in which alcohol use was involved. All these arrests do not involve different individuals. Public drunkenness, for example, accounts for about half of all arrests in urban areas. Most public drunkenness arrests involve persons such as vagrants or street people who are being repeatedly arrested and released.

For such individuals, jail is a "revolving door." In general, a relatively small proportion of the drinking population accounts for the majority of alcohol-related arrests.

Economic Effects

While the alcoholic beverage industry is prospering from the sales of its products and government is benefiting from alcohol-related tax revenues, alcohol abuse and alcoholism are costly to business, government, and (of course) individuals. Earlier we mentioned federal government estimates of over $184 billion in costs annually. Many would consider this conservative. For example, health-care delivery costs have risen markedly in recent years, and it has been argued that the degree to which alcohol produces or contributes to people's health problems may be greatly underestimated (U.S. Department of Health and Human Services 1993).

Reduced job productivity among members of the labor force due to drinking costs the U.S. economy more than $129 billion, or 70 percent of the $184 billion in total costs each year (www.niaaa.nih.gov). Most of this is due to absenteeism, accidents, and inefficiency. Almost 13 percent, about $23 billion, goes to pay for medical problems people suffer as a consequence of drinking, including the treatment of alcoholism. Anywhere from 25 to 40 percent of all patients in U.S. general hospital beds (except those in maternity or intensive care) are being treated for alcohol-related problems (www.marininstitute.org). Almost 20 percent of the costs, or over $36 billion, is attributable to premature deaths involving drinking (e.g., from accidents or disease).

Beyond these costs that are included in the calculation of the monetary cost of alcoholism, other additional costs are associated with the care of those born with fetal alcohol syndrome, damage to property from alcohol-related incidents, alcohol-attributable administration of welfare and criminal justice programs, and lost productivity of imprisoned perpetrators and victims of alcohol-related crimes. All told, these add almost $27 billion to the costs of alcohol abuse and alcoholism (www.niaaa.nih.gov).

The conservative estimate of $184 billion annually represents financial resources lost to society that could have been used for other purposes. The overall economic costs of alcoholism and alcohol abuse in general clearly dwarf the amounts being spent to combat this micro problem.

Types of Treatment

Several different kinds of treatment are used in cases of alcoholism. These treatment procedures are directed at altering the physical and/or mental state of the alcoholic. Most of them fall within the context of the medical model, in which the alcoholic is considered ill and in need of being cured. Instead of attacking the societal conditions that may help produce and sustain alcoholism, efforts are made to help the drinker function within the prevailing order (U.S. Department of Health and Human Services 1993).

The "cure rate" for alcoholism is not very high. When we use abstinence for more than 3 or 5 years as the criterion for cure, fewer than 20 percent of those treated are cured. If, on the other hand, the criterion is the ability of the alcoholic to maintain control over drinking *most* of the time, the cure rate approaches two-thirds of those treated. Moreover, treatment outcomes appear to be highly correlated with such factors as social class. Among socially stable middle-class alcoholics, treatment outcomes are relatively successful. Among the lower socioeconomic strata, the rate of success tends to be quite low.

The chances for cure depend on the severity of the impact of alcohol on the individual. People who have not been severely affected are much more likely to control their drinking. Persons placed in mental hospitals to be treated for alcoholic psychoses, on the other hand, have only 1 chance in 10 of being cured.

These statistics come from agencies and institutions involved in treatment (see Table 17.3). It is difficult to know if their claims of successful treatment are real or somewhat inflated. Moreover, an estimated 85 percent of the millions of alcoholics and problem drinkers never come into contact with treatment facilities. So it is possible that those who are treated are either more—or less—amenable to "cure" than the untreated.

Physiological Treatment

Alcoholics who suddenly stop drinking often suffer from withdrawal symptoms, in which the body, having adjusted to large amounts of alcohol, reacts to the shock of abstinence. Common withdrawal symptoms include trembling, nausea, nervousness, and inability to sleep. Some

Table 17.3	Substance Abuse Treatment Services: 2003	
Primary focus		**Number**
Facilities		
Total		13,690
Type of care		
Substance abuse treatment services		8,386
Mental health services		1,168
General health care		249
Both substance abuse and mental health care		3,619
Other		273
Clients		
Total		1,091,816
Type of care		
Substance abuse treatment services		743,971
Mental health services		56,159
General health care		17,766
Both substance abuse and mental health care		254,986
Other		18,934
Type of Care and Type of Problem		
Outpatient rehab		956,245
Outpatient detoxification		11,761
24-hour rehab		107,695
24-hour detoxification		16,115
Drug only		358,165
Alcohol only		221,800
Both alcohol and drug		511,851
Total with a drug problem*		870,016
Total with an alcohol problem**		733,651

*The sum of clients with a drug problem and clients with both diagnoses.
**The sum of clients with an alcohol problem and clients with both diagnoses.

Source: U.S. Department of Commerce, Bureau of the Census, *Statistical Abstract of the United States, 2004/2005* (Washington, DC: U.S. Government Printing Office, 2005), p. 124.

alcoholics suffer from the DTs, delirium tremens, when they stop drinking. The DTs are often characterized by nightmarish hallucinations, serious convulsions, and feverishness. The individual may be terror-stricken, convinced that snakes or insects are crawling all over his or her body.

The most common method of dealing with withdrawal symptoms is to provide the alcoholic with tranquilizers, a balanced intake of liquids and solids, and bed rest. Once the individual's bodily system has undergone detoxification (i.e., is cleansed of alcohol), further medical treatments may be undertaken to handle physical and mental problems that remain.

Detoxification, or the drying out of an alcoholic, is not the same as eliminating the desire to drink. Thus, further treatment often consists of drugging alcoholics with tranquilizers in the hope of relieving this desire. The difficulty here is that the tranquilizing drugs may themselves be no more than alcohol substitutes. The alcoholic simply seeks escape from reality through drug treatment.

Attempts have been made to cure alcoholism by using a drug (disulfiram, or Antabuse) that induces a deep, reflexive aversion to drinking. The deterrent drug causes headaches, violent nausea, and other physical discomforts whenever alcohol is ingested. The idea is to condition the alcoholic to associate drinking with physical agony and thus to promote abstinence. Deterrent drugs can be used only if the alcoholic is willing to be subjected to such unpleasant treatment. Also, some alcoholics manage to drink themselves beyond the deterrent effects. While deterrent drugs may create an aversion to alcohol, they do not necessarily remove the desire to escape reality.

In general, the physiological approach to treatment does not guarantee abstention from alcohol or the production of "cured" alcoholics. For such reasons, psychologically oriented treatments have also been developed to deal with this "illness."

Psychological Treatment

Psychological treatments for alcoholism are based on the premise that underlying character disorders or weaknesses cause the individual to drink. A variety of approaches are in use. At one extreme, therapists have experimented with LSD in order to produce unusual hallucinations and other mental experiences with the hope that alcoholics will gain insights while under the influence of the drug. The results of such experiments have been minimal.

At the other extreme is psychotherapy, in which alcoholics receive individual counseling and are encouraged to contemplate and talk about the deep-seated reasons why they drink. Efforts are made to urge the alcoholic to overcome the psychological problems for which drinking is thought to provide an escape. Psychotherapy is very expensive. And many persons who face problems in living find such attempts to suggest that they are to blame for their own troubles less than helpful.

Group therapy often takes place in hospitals, churches, and mental institutions. One organization that claims a high level of success in fostering abstention is Alcoholics Anonymous (AA) (Katz 1991; Nace 1987). In group therapy, the alcoholic is encouraged to talk honestly with other persons who are trying to or have managed to abstain. The alcoholic thus finds others who have been "saved" from the harmful effects of drinking and enjoys the fellowship of a sympathetic group. Alcoholics Anonymous encourages alcoholics to put themselves in the hands of a higher power and to take encouragement from the experiences and expectations of other AA participants. Although several hundred thousand people are currently involved with AA, the spiritual orientation is not attractive to many other alcoholics. Though it claims great success with those who seek out its services, AA—like alcoholism treatment programs generally—touches only a small percentage of those thought to be alcoholics or problem drinkers.

What Treatment Works Best?

As is evident from our discussion of treatment statistics and practices, no one really knows how to "cure" alcoholism. According to the National Institute on Alcohol Abuse and Alcoholism (U.S. Department of Health, Education, and Welfare, 1974:24): "There is no evidence that any particular type of therapist—physician, clergyman, Alcoholics Anonymous member, psychiatrist, psychologist, or social worker—will have better results than another. The chances of a successful outcome apparently depend more on the combination of right patient and right treatment."

Existing approaches to treatment fail to take into account the possibility that alcoholism may be a response to societal conditions that do harm to people. Unless these conditions are dealt with, it can be very difficult for alcoholics and problem drinkers to confront life in a sober state. According to Joel Fort and Christopher T. Cory (1975:61): "Drug use may be a way for society to keep people with dissatisfactions and frustrations doped up so that they cannot challenge society to eliminate injustice, oppression, political corruption, boring jobs, and unfair economic conditions."

In other words, these experts believe that alcohol and other drugs facilitate users' escapism, diverting people from struggling against the kinds of problems analyzed in the first part of this book. Presumably, the more people who seek escape from reality and from societal conditions that are intolerable, the more likely it is that such conditions will continue.

Summary

The term *drug* is subject to a wide variety of meanings and uses—scientific, medical, and legal. In actuality, there is no single quality that would distinguish substances designated as drugs from nondrugs. Any and all substances that are designated as drugs are socially defined as such. So-called problem drugs (e.g., marijuana and heroin) differ from other drug and nondrug substances in that they have a different and more negative social definition. Social definitions frequently change with time, and different groups commonly disagree over such definitions.

Among the most used problem drugs are marijuana, heroin, cocaine, LSD, PCP, amphetamines, and club drugs. Marijuana is the most widely used illegal substance in the United States. Less public concern has been expressed over the high consumption of legal prescription and over-the-counter psychoactive drugs than over illegal substances. The forces underlying this high consumption include the pharmaceutical industry, which constantly seeks out new markets and encourages increased use of existing drugs, and medical practitioners, who often prescribe psychoactive drugs to patients who have no easily diagnosable physical ailment. Many people have come to believe that drug taking is an acceptable and effective way of dealing with problems in living. Despite the hazards they pose, prescribed and over-the-counter drugs are rarely considered part of the drug problem in the United States.

There are a number of explanations for why people use psychoactive drugs. Illegal drug use has been said to stem from manipulation of people by drug pushers, moral or mental weaknesses of users, and a cultural environment that extols drug use in general. Each of these explanations is open to criticism. Most recent sociological explanations emphasize that illegal drug use is learned behavior. Peers, and to a lesser extent parents, are important influences and sources of knowledge about drug use. Widespread use of both illegal and legal psychoactive substances may be a response to harmful societal conditions, a false palliative but nonetheless one that helps make an otherwise unbearable existence bearable.

Concern has been expressed over the use of drugs for social control purposes. Drugs have been administered to schoolchildren, inmates of mental hospitals and prisons, and elderly persons in nursing homes. Drugs have been used to make such persons more "manageable." Political use of drugs extends to experimentation for covert intelligence purposes.

Use and abuse of anabolic steroids, particularly among athletes, is increasingly widespread. Both students and professional athletes find themselves in a hypercompetitive environment in which tremendous amounts of money are at stake. Steroids become perceived as a quick way to build muscle and enhance performance. School administrators, Congress, and professional sports commissions are only slowly coming to appreciate the extent of steroid use among athletes and the long-term dangers it poses.

The use of alcohol and, to a lesser extent, tobacco, is a popular and acceptable activity in U.S. society. Alcohol is a drug, although many people do not think of it in this way. Many heavy drinkers use it in attempts to relieve depression and to escape problems in living that are intolerable when faced in a state of sobriety. One out of seven drinkers, some 15 million people, use this drug so heavily that they may be considered an alcohol abuser or an alcoholic.

Experts disagree about what alcoholism is and why it exists, but most, using the medical model, blame the drinker for his or her own plight. Treatment approaches, both physiological and psychological, generally operate within the context of the medical model and attempt to alter the drinking behavior that is in question. Such approaches to alcoholism and alcohol abuse tend to bypass processes by which people are labeled alcoholics and do not take into consideration the societal conditions that may provoke people to become problem drinkers.

Meanwhile, massive costs are generated as a consequence of such drinking behavior—both for the individual drinker and for U.S. society as a whole. But despite these costs, the alcoholic beverage industry continues to promote and profit from the drug it markets, and the government amasses huge tax revenues from alcohol production and use. Resources devoted to combating the costs associated with the U.S. population's drinking practices are negligible in comparison with the profits and tax revenues collected. And alcoholism remains this society's number one health problem and a self-harmful means of escapism from the status quo.

Not all drugs are harmful, and many are known to have extremely beneficial effects. Drugs may be used to heighten human wellbeing or to thwart it.

Key Terms

Discussion Questions

1. What arguments could be made for and against legalizing all so-called problem drugs and leaving the choice of use up to individuals? Would the argument be the same for marijuana, cocaine, heroine, steroids, and club drugs? Why or why not?

2. Obtain copies of magazine or medical journal advertisements for over-the-counter or prescribed psychoactive drugs. What might be said about the content of these advertisements? Are the sources of the problems to which they are directed necessarily medical? Should prescription drugs be advertised in popular magazines or on television? Why or why not?

3. Visit a drug rehabilitation center or a meeting of Alcoholics Anonymous. On the basis of what you learn there, assess the role of alcohol and other drugs in the lives of those seeking help and the reasons they became abusers. Compare your impressions with those of your classmates.

4. Does anyone you know appear to meet the criteria for being an alcoholic or a problem drinker? How would you explain this person's drinking behavior? What are the obstacles to changing this individual's behavior?

5. Examine a sample of advertisements for alcoholic beverages and nicotine products. What do these advertisements suggest, directly or indirectly, about the types of people who drink and smoke? What do they suggest about the benefits of alcohol and nicotine use? What facts from this chapter do these ads systematically ignore?

6. If you normally drink or use drugs at parties, bars, and the like, arrive at one of these settings late in the evening completely sober. How does the behavior of others appear to you when you stand back and view it as an uninvolved observer?

Suggested Readings

Currie, Elliott. *Reckoning* (New York: Hill and Wang, 1993).

Addresses the failure of the law enforcement approach to illegal drug use and calls for major changes in social and economic policies to reduce people's need to use or sell drugs.

Goode, Erich. *Drugs in American Society.* 5th ed. (New York: McGraw-Hill, 1999).
The contributions made by the alcoholic
Comprehensive assessment of what is known about the nature and extent of drug use and abuse, including alcohol.

Jacobson, Michael, George Hacker, and Robert Atkins. *The Booze Merchants* (Washington, DC: Center for Science in the Public Interest, 1983).
The contributions made by the alcoholic beverage industry in promoting drinking as desirable behavior.

Normand, Jacques, Richard O. Lempert, and Charles P. O'Brien, eds. *Under the Influence* (Washington, DC: National Academy Press, 1994).
An assessment of the nature and extent of drug use by members of the U.S. workforce and implications for employers.

Reinerman, Craig, and Harry Gene Levine, eds. *Crack in America: Demon Drugs and Social Justice* (Berkeley, CA: University of California Press, 1997).
Sociological treatment of the history of cocaine and crack cocaine in the United States as an analytical filter for understanding broader drug and drug policy issues. The book offers analyses of the differential impact of the drug and drug control policy on the basis of race and class, and offers a comparative international assessment of why the drug has had less of a severe effect in other countries.

U.S. Department of Health and Human Services. *Alcohol and Health.*
Periodic special report to the Congress summarizing research findings bearing on alcohol use and abuse, costs of abuse to U.S. society, and developments in treatment.

Wechsler, Henry, and Bernice Wuethrich. *Dying to Drink: Confronting Binge Drinking on College Campuses* (New York: Rodale Books, 2003).
An analysis of underage and binge drinking on college campuses, where alcoholic abuse is often considered by students as a rite of passage rather than a potentially lethal activity. The book contains individual accounts and testimonials of campus binge drinking.

chapter 18

Suicide

Members of U.S. society should be at peace with themselves and with one another. The social factors that provoke suicide should be absent.

By the time you finish reading this chapter, two or three people in the United States will have killed themselves. According to official statistics, almost 31,000 people committed **suicide** in 2002 (U.S. Bureau of the Census 2005:80). The National Institute of Mental Health (NIMH) estimates that anywhere from 8 to 25 suicides are attempted for every suicide death (www.nimh.gov/suicideprevention/suifact.cfm). Many of those who attempt suicide will try again in the future. On the assumption that the lives of each touched a half dozen others at the time of their attempt, some 46 million people in the United States have had to handle the experience of a person close to them seeking to end her or his own life (Clines 1993).

Means of suicide range from the straightforwardly grim to the unexpectedly bizarre. People shoot and slash themselves, ingest poisonous substances, overdose on drugs, asphyxiate themselves with gas or plastic bags, jump from high places, hang themselves, leap in front of trains, electrocute and drown themselves, swallow dangerous objects, tear themselves apart with explosives, pilot speeding vehicles into crashes, and burn themselves. Those who survive suicide attempts are often maimed or disabled.

Most of us think of suicide, in the abstract, as an unnatural act, probably related to mental illness. How could a sane person choose death over life? The whole idea is distasteful to contemplate and difficult to condone. As with many other forms of socially unpleasant behavior, people tend to blame the victim for his or her own plight.

In more concrete situations, where the suicidal individual is known, friends and family are likely to react with shock and self-blame. Asking themselves whether there was something they could have done to avert the tragedy, they try to assuage their sense of guilt and rationalize what has happened. Family members attempt to limit public attention to the death, for in this society suicide is considered a shamefully unfortunate affair (Dunne et al. 1987; Fine 1999).

587

Suicide is the 11th-leading cause of death in the United States, and the 3rd-leading cause of death among young people between the ages of 15 and 24 years old (www.nimh.gov/suicide prevention/suifact.cfm). Yet despite the frequency with which self-inflicted deaths occur in U.S. society, such deaths generate a great deal of confusion and uncertainty. When people are confronted with suicide, the first question they ask is "Why?" This same question has preoccupied social scientists for decades; it is a central concern of this chapter. In the following pages we focus on the nature and extent of suicide, efforts to explain suicide, and approaches to suicide prevention.

The Nature and Extent of Suicide

Before any social phenomenon can be explained, it must be carefully defined. We have already seen the problems involved in defining such phenomena as crime, mental illness, and alcoholism. Similar difficulties arise in any discussion of suicide.

The Concept of Suicide

What exactly should someone interested in explaining suicide choose to study? Should suicide research be limited to those who succeed in killing themselves? Or should researchers also study those who attempt to kill themselves but fail? Furthermore, many persons threaten to kill themselves and, at least in some cases, follow such threats with suicide attempts. Others express, directly or indirectly, suicidal thoughts. Should these forms of behavior be of major concern to someone interested in explaining suicide?

As a result of such questions, social scientists have attempted to categorize various forms of suicidal behavior. Such categorization raises the issue of *intent*. Is it not important to understand the intentions of persons who engage in one or another form of suicidal behavior (Shneidman 1995)? For example, researchers believe that some completed suicides are actually accidental deaths caused by errors of judgment. This would be the case when a person who takes an overdose of drugs, expecting to be discovered and saved from death, is not found in time. Shouldn't such deaths be distinguished from suicides in which the intent to die is clear? Or, to take another example, some attempted suicides are staged events. An attempt may be superficial or ambivalent, involving a method of self-harm that is unlikely to cause death. Should not such attempts be distinguished from those that appear serious and potentially lethal?

Intent is closely related to the issue of *consciousness*. Here the question is whether individuals realize that their actions may bring about their demise. Many suicides are both intentional and consciously planned; the person carefully chooses the method, time, and circumstances. In other cases the degree of consciousness is less clear. For example, when individuals kill themselves while under the influence of alcohol or other drugs, we may have no way of knowing whether they are really conscious of the possible outcome of their actions.

To complicate things even more, many people die as a consequence of taking risks with their own personal welfare. For example, medical experts claim that heavy cigarette smokers and drinkers are slowly killing themselves. Although the average person may not categorize heavy smoking or drinking as suicidal behavior, social scientists must deal with these phenomena in terms of their potential lethality for the individuals involved. Is such self-harm a form of suicidal behavior? If so, is it intentional? Is it conscious self-harm (Farberow 1980)? What about death row inmates who refuse to seek appeals to prevent their execution? Does their time on death row reduce their ability to make a deliberate, carefully considered decision (see

Chapter 16). Or consider **suicide by cop,** in which individuals engage in behaviors that provoke officers into drastic, sometimes lethal measures to disarm an apparently threatening person (Lindsay and Lester 2004): Is an individual's death the intention, or is the death an outcome of the person's risky, illegal, or threatening behavior? Consider, too, politically motivated suicides, such as suicide bombers.

In sum, those interested in explaining suicide continue to face challenges in categorizing suicidal behavior and in figuring out how to take the issue of intent into account. For the most part, sociologists have focused on completed suicides, frequently using official statistics gathered by agencies of government. In the next section we look at some of the limitations of these statistics as well as some of the patterns of suicidal behavior.

Suicide Statistics

As in the areas of unemployment and crime, statistics on suicide are collected by agencies of government. The government calculates the frequency of deaths by suicide, as compared to deaths from other causes (see, for example, Table 18.1). Government data also include information on the age, sex, and race of persons who take their own lives.

In this society, a physician ordinarily ascertains cause of death. When there is doubt about the cause of death, a coroner or medical examiner usually conducts an inquiry. In all cases, the death certificate classifies the death as natural, accidental, homicide, or suicide. Death certificates provide the basis for official statistics.

Social scientists have long been concerned about the reliability of official statistics, suspecting that they underestimate the frequency of suicide (Douglas 1967; O'Carroll 1989; Pescosolido and Mendelsohm 1986). The cause of death listed on death certificates reflects the judgment of the physicians and other medical professionals assigned to ascertain causes of death. Social scientists do not know how these individuals choose to define suicide or whether they agree on a common definition. Moreover, it is suspected that doctors classify some suicides as deaths from other causes to spare the feelings of the victims' families or even to assist their heirs in avoiding problems with life insurance companies.

Often, it is extremely difficult to be positive that suicide is the cause of death. For example, an elderly person is found dead after taking the wrong dosages of prescribed medicines. Was this a failure of memory or judgment, or a suicide? Could it have been a homicide, set up to look like a suicide? A young person is found shot to death. It looks accidental, but perhaps the family concealed a suicide note. Or did the victim purposely manage the circumstances of death to make it look accidental? Could the individual have been murdered? A middle-age individual dies in a single-car automobile accident. Did alcohol cause this person to misjudge speed and road conditions? Or did it simply give the person courage to go through with a suicidal act? Or did someone tamper with the car?

It is probable that many suicides are attributed to accidental causes each year—whether intentionally or through error. There is no way of knowing how extensive such underreporting is or whether it is systematically skewed in a particular direction. (For example, are the wealthy more prone to hide the fact of suicide, or more likely to gain the cooperation of authorities in doing so, than the poor?) With such cautions in mind, we will briefly examine the statistical picture.

▲ General Population

As we mentioned earlier, nearly 31,000 people in the United States killed themselves in 2002. This is a rate of about 11 suicides per 100,000 people. As the 11th-leading cause of death, suicides are less frequent than deaths from diabetes but substantially more frequent than deaths from homicide or AIDS (U.S. Bureau of the Census

| Table 18.1 | Death Rates from Accidents and Violence, 1970–2002* |

	White								Black							
	Male				Female				Male				Female			
Cause of death	1970	1980	1992	2002	1970	1980	1992	2002	1970	1980	1992	2002	1970	1980	1992	2002
Total	**101.9**	**97.1**	**76.2**	**25.5**	**42.4**	**36.3**	**30.4**	**6.8**	**183.2**	**154.0**	**134.5**	**48.1**	**51.7**	**42.6**	**36.7**	**8.6**
Motor vehicle accidents	39.1	35.9	22.4	22.4	14.8	12.8	10.2	10.2	44.3	31.1	24.0	21.6	13.4	8.3	8.8	8.0
All other accidents	38.2	30.4	23.4	28.0	18.3	14.4	12.4	17.2	63.3	46.0	30.9	26.4	22.5	18.6	12.7	11.7
Suicide	18.0	19.9	21.2	19.9	7.1	5.9	5.1	4.8	8.0	10.3	12.0	9.1	2.6	2.2	2.0	1.6
Homicide	6.8	10.9	9.1	5.2	2.1	3.2	2.8	2.0	67.6	66.6	67.5	38.4	13.3	13.5	13.1	7.1

*Rates per 100,000 population.

Source: U.S. Department of Commerce, Bureau of the Census, *Statistical Abstract of the United States, 1989* (Washington, DC: U.S. Government Printing Office, 1989), p. 83; U.S. Department of Commerce, Bureau of the Census, *Statistical Abstract of the United States, 1995* (Washington, DC: U.S. Government Printing Office, 1995), p. 99; Centers for Disease Control, National Center for Injury Prevention and Control, available at http://webappa.cdc.gov/cgi-bin/broker.exe.

2005:80). The overall suicide rate has been fairly constant over the last 25 years but has shown a slight rising trajectory. (Of course, there is no way of knowing whether the actual suicide rate—as opposed to the official rate—has been rising.) No reliable statistics are available regarding the proportion of suicide attempts, but a rough ratio of 10 attempts to each completed suicide is thought to exist. This would mean that some 310,000 persons attempt to kill themselves each year.

▲ Age

In general, the probability that persons will commit suicide increases with advancing age (Table 18.2). The relationship between aging and suicide is most marked for white men; the suicide rate among white males increases fairly steadily for all age groups up through those 65 and older. And white males account for 73 per-

cent of all suicide deaths (National Institute of Mental Health, available at www.nimh.gov/suicidepreventionasuifact.cfm). The pattern for white women is slightly different; their suicide rate tends to drop off in their 60s, after reaching a peak in the 40s and 50s (Bender 2000; Coren and Hewitt 1999). Suicide and age correlate differently for people of color. Among African Americans, for example, suicide is at its peak among young adults ages 25 to 44.

With regard to attempted suicides (also referred to as **parasuicides**), the rate is much higher among the young than among the elderly. Older people have fewer attempts but are more likely to be successful, since they are likely to use more lethal methods. But changes may be under way, as a higher percentage of suicides among the young involve firearms, perhaps reflecting the increased accessibility of guns kept in residences or available on the streets (Leary 1995).

Table 18.2	Suicide Rates, by Sex, Race, and Age Group: 2002*				
		Male		**Female**	
Age	Total[†]	White	Black	White	Black
All ages[§]	11.0	19.9	9.1	4.8	1.5
15 to 24 years old	9.9	17.7	11.3	3.1	1.7
25 to 44 years old	14.0	24.0	15.1	6.6	2.4
45 to 64 years old	14.9	25.9	9.6	7.5	2.1
65 years and over	15.6	34.2	11.7	4.3	1.1

*Rates per 100,000 population.
[†]Includes other races not shown separately.
[§]Includes other age groups not shown separately.

Source: National Center for Health Statistics, *Health, United States, 2004,* available at www.cdc.gov.

In recent years an increase in suicide rates among young people has generated substantial attention and deep concern (Borst and Borst 1994; Manor, Vincent, and Tyano 2004; Rutter and Behrendt 2004). The overall rate for adolescents and young adults nearly tripled between 1950 and 2002. In 2002 alone 4,274 children, teenagers, and young adults under age 25 killed themselves, constituting almost 14 percent of all recorded suicides (Centers for Disease Control, available at webappa.cdc.gov/cgi-bin/broker. exe). Suicide is the third-leading cause of death for children and young adults aged 10 to 24.

Among the young people who take their own lives, bisexual, gay male, and lesbian youths are most likely to do so. They are two to three times as likely to complete suicide than heterosexual youths, and it is estimated that they constitute 30 percent of all adolescent suicides (Gibson 1989). There is nothing about being bisexual or homosexual that causes suicide. Rather, researchers have found that societal attitudes toward and treatment of homosexuals create enormous problems for adolescents who suspect or know their sexual orientation is not in line with the dominant heterosexual norm. Such youth often are forced to hide their orientations from others, including their families and peers, and many fear or are subject to expressions of homophobia and homohatred ranging from verbal abuse to physical violence (see Chapter 9). The stress that results is a major risk factor for suicide (Hershberger and D'Augelli 1995; Savin-Williams 1995).

▲ College Students

Periodically, much is made in newspapers and the popular press about young adults committing suicide on college campuses. The perception that college students are at high risk for suicide resurfaced when a wrongful death suit was filed on behalf of the bereaved family of a student who committed suicide in 2000 at Massachusetts Institute of Technology. However, data indicate that college students are actually far less likely to commit suicide than their age peers who are not students. Students have a suicide rate of 7.5 per 100,000, compared with a rate of 15 per 100,000 among their nonstudent age peers (Silverman et al. 1997). There are several likely reasons for this notable contrast. For one thing, while college life can be stressful, particularly at highly competitive elite universities, campus infrastructures typically contain support systems that are designed to identify students at risk and provide a variety of helpful services to them. Moreover, campus prohibitions against firearms possession contribute to a reduction in suicide attempts. The vast majority of suicides use a gun: 74 percent of men and 31 percent of women carried out their suicides using firearms (www.merck.com). Restrictions against possession of firearms on campus clearly reduce that number. Instead of using guns, students are more likely to jump from buildings, hang themselves, or swallow lethal chemicals (www.psychiatrictimes.com).

Yet, although the suicide rate among college students is lower than the rate among their nonstudent age peers, suicide ranks as the second-leading cause of death among students in the United States (Jamison 1999). In one study, 85 percent of counseling center directors reported a significant increase in serious psychological problems among college students over the preceding five years; more than half reported an increase in self-injury (Gallagher, Sysko, and Zhang 2001). Observers often assume that the stressful challenges of higher education trigger unbearable levels of frustration leading to suicide. However, while it is true that the demands of college can be highly stressful, researchers suggest that the stress in and of itself does not cause suicide; rather, the stress can be a deciding factor for students who are vulnerable to begin with.

One key factor in campus suicides appears to be social isolation. Suicide rates are higher among international students, for whom integration into campus life may be complicated by cultural differences. Social isolation is the key factor among native born students' suicides, many of whom are typically highly depressed and withdrawn. Suicide is also more likely among those who take more than four years to complete a degree, a finding that researchers suggest may be because many of these are students whose college career has been interrupted by bouts with serious depression (www.afsp.org).

▲ Sex

Men complete suicide far more frequently than women, at a ratio of roughly four to one (Lester 1988). On the other hand, suicide attempts are thought to be far more common among women. For reasons not fully understood, methods of suicide differ between the sexes, just as they do between the old and the young. Men are most likely to choose such violent techniques as shooting and hanging, whereas women are more prone to use drugs, poisons, and gas. In recent years, both men's and women's use of firearms has been on the decrease (see Table 18.3).

▲ Race and Ethnicity

According to official statistics, the suicide rate among whites is normally twice as high as that among racial minorities such as African Americans and Latinos. But there are some important variations. For example, while the suicide rate is lower for African Americans than for whites in the southern United States, the opposite is true in the northern states. It has also been noted that the suicide rate is inordinately high among Native American youth in comparison to white adolescents (National Center for Health Statistics 2004).

▲ Religion

Overall, suicide is more frequent among Protestants than among either Jews or Roman Catholics. However, it is suspected that there are variations among particular Protestant denominations. It is possible that some Protestant denominations have lower rates than Jews and Roman Catholics.

| Table 18.3 | Suicides, by Sex and Method Used: 1970 to 2002 |

Method	Male							Female						
	1970	1980	1985	1990	1991	1992	2002	1970	1980	1985	1990	1991	1992	2002
Total	**16,629**	**20,505**	**23,145**	**24,724**	**24,769**	**24,457**	**25,409**	**6,851**	**6,364**	**6,308**	**6,182**	**6,041**	**6,027**	**6,246**
Firearms*	9,704	12,937	14,809	16,285	16,120	15,802	15,045	2,068	2,459	2,554	2,600	2,406	2,367	2,063
Percent of total	58	63	64	66	65	65	59	30	39	41	42	40	39	33
Poisoning†	3,299	2,997	3,319	3,221	3,316	3,262	3,097	3,285	2,456	2,385	2,203	2,228	2,233	2,389
Hanging and strangulation§	2,422	2,997	3,532	3,688	3,751	3,822	5,385	831	694	732	756	810	856	1,107
Other¶	1,204	1,574	1,485	1,530	1,582	1,571	251	667	755	637	623	597	571	64

*Includes explosives in 1970.

†Includes solids, liquids, and gases.

§Includes suffocation.

¶Beginning 1980, includes explosives.

Source: U.S. Department of Commerce, Bureau of the Census, *Statistical Abstract of the United States, 1995* (Washington, D.C.: U.S. Government Printing Office, 1995), p. 99; Center for Disease Control, National Center for Injury Prevention and Control, available at http://webappa.cdc.gov/cgi-bin/broker.exe.

▲ Marital Status

A correlation between suicide rates and marital status has long been noted in official statistics. Single persons are twice as likely as married persons to complete the act of suicide. The widowed and divorced also kill themselves more frequently than the married. These generalizations must be qualified by noting variations. For example, the rate of suicide among young married persons is higher than among young people who are single. Among the elderly, suicide is more frequent among those who are married than among those who are widowed.

▲ Place of Residence

In the past decades, official statistics generally showed higher rates for cities than for rural areas. But suicide is not an urban phenomenon. Today the urban-rural differences are very small. There are also differences in the rates prevailing in particular cities and in different regions of the country. For example, San Francisco has a higher suicide rate than virtually any other U.S. city, and its Golden Gate Bridge alone has been the site for about 1,000 known suicides since it was built in 1937 (Stryker 1995). The western states in general tend to have higher suicide rates than other regions.

▲ Occupation

Even when they are available, official statistics relating suicide rates to occupation are not easy to interpret. Standard occupational categories are not used on death certificates, thus making comparisons between occupations difficult. In some cases, the occupation of the deceased may be unknown. Or those charged with filling out death certificates may simply put down the last known occupation. This could be misleading, for a person could be unemployed or employed in a different job than usual at the time of death. Thus, it is not surprising that the findings of studies attempting to correlate suicide rates with occupation have been contradictory. Nevertheless, evidence suggests that suicide is more frequent among the unemployed than among jobholders—at least for men (Platt 1984). In addition, certain professions (such as psychiatry) appear to have unusually high rates.

Statistical Trends

As mentioned earlier, suicide rates have shown a slight tendency to rise in recent years, perhaps reflecting the higher rates among young adults, youth, and children. While the situation of the latter has received widespread attention, some experts believe that too little notice is being taken of the possibility of significant increases occurring in the rate of self-inflicted deaths among our elders (Knowlton 2000; McIntosh 1992a).

We have seen that the suicide rate advances with age, such that older people in the United States (particularly white males) are more likely to take their lives than younger persons. The average age of members of the U.S. population has been increasing as the proportion of the population that is approaching old age (or has achieved it) has been going up. Older members of the post–World War II "baby boom" (those born between 1946 and 1964) are now reaching their 60s. Many more older people in the United States are expected to take their lives as a reflection of demographic change.

But while the numbers of suicides may increase simply because there are more elders, will the suicide rate itself also increase for the older population? Those who believe the answer is yes point to comparatively high rates of depression and suicidal behavior among baby boomers at younger ages, suggesting levels of stress within this population that may be manifested in high rates of suicide among those who survive into old age. Such predictions have generated some controversy. In reviewing this controversy, John L. McIntosh (1992a:327) notes that our ability to predict the future behavior of our elders may be affected by

future attitudes, health and disease control, economic conditions, treatment of mental health problems and disorders such as depression and Alzheimer's disease, the development of programs targeted specifically to older adults who are suicidal . . . [and] biological, medical, and technological knowledge advances will also be among those factors that must be considered.

Explanations for Suicide

There are many types of explanations for why people kill themselves. Such explanations can be categorized as physiological, psychological, and sociological. Most of them focus on completed suicides, rather than on other forms of suicidal behavior (Lester 1990, 2000).

Physiological Explanations

There has been an ongoing controversy about whether the act of suicide is confined to the human species (Lester 2000). Those who argue that other species engage in suicide sometimes point to the lemming, a mouselike rodent native to Sweden and Norway. It is believed that, during their semiannual migrations, lemmings pursue a straight path to their destinations, sometimes falling off cliffs or drowning. Those who dispute the idea that animals commit suicide usually point out that only human beings show evidence of intent. We have no wish to enter this debate, but we must point out that it exists.

Researchers have attempted to determine if people who kill themselves differ physiologically from those who show no sign of suicidal behavior (Lester 2000). For example, researchers have asked if those who kill themselves are less likely to be physically healthy than nonsuicidal individuals. Some studies have found this to be the case, whereas others have uncovered no relationship between health and suicidal behavior. This question thus remains open.

It is true that people with certain health problems or disabilities are at greater risk for suicide than members of the general population, but the "cause" of suicide for such persons is not physiological. People with AIDS, for example, kill themselves at a rate that is higher than for people with other chronic diseases and at a rate that may be 10 to 20 times that of the general population. AIDS is debilitating and fatal, and as one researcher has pointed out, "there are just tremendous psychosocial stresses associated with AIDS—financial insecurity, homelessness, joblessness, social isolation" (Kolata 1994:C1; see also Werth 1995). These stresses are an important element in placing people with AIDS at special risk for suicide.

Other investigators have tried to determine if there are differences in physical traits, such as weight, between those who commit suicide and those who do not. It has been found that individuals who are disposed toward suicide are often overweight or underweight. However, such individuals could have lost or gained weight on the way toward completing the suicide act. Hormonal and chemical imbalances have also been investigated. Researchers have theorized that such imbalances are more likely to be present in those who kill themselves than in nonsuicidal persons. The findings of such research have been mixed, and no hard conclusions may be drawn from them.

Research has focused on the possibility that individuals inherit the potential to commit suicide. Though suicide has been unusually frequent in certain families, investigators have no way of determining whether this is a result of environmental experiences or genetic

The suicide rate for young people in general, and for young males in particular, has been on the increase. In this sad photograph, a young man holds a pistol in his hands against his head as he contemplates whether or not to go through with it.

factors. Thus, research in this area remains inconclusive.

The claim has been made that the majority of persons who commit suicide are, in part due to biological deficiencies, incapable of coping with stresses associated with their environment. Such persons, whose life-threatening behaviors are alleged to be a form of "gene expression," are said to carry little potential for making contributions to society. One proponent of this view has stated that suicide "may benefit the larger society because it extracts from the population individuals consuming resources but without productive and reproductive potential" (de Catanzaro 1981:143).

These and other efforts to explain suicide in terms of physiological traits all have one thing in common: They focus almost entirely on the constitution of individuals, and they tend to ignore the world in which suicidal individuals live. If most suicides are intentional acts, then explanations must take into account the fact that people have minds. Psychologists have tried to provide alternatives to physiological explanations by speculating on the personality traits of those who take their own lives.

Psychological Explanations

The mental makeup of persons who kill themselves is often difficult to ascertain. Frequently, researchers must rely on suicide notes or on people who knew the individuals. Occasionally, information on their state of mind is available from the records of medical and mental health practitioners. The reliability of all such information is open to question, but it has formed the basis for a number of theories on the psychological traits of those who commit suicide (Lester 2000).

For example, some psychologists have suggested that suicide-prone individuals are likely to have suffered from parental deprivation when young. Various forms of deprivation are said to be related to suicide, including the death or absence of parents and parental indifference to childhood needs. Deprivation, it is thought, disrupts the normal psychological development of children and provokes suicidal tendencies.

Others have claimed that suicide indicates—and is a result of—aggression that is directed inward. Children presumably learn to internalize aggressive impulses, rather than express them outwardly, as a result of parental disciplinary practices. In particular, parents who punish their children psychologically rather than physically

are thought to foster inwardly directed aggression. Some theorists believe that all people have both an instinct for self-preservation and an instinct for self-destruction (the so-called death instinct). Suicide is said to represent a breakthrough of the death instinct, a process most likely to occur among individuals who are suffering from mental problems.

It has also been postulated that persons who kill themselves are excessively rigid in their thinking and/or illogical in their reasoning and thought processes. These are considered mental disabilities that interfere with relations with other people and that deny the individual the flexibility needed to deal with everyday life. Suicide is the result.

Suicide has also been portrayed as stemming from a desire to manipulate others—perhaps to invoke love and attention. According to this theory, suicide is a cry for help from persons powerless to proceed in any other way. Alternatively, it has been suggested that suicide is an effort to hurt other people—a means of communicating deep-felt hostility or of exercising revenge.

Finally, mental illness is frequently invoked as a psychological explanation for suicide. In particular, it is thought that depressive psychoses are closely linked with suicidal behavior (Lester 2000).

Explanations for suicide that are limited to the mental state of individuals, while provocative, ignore the social context within which people kill themselves. The trend in **suicidology** (the study of suicide) is away from purely psychological interpretations of the act. Researchers are now more likely to see suicide as the outcome of an individual's biography or **suicide career** (Maris 1981) and to ask "how psychic, social, and cultural factors are interwoven to produce suicidal behavior in people from very different backgrounds" (Hendin 1982:18). The importance of societal context and group membership in helping to produce and determine motivations for suicide is underscored by research on suicidal behavior in other societies (Farberow 1975; Minois 2001). (See Table 18.4.)

Sociological Explanations

Sociological explanations for suicide attempt to remedy the psychologists' omissions, but (unfortunately) often at the cost of ignoring the individual. Sociologists are much more concerned with explaining variations in suicide rates, such as those that appear in official statistics.

▲ Social Integration Theory

The starting point for virtually all sociological explanations for suicide is a theory put forth by French sociologist Émile Durkheim (1951). Writing in 1897, Durkheim tried to demonstrate that the character of a society determined the probability that people would be pushed toward committing suicide. According to Durkheim's **social integration theory,** suicide could not be explained by physiological traits or psychological variables. Instead, one must look at the social forces impinging on and shaping the lives of the members of any given society. In Durkheim's view, the presence or absence of these forces accounted for variations in suicide rates.

According to Durkheim, suicide is related to the degree to which a society is *integrated*— in other words, the degree to which members of a society share common ideas and goals and sense their ties with one another. Where integration is low, **egoistic suicides**—due to the absence

There is very little reliable information on the personal or psychological motivations of persons who take their own lives. Even when suicide victims leave suicide notes, it is often difficult to determine their real reasons for killing themselves.

of meaningful social relationships or a sense of belonging—will be frequent. This is illustrated by the higher rates of suicide among international students in the United States compared with their U.S. peers. Conversely, where integration is high, individuals will be likely to willingly give up their lives for the group, committing **altruistic suicides.** Such self-sacrifices might take place in times of war or as part of religious rituals. It is also illustrated by the example of suicide bombers (more on this later).

Durkheim also argued that **social regulation** plays a role in generating suicidal behavior. In a society with a high degree of control over its members' emotions and motivations,

Table 18.4	**Suicide Rates, by Nation and Sex**											
Sex	United States 2000	Australia 2001	Austria 2002	Canada 2000	Denmark 1999	France 1999	Germany 2001	Italy 2000	Japan 2000	Netherlands 2000	Poland 2001	Sweden 2001	United Kingdom[†] 1999
Male	17.1	20.1	30.5	18.4	21.4	26.1	20.4	10.9	35.2	12.7	26.7	18.9	11.8
Female	4.0	5.3	8.7	5.2	7.4	9.4	7.0	3.5	13.4	6.2	4.3	8.1	3.3

[Rate per 100,000 population. Includes deaths resulting indirectly from self-inflicted injuries. Deaths classified according to the ninth revision of the International Classification of Diseases (I.C.D.)]

[†]*England and Wales only.*

Source: World Health Organization, available at www.who.int/mental_health/prevention/suicide/en/Figures_web0604_table.pdf.

fatalistic suicide will occur. That is, people kill themselves out of a sense of overmanipulation or of hopelessness about altering their life conditions. Conversely, in a society that provides few guidelines for its members' feelings and inclinations, thereby leaving people unregulated or uncontrolled, **anomic suicide** will take place.

Because Durkheim did not provide measures of integration and social regulation, it has proved difficult to test his arguments. Nonetheless, many sociologists have been influenced by his ideas in developing their own explanations. For example, French sociologist Maurice Halbwachs (1930; see Douglas 1967:124–31) theorized that suicide is a function of social isolation. According to Halbwachs, suicide occurs most frequently among individuals who lack stable and enduring relationships with others. Since such social isolation is presumably more common among city dwellers than among rural people, said Halbwachs, suicide rates should be higher in cities. Writing in 1930, Halbwachs found that the data on suicide rates available to him supported his hypothesis. Today, however, there is no significant difference between urban and rural suicide rates—at least in the United States—so the social isolation thesis does not appear helpful.

▲ Class and Status Perspective

Borrowing some of Durkheim's ideas, Elwin H. Powell (1958) proposed an explanation that relates suicide to the status of different groups in U.S. society. Powell hypothesized that suicide rates would be highest in the lower and upper classes. He reasoned that individuals at the bottom of the class structure would be prone to suicide because they were dissociated from the larger society and had little hope of achieving cultural success goals. The upper class, in his view, was so "enveloped" in these goals that many individuals could not find personal reasons for living. Using occupational data from suicide records in Tulsa, Oklahoma, Powell found support for his hypothesis. However, other studies have not found any consistent correlations between occupational status and suicide rates (Lester 2000), and Powell's explanation is open to question.

Sociologists Andrew Henry and James Short (1954) have also investigated the relationship between status and suicide. These researchers suggested that higher-status groups were least likely to be characterized by strong "relational systems" among their members. In other words, their emotional ties were weak. Society, they felt, places few "external constraints"—pressures toward conformity—on the behavior of high-status people. Henry and Short hypothesized that suicide rates would vary directly with social status. Thus, groups to which they assigned high status (men, whites, the affluent, the unmarried) could be expected to have the highest rates of suicide. In general, the statistics they mobilized supported their hypothesis. But there have been criticisms of Henry and Short's work. For example, how does one explain the high suicide rates that seem to prevail among African Americans residing in the north in comparison to whites? Such variations in the overall statistics on suicide rates are not easily handled within the framework of Henry and Short's explanation. Also, do unmarried people really have higher status than married people in U.S. society? Although this assumption fits with Henry and Short's statistical findings on suicide rates, it does not make much sense.

Some data suggest an indirect relationship between class membership and suicide; that is, the higher the class position, the lower the suicide rate. The rate of suicide appears to be highest among the poor (Lampert et al. 1984; Stack 1982). Stress, depression, and feelings of hopelessness associated with economic deprivation may account for this; however, such a conclusion requires quite a bit more empirical research.

▲ Role Incompatibility

Other sociologists have hypothesized that suicide rates are related to people's ability to carry out the roles society assigns them. Jack Gibbs and Walter Martin (1964) have pointed out that people must sometimes fill several roles simultaneously; that is, often they have to meet the demands and expectations of a variety of groups. If all these roles are compatible with one another, **status integration** is said to exist, and suicide is unlikely. On the other hand, if the roles are incompatible—if individuals are confronted with conflicting demands and expectations—suicide will be more frequent. In this case, individuals become more suicide-prone because they are unable to satisfy others,

and their social relationships with other people weaken. The problem with this explanation is that there is no objective way of measuring the role incompatibility of those who have committed suicide. Instead, we can only assume that role conflict is highest among those who kill themselves. Thus, a crucial aspect of Gibbs and Martin's explanation remains difficult to demonstrate.

▲ Societal Reaction

Another sociological explanation for variations in suicide rates holds that societal reaction to suicide is of key importance (Farber 1968). According to this explanation, where members of a society accept or condone acts of suicide, rates will be high; and where suicide is condemned, rates will be low. In other words, the cultural values of a group can either deter or facilitate self-destruction. Proponents of this explanation point to the fact that suicide rates among Roman Catholics, who explicitly condemn suicide, are much lower than suicide rates among Protestants, who do not condemn it as strongly. But the societal reaction theory is not helpful in shedding light on other variations in suicide rates. For example, there is no reason to believe that people in the United States are more accepting of suicide among men than among women, among the old as opposed to the young, or among the poor as opposed to the affluent.

▲ The Meaning of Suicide

The failure of sociologists to explain variations in suicide rates should be evident. Despite the hints provided by Durkheim and the efforts by many sociologists to reformulate and test his ideas, existing explanations are inadequate. Recognizing this, and concerned by sociologists' willingness to use questionable official statistics to test their hypotheses about suicide, Jack Douglas (1971) proposed an entirely different approach, based on the "meaning" of suicide to persons who take their lives.

In effect, Douglas has called for investigation of the motives or intentions that underlie individual acts of suicide, a sociological point of view more recent sociologists refer to as **standpoint theory** (Smith 1999). In calling for sociologists to study the meaning of suicide, he has suggested that research should focus on the goals and objectives that suicidal persons are trying to fulfill through their behavior. In other words, we should view those who die by suicide as actors, rather than as those who have been acted upon by society.

In Douglas's view, the meaning of suicide can best be ascertained by examining a sample of individual cases. Researchers can document patterns of verbal and nonverbal communication of the suicide victim and of any others involved in the death situation. Douglas attempted to illustrate how this might be done. However, he was forced to rely on published case reports, thereby opening up the question of the reliability of such reports and of those who wrote them. Nevertheless, Douglas is one of the few sociologists who have examined the social determinants of individual suicides, rather than searching for explanations for variations in suicide rates.

▲ Suicide and Imitation

In recent years some sociologists have theorized that news stories about suicide and suicide fatalities foster imitative behaviors, or **copycat suicides.** Several studies have examined the effects of newspaper accounts and found that suicides increase in the aftermath of such reporting (Lester 2000). For example, Steven Stack (1987) demonstrated that highly publicized suicide stories involving celebrities with whom many people identify seem to foster suicide deaths. In particular, deaths of political heroes and entertainers have such an effect. The reasons remain speculative, and no one knows whether such imitative suicides represent any more than a tiny minority of the total suicides that occur.

In response to so-called epidemics of suicide among clusters of adolescents in different communities around the country, some have asked if suicide can be considered "contagious." Suicide, it is thought, may contain an imitative component for some adolescents. Researchers have found evidence that "exposure to the suicide or suicidal behavior of one or more persons influences others to commit suicide" (*Morbidity and Mortality Weekly Report* 1994:13), and that such influence seems to be particularly strong for adolescents. Sources of influence include the reporting that takes place in the news media, as well as school and community expressions of grief. To discourage contagion, experts now recommend that the media, community, and schools limit the attention given to suicides to avoid even indirectly sensationalizing, glorifying, or legitimizing this behavior.

Other Explanations

Investigators have studied many factors in a search for correlates of overall suicide rates (Lester 2000). For example, suicide rates tend to vary in accordance with the days of the week and month. More suicides occur on Mondays than on other days, and most suicides take place early in the month. Suicides also tend to take place in the spring and in the fall. But such temporal variations often do not always hold when researchers look at suicides by race, sex, residence, and so forth. The reasons why are not known.

At times researchers have investigated some rather unusual factors, hoping that they will shed some light on suicide rates. For example, research has been conducted to determine the relationship between suicide rates and phases of the moon, as well as any correlations between suicide and people's birthdays and astrological signs. No consistent relationships have been discovered.

The Unanswerable Question: Why?

Despite the accumulation of statistical data and other evidence bearing on completed suicides, social scientists continue to debate the causes of this phenomenon. Almost 30 years ago one expert in suicidology, Louis Wekstein (1979:13), noted that "research to date has neither unearthed nor revealed what possesses some individuals to effectuate their own demise and why such a desperate course of action is dictated." His statement is still very true today.

A major problem that continues to plague researchers is the quantity and quality of the data with which they have to work. Only recently have sociologists begun to mobilize studies that allow sufficient data to be generated to begin shedding more light on suicide. Nonetheless, the basic question of "Why?" may continue to elude social scientists for some time to come.

The Question of Attempted Suicide

As we noted earlier, most of the efforts to explain suicide have been limited to completed suicides, ignoring the question of attempted suicide or *parasuicide* (Kreitman 1977). Yet an estimated 10 times as many persons are thought to make unsuccessful suicide attempts. Perhaps 5 million people in the United States are currently living after having made one or more attempts to die. Unfortunately there are no official statistics on attempted suicides; available information generally comes from hospitals and/or from physicians. These people probably never hear of a significant number of cases. For example, an act of attempted suicide may result in only minor injury. Many such attempts may be intentionally concealed. Finally, it may be difficult to judge whether an attempted suicide has indeed taken place (as opposed, for example, to an accident). Thus our knowledge of attempted

suicide remains very limited, as do explanations for it.

Women are more likely to attempt suicide than men, and women who attempt suicide are likely to be younger than men who do so. Women are also more likely to make repeated attempts than men and to use less lethal methods. Attempts are thought to be most frequent among housewives, in comparison with other groups of women (Jack 1992).

Researchers have not been able to explain these differences between the sexes. Some have suggested that women use less lethal methods because they are less aggressive or more concerned with their appearance after death than men. It has been hypothesized that women often survive suicide attempts because they are the biologically "stronger sex" (which probably means that women generally live longer than men). But none of these observations gets at the question of why so many women attempt suicide in the first place.

One of the few other things we know is that attempted suicide is apparently correlated with age. The average age of persons who attempt suicide is much younger than the average age of those who complete suicide. Estimates are that for every completed suicide among adolescents there may be 200 to 300 attempted suicides. By contrast, among the elderly it is estimated that there are four attempts to every completed suicide (McIntosh 1992b). Again, there is a difference in lethality of methods, with adolescents tending to use the least lethal methods. Moreover, it is thought that suicidal behavior among the young is more likely to be impulsive and less likely to be premeditated. As with women, there is no real consensus about why the young attempt suicide so frequently.

The lack of reliable statistical information hampers our knowledge of attempted suicides. Also, there is disagreement over whether completed and attempted suicides involve the same types of people. Do people who attempt suicide and those who complete it make up two distinct groups possessing quite different characteristics? Since most persons who complete suicide have made one or more previous attempts, but relatively few who attempt suicide ultimately kill themselves, researchers have taken a middle position. It is thought that two distinct groups do exist, but that their memberships overlap to some degree. Thus, one can learn little about one of these groups by studying the other. But some researchers believe that this position is erroneous, arguing that more information about both attempted and completed suicides is crucial to an understanding of each (Maris et al. 1992).

Suicide Prevention

At the start of this chapter, we noted that most people in the United States view suicide as an unnatural and abnormal act, possibly linked with mental illness. This view, which draws attention away from the societal context within which people move toward suicide, underlies suicide prevention programs. They view the individual as the problem, not the society. In this section we look at these programs and consider the debate over whether people have the right to choose death over life.

Suicide Prevention Centers

Approaches to preventing suicide range from counseling by clergy and mental health practitioners to pleas by police officers called to the scene of suicide attempts. In the last several decades, communities around the country have instituted organized efforts to prevent suicide, setting up suicide prevention centers and other crisis projects that try to assist troubled people.

Suicide prevention centers vary greatly in size, resources, and services, and their effectiveness is very difficult to assess (Neimeyer and Pfeiffer 1994). Even as more centers have opened, many with the help of governmental financing, the overall number of suicides in the United

States has been increasing. It is possible that the presence of such centers—particularly the research involvement of a few—has promoted more careful investigations and record keeping on causes of deaths. Thus, instead of an increase in suicides, we could simply be seeing better detection and recording by medical officials.

Research on the effectiveness of suicide prevention centers indicates that their presence does have some effect on the rates of suicide, although the effect is not a strong one. Such centers have tended to be set up in states with high suicide rates. Those states with more suicide prevention centers and more centers per capita have been found to have experienced less of a rate increase than other states (Lester 1991, 1993). Although suicide prevention centers have not made a dramatic dent in the number of suicides that occur, their services are no doubt of assistance to those with whom they interact.

Suicide prevention centers seek to keep people from taking their lives by being ready to assist anyone who voluntarily contacts them. Thus, such centers probably come into contact with or learn of only a small percentage of those who attempt and/or complete suicide. Their effectiveness therefore depends largely on how well they handle this minority.

Often workers at suicide prevention centers have very limited contact with potentially suicidal individuals, perhaps just a telephone conversation with the person or concerned family members or friends. Workers thus must rely on guidelines to help them determine how to approach the cases at hand. For example, some centers use a version of guidelines developed by psychologist Edwin S. Shneidman (1968), one of the founders of the well-known Los Angeles Suicide Prevention Center:

1. Persons who are contemplating suicide wish to be stopped or rescued before death. They are mentally torn between wanting to live and wanting to die and can be pushed toward living.

2. Contemplation of suicide occurs during a period of extreme crisis that may be relatively brief in duration. If the suicidal individual can be gotten through the crisis, the probability of suicide is minimized.

3. Persons who are about to kill themselves are almost always fully conscious of their intentions, although they may not communicate these intentions directly. Few people are unconscious of their intentions.

4. Suicidal behavior usually stems from a sense of isolation and is an act to stop an intolerable existence. Since people define "intolerable" differently, prevention efforts must take into account the perspective of the potential suicide.

Shneidman (1987) has pointed out that almost all those who kill themselves drop **prodromal clues** before doing so. That is, they signal their suicidal thoughts to others, often days or weeks before taking steps to die. Such clues may be verbal, involving direct or indirect statements of suicidal intentions. Or they may be behavioral, as when an individual makes a will and sets affairs in order, or actually makes a "practice run" in planning death. Prodromal clues may also be situational; for example, an individual is obviously caught up in conditions involving a great deal of stress-produced anxiety. Finally, the clues may be "prodromatic"; that is, a person appears to be deeply depressed, disoriented, or defiant. Though some persons kill themselves on impulse, Shneidman suggests that even in such cases some kind of warning is given beforehand. In Shneidman's view, perhaps 80 percent of those who take their own lives communicate intent. The problem is that the communications may go unrecognized or even ignored.

After suicide prevention center workers have used these or other guidelines and have decided that an individual who phones is suicidal, they ordinarily try to talk the person through the crisis period. They may attempt to convince the

individual to seek out counseling or therapy. If they learn the identity of the individual, they may contact family, friends, or others who can intervene and secure assistance for the suicide-prone person. Therapy typically involves psychiatric treatment and/or drugs. In extreme cases, the suicidal individual may be involuntarily hospitalized for observation and treatment.

The ultimate goal of suicide prevention centers and other treatment services is to enable people to function in the prevailing social order. Thus, suicide prevention and therapy do not touch on the question of social changes that might reduce the frequency of self-initiated deaths. Speaking from a sociological perspective, Jack P. Gibbs (1971:311–12) stated:

If any theory on the suicide rate is valid, then conceivably the volume of suicide could be reduced substantially by deliberate social change. However, most theories deal with such basic structural components of society that few policymakers would contemplate making changes, let alone succeed. Further, neither policymakers nor the public is likely to view the "cost" of suicide as sufficiently great to justify undertaking any major remedial action. So in the final analysis, there appears to be only one way to reduce the incidence of suicide, and that is by instituting prevention programs that focus on individual cases.

We cannot share Gibbs's pessimism about the possibility of social changes that will reduce suicide. To write this possibility off, as Gibbs does, is to ensure that such changes will never take place.

Rational Suicide: Is There a Right to Die?

As mentioned, the goal of suicide prevention programs is the preservation of individual lives, no matter what the circumstances. Workers in such programs believe that they know what is

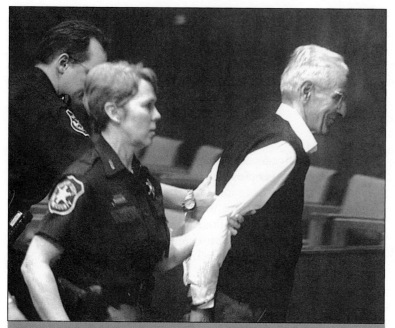

Should doctors be permitted to assist terminally ill patients who wish to take their own lives? This issue has been debated nationally in response to the actions of Dr. Jack Kevorkian, a retired Michigan pathologist. Dr. Kevorkian assisted in the suicides of several people in defiance of legislative attempts to ban doctor-assisted suicides in that state. Here, he is being arrested for violating that ban.

best for the suicide-prone. The basic precept of suicide prevention is that life is preferable to death and suicide is a form of deviant behavior that must be fought.

Contrasted to these beliefs is the fact that many members of our society seem to find good reason to kill themselves. Psychologist David Lester (1972:325–26) put it this way: "Suicide is a way of living, a way of coping with problems that arise from living, and for many people it is a way of achieving a better life or avoiding a worse life." Though we can all appreciate the pro-life thrust of suicide prevention efforts, it seems valid to consider whether people also have a right to die. A related question is whether there are circumstances under which suicide is rational behavior and efforts to prevent it irrational. Though we cannot provide definitive answers to these

questions, we believe them worthy of consideration.

Despite the voluminous literature on suicide, most experts believe that it must be prevented—if only to keep from losing persons who might otherwise make a contribution to society. But in recent years a debate has arisen in the United States and elsewhere around what has been called **rational suicide** (Szasz 1986). This term was used more than 30 years ago by Jacques Choron (1972), who defined it as suicidal behavior on the part of those who are mentally normal (so far as can be judged), whose reasoning powers are not impaired, and whose motives can be considered justified. To Choron (1972:97), justification refers to "approval by contemporaries, in the sense of their agreeing that in similar circumstances they might have done the same thing." With regard to such persons, it could be argued that suicide prevention efforts are misdirected or inappropriate. Perhaps, some now say, their decisions should be accepted (Singer 1995; Werth 1995).

▲ Political Suicide

One form of rational suicide can be termed **political suicide,** or the intentional taking of one's own life for political reasons (Crosby, Rhee, and Holland 1997). An increasing number of individuals have intentionally strapped explosives to their own bodies to detonate them in crowded markets, buses, trains, clubs, and cafés. Others have deliberately planned, trained, and executed strategies that required them to pilot fully fueled planes into the World Trade Center and the Pentagon in the infamous September 11,

2001, bombings. In the past two decades, at least 300 suicide attacks have occurred, involving 15 different terrorist organizations and 15 nations around the world as part of organized protests (Poland 2003).

Clearly, these actions guarantee the death of the individual engaged in the missions, but they also are calculated to exact as high a toll on others as possible and to plunge the population into chaos and vulnerability. The point of the suicide is a political statement or objective, not just the end of the individual suicide's own life. Studies indicate that these are not impulsive actions or the last resort of mentally ill individuals. Rather, these are rationally planned, carefully strategized, and enacted by individuals, often as members of a political organization.

For some, the suicide mission is an act of religious faith: To sacrifice one's life in the name of the cause is an act of **martyrdom** that will be justly rewarded in the afterlife. In some instances, surviving family members of the martyr are rewarded in the here and now monetarily by the sponsoring organization or state. In such cases, a strong connection to one's faith or to political organizations devoted to resisting what they see as oppression actually enhances the chances of suicide rather than acting, as Durkheim predicted, as a deterrent (Pedahzur, Perliger, and Weinberg 2003).

Participation in suicide missions in the name of the cause, then, becomes a rational decision by individuals who firmly believe in the goals of the group and are convinced of the power of suicide as a political strategy. This is not unlike members of the military who have intentionally put themselves in situations of almost certain death in the name of sacrifice for one's country or loyalty to cause. In either case, the act constitutes a political suicide, undertaken consciously and deliberately in the name of a political objective.

▲ Euthanatic Suicide

The debate over the notion and acceptability of rational suicide by the terminally ill has received impetus from the mass media attention given to the actions of Dr. Jack Kevorkian, a retired pathologist who began assisting people to die in Michigan in 1990 and had helped more than 30 by 1996. Dr. Kevorkian's **assisted suicides** involved men and women suffering from terminal illnesses who have expressed a wish to end their lives. He provided them with the means to painlessly kill themselves using simple technology that the media sensationalized as a "suicide machine." Michigan courts have ruled that people have no constitutional right to assisted suicide and found it to be illegal under Michigan common law, a ruling the U.S. Supreme Court refused to review. Despite legal actions to block him, Dr. Kevorkian went ahead with his activities, even opening up a clinic where people from other states could come to die. Public opinion polls in Michigan indicated a good deal of public support for his assisted suicides (*Los Angeles Times* 1995; Peterson, 1995).

The philosophy or ideology of suicide prevention leaves no room for rational suicides of any type. When their intentions become known, people with terminal illnesses who express the wish to commit suicide are typically the focus of attempts to preserve their lives. But alternative ways of thinking are being entertained. And medical personnel do frequently take actions or avoid taking actions so as to hasten the deaths of suffering people, even if they do not assist in self-inflicted deaths. However, more and more doctors are discussing the desirability of legitimizing and establishing guidelines for physician-assisted suicide (Quill 1994).

Physician-assisted suicides (as well as **euthanasia** or **mercy killing**) became legal in the Netherlands in 1993, and the Oregon state legislature passed a law permitting assisted suicides in 1994. In Oregon, doctors may prescribe lethal drugs for patients judged to be in their last 6 months of life. While public opinion polls indicate that people in the United States are generally supportive of assisted suicide for those who are suffering and are terminally ill, laws like that in Oregon have not been successfully introduced or passed in other states. Critics, such as suicidologist Herbert Hendin, see such legislation as encouraging people to prematurely choose death over life and as opening up all kinds of opportunities for abuse (Hendin 1995a, 1995b).

Suicide prevention workers are sometimes faced with elderly and/or severely ill persons who indicate intentions to undertake **euthanatic suicide**—in Choron's terms, "easy dying." In such cases, asks Choron (1972:104–5): "Should not the multitudes who die painfully and miserably each year be allowed to decide for themselves what is best for them?" In our society, this question is being more widely debated. The idea that the right to die should be legally protected, and that the means for a quick and painless death should be provided to people on request, is highly controversial. Meanwhile, many persons do undertake "easy dying" without legal sanction—often unsuccessfully or by violent means:

It would be too much to expect that resistance to the idea of euthanatic suicide will be easily overcome. The most important step in that direction is the realization that considering suicide the wrong cure for the ills of the living does not necessarily exclude the possibility that it may be the right cure for the ills of the dying. (Choron 1972:106)

Some would argue that the right to take one's life belongs to any who are terminally ill, while others would extend it to those who are aging. Still others would extend this right to any who prefer death over life. There are those who go so far as to advocate support, encouragement, and even technical help to potential suicides. Handbooks have been published to educate people about the various methods available to kill themselves, thus helping to intensify the debate (Humphry 1992).

We have not presented this discussion because we are against suicide prevention or because we favor the right to die. But in the absence of societal changes that might reduce the volume of suicide, much of it might be viewed as rational. Only when we begin to search for the rational components of self-initiated death—its "meaning," in sociologist Jack Douglas's terms—will more people begin to ask: What is it about the organization and operation of U.S. society that leads so many to suicidal behavior? We must begin to ask this question if, at some future time, thousands of people are to avoid concluding:

In this life it's not difficult to die. To make life is more difficult by far. (Mayakovsky 1965:350)

Summary

Each year tens of thousands of people in the United States take their own lives. Official statistics no doubt underreport the actual number of suicides. Often it is difficult to determine the actual cause of a person's death. Moreover, the fact of suicide may be concealed and death attributed to other causes. There is no way to know how extensive underreporting is.

Official statistics indicate that the suicide rate has been relatively constant over the years, although increases have occurred recently (especially among young people). Older adults are more likely to take their lives than the young, men more than women, whites more than racial minority group members, and Protestants more than Catholics or Jews. Single, widowed, and divorced persons commit suicide at a higher rate than those who are married and living with their mates. City dwellers take their lives at about the same rate as rural residents. Data on occupations and suicide are mixed, but it is thought that the unemployed have higher rates than the employed.

A variety of explanations have been offered for why people kill themselves. Some researchers have sought to find indications that those who commit suicide differ physically from others and have suggested that genetic factors are involved. Others have offered explanations based on the presumed mental states of suicide victims, suggesting that such persons are mentally abnormal. Finally, it has been suggested that societal forces are involved in pushing people toward suicide and that suicide may have a special social and cultural meaning to its victims.

Attempted suicide is thought to be 10 times more frequent than completed suicide. Unfortunately, there are no official statistics on suicide attempts. It is known that women and the young make the most attempts and that they tend to use less lethal methods than men and older adults. There is controversy over whether completed and attempted suicides involve the same types of people.

In the last few decades, communities across the country have instituted organized efforts to prevent suicide. Suicide prevention centers have been established, but their effectiveness in lowering suicide rates has been limited. Such centers probably come into contact with or learn of only a small percentage of those who attempt and/or complete suicide. However, prevention efforts are not uncontroversial, and may indeed be inappropriate or irrelevant when it comes to rational suicides. While efforts to prevent suicides go on, some have suggested that people might have a right to choose death over life. Are there not circumstances under which suicide is rational behavior and efforts to prevent it irrational?

Key Terms

Discussion Questions

1. What are the attitudes of people you know toward those who would attempt or complete the act of suicide? To what degree do you share these attitudes?

2. Do you think people should have the right to take their own lives if they wish? If so, should this be an absolute right or are there certain conditions you would attach?

3. If you assist a person in committing a suicidal act, you may be accused of a crime. Can you think of any circumstances under which you would violate the law in this way?

4. Your doctor tells you that by quitting smoking and losing excess weight you may add years to your life. You fail to heed your doctor's advice. Is this the same as committing suicide? Why?

5. According to official statistics, the suicide rate among African American adolescents and children has been increasing dramatically. Speculate on why this is the case.

6. Visit a local suicide or crisis prevention center that often handles calls from persons who are potentially suicidal. On the basis of what the staff is able to tell you about the content of such calls, develop your own explanation for why people kill themselves. (Remember, however, that the center may have contact with only a small percentage of potential suicides.)

Suggested Readings

Emanuel, Linda L., ed. *Regulating How We Die: The Ethical, Medical, and Legal Issues Surrounding Physician-Assisted Suicide* (Cambridge, MA: Harvard University Press, 1998).
Anthology of clashing viewpoints on euthanatic suicide.

Faberow, Norman L., ed. *The Many Faces of Suicide* (New York: McGraw-Hill, 1980).
Consideration of a variety of self-destructive behaviors not commonly classified as "suicide."

Hendin, Herbert. *Suicide in America.* 2d ed. (New York: W. W. Norton, 1995).
Overview of the nature and dimensions of the problem of suicide in the United States and issues surrounding the "right to die."

Lester, David. *Why People Kill Themselves.* 4th ed. (Springfield, IL: Charles C. Thomas, 2000).
Summaries of research findings on suicidal behavior (supplements the contents of the 1972, 1983, and 1992 editions).

Long, Robert Emmet, ed. *Suicide* (New York: H. W. Wilson Company, 1995).
Articles on various aspects of suicide, with special attention to youth suicide.

Maris, Ronald W., Alan L. Berman, John T. Maltsberger, and Robert I. Yufit, eds. *Assessment and Prediction of Suicide* (New York: Guilford Press, 1992).
Addresses issues that arise in defining suicidal behavior and in determining the characteristics of those who are most likely to take their own lives.

Slaby, Andrew, and Lili Frank Garfinkel. *No One Saw My Pain: Why Teens Kill Themselves.* (New York: W.W. Norton, 1996).
Case studies of eight families whose child committed suicide, with the common observation that hints of their child's intent were dismissed or overlooked.

glossary

A

abuse The use of force or violent language against a person.

abusive violence Violence in a family that is considered serious enough to cause physical harm.

academic boot camp Term referring to kindergarten in which educators work to teach the student role (behaviors and attitudes) to children.

academic track A plan of study and instruction for students grouped on the basis of the presumption that their past classroom performance and standardized test scores are valid indicators of their ability and potential; for example, schools may divide students into academic (college-bound) and vocational (employment-bound) tracks.

acquaintance rape/date rape The terms referring to sexual coercion or abuse by an assailant who is known to the victim.

activity theory An interactionist theory of aging that argues that elderly people who remain active and socially involved will be best-adjusted.

affirmative action Regulations requiring that employers or educational institutions not discriminate in hiring or enrollment and that they take positive steps to increase the number of members of racial minority groups and women in their applicant pools.

age consciousness Awareness of common interests based on age, often prompting attempts to advance these interests through societywide mobilization.

ageism Prejudice and discrimination based on a person's age.

aggravated assault Any of various assaults that are more serious than a common assault, especially one performed with intent to commit a crime.

alcohol dependence Alcoholism; refers to a disease that is characterized by abnormal alcohol-seeking behavior that leads to impaired control over drinking.

alcoholic personality Alcoholics who are presumably maladjusted, immature, dependent on others, negative in their views of themselves, suffering from guilt feelings, and incapable of tolerating tension and frustration.

alcoholics Persons who exhibit numerous symptoms of problem drinking.

alienation A condition of estrangement or disassociation from family or society.

anomic suicide Suicide as a result of weak social integration or contradictory messages given to an individual by the social group or groups they belong to.

anomie A sense of disorientation felt in a society when social control of individual behavior is ineffective.

anomie theory The theory that many forms of deviance are caused by a disjunction between society's goals and the approved means to achieve these goals.

assimilation Forsaking one's own cultural traditions in order to become part of a different culture.

assisted suicides Completion of suicide by a terminally ill or suffering individual with the aid of a physician or other clinician.

Attention Deficit Hyperactivity Disorder (ADHD) A type of impaired brain function which causes a lack of attention and increased hyperactivity.

B

binge drinking Five or more drinks on the same occasion at least once per month.

biology is destiny The idea that women's and men's different physical characteristics, reproductive roles, and hormones predetermine characteristics like intelligence, strength, temperament, leadership abilities, and emotions.

birthrate Number of live births per 1,000 population in a given year.

bisexual People who find themselves sexually attracted to members of both sexes.

borderless crimes Violations of law which transcend national boundaries.

brain drain Migration of skilled workers and professionals who are needed in their home countries to other nations.

bureaucracy A component of formal organization that uses rules and hierarchical ranking to achieve efficiency.

business dominance perspective The view that the state is not a neutral arbiter of the common good because capitalists have captured it and use it to further their own interests.

C

capitalist economy An economic system characterized by an arrangement of production in which workers cooperate to produce wealth that is then privately owned by whoever hired the workers.

capital punishment The death penalty; execution by the state.

catastrophic leave policy A policy allowing workers to donate accumulated vacation, personal, and sick days to an account for use by a fellow employee facing a devastating family crisis.

child abuse The use of violence against a child by adults, especially those in positions of authority over the child, such as a parent/guardian or other family member, teacher, religious or community leader, police, etc.

child support Court-ordered payment by the noncustodial parent to the custodial parent or guardian after divorce or separation.

claims process Political process of moving the socially constructed line between the natural and biological aspects of gender.

clearcutting Practice of logging in which large areas are stripped of all trees.

club drugs Substances commonly used by young adults and teenagers at dance clubs, bars, and raves.

comparable worth A policy in which people who perform similar work requiring similar skills and training receive the same wages.

competitive individualism The belief that individuals are completely responsible for their own economic condition so that economic success (wealth) or failure (poverty) is the result of individual effort.

computer crime Illegal activity involving the use of or attacks against computers.

conflict theory of legal change Theory that alterations in laws are rooted in conflicts between groups or social classes.

containment theory A social-psychological explanation that suggests that deviant behavior is limited in society because of internal (personal) and external (societal) controls that contain the behavior of individuals.

contingency work force Workers who are hired for temporary, part-time, or "contracted" employment only for the duration of the project.

copycat suicides A duplication of another suicide that the person attempting suicide learned of from either local knowledge or media coverage.

corporate capitalism A capitalist economy in which a few large firms dominate most product and service activities.

corporate crimes Violations of the law that are matters of institutional practice or standard operating procedures that largely benefit the corporation or organization.

corporatization of medicine A trend in health care in which large private firms have entered the health-care services field for the purpose of making a profit.

correctional-industrial complex Structure in which various vested interests benefit from corrections institutions—from politicians who are elected on platforms of "getting tough on crime" to the construction companies and manufacturers that contract to build, equip, and supply the burgeoning prisons.

crime Acts that are intentional, inexcusable or indefensible, in violation of an existing law, and punishable by the state.

crime problem Violations such as larceny, burglary, robbery, auto theft, assault, rape, murder, and arson viewed by members of society as serious and problematic.

crime rates The ratio of crimes in an area to the population of that area; nationally, expressed per 100,000 population per year.

critical approach An approach to the study of society which examines societal, group, and institutional arrangements that often privilege the interests of some members of society and harm others.

cultural theory of drug use The idea that people will use illegal drugs when they have the opportunity to do so.

culture of poverty The theory that certain groups and individuals tend to persist in a state of poverty because they have distinct beliefs, values, and ways of behaving that are incompatible with economic success.

custodial parent The parent who takes over the legal responsibility for the child/children.

D

date rape The use of force to compel the victim to engage in a sexual act with someone the victim knows or is familiar with.

death rate The number of deaths per 1,000 population in a given year.

death row A cellblock in a prison whose prisoners sentenced to the death penalty await their execution.

death row syndrome Situation in which an extended stay on death row can reduce prisoners' will to live and can actually convince them of their own guilt even if they are innocent.

deindustrialization A practice of systematic withdrawal of investment in productive facilities such as factories and plants from specific geographic areas.

deinstitutionalization A practice of releasing psychiatric patients from mental institutions into local communities.

delinquent subcultures "Support groups" or gangs formed by youths due to the gap between cultural success goals and opportunities to pursue these.

democracy A system of government where citizens have equal legal rights to vote in free elections.

differential association theory A social-psychological explanation for deviant behavior that suggests that such behavior results from an individual associating with people who are already disposed toward deviant behavior.

disengagement theory the view that it is natural for all elderly people to withdraw from the social roles they occupied when they were younger because of inevitable biological and psychological decline.

disinformation Deliberately inaccurate or false information designed to create divisions within and between groups or to create false public perceptions.

divorce rate The number of divorces per 1,000 persons in the population.

domestic code The view that assumes that men will work and support women and children who remain in the home.

double or triple shift A situation in which women who work full time also perform most or all of the domestic chores at home (double shift), as well as informal or voluntary work in the community (triple shift).

downsizing Practice of employers consolidating or eliminating positions as part of deindustrialization.

drive-through deliveries Practice of hospitals in which mothers and newborns are released quickly from the hospital following birth, often the result of cost-cutting by insurance companies.

drug Any substance other than food which by its chemical nature affects the structure or function of the living organism.

dry communities Places where the sale of alcoholic beverages is illegal.

dual labor market Labor market structure in which men and women commonly are employed in distinctly different job categories.

E

ecosystem A self-sustaining community within a natural environment in which each living organism serves functions that have a bearing on the system as a whole.

ectomorphs Thin and fragile individuals with introverted personalities.

ego As described by Freud, the rational self that controls the urges of the individual.

egoistic suicides Suicides due to the absence of meaningful social relationships or a sense of belonging.

elder abuse Physical and/or mental violence against elders by members of their own families or households.

electronic vandalism Acts of criminals who hack into computer systems, send e-mails spreading viruses, and damage programs.

endomorphs Soft and fat individuals with submissive personalities.

environmental abuse Human activities that harm the environment, from dirtying the atmosphere to depleting irreplaceable resources.

environmental racism The dumping of toxic wastes in racial minority communities to a disproportionate degree compared to dumping in other areas..

ethnic group People who share a national origin and distinctive cultural patterns.

euthanasia or mercy killing The act of bringing about a quick and painless death to a terminally ill and suffering person.

euthanatic suicide The active acceleration of a "good" death by use of drugs etc., whether by oneself or with the aid of a doctor.

experimental research Research conducted to determine how a particular person or group is affected by different types of treatment or conditions selected by the researcher.

F

fall from grace Term used to describe the serious decline in a middle class person's standard of living, often the result of downsizing or other workplace changes beyond the individual's control.

fatalistic suicide People kill themselves out of a sense of over manipulation or of hopelessness about altering their life conditions.

feminist movement A social movement fostering awareness of the sources of gender inequality.

feminization of poverty A situation in which a growing percentage of the poor live in female-headed households; subtly suggests that women choose to be poor and stay on welfare or somehow bring poverty on themselves.

fetal alcohol syndrome Refers to certain birth defects, and serious, life-long mental and emotional impairments that may be suffered by a fetus as the result of heavy alcohol consumption by its mother during pregnancy.

field research Research conducted at the place where the subjects are located so that the researcher may gain information through first-hand observation.

flextime An arrangement that allows employees to set their own schedules (starting and quitting time) to accommodate demands outside employment.

functional psychoses A condition in which thought, behavior, and emotion are disturbed without known pathological changes in tissues or the conditions of the brain.

G

gatekeeper A person or system controlling access and opportunities; e.g., in education.

gateway drug A habit-forming substance whose use may precede the abuse of drugs that are more addictive or more dangerous.

gender The category of masculine or feminine, determined by societal expectations for behavior and ways of relating to others based on sex.

genocide The systematic extermination of an entire people or nation by dominants in society who consider themselves to be biologically or culturally superior.

glass ceiling An invisible barrier that blocks the promotion of a qualified individual in a work environment because of the individual's gender, race, or ethnicity.

graying of America A trend in which the population of American elderly people is increasing.

greenhouse effect An increase in the earth's temperature that results when carbon dioxide is released and trapped in the atmosphere; occurs, for example, when fossil fuels are burned.

group problems Social problems that affect the life chances of millions of people based on their ascribed statuses, particularly class and poverty, racial and ethnic heritages, gender, sexual orientation, and age.

gun control Regulation of the sale and use of rifles and handguns.

H

heteronormativity A social construction that privileges heterosexuality as the norm governing the treatment of individuals and their status and participation in society.

heterosexism Discrimination or prejudice against lesbians, gay men, and bisexuals by heterosexual people.

home schooling The practice of teaching children in the home as an alternative to attending public or private elementary or high school.

homohatred Occurs when members of the heterosexual majority display prejudicial attitudes and engage in discriminatory actions that demonstrate their dislike of and contempt for persons who are gay.

homophobia The fear of and prejudice against homosexuality.

I

id As described by Freud, a primitive, almost feral self that compels individuals to focus on their own personal pleasure.

identity theft Stealing the identity of others by using their credit card, driver's license, social security or other personal identification numbers.

illicit drugs Substances that have been formally declared by the government as illegal.

illiteracy The lack of ability to read and write well enough to succeed in society.

impoverishment of women and children A term that refers to institutional forces that systematically make women and children poor.

impression management Refers to the altering of the presentation of the self in order to create distinctive appearances and satisfy particular audiences.

imprisonment binge The policy of placing increasing numbers of people in prisons.

income Money received in the form of hourly wages or annual salaries, or government benefits, or return on investments.

index offenses Serious law violations counted by Justice Department for its annual Uniform Crime Reports.

index of segregation The simple, single measure of the level of sex segregation in occupations which tells us what it would take to achieve an equal distribution of female and male workers throughout the occupational classifications.

individualistic, psychological theory The idea that individuals use illegal drugs because they have psychological deficiencies, character disorders, or personal maladjustments. According to this theory, "normal" people are not attracted to such drugs even when they are available.

individual problems Personal difficulties which arise from the action of individuals; such personal problems are commonly within the control of individuals.

infant mortality rate The number of deaths of infants under one year of age per 1,000 live births in a given year.

informal organization A social structure that emerges spontaneously as people interact in bureaucratic or formal organizational settings.

insanity The condition of being in some way mentally "out of touch" with the real world or with "normal" human functioning, often assumed to be a result of a mental illness.

institution Refers to an organizational structure created to perform certain services or tasks within a society.

institutional problems Social problems that derive from the way that social institutions are arranged to address the basic needs of social survival.

institutional racism Racial prejudice or discrimination embedded in the routine functioning of societal institutions.

institutional sexism Prejudicial or discriminatory practices that foster advantages for males and that accompany the routine operations of societal institutions.

involuntary part-time workers People who need and want full time jobs but can only find part-time work.

J

job satisfaction The measure given by the employee rating the content of the job, the resources to do it well, a chance to realize one's talents, and also pay.

justice juggernaut Correctional-industrial complex relations that have become so strong as to be difficult to control.

juvenile delinquents Individuals in trouble with the law between seven and sixteen or eighteen years of age, often considered to be less responsible for their behavior than adults.

L

labeling theory A theory of deviance that draws attention to how people come to be labeled as deviants and the impact of this label on such individuals and their subsequent behavior.

labor force Consists of people who are sixteen years of age or older (with the exception of inmates of institutions) who have a full-time or part-time job or have been actively seeking work in the four-week period prior to the Labor Department's monthly unemployment survey.

latent functions An unintended and sometimes unrecognized results that are produced as institutions carry out their manifest functions.

learned behavior theory The theory that people learn attitudes and modes of behavior through social interaction.

legal drugs Prescription and over-the-counter drugs.

life expectancy The average number of years a group of people all born in the same year are expected to live.

M

macro problems Large-scale social problems arising out of societal dynamics, inequalities between groups, and the failure of institutions to meet people's needs; systemic conditions that limit the life chances of millions of people.

mala in se Crimes that are considered evil in and of themselves.

male chauvinism A form of sexism through which men express the belief that males are superior to females and have a right to insist on the subordination of females.

malingering The purposeful exaggeration of physical or psychological complaints in order to receive some kind of reward.

malthusian logic The argument that population growth produces poverty.

managed care A system in which large health insurance companies impose strict limits on the types and amounts of services they will cover.

manifest functions The basic social needs an institution is intended to address.

marital dissolution Breakup of a marriage because of divorce, desertion, or death.

marketability The demand for a workforce members' labor by public and private employers.

martyrdom The sacrifice of one's life in the name of a cause.

masculinization of wealth The notion that institutional arrangements systematically reward men economically more than women.

massification Process in which the public becomes increasingly unable to define and act on its own political interests because of manipulation by the powerful.

"Mcdonaldization" of health care The trend in health care in which hospitals in the United States are increasingly being run for profit.

medical-industrial complex Set of power relations in the health care industry which privilege profit-making interests over nonprofit interests; has typically encouraged increases in the number of investor-owned, for-profit private hospitals; growth in the size of firms that lease or own hospitals that are run as chains; expansion of for-profit operators of health care plans; private investor and corporate expansion into nursing homes, home health services, and local surgical centers and clinics; and movement by investor-owned hospitals into such areas as private health insurance.

medical model The theory that mental troubles are matters of health, rather than the result of demonic "possession," moral defectiveness, or witchcraft.

mental illness A disorder of the brain that disrupts a person's thinking, feeling, and ability to interact with others.

mental illness as political event The notion that those with medical, legal, and moral authority are in a position to cast an individual into the role of sick person.

meritocracy A system in which individuals' gain rewards based entirely on their efforts and merit.

mesomorphs Muscular and tough individuals with assertive personalities.

micro problems Behaviors on the part of individuals that are self-harmful and/or harmful to others; e.g., criminal behavior, alcoholism, and suicide, may be caused or set in motion by macro problems.

militarized Congress Situation in which military expenditures are privileged in Congress relative to other budgetary demands because of the political, social, and economic relationships between many members of Congress and the military.

military-industrial complex A group, composed of the uniformed military, the aerospace-defense industry, the civilian national security managers, and the U.S. Congress, that works to advance the interests of each member while simultaneously promoting and reinforcing the interests of the others.

minimal brain dysfunction A condition characterized by behavioral and learning disorders.

minority An ethnic, racial, religious, or other group having little power or representation relative to other groups within a society.

model minority A minority group whose members are noted by the general public of the country in which they reside for typically achieving a higher degree of success than other minorities in business, income-earning potential, education, and other factors, presumably as a result of their cultural values rather than structural advantages.

mommy track A career path determined by work arrangements offering mothers certain benefits, such as flexible hours, but usually providing them with fewer opportunities for advancement.

mood disorders A condition where the prevailing emotional mood is distorted or inappropriate to the circumstances.

mortification Discipline of the body and the mind by self-denial or self-inflicted deprivation.

murder and non-negligent manslaughter The willful killing of another person, as determined by police investigation.

N

national health service Policy in which the provision of health care services is the direct responsibility of government and is not left to the private economic marketplace.

national security managers Government officials who control foreign policy and intelligence.

negative income tax A method of tax reform to raise the income of the poor by direct cash subsidies from the government.

neocolonialism Continuing control of former colonies by foreign countries.

net worth tax A policy that would tax the wealth of millionaire families and provide special tax reductions for less affluent families. The net result would be a gradual reduction in the concentration of wealth among the rich.

neurosis Any of various mental or emotional disorders, such as hypochondria or neurasthenia, arising from no apparent organic lesion or change and involving symptoms such as insecurity, anxiety, depression, and irrational fears, but without psychotic symptoms such as delusions or hallucinations.

new poor Highly educated people with a strong income who have never been poor before but who are suddenly thrust into poverty due to downsizing, deindustrialization, and globalization.

nonmarital births Births to unwed mothers.

normal violence Violence in a family such as spanking that is tolerated and accorded legitimacy.

O

officer class Professional career officers who command vast military bureaucracies.

organic psychoses Serious mental illness due to physical damage to the brain or chemical imbalances in a person's system.

organizational adult The team-oriented person who fits well into nonschool bureaucracies, such as corporations, the military, and the government.

organization child The child who is most comfortable when those in authority provide supervision, guidance, and roles to be fulfilled.

organized crime The group and its efforts that regulates relations between criminal enterprises involved in illegal activities, including prostitution, gambling, and the smuggling and sale of drugs.

outsourcing A practice used by companies to reduce costs by transferring or subcontracting portions of work to outside suppliers and producers rather than performing it internally.

P

parasuicide A suicide attempt which does not result in death.

pauperization of motherhood A concept that explicitly refers to institutional forces that have impoverished women and children.

pentagon capitalism The cooperative economic relationship between the private aerospace-defense industry and the Department of Defense.

personal racism The racial prejudice or discrimination expressed by individuals or small groups of people.

personal troubles Matters involving a person's character and his or her relations with others over which the individual has control.

plea bargaining A process by which an agreement between the prosecutor of a case and a defendant is negotiated.

pluralist perspective The theory that competing interest groups or elites coexist, cooperate, and maintain a balance of power to create government in the common good.

political action committees Committees formed by business, labor, or other special-interest groups to raise money and make contributions to the campaigns of political candidates whom they support.

political alienation Belief that the electoral process does not address issues that are vitally important leading individuals to not participate.

political apathy Lack of caring about the outcome of an election or other political process.

political crime Illicit acts undertaken with the intention of affecting political policies or processes or the political system as a whole.

political legitimacy crisis Situation in which citizens widely cease accepting the existing leadership or political structure as effective or viable.

political riots Mass civil disturbances involving the indiscriminate use of force and the extensive violation of constitutional rights, often by social control agents such as police, military, or national guard.

political suicide The intentional taking of one's own life for political reasons or objectives.

population explosion The geometric expansion of a population, especially the unchecked growth in human population resulting from a decrease in infant mortality and an increase in longevity.

population growth rate The rate at which the number of individuals in a population increases.

postpartum depression Psychological depression which may affect new mothers after they give birth.

posttraumatic stress syndrome A common anxiety disorder that develops after exposure to a terrifying event or ordeal in which grave physical harm occurred or was threatened.

poverty The economic state in which people are either materially deprived of the basics of survival or are materially deprived in comparison with the majority of the population.

power elite theory Theory that the people who fill the command positions of strategically important institutions, such as the state, the corporate economy, and the military come from a single group and share a single world view.

presenting culture Patients' prior sense of who they are before they enter a mental health-care institution.

primary sector That part of a modern economy based on the extraction of natural resources directly from the natural environment—includes such areas as mining and agricultural production.

problem drinker Anyone who has any of these symptoms: frequent bouts of intoxication, binge drinking, physical dependence on and loss of control over alcohol, psychological dependence on drinking, ruptured relations with family or friends, employment difficulties associated with alcohol use on or off job, involvement in accidents or in trouble with law due to alcohol, and health or financial problems due to drinking.

prodromal clues   Signal of suicidal thoughts to others, days or weeks before taking steps to die.

psychoactive substances   Drugs that may affect the minds of those who consume them.

psychoanalytic explanation   Point of view that explains crime as the outcome of unconscious motivations arising within certain troubled individuals.

psychological dependence   Reliance on alcohol or other drugs to relieve depression or escape problems in living.

psychoses   Serious mental disorders that involve a failure to distinguish between internal and external reality, such that the affected people cannot function effectively in social life.

public issues   Problems that are typically widespread and pervasive and beyond individuals' control, affecting large proportions of the population.

pushouts/throwaway children   Children or teenagers who have been rejected, ejected, or abandoned by parents or guardians.

R

race   A category into which people are assigned based on the social meaning and significance given to certain physical (and sometimes cultural) characteristics of members of a society's population.

race to the bottom   A globalization trend of searching for the cheapest, most exploitable labor while destroying jobs and living wages in nations.

racial formation   According to Omi and Winant, the process in which the dominant groups in society establish the content and importance of racial categories.

racism   A complex set of beliefs and practices that treat some groups of human beings as inherently or genetically inferior to others.

radical feminists   Women who seek liberation from all roles associated with male dominance.

rational suicide   Suicidal behavior on the part of those whose reasoning powers are not impaired, and whose motives can be considered justified or reasoned.

raves   All-night events where young people dance to modern electronic music and sometimes take illegal drugs.

reductionism   A process that reduces complex ideas or information to simple terms; for example, people who attribute deviant behavior to physiological or psychological reasons only and do not consider larger societal influences are practicing reductionism.

reinforcement   Systems of rewards or punishments designed to affect behavior.

residual deviance   Behavior that is so unusual or unthinkable that it falls under the category of mental illness.

resource depletion   The total decrease in the amount of natural materials available for use by humans and other living beings.

reverse discrimination   Discrimination against members of a dominant or majority group, especially when resulting from policies established to correct discrimination against members of a minority or subordinate group.

S

sandwich generation   Generation of adults caring for both elders and children.

scapegoating   Situation in which members of society who are frustrated by crises blame another group as responsible, which can lead to violence and genocide.

schizophrenia   A serious mental disturbance in which an individual typically has delusions or hallucinations and a distorted sense of reality.

seasonal affective disorder   A form of depression occurring at certain seasons of the year, especially when the individual has limited exposure to sunlight.

secondary sector   Manufacturing.

second shift   See *double shift*.

self-fulfilling prophecy   The phenomenon in which people achieve to the level expected of them rather than to the level of which they may actually be capable.

seller theory   The idea that drug use is a result of the inability of law enforcement agencies to exercise control over supplies of illegal substances and of the ability of sellers to exert wily promotional and sales tactics on innocent nonusers.

sex The category of male or female, determined by fundamental biological characteristics.

social disorganization approach The perspective that focuses on the influence of the social environment in explaining deviance.

social integration theory The perspective that suicide is not best explained by physiological traits or psychological variables but rather by the failure of individuals to become effectively linked to the rest of society.

social pathology approach The approach, popular during the nineteenth and early twentieth centuries, that focused on the influence of biological or psychological deficiencies on deviant behavior of individuals.

social regulation A practice in which society has a high degree of control over its members' emotions and motivations.

socialist feminists People who argue that female liberation can only be achieved by working to end both the economic and cultural sources of women's oppression.

societal problems Social structures that have a vast impact on how societies operate and the negative effect of this on the life chances of millions of people.

societal reaction See *labeling theory.*

soft money Political donations made in such a way as to avoid federal regulations or limits, such as donating to a party organization rather than to a particular candidate or campaign.

spouse abuse Domestic violence, where physical or sexual abuse is perpetuated by one spouse upon another.

standpoint theory The approach that investigates the motives or intentions that underlie individual acts of suicide.

status frustration Alienation felt by lower-class youth who feel unfairly discriminated against by middle-class society.

status integration Situation in which the many roles people must play simultaneously are compatible with one another, making suicide unlikely.

stigma A negative mark that discredits or devalues a person's or group's worth.

structuralist perspective An approach that focuses on the ways societies are organized so as to contribute to the creation of social problems.

structural transformation of the economy The shift in the economy from emphasizing primarily goods production to emphasizing service sector employment.

suicide A death caused by a person choosing to end his or her own life.

suicide by cop Situation in which an individual deliberately provokes law enforcement agents to use drastic, sometimes lethal measures to disarm an apparently threatening person.

suicide career Individual pattern of multiple suicide attempts.

suicidology The study of suicide.

superego As described by Freud, the conscience that functions as the restraining force of the id and the ego, reinforcing the limiting rules of social behavior.

survey research A type of research in which the participants fill out a questionnaire or answer questions in person or over the phone.

sweatshops Places in which workers (including children) toil in overcrowded, unsafe conditions for below-poverty wages, with mandatory but unpaid overtime, and with few or no protections.

T

terrorism The use of violence as a strategy to gain political objectives, often by individuals or groups who have relatively little power otherwise.

tertiary sector That part of an economy that provides services (nursing homes, psychological counseling, and so forth)—engaged in by both private and government entities.

theory of the social reality of crime Approach that examines crimes as a product of law or an outcome of structured opportunities, learning experiences, interpersonal relations, and self-conceptions; those whose behaviors are defined as crimes will see themselves as criminals and act in response to fulfill that role.

tooth fairy approach The idea that students are encouraged to view and celebrate the political status quo as an idealized state of affairs.

total institutions Institutions in which individuals are completely isolated from the rest of society for an extended period of time; for example, mental institutions.

tracks Specific curriculum groups in which students are placed based on test scores and other criteria; see *academic tracking*.

traditional crime Common crime.

transnational capitalist class A group of owners of the means of production whose activities transcend national boundaries.

U

underemployment Situation in which individuals are employed at jobs that do not fully utilize their skills, that pay less than a living wage, or that do not offer opportunities for full-time employment.

unemployment The inability of workers to find paid work.

unemployment compensation A federal policy in which workers who lose their jobs through no fault of their own are eligible to temporarily receive a percentage of their former wages.

universal health insurance Policy by which all of society's members are covered by a comprehensive program of health insurance, regardless of their individual ability to pay.

V

victimless crimes Violation of law in which there is presumably no other person (aside from the offender) victimized, such as drug-taking or illegal gambling.

vocational track An educational program of study for students presumed by educators to be destined for physical labor rather than higher education.

W

war An organized, armed conflict between nations.

wealth A person's material assets, including land, stocks, and other types of property.

welfare queen The stereotypical woman who lives off the public dole indefinitely, refusing to work, having more children in order to increase her benefits, and acting as a financial drain on public resources.

welfare reform A policy in which individuals are held to greater responsibility for escaping their own poverty, and which provides much more limited benefits and for shorter periods of time than was previously allowed.

wet communities Places where the sale of alcohol is legal.

white-collar crime Violations of the law by individuals in the course of their occupations or professions and that benefit them.

work Any activity that produces something of value for other people.

world of unfreedom Description of institutions where patients have little control over what happens to them.

references

A

AARP. 2003. Working in Retirement Survey. April 9–June 5.

Abadinsky, Howard. 2004. *Drugs: An Introduction.* 5th ed. Belmont, CA: Thomson Wadsworth.

Abbott, Franklin, ed. 1998. *Boyhood, Growing Up Male: A Multicultural Anthology.* Madison: University of Wisconsin Press.

ABC News/*Washington Post.* 2003. Survey done October 9–13.

ABC News/*Washington Post* **Poll.** 2003. October 26–29.

Abramovitz, Mimi. 1988. *Regulating the Lives of Women.* Boston, MA: South End Press.

————. 2000. *Under Attack, Fighting Back: Women and Welfare in the United States.* New York: Monthly Review Press.

Ackerman, Robert J. 1978. *Children of Alcoholics.* Holmes Beach, FL: Learning Publications.

Acuña, Rodolfo. 1988. *Occupied America.* 4th ed. New York: Harper and Row.

Adam, Barry. 1987. *The Rise of a Gay and Lesbian Movement.* Boston: Twayne.

Adams, Jane Meredith. 2002. "Medical Marijuana Users Sue U.S. Officials." *Chicago Tribune,* October 10, p. 12.

Adler, Freda, Gerhard O. W. Mueller, and William S. Laufer. 1995. *Criminology.* 2d ed. New York: McGraw-Hill.

————. 2003. *Criminology.* 5th ed. New York: McGraw-Hill.

Adler, Nancy E., and Jeanne M. Tschann. 1993. "Conscious and Preconscious Motivation for Pregnancy among Female Adolescents." Pp. 144–58 in *The Politics of Pregnancy: Adolescent Sexuality and Public Policy,* edited by Annette Lawson and Deborah L. Rhode. New Haven, CT: Yale University Press.

Aftandilian, Dave. 1999. "Noise Pollution." *Conscious Choice* (June), available at www.consciouschoice. com/note/note1206.html.

Aguirre, Adelberto Jr., and Jonathan Turner. 2004. *American Ethnicity: The Dynamics and Consequences of Discrimination.* New York: McGraw-Hill.

Aiken, Michael, Louis Ferman, and Harold L. Sheppard. 1968. *Economic Failure, Alienation, and Extremism.* Ann Arbor: University of Michigan Press.

Aizcorbe, Ana M., Arthur B. Kennickell, and Kevin B. Moore. 2003. "Recent Changes in U.S. Family Finances: Evidence from the 1998 and 2001 Survey." *Federal Reserve Bulletin* 89 (January), available at http://www.federalreserve. gov/pubs/bulletin/2003/ 03bulletin.htm#jan.

Akers, Ronald L. 1973. *Deviant Behavior.* Belmont, CA: Wadsworth.

Albanese, Jay S. 1994. "Models of Organized Crime." Pp. 77–90 in *Handbook of Organized Crime in the United States,* edited by Robert J. Kelly, Ko-Lin Chin, and Rufus Schatzberg. Westport, CT : Greenwood Press.

Alcohol Health and Research World, II. 1986/1987. Special issue devoted to drinking practices among different racial and ethnic minority groups (Winter).

Alderman, Lesley. 1995. "Here Comes the Four-Income Family." *Money,* February, pp. 149–55.

Alford, Robert R., and Roger Friedland. 1985. *Powers of Theory: Capitalism, the State, and Democracy.* Cambridge, England: Cambridge University Press.

Allen, Robert L. 1969. *Black Awakening in Capitalist America.* Garden City, NY: Doubleday.

Alston, Dana, ed. 1990. *We Speak for Ourselves: Social Justice, Race, and Environment.* Washington, DC: Panos Institute.

Alter, Jonathan. 2000. "The Death Penalty on Trial." *Newsweek,* June 12, pp. 24–34.

American Association of University Women. 1992. *How Schools Shortchange Girls.* Washington, DC: AAUW Educational Foundation.

American Civil Liberties Union. 1999. "Overview of Lesbian and Gay Parenting, Adoption and Foster Care." April 6; available at http://archive.aclu.org/issues/gay/ parent.html.

American Civil Liberties Union. 2000–present. Available at www.aclu.org.

American Psychiatric Association. 2000. *Diagnostic and Statistical Manual of Mental Disorders: DSM-IV-TR.* 4th ed. Washington, DC: Author.

American Savings Council. 2004. "Retirement Survey 2004." January 2–February 2.

Amneus, Daniel. 1979. *Back to Patriarchy.* New Rochelle, NY: Arlington.

Amott, Teresa. 1993. *Caught in the Crisis: Women and the U.S. Economy Today.* New York: Monthly Review Press.

———— **and Julie A. Matthaei.** 1996. *Race, Gender and Work: A Multicultural Economic History of Women in the United States.* Rev. ed. Boston: South End Press.

Andersen, Margaret L. 2003. *Thinking about Women.* 6th ed. New York: Allyn and Bacon.

Anderson, Kristin L., and Debra Umberson. 2001. "Gendering Violence: Masculinity and Power in Men's Accounts of Domestic Violence." *Gender and Society* 15 (3): 358–80.

Anderson, Tammy L. 1998. "A Cultural Identity Theory of Drug Abuse." *Sociology of Crime, Law, and Deviance* 1:233–62.

Annals of the American Academy of Political and Social Science. 1985. Special Edition: "The Insanity Defense." 477 (January).

Anspaugh, Lynn R., Robert J. Catlin, and Marvin Goldman. 1988. "The Global Impact of the Chernobyl Reactor Accident." *Science* 242 (December 16): 1513.

Apple, Michael W. 2000. "Away with All Teachers: The Cultural Politics of Home Schooling." *International Studies in Sociology of Education* 10 (1): 61–80.

————. 2004. *Ideology and Curriculum.* 3d ed. New York: Routledge.

———— **and Linda K. Christian-Smith, eds.** 1991. *The Politics of the Textbook.* New York: Routledge.

Applebaum, Richard P. 1989. "The Affordability Gap." *Social Policy* 19 (May/June): 7.

Arendell, Terry. 1986. *Mothers and Divorce.* Berkeley: University of California Press.

————. 1987. "Women and the Economics of Divorce in the United States." *Signs* 13 (Autumn): 121–35.

————. 1995. *Fathers and Divorce.* Thousand Oaks, CA: Sage.

Armaline, William D., Kathleen S. Farber, and Shan Nelson-Rowe. 1994. "Reading Class: Marxist Theories of Education." Pp. 178–206 in *From the Left Bank to the Mainstream,* edited by Patrick McGuire and Donald McQuarie. Dix Hills, NY: General Hall.

Armstrong, Louise. 1993. *And They Call It Help: The Psychiatric Policing of America's Children.* Reading, MA: Addison-Wesley.

Aronowitz, Stanley, and William DiFazio. 1994. *The Jobless Future: Sci-Tech and the Dogma of Work.* Minneapolis: University of Minnesota Press.

———— **and Henry A. Giroux.** 1993. *Education Still under Siege.* 2d ed. Westport, CT: Bergin and Garvey.

Ascenzi, Joseph. 2000. "Toxics Suit Cites PG&E in 4 Deaths; Action by 56 Plaintiffs Says Toxic Water Used to Fill Swimming Pools." The Business Press/California; available at www.fumento.com/buspress.html.

Ashmore, Harry. 1982. *Hearts and Minds.* New York: McGraw-Hill.

Auerbach, Judith D., Christina Wypijewska, and H. Keith H. Brodie, eds. 1994. *AIDS and Behavior.* Washington, DC: National Academy Press.

Ayers, William, Bernadine Dohrn, and Rick Ayers. 2001. *Zero Tolerance: Resisting the Drive for Punishment in Our Schools.* New York: The New Press.

B

Bacon, Betty, ed. 1988. *How Much Truth Do We Tell the Children? The Politics of Children's Literature.* Minneapolis, MN: MEP Publications.

Baker, Daniel B., Sean O'Brien Strub, and Bill Henning. 1995. *Cracking the Corporate Closet.* New York: Harper Business.

Bales, Kevin. 1999. *Disposable People: New Slavery in the Global Economy.* Berkeley: University of California Press.

Banfield, Edward C. 1970. *The Unheavenly City.* Boston: Little, Brown.

————. 1974. *The Unheavenly City Revisited.* Boston: Little, Brown.

Banks, Michael H., and Debra Roker. 1994. "The Political Socialization of Youth: Exploring the Influence of the School Experience." *Journal of Adolescence* 17:3–15.

Barak, Gregg, Jeanne M. Flavin, and Paul S. Leighton. 2001. *Class, Race, Gender, and Crime.* Los Angeles: Roxbury.

Baran, Paul A., and Paul M. Sweezy. 1969. *Monopoly Capital.* New York: Monthly Review Press.

Barlett, Donald, and James B. Steele. 1992. *America: What Went Wrong?* Kansas City: Andrews and McMeel.

————. 1994. *America: Who Really Pays the Taxes?* New York: Simon and Schuster.

————. 2004. *Critical Condition: How Health Care in America Became Big Business—and Bad Medicine.* New York: Doubleday.

Barnet, Richard J. 1969. *The Economy of Death.* New York: Atheneum.

————. 1981. *The Lean Years.* New York: Simon and Schuster.

———— **and John Cavanagh.** 1994. *Global Dreams: Imperial Corporations and the New World Order.* New York: Simon and Schuster.

Barringer, Felicity. 1993. "School Hallways as Gantlets of Sexual Taunts." *The New York Times,* June 2, p. B7.

Bartfeld, Judi. 2000. "Child Support and the Postdivorce Economic Well-Being of Mothers, Fathers, and Children." *Demography* 37 (2): 203–13.

Barthel, Diane. 1988. *Putting on Appearances: Gender and Advertising.* Philadelphia: Temple University Press.

Bass, Ellen, and Louise Thornton, eds. 1982. *I Never Told Anyone.* New York: Harper and Row.

Bass, Scott A. 1995. *Older and Active: How Americans over 55 Are Contributing to Society.* New Haven, CT : Yale University Press.

BBC News. 1999. "Doubt Cast on 'Gay Gene.'" April 23; available at http://news.bbc.co.uk/1/hi/sci/tech/325979.stm.

Beaulieu, Lionel J. 1998. "Welfare Reform: An Overview of Key Provisions." *Southern Rural Development Center Information Brief* 1 (January): 1–3.

Becker, Howard S. 1953. "Becoming a Marijuana User." *American Journal of Sociology* 59 (November): 235–42.

———. 1963. *Outsiders.* New York: The Free Press.

———. 1973. "Consciousness, Power, and Drug Effects." *Society* 10 (May–June): 31.

Beckman, Peter R., Paul Crumlish, Michael Dobkowski, and Steven Lee. 1989. *The Nuclear Predicament.* Englewood Cliffs, NJ: Prentice Hall.

Begley, Sharon. 1995. "Deliver, Then Depart." *Newsweek,* July 10, p. 62.

Beirne, Piers, and James Messerschmidt. 1995. *Criminology,* 2d ed. Fort Worth, TX: Harcourt Brace.

Belkin, Aaron, and Geoffrey Bateman. 2003. *Don't Ask, Don't Tell: Debating the Gay Ban in the Military.* Boulder, CO: Lynne Rienner.

Bell, R. E. 2002. "The Prosecution of Computer Crime." *Journal of Financial Crime* 9 (4): 308–25.

Bellanca, James, and Elizabeth Swartz, eds. 1993. *The Challenge of Detracking.* Palatine, IL: IRI/Skylight Publishing.

Bender, Mary. 2000. "Suicide and Older African-American women." *Mortality* 5 (2): 158–70.

Benefield, Robert L. 1996. "Who Loses Coverage and for How Long?" *Current Population Reports P70-54.* Washington, DC: U.S. Bureau of the Census.

Benjamin, Lois. 1991. *The Black Elite.* Chicago: Nelson-Hall Publishers.

Bennett, Kathleen de Marrais, and Margaret LeCompte. 1990. *The Way Schools Work.* New York: Longman.

———. 1998. *The Way Schools Work.* 3d ed. New York: Longman.

Bensman, David, and Roberta Lynch. 1987. *Rusted Dreams.* New York: McGraw-Hill.

Berg, Ivar. 1970. *Education and Jobs.* New York: Praeger.

Berger, Joseph. 1988. "Price of Illiteracy Translates into Poverty and Humiliation." *The New York Times,* September 6, p. A1.

Berheide, Catherine W. 1992. "Women Still 'Stuck' in Low-Level Jobs." *Women in Public Services: A Bulletin for the Center for Women in Government* 3 (Fall): 2–4.

Berlet, Chip. 1994. "The Right Rides High." *The Progressive* 58 (October): 22–29.

——— **and Matthew N. Lyons.** 1995. "Militia Nation." *The Progressive* 59 (June): 22–25.

Berman, Daniel. 1978. *Death on the Job.* New York: Monthly Review Press.

Bernard, Jessie. 1971. "The Paradox of the Happy Marriage." Pp. 145–62 in *Woman in Sexist Society,* edited by Vivian Gornick and Barbara

K. Moran. New York: Mentor Books.

Bernstein, Deborah S. 1992. *Pioneers and Homemakers: Jewish Women in Pre-State Israel.* Albany: State University of New York Press.

Bernstein, Robert A. 2003. *Straight Parents, Gay Children.* Rev. and updated ed. New York: Thunder's Mouth Press.

Bhugra, Dinesh, ed. 1996. *Homelessness and Mental Health.* New York: Cambridge University Press.

Billings, Dwight B., and Kathleen M. Blee. 2000. *The Road to Poverty: The Making of Wealth and Hardship in Appalachia.* New York: Cambridge University Press.

Billy, John O. G., Koray Tanger, William Grady, and Daniel Klepinger. 1993. "The Sexual Behavior of Men in the United States." *Family Planning Perspectives* 25 (March–April): 52–60.

Bingham, Kennetha J. 1994. "Watercide: Are We Killing Our Water?" *Current Health* (November): 19–21.

Binstock, Robert H. 1993. "Older People and Health Care Reform." *American Behavior Scientist* 36 (July/August): 823–40.

Bird, Caroline. 1969. *Born Female.* New York: Pocket Books.

Bischak, Gregory A., ed. 1991. *Toward a Peace Economy in the United States.* New York: St. Martin's Press.

Black Enterprise. 1993. "Small Businesses Get Shortchanged." 24 (November): 28.

Blackstock, Nelson. 1976. *COINTELPRO: The FBI's Secret War on Political Freedom.* New York: Vintage Books.

Blackwood, Evelyn, ed. 1986. *The Many Faces of Homosexuality:*

Anthropological Approaches to Homosexual Behavior. New York: Harrington Park Press.

Blau, Francine D., and Anne E. Winkler. 1989. "Women in the Labor Force: An Overview." Pp. 265–86 in *Women: A Feminist Perspective,* 4th ed., edited by Jo Freeman. Mountain View, CA: Mayfield.

Blau, Joel. 1999. *Illusions of Prosperity: America's Working Families in an Age of Economic Insecurity.* New York: Oxford University Press.

Blau, Peter M., and Marshall W. Meyer. 1971. *Bureaucracy in Modern Society.* 3d ed. New York: Random House.

Blauner, Robert. 1972. *Racial Oppression in America.* New York: Harper and Row.

Bloch, Farrell. 1995. "Affirmative Action Hasn't Helped Blacks." *Wall Street Journal,* March 1, p. A14.

Bluestone, Barry, and Bennett Harrison. 1982. *The Deindustrialization of America.* New York: Basic Books.

Blum, Richard H. et al. 1972. *Horatio Alger's Children.* San Francisco: Jossey-Bass.

Blumberg, Paul. 1980. *Inequality in an Age of Decline.* New York: Oxford University Press.

Blumenfeld, Warren. 1992. *Homophobia: How We All Pay the Price.* Boston: Beacon Press.

———— **and Diane Raymond.** 1993. *Looking at Gay and Lesbian Life.* Expanded ed. Boston: Beacon Press.

Board of Inquiry into Hunger and Malnutrition. 1968. *Hunger U.S.A.: A Report by the Citizen's Board of Inquiry into Hunger and Malnutrition in the United States.* Boston: Beacon Press, 1968.

Bocij, Paul, and LeRoy McFarlane. 2003. "The Internet: A Discussion of Some New and Emerging Threats to Young People." *Police Journal* 76 (1): 3–13.

Bock, Alan. 1982. *The Ecology Action Guide.* New York: Pyramid Books.

Boessenkool, Antonie. 2004. "Gender Gap Widens with Higher Salaries." *The Washington Times,* June 4; available at www.washingtontimes.com.

Bogdanich, Walt. 1991. *The Great White Lie: How America's Hospitals Betray Our Trust and Endanger Our Lives.* New York: Simon and Schuster.

Boggs, Carl. 1995. "Rethinking the Sixties Legacy." Pp. 331–55 in *Social Movements,* edited by Stanford M. Lyman. New York: New York University Press.

Boies, John L. 1994. *Buying for Armageddon: Business, Society, and Military Spending Since the Cuban Missile Crisis.* New Brunswick, NJ: Rutgers University Press.

Bond, James T. 1994. *Preliminary Examination of the Contingent Workforce.* Washington, DC: Families and Work Institute.

Borst, Noam, and Sophie Borst, eds. 1994. *Children, Youth, and Suicide.* San Francisco: Jossey-Bass.

Boulding, Elise. 1976. *The Underside of History.* Boulder, CO: Westview Press.

Bottomore, T. B., and Maximilien Rubel, eds. 1964. *Karl Marx: Selected Writings.* New York: McGraw-Hill.

Bowd, A. D. 2003. "Stereotypes of Elderly Persons in Narrative Jokes." *Research on Aging* 25 (1): 3–21.

Bowles, Samuel. 1972. "Getting Nowhere: Programmed Class Stagnation." *Society* 9 (June): 43.

————. 1974. "Unequal Education and the Reproduction of the Social Division of Labor." Pp. 17–43 in *The Education Establishment,* edited by Elizabeth L. Useem and Michael Useem. Englewood Cliffs, NJ: Prentice Hall.

———— **and Herbert Gintis.** 1976. *Schooling in Capitalist America.* New York: Basic Books.

————, **David M. Gordon, and Thomas E. Weisskopf.** 1984. *Beyond the Wasteland.* Garden City, NY : Anchor Books.

Bowser, Benjamin P., Gale S. Auletta, and Terry Jones. 1993. *Confronting Diversity Issues on Campus.* Newbury Park, CA: Sage.

Bowser, Benjamin P., and Raymond G. Hunt, eds. 1981. *Impacts of Racism on White Americans.* Beverly Hills, CA: Sage.

Boyer, Debra, and David Fine. 1992. "Sexual Abuse as a Factor in Adolescent Pregnancy and Child Maltreatment." *Family Planning Perspectives* 24 (January/February): 4–19.

Braginsky, Benjamin, Dorthea Braginsky, and Kenneth Ring. 1969. *Methods of Madness.* New York: Holt, Rinehart and Winston.

Braude, Lee. 1975. *Work and Workers.* New York: Praeger.

Braverman, Harry. 1974. *Labor and Monopoly Capital.* New York: Monthly Review Press.

Brecher, Jeremy, Tim Costello, and Brendan Smith. 2000. *Globalization from Below: The Power of Solidarity.* Cambridge, MA: South End Press.

Brennan, Patricia A., S. A. Mednick, and J. Volavka. 1995. "Biomedical Factors in Crime." Pp. 65–90 in *Crime,* edited by James Q. Wilson and Patricia A. Brennan. San Francisco: ICS Press.

Brennan, Tim, David Huizinga, and Delbert S. Elliott. 1978. *The Social Psychology of Runaways.* Lexington, MA: Lexington Books.

Brenner, M. Harvey. 1973. *Mental Illness and the Economy.* Cambridge, MA: Harvard University Press.

———. 1977. "Personal Stability and Economic Security." *Social Policy* 8 (May/June): 2–4.

Briggs, David. 2003. "Environmental Pollution and the Global Burden of Disease." *British Medical Bulletin* 68:1–24.

Brimelow, Peter. 1995. *Alien Nation: Common Sense about America's Immigration Disaster.* New York: Random House.

Brimmer, Andrew F. 1992. "A Cross to Bear." *Black Enterprise* 22 (May): 44–45.

Brint, Steven, and Jerome Karabel. 1989. *The Diverted Dream.* New York: Oxford University Press.

Brodeur, Paul. 1974. *Expendable Americans.* New York: Viking Press.

Brody, Jane E. 2001. "An Old Enemy, Smoking, Hangs Tough." *New York Times*, December 11, p. D7.

Bromberg, Walter. 1948. *Crime and the Mind.* Philadelphia: J. B. Lippincott.

Bronzaft, Arline. 1993. "Noise Annoys." *E: The Environmental Magazine* (March/April): 16+.

Brooks, Gary R. 1991. "Men's Studies and Psychotherapy: A Current Perspective on the Status of the Men's Movement." *The Psychotherapy Bulletin* 26 (Summer): 19–21.

Brown, J. Larry. 1987. "Hunger in the U.S." *Scientific American* 256 (February): 37.

Brown, Lester R. 1987. "Analyzing the Demographic Trap." Pp. 20–37 in *State of the World 1987,* Worldwatch Institute. New York: W. W. Norton.

———. 2000. *State of the World 2000.* New York: W. W. Norton.

——— **and Christopher Flavin.** 1988. "The Earth's Vital Signs," in

Worldwatch Institute, *State of the World, 1988.* New York: W. W. Norton.

Brown, Michael. 1980. *Laying Waste: The Poisoning of America by Toxic Chemicals.* New York: Pantheon Books.

Brown, Thomas C. 1999. "Past and Future Freshwater Use in the United States: A Technical Document Supporting the 2000 USDA Forest Service RPA Assessment." General Technical Report RMRS-GTR-39. Fort Collins, CO: U.S. Department of Agriculture, Forest Service, Rockey Mountain Research Station. Available at www.fsfed.us.

Brownmiller, Susan. 1975. *Against Our Will.* New York: Simon and Schuster.

Bruck, David. 1983. "Decisions of Death." *The New Republic* 189 (December 12): 18–21.

Bryant, Bunyan, and Paul Mohai, eds. 1992. *Race and the Incidence of Environmental Hazards.* Boulder, CO: Westview Press.

Budig, Michelle J., and Paula England. 2001. "The Wage Penalty for Motherhood." *American Sociological Review* 66 (2): 204–25.

Bullard, Robert D. 1993. *Confronting Environmental Racism: Voices from the Grassroots.* Boston: South End Press.

Bullard, Robert D. ed. 1997. *Unequal Protection: Environmental Justice and Communities of Color.* San Francisco: Sierra Club Books.

Burchell, Brendan J., Diana Day, Maria Hudson, David Ladipo, Roy Makelow, Jane P. Nolan, Hannah Reed, Ines C. Wichert, and Frank Wilkinson. 1999. *Job Insecurity and Work Intensification: Flexibility and the Changing Boundaries of Work.* York, England: Joseph Rowntree Foundation, YPS,

http://www.jrf.org.uk/knowledge/findings/socialpolicy/849.asp.

Busch, Noeel Bridget, Holly Bell, Norma Hotaling, and Martin A. Monto. 2002. "Male Customers of Prostituted Women: Exploring Perceptions of Entitlement to Power and Control and Implications for Violent Behavior Toward Women." *Violence Against Women* 8 (September): 1093–1112.

BusinessWeek. 1984. *The Reindustrialization of America.* New York: McGraw-Hill.

Butler, Robert N. 1975. *Why Survive? Being Old in America.* New York: Harper and Row.

Buxton, Amity Pierce. 1994. *The Other Side of the Closet: The Coming-Out Crisis for Straight Spouses and Their Families.* Rev. ed. New York: John Wiley.

C

Cagin, Seth, and Philip Dray. 1993. *Between Earth and Sky: How CFCs Changed Our World and Endangered the Ozone Layer.* New York: Pantheon.

Cahalan, Don. 1970. *Problem Drinkers.* San Francisco: Jossey-Bass.

———, **Ira H. Cisin, and Helen M. Crossley.** 1969. *American Drinking Practices.* New Brunswick, NJ: Rutgers Center of Alcohol Studies.

——— **and Robin Room.** 1974. *Problem Drinking among American Men.* New Brunswick, NJ: Rutgers Center of Alcohol Studies.

Cahn, Sidney. 1970. *The Treatment of Alcoholics.* New York: Oxford University Press.

Calavita, Kitty, and Henry N. Pontell. 1991. "Other People's Money Revisited: Collective Embezzlement in the Savings and

Loan and Insurance Industries." *Social Problems* 38:94–112.

Callahan, Raymond. 1962. *Education and the Cult of Efficiency.* Chicago: University of Chicago Press.

Canada, Geoffrey. 1995. *Fist Stick Knife Gun.* Boston: Beacon Press.

Carnoy, Martin, and Henry M. Levin. 1985. *Schooling and Work in the Democratic State.* Stanford, CA: Stanford University Press.

Casey, Timothy J. 1998. "Welfare Reform and Its Impact in the Nation and in New York." New York: Federation of Protestant Welfare Agencies, Inc.; available at http://www.wnylc.net/web/welfare-law/resource-material/welrefor.htm

Cashmore, Ellis, and Eugene McLaughlin, eds. 1991. *Out of Order? Policing Black People.* New York: Routledge.

Catalano, Shannan N. 2004. *Sourcebook of Criminal Justice Statistics, 2003.* Washington, DC: U.S. Government Printing Office; available at www.ojp.usdoj.gov.

Cavalluzzo, Ken, and John Wolken. 2002. "Small Business Loan Turndowns, Personal Wealth and Discrimination." Washington, DC: Federal Reserve System Board of Governors.

Cavell, Lori J. 2000. "Graduate Student Unionization in Higher Education." ERIC Clearinghouse on Higher Education, Washington, DC, 2000.

CBS News/*New York Times* Poll. 2003. July 13–27.

Centers for Disease Control and Prevention. 2002. "Summary Health Statistics for U.S. Adults: National Health Interview Survey, 1997." *Vital and Health Statistics*, Series 10, No. 205 (May): 53.

Chace, James. 1984. *Endless War.* New York: Vintage Books.

Chamberlin, Judi. 1978. *On Our Own.* New York: Hawthorne Books.

Chambliss, William J. 1974. "The State, the Law, and the Definition of Behavior as Criminal or Delinquent." Pp. 7–43 in *Handbook of Criminology,* edited by Daniel Glaser. Chicago: Rand McNally.

_____ **and Robert Seidman.** 1982. *Law, Order, and Power.* Reading, MA: Addison-Wesley.

Charen, Mona. 1995. "The World of Teen Sex Is No Playground." *Hartford Courant,* August 11, p. A15.

Chase, Allan. 1977. *The Legacy of Malthus.* New York: Alfred A. Knopf.

Chatterjee, Pratap, and Matthias Finger. 1994. *The Earth Brokers: Power, Politics and World Development.* New York: Routledge.

Cherlin, Andrew J. 1981. *Marriage, Divorce, Remarriage.* Cambridge, MA: Harvard University Press.

_____. 1992. *Marriage, Divorce, Remarriage: Social Trends in the United States.* Cambridge, MA: Harvard University Press.

Chesler, Phyllis. 1971. "Patient and Patriarch: Women in the Psychother-apeutic Relationship." Pp. 362–63 in *Woman in Sexist Society*, edited by Vivian Gornick and Barbara K. Moran. New York: Mentor Books.

_____. 1997. *Women and Madness,* reprint edition. New York: Four Walls Eight Windows.

Chi, Keon S. 1988. "Comparable Worth in State Government." Pp. 109–23 in *Comparable Worth, Pay Equity, and Public Policy,* edited by Rita Mae Kelly and Jane Bayes. Westport, CT : Greenwood Press.

Chirot, Daniel. 1977. *Social Change in the Twentieth Century.* Orlando, FL: Harcourt Brace Jovanovich.

Chivian, Eric , Susanna Chivian, Robert Jay Lifton, and John E.

Mack, eds. 1982. *Last Aid: The Medical Dimension of Nuclear War.* San Francisco: W. H. Freeman.

Chomsky, Noam. 1982. *Towards a New Cold War.* New York: Pantheon.

_____. 1991. *Media Control: The Spectacular Achievements of Propaganda.* Westfield, NJ: Open Media.

Choron, Jacques. 1972. *Suicide.* New York: Charles Scribner's Sons.

Christiani, David C. 1993. "Urban and Transboundary Air Pollution: Human Health Consequences." Pp. 13–30 in *Critical Condition: Human Health and the Environment,* edited by Eric Chivian, Susanna Chivian, Robert Jay Lifton, and John E. Mack. Cambridge, MA: MIT Press.

Christie, Ian. 1992. "Social and Political Aspects of Global Warming." *Futures* 24 (January–February): 83–90.

Church, George. 1988. "Beltway Bandits at Work in the Pentagon," *Time,* July 4, pp. 22–23.

Churchill, Ward, and Jim Vander Wall. 1990. *The Cointelpro Papers: Documents from the FBI's Secret Wars against Dissent.* Boston: South End Press.

Cimons, Marlene. 1990. "GAO Cites Bias in Health Research." *Los Angeles Times,* June 19, p. A20.

Clapp, Jennifer. 2001. *Toxic Exports: The Transfer of Hazardous Wastes From Rich to Poor Countries.* Ithaca, NY: Cornell University Press.

Clark, Ramsey, Brian Becker, Joyce Chediac, Francis Kelly, Michael Ratner, and Paul Walker. 1992. *War Crimes: A Report on U.S. War Crimes against Iraq.* Washington, DC: Maison Neuve Press.

Clarke, Caroline V. 1994. "Downsizing Trounces Diversity." *Black Enterprise* 24 (February): 69–70.

Clarke, Kevin. 1993. "Growing Hunger." *Utne Reader* (November/December): 63.

Clausen, John A. 1976. "Drug Use." In *Contemporary Social Problems,* 4th ed., edited by Robert K. Merton and Robert Nisbet. New York: Harcourt Brace Jovanovich.

Clawson, Dan. 1980. *Bureaucracy and the Labor Process: The Transformation of U.S. Industry, 1860–1920.* New York: Monthly Review Press.

———, **Alan Neustadtl, and Mark Weller.** 1998. *Dollars and Votes: How Business Campaign Contributions Subvert Democracy.* Philadelphia: Temple University Press.

Clift, Eleanor. 1992. "How the Candidates Play to Gays." *Newsweek,* September 14, p. 40.

Clinard, Marshall B., and Robert F. Meier. 1992. *Sociology of Deviant Behavior.* 8th ed. Fort Worth, TX: Harcourt Brace Jovanovich.

——— **and G. C. Yeager.** 1980. *Corporate Crime.* New York: The Free Press.

Clines, Francis X. 1993. "A Fatal Silence and a Chance to Address It." *New York Times,* August 22, Section I, p. 33.

Cloward, Richard A., and Lloyd E. Ohlin. 1960. *Delinquency and Opportunity.* New York: The Free Press.

Cochrane, Michelle. 2003. *When AIDS Began: San Francisco and the Making of an Epidemic.* New York: Routledge.

Cockerham, William C. 2003. *Medical Sociology.* 9th ed. Englewood Cliffs, NJ: Prentice Hall.

Cohen, Albert K. 1955. *Delinquent Boys.* New York: The Free Press.

Cohen, David K., and Marvin Lazerson. 1972. "Education and the Corporate Order." *Socialist Revolution* (March–April): 47–72.

Cohen, Joshua, and Joel Rogers. 1983. *On Democracy.* New York: Penguin Books.

Cohen, Mitchell. 1990. "Toxic Imperialism: Exporting Pentagonorrhea." *Z Magazine* (October): 78–79.

Coleman, James. 1961. *The Adolescent Society.* New York: The Free Press.

Coleman, James William. 1995. *The Criminal Elite.* 3d ed. New York: St. Martin's Press.

———. 2001. *The Criminal Elite: The Sociology of White Collar Crime.* 5th ed. New York: Worth Publishers.

———, **and John Hagan.** 1994. *Crime and Disrepute.* Thousand Oaks, CA: Pine Forge Press.

Collins, R. Lorraine, Kenneth E. Leonard, and John S. Searles, eds. 1990. *Alcohol and the Family: Research and Clinical Perspectives.* New York: Guilford Press.

Coltrane, Scott, and Michele Adams. 2001. "Men, Women, and Housework." Pp. 145–54 in *Gender Mosaics: Social Perspectives,* edited by Dana Vannoy. Los Angeles: Roxbury.

Commoner, Barry. 1974. *The Closing Circle.* New York: Bantam Books.

Comstock, Gary. 1991. *Violence against Gay Men and Lesbians.* New York: Columbia University Press.

Connell, R. W. 1992. "A Very Straight Gay: Masculinity, Homosexual Experience, and the Dynamics of Gender." *American Sociological Review* 57 (December): 735–51.

Conrad, Peter, and Joseph W. Schneider. 1992. *Deviance and Medicalization.* Expanded ed. Philadelphia: Temple University Press.

Conte, Jon R. 1993. "Sexual Abuse of Children." Pp. 56–85 in *Family Violence,* edited by Robert L. Hampton, Thomas P. Gullotta, and Gerald R. Adams. Newbury Park, CA: Sage.

Conway, M. Margaret, David W. Ahern, and Gertrude A. Steuernagel. 1995. *Women and Public Policy.* Washington, DC: Congressional Quarterly.

Cook, Christopher. 2000. "Temps Demand a New Deal." *The Nation,* March 27, pp. 13–19.

Cook, Fred J. 1962. *The Warfare State.* New York: Macmillan.

Cook, Philip J., and Mark H. Moore. 1995. "Gun Control." Pp. 270–71 in *Crime,* edited by James Q. Wilson and Joan Petersilia. San Francisco: ICS Press.

Cookson, Peter, and Caroline Persell. 1985. *Preparing for Power: America's Elite Boarding Schools.* New York: Harper and Row.

Coons, John E., and Stephen D. Sugarman. 1991. "The Private School Option in Systems of Education Choice." *Educational Leadership* 48 (4): 54–56.

Cooper, Mary H. 1988. "The Business of Illicit Drugs." *Editorial Research Report* 1 (May 20): 266–67.

Cooperative Commission on the Study of Alcoholism. 1967. *Alcohol Problems.* New York: Oxford University Press.

Coren, Stanley, and P. L. Hewitt. 1999. "Sex Differences in Elderly Suicide Rates: Some Predictive Factors." *Aging and Mental Health* 3 (2): 112–18.

Corrigan, Patrick, and Robert Lundin. 2001. *Don't Call Me Nuts: Coping with the Stigma of Mental Illness.* Tinley Park, IL: Recovery Press.

Cose, Ellis. 1993. *The Rage of a Privileged Class.* New York: HarperCollins.

Costanzo, Mark, and Lawrence T. White. 1994. "An Overview of the Death Penalty and Capital Trials." *Journal of Social Issues* 50 (Summer): 1–18.

Cott, Nancy F. 1987. *The Grounding of Modern Feminism.* New Haven, CT: Yale University Press.

Council on Environmental Quality. 1970. *First Annual Report, August 1970.* Washington, DC: U.S. Government Printing Office.

Council on Environmental Quality and Department of State. 1980. *The Global 2000 Report to the President,* Vol. 1. Washington, DC: U.S. Government Printing Office.

Craypo, Charles, and Bruce Nissen, eds. 1993. *Grand Designs: The Impact of Corporate Strategies on Workers, Unions, and Communities.* Ithaca, NY : ILR Press.

Crispell, Diane. 1994. "Getting Home." *American Demographics* (January):55.

Crittenden, Ann. 2001. *The Price of Motherhood: Why the Most Important Job in the World is Still the Least Valued.* New York: Metropolitan Books.

Crosby, Kevin, Joong-oh Rhee, and Jimmie Holland. 1977. "Suicide by Fire: A Contemporary Method of Political Protest." *International Social Psychology* 23:60–69.

Crossette, Barbara. 1994. "Ten Years After the Gas, No End in Tears." *New York Times,* December 11, Section 4, p. 5.

———.1995. "Treaty Aimed at Halting Spread of Nuclear Weapons Extended," *New York Times,* May 12, pp. A1, A10.

Cuklanz, Lisa M. 2000. *Rape on Prime Time: Television, Masculinity, and Sexual Violence.* Philadelphia: University of Pennsylvania Press.

Cumming, Elaine, and William E. Henry. 1961. *Growing Old: The Process of Disengagement.* New York: Basic Books.

Cummings, Scott, ed. 1988. *Business Elites and Urban Development.* Albany: State University of New York Press.

Cummings, Scott, and Del Taebel. 1978. "The Economic Socialization of Children." *Social Problems* 26 (December): 198–210.

Currie, Elliott. 1993. *Reckoning: Drugs, the Cities, and the American Future.* New York: Hill and Wang.

D

Daly, Kathleen. 1994. *Gender, Crime, and Punishment.* New Haven, CT : Yale University Press.

Daniels, Lee A. 1988. "Illiteracy Seen as Threat to U.S. Economic Edge." *New York Times,* September 7, p. B8.

Daniels, Norman. 1995. *Seeking Fair Treatment: From the AIDS Epidemic to National Health Care Reform.* New York: Oxford University Press.

Darnay, Arsen J., ed. 1994. *Statistical Record of Older Americans.* Detroit: Gale Research Inc., 1994.

Darnton, John. 1994. "'Lost Decade' Drains Africa's Vitality." *New York Times,* June 19, p. A10.

D'Augelli, Anthony R. 1989. "Lesbians' and Gay Men's Experiences of Discrimination and Harassment in a University Community." *American Journal of Community Psychology* 17 (June): 317–21.

Davey, Joseph Dillon. 1995. *The New Social Contract: America's Journey from a Welfare State to a Police State.* Westport, CT: Praeger.

Davis, Karen, and Diane Rowland. 1990. "Uninsured and Underserved: Inequities in Health Care in the United States." In *The Sociology of Health and Illness,* 3d. ed., edited by Peter Conrad and Rochelle Kern. New York: St. Martin's Press.

de Beauvoir, Simone. 1973. *The Coming of Age.* New York: Warner Books.

de Catanzaro, Denys. 1981. *Suicide and Self-Damaging Behavior: A Sociobiological Perspective.* New York: Academic Press.

De Graaf, John, ed. 2003. *Take Back Your Time: Fighting Overwork and Time Poverty in America.* San Francisco: Berrett-Koehler.

DeGruijl, Frank R. 1995. "Impacts of a Projected Depletion of the Ozone Layer." Available at www.gcrio.org/CONSEQUENCES/ summer95/impacts.html.

Del Boca, Frances K. 1994. "Sex, Gender, and Alcoholic Typologies." Pp. 34–48 in *Types of Alcoholics,* edited by Thomas F. Babor, Victor Hesselbrock, Roger E. Meyer, and William Shoemaker. New York: New York Academy of Sciences.

Demo, David H., and Lawrence H. Ganong. 1994. "Divorce." Pp. 197–218 in *Families and Change: Coping with Stressful Events,* edited by Patrick C. McKenry and Sharon J. Price. Thousand Oaks, CA: Sage.

DeNavas-Walt, Carmen, Bernadette D. Proctor, and Robert J. Mills. 2004. "Income, Poverty, and Health Insurance Coverage in the United States: 2003." *Current Population Reports P60-226.* Washington, DC: U.S. Bureau of Census, Government Printing Office.

Dennis, Jessica M., Ross D. Parke, Scott Coltrane, Jan Blacher, and Sharon A. Borthwick-Duffy. 2003. "Economic Pressure, Maternal Depression, and Child Adjustment in Latino Families: An Exploratory Study." *Journal of Family and Economic Issues* 24 (2): 183–202.

Des Jarlais, Don C., and Samuel R. Friedman. 1994. "AIDS and the Use of Injected Drugs." *Scientific American* 270 (February): 82–88.

Deudney, Daniel, and Christopher Flavin. 1983. *Renewable Energy.* New York: W. W. Norton.

Deutch, John. 1995. Defense Department briefing (January 3). Washington, DC: Federal News Service.

Devall, Bill, ed. 1995. *Clearcut: The Tragedy of Industrial Forestry.* San Francisco: Sierra Club.

"Discrimination Based on Sexual Orientation." Available at www.nolo.com/lawcenter.

Dohrenwend, Bruce P., and Barbara S. Dohrenwend. 1969. *Social Status and Psychological Disorder.* New York: John Wiley.

Dollinger, Sol, and Genora Johnson Dollinger. 2000. *Not Automatic: Women and the Left in the Forging of the Auto Workers' Union.* New York: Monthly Review Press.

Domhoff, G. William. 1967. *Who Rules America?* Englewood Cliffs, NJ: Prentice Hall.

———. 1990. *The Power Elite and the State: How Policy Is Made in America.* New York: Aldine De Gruyter.

———. 1995. "Who Rules America?" Pp. 32–47 in *American Society and Politics,* edited by Theda Skocpol and John L. Campbell. New York: McGraw-Hill.

———. 2002. *Who Rules America? Power and Politics.* 4th ed. New York: McGraw-Hill.

——— **and Hoyt B. Ballard, eds.** 1968. *C. Wright Mills and the Power Elite.* Boston: Beacon Press.

Donner, Frank. 1980. *The Age of Surveillance.* New York: Alfred A. Knopf.

Donovan, James A. 1970. *Militarism, U.S.A.* New York: Charles Scribner's Sons.

Doob, Christopher Bates. 1993. *Racism: An American Cauldron.* New York: HarperCollins.

Dougherty, Kevin J. 1994. *The Contradictory College.* Albany: State University of New York Press.

Douglas, Jack D. 1967. *The Social Meanings of Suicide.* Princeton, NJ: Princeton University Press.

———. 1971. "The Sociological Analysis of Social Meanings of Suicide." Pp. 121–51 in *The Sociology of Suicide,* edited by Anthony Giddens. London: Frank Cass.

Drucker, Jane. 2001. *Lesbian and Gay Families Speak Out: Understanding the Joys and Challenges of Diverse Family Life.* Cambridge, MA: Perseus.

Dudley, Kathryn Marie. 1994. *The End of the Line: Lost Jobs, New Lives in Postindustrial America.* Chicago: The University of Chicago Press.

Dugdale, Richard L. 1877. *The Jukes.* New York: G. P. Putnam's Sons.

Duncan, Greg J. 1984. *Years of Poverty, Years of Plenty.* Ann Arbor: University of Michigan, Institute for Social Research.

———, **Timothy M. Smeeding, and William Rodgers.** 1992. "The Incredible Shrinking Middle Class." *American Demographics* (May): 34–38.

Dunlap, David W. 1994. "Survey Details Gay Slayings Around U.S." *New York Times,* December 21, p. D21.

Dunne, Edward, John McIntosh, and Karen Dunne-Maxim, eds. 1987. *Suicide and Its Aftermath.* New York: W. W. Norton.

Durkheim, Émile. 1951. *Suicide.* Translated by John A. Spaulding and George Simpson. New York: The Free Press.

———. 1965. *The Division of Labor in Society.* New York: The Free Press.

Dutton, Diane B. 1986. "Social Class, Health, and Illness." Pp. 31–62 in *Applications of Social Science to Clinical Medicine and Health Policy,* edited by Linda H. Aiken and David Mechanic. New Brunswick, NJ: Rutgers University Press.

Dye, Thomas R. 1995. *Who's Running America?* 6th ed. Englewood Cliffs, NJ: Prentice Hall.

———. 2002. *Who's Running America? The Bush Reconstruction.* Upper Saddle River, NJ: Prentice Hall.

——— **and L. Harmon Ziegler.** 1972. *The Irony of Democracy.* 2d ed. Belmont, CA: Duxbury Press.

E

Eccles, Jacquelynne S., Janis E. Jacobs, and Rena D. Harold. 1990. "Gender Role Stereotypes, Expectancy Effects and Parents' Socialization of Gender Differences." *Journal of Social Issues* 46 (1990): 183–201.

Eckholm, Erik P. 1977. *The Picture of Health.* New York: W. W. Norton.

———. 1982. *Down to Earth: Environment and Human Needs.* New York: W. W. Norton.

———. 1994. "While Congress Remains Silent, Health Care Transforms Itself." *New York Times,* December 18, pp. 4, 34.

The Economist. 2001. "Stumbling in the Dark." July 26. Available at www.economist.com.

Edelhertz, Herbert. 1970. *Nature, Impact, and Prosecution of White Collar Crime.* Washington, DC: U.S. Government Printing Office.

Edelman, Marian Wright. 1988. "Growing Up Black in America." P. 154 in *Crisis in American Institutions,* 7th ed., edited by Jerome H. Skolnick and Elliott Currie. Glenview, IL: Scott, Foresman, 1988.

Edsall, Thomas Byrne, and Mary D. Edsall. 1992. *Chain Reaction: The Impact of Race, Rights, and Taxes on American Politics.* New York: W. W. Norton.

Edson, Lee. 1994. "The Biggest Chill." *Across the Board* (March): 36–40.

Edwards, Richard. 1979. *Contested Terrain.* New York: Basic Books.

Ehrenreich, Barbara. 1983. *The Hearts of Men.* Garden City, NY: Anchor Doubleday.

_____. 1986. "Is the Middle Class Doomed?" *New York Times Magazine,* September 7, p. 44.

_____. 2001. *Nickel and Dimed: On (Not) Getting By in America.* New York: Metropolitan Books.

Ehrhart, Julie K., and Bernice R. Sandler. 1985. *Campus Gang Rape: Party Games?* Washington, DC: Association of American Colleges.

Eitzen, D. Stanley, and Maxine Baca Zinn. 2000. "The Missing Safety Net and Families: A Progressive Critique of the New Welfare Legislation." *Journal of Sociology and Social Welfare* 27 (1): 53–72.

_____, eds. 1989. *The Reshaping of America: Social Consequences of the Changing Economy.* Englewood Cliffs, NJ: Prentice Hall.

_____. 2003. *Social Problems.* 9th ed. Boston: Allyn and Bacon.

Ellsworth, Pheobe C., and Samuel R. Gross. 1994. "Hardening of the Attitudes: Americans' Views on the Death Penalty." *Journal of Social Issues* 50 (Summer): 19–52.

England, Paula. 1992. *Comparable Worth: Theories and Evidence.* Hawthorne, NY : Aldine De Gruyter.

Environmental Protection Agency. 1991. *National Air Quality and Emissions Trends Report, 1990.* Research Triangle Park, NC: Author.

Epstein, Gerald, Julie Graham, and Jessica Nembhard, eds. 1993. *Creating a New World Economy: Forces of Change and Plans for Action.* Philadelphia: Temple University Press.

Epstein, Samuel S., Lester R. Brown, and Carl Pope. 1982. *Hazardous Waste in America.* San Francisco: Sierra Club Books.

Eskridge, William N. Jr. 1996. *The Case for Same-Sex Marriage: From Sexual Liberty to Civilized Commitment.* New York: The Free Press.

Essed, Philomena. 1991. *Understanding Everyday Racism.* Newbury Park, CA: Sage.

Essman, Elliot. 2002. "Life in the USA: Retirement and Aging Attitudes." Available at www.lifeintheusa.com.

Evans, Nancy J., and Vernon A. Wall, eds. 1991. *Beyond Tolerance: Gays, Lesbians, and Bisexuals on Campus.* Alexandria, VA.: American College Personnel Association.

Evans, Sara. 1980. *Personal Politics: The Roots of Women's Liberation in the Civil Rights Movement and the New Left.* New York: Random House.

Everhart, Robert B. 1983. "Classroom Management, Student Opposition, and the Labor Process." Pp. 169–92 in *Ideology and Practice in Schooling,* edited by Michael W.

Apple and Lois Weis. Philadelphia: Temple University Press.

Ewen, Stuart. 1976. *Captains of Consciousness.* New York: McGraw-Hill.

_____ and Elizabeth Ewen. 1982. *Channels of Desire.* New York: McGraw-Hill.

F

Farber, Maurice L. 1968. *Theory of Suicide.* New York: Funk and Wagnalls.

Farberow, Norman L., ed. 1980. *The Many Faces of Suicide: Indirect Self-Destructive Behavior.* New York: McGraw-Hill.

_____. 1975. *Suicide in Different Cultures.* Baltimore: University Park Press.

Faris, Robert E. L., and H. Warren Dunham. 1939. *Mental Disorders in Urban Areas.* Chicago: University of Chicago Press.

Fausto-Sterling, Anne. 1985. *Myths of Gender: Biological Theories about Women and Men.* New York: Basic Books.

Feagin, Joe R. 1991. "The Continuing Significance of Race: Antiblack Discrimination in Public Places." *American Sociological Review* 56: 101–16.

Feagin, Joe R., and Clairece Booher Feagin. 1986. *Discrimination American Style.* 2d ed. Malabar, FL: Krieger.

_____. 2005. *Racial and Ethnic Relations.* 7th ed. Englewood Cliffs, NJ: Prentice Hall.

Feagin, Joe R., and Melvin P. Sikes. 1994. *Living with Racism: The Black Middle Class Experience.* Boston: Beacon Press.

Feagin, Joe R., and Vera Hernan. 1995. *White Racism: The Basics.* New York: Routledge.

Federal Glass Ceiling Commission. 1995. *Good for Business: Making Full Use of the Nation's Human Capital.* Washington, DC: U.S. Government Printing Office.

Federal Times. 2004. "OSC to Study Whether Bias Law Covers Gays." March 15; available at http://daily.misleader.org.

Feltey, Kathryn M. 2001. "Gender Violence: Rape and Sexual Assault." Pp. 363–73 in *Gender Mosaics: Social Perspectives,* edited by Dana Vannoy. Los Angeles: Roxbury.

Fernandez, Ronald. 1994. *Prisoners of Colonialism.* Monroe, ME: Common Courage Press.

Fernando, Suman, ed. 1995. *Mental Health in a Multi-Ethnic Society: A Multi-Disciplinary Handbook.* New York: Routledge.

Ferner, Miker. 1995. "View from Toledo." *The Nation,* February 13, p. 188.

Ferree, Myra Marx. 1983. "Housework: Rethinking the Costs and Benefits." Pp. 148–67 in *Families, Politics, and Public Policy,* edited by Irene Diamond. New York: Longman.

————— **and Beth B. Hess.** 2000. *Controversy and Coalition: The New Feminist Movement across Three Decades of Change.* Rev. ed. New York: Routledge.

————— **and Patricia Yancey Martin, eds.** 1995. *Feminist Organizations: Harvest of the New Women's Movement.* Philadelphia: Temple University Press.

Feyerick, Debby. 1998. "Baby Boomers Feeling Strain of Caring for Older Parents." Available at www.cnn.com/health/9807/31/edler.care.

Fialka, John J. 1992. *Hotel Warriors: Covering the Gulf War.* Baltimore: Johns Hopkins University Press.

Fields, Jason. 2003. "Children's Living Arrangements and Characteristics: March 2002." *Current Population Reports P20-547.* Washington, DC: U.S. Bureau of the Census.

Findlen, Barbara. 1995. "Is Marriage the Answer?" *Ms.,* May/June 1995, pp. 86–91.

Fine, Carla. 1999. *No Time to Say Goodbye: Surviving the Suicide of a Loved One.* New York: Doubleday/Main Street Books.

Fine, Michelle. 1991. *Framing Dropouts: Notes on the Politics of an Urban Public High School.* Albany: State University of New York Press.

Fink, Paul Jay, and Allan Tasman, eds. 1992. *Stigma and Mental Illness.* Washington, DC: American Psychiatric Press.

Finkelhor, David. 1979. *Sexually Victimized Children.* New York: The Free Press.

—————. 1982. "Sexual Abuse: A Sociological Perspective." *Child Abuse and Neglect* 6:99.

—————. 1984. *Child Sexual Abuse.* New York: The Free Press.

—————, **Gerald Hotaling, and Andrea Sedlak.** 1990. *Missing, Abducted, Runaway, and Thrownaway Children in America.* Washington, DC: U.S. Department of Justice.

Fischer, David H. 1981. *Growing Old in America.* New York: Oxford University Press.

Fisher, David E. 1990. *Fire and Ice.* New York: Harper and Row.

Fitzpatrick, James. 1987. *Puerto Rican Americans.* 2d ed. Englewood Cliffs, NJ: Prentice Hall.

Flexner, Eleanor. 1973. *Century of Struggle.* New York: Atheneum.

Folbre, Nancy. 1985. "The Pauperization of Motherhood: Patriarchy and Public Policy in the U.S." *Review of Radical Political Economics* 16 (4): 72–88.

Foner, Philip S., ed. 1970. *The Black Panthers Speak.* Philadelphia: J. B. Lippincott.

Foot, Hugh C., Michelle Morgan, and Rosalyn Shute, eds. 1990. *Children Helping Children.* New York: John Wiley.

Form, William H., and Joan Rytina. 1969. "Ideological Beliefs on the Distribution of Power in the United States." *American Sociological Review* 34 (February): 19–31.

Forster, Bruce A. 1993. *The Acid Rain Debate.* Ames: Iowa State University Press.

Fort, Joel. 1969. *The Pleasure Seekers.* Indianapolis: Bobbs-Merrill.

—————. 1973. *Alcohol: Our Biggest Drug Problem.* New York: McGraw-Hill.

————— **and Christopher T. Cory.** 1975. *American Drugstore.* Boston: Educational Associates.

Foster, Catharine. 1988. "OVE RCOM INGIL LITE RACY." *Christian Science Monitor,* September 8, pp. 14–15.

Foucault, Michel. 1965. *Madness and Civilization.* New York: Random House.

Franklin, John Hope, and Alfred A. Massis Jr. 2000. *From Slavery to Freedom.* 8th ed. New York: McGraw-Hill.

Fraser, Steven, ed. 1995. *The Bell Curve Wars: Race, Intelligence, and the Future of America.* New York: Basic Books.

Freeman, Jo. 1973. "The Origins of the Women's Liberation Movement." *American Journal of Sociology* 78 (January): 792–811.

Freidson, Eliot. 1970. *Professional Dominance: The Social Structure of Medical Care.* New York: Atherton Press.

Freire, Paulo. 1970. *Pedagogy of the Oppressed.* New York: Continuum.

Freud, Sigmund. 1963. *Sexuality and the Psychology of Love.* New York: Collier.

Friedan, Betty. 1981. *The Second Stage.* New York: Summit Books.

_____. 1984. *The Feminine Mystique.* New York: Dell.

Friedenberg, Edgar Z. 1965. *Coming of Age in America.* New York: Vintage Books.

Friends of the Earth. 1982. *Ronald Reagan and the American Environment.* San Francisco: Friends of the Earth Books.

Fromm, Erich. 1955. *The Sane Society.* Greenwich, CT : Fawcett.

Fuller, Richard C., and Richard R. Myers. 1941. "The Natural History of a Social Problem." *American Sociological Review* 6 (June): 320–28.

G

Gabriel, Trip. 1995. "How Marriages Unravel When One Spouse Is Gay." *The New York Times,* April 23, p. A1.

Gallagher, R.P., H.B. Sysko, and B. Zhang. 2001. *National Survey of Counseling Center Directors.* Alexandria, VA: International Association of Counseling Services, Inc.

Gallup Poll. 2003. March 24–25.

_____. 2004. January 12–15.

_____. 2004. April 5–8.

Gallup Organization. 2003. Gallup/CNN/*USA Today* Poll. June 9–10.

Garber, Marjorie. 1995. *Vice Versa: Bisexuality and the Eroticism of Everyday Life.* New York: Simon and Schuster.

Garner, Abigail. 2004. *Families Like Mine: Children of Gay Parents Tell It Like It Is.* New York: HarperCollins.

Garrow, David J. 1983. *The FBI and Martin Luther King.* New York: Penguin Books.

Gartner, Alan, Colin Greer, and Frank Riessman, eds. 1973. *After Deschooling What?* New York: Harper and Row.

Gault, Barbara, and Annisah Um'rani. 2000. "The Outcomes of Welfare Reform for Women." *Poverty and Race* 9 (4): 1–6.

Gaw, Albert C., ed. 1993. *Culture, Ethnicity, and Mental Illness.* Washington, DC: American Psychiatric Press.

Gelbspan, Ross. 1991. *Break-ins, Death Threats, and the FBI.* Boston: South End Press.

Gelles, Richard. 1985. "Family Violence." *Annual Review of Sociology* 11:347–67.

_____ **and Donileen R. Loseke, eds.** 1993. *Current Controversies on Family Violence.* Newbury Park, CA: Sage.

_____ **and Murray A. Straus.** 1988. *Intimate Violence.* New York: Simon and Schuster.

Gerike, Ann E. 1990. "On Gray Hair and Oppressed Brains." Pp. 35–46 in *Women, Aging and Ageism,* edited by Evelyn R. Rosenthal. New York: The Haworth Press.

Gerson, Kathleen. 1993. *No Man's Land: Men's Changing Commitments to Family and Work.* New York: Basic Books.

Gerstein, Dean R., and Lawrence W. Green, eds. 1993. *Preventing Drug Abuse: What Do We Know?* Washington, DC: National Academy Press.

Gerth, H. H., and C. Wright Mills, eds. 1968. *From Max Weber.* New York: Oxford University Press.

Geyman, John. 2003. *Falling through the Safety Net: Americans without Health Insurance.* San Francisco: Common Courage Press.

Gibbons, Don C. 1991. *Society, Crime, and Criminal Behavior.* 6th ed. Englewood Cliffs, NJ: Prentice Hall.

Gibbs, Jack P. 1971. "Suicide." Pp. 311–12 in *Contemporary Social Problems,* 3d ed., edited by Robert K. Merton and Robert Nisbet. New York: Harcourt Brace Jovanovich.

_____ **and Walter T. Martin.** 1964. *Status Integration and Suicide.* Eugene: University of Oregon Press.

Gibson, Margaret A., and John U. Ogbu, eds. 1991. *Minority Status and Schooling.* New York: Garland.

Gibson, Paul. 1989. "Gay Male and Lesbian Youth Suicide." Pp. 110–42 in U.S. Department of Health and Human Services, *Report of the Secretary's Task Force on Youth Suicide,* Vol. 3. Washington, DC: U.S. Government Printing Office.

Gifford, A. L., W. E. Cunningham, K. C. Heslin, R. M. Andersen, T. Nakazono, D. K. Lieu, M. F. Shapiro, and S. A. Bozzette. 2002. "Participation in Research and Access to Experimental Trials by HIV-Infected Patients." *New England Journal of Medicine* 346 (May): 1373–82.

Gillett, J. W., J. B. Johnson, D. G. Arey, R. Constanza, I. J. Tinsley, J. S. Weis, and A. F. Yanders. 1992. "The Need for an Integrated Urban Environmental Policy." *Journal of Urban Affairs* 14 (3–4): 377–98.

Gimpel, James G. 2003. *Cultivating Democracy: Civic Environments and Political Socialization in America.* Washington, DC: Brookings Institution Press.

Gist, Yvonne J., and Lisa I. Hetzel. 2004. "We the People: Aging in the United States." Washington, DC: U.S. Census Bureau 2000 Special Reports.

Glasberg, Davita Silfen. 1989. *The Power of Collective Purse Strings.* Berkeley: University of California Press.

Glass, Jennifer L., and Sara Beth Estes. 1997. "The Family Responsive Workplace." *Annual Review of Sociology* 23:289–313.

Glassner, Barry. 1988. *Bodies.* New York: Putnam.

Glenmullen, Joseph. 2001. *Prozac Backlash: Overcoming the Dangers of Prozac, Zoloft, Paxil, and Other Antidepressants with Safe, Effective Alternatives.* New York: Simon and Schuster.

Global AIDS Action Network. 2002. "Missing: U.S. Strategy and Exemplary Leadership on Global AIDS." The Global AIDS Accountability and Consensus Project Communique; available at www.icrw.org/doc/globalaids_communique_final_1002.doc.

Goddard, Henry H. 1914. *The Kallikak Family.* New York: Macmillan.

Goffman, Erving. 1961. *Asylums.* Garden City, NY: Anchor Books.

Gold, David A., Clarence Y. H. Lo, and Erik Olin Wright. 1975. "Recent Developments in Marxist Theories of the Capitalist State." *Monthly Review* 27 (October): 29–43.

Goldberg, Edward D. 1976. *The Health of the Oceans.* Paris: UNESCO Press.

Goldberg, Steven. 1973. *The Inevitability of Patriarchy.* New York: William Morrow.

Goldstein, Arnold A. 1993. "The Elderly Population." *Population Profile of the United States.* Washington, DC: U.S. Bureau of the Census, U.S. Government Printing Office.

Goldstein, Richard, and Stephen M. Sachs, eds. 1983. *Applied Poverty Research.* Totowa, NJ: Rowman and Allanheld.

Goode, Erich. 1999. *Drugs in American Society.* 5th ed. New York: McGraw-Hill.

Goodlad, John I. 1984. *A Place Called School.* New York: McGraw-Hill.

Gordon, Diana R. 1990. *The Justice Juggernaut.* New Brunswick, NJ: Rutgers University Press.

Gordon, Linda. 1994. "How 'Welfare' Became a Dirty Word." *Chronicle of Higher Education,* July 20, pp. B1–B2.

Gordon, Margaret T., and Stephanie Riger. 1988. *The Female Fear.* New York: The Free Press.

Goring, Charles. 1913. *The English Convict.* London: H. M. Stationery Office.

Gossett, Thomas F. 1965. *Race: The History of an Idea in America.* New York: Schocken Books.

Gould, Stephen J. 1996. *The Mismeasure of Man.* Rev. ed. New York: W. W. Norton.

Gould, William B. 1977. *Black Workers in White Unions.* Ithaca, NY: Cornell University Press.

Gould, W. T. S., and A. M. Findlay, eds. 1994. *Population Migration and the Changing World Order.* Chichester, England, and New York: John Wiley.

Grabosky, Peter. 2000. "Computer Crime in a Borderless World." *International Annals of Criminology* 38 (1/2): 67–92.

———. 2001. "Computer Crime: A Criminological Overview." *Forum on Crime and Society* 1 (1): 35–53.

Gracey, Harry L. 1972a. "Learning the Student Role: Kindergarten as Academic Boot Camp." Pp. 243–54 in *Readings on Introductory Sociology,* 2d ed., edited by Dennis H. Wrong and Harry L. Gracey. New York: Macmillan.

———. 1972b. *Curriculum and Craftsmanship.* Chicago: University of Chicago Press.

Graig, Laurene A. 1999. *Health of Nations: An International Perspective on U.S. Health Care Reform.* 3d ed. Washington, DC: Congressional Quarterly Books.

Grall, Timothy S. 2003. "Custodial Mothers and Fathers and Their Child Support: 2001." *Current Population Reports P60-225.* Washington, DC: U.S. Bureau of the Census.

Granfield, Mary. 1991. "Having It All in America Today." *Money,* October, p. 124.

Grau, Gunter, ed. 1995. *Hidden Holocaust? Gay and Lesbian Persecution in Germany, 1933–45.* Translated by Patrick Camiller. Chicago: Fitzroy Dearborn.

Greenberg, David F. 1988. *The Construction of Homosexuality.* Chicago: University of Chicago Press.

———, **ed.** 1993. *Crime and Capitalism: Readings in Marxist Criminology.* Expanded ed. Philadelphia: Temple University Press.

Greenberger, Marcia. 1980. "The Effectiveness of Federal Law Prohibiting Sex Discrimination in the United States." Pp. 108–128 in *Equal Employment Policy for Women,* edited by Ronnie S. Ratner. Philadelphia: Temple University Press.

Greenhouse, Linda. 1989. "Supreme Court, 5–4, Narrowing *Roe v. Wade,* Upholds Sharp State Limits on Abortions." *New York Times,* July 4, p. A1.

———. 1995. "By 5–4, Justices Cast Doubts on U.S. Programs That Give Preferences Based on Race." *New York Times,* June 13, p. A1.

Greer, Colin. 1972. *The Great School Legend.* New York: Basic Books.

Gregory, Raymond F. 2001. *Age Discrimination in the American Workplace: Old at a Young Age.* New Brunswick, NJ: Rutgers University Press.

Grier, William H., and Price M. Cobbs. 1968. *Black Rage.* New York: Basic Books.

Gronfein, William. 1985. "Psychotropic Drugs and the Origins of Deinstitutionalization." *Social Problems* 32 (June): 437–54.

Grunseit, Anne, Susan Kippax, Peter Aggleton, Mariella Baldo, and Gary Slutkin. 1997. "Sexuality Education and Young People's Sexual Behavior: A Review of Studies." *Journal of Adolescent Research* 12 (4): 421–53.

Guevremont, D. C., G. J. DuPaul, and R. A. Barkley. 1992. "Diagnosis and Assessment of Attention Deficit Hyperactivity Disorder in Children." *Journal of School Psychology* 28:51–78.

Guttmacher, Alan. 1989. *Teenage Pregnancy in the United States: The Scope of the Problem and State Responses.* New York: Alan Guttmacher Institute.

———. 1999. *Sex and America's Teenagers.* New York: Alan Guttmacher Institute; available at www.agi-usa.org.

Gyorgy, Anna. 1979. *No Nukes.* Boston: South End Press.

H

Hacker, Andrew. 1992. *Two Nations: Black and White, Separate, Hostile, Unequal.* New York: Charles Scribner's Sons.

Hacker, Helen M. 1951. "Women as a Minority Group." *Social Forces* 30: 60–69.

Hagan, John, and Patricia Parker. 1985. "White-Collar Crime and Punishment: The Class Structure and Legal Sanctioning." *American Sociological Review* 50:302–15.

Halbwachs, Maurice. 1930. *Les Causes du Suicide.* Paris: Atcan, 1930.

Halvorson, George. 1993. *Strong Medicine.* New York: Random House.

Hamid, Ansley. 1998. *Drugs in America: Sociology, Economics, and Politics.* Sudbury, MA: Jones and Bartlett.

Hamilton, Charles, and Stokely Carmichael. 1967. *Black Power: The Politics of Liberation in America.* New York: Vintage Books.

Hamilton, Jon. 1995. "AIDS: Where Are We Now?" *American Health,* May, pp. 52–57.

Hamm, Mark S. 1993. *American Skinheads: The Criminology and Controls of Hate Crime.* Westport, CT: Praeger.

Hampton, Robert L., Thomas P. Gullotta, and Gerald R. Adams, eds. 1993. *Family Violence.* Newbury Park, CA: Sage.

Haney Lopez, Ian F. 1996. *White By Law: The Legal Construction of Race.* New York: New York University Press.

Hanson, Thomas L., Sara S. McLanahan, and Elizabeth Thomson. 1998. "Windows on Divorce: Before and After." *Social Science Research* 27 (3): 329–49.

Harlow, Enid, David Matas, and Jane Rocamoral, eds. 1995. *The Machinery of Death.* New York: Amnesty International USA.

Harrington, Michael, and Mark Levinson. 1985. "The Perils of a Dual Economy." *Dissent* (Fall): 417–26.

Harris, Charles S. 1978. *Fact Book on Aging: A Profile of America's Older Population.* Washington, DC: National Council on the Aging.

Harris Poll. 1991. April 21.

———. 2003. October 14–19.

———. 2003. December 10–16.

Hartley, Jean, Dan Jacobson, Bert Klandermans, and Tinka Van Vuuren. 1991. *Job Insecurity: Coping with Jobs at Risk.* Newbury Park, CA: Sage.

Hartman, Betsy. 1995. *Reproductive Rights and Wrongs: The Global Politics of Population Control.* Rev. ed. Boston: South End Press.

Hartman, David W. 2000. "Policy Implications from the Study of the Homeless." *Sociological Practice* 2 (2): 57–76.

Hartmann, Heidi. 1994. "Women Working a Third Shift." *Working Woman,* December, p. 16.

Harty, Sheila. 1979. *Hucksters in the Classroom: A Review of Industry Propaganda in the Schools.* Washington, DC: Center for Study of Responsive Law.

Haynes, Dina Francesca. 2004. "Used, Abused, Arrested, and Deported: Extending Immigration Benefits to Protect the Victims of Trafficking and to Secure the Prosecution of Traffickers." *Human Rights Quarterly* 26 (2): 221–72.

Heckscher, Charles. 1995. *White-Collar Blues: Management Loyalties in an Age of Corporate Restructuring.* New York: Basic Books.

Heilbroner, Robert L. 1991. *An Inquiry into the Human Prospect.* Rev. ed. New York: W. W. Norton.

———. 1996. *An Inquiry into the Human Prospect, Updated and Reconsidered for the Nineteen Nineties.* New York: W. W. Norton.

Hendin, Herbert. 1982. *Suicide in America.* New York: W. W. Norton.

———. 1995a. "Assisted Suicide, Euthanasia, and Suicide Prevention: The Implications of the Dutch Experience." *Suicide and*

Life-Threatening Behavior 25 (Spring): 193–204.

———. 1995b. *Suicide in America.* 2d ed. New York: W. W. Norton.

Henry, Andrew F., and James F. Short Jr. 1954. *Suicide and Homicide.* New York: The Free Press.

Henry, Jules. 1965. *Culture against Man.* New York: Vintage Books.

Heredia, Christopher. 2001. "Hate Crimes against Gays on Rise Across U.S." *San Francisco Chronicle*, April 13, p. A19; available at www.ntac.org/news/01/04/15sf.html.

Herek, Gregory M., and Kevin T. Berrill, eds. 1992. *Hate Crimes: Confronting Violence against Lesbians and Gay Men.* Newbury Park, CA: Sage.

Herman, Edward S. 1987. "U.S. Sponsorship of International Terrorism: An Overview." *Crime and Social Justice* 27–28:1–31.

Heron, Ann. 1995. *Two Teenagers in Twenty: Writings by Gay and Lesbian Youth.* Los Angeles: Alyson Publications.

Herrnstein, R. J. 1995. "Criminogenic Traits." Pp. 39–63 in *Crime,* edited by James Q. Wilson and Patricia A. Brennan. San Francisco: ICS Press.

——— **and Charles Murray.** 1994. *The Bell Curve: Intelligence and Class Structure in American Life.* New York: Basic Books.

Hershberger, Scott L., and Anthony R. D'Augelli. 1995. "The Impact of Victimization on the Mental Health and Suicidality of Lesbian, Gay, and Bisexual Youths." *Developmental Psychology* 31: 65–74.

Hershey, Robert D. Jr. 1983. "Women's Pay Fight Shifts to Comparable Worth." *New York Times,* November 1, p. A15.

Hewes, Richard, and Robert Brewin. 1979. *The Tranquilizing of*

America. New York: Harcourt Brace Jovanovich.

Hightower, Jim. 2002. "How Wal-Mart Is Remaking Our World." *Hightower Lowdown,* April 26; available at www.alternet.org.

Hilgartner, Stephen, and Charles L. Bosk. 1988. "The Rise and Fall of Social Problems: A Social Arenas Model." *American Journal of Sociology* 94 (July): 53–78.

Hilts, Philip J. 1995. "U.S. Convenes Grand Jury to Look at Tobacco Industry." *New York Times,* July 26, pp. A1.

Himmelstein, Jerome L. 1990. *To the Right: The Transformation of American Conservatism.* Berkeley: University of California Press.

Hochschild, Adam. 1994. "Changing Colors." *Mother Jones,* May/June, pp. 55–58.

Hochschild, Arlie R. 1975. "Disengagement Theory: A Critique and Proposal." *American Sociological Review* 40 (1975): 553–69.

———. 1997. *The Time Bind: When Work Becomes Home and Home Becomes Work.* New York: Metropolitan Books.

——— **and Anne Machung.** 1997. *The Second Shift: Inside the Two-Job Marriage.* New York: Avon Books.

Hoffman, Andrew J. 1995. "An Uneasy Rebirth at Love Canal." *Environment* (March): 4–9.

Hoffman, Bruce. 1995. "'Holy Terror': The Implications of Terrorism Motivated by a Religious Imperative." *Studies in Conflict and Terrorism* 18 (4): 271–84.

Hoff-Wilson, Joan. 1987. "The Unfinished Revolution: Changing Legal Status of Women." *Signs* 13 (Autumn): 7–36.

Hofstadter, Richard. 1965. *Social Darwinism in American Thought.* Rev. ed. Boston: Beacon Press.

Hohenemser, Christopher, and Ortwin Renn. 1988. "Chenobyl's Other Legacy." *Environment* 30 (April): 5.

Holden, Karen C., and Pamela J. Smock. 1991. "The Economic Costs of Marital Dissolution: Why Do Women Bear a Disproportionate Cost?" *Annual Review of Sociology* 17: 51–78.

Hollingshead, August B., and Fredrick C. Redlich. 1958. *Social Class and Mental Illness.* New York: John Wiley.

Holmes, Steven A. 1994. "Ranks of Inmates Reach One Million in a 2-Decade Rise." *New York Times,* October 28, pp. A1.

———. 1995. "Clinton Backs Bill to Protect Homosexuals from Job Bias." *New York Times,* October 20, p. A1.

Honderich, Kiaran. 1993. "Cocaine Capitalism." Pp. 123–39 in *Creating a New World Economy: Forces of Change and Plans for Action,* edited by Gerald Epstein, Julie Graham, and Jessica Nembhard. Philadelphia: Temple University Press.

Hood, Jane C., ed. 1993. *Men, Work, and Family.* Newbury Park, CA: Sage.

Hooks, Gregory. 1991. *Forging the Military Industrial Complex.* Urbana: University of Illinois Press.

Horrigan, Michael W., and Steven E. Haugen. 1988. "The Declining Middle-Class Thesis." *Monthly Labor Review* 111 (May): 3–13.

Horton, John. 1966. "Order and Conflict Theories of Social Problems." *American Journal of Sociology* 31 (March): 701–13.

Horwitz, Tony. 1994. "Mr. Eden Profits from Watching His Workers' Every Move." *Wall Street Journal,* December 1, p. A9.

Houppert, Karen. 1999. "You're Not Entitled! Welfare 'Reform' Is Leading to Government Lawlessness."

The Nation, October 25, pp. 11–18.

Howell, David R. 1994. "The Skills Myth." *The American Prospect,* Summer, p. 86.

Howey, Noelle, Ellen Samuels, Margarethe Cammermeyer, and Dan Savage. 2000. *Out of the Ordinary: Essays on Growing Up with Gay, Lesbian, and Transgender Parents.* Sacramento, CA: Stonewall Inn Editions.

Huber, Joan, and William Form. 1973. *Income and Ideology.* New York: The Free Press.

Huber, Melissa S., and Ellen Ernst Kosser. 1999. "Community Distress Predicting Welfare Exits: The Under-Examined Factor for Families in the United States." *Community, Work and Family* 2 (2): 173–86.

Hughes, John R. 1990. "Nicotine Abstinence Effects." P. 123 in *Problems of Drug Dependence, 1989,* edited by Louis S. Harris. Rockville, MD: NIDA.

Human Rights Watch. 2000. *United States: Stark Race Disparities in Drug Incarceration.* New York: HRW.

———. 2001. "Hatred in the Hallways: Violence and Discrimination against Lesbian, Gay, Bisexual, and Transgender Students in U.S. Schools." Available at www.hrw.org/reports/2001/uslgbt/.

Humphry, Derek. 1992. *Final Exit: The Practicalities of Self-Deliverance and Assisted Suicide for the Dying.* New York: Dell.

Hunter, Nan D., Sherryl E. Michaelson, and Thomas B. Stoddard. 2004. *The Rights of Lesbians and Gay Men.* 4th ed. Carbondale: Southern Illinois University Press.

Huxley, Aldous. 1970. *Brave New World.* London: Chatto and Windus.

I

Ifill, Gwen. 1989. "Homelessness Takes Hold as National Issue." *Washington Post,* February 5, p. A4.

Illich, Ivan. 1971. *Deschooling Society.* New York: Harrow Books.

Inhetveen, Heide. 1998. "Women Pioneers in Farming: A Gendered History of Agricultural Progress." *Sociologia Ruralis* 38 (3): 265–84.

Institute of Medicine. 2002. *Unequal Treatment: Confronting Racial and Ethnic Disparities in Health Care.* Washington, DC: National Academy Press.

Intergovernmental Panel on Climate Change. 2001. *Climate Change, 2001: IPCC Third Assessment Report.* New York: United Nations; available at www.grida.no/climate/ipcc_tar.

IPSOS-Public Affairs Poll. 2004. February 20–22.

Irvine, Jacqueline Jordon. 1991. *Black Students and School Failure.* New York: Greenwood Press.

Irwin, John, and James Austin. 1994. *It's About Time: America's Imprisonment Binge.* Belmont, CA: Wadsworth.

Isaac, Rael Jean, and Virginia C. Armat. 1990. *Madness in the Streets: How Psychiatry and the Law Abandoned the Mentally Ill.* New York: The Free Press.

J

Jack, Raymond. 1992. *Women and Attempted Suicide.* Hove, East Sussex, United Kingdom: Lawrence Erlbaum.

Jacobs, James B., Christopher Panarella, and Jay Worthington. 1994. *Busting the Mob.* New York: New York University Press.

Jacobs, Janet L. 1994. "Gender, Race, Class, and the Trend Toward Early Motherhood." *Journal of Contemporary Ethnography* 22 (January): 442–62.

Jacobson, Michael, George Hacker, and Robert Atkins. 1983. *The Booze Merchants.* Washington, DC: Center for Science in the Public Interest.

Jaggar, Alison M. 1983. *Feminist Politics and Human Nature.* Totowa, NJ: Rowman and Allanheld.

James, M. Annette, ed. 1992. *The State of Native America.* Boston: South End Press.

Jamison, K. R. 1999. *Night Falls Fast.* New York: Vintage Books.

Japsen, Bruce. 2005. "Analysis Shows Jump in Hospital Mergers." *Chicago Tribune,* February 10.

Jellinek, E. M. 1960. *The Disease Concept of Alcoholism.* New Haven, CT: Hillhouse Press.

Jensen, Carl J. III. 2001. "Beyond the Tea Leaves: Futures Research and Terrorism." *American Behavioral Scientist* 44 (6): 914–36.

Jet. 1995. "Who Benefits Most from Affirmative Action?" March 20, pp. 8–10.

Johnson, Bruce D. 1973. *Marijuana Users and Drug Subcultures.* New York: John Wiley.

Johnson, Dirk. 1994. "Family Struggles to Make Do after Fall from Middle Class." *New York Times,* March 11, p. A1.

Johnson, Fenton. 1992. "In the Fields of King Coal." *New York Times Magazine,* November 22, pp. 30–32.

Johnston, Lloyd D., Patrick M. O'Malley, Gerald Bachman, and John Schulenberg. 2004a. "Overall Teen Drug Use Continues Gradual Decline; But Use of Inhalants Rises." University of Michigan News and Information Services, Ann Arbor, MI; available at www.monitoringthefuture.org.

———. 2004b. *National Survey Results on Drug Use from the Monitoring the Future Study.* Available at www.nida.nih.gov.

Johnston, R., ed. 1977. *Marine Pollution.* Orlando, FL: Academic Press.

Journal of Social Issues. 1994. Special Issue. Summer.

K

Kaestle, Carl F., Helen Damon-Moore, Lawrence Stedman, and Katherine Tinsley. 1991. *Literacy in the United States.* New Haven, CT : Yale University Press.

Kanter, Rosabeth Moss. 1972. "The Organization Child: Experience Management in a Nursery School." *Sociology of Education* 45 (Spring): 186–211.

Kaplan, Fred. 1982. *Wizards of Armageddon.* New York: Simon and Schuster.

Kaplan, Howard B. 1972. *The Sociology of Mental Illness.* New Haven, CT: College and University Press.

Karabel, Jerome. 1972. "Community Colleges and Social Stratification," *Harvard Educational Review* 42 (November): 55.

Kardiner, Abram, and Lionel Ovesey. 1951. *The Mark of Oppression.* Cleveland: World Publishing.

Katz, Arthur M. 1982. *Life after Nuclear War.* Cambridge, MA: Ballinger.

Katz, Ernest. 1991. *Not God: A History of Alcoholics Anonymous.* Center City, MN: Hazeldon Educational Services.

Katz, Michael. 1971. *Class, Bureaucracy, and Schools.* New York: Praeger.

Kaufman, Irving R. 1982. "The Insanity Pleas on Trial." *New York Times Magazine* 131 (August 8): 18.

Kavaler, Lucy. 1978. *The Dangers of Noise.* New York: Crowell.

Kay, Emanuel. 1974. "Middle Management." Pp. 106–126 in *Work and the Quality of Life,* edited by James O'Toole. Cambridge, MA: MIT Press.

Kaysen, Susanna. 1994. *Girl, Interrupted.* New York: Vintage Books.

Keller, Mark. 1958. "Alcoholism: Nature and Extent of the Problem." *Annals of the American Academy of Political and Social Science* 315 (January): 1.

Kelly, Rita Mae, and Jane Bayes. 1988. "Comparable Worth and Pay Equity: Issues and Trends." In *Comparable Worth, Pay Equity, and Public Policy,* edited by Rita Mae Kelly and Jane Bayes. Westport, CT: Greenwood Press.

Kelly, Robert J., Ko-Lin Chin, and Rufus Schatzberg, eds. 1994. *Handbook of Organized Crime in the United States.* Westport, CT: Greenwood Press.

Kennickell, Arthur B. 2003. "A Rolling Tide: Changes in the Distribution of Wealth in the U.S., 1989–2001." *Survey of Consumer Finances,* U.S. Federal Reserve; available at www.federalreserve. gov/pubs/oss/ oss2/scfindex.html.

Kerbo, Harold R. 2003. *Social Stratification and Inequality.* 5th ed. New York: McGraw-Hill.

Kesey, Ken. 1962. *One Flew over the Cuckoo's Nest.* New York: Signet.

Kessler-Harris, Alice. 1980. *Women Have Always Worked: A Historical Overview.* New York: Feminist Press.

Kilborn, Peter T. 1995a. "For Many in Work Force, 'Glass Ceiling' Still Exists." *New York Times,* March 16, p. A22.

———. 1995b. "In New Work World, Employers Call All the Shots." *New York Times,* July 3, p. A1.

Kimmel, Michael S. 1989. "From Pedestals to Partners: Men's Responses to Feminism." Pp. 531–94 in *Women: A Feminist Perspective,* 4th ed., edited by Jo Freeman. Mountain View, CA: Mayfield Publishing Company.

———. 1992. *Against the Tide: Pro-Feminist Men in the United States.* Boston: Beacon Press.

——— **and Michael A. Messner, eds.** 2003. *Men's Lives.* 6th ed. New York: Allyn and Bacon.

Kingsolver, Barbara. 1989. *Holding the Line: Women in the Great Arizona Mine Strike of 1983.* Ithaca, NY: ILR Press.

Kinsella, Kevin G. 1994. "An Aging World Population." *World Health* 4 (July–August): 6.

Kinsey, Alfred C., Wardell E. Pomeroy, and Clyde E. Martin. 1948. *Sexual Behavior in the Human Male.* Philadelphia: W. B. Saunders.

———, ———, **and Martin Gebhard.** 1953. *Sexual Behavior in the Human Female.* Philadelphia: W. B. Saunders.

Kirk, Margaret O. 1995. "When Surviving Just Isn't Enough." *New York Times,* June 25, Section F, p. 11.

Kirk, Marshall and Hunter Madsen. 1989. *After the Ball: How America Will Conquer Its Fear and*

Hatred of Gays in the 90's. New York: Plume.

Kirk, Stuart A., and Herb Kutchins. 1992. *The Selling of DSM: The Rhetoric of Science in Psychiatry.* New York: Aldine de Gruyter.

Kirschenman, Joleen, and Kathryn Neckerman. 1991. "'We'd Love to Hire Them, But . . . ': The Meaning of Race for Employers." Pp. 203–32 in *The Urban Underclass,* edited by Christopher Jencks and Paul Peterson. Washington, DC: The Brookings Institution.

Kissick, William L. 1994. *Medicine's Dilemmas.* New Haven, CT: Yale University Press.

Kitano, Harry H. L., and Roger Daniels. 2000. *Asian Americans: Emerging Minorities.* 3d ed. Englewood Cliffs, NJ: Prentice Hall.

Klare, Michael T. 1972. *War Without End.* New York: Vintage Books.

———. 1981. *Beyond the "Vietnam Syndrome."* Washington, DC: Institute for Policy Studies.

———. 1984. *American Arms Supermarket.* Austin: University of Texas Press.

———. 1991. "Behind Desert Storm: The New Military Paradigm." *Technology Review* (May/June): 28–36.

———. 1993a. "The Next Great Arms Race." *Foreign Affairs* 72 (Summer): 136–52.

———. 1993b. "The Two-War Strategy." *The Nation,* October 4, p. 348.

———. 1995a. *Rogue States and Nuclear Outlaws: America's Search for a New Foreign Policy.* New York: Hill and Wang.

———. 1995b. "The New 'Rogue State' Doctrine." *The Nation,* May 8, pp. 625–26.

——— **and Peter Kornbluh, eds.** 1988. *Low Intensity Warfare: Counterinsurgency, Proinsurgency,*

and Antiterrorism in the Eighties. New York: Pantheon Books.

Klatch, Rebecca E. 1988. *Women of the New Right.* Philadelphia: Temple University Press.

Kleck, Gary. 1991. *Point Blank: Guns and Violence in America.* New York: Aldine de Gruyter.

——— **and Karen McElrath.** 1991. "The Effects of Weaponry on Human Violence." *Social Forces* 69: 669–92.

Kleinke, J. D. 2001. *Oxymorons: The Myth of a U.S. Health Care System.* New York: Jossey-Bass.

Knowles, Louis L., and Kenneth Prewitt, eds. 1969. *Institutional Racism in America.* Englewood Cliffs, NJ: Prentice Hall.

Knowlton, Lesli. 2000. "Treating Suicidal Elders." *Geriatric Times* 1(3); available at www.geriatrictimes.com.

Kolata, Gina. 1994. "AIDS Patients Seek Solace in Suicide but Many Risk Added Pain in Failure." *New York Times,* June 14, pp. C1+.

———. 1995. "New Picture of Who Will Get AIDS Is Crammed with Addicts." *New York Times,* February 28, p. C3.

Koppelman, Andrew. 1995. "No Fantasy Island." *The New Republic,* August 7, pp. 22–24.

Korem, Dan. 1994. *Suburban Gangs: The Affluent Rebels.* Richardson, TX: International Focus Press.

Kozol, Jonathan. 1985. *Illiterate America.* Garden City, NY : Anchor Press/Doubleday.

———. 1991. *Savage Inequalities.* New York: Crown.

———. 2005. *The Shame of the Nation: The Restoration of Apartheid Schooling in America.* New York: Crown.

Kposowa, Augustine J., Glenn T. Tsunokai, and Edgar W. Butler. 2002. "The Effects of Race and Ethnicity on Schizophrenia:

Individual and Neighborhood Contexts." *Race, Gender, and Class* 9 (1): 33–54.

Kramer, Peter D. 1997. *Listening to Prozac.* New York: Penguin Books.

Kreider, Rose M., and Jason M. Fields. 2002. "Number, Timing, and Duration of Marriages and Divorces, 1996." *Current Population Reports P70-80.* Washington, DC: U.S. Bureau of the Census.

Kreitman, Norman. 1977. *Parasuicide.* New York: Wiley.

Kumamoto, Robert. 1991. "Diplomacy from Below: International Terrorism and American Foreign Relations, 1945–1962." *Terrorism* 14 (1): 31–48.

Kuntz, Tom. 1994. "Killings, Legal and Otherwise, around the U.S." *New York Times,* December 4, p. D3.

L

Lacey, Marc. 1992. "Death Toll from L.A. Riots Is Lowered to 51." *Los Angeles Times,* August 12, p. A1.

LaFree, Gary. 1989. *Rape and Criminal Justice: The Social Construction of Sexual Assault.* Belmont, CA: Wadsworth.

Laing, R. D. 1967. *The Politics of Experience.* New York: Ballantine Books.

Lamb, Richard H., and Linda E. Weinberger, eds. 2001. *New Directions for Mental Health Services, Deinstitutionalization: Promise and Problems.* Hoboken, NJ: Jossey-Bass.

Lampert, Dominique, Lan Bourque, and John Kraus. 1984. "Occupation and Suicide." *Suicide and Life-Threatening Behavior* 14 (4): 254–69.

Lamphere, Louise, Alex Stepick, and Guillermo Grenier, eds. 1994.

Newcomers in the Workplace: Immigrants and the Restructuring of the U.S. Economy. Philadelphia: Temple University Press.

Lamphere, Louise, Patricia Zavella, Felipe Gonzales, and Peter B. Evans. 1993. *Sunbelt Working Mothers: Reconciling Family and Factory.* Ithaca, NY : Cornell University Press.

Landry, Mim J. 1994. *Understanding Drugs of Abuse.* Washington, DC: American Psychiatric Press.

Lapp, Richard E. 1968. *The Weapons Culture.* New York: W. W. Norton.

Lappé, Frances Moore, and Joseph Collins. 1979. *Food First: Beyond the Myth of Scarcity.* Rev. ed. New York: Ballantine Books.

————. 1981. *Food First.* Rev. ed. New York: Ballantine Books.

————.1986. *World Hunger: Twelve Myths.* New York: Grove Press.

Lappe, Frances Moore, Joseph Collins, and Peter Rosset. 1986. *World Hunger: Twelve Myths.* New York and San Francisco: Grove Press/Food First Books.

———— **and Rachel Schurman.** 1990. *Taking Population Seriously.* San Francisco: Institute for Food and Development Policy.

Larson, Jeffrey H., Stephan M. Wilson, and Rochelle Beley. 1994. "The Impact of Job Insecurity on Marital and Family Relationships." *Family Relations.* 43: 138–143.

Larson, Luke J. 2004. "The Foreign-Born Population in the United States: 2003." *Current Population Reports P20-551.* Washington, DC: U.S. Bureau of the Census, U.S. Government Printing Office.

Lasley, Paul, F. Larry Leistritz, Linda M. Labao and Katherine Meyer. 1995. *Beyond the Amber Waves of Grain: An Examination of Social and Economic Restructuring in the Heartland.* Boulder, CO: Westview Press.

Laumann, Edward O., John H. Gagnon, Robert T. Michael, and Stuart Michaels. 1994. *The Social Organization of Sexuality in the United States.* Chicago: University of Chicago Press.

Laurier, Joanne. 2004. "U.S. Consumer Debt Reaches Record Levels." International Committee of the Fourth International, January 15, 2004; available at www.wsws.org.

Lazerson, Marvin. 1973. "Revisionism and American Educational History." *Harvard Educational Review* 43 (May): 269–83.

Leary, Warren E. 1995. "Young People Who Try Suicide May Be Succeeding More Often." *New York Times,* April 21, p. A15.

Leckie, Robert. 1992. *The Wars of America.* New York: Harper Collins.

Leidner, Robin. 1993. *Fast Food, Fast Talk: Service Work and the Routinization of Everyday Life.* Berkeley: University of California Press.

Lemann, Nicholas. 1995. "Taking Affirmative Action Apart." *The New York Times Magazine,* June 11, pp. 36–43.

Lemert, Edwin. 1967. *Human Deviance, Social Problems, and Social Control.* Englewood Cliffs, NJ: Prentice Hall.

Lennard, Henry L., Leon J. Epstein, Arnold Bernstein, and Donald Ransom. 1971. *Mystification and Drug Misuse.* San Francisco: Jossey-Bass.

Lens, Sidney. 1970. *The Military-Industrial Complex.* Philadelphia: Pilgrim Press.

Leontief, Wassily W. 1982. "The Distribution of Work and Income." *Scientific American* 247 (September): 188–90.

Lerman, Robert I., and Theodora J. Ooms, eds. 1993. *Young Unwed Fathers: Changing Roles and Emerging Policies.* Philadelphia: Temple University Press.

———— **and Harold Salzman** 1988. "Deskilling and Declassing: Whither the Middle Stratum?" *Society* (September/October): 60–66.

Lester, David. 1972. *Why People Kill Themselves.* Springfield, IL: Charles C. Thomas.

————. 1988. *Why Women Kill Themselves.* 2d ed. Springfield, IL: Charles C. Thomas.

————. 1990. *Understanding and Preventing Suicide.* Springfield, IL: Charles C. Thomas.

————. 1991. "Do Suicide Prevention Centers Prevent Suicide?" *Homeostasis in Health and Disease* 33 (December): 190–94.

————. 1993. "The Effectiveness of Suicide Prevention Centers." *Suicide and Life-Threatening Behavior* 23 (Fall): 263–67.

————. 2000. *Why People Kill Themselves.* 4th ed. Springfield, IL: Charles C. Thomas.

Lev, Michael A. 2000. "China's One-Child Rule: 'The Next Generation.'" *Hartford Courant,* May 1, p. B7.

Levi, Michael. 1998. "Offender Organization and Victim Responses: Credit Card Fraud in International Perspective." *Journal of Contemporary Criminal Justice* 14 (4): 368–83.

Levin, Jack, and Arnold Arlucke. 1983. "Our Elderly's Fate." *New York Times,* September 29, p. A31.

———— **and William C. Levin.** 1980. *Ageism: Prejudice and Discrimination against the Elderly.* Belmont, CA: Wadsworth.

_____ **and Jack McDevitt.** 1993. *Hate Crimes: The Rising Tide of Bigotry and Bloodshed.* New York: Plenum.

Levine, Murray. 1981. *The History and Politics of Community Mental Health.* New York: Oxford University Press.

Levine, Suzanne Braun. 2000. *Father Courage: What Happens When Men Put Family First.* New York: Harcourt.

Levison, Andrew. 1974. *The Working-Class Majority.* New York: Coward, McCann and Geoghegan.

Lewis, Dan A., Stephanie Riger, Helen Rosenberg, Hendrik Wagenaar, Arthur Lurigio, and Susan Reed. 1991. *Worlds of the Mentally Ill: How Deinstitutionalization Works in the City.* Carbondale: University of Illinois Press.

Lewis, Michael. 1978. *The Culture of Inequality.* New York: New American Library.

Lewis, Oscar. 1959. *Five Families: Mexican Case Studies in the Culture of Poverty.* New York: Basic Books.

Lewontin, Richard C., Steven Rose, and Leon J. Kamin. 1984. *Not in Our Genes: Biology, Ideology, and Human Nature.* New York: Pantheon Books.

Lichtenstein, Kenneth, and Ira Helfand. 1993. "Radiation and Health: Nuclear Weapons and Nuclear Power." Pp. 93–121 in *Critical Condition: Human Health and the Environment,* edited by Eric Chivian, Michael McCally, Howard Hu, and Andrew Haines. Cambridge, MA: MIT Press.

Liebow, Elliot. 1967. *Tally's Corner.* Boston: Little, Brown.

_____. 1993. *Tell Them Who I Am: The Lives of Homeless Women.* New York: The Free Press.

Liem, Ramsay, and Joan Liem. 1988. "Psychological Effects of Unemployment on Workers and Their Families." *Journal of Social Issues* 44: 87–105.

_____ **and Paula Rayman.** 1982. "Health and Social Costs of Unemployment." *American Psychologist* 37 (October): 1116–23.

Ligos, Melinda. 2000. "The Fear of Taking Paternity Leave." *New York Times,* May 31, p. G1.

Lindorff, Dave. 1992. *Marketplace Medicine.* New York: Bantam Books.

Lindsay, Mark, and David Lester. 2004. *Suicide by Cop: Committing Suicide by Provoking Police to Shoot You.* Amityville, NY: Baywood.

Link, Bruce G., Francis T. Cullen, James Frank, and John F. Wozniak. 1987. "The Social Rejection of Former Mental Patients: Understanding Why Labels Matter." *American Journal of Sociology* 92 (May): 1461–1500.

Lips, Hilary M. 1989. "Gender-Role Socialization." Pp. 202–5 in *Women: A Feminist Perspective,* 4th ed., edited by Jo Freeman. Mountain View, CA: Mayfield.

Lipset, Seymour Martin. 1990. *Continental Divide: The Values and Institutions of the United States and Canada.* New York, London: Routledge.

_____ **and William Schneider.** 1983. *The Confidence Gap: Business, Labor, and Government in the Public Mind.* New York: The Free Press.

Little, Charles E. 1992. *Hope for the Land.* New Brunswick, NJ: Rutgers University Press.

Lorber, Judith. 1994. *Paradoxes of Gender.* New Haven, CT : Yale University Press.

_____. 1996. "Beyond the Binaries: Depolarizing the Categories of Sex, Sexuality, and Gender." *Sociological Inquiry* 66:143–59.

Los Angeles Times. 1995. "Kevorkian Opens Clinic, Attends 24th Death." June 27, p. A10.

Losen, D. J., and G. Orfield. 2002. *Racial Inequity in Special Education.* Cambridge, MA: Civil Rights Project, Harvard University.

Louis Harris and Associates. 1991. *Public Attitudes toward People with Disabilities.* Washington, DC: National Organization on Disability.

Lucas, Samuel R. 1999. *Tracking Inequality: Stratification and Mobility in American High Schools.* New York: Columbia University Teachers College Press.

Luker, Kristin. 1984. *Abortion and the Politics of Motherhood.* Berkeley: University of California Press.

Lynch, Michael J. 1994. "Rediscovering Criminology: Lessons from the Marxist Tradition." Pp. 263–65 in *From the Left Bank to the Mainstream,* edited by Patrick McGuire and Donald McQuarie. Dix Hills, NY: General Hall.

Lyter, Deanna M., Melissa Sills, and Gi-Taik Oh. 2002. "Children in Single Parent Families Living in Poverty Have Fewer Supports After Welfare Reform." Institute for Women's Policy Research; available at www.iwpr.org.

M

Maas, Peter. 1968. *The Valachi Papers.* New York: G. P. Putnam's Sons.

MacArthur, John R. 1992. *Second Front: Censorship and Propaganda in the Gulf War.* New York: Hill and Wang.

Macedo, Donald. 1994. *Literacies of Power: What Americans Are Not Allowed to Know.* Boulder, CO: Westview Press.

MacLean, Nancy. 1994. *Behind the Mask of Chivalry.* New York: Oxford University Press.

Magaziner, Ira C., and Robert B. Reich. 1983. *Minding America's Business.* New York: Vintage Books.

Magdoff, Harry. 1969. *The Age of Imperialism.* New York: Monthly Review Press.

————. 1978. *Imperialism: From the Colonial Age to the Present.* New York: Monthly Review Press.

Maher, Timothy. 1998. "Environmental oppression: Who is targeted for toxic exposure?" *Journal of Black Studies* 28(3):357-67.

Mahmud, Simeen, and Anne M. Johnston. 1994. "Women's Status, Empowerment, and Reproductive Outcomes." Pp. 151–59 in *Population Policies Reconsidered: Health, Empowerment, and Rights,* edited by Gita Sen, Adrienne Germain, and Lincoln C. Chen. Boston: Harvard Series on Population and International Health.

Malinchak, Alan A. 1980. *Crime and Gerontology.* Englewood Cliffs, NJ: Prentice Hall.

Mandel, Elizabeth, and Beryl Sinclair. 2002. "Pioneers of Production: Women Industrial Workers in World War II." *Journal of Women's History* 14 (2): 158–61.

Manderscheid, Ronald W., and Marilyn J. Henderson. 2001. *Mental Health, United States 2000.* Washington, DC: Center for Mental Health Services, Department of Health and Human Services.

Manheimer, Ronald J., ed. 1994. *Older American Almanac.* Detroit: Gale Research.

Mann, Coramae Richey. 1993. *Unequal Justice: A Question of Color.* Bloomington: Indiana University Press.

Manning, Robert D. 2000. *Credit Card Nation: The Consequences of America's Addiction to Credit.* New York: Basic Books.

Manor, Iris, Michel Vincent, and Sam Tyano. 2004. "The Wish to Die and the Wish to Commit Suicide in the Adolescent: Two Different Matters?" *Adolescence* 39 (154): 279–93.

Mansbridge, Jane J. 1986. *Why We Lost the E.R.A.* Chicago: University of Chicago Press.

Marcus, Eric. 1993. *Is It a Choice?: Answers to 300 of the Most Frequently Asked Questions about Gays and Lesbians.* New York: HarperCollins.

Marger, Martin N. 1987. *Elites and Masses.* 2d ed. Belmont, CA: Wadsworth.

Margolis, Richard J. 1988. "Our Closet Youth Institutions." *The New Leader* 71 (March 21): 16–17.

————. 1990. *Risking Old Age in America.* Boulder, CO: Westview Press.

————. 1992. "Voiceless Children: Juvenile Detention in the U.S." *Education Digest* 57 (March): 37–41.

Marine, Gene. 1969. *America the Raped.* New York: Simon and Schuster.

Maris, Ronald W. 1981. *Pathways to Suicide.* Baltimore: Johns Hopkins University Press.

————, **Alan L. Berman, John T. Maltsberger, and Robert I. Yufit, eds.** 1992. *Assessment and Prediction of Suicide.* New York: Guilford Press.

Markusen, Ann R., Scott Campbell, Peter Hall, and Sabrina Deitrick. 1991. *The Rise of the Gunbelt: The Military Remapping of Industrial America.* New York: Oxford University Press.

———— **and Joel Yudken.** 1992. *Dismantling the Cold War Economy.* New York: Basic Books.

Martin, Jack K., Bernice A. Pescosolido, and Steven A. Tuch. 2000. "Of Fear and Loathing: The Role of 'Disturbing Behavior,' Labels, and Causal Attributions in Shaping Public Attitudes Toward People with Mental Illness." *Journal of Health and Social Behavior* 41 (2): 208–23.

————, **Steven A. Tuch, and Paul M. Roman.** 2003. "Problem Drinking Patterns among African Americans: The Impact of Reports of Discrimination, Perceptions of Prejudice, and 'Risky' Coping Strategies." *Journal of Health and Social Behavior* 44 (3): 408–25.

Martin, M. Kay, and Barbara Voorhies. 1975. *Female of the Species.* New York: Columbia University Press.

Massachusetts Governor's Commission on Gay and Lesbian Youth. 1993. *Making Colleges and Universities Safe for Gay and Lesbian Students.* Boston: Office of the Governor of Massachusetts.

Massey, Douglas, and Nancy Denton. 1998. *American Apartheid: Segregation and the Making of the Underclass.* Cambridge, MA: Harvard University Press.

Matthews, David. 1993. "Why Students Hate Politics." *Education Digest* 59 (September): 49–51.

Matthews, Dawn D., ed. 2004. *Child Abuse Sourcebook: Basic Consumer Health Information about the Physical, Sexual, and Emotional Abuse of Children.* Detroit: Omnigraphics.

Maume, David J., Jr. 2001. "Work-Family Conflict: Effects for Job Segregation and Career Perceptions." Pp. 240–48 in *Gender Mosaics: Social Perspectives,* edited by Dana Vannoy. Los Angeles: Roxbury.

May, Richard. 1994. *1993 Poverty and Income Trends.* Washington, DC: Center on Budget and Policy Priorities.

Mayakovsky, Vladimir Vladimirovich. 1965. "To Sergei Yessenin." P. 350 in *Mayakovsky,* translated and edited by Herbert Marshall. New York: Hill and Wang.

Mayer, Jane, and Jill Abramson. 1994. *Strange Justice: The Selling of Clarence Thomas.* Boston: Houghton Mifflin.

Maynard, Rebecca. A., ed. 1996. *Kids Having Kids: A Robin Hood Foundation Special Report on the Costs of Adolescent Childbearing.* New York: The Robin Hood Foundation.

McAuliffe, William E., and Roberta A. Gordon. 1974. "A Test of Lindesmith's Theory of Addiction." *American Journal of Sociology* 79 (January): 795–840.

McCarthy, Cameron, and Warren Crichlow, eds. 1993. *Race, Identity, and Representation in Education.* New York: Routledge.

McCarthy, John, and William Yancey. 1971. "Uncle Tom and Mr. Charlie: Metaphysical Pathos in the Study of Racism and Personal Disorganization." *American Journal of Sociology* 76 (January): 648–72.

McCoy, Frank. 1994. "We're in the (White) House!" *Black Enterprise* 24 (March): 20.

McGarity, Thomas D., and Sidney A. Shapiro. 1993. *Workers at Risk.* Westport, CT : Praeger.

McGowan, William. 1993. "Class Ads." *Scholastic Update* 125 (May 7): 14–15.

McIntosh, John L. 1992a. "Older Adults: The Next Suicide Epidemic." *Suicide and Life-Threatening Behavior* 22 (Fall): 322–32.

———. 1992b. "Epidemiology of Suicide in the Elderly." *Suicide and Life-Threatening Behavior* 22 (Spring): 15–35.

McKee, David J., ed. 1994. *Tropospheric Ozone: Human Health and Agricultural Impacts.* Boca Raton, FL: Lewis Publishers.

McKeown, Thomas. 1994. "Determinants of Health." Pp. 6–13 in *The Nation's Health,* 4th ed., edited by Philip R. Lee and Carroll L. Estes. Boston: Jones and Bartlett.

McKinlay, John B., and Sonja M. McKinlay. 2000. "Medical Measures and the Decline of Mortality." Chapter 1 in *The Sociology of Health and Illness,* 6th ed., edited by Peter Conrad and Rochelle Kern. New York: Worth.

McLanahan, Sara, and Gary Sandefur. 1994. *Growing Up with a Single Parent: What Hurts, What Helps.* Cambridge, MA: Harvard University Press.

McLeod, Jay. 1995. *Ain't No Makin' It.* Rev. ed 1995. Boulder, CO: Westview Press.

McManus, Patricia A., and Thomas A. DiPrete. 2001. "Losers and Winners: The Financial Consequences of Separation and Divorce for Men." *American Sociological Review* 66 (2): 246–68.

McQuarie, Donald, and Patrick McGuire, eds. 1994. *From the Left Bank to the Mainstream: Historical Debates and Contemporary Research in Marxist Sociology.* Dix Hills, NY: General Hall.

Mead, Lawrence M. 1992. *The New Politics of Poverty.* New York: Basic Books.

Mead, Margaret. 1935/1963. *Sex and Temperament in Three Societies.* New York: William Morrow.

Mechanic, David. 1969. *Mental Health and Social Policy.* Englewood Cliffs, NJ: Prentice Hall.

Medbroadcast. 2004. "Stuck in the Middle: Mental Health of Mid-Level Managers Shakiest, CEOs Fret." March 28; available at www.medbroadcast.com.

Medoff, Peter, and Holly Sklar. 1994. *Streets of Hope: The Fall and Rise of an Urban Neighborhood.* Boston: South End Press.

Megan, Kathleen. 1994. "Sex Harassment Cases Taking Years to Resolve." *Hartford Courant,* October 2, p. A1.

Mellor, Earl F., and William Parks II. 1988. "A Year's Work: Labor Force Activity from a Different Perspective." *Monthly Labor Review* 111 (September): 17.

Melman, Seymour. 1965. *Our Depleted Society.* New York: Holt, Rinehart and Winston.

———. 1974. *The Permanent War Economy.* New York: Simon and Schuster.

———. 1970. *Pentagon Capitalism: The Political Economy of War.* New York: McGraw-Hill.

Merry, Sally Engle. 2002. "Governmentality and Gender Violence in Hawai'i in Historical Perspective." *Social and Legal Studies* 11 (1): 81–111.

Merton, Robert K. 1938. "Social Structure and Anomie." *American Sociological Review* 3 (October): 672–82.

———. 1957. *Social Theory and Social Structure.* New York: The Free Press.

———. 1964. *Social Theory and Social Structure.* Rev. ed. New York: The Free Press.

Meyer, Cheryl L., Michelle Oberman, Kelly White, Michelle Rone, Priya Batra, and Tara C. Proano. 2001. *Mothers Who Kill Their Children: Understanding the Acts of Moms from Susan Smith to the "Prom Mom."* New York: NYU Press.

Milbank, Dana. 1991. "Hooked on Plastic: Middle-Class Family Takes a Harsh Cure for Credit-Card Abuse." *Wall Street Journal,* January 8.

Milburn, Michael A., Roxanne Mather, and Sheree D. Conrad. 2000. "The Effects of Viewing R-Rated Movie Scenes That Objectify Women on Perceptions of Date Rape." *Sex Roles* 43 (9–10): 645–64.

Miliband, Ralph. 1969. *The State in Capitalist Society.* New York: Basic Books.

Miller, Neil. 1995. *Out of the Past: Gay and Lesbian History from 1869 to the Present.* New York: Vintage Books.

Miller, S. M., and Eliot G. Mishler. 1959. "Social Class, Mental Illness, and American Psychiatry." *Milbank Memorial Fund Quarterly* 37 (April): 1–26.

Miller, Walter B. 1958. "Lower Class Culture as a Generating Milieu of Gang Delinquency." *Journal of Social Issues* 14 (3): 5–19.

Mills, C. Wright. 1943. "The Professional Ideology of Social Pathologists." *American Journal of Sociology* 49 (September): 165–80.

———. 1951. *White Collar.* New York: Oxford University Press.

———. 1956. *The Power Elite.* New York: Oxford University Press.

———. 1959. *The Sociological Imagination.* New York: Oxford University Press.

Mills, Robert J. 2001. "Health Insurance Coverage: 2000." *Current Population Reports, P60-215.* Washington, DC: U.S. Census Bureau, U.S. Government Printing Office.

Minois, Georges. 2001. *History of Suicide: Voluntary Death in Western Culture.* Translated by Lydia G. Cochrane. Baltimore, MD: Johns Hopkins University Press.

Mishel, Lawrence, and Jared Bernstein. 2003. *The State of Working America 2002–2003.* Ithaca, NY: Cornell University Press.

Moen, Phyllis. 1992. *Women's Two Roles: A Contemporary Dilemma.* New York: Auburn House.

Mohr, Richard D. 1994. *A More Perfect Union: Why Straight America Must Stand Up for Gay Rights.* Boston: Beacon Press.

Monto, Martin A. 2004. "Female Prostitution, Customers, and Violence." *Violence Against Women* 10 (2): 160–88.

Moody, Harry R. 2002. *Aging: Concepts and Controversies.* 4th ed. Thousand Oaks, CA: Pine Forge Press.

Moore, Jack B. 1993. *Skinheads Shaved for Battle.* Bowling Green, Ohio: Bowling Green State University Popular Press.

Moore, Molly. 1994. "The Second Disaster in Bhopal." *Business and Society Review* (Winter): 26–28.

Moore, Robert B. 1995. "Racism in the English Language." Pp. 376–86 in *Race, Class, and Gender in the United States,* 3d ed., edited by Paula S. Rothenberg. New York: St. Martin's Press.

Moore, Stanley W., James Care, and Kenneth A. Wagner. 1985. *The Child's Political World.* New York: Praeger.

Morbidity and Mortality Weekly Report. 1994. "Suicide Contagion and the Reporting of Suicide: Recommendations from a National Workshop." 43 (April 22): 13.

———. 1995. "Suicide among Children, Adolescents, and Young Adults—United States, 1980–1992." 44 (April 21): 289.

Morrison, Toni, ed. 1992. *Race-ing Justice, En-gendering Power.* New York: Pantheon Books.

Ms. 1995. Special Report on Abortion. (May/June).

Muller, Charlotte. 1972. "The Overmedicated Society." *Science* 176 (May 5): 488–92.

Munro, Neil. 2001. "Internet-Based Financial Services: A New Laundry?" *Journal of Financial Crime* 9 (2): 134–52.

Murdoch, William W. 1980. *The Poverty of Nations.* Baltimore, MD: Johns Hopkins University Press.

Musick, Judith S. 1993. *Young, Poor, and Pregnant: The Psychology of Teenage Motherhood.* New Haven, CT: Yale University Press.

Musto, David F. 1999. *The American Disease: Origins of Narcotic Control.* 3d ed. New York: Oxford University Press.

Myers, Jerome K., and Lee L. Bean. 1968. *A Decade Later: A Follow-Up of Social Class and Mental Illness.* New York: John Wiley.

N

Nace, Edgar P. 1987. *The Treatment of Alcoholism.* New York: Brunner/Mazel.

Nathanson, Constance A. 1991. *Dangerous Passage: The Social Control of Sexuality in Women's Adolescence.* Philadelphia: Temple University Press.

National Advisory Commission on Civil Disorders. 1968. *Report of the National Advisory Commission on Civil Disorders.* Washington, DC: U.S. Government Printing Office.

National Center for Education Statistics. 2003. *Digest of Education Statistics, 2002.* Washington, DC: U.S. Government Printing Office; available at http://nces.ed.gov.

National Center for Health Statistics. 2001. *Health, U.S.A.: 2001.* Hyattsville, MD: Author.

———. 2004. *Health, United States, 2004.* Washington, DC: U.S. Government Printing Office.

National Center for Injury Prevention and Control. 2004. "Youth Violence." Washington, DC: U.S. Centers for Disease Control; available at www.cdc.gov.

National Center on Education and the Economy. 1990. *America's Choice: High Skills or Low Wages.* Rochester, NY: Author.

National Commission on Employment and Unemployment Statistics. 1979. *Counting the Labor Force.* Washington, DC: U.S. Government Printing Office.

National Commission on Marijuana and Drug Abuse. 1973. *Drug Use in America.* Washington, DC: U.S. Government Printing Office.

National Education Association. 2004. "Vouchers." Available at www.nea.org.

National Institute of Mental Health. 1972. *Alcohol and Alcoholism.* Rev. ed. Washington, DC: U.S. Government Printing Office.

National Institute on Aging. 2003. *Alzheimer's Disease Fact Sheet.* Available at http://adear.niapublications.org.

National Institute on Alcohol Abuse and Alcoholism. 1988. "Alcohol and Aging." *Alcohol Alert* 1 (October): 1–4.

National Institute on Drug Abuse. 1988/1989. "AIDS Is Spreading at Same Rate in Heterosexuals." *National Institute on Drug Abuse Notes* 3 (Winter): 14.

_____. 1989. "NIDA Outreach Demonstration." *National Institute on Drug Abuse Notes* 4 (Spring/Summer): 1.

_____. 2004. *Marijuana: Facts Parents Need to Know.* Available at www.nida.nih.gov.

Nava, Michael, and Robert Dawidoff. 1994. *Created Equal: Why Gay Rights Matter to America.* New York: St. Martin's Press.

Navarro, Vincente. 1993. *Dangerous to Your Health: Capitalism in Health Care.* New York: Monthly Review Press.

NBC News/*Wall Street Journal* Poll. 2004. January 10–12.

Neier, Aryeh. 2004. "Zimbabwe's Despot Watches His People Starve." *International Herald Tribune;* available at www.iht.com.

Neimeyer, Robert A. and Angela M. Pfeiffer. 1994. "Evaluation of Suicide Intervention Effectiveness." *Death Studies* 18 (March–April): 131–166.

Nellis, Muriel. 1980. *The Female Fix.* Boston: Houghton Mifflin.

Nelson, Bryce. 1983. "Despair among Jobless." *New York Times,* April 2, p. 25.

Nelson, Jack and Robert Ostrow. 1972. *The FBI and the Berrigans.* New York: Coward, McCann and Geoghegan.

Neubeck, Kenneth J. and Noel Cazanave. 2001. *Welfare Racism: Playing the Race Card Against America's Poor.* New York: Routledge.

_____ **and Jack L. Roach.** 1981. "Income Maintenance Experiments, Politics and the Perpetuation of Poverty." *Social Problems* 28 (February): 308–20.

_____ **and Davita Silfen Glasberg.** 2005. *Sociology: Diversity, Conflict, and Change.* New York: McGraw-Hill.

Newman, Katherine S. 1993. *Declining Fortunes: The Withering of the American Dream.* New York: Basic Books.

_____. 1999. *Falling from Grace: The Experience of Downward Mobility in the American Middle Class.* New York: The Free Press.

_____ **and Chauncy Lennon.** 1995. "The Job Ghetto." *The American Prospect* (Summer): 66–67.

Newsweek. 1972. "Crisis Named Eagleton." August 7, pp. 12–16.

_____. 1985. "Abusing the Elderly." September 23, p. 75.

_____. 1988. "The Risk from Radon." September 26, p. 69.

_____. 1993a. The Clinton Solution." September 20, pp. 30–32.

_____. 1993b. "The Clinton Cure." October 4, pp. 36–38.

New York Times. 1983. "A Study of Patterns in Family Violence." June 8, p. C14.

_____. 1988. "FBI Documents Show Surveillance of Hundreds of Groups and Individuals." January 28, p. A1.

_____. 1990. "Racial Harm Is Found in Schools' Tracking." September 20, p. A14.

_____. 1993. "14-Year Cleanup at Three Mile Island Concludes." August 15, Section 1, p. 15.

_____. 1994a. "Pulse: Free Trade and Job Losses." November 28, p. B1.

_____. 1994b. "U.S. Study Shows Half of Food-Stamp Recipients Are Children." November 25, p. A25.

_____. 1995a. "Malnutrition Hits Many Elderly." July 3, p. A28.

_____. 1995b. "Reverse Discrimination Complaints Rare, Labor Study Shows." March 31, p. A23.

_____. 1999. Poll, July 17–19.

Nicholson, Sean, and Mark V. Pauly. 2001/2002. "Community Benefits: How Do For-Profit and Nonprofit Hospitals Measure Up?" *LDI Issue* Brief 6(4); available at www.upenn.edu/ldi/issuebrief.

Noble, David. 2001. *Digital Diploma Mills.* New York: Monthly Review Press.

Normand, Jacques, Richard O. Lempert, and Charles P. O'Brien, eds. 1994. *Under the Influence? Drugs and the American Work Force.* Washington, DC: National Academy Press.

Norris, Donald F., and Lyke Thompson, eds. 1995. *The Politics of Welfare Reform.* Thousand Oaks, CA: Sage.

Nuwer, Hank. 2002. *Wrongs of Passage: Fraternities, Sororities, Hazing, and Binge Drinking.* Bloomington: Indiana University Press.

O

Oakes, Jeannie. 1985. *Keeping Track: How Schools Structure Inequality.* New Haven, CT : Yale University Press.

_____. 1993. "Tracking, Inequality, and the Rhetoric of Reform: Why Schools Don't Change." Pp. 85–102 in *Critical Social Issues in American Education,* edited by H. Svi Shapiro and David E. Purpel. New York: Longman.

_____. 1994. "More Than Misapplied Technology." *Sociology of Education* (April): 79–91.

_____ **and Martin Lipton.** 1994. "Tracking and Ability Grouping: A Structural Barrier to Access and Achievement." Pp. 187–204 in *Access to Knowledge,* edited by John I. Goodlad and Pamela Keating. New York: College Entrance Examination Board.

O'Carroll, Patrick W. 1989. "A Consideration of the Validity and Reliability of Suicide Mortality Data." *Suicide and Life-Threatening Behavior* 19 (1): 1–16.

O'Connell, Martin. 1993. *Where's Papa? Father's Role in Child Care.* Washington, DC: Population Reference Bureau.

O'Connor, James. 1973. *The Fiscal Crisis of the State.* New York: St. Martin's Press.

Office of National Drug Control Policy. 2000. "What America's Users Spend on Illegal Drugs, 1988–1998." Available at www.whitehousedrugpolicy.gov/publications/drugfact.

Ogbu, John U. 1978. *Minority Education and Caste.* New York: Academic Press.

Okihiro, Gary Y. 1993. "The Victimization of Asians in America." *The World and I,* April 1993, pp. 397–413.

Olson, Laura K. 1982. *The Political Economy of Aging.* New York: Columbia University Press.

O'Malley, Suzanne. 2004. *Are You There Alone? The Unspeakable Crime of Andrea Yates.* New York: Simon and Schuster.

Omi, Michael, and Howard A. Winant. 1994. *Racial Formation in the United States: From the 1960s to the 1990s.* New York: Routledge.

Orenstein, Peggy. 1994. *School Girls: Young Women, Self-Esteem and the Confidence Gap.* New York: Doubleday.

Orfield, Gary, and Mindy Kornhaber, eds. 2001. *Raising Standards or Raising Barriers? Inequality and High Stakes Testing in Education.* Washington, DC: Century Foundation Press.

Ostrander, Susan. 1984. *Women of the Upper Class.* Philadelphia: Temple University Press.

P

Page, Reba Neukon. 1991. *Lower-Track Classrooms.* New York: Teachers College Press.

Pahl, Raymond E., ed. 1988. *On Work: Historical, Comparative and Theoretical Approaches.* London: Basil Blackwell.

Palen, J. John. 2001. *Social Problems for the Twenty-First Century.* New York: McGraw-Hill.

Palmore, Erdman B. 1999. *Ageism: Negative and Positive.* 2d ed. New York: Springer.

Pappas, Gregory. 1989. *The Magic City: Unemployment in a Working-Class Community.* Ithaca, NY: Cornell University Press.

Parenti, Michael. 1994. *Land of Idols: Political Mythology in America.* New York: St. Martin's Press.

_____. 1995. *Democracy for the Few.* 6th ed. New York: St. Martin's Press.

Parsons, Talcott. 1955. "The American Family: Its Relationship to Personality and to the Social Structure." Pp. 21–31, in *Family, Socialization, and Interaction Process,* edited by Talcott Parsons and Robert F. Bales. New York: The Free Press.

Pascall, Glenn R., and Robert D. Lamson. 1991. *Beyond Guns and Butter.* Washington, DC: Brassey's (US), Inc.

Pear, Robert. 1987. "Number of Blacks in Top Jobs in Administration Off Sharply." *New York Times,* March 22, p. A1.

Peart, Karen N. 1994. "Three Deadly Legacies." *Scholastic Update,* April 15, p. 21.

Peattie, Lisa, and Martin Rein. 1983. *Women's Claims: A Study in Political Economy.* New York: Oxford University Press.

Pedahzur, Ami, Arie Perliger, and Leonard Weinberg. 2003. "Altruism and Fatalism: The Characteristics of Palestinian Suicide Terrorists." *Deviant Behavior* 24 (4): 405–23.

Perrucci, Robert. 1974. *Circle of Madness.* Englewood Cliffs, NJ: Prentice Hall.

Perry, Melissa J. 1996. "The Relationship between Social Class and Mental Disorder." *The Journal of Primary Prevention* 17 (1): 17–30.

Pescosolido, Bernice, and Robert Mendelsohn. 1986. "Social Causation or Social Construction of Suicide?" *American Sociological Review* 51 (February): 80–101.

Peters, Stefanie Doyle, Gail Elizabeth Wyatt, and David Finkelhor. 1986. "Prevalence." Pp. 15–59 in *A Sourcebook on Child Sexual Abuse,* edited by David Finkelhor et al. Beverly Hills, CA: Sage.

Peterson, Iver. 1995. "In One Doctor's Way of Life, a Way of Death." *New York Times,* May 21, p. 14.

Peterson, Wallace C. 1994. *Silent Depression: The Fate of the American Dream.* New York: W. W. Norton.

Pettigrew, Thomas F. 1964. *A Profile of the Negro American.* Princeton, NJ: D. Van Nostrand Company.

Pfost, Donald R. 1987. "Reagan's Nicaraguan Policy: A Case Study of Political Deviance and Crime." *Crime and Social Justice* 27–28: 66–87.

Pharr, Suzanne. 1995. "Homophobia as a Weapon of Sexism." Pp. 481–90 in *Race, Class, and Gender in the United States,* 3d ed., edited by Paula S. Rothenberg. New York: St. Martin's Press.

Phillips, Kevin. 1990. *The Politics of Rich and Poor.* New York: Random House.

———. 1993. *Boiling Point: Democrats, Republicans, and the Decline of Middle-Class Prosperity.* New York: HarperCollins.

Physician Task Force on Hunger in America. 1985. *Hunger in America: The Growing Epidemic.* Middletown, CT: Wesleyan University Press.

Pilisuk, Marc, and Thomas Hayden. 1965. "Is There a Military-Industrial Complex Which Prevents Peace? Consensus and Countervailing Power in Pluralistic Society." *Journal of Social Issues* 21 (July): 67–117.

Pillemer, Karl, and David Finkelhor. 1989. "Causes of Elder Abuse." *American Journal of Orthopsychiatry* 59 (April): 179–87.

Piven, Frances Fox. 1995. "Poorhouse Politics." *The Progressive,* February, pp. 22–24.

——— and Richard A. Cloward. 1993. *Regulating the Poor.* Updated ed. New York: Vintage Books.

——— and Richard A. Cloward. 2000. *Why Americans Still Don't Vote: And Why Politicians Want It That Way.* Boston: Beacon Press.

Plant, Richard. 1986. *The Pink Triangle: The Nazi War against Homosexuals.* New York: Henry Holt.

Platt, Stephen. 1984. "Unemployment and Suicidal Behavior." *Social Science and Medicine* 19 (2): 93–115.

Poland, James M. 2003. "Suicide Bombers: A Global Problem." *Humboldt Journal of Social Relations* 27 (2): 100–35.

Powell, Douglas H., and Paul F. Driscoll. 1973. "Middle Class Professionals Face Unemployment." *Society* 10 (January/February): 18–26.

Powell, Elwin H. 1958. "Occupation, Status, and Suicide." *American Sociological Review* 23 (April): 131–140.

President's Commission on Law Enforcement and Administration of Justice. 1968. *The Challenge of Crime in a Free Society.* New York: Avon Books.

President's Commission on Mental Health. 1978. *Report to the President.* Washington, DC: U.S. Government Printing Office.

President's Commission on Organized Crime. 1986a. *The Impact: Organized Crime Today.* Washington, DC: U.S. Government Printing Office

———. 1986b. *The Edge: Organized Crime, Business, and Labor Unions.* Washington, DC: U.S. Government Printing Office.

Price, Barbara R., and Natalie J. Sokoloff, eds. 2003. *The Criminal Justice System and Women: Offenders, Prisoners, Victims, and Workers.* New York: McGraw-Hill.

Price-Bonham, Sharon, David W. Wright, and Joe F. Pittman. 1983. "Divorce: A Frequent 'Alternative' in the 1970s." Pp. 125–46 in *Contemporary Families and Alternative Lifestyles,* edited by Eleanor D. Macklin and Roger H. Rubin. Beverly Hills, CA: Sage.

Princeton Survey Research. 1994. "Worker Representation and Participation Survey." September 15–October 13.

Princeton Survey Research Associates/*Newsweek* Poll. 2003. October 9–10.

Proctor, Bernadette, and Joseph Dalaker. 2003. "Poverty in the United States: 2002." *Current Population Report P60-222.* Washington, DC: U.S. Bureau of the Census, Government Printing Office.

Providence Journal. 2004. "State: Providers of Home Daycare Eligible for Union." March 30; available at www.projo.com.

Psychology Today. 1987. "Date Rape: Familiar Strangers." (July): 10.

———. 1992. "Not So Hot for Tots." 25 (September/October): 15.

Q

Quadagno, Jill. 1994. *The Color of Welfare: How Racism Undermined the War on Poverty.* New York: Oxford University Press.

Quill, Timothy E. 1994. "Physician-Assisted Death: Progress or Peril." *Suicide and Life-Threatening Behavior* 24 (Winter): 315–25.

Quinn, Robert P., and Graham L. Staines. 1979. *The 1977 Quality of Employment Survey: Descriptive Statistics with Comparison Data from the 1969–70 and 1972–73 Surveys.* Ann Arbor: University of Michigan, Institute for Social Research.

Quinney, Richard. 1970. *The Social Reality of Crime.* Boston: Little, Brown.

Quint, Michael. 1995. "Merger to Create Largest Company for Health Plans." *New York Times,* June 27, p. A1.

R

Radelet, Michael L., Hugo Adam Bedau, and Constance E. Putnam. 1992. *In Spite of Innocence: Erroneous Convictions in Capital Cases.* Boston: Northeastern University Press.

Rainwater, Lee, and William L. Yancey. 1967. *The Moynihan Report and the Politics of Controversy.* Cambridge, MA: MIT Press.

Ramasubbu, K., H. Gurm, and D. Litaker. 2001. "Gender Bias in Clinical Trials: Do Double Standards Still Apply?" *Journal of Women's Health and Gender-Based Medicine* 10 (October): 757–64.

Rank, Mark Robert. 1995. *Living on the Edge: The Realities of Welfare in America.* New York: Columbia University Press.

Ratcliff, Katherine Strother, ed. 2002. *Women and Health: Power, Technology, and Inequality in a Gendered World.* Boston: Allyn and Bacon.

Ravitch, Diane. 1978. *The Revisionist Revised.* New York: Basic Books.

Raymend, Joan. 2001. "Business Strategists Beware: The Shortage of Skilled Labor Is Here to Stay—Sonsequences of Today's Students' Poor Math, Science Skills." *Forecast* (March); available at http://articles.findarticles.com.

Read, Piers Paul. 1993. *Ablaze: The Story of the Heroes and Victims of Chernobyl.* New York: Random House.

Reckless, Walter C. 1961. *The Crime Problem.* New York: Appleton-Century-Crofts.

Redick, Richard W. et al. 1992. "Specialty Mental Health System Characteristics." *Mental Health, United States, 1992.* Washington, DC: U.S. Government Printing Office.

Regenstein, Lewis. 1982. *America the Poisoned.* Washington, DC: Acropolis Books.

Regier, D. A., W. E. Narrow, D. S. Rae, R. W. Manderscheid, B. Z. Locke, and F. K. Goodwin. 1993. "The De Facto U.S. Mental and Addictive Disorders Service System." *Archives of General Psychiatry* 50 (February): 85–94.

Reich, Michael. 1978. "The Development of the Wage-Labor Force." In *The Capitalist System,* 2d ed., edited by Richard C. Edwards, Michael Reich, and Thomas B. Weisskopf. Englewood Cliffs, NJ: Prentice Hall.

Reich, Robert. 1991. *The Work of Nations: Preparing Ourselves for 21st-Century Capitalism.* New York: Alfred A. Knopf.

————. 1994. "Jobs: Skills before Credentials." *Wall Street Journal,* February 2, p. A18.

Reiman, Jeffrey. 2003. *The Rich Get Richer and the Poor Get Prison.* 7th ed. New York: Allyn and Bacon.

Reinerman, Craig, and Harry Gene Levine, eds. 1997. *Crack in America: Demon Drugs and Social Justice.* Berkeley: University of California Press.

Repetto, Robert. 1995. *The "Second India" Revisited.* Washington, DC: World Resources Institute.

Reskin, Barbara F., and Heidi I. Hartmann, eds. 1986. *Women's Work, Men's Work: Sex Segregation on the Job.* Washington, DC: National Academy Press.

Reskin, Barbara, and Irene Padavic. 1994. *Women and Men at Work.* Thousand Oaks, CA: Pine Forge Press.

Rich, Cynthia, and Barbara Macdonald. 2001. *Look Me in the Eye: Old Women, Aging and Ageism.* San Francisco: Spinsters Book Company.

Rich, John M., and Joseph L. DeVitis. 1992. *Competition in Education.* Springfield, IL: Charles C Thomas.

Rider, Barry A. K. 2001. "Cyber-Organized Crime: The Impact of Information Technology on Organized Crime." *Journal of Financial Crime* 8 (4): 332–46.

Ridgeway, James. 1991. *Blood in the Face.* New York: Thunder's Mouth Press.

Riegel, Sarah. 2001. "The Home Schooling Movement and the Struggle for Democratic Education." *Studies in Political Economy* 65 (Summer): 91–116.

Riesman, David. 1961. *The Lonely Crowd,* abridged ed. New Haven, CT: Yale University Press.

Rifkin, Jeremy. 1995a. "After Work: A Blueprint for Social Harmony in a World without Jobs." *Utne Reader,* May–June, p. 58.

————. 1995b. *The End of Work: The Decline of the Global Labor Force and the Dawn of the Post-Market Era.* New York: G. P. Putnam's Sons.

Riley, Richard W. 1994. "Curbing Youth Violence." *USA Today,* January, pp. 36–38.

Rimmerman, Craig A. 1996. *Gay Rights, Military Wrongs: Political Perspectives on Lesbians and Gays in the Military.* New York: Garland.

Riordan, Michael, ed. 1982. *The Day after Midnight.* Palo Alto, CA: Cheshire Books.

Rist, Ray C. 1970. "Student Social Class and Teacher Expectations." *Harvard Educational Review* 40 (August): 411–51.

————. 1973. *The Urban School: A Factory for Failure.* Cambridge, MA: MIT Press.

————. 1977. "On Understanding the Processes of Schooling." Pp. 292–305 in *Power and Ideology in Education,* edited by Jerome Karabel and A. H. Halsey. New York: Oxford University Press.

Ritzer, George. 1995. *Expressing America: A Critique of the Global Credit Card Society.* Thousand Oaks, CA: Pine Forge Press.

————. 1996. *The McDonaldization of Society.* Rev. ed. Thousand Oaks, CA: Pine Forge Press.

———— **and Douglas J. Goodman.** 2003. *Sociological Theory.* 6th ed. New York: McGraw-Hill.

Rivlin, Leanne G. 1986. "A New Look at the Homeless." *Social Policy* 16 (Spring): 4.

Robertson, Ian. 1987. *Sociology.* 3d ed. New York: Worth.

Robinson, Daniel N. 1996. *Wild Beasts and Idle Humours: The Insanity Defense from Antiquity to the Present.* Cambridge, MA: Harvard University Press.

Robinson, Randall. 2001. *The Debt: What America Owes to Blacks.* New York: Dutton Books.

Rochefort, David A. 1997. *From Poorhouses to Homelessness: Policy Analysis and Mental Health Care.* 2d ed. New York: Auburn House.

Romero, Mary. 1992. *Maid in the U.S.A.* New York: Routledge.

Roper Organization. 1990. "Human Sexuality Poll." September.

Roschelle, Anne R. 1999. "Gender, Family Structure, and Social Structure: Racial Ethnic Families in the United States." Pp. 311–40 in *Revisioning Gender,* edited by Myra Marx Ferree, Judith Lorber, and Beth B. Hess. Thousand Oaks, CA: Sage.

Rose, Douglas D., ed. 1992. *The Emergence of David Duke and the Politics of Race.* Chapel Hill: University of North Carolina Press.

Rosen, Ellen Israel. 1987. *Bitter Choices: Blue Collar Women in and out of Work.* Chicago: University of Chicago Press.

————. 2002. *Making Sweatshops: The Globalization of the U.S. Apparel Industry.* Berkeley: University of California Press.

Rosen, George. 1968. *Madness in Society.* Chicago: University of Chicago Press.

Rosenbaum, Walter A. 1991. *Environmental Politics and Policy.* 2d ed. Washington, DC: Congressional Quarterly Press.

Rosenhan, David L. 1973. "On Being Sane in Insane Places." *Science* 179 (January): 19.

Rosoff, Stephen M., Henry N. Pontell, and Robert H. Tillman. 2004. *Profit Without Honor: White Collar Crime and the Looting of America.* 3d ed. Upper Saddle River, NJ: Prentice Hall.

Rosow, Irving. 1976. "And Then We Were Old." In *Growing Old in America,* edited by Beth B. Hess. New Brunswick, NJ: Transaction Books.

Ross, Irwin. 1993. "Inside the Biggest Pentagon Scam." *Fortune,* January 11, pp. 88–89.

Ross, Kenneth W. 1985. "Political Education Is Needed in Our Schools." *Education Digest* 50 (February): 59–61.

Ross, Robert, and Graham L. Staines. 1972. "The Politics of Analyzing Social Problems." *Social Problems* 20(Summer): 18–40.

Ross, Stephen L., and John Yinger. 2002. *The Color of Credit: Mortgage Discrimination, Research Methodology, and Fair-Lending Enforcement.* Cambridge, MA: MIT Press.

Rossi, Peter H. 1988. *Without Shelter.* New York: Unwin Hyman.

————, **J. Wright, G. A. Fischer, and G. Willis.** 1987. "The Urban Homeless: Estimating Size and Composition." *Science* 235 (March 13): 1336–41.

Roszak, Theodore. 1969. *The Making of a Counter Culture.* Garden City, NY : Anchor Books.

Rubin, Lillian. 1994. *Families on the Fault Line: America's Working Class Speaks about the Family, the Economy, Race, and Ethnicity.* New York: Harper Perennial.

Rubington, Earl, and Martin S. Weinberg, eds. 2002. *The Study of Social Problems.* 6th ed. New York: Oxford University Press.

Ruiz, Dorothy S. 1990. *Handbook of Mental Health and Mental Disorder among Black Americans.* New York: Greenwood Press.

Rush, Florence. 1980. *The Best Kept Secret: Sexual Abuse of Children.* New York: McGraw-Hill.

Russell, Diana E. H. 1986. *The Secret Trauma: Incest in the Lives of Girls and Women.* New York: Basic Books.

Russell, Denise. 2000. *Women, Madness, and Medicine.* Cambridge, England: Polity Press.

Russo, N. F. 1990. "Forging Priorities for Women's Mental Health." *American Psychologist* 45:368–73.

Rust, Paula C. 1992. "The Politics of Sexual Identity." *Social Problems* 39 (November): 366–86.

Rutter, Philip A., and Andrew E. Behrendt. 2004. "Adolescent Suicide Risk: Four Psychosocial Factors." *Adolescence* 38 (154): 295–302.

Ryan, William. 1976. *Blaming the Victim.* Rev. ed. New York: Vintage Books.

S

Sabbag, Robert. 1994. "The Cartels Would Like a Second Chance." *Rolling Stone,* May 5, pp. 35–37.

SADD, Liberty Mutual Group and Atlantic Marketing Research Company. 2001. Survey done February.

Sadker, Myra, and David Sadker. 1994. *Failing at Fairness: How America's Schools Cheat Girls.* New York: Scribner.

Sagan, Carl, and Richard Turco. 1990. *A Path Where No Man Thought: Nuclear Winter and the End of the Arms Race.* New York: Random House.

Santiago-Irizarry, Vilma. 2001. *Medicalizing Ethnicity: The Construction of Latino Identity in Psychiatric Settings.* Ithaca, NY: Cornell University Press.

Savin-Williams, Ritch C. 1995. "Verbal and Physical Abuse as Stressors in the Lives of Lesbian, Gay Male, and Bisexual Youths." Pp. 28–50 in *Suicide,* edited by Robert Emmet Long. New York: H. W. Wilson.

Schafer, Walter E., Carol Olexa, and Kenneth Polk. 1970. "Programmed for Social Class: Tracking in High School." *Transaction* 7 (October): 39–46.

Schauer, Frederick. 2003. *Profiles, Probabilities, and Stereotypes.* Cambridge, MA: Belknap Press.

Scheff, Thomas J. 1999. *Being Mentally Ill.* 3d ed. Chicago: Aldine De Gruyter.

Schmalz, Jeffrey. 1993. "Survey Stirs Debate on Number of Gay Men in U.S." *New York Times,* April 16, p. A20.

Schoendorf, Kenneth C., C. J. R. Hogue, J. C. Kleinman, and D. Rowley. 1992. "Mortality among Infants of Black as Compared with White College-Educated Parents." *New England Journal of Medicine* 326 (June): 1522–26.

Schor, Juliet. 1991. *The Overworked American: The Unexpected Decline of Leisure.* New York: Basic Books.

Schrag, Peter. 1978. *Mind Control.* New York: Pantheon Books.

Schram, Sanford F., and Samuel H. Beer, eds. 1999. *Welfare Reform: A Race to the Bottom?* Washington, DC: Woodrow Wilson Center Press.

Schroedel, Jean R., and Ronnie J. Steinberg, eds. 1985. *Alone in a Crowd.* Philadelphia: Temple University Press.

Schultz, James H. 1980. *The Economics of Aging,* 2d ed. Belmont, CA: Wadsworth.

Schur, Edwin M. 1983. *Labeling Women Deviant: Gender, Stigma, and Social Control.* New York: McGraw-Hill.

———— **and H. A. Bedeau.** 1974. *Victimless Crimes: Two Sides of a Controversy.* Englewood Cliffs, NJ: Prentice Hall.

Schwarz, John E. and Thomas J. Volgy. 1993. "Above the Poverty Line—But Poor." *The Nation,* February 13, pp. 191–92.

————. 1992. *The Forgotten Americans.* New York: W. W. Norton.

Schwartz-Nobel, Loretta. 2002. *Growing Up Empty: The Hunger Epidemic in America.* New York: HarperCollins.

Science. 1988. "Indoor Radon: The Deadliest Pollutant." 240 (April 29): 606–8.

Scott, Ellen K., Andrew S. London, and Nancy A. Myers. 2002. "Dangerous Dependencies: The Intersection of Welfare Reform and Domestic Violence." *Gender and Society.* 16(6):878-897.

Scott, James C. 1985. *Weapons of the Weak: Everyday Forms of Peasant Resistance.* New Haven, CT: Yale University Press.

Scull, Andrew T. 1977. *Decarceration.* Englewood Cliffs, NJ: Prentice Hall.

Seccombe, Karen. 1999. *"So You Think I Drive a Cadillac?" Welfare Recipients' Perspectives on the System and Its Reform.* Boston: Allyn and Bacon.

Seidman, David, and Michael Conzens. 1974. "Getting the Crime Rate Down: Political Pressure and Crime Reporting." *Law and Society Review* 8 (Spring): 457–93.

Seidman, Steven. 2004. *Beyond the Closet: The Transformation of Gay and Lesbian Life.* New York: Routledge.

Sen, Amartya. 2000. *Development as Freedom.* New York: Anchor Books.

Sen, Gita, Adrienne Germain, and Lincoln C. Chen, eds. 1994. *Population Policies Reconsidered: Health, Empowerment, and Rights.*

Boston: Harvard Series on Population and International Health.

Sennett, Richard, and Jonathan Cobb. 1972. *The Hidden Injuries of Class.* New York: Vintage Books.

Serafica, Felicisima C., Andrew Schwebel, Richard Russell, Paul Isaac, and Linda Myers. 1990. *Mental Health of Ethnic Minorities.* New York: Praeger.

Shah, Saleem A., and Loren H. Roth. 1974. "Biological and Psychophysiological Factors in Criminality." Pp. 101–73 in *Handbook of Criminology,* edited by Daniel Glaser. Chicago: Rand McNally.

Shane, Paul G. 1989. "Changing Patterns among Homeless and Runaway Youth." *American Journal of Orthopsychiatry* 59 (April): 208–14.

Shapiro, Joseph P. 1995. "An Epidemic of Fear and Loathing." *U.S. News & World Report,* May 8, p. 38.

Shapiro, Laura. 1994. "How Hungry Is America?" *Newsweek,* March 14, pp. 58–59.

Sharp, Deanna L., Joan M. Hermsen, and Jodi Billings. 2002. "Factors Associated with Having Flextime: A Focus on Married Workers." *Journal of Family and Economic Issues* 23 (1): 51–72.

Shaw, Clifford, and Henry McKay. 1942. *Juvenile Delinquency and Urban Areas.* Chicago: University of Chicago Press.

Sheehan, Susan. 1983. *Is There No Place on Earth for Me?* New York: Vintage Books.

Sheldon, William H. 1949. *The Varieties of Delinquent Youth.* New York: Harper and Row.

Sheley, Joseph A., ed. 1999. *Criminology: A Contemporary Handbook.* 3d ed. Belmont, CA: Wadsworth.

Shelton, Beth Anne, and Rebecca E. Dean. 2001. "Divorce Trends and Effects for Women and Men." Pp. 216–26 in *Gender Mosaics: Social Perspectives,* edited by Dana Vannoy. Los Angeles: Roxbury.

Sheppard, Harold L., and Neal Herrick. 1972. *Where Have All the Robots Gone?* New York: The Free Press.

Sheridan, Pamela, Judi Solomont, Neil Kowall, and Jeffrey Hausdorff. 2003. "Influence of Executive Function on Locomotor Function: Divided Attention Increases Gait Variability in Alzheimer's Disease." *Journal of the American Geriatrics Society* 51 (11): 1633–37.

Sherman, Suzanne, ed. 1992, *Lesbian and Gay Marriage: Private Commitments, Public Ceremonies.* Philadelphia: Temple University Press.

Sherrill, Robert. 1995. "The Madness of the Market." *The Nation,* January 9/16, p. 49.

Shifman, Pamela, Esohe Aghatise, Colette DeTroy, Ruchira Gupta, and Aida Santos. 2003. "Trafficking and Women's Human Rights in a Globalised World." *Gender and Development* 11 (1): 125–32.

Shilts, Randy. 1987. *And the Band Played On: Politics, People, and the AIDS Epidemic.* New York: St. Martin's Press.

———. 1993. *Conduct Unbecoming: Lesbians and Gays in the U.S. Military.* New York: St. Martin's Press.

Shinn, Marybeth, and Colleen Gillespie. 1994. "The Roles of Housing and Poverty in the Origins of Homelessness." *American Behavioral Scientist* 37 (February): 505–21.

Shneidman, Edwin. 1968. "Preventing Suicide." Pp. 255–6 in *Suicide,* edited by Jack P. Gibbs. New York: Harper and Row.

———. 1987. "At the Point of No Return." *Psychology Today* 21 (March): 55–58.

———. 1995. *Definition of Suicide (Master Work).* Lanham, MD: Jason Aronson.

Shorris, Earl. 2001. *Latinos: A Biography of the People.* New York: Longman.

Shulman, Seth. 1992. *The Threat at Home: Confronting the Toxic Legacy of the U.S. Military.* Boston: Beacon Press.

Sickmund, Melissa. 1990. "Runaways in Juvenile Courts." *Juvenile Justice Bulletin* (November): 1–7.

Sidel, Ruth. 2000. "The Enemy Within: The Demonization of Poor Women." *Journal of Sociology and Social Welfare* 27 (1): 73–84.

Sidel, Victor W., and Ruth Sidel. 1990. "Health Care and Medical Care in the United States." In *The Sociology of Health and Illness,* edited by Peter Conrad and Rochelle Kern. New York: St. Martin's Press.

Siegel, Jacob S. 1993. *A Generation of Change: A Profile of America's Older Population.* New York: Russell Sage Foundation.

Silberman, Charles E. 1970. *Crisis in the Classroom.* New York: Vintage Books.

Silverman, Bertram, and Murray Yanowitch, eds. 1974. *The Worker in "Post-Industrial" Capitalism.* New York: The Free Press.

Silverman, M. M., P. M. Meyer, F. Sloane, M. Raffel, and D. M. Pratt. 1997. "The Big Ten Student Suicide Study: A 10-Year Study of Suicides on Midwestern University Campuses." *Suicide Life Threat Behavior* 27 (3): 285–303.

Silverstein, Brett. 1995. *Cost of Competence: Why Inequality Causes Depression, Eating Disorders, and*

Illness in Women. New York: Oxford University Press.

Simon, David R. 2001. *Elite Deviance.* 7th ed. Boston: Allyn and Bacon.

Simon, Rita James. 1975. *Women and Crime.* Lexington, MA: D. C. Heath.

Simon, Rita J., and David E. Aaronson, eds. 1988. *The Insanity Defense: A Critical Assessment of Law and Policy in the Post-Hinckley Era.* New York: Praeger.

Singer, Bennett L., and David Deschamps. 1994. *Gay and Lesbian Stats: A Pocket Guide of Facts and Figures.* New York: The New Press.

Singer, Peter. 1995. *Rethinking Life and Death.* New York: St. Martin's Press.

Skerry, Peter. 1993. *Mexican Americans: The Ambivalent Minority.* New York: The Free Press.

Sklair, Leslie. 1991. *Sociology of the Global System.* Baltimore, MD: Johns Hopkins University Press.

———. 1995. *Sociology of the Global System.* 2d ed. Baltimore: Johns Hopkins University Press.

Sklar, Holly. 1995. *Chaos or Community? Seeking Solutions, Not Scapegoats for Bad Economics.* Boston: South End Press.

———. 2002. "Poverty Up, Income Down, Except for Top 5 Percent"; available at www.inequality.org.

Skocpol, Theda, and John L. Campbell, eds. 1995. *American Society and Politics.* New York: McGraw-Hill.

Small, Meredith F. 1993. "The Gay Debate: Is Homosexuality a Matter of Choice or Chance?" *American Health,* 12 (March): 70.

Small, Stephen A., and Tom Luster. 1994. "Adolescent Sexual Activity: An Ecological, Risk-Factor Approach" *Journal of Marriage and the Family* 56 (February): 181–92.

Smedley, Audrey. 1998. *Race in North America: Origin and Evolution of a Worldview Press.* 2d ed. Boulder, CO: Westview Press.

Smil, Vaclav. 1990. "Planetary Warming: Realities and Responses." *Population and Development Review* 16 (March): 1–29.

Smith, Dorothy. 1999. *Writing the Social: Critique, Theory, and Investigations.* Toronto: University of Toronto Press.

Smith, Lee. 1993. "Can Defense Pain Be Turned to Gain?" *Fortune,* February 8, p. 84.

———. 1994. "Burned-Out Bosses." *Fortune,* July 25, p. 45.

Smith, Samuel. 1911. *Social Pathology.* New York: Macmillan.

Smolowe, Jill. 1995. "Enemies of the State." *Time,* May 8, p. 60.

Snow, David. 1993. *Down on Their Luck: A Study of Homeless Street People.* Berkeley: University of California Press.

Society. 1994a. "Counting Homelessness." 32 (November/December): 2–3.

———. 1994b. "Survey of Adult Literacy." (January/February): 2–3.

Society for Neuroscience. 2002. *Brain Facts: A Primer on the Brain and Nervous System.* Washington, DC: Author.

Soroka, Michael P., and George J. Bryjak. 1999. *Social Problems: A World at Risk.* Boston: Allyn and Bacon.

Southern Poverty Law Center. 1991. *The Ku Klux Klan: A History of Racism and Violence.* 4th ed. Montgomery, AL: Author.

———. 1995a. "Aryan Nations: A Long History of Hate and Violence." *Klanwatch Intelligence Report* (March 1995): 7.

———. 1995b. "Hate Movement Shifts Tactics in 1994: Klan Groups Fall; Aryan Nations, Militias and

States Rights Organizations Rise." *Klanwatch Intelligence Report* (March): 9–11.

Soyer, Daniel. 1999. "Garment Sweatshops, Then and Now." *New Labor Forum* 4 (Spring–Summer): 35–46.

Spitzer, Robert J. 1995. *The Politics of Gun Control.* Chatham, NJ: Chatham House Publishers.

Spring, Joel H. 1972. *Education and the Rise of the Corporate State.* Boston: Beacon Press, 1972.

Squires, Gregory D. 1994. *Capital and Communities in Black and White.* Albany: State University of New York Press.

Srole, Leo, Thomas S. Langner, Marvin K. Opler, and Thomas A. C. Rennie. 1962. *Mental Health in the Metropolis.* New York: McGraw-Hill.

Stack, Carol B. 1974. *All Our Kin.* New York: Harper and Row.

Stack, Steven. 1978. "Ideological Beliefs on the American Distribution of Opportunity, Power, and Rewards." *Sociological Focus* 11 (August): 221–33.

———. 1982. "Suicide: A Decade Review of the Sociological Literature." *Deviant Behavior* 4: 41–66.

———. 1987. "Celebrities and Suicide." *American Sociological Review* 52 (June): 401–12.

Staines, Graham L., and Robert P. Quinn. 1979. "American Workers Evaluate the Quality of Their Jobs." *Monthly Labor Review* 102 (January): 3–12.

Staples, Robert. 1986. *The Urban Plantation.* San Francisco: Black Scholars Press.

Starr, Linda. 1998. "From Billboard to Chalkboard: Advertising Creeps into the Classroom." *Education World;* available at www.education-world.com.

Starr, Paul. 1982. *The Social Transformation of American Medicine.* New York: Basic Books.

Steadman, Henry J., Margaret McGreevy, Joseph Morrissey, Lisa Callahan, Pamela Clark Robbins, and Carmen Cirincione. 1993. *Before and After Hinckley: Evaluating Insanity Defense Reform.* New York: Guilford.

Steffensmeier, Darrell, and Michael Cobb. 1981. "Sex Differences in Urban Arrest Patterns, 1934–1979." *Social Problems* 29 (October): 37–49.

Steil, Janice M. 1989. "Marital Relationships and Mental Health: The Psychic Costs of Inequality." Pp. 138–48 in *Women: A Feminist Perspective,* 4th ed., edited by Jo Freeman. Mountain View, CA: Mayfield.

Steinmetz, Suzanne K. 1987. "Elderly Victims of Domestic Violence." Pp. 126–41 in *The Elderly: Victims and Deviants,* edited by Carl D. Chambers, John H. Lindquist, O. Z. White, and Michael T. Harter. Athens: Ohio University Press.

Stevens, Mitchell L. 2001. *Kingdom of Children: Culture and Controversy in the Homeschooling Movement.* Princeton, NJ: Princeton University Press.

Stevens, William K. 1994. "Green Revolution Is Not Enough, Study Find." *New York Times,* September 6, p. C11.

Stevenson, Michael R., and Jeanine Cogan, eds. 2003. *Everyday Activism: A Handbook for Lesbian, Gay, and Bisexual People and Their Allies.* New York: Routledge.

Stewart, John Massey, ed. 1992. *The Soviet Environment: Problems, Policies, and Politics.* Cambridge, England: Cambridge University Press.

Stiffman, Arlene Rubin. 1989. "Physical and Sexual Abuse in Runaway Youths." *Child Abuse and Neglect* 13: 417–26.

Stratton, Joanna. 1982. *Pioneer Women.* Washington, DC: Touchstone Press.

Straus, Murray A. 1980. "A Sociological Perspective on Violence in the Family." Pp. 7–31 in *Violence and the Family,* edited by Maurice R. Green. Boulder, CO: Westview Press.

———, Richard J. Gelles, and Suzanne K. Steinmetz, 1980. *Behind Closed Doors: Violence in the American Family.* Garden City, NY: Anchor Books.

Strickland, Bonnie R. 1995. "Research on Sexual Orientation and Human Development." *Developmental Psychology* 31 (January): 137–140.

Stryker, Jeff. 1995. "An Awful Milestone for the Golden Gate Bridge." *New York Times,* July 9, p. D3.

Stubbing, Richard A., and Richard A. Mendel. 1986. *The Defense Game.* New York: Harper and Row.

Summer, Laura, and Isaac Shapiro. 1994. *Trends in Health Insurance Coverage, 1987–1993.* Washington, DC: Center on Budget and Policy Priorities.

Suplee, Curt. 1995. "Study Lends Credence to Theory of 'Gay Gene.'" *Hartford Courant,* October 31, pp. A1, A5.

Sutherland, Edwin H. 1940. "White-Collar Criminality." *American Sociological Review* 5 (February): 1–12.

———. 1949. *White Collar Crime.* New York: Dryden Press.

——— and Donald R. Cressey. 1974. *Criminology.* 9th ed. Philadelphia: J. B. Lippincott.

Szasz, Thomas S. 1984. *The Myth of Mental Illness* Rev. ed. New York: Perennial Currents.

———. 1986. "The Case against Suicide Prevention." *American Psychologist* 41: 806–12.

———. 1991. *Ideology and Insanity.* Syracuse, NY: Syracuse University Press.

———. 1994. *Cruel Compassion: Psychiatric Control of Society's Unwanted.* New York: John Wiley.

———. 1997. *Insanity: The Idea and Its Consequences.* Syracuse, NY: Syracuse University Press.

Szulc, Tad. 1977. "CIA's Electric Kool-Aid Acid Test." *Psychology Today* 11 (November): 92–94.

T

Tanzer, Michael. 1971. *The Sick Society.* New York: Holt, Rinehart.

Taylor, Ian. 1999. *Crime in Context: A Critical Criminology of Market Societies.* Boulder, CO: Westview Press.

Taylor, Ronald L. 1976. "Psychosocial Development among Black Children and Youth." *American Journal of Orthopsychiatry* 46 (January): 4–19.

———, ed. 1995. *African-American Youth: Their Social and Economic Status in the United States.* Westport, CT: Praeger.

Taylor, Shawn. 2003. "Time to Give: Workers Donating Paid Hours Off to Colleagues in Need." *Hartford Courant,* March 10, p. E1.

Teixeira, Ruy. 1992. *The Disappearing American Voter.* Washington, DC: Brookings Institution.

Testa, Mark F. 1992. "Racial and Ethnic Variation in the Early Life Course of Adolescent Welfare Mothers." Pp. 89–112 in *Early*

Parenthood and Coming of Age in the 1990s, edited by Margaret K. Rosenheim and Mark F. Testa. New Brunswick, NJ: Rutgers University Press.

Theodoris, Athan, ed. 1991. *From the Secret Files of J. Edgar Hoover.* Chicago: I. R. Dee.

Thomas, William I., and Florian Znaniecki. 1927. *The Polish Peasant in Europe and America.* New York: Alfred A. Knopf.

Thomson, Allison. 1995. "The Contingent Workforce." U.S. Department of Labor, Bureau of Labor Statistics, *Occupational Outlook Quarterly* (Spring): 45–48.

Thorne, Barrie. 1993. *Gender Play: Girls and Boys in School.* New Brunswick, NJ: Rutgers University Press.

Thornton, Russell. 1987. *American Indian Holocaust and Survival.* Norman: University of Oklahoma Press.

Thurow, Lester C. 1987. "A Surge in Inequality." *Scientific American* 256 (May): 30–37

Time. 1977. "Mind-Bending Disclosures: CIA Testing." August 15, p. 9.

———. 1993. "Fighting Off Doomsday." June 21, p. 38.

Time/CNN. 2002. *Time/CNN/Harris Interactive Poll.* December 17–18.

Tomaskovic-Devey, Donald. 1993. *Gender and Racial Inequality at Work.* Ithaca, NY: ILR Press.

Tonry, Michael. 1996. *Malign Neglect: Race, Crime, and Punishment in America.* New York: Oxford University Press.

Torres, Aida, and Jacqueline D. Forrest. 1988. "Why Do Women Have Abortions?" *Family Planning Perspectives* 20 (July/August): 169–76.

Torrey, E. Fuller. 1998. *Out of the Shadows: Confronting America's Mental Illness Crisis.* Hoboken, NJ: Wiley.

Tower, Cynthia Crosson. 1996. *Understanding Child Abuse and Neglect.* 3d ed. Boston: Allyn and Bacon.

Tucker, Jerry. 1974. *The Experience of Politics.* San Francisco: Canfield Press.

Turner, Margaret Austin, Michael E. Fix, and Raymond J. Struyk. 1991. *Opportunities Denied, Opportunities Diminished: Racial Discrimination in Hiring.* Washington, DC: Urban Institute Press.

2003 Values Update Survey. 2003 Princeton Survey Research Associates, July 14–August 5.

Tyrer, Peter, and Derek Steinberg. 1998. *Models for Mental Disorders: Conceptual Models in Psychiatry.* 3d ed. New York: John Wiley.

U

Uchitelle, Louis, and N. R. Kleinfield. 1996. "On the Battlefields of Business, Millions of Casualties." *New York Times,* March 3, p. A1.

United Nations. 1991. *The Impact of the War on Iraq.* New York: United Nations.

———. 1992. "Down to Basics: Food, Water, Sanitation." *UN Chronicle* (September): 56.

———. 2000. *Human Development Report, 2000.* New York: Oxford University Press.

———. 2002. *UNDP/UNICEF 2002 Report*; available at www.chernobyl.info.

———. 2003a. *United Nations Statistical Yearbook*; available at www.unhcr.org.

———. 2003b. *World Population Prospects: The 2002 Revision.* Vol. I.

United Nations Children's Fund. 1995. *The State of the World's Children, 1995.* New York: Oxford University Press.

———. 2002. *The State of the World's Children, 2002.* New York: Oxford University Press.

United Nations Population Fund. 1993. *The State of the World Population 1993: The Individual and the World: Population, Migration and Development in the 1990s.* New York: Author.

United Way of New York City. 1995. *Low-Income Populations in New York City: Economic Trends and Social Welfare Programs, 1994.* New York: United Way.

Unks, Gerald, ed. 1995. *The Gay Teen.* New York: Routledge.

Ursano, Robert J., and Ann E. Norwood, eds. 1996. *Emotional Aftermath of the Persian Gulf War: Veterans, Families, Communities, and Nations.* Arlington, VA: American Psychiatric Association.

U.S. Bureau of the Census. 1971. *Minority-Owned Business: 1969.* Washington, DC: U.S. Government Printing Office.

———. 1995. *Statistical Abstract of the United States, 1994.* Washington, DC: U.S. Government Printing Office.

———. 2004. *Statistical Abstract of the United States, 2003.* Washington, DC: U.S. Government Printing Office.

———. 2005. *Statistical Abstract of the United States, 2004–2005.* Washington, DC: U.S. Government Printing Office.

U.S. Commission on Civil Rights. 1981a. *Affirmative Action in the 1980s: Dismantling the Process of Discrimination.* Washington, DC: U.S. Government Printing Office.

———. 1981b. *With All Deliberate Speed, 1954–1980.* Washington, DC: U.S. Government Printing Office.

———. 1983. *Equal Opportunity in Presidential Appointments.* Washington, DC: U.S. Government Printing Office.

U.S. Conference of Mayors. 1994. *Needle Exchange: Moving beyond the Controversy.* Washington, DC: Author.

———. 2002. "A Status Report on Hunger and Homelessness in America's Cities, 2002."

U.S. Congress, House. 1992a. Select Committee on Aging, *Alzheimer's Disease: The Time Bomb in Our Health Care System.* Washington, DC: U.S. Government Printing Office.

———. 1992b. Select Committee on Hunger, *Hunger in America: Who Cares?* Washington, DC: U.S. Government Printing Office.

———. 2004. "Everyday Low Wages: The Hidden Price We All Pay For Wal-Mart." Report for the Committee on Education and the Workforce. Washington, DC: U.S. Government Printing Office.

U.S. Congress, Senate. 1980. Committee on the Judiciary, *Homeless Youth: The Saga of Pushouts and Throwaways in America.* Washington, DC: U.S. Government Printing Office.

———. 1990. Committee on Labor and Human Services, *Street Kids— Homeless and Runaway Youth.* Washington, DC: U.S. Government Printing Office.

———. 1992. Committee on Environment and Public Works, *Effects of the Accident at the Chernobyl Nuclear Power Plant.* Washington, DC: U.S. Government Printing Office.

———. 1993. Committee on Labor and Human Resources, *Recess from Violence: Making Our Schools Safe.* Washington, DC: U.S. Government Printing Office.

———. 1994. Committee on Labor and Human Resources, *Hearing on the Employment Non-Discrimination Act of 1994.* Washington, DC: U.S. Government Printing Office.

———. 1999. Committee on Health, Education, Labor and Pensions, *Hearing on School Safety: Making Our Schools Safer.* May 6, available at http://enzi.senate.gov.

———. 2002. "Identity Theft: The Nation's Fastest Growing Crime Wave Hits Seniors." Hearing before the Special Committee on Aging of the United States, July 18. Washington, DC: Government Printing Office.

U.S. Department of Commerce. 2004. "Alcoholic Beverages and Tobacco Products: 2002." Available at www.census.gov.

U.S. Department of Education. 1993. National Center for Educational Statistics, *Adult Literacy in America: A First Look at the Results of the National Adult Literacy Survey.* Washington, DC: U.S. Government Printing Office.

———. 1998. National Center for Educational Statistics, "Descriptive Summary of 1995–96 Beginning Postsecondary Students." Washington, DC: Government Printing Office.

———. 2001. National Center for Education Statistics, *Dropout Rates in the United States, 2000.* Washington, DC: U.S. Government Printing Office; available at http://nces.ed.gov.

———. 2002. *The Condition of Education, 2002.* Washington, DC: Government Printing Office.

U.S. Department of Health, Education, and Welfare. 1973. *Work in America.* Report of a Special Task Force to the Secretary of Health, Education, and Welfare. Washington, DC: U.S. Government Printing Office.

———. 1974. *Facts about Alcohol and Alcoholism.* Washington, DC: U.S. Government Printing Office.

U.S. Department of Health and Human Services. 1981. *Alcohol and Health: Fourth Special Report to the U.S. Congress.* Washington, DC: U.S. Government Printing Office.

———. 1983. *Overview of The Seattle-Denver Income Maintenance Final Report.* Washington, DC: U.S. Government Printing Office.

———. 1987. *Alcohol and Health: Sixth Special Report to the U.S. Congress.* Washington, DC: U.S. Government Printing Office.

———. 1989. *Methamphetamine Abuse in the United States.* Washington, DC: U.S. Government Printing Office.

———. 1993. *Alcohol and Health: Eighth Special Report to the U.S. Congress.* Washington, DC: U.S. Government Printing Office.

———. 1998. *Facts about Heart Disease and Women.* Bethesda, MD: National Institutes of Health.

———. 2002a. *Income of the Aged Chartbook, 2001.* Washington, DC: U.S. Government Printing Office.

———. 2002b. "Results from the 2002 National Survey on Drug Use and Health: National Findings." Available at www.oas.samhsa.gov.

———. 2004. *National Health Interview Survey, 2004.* Washington, DC: U.S. Government Printing Office; available at www.cdc.gov/nchs/about/major/nhis/released200412.htm.

U.S. Department of Justice. 2003. *Criminal Victimization in the United States, 2002 Statistical Tables.* Washington, DC: Government Printing Office.

———. 2004. *Uniform Crime Reports for the United States, 2003.* Washington, DC: U.S. Government Printing Office.

U.S. Department of Labor. 1991. *A Report on the Glass Ceiling Initiative.* Washington, DC: U.S. Government Printing Office.

U.S. Department of State. 1961. *Bulletin,* Vol. 44: February 6.

U.S. Environmental Protection Agency. 1992. *A Citizen's Guide to Radon.* 2d ed. Washington, DC: U.S. Government Printing Office.

———. 1993. *Radon: The Health Threat with a Simple Solution.* Washington, DC: U.S. Government Printing Office.

———. 2004. "Acid Rain." Available at www.epa.gov/airmarkets/acidrain.

"U.S. Finds Heavy Toll of Rapes on Young." 1994. *New York Times,* June 23, p. A13.

U.S. General Accounting Office. 1982. *Advances in Automation Prompt Concern over Increased*

U.S. News & World Report. 1972. "Eagleton's Own Story of His Health Problems." August 7, pp. 16–17.

———. 1988. "Lethal Leaks in the Roof of the World." March 28, p. 10.

U.S. Senate, Subcommittee on Terrorism, Narcotics, and International Operations of the Committee on Foreign Relations. 1989. *Drugs, Law Enforcement, and Foreign Policy.* Washington, DC: U.S. Government Printing Office.

Ussher, Jane M. 1992. *Women's Madness: Misogyny or Mental Illness?* Amherst: University of Massachusetts Press.

U.S. Surgeon General. 2001. *Mental Health, Culture, Race, and Ethnicity: A Supplement to Mental Health, A Report of the Surgeon General.* Washington, DC: Government Printing Office.

U.S. Unemployment. Washington, DC: U.S. Government Printing Office.

V

Vedder, Richard K. 1982. *Robotics and the Economy.* Washington, DC: U.S. Government Printing Office.

Verhovek, Sam Howe. 1995. "Across the U.S., Executions Are Neither Swift Nor Cheap." *The New York Times,* February 22, p. A1.

Violas, Paul. 1978. *The Training of the Urban Working Class.* Chicago: Rand McNally.

W

Wagner, Travis. 1994. *In Our Backyard: A Guide to Understanding Pollution and Its Effects.* New York: Van Nostrand Reinhold.

Wahl, Otto F. 1999. *Telling Is Risky Business: The Experience of Mental Illness Stigma.* New Brunswick, NJ: Rutgers University Press.

Wald, Patricia M., and Peter Barton Hutt. 1972. "The Drug Abuse Survey Project." In *Dealing with Drug Abuse,* edited by Patricia M. Wald, Peter Baron-Hutt, James V. DeLong, Peter A. Wilson, John F. Holahan, and Annette Abrams. New York: Praeger.

Wallace, Betty, and William Graves. 1995. *Poisoned Apple: The Bell-Curve and How Our Schools Create Mediocrity and Failure.* New York: St. Martin's Press.

Wallace, Steven P., John B. Williamson, Rita, Gaston Lung, and Lawrence A. Powell. 1991. "A Lamb in Wolf's Clothing? The Reality of Senior Power and Social Policy." Pp. 95–114 in *Critical Perspectives on Aging: The Political*

and Moral Economy of Growing Old, edited by Meredith Minkler and Carroll L. Estes. Amityville, NY : Baywood.

Wallerstein, Immanuel. 1979. *The Capitalist World-Economy.* Cambridge, England: Cambridge University Press.

Wallerstein, Judith S., and Sandra Blakeslee. 1989. *Second Chances.* New York: Ticknor and Fields.

———. 2001. *The Unexpected Legacy of Divorce: The 25 Year Landmark Study.* New York: Hyperion.

Wallerstein, Judith S., and Joan B. Kelly. 1980. *Surviving the Breakup.* New York: Basic Books.

Walters, Donna K. H. 1995. "Study Shows More Women Being Providers." *Hartford Courant,* May 11, p. A1.

Warner, Jennifer. 2003. "Job Stress Affects Workers' Mental and Physical Health." WebMD Medical News (November 4); available at http://my.webcd.com.

Warner, Leslie Maitland. 1986. "U.S. Study on Adult Literacy Finds the Results Are Mixed." *New York Times,* September 26, p. D27.

Washington Post. 1995. "Road to Justice Needs Shortening, Report Says." June 24, p. A21.

———. 2000. "Gay Rights Information Taken Off Site." February 18; available at http://daily.misleader.org.

Wasserman, Harvey, and Norman Solomon. 1982. *Killing Our Own: Disaster of America's Experience with Atomic Radiation.* New York: Dell.

Wattenberg, Martin P. 2002. *Where Have All the Voters Gone?* Cambridge, MA: Harvard University Press.

Weber, Max. 1968. *Economy and Society.* Translated by Ephraim

Banks for Reconstruction and Development.

World Resources Institute. 2004. *Environmental Almanac.* Boston: Houghton Mifflin.

Worley, Jennifer Campbell, and Dana Vannoy. 2001. "The Challenge of Integrating Work and Family Life." Pp. 165–73 in *Gender Mosaics: Social Perspectives,* edited by Dana Vannoy. Los Angeles: Roxbury.

Wright, James D., and Peter H. Rossi. 1994. *Armed and Considered Dangerous: A Survey of Felons and Their Firearms.* Expanded ed. New York: Aldine de Gruyter.

Y

Yates, Michael D. 1994. *Longer Hours, Fewer Jobs: Employment and Unemployment in the United States.* New York: Monthly Review Press.

Z

Zedlewski, Sheila R., Roberta O. Barnes, Martha R. Burt, Timothy D. McBride, and Jack A. Meyer. 1990. *The Needs of the Elderly in the 21st Century.* Washington, DC: Urban Institute Press.

Zelnick, Melvin, and John F. Kantner. 1979. "Reasons for Nonuse of Contraception by Sexually Active Women Aged 15–19." *Family Planning Perspectives* 11 (September/October): 290–96.

Ziegler, Harmon, and Wayne Peak. 1970. "The Political Functions of the Educational System." *Sociology of Education* 43 (Spring): 129–42.

Zimring, Franklin E. 2004. *The Contradictions of American Capital Punishment.* New York: Oxford University Press.

Zweigenhaft, Richard L., and G. William Domhoff. 1998. *Diversity in the Power Elite: Have Women and Minorities Reached the Top?* New Haven, CT: Yale University Press.

Fischoff et al. New York: Bedminster Press.

Wechsler, Henry, and Bernice Wuethrich. 2003. *Dying to Drink: Confronting Binge Drinking on College Campuses.* New York: Rodale Books.

_____, A. Davenport, G.W. Dowdall, B. Moeykens, and S. Castillo. 1994. "Health and Behavioral Consequences of Binge Drinking in College." *Journal of the American Medical Association* 272 (December 7): 1676.

Weeks, Jeffrey. 2003. *Sexuality.* 2d ed. New York: Routledge.

Weinberg, Martin S., Colin J. Williams, and Douglas W. Pryor. 1994. *Dual Attraction: Understanding Bisexuality.* New York: Oxford University Press.

Weisberg, Barry. 1971. *Beyond Repair.* Boston: Beacon Press.

Weissert, Carol S., and William G. Weissert. 2002. *Governing Health: The Politics of Health Policy.* 2d ed. Baltimore, MD: Johns Hopkins University Press.

Weissman, Joel S., and Arnold M. Epstein. 1994. *Falling through the Safety Net.* Baltimore, MD: Johns Hopkins University Press.

Weitzman, Lenore J. 1985. *The Divorce Revolution: The Unexpected Consequences for Women and Children in America.* New York: The Free Press.

Wekstein, Louis. 1979. *Handbook of Suicidology.* New York: Brunner/Mazel.

Wellburn, Allan. 1994. *Air Pollution and Climate Change: The Biological Impact.* 2d ed. New York: John Wiley.

Wellman, David T. 1993. *Portraits of White Racism.* Cambridge: Cambridge University Press.

Werth, James L. Jr. 1995. "Rational Suicide Reconsidered: AIDS as an

Impetus for Change." *Death Studies* 19: 65–80.

West, Candace, and Don Zimmerman. 1987. "Doing Gender." *Gender and Society* 1 (June): 125–51.

West, Robin. 1985. *Memory Fitness Over 40.* Gainesville, FL: Triad.

_____ and Monica Yassuda. 2004. "Aging and Memory Control Beliefs: Performance in Relation to Goal Setting and Memory Self-Evaluation." *Journals of Gerontology (Series B—Psychological Sciences and Social Sciences)* 59B (2): 56–65.

Wheeler, David L. 1993. "Study of Lesbians Rekindles Debate over Biological Basis for Homosexuality." *Chronicle of Higher Education* (March 17): A6.

Wheelock, Anne. 1992. *Crossing the Tracks: How "Untracking" Can Save America's Schools.* New York: The New Press.

_____. 1994. *Alternatives to Tracking and Ability Grouping.* Arlington, VA: American Association of School Administrators.

White, O. Z. 1987. "Our Prejudices against the Elderly." Pp. 1–12 in *The Elderly: Victims and Deviants,* edited by Carl D. Chambers, John H. Lindquist, O.Z. White, and Michael T. Harter. Athens: Ohio University Press.

Wiggins, Lynne M. 2002. "Corporate Computer Crime: Collaborative Power in Numbers." *Federal Probation* 66 (3): 19–29.

Willhelm, Sidney. 1983. *Black in a White America.* Cambridge, MA: Schenkman Books.

Williams, Mary E., ed. 2001. *The Death Penalty: Opposing Viewpoints.* San Diego, CA: Greenhaven Press.

Williams, William Appleman. 1980. *Empire as a Way of Life.*

New York: Oxford Univei Press.

Wills, Garry. 1995. "The Revolutionaries." *The Nev Review,* August 10, pp. 50

Wilson, Edward O. 1979 *Human Nature.* New York Books.

Wilson, William Julius. *Truly Disadvantaged.* Chi University of Chicago Pre

Winfeld, Liz, and Susan 2001. *Straight Talk About Workplace.* 2d ed. Bingha Harrington Park Press.

Wise, David. 1976. *The A Police State.* New York: R House.

Wolf, Naomi. 1991. *The E Myth: How Images of Bea Used against Women.* New William Morrow.

Wolff, Edward N. 1995. *7 A Study of the Increasing I of Wealth in America.* New Twentieth Century Fund.

Women's E-News. 2002. ' Share of Housework Rema Same Since 1985." March available at www.womense

Women's Voices, Women' **Survey.** 2003. October 23– November 19.

Woods, James D. 1993. *Th Corporate Closet: The Proj Lives of Gay Men in Ameri* York: The Free Press.

Woog, Dan. 1995. *School's Impact of Gay and Lesbian America's Schools.* Boston: Publications.

_____. 2001. *Gay Men, Sti Jobs.* Los Angeles: Alyson Publications.

World Bank. 2003. *World Development Indicators.* Washington, DC: World Bar

World Development Indica 2002. Washington, DC: Inte

photo credits

name index

subject index